ARGUING ABOUT THE MIND

'I think this is brilliant. In conception and execution, the anthology does something which is both original and needed as a teaching resource. Instead of taking tired old routes, the editors motivate the philosophical questions in a fresh and illuminating way, with an excellent choice of readings based around problems which will have occurred to most thoughtful philosophy students.'

Tim Crane, *University College London, UK*

'An excellent, comprehensive selection of key papers that are accessible to entry-level students.'
Ron Chrisley, *University of Sussex, UK*

Arguing About the Mind is a highly accessible, engaging introduction to the core questions in the philosophy of mind. This fresh, bold and exciting collection offers a selection of thought-provoking articles that examine a broad range of issues from the mind/body relation to animal and artificial intelligence.

The editors assemble some of the most influential and controversial contributions of key philosophers in the field including David Chalmers, Thomas Nagel, Daniel Dennett and Alan Turing, and challenge the reader to reflect on debates on:

- the problem of consciousness
- the nature of the mind
- the relationship between the mind, body and world
- the notion of selfhood
- pathologies and behavioural problems
- animal, machine and extra-terrestrial intelligence

The articles chosen are clear, interesting and free from unnecessary jargon. The editors provide lucid introductions to each section in which they give an overview of the debate and outline the arguments of the papers. *Arguing About the Mind* is an original and stimulating reader for students new to the philosophy of mind.

Brie Gertler is Associate Professor of Philosophy at the University of Virginia, USA.

Lawrence Shapiro is Professor of Philosophy at the University of Wisconsin-Madison, USA.

ARGUING ABOUT PHILOSOPHY

This exciting and lively series introduces key subjects in philosophy with the help of a vibrant set of readings. In contrast to many standard anthologies which often reprint the same technical and remote extracts, each volume in the Arguing About Philosophy series is built around essential but fresher philosophical readings, designed to attract the curiosity of students coming to the subject for the first time. A key feature of the series is the inclusion of well-known yet often neglected readings from related fields, such as popular science, film and fiction. Each volume is edited by leading figures in their chosen field and each section carefully introduced and set in context, making the series an exciting starting point for those looking to get to grips with philosophy.

ARGUING ABOUT METAETHICS
Edited by Andrew Fisher and Simon Kirchin

ARGUING ABOUT THE MIND
Edited by Brie Gertler and Lawrence Shapiro

Forthcoming titles:

ARGUING ABOUT METAPHYSICS
Edited by Michael Rea

ARGUING ABOUT KNOWLEDGE
Edited by Duncan Pritchard and Ram Neta

ARGUING ABOUT ART 3RD EDITION
Edited by Alex Neill and Aaron Ridley

ARGUING ABOUT THE MIND

Edited by Brie Gertler and
Lawrence Shapiro

Routledge
Taylor & Francis Group

NEW YORK AND LONDON

First published 2007
by Routledge
270 Madison Avenue, New York, NY 10016

Simultaneously published in the UK
by Routledge
2 Milton Park Square, Milton Park, Abingdon, OX14 4RN

Reprinted 2010

Routledge is an imprint of the Taylor & Francis Group, an informa business

Typeset in Sabon and Frutiger by Taylor & Francis Books Ltd
Printed and bound in Great Britain by CPI Antony Rowe, Chippenham, Wiltshire

British Library Cataloguing in Publication Data
A catalogue record for this book is available from the British Library

Library of Congress Cataloging in Publication Data
Arguing about the mind / edited by Brie Gertler and Lawrence Shapiro.
p. cm.
ISBN-13: 978-0-415-77162-7 (hardback : alk. paper)
ISBN-13: 978-0-415-77163-4 (pbk. : alk. paper) 1.
Philosophy of mind. 2. Consciousness. 3. Mind and body. I. Gertler,
Brie. II. Shapiro, Lawrence A.
BD418.3.A74 2007
128'.2–dc22

2006031915

ISBN10: 0-415-77162-5 (hbk)
ISBN10: 0-415-77163-3 (pbk)

ISBN13: 978-0-415-77162-7 (hbk)
ISBN13: 978-0-415-77163-4 (pbk)

CONTENTS

Acknowledgements   x

1 Introduction   1

PART 1
Consciousness: what is the problem?   **3**

2 The problem of consciousness   12
   JULIAN JAYNES

3 The puzzle of conscious experience   15
   DAVID CHALMERS

4 The Hornswoggle problem   27
   PATRICIA S. CHURCHLAND

5 The incompleteness of objective reality   36
   THOMAS NAGEL

6 Science and the phenomenal   50
   JENANN ISMAEL

PART 2
Consciousness: how should it be studied?   **57**

7 Science, publicity, and consciousness   64
   ALVIN I. GOLDMAN

CONTENTS

8 Who's on first? Heterophenomenology explained   81
   DANIEL DENNETT

9 Three facets of consciousness   94
   D. W. SMITH

PART 3
Is the mind physical?   **109**

10 An argument for dualism   117
    W. D. HART

11 The case for materialism   125
    DAVID PAPINEAU

12 What is the soul?   133
    BERTRAND RUSSELL

13 Post-physicalism   136
    BARBARA MONTERO

PART 4
**How is your mind related to your body? How is it related
to the world?**   **157**

14 Meditations   164
    RENÉ DESCARTES

15 Bodily awareness and the self   170
    BILL BREWER

16 The extended mind   180
    ANDY CLARK AND DAVID CHALMERS

17 Overextending the mind?   192
    BRIE GERTLER

CONTENTS

PART 5
What is the self?   **207**

18 Brain bisection and the unity of consciousness   214
    THOMAS NAGEL

19 Divided minds and the nature of persons   229
    DEREK PARFIT

20 The self as a center of narrative gravity   237
    DANIEL DENNETT

21 Against narrative   248
    GALEN STRAWSON

22 There is no problem of the self   262
    ERIC T. OLSON

PART 6
What can pathological cases teach us about the mind?   **279**

23 The unbearable likeness of being   285
    V. S. RAMACHANDRAN AND SANDRA BLAKESLEE

24 Reconceiving delusion   299
    G. LYNN STEPHENS AND GEORGE GRAHAM

25 Does the autistic child have a 'theory of mind'?   310
    SIMON BARON-COHEN, ALAN M. LESLIE, AND UTA FRITH

26 Autism and the "theory of mind" debate   319
    ROBERT M. GORDON AND JOHN A. BARKER

27 Autism as mind-blindness: an elaboration and partial defence   333
    PETER CARRUTHERS

28 Free will, moral responsibility and ADHD   352
    GORDON TAIT

29 Alcohol addiction and responsibility attributions   372
    FERDINAND SCHOEMAN

PART 7
How can we know whether—and what—non-human animals think?   389

30 How to read minds in behaviour: a suggestion from a philosopher   396
    JONATHAN BENNETT

31 The mental lives of non-human animals   407
    JOHN DUPRÉ

32 Can animals empathize? Yes   424
    GORDON GALLUP, JR.

33 Can animals empathize? Maybe not   431
    DANIEL POVINELLI

34 Apes with language   439
    SUE SAVAGE RUMBAUGH, STUART SHANKER AND TALBOT J. TAYLOR

35 Behind the ape's appearance: escaping anthropocentrism in the study of
    other minds   451
    DANIEL POVINELLI

PART 8
Can machines think?   465

36 Computing machinery and intelligence   471
    A.M. TURING

37 Minds, brains, and programs   495
    JOHN R. SEARLE

38 The curious case of the Chinese room   514
    J. COPELAND

39 Can machines think?   532
    DANIEL DENNETT

CONTENTS

40 Subcognition and the limits of the Turing test 548
ROBERT M. FRENCH

PART 9
Is there intelligent life on other planets? 561

41 The Drake equation 567
ROBERT NAEYE

42 Can SETI succeed? Not likely 569
ERNST MAYR

43 The abundance of life-bearing planets 574
CARL SAGAN

44 Response to Sagan 579
ERNST MAYR

45 Response to Mayr 581
CARL SAGAN

46 The decoding problem: do we need to search for extra terrestrial
intelligence to search for extraterrestrial intelligence? 583
NEIL TENNANT

Index 598

ACKNOWLEDGEMENTS

Julian Jaynes. Excerpts from *The Origin of Consciousness in the Breakdown of the Bicameral Mind*. © 1976, 1990. Reprinted by permission of the estate of Julian Jaynes and Houghton Mifflin Company. All rights reserved.

David Chalmers. "The Puzzle of Conscious Experience", in *Scientific American* Dec. 1995, 62–68. (http://consc.net/papers/puzzle.pdf). Reproduced by kind permission of the author.

Patricia Churchland. "The Hornswoggle Problem", in *Journal of Consciousness Studies* 3, 5–6, 1996, 402–8. © Imprint Academic, Exeter, UK.

Thomas Nagel. "Mind", in *The View from Nowhere*, Oxford University Press, 1986. Reprinted by permission of the author, Oxford University Press and Oxford University Press, Inc.

Jenann Ismael. "Science and the Phenomenal", in *Philosophy of Science* 66, 1999, 351–69. Reproduced by permission of the publisher, The University of Chicago Press, and the author. A revised and extended version of this article is to be published in *The Situated Self*, Oxford University Press, New York, 2006.

Alvin Goldman. "Science, Publicity, and Consciousness", in *Philosophy of Science* 64, 1997, 525–45. Reproduced by permission of the publisher, The University of Chicago Press, and the author.

Daniel Dennett. "Who's on First? Heterophenomenology Explained", in *Journal of Consciousness Studies* 10, 9–10, 2003, 19–30. © Imprint Academic, Exeter, UK.

D. W. Smith. "Three Facets of Consciousness", in *Axiomathes* 12, 2001, 55–85. With kind permission from Springer Science and Business Media.

W. D. Hart. Excerpts from *Engines of the Soul*, © 1988 Cambridge University Press. Reproduced with permission of the author and publisher.

David Papineau. "The Case for Materialism", in *Thinking about Consciousness*, Oxford University Press, 2002. Reprinted by permission of the author, Oxford University Press and Oxford University Press, Inc.

Bertrand Russell. "What is the Soul?" 1928, from *In Praise of Idleness*, 2nd edn., ©
2004 The Bertrand Russell Peace Foundation Ltd. Reproduced by permission of
Taylor & Francis Books, Ltd.

Barbara Montero. "Post-Physicalism", in *The Journal of Consciousness Studies* 8, 2,
2001, 61–80. © Imprint Academic, Exeter, UK.

John Cottingham and Bernard Williams (trans.) *Descartes: Meditations on First Philosophy With Selections from the Objections and Replies*, 1996, © Cambridge University Press, reproduced with permission.

Bill Brewer. "Bodily Awareness and the Self", in J. Bermudez, A.J. Marcel and N. Eilan
(eds.), *The Body and The Self*. Cambridge, Mass: MIT Press. © 1995 by the Massachusetts Institute of Technology. Reproduced with permission.

Andy Clark and David Chalmers. "The Extended Mind", in *Analysis* 58, 1998, 10–23.
Reproduced with permission from Blackwell Publishing and the authors.

Thomas Nagel. "Brain Bisection and the Unity of Consciousness", in *Synthese* 23,
1971, 396–413. With kind permission from Springer Science and Business Media.

Derek Parfit. "Divided Minds and the Nature of Persons", in Blakemore and Greenfield
(eds.) *Mindwaves*. Oxford: Blackwell, 1987. Reproduced with permission from
Blackwell Publishing.

Daniel Dennett. "The Self as a Center of Narrative Gravity", in F. Kessel, P. Cole and D.
Johnson (eds.) *Self and Consciousness: Multiple Perspectives*, 1992. Hillsdale, NJ:
Erlbaum. Reproduced by kind permission of the author and publisher.

Galen Strawson. "Against Narrative", from the *Times Literary Supplement* October 15
2004. This paper is an abridgement of a longer paper called "Against Narrativity",
published in *The Self*, edited by G. Strawson (Oxford, Blackwell, 2005). Reproduced
with permission.

Eric Olson. "There is no Problem of the Self", in *Journal of Consciousness Studies* 5, 5–
6, 1998, 645–57. © Imprint Academic, Exeter, UK.

Vilayanur S. Ramachandran and Sandra Blakeslee. "The Unbearable Likeness of Being",
chapter 8 of *Phantoms in the Brain*. Reprinted by permission of HarperCollins Publishers Ltd. © V.S. Ramachandran and Sandra Blakeslee, 1998.

G. Lynn Stephens and George Graham. "Reconceiving Delusion", in *International
Review of Psychiatry* 16, 2004, 236–41. Reproduced by kind permission of the
authors and publisher.

Simon Baron-Cohen, Alan Leslie and Uta Frith. "Does the Autistic Child have a 'Theory
of Mind'", *Cognition* 21, 1985, 37–46.

Robert Gordon and John Barker. "Autism and the 'theory of mind' debate", in G.
Graham and L. Stephens (eds.) *Philosophical Psychopathology: A Book of Readings*,
Cambridge: MIT Press. © 1994 by the Massachusetts Institute of Technology.
Reproduced with permission.

Peter Carruthers. "Autism as Mind-Blindness: An Elaboration and Partial Defence", in Carruthers, P. and Smith, P. (eds.) *Theories of Theories of Mind*. © 1996 Cambridge University Press reproduced with permission of the author and publisher.

Gordon Tait. "Free Will, Moral Responsibility and ADHD", *International Journal of Inclusive Education* 7, 2003, 429–46. Reproduced by kind permission of the author and publisher.

Ferdinand Schoeman. "Alcohol Addiction and Responsibility Attributions", in G. Graham and L. Stephens (eds.) *Philosophical Psychopathology: A Book of Readings*, Cambridge: MIT Press. © 1994 by the Massachusetts Institute of Technology. Reproduced with permission.

Jonathan Bennett. "How to Read Minds in Behaviour: A Suggestion from a Philosopher", in A. Whiten (ed.) *Natural Theories of Mind: Evolution, Development and Simulation of Everyday Mind Reading* (Oxford: Basil Blackwell Ltd.). © 1993. Reproduced with permission from Blackwell Publishing.

John Dupré. "The Mental Lives of Nonhuman Animals", in M. Bekoff and D. Jamieson (eds.) *Readings in Animal Cognition*, Cambridge: MIT Press. © 1996 by the Massachusetts Institute of Technology. Reproduced with permission.

Gordon Gallup. "Can Animals Empathize? Yes", *Scientific American* 9, 1998, 66–71. Reprinted with permission. © 1998 by Scientific American, Inc. All rights reserved.

Daniel Povinelli. "Can Animals Empathize? Maybe Not", *Scientific American* 9, 1998, 67–75. Reprinted with permission. © 1998 by Scientific American, Inc. All rights reserved.

Sue Savage Rumbaugh, Stuart Shanker and Talbot Taylor. "Apes with Language", *Critical Quarterly* 38, 1996, 45–56. Reproduced with permission from Blackwell Publishing.

Daniel Povinelli. "Of Apes and Men", in *Daedalus* 133, 1, 2004, 29–41. © 2004 by the American Academy of Arts and Sciences.

Alan Turing. "Computing Machinery and Intelligence", in *Mind* 59, 1950, 433–60. Reprinted by permission of Oxford University Press and the author.

John Searle. "Minds, Brains, and Programs", in *Behavioral and Brain Sciences* 3, 1980, 417–24. © 1980 Cambridge University Press, reprinted with permission.

Jack Copeland. "The Curious Case of the Chinese Room", chapter 6 in *Artificial Intelligence: A Philosophical Introduction* (Oxford: Basil Blackwell Ltd.). © 1993. Reproduced with permission from Blackwell Publishing.

Daniel Dennett. "Can machines think?" in M. Shafto (ed.) *How We Know: Nobel Conference XX*. © 1986 by Gustavus Adolphus College. Reprinted by permission of HarperCollins Publishers.

Robert French. "Subcognition and the Limits of the Turing Test", in *Mind* 99, 1990, 53–65. Reprinted by permission of Oxford University Press and the author.

Robert Naeye. "The Drake Equation", in *Mercury*, 32, 6, 2003, 20. Reproduced by kind permission of the author and journal.

Ernst Mayr. "Can SETI Succeed? Not Likely", *Bioastronomy News*, 7, 3, 1995. Reproduced by permission of The Planetary Society.

Carl Sagan. "The Abundance of Life-Bearing Planets", *Bioastronomy News*, 7, 4, 1995. Reproduced by permission of The Planetary Society.

Ernst Mayr. "Response to Sagan." Reproduced by permission of The Planetary Society.

Carl Sagan. "Response to Mayr." Reproduced by permission of The Planetary Society.

Neil Tennant. "The Decoding Problem: Do We Need to Search for Extra Terrestrial Intelligence to Search for Extraterrestrial Intelligence?", in S. Kingsley (ed.), *SPIE Proceedings Volume 1867*. © 1993. Reproduced by kind permission of the author and SPIE.

Every effort has been made to trace and contact copyright holders. The publishers would be pleased to hear from any copyright holder not acknowledged here so that this section may be amended at the earliest opportunity.

We are grateful to Athena Skaleris for help in correcting proofs, and to George Graham and Eric Margolis for advice on some of the selected readings. Thanks also to Tony Bruce for initiating this project, Priyanka Pathak for guiding us through the process, and Geraldine Martin and Nick Barnett for their careful editing.

1

INTRODUCTION
Arguing About the Mind

The mind holds a special interest for philosophers. Of course, the mind is implicated in every area of philosophy, as it is what we *use* to philosophize. But the mind also harbors mysteries – about how consciousness relates to the physical world, whether we might someday construct artificial minds, what one's mind contributes to one's self, whether human thought is on a par with animal cognition – that make it an irresistible target for philosophers in its own right.

You may wonder whether a philosopher has anything interesting to say about these questions. After all, they seem to fall within the purview of empirical science: cognitive psychology, neuroscience, linguistics, animal ethology, and computer science. Investigators in these areas develop an understanding of the mind through laboratory experiments and other means of empirical research. But according to a widespread stereotype, the only tool available to philosophers is reflection: they are like Rodin's thinker, staring fixedly into the middle distance, trying to unravel abstract enigmas through pure thought.

What, then, can the philosopher contribute to an understanding of the mind? The articles in this volume provide a range of answers to this question. They exhibit philosophers at work, using distinctively philosophical methods to develop a variety of theories about how the mind operates, and how it relates to the non-mental world. They also present empirical work that both informs philosophical reflection on the mind and raises new issues for further philosophical scrutiny.

Together, these articles comprise a fresh approach to the philosophy of mind, introducing philosophical thought on questions about the mind that most of us pondered long before we took a philosophy course. The topics include issues squarely within the philosophical tradition, such as the relation between mind and body, and the nature of the self; but they also encompass more cutting-edge concerns, such as the lessons to be learned from mental pathologies, and the existence (and character) of animal or artificial intelligence. In assembling the anthology, we chose articles that are accessible, intrinsically interesting, and free from unnecessary jargon.

Each of the nine sections begins with a clear, engaging introduction to the questions it covers. The section introductions provide an overview of the topic at hand, and include questions to think about and suggestions for further reading. Although the nine sections of the book cover distinct topics and can be read in any order, they are also connected to each other in ways that the section introductions explain.

As you read this book, we are confident that you will experience the type of intellectual exhilaration that has spurred us and others to join the search for a deeper understanding of the mind and its place in the world.

Part 1

CONSCIOUSNESS

What is the problem?

O, what a world of unseen visions and heard silences, this insubstantial country of the mind!

So begins Julian Jaynes' dramatic depiction of conscious experience, the phenomenon at the core of philosophical inquiry into the mind. The passage seems intended to confuse. How can visions go unseen, silences be heard, a country lack substance? But the implication is clear. In attending to our stream of consciousness, we are aware of something that stands in stark opposition to the world perceived with eyes and ears – the shared, external world that Jaynes calls 'kickable reality'.

Philosophers describe this opposition in a variety of ways.

Consciousness is:	Whereas the rest of reality is:
Private	Public
Subjective	Objective
Inner	Outer
Introspectible	Perceptible
Ineffable	Describable

While most philosophers agree that consciousness has at least some of these distinctive features, there is a great deal of controversy about the ultimate significance of these contrasts. The *problem of consciousness* arises from the fact that the physical sciences seem to address only the aspects of reality that have the features listed on the right. How then can conscious experience, which has the special features listed on the left, be explained within the theories those sciences generate? The problem of consciousness is the challenge of showing how a unified, broadly scientific account of reality can accommodate the phenomena of conscious experience.

Let us consider, in more detail, why conscious experience may appear to fall outside the scope of ordinary scientific explanation. One reason is that the physical sciences begin with the data of perception: what we see, hear, touch, etc. By contrast, conscious experience is not itself *perceived*. To appreciate this point, imagine a purple giraffe. In performing this imaginative exercise, you do not *see* a giraffe; for example, you need not use your eyes to perform the exercise. Rather, the visual picture of the giraffe forms, to borrow Jaynes' phrase, an 'unseen vision'. Of course, there are similarities between visually perceiving a giraffe and imagining one: both seem to involve a representation of a giraffe that is *visual* (in a loose sense). This similarity is sometimes expressed by saying that, in imagining, we 'see with the mind's eye'. But this is a merely metaphorical use of 'see'. Perception is not imagination, and what is imagined should not be confused with what is perceived. Presumably, no one has perceived – and, possibly, no one ever will perceive – a purple giraffe.

This brings us to another feature of conscious experience that makes it appear to transcend the domain of physical science: its *privacy*. While ordinary objects (like giraffes) can, at least in principle, be observed equally well by various people, conscious experience is *private*, in the sense that each of us can directly observe only her own experience. Two persons may simultaneously imagine a purple giraffe, but each has a kind of access to her own mental picture of a giraffe that is unavailable to the other. This type of privacy threatens to put conscious experience beyond the reach of the ordinary methods of physical science, which arguably require that data be available to (and confirmed by) multiple observers.[1]

Historically, most philosophers have denied that the physical sciences will explain conscious experience. For they have regarded conscious experience as belonging to a *soul* that differs markedly from physical reality, in being spiritual rather than physical. The belief that the mental is non-physical is known as *dualism*, for it implies a duality of substances or properties: the mental and the physical. Dualism was often accompanied by the belief that the soul was unrestricted, not subject to the scientific laws of nature that govern the body.[2] In fact, according to a central idea in many philosophical and religious traditions, it is only because the soul's operations lie beyond the reach of natural laws that human decisions can be genuinely free.

This historically influential position has now been widely abandoned. Most contemporary thinkers believe that conscious experience will ultimately be explained by ordinary physical science. On the weakest version of this *physicalist* view, the claim is just that physical science will someday, somehow account for conscious experience; on the strongest version, it is that we already have a significant scientific explanation of consciousness in hand. Between these extremes lies the belief that some particular aspect of our current understanding of the brain and its cognitive architecture will eventually provide the basis for a comprehensive account of consciousness, though it has not yet done so.

Still, some contemporary philosophers have challenged this optimism about physical science. Unlike their historical predecessors, today's leading dualists do not use religiously based arguments in opposing physical explanations of consciousness. Rather, they adopt a naturalistic approach to conscious experience. They treat the special features of consciousness as data, and aim to show that physical theories could not possibly explain these data.

If physical science cannot explain consciousness, then we must abandon a cherished modern belief: that a comprehensive account of reality is within the purview of the physical sciences, broadly construed. The stakes in this debate thus seem extremely high. However, many contemporary dualists hold that the costs of relinquishing this belief are not so very great, for we can maintain a scientific worldview while recognizing that the physical sciences cannot provide an exhaustive theory of the world.

The current section of this book contains arguments on both sides of this issue. The first author is Jaynes, who notes that the problem of consciousness has been with us for centuries. He argues that, while each generation uses its own metaphors to understand consciousness, these historical antecedents have not yielded progress on the basic problem. Nor does he expect that an exclusively scientific approach will ever solve the problem: for instance, he argues that no purely neuroscientific understanding of the brain could even uncover the presence of consciousness, let alone reveal its nature or purpose. So Jaynes is pessimistic about the prospects for explaining consciousness in physical science terms.

This conclusion is embraced and extended by David Chalmers. Chalmers argues that those who cite progress on the problem of consciousness, and are therefore sanguine about solving that problem, are in fact mistaken about the problem itself. Developments in neuroscience and cognitive science have facilitated progress only on what he calls the *Easy Problems* of consciousness, such as how perceptual information processed in different faculties is integrated into a unified representation of an object. The Easy Problems concern aspects of consciousness that lack the special features described above. The problem that arises from these special features – what I referred to simply as 'the problem of consciousness' – Chalmers labels the *Hard Problem*.

Chalmers is not merely agnostic about this problem. He believes that there are strong reasons to doubt that conscious experience can be explained within the framework of physical science. Our concepts of the physical are, he says, tied to the 'structures and functions' of physical systems. Since conscious experience is not a matter of structures and functions, it is beyond the domain of physical science, which is exclusively concerned with these. However, Chalmers is himself naturalistically inclined. He does not interpret conscious experience as a supernatural or extra-scientific phenomenon; rather, he proposes that it is a fundamental, irreducible feature of reality. (Other such fundamental features include space-time, mass, and charge.) We have every reason to expect that this feature will be law-governed, though the relevant laws will not be purely physical laws. They may instead be psychophysical laws, which relate fundamentally conscious features of reality to non-conscious ones.

Patricia Churchland emphatically rejects Chalmers' claim that physical science cannot explain consciousness. She contends that this claim depends on a relatively static interpretation of the limits of physical science. But, she observes, physical science is constantly evolving, so we may eventually revise our estimation of its limits. This objection also casts doubt on Chalmers' distinction between Easy and Hard Problems, since which problems *appear* hard, and which appear easy, depends on our current understanding of physical science's proper domain.

Of course, Chalmers does not simply assume that physical science has certain limits; he reaches this conclusion through thought experiments that suggest a disparity between our concepts of physical states and our concepts of conscious states. Churchland criticizes Chalmers' use of thought experiments, claiming that these show, at most, that we cannot *imagine* an explanation of consciousness that uses the terms and methods of physical science. Our inability to imagine this is, on her view, "a rather uninteresting psychological fact about *us*, not an interesting metaphysical fact about the world". After all, previous generations seemed unable to imagine how purely physical features could constitute *life*, but advances in biochemistry have dissolved this mystery. In response, Chalmers could maintain that the issue about consciousness differs importantly from the issue about life, in that an organism's being alive is a matter of structure and function. But Churchland would likely contend that this understanding of *life* occurred only as a result of the relevant advances in biochemistry.

The basic point of contention between Chalmers and Churchland centers on this question: is our current understanding of consciousness and physical science sufficiently well developed to allow us to determine whether physical science could ultimately provide an explanation of consciousness? Chalmers believes that it is, for he thinks that we have a fairly accurate grasp of the concepts – 'consciousness', 'structure', 'function', 'physical', etc. – that define the problem of consciousness. Churchland maintains that Chalmers' conclusion is unwarranted because we do not yet possess an adequate grasp of the physical (etc.).

The problem of consciousness stems, at least in large part, from the contrast between the mind's *subjective* nature and the seemingly *objective* nature of other aspects of reality. Thomas Nagel's chapter examines this contrast. On his view, attempts to explain the mind in purely physical terms are misguided. For they rely on an overly narrow conception of objectivity, one that wrongly assumes that objective reality can be completely captured in the terms of physical science. He labels this 'the physical conception of objectivity', and claims that it springs from the idea that only what can be understood in a particular way – namely, what can be given a familiar physical science explanation – actually exists. The special emphasis placed on a particular way of understanding reality gives pride of place to the *thinker*. Nagel points out that this result is ironic: it amounts to forcing reality to conform to the thinker, whereas physicalists allegedly seek to assimilate the thinker to the rest of reality. For this reason, Nagel sees attempts to explain the mind in terms of physical science as 'idealist', in that they yield a picture of reality that derives from the categories and methods used by thinkers to understand their world.

But while Nagel rejects the physical conception of objectivity, he believes that the only way to advance our understanding of the mind is to try to capture the mental within *some* objective conception of the world. He does not advocate this approach because he thinks it will succeed; he recommends that we should pursue an objective conception of the mind in part because he thinks it will be instructive to see exactly how far this approach takes us, and where, precisely, it fails. And he is confident that it will fail, and that there will forever remain a residue of subjectivity that cannot be comprehended within an objective framework. In his words: "Reality is not just objective reality."

Here is an exercise that illustrates why the subjective cannot be reduced to the objective. Imagine that you know all of the objective features of someone's experience: you know that she is sitting in a room in which coffee is being brewed, you know that her olfactory system is working properly, you know what neurophysiological events are occurring in her brain, etc. This information may allow you to infer that she is now smelling coffee. But all of these objective facts will not tell you the intrinsic nature of her experience, that is, *what it's like* (for her) to smell the coffee. (Of course, you might try to determine this by drawing on similar experiences you've had, and imagining the smell of coffee – but to do that is already to adopt a *subjective* viewpoint on the experience.) This suggests that the subjective viewpoint is necessary to grasp what philosophers call the *phenomenal* character of experience, e.g., *what it's like* to smell coffee. At its most basic, the point here does not concern how I *know* that others have certain experiences. Instead, it concerns the subjective *nature* of experience.

The existence of irreducibly subjective facts poses a problem for physicalism. The physical seems to be graspable 'objectively', regardless of any particular viewpoint. This means that if conscious experiences are completely physical, an objective understanding of them will not leave anything out. But the previous exercise suggests that an objective understanding *does* leave something out, namely, *what it's like* to undergo the experience. These facts about conscious experiences thus seem irreducibly subjective, and hence do not seem to be *physical* facts.

Jenann Ismael hopes to defend physicalism from this threat. She accepts that conscious experience involves a type of subjectivity that is irreducible to objective features of the physical world. But she discounts the significance of this irreducibility. On her view, it is a trivial consequence of the fact that "the physical is *essentially* impersonal". Her defense of physicalism uses an analogy between conscious experience and spatial location. While purely objective information will not allow me to know where I am spatially located, this does not mean that 'here' names a special (non-physical) place; it simply refers to a place to which I bear a special *relation*. Similarly, she says, while purely objective information will not allow me to know what it's like to undergo a particular experience, this does not mean that experiences are special; it simply means that I bear a special *relation* to my experiences.

Does the irreducibly subjective character of our experience cast doubt on physicalism? Ismael correctly points out that other features of us, including our spatial location, are also irreducibly subjective. And she is surely correct that this does not tempt us to reject physicalism about spatial location. Still, one might argue that the case of conscious experience represents the basic subjective fact, and cases like 'here' are subjective only in a way that derives from the subjectivity of consciousness. As soon as

I undergo any conscious experience, I can think of 'here' in relation to it: for instance, if I undergo a visual experience of a lake, I may think of 'here' as 'on the edge of *this* lake'. And even if my only conscious experience is imagining a purple giraffe, I may think of 'here' as the place where *this* experience is occurring. According to this line of argument, the comparison to spatial location does not neutralize the threat that subjectivity poses to physicalism.

QUESTIONS TO THINK ABOUT

1   Jaynes observes that historical understandings of consciousness followed trends in science: e.g., in the 19th century, the rise of geology led to the notion that the mind is composed of "layers which recorded the past of the individual". Do you think that trends in science continue to influence how we understand the mind? If so, what, if anything, does this imply about our best current theory of consciousness?

2   Chalmers' argument depends on our concepts of consciousness and the physical. Is it legitimate to argue from how we conceptualize something to conclusions about its basic nature? Are there alternatives to this sort of argument, or must all investigations be constrained by some conception of the object of inquiry?

3   Churchland cites the discovery that *life* was physically explainable as a reason for optimism about a physical explanation of consciousness. Do you agree? If so, why? If not, how does our current situation regarding consciousness differ from the previous situation regarding life?

4   Nagel argues that the physical conception of objectivity is unprincipled. What sort of conception of objectivity might replace this one? In the end, what does it mean to say that a fact is *objective*?

5   According to Ismael, the subjectivity of consciousness is on a par with certain features of one's spatial location. Imagine a world with no conscious beings. Would such a world contain the features of spatial location that Ismael describes? Does your answer to this question help you to determine whether the irreducibility of the subjective is a problem for explaining consciousness?

NOTES

1 Part 2 of the current volume addresses this controversy about privacy and scientific method.
2 Laws of nature include the law of gravity, the law of inertia, etc. It was historically assumed – and many philosophers still hold – that all laws of nature are *physical*, in that they govern only physical objects and events.

FURTHER READING

Koch, C. "Introduction to the Study of Consciousness". Chapter 1 of his *The Quest for Consciousness*. Englewood, CO: Roberts & Company Publishers. Available online at http://www.questforconsciousness.com/chapter1.pdf.

Lycan, W. G. "Subjectivity". Chapter 7 of his *Consciousness*. Cambridge, MA: MIT Press, 1987.

McGinn, C. *The Problem of Consciousness*. Oxford: Blackwell, 1991.

Perry, J. "The Problem of the Essential Indexical". *Noûs* 13:3–21, 1979. Reprinted in *The Problem of the Essential Indexical and other Essays*. Oxford: Oxford University Press, 1993.

Searle, J. *The Rediscovery of the Mind*. Cambridge, MA: MIT Press, 1992.

Shear, J. (ed.) *Explaining Consciousness: the hard problem*. Cambridge, MA: MIT Press, 1999.

2

THE PROBLEM OF CONSCIOUSNESS

Julian Jaynes

O, what a world of unseen visions and heard silences, this insubstantial country of the mind! What ineffable essences, these touchless rememberings and unshowable reveries! And the privacy of it all! A secret theater of speechless monologue and prevenient counsel, an invisible mansion of all moods, musings, and mysteries, an infinite resort of disappointments and discoveries. A whole kingdom where each of us reigns reclusively alone, questioning what we will, commanding what we can. A hidden hermitage where we may study out the troubled book of what we have done and yet may do. An introcosm that is more myself than anything I can find in a mirror. This consciousness that is myself of selves, that is everything, and yet nothing at all – what is it?

And where did it come from?

And why?

Few questions have endured longer or traversed a more perplexing history than this, the problem of consciousness and its place in nature. Despite centuries of pondering and experiment, of trying to get together two supposed entities called mind and matter in one age, subject and object in another, or soul and body in still others, despite endless discoursing on the streams, states, or contents of consciousness, of distinguishing terms like intuitions, sense data, the given, raw feels, the sensa, presentations and representations, the sensations, images, and affections of structuralist introspections, the evidential data of the scientific positivist, phenomenological fields, the apparitions of Hobbes, the phenomena of Kant, the appearances of the idealist, the elements of Mach, the phanera of Peirce, or the category errors of Ryle, in spite of all of these, the problem of consciousness is still with us. Something about it keeps returning, not taking a solution.

It is the difference that will not go away, the difference between what others see of us and our sense of our inner selves and the deep feelings that sustain it. The difference between the you-and-me of the shared behavioral world and the unlocatable location of things thought about. Our reflections and dreams, and the imaginary conversations we have with others, in which never-to-be-known-by-anyone we excuse, defend, proclaim our hopes and regrets, our futures and our pasts, all this thick fabric of fancy is so absolutely different from handable, standable, kickable reality with its trees, grass, tables, oceans, hands, stars – even brains! How is this possible? How do these ephemeral existences of our lonely experience fit into the ordered array of nature that somehow surrounds and engulfs this core of knowing?

Men have been conscious of the problem of consciousness almost since consciousness began. And each age has described consciousness in terms of its own theme and concerns. In the golden age of Greece, when men traveled about in freedom while slaves did the work, consciousness was as free as that. Heraclitus, in particular, called it an enormous space whose boundaries, even by traveling along every path, could never be found out. A millennium later, Augustine among the caverned hills of Carthage was astonished at the "mountains and hills of my high imaginations," "the plains and caves and caverns of my memory" with its recesses of "manifold and spacious chambers, wonderfully furnished with unnumberable stores." Note how the metaphors of mind are the world it perceives.

The first half of the nineteenth century was the age of the great geological discoveries in which the record of the past was written in layers of the earth's crust. And this led to the popularization of the idea of consciousness as being in layers which recorded the past of the individual, there being deeper and deeper layers until the record could no longer be read. This emphasis on the unconscious grew until by 1875 most psychologists were insisting that consciousness was but a small part of mental life, and that unconscious sensations, unconscious ideas, and unconscious judgments made up the majority of mental processes.

In the middle of the nineteenth century chemistry succeeded geology as the fashionable science, and consciousness from James Mill to Wundt and his students, such as Titchener, was the compound structure that could be analyzed in the laboratory into precise elements of sensations and feelings.

And as steam locomotives chugged their way into the pattern of everyday life toward the end of the nineteenth century, so they too worked their way into the consciousness of consciousness, the subconscious becoming a boiler of straining energy which demanded manifest outlets and when repressed pushed up and out into neurotic behavior and the spindling camouflaged fulfillments of going-nowhere dreams.

There is not much we can do about such metaphors except to state that that is precisely what they are . . . .

. . . We can only know in the nervous system what we have known in behavior first. Even if we had a complete wiring diagram of the nervous system, we still would not be able to answer our basic question. Though we knew the connections of every tickling thread of every single axon and dendrite in every species that ever existed, together with all its neurotransmitters and how they varied in its billions of synapses of every brain that ever existed, we could still never – *not ever* – from a knowledge of the brain alone know if that brain contained a consciousness like our own. We first have to start from the top, from some conception of what consciousness is, from what our own introspection is. We have to be sure of that, before we can enter the nervous system and talk about its neurology.

We must therefore try to make a new beginning by stating what consciousness is. We have already seen that this is no easy matter, and that the history of the subject is an enormous confusion of metaphor with designation . . . .

3

THE PUZZLE OF CONSCIOUS EXPERIENCE

David Chalmers

Conscious experience is at once the most familiar thing in the world and the most mysterious. There is nothing we know about more directly than consciousness, but it is extraordinarily hard to reconcile it with everything else we know. Why does it exist? What does it do? How could it possibly arise from neural processes in the brain? These questions are among the most intriguing in all of science.

From an objective viewpoint, the brain is relatively comprehensible. When you look at this page, there is a whir of processing: photons strike your retina, electrical signals are passed up your optic nerve and between different areas of your brain, and eventually you might respond with a smile, a perplexed frown or a remark. But there is also a subjective aspect. When you look at the page, you are conscious of it, directly experiencing the images and words as part of your private, mental life. You have vivid impressions of the colors and shapes of the images. At the same time, you may be feeling some emotions and forming some thoughts. Together such experiences make up consciousness: the subjective, inner life of the mind.

For many years, consciousness was shunned by researchers studying the brain and the mind. The prevailing view was that science, which depends on objectivity, could not accommodate something as subjective as consciousness. The behaviorist movement in psychology, dominant earlier in [the twentieth] century, concentrated on external behavior and disallowed any talk of internal mental processes. Later, the rise of cognitive science focused attention on processes inside the head. Still, consciousness remained off-limits, fit only for late-night discussion over drinks.

Over the past several years, however, an increasing number of neuroscientists, psychologists and philosophers have been rejecting the idea that consciousness cannot be studied and are attempting to delve into its secrets. As might be expected of a field so new, there is a tangle of diverse and conflicting theories, often using basic concepts in incompatible ways. To help unsnarl the tangle, philosophical reasoning is vital.

The myriad views within the field range from reductionist theories, according to which consciousness can be explained by the standard methods of neuroscience and psychology, to the position of the so-called mysterians, who say we will never understand consciousness at all. I believe that on close analysis both of these views can be seen to be mistaken and that the truth lies somewhere in the middle.

Against reductionism I will argue that the tools of neuroscience cannot provide a full account of conscious experience, although they have much to offer. Against mysterianism I will hold that consciousness might be explained by a new kind of theory. The full details of such a theory are still out of reach, but careful reasoning and some educated inferences can reveal something of its general nature. For example, it will probably involve new fundamental laws, and the concept of information may play a central role. These faint glimmerings suggest that a theory of consciousness may have startling consequences for our view of the universe and of ourselves.

THE HARD PROBLEM

Researchers use the word "consciousness" in many different ways. To clarify the issues, we first have to separate the problems that are often clustered together under the name. For this purpose, I find it useful to distinguish between the "easy problems" and the "hard problem" of consciousness. The easy problems are by no means trivial—they are actually as challenging as most in psychology and biology—but it is with the hard problem that the central mystery lies.

The easy problems of consciousness include the following: How can a human subject discriminate sensory stimuli and react to them appropriately? How does the brain integrate information from many different sources and use this information to control behavior? How is it that subjects can verbalize their internal states? Although all these questions are associated with consciousness, they all concern the objective mechanisms of the cognitive system. Consequently, we have every reason to expect that continued work in cognitive psychology and neuroscience will answer them.

The hard problem, in contrast, is the question of how physical processes in the brain give rise to subjective experience. This puzzle involves the inner aspect of thought and perception: the way things feel for the subject. When we see, for example, we experience visual sensations, such as that of vivid blue. Or think of the ineffable sound of a distant oboe, the agony of an intense pain, the sparkle of happiness or the meditative quality of a moment lost in thought. All are part of what I call consciousness. It is these phenomena that pose the real mystery of the mind.

To illustrate the distinction, consider a thought experiment devised by the Australian philosopher Frank Jackson. Suppose that Mary, a neuroscientist in the 23rd century, is the world's leading expert on the brain processes responsible for color vision. But Mary has lived her whole life in a black-and-white room and has never seen any other colors. She knows everything there is to know about physical processes in the brain—its biology, structure and function. This understanding enables her to grasp all there is to know about the easy problems: how the brain discriminates stimuli, integrates information and produces verbal reports. From her knowledge of color vision, she knows how color names correspond with wavelengths on the light spectrum. But there is still something crucial about color vision that Mary does not know: what it is like to experience a color such as red. It follows that there are facts about conscious experience that cannot be deduced from physical facts about the functioning of the brain.

Indeed, nobody knows why these physical processes are accompanied by conscious experience at all. Why is it that when our brains process light of a certain wavelength, we have an experience of deep purple? Why do we have any experience at all? Could not an unconscious automaton have performed the same tasks just as well? These are questions that we would like a theory of consciousness to answer.

IS NEUROSCIENCE ENOUGH?

I am not denying that consciousness arises from the brain. We know, for example, that the subjective experience of vision is closely linked to processes in the visual cortex. It is the link itself that perplexes, however. Remarkably, subjective experience seems to emerge from a physical process. But we have no idea how or why this is.

Given the flurry of recent work on consciousness in neuroscience and psychology, one might think this mystery is starting to be cleared up. On closer examination, however, it turns out that almost all the current work addresses only the easy problems of consciousness. The confidence of the reductionist view comes from the progress on the easy problems, but none of this makes any difference where the hard problem is concerned.

Consider the hypothesis put forward by neurobiologists Francis Crick of the Salk Institute for Biological Studies in San Diego and Christof Koch of the California Institute of Technology. They suggest that consciousness may arise from certain oscillations in the cerebral cortex, which become synchronized as neurons fire 40 times per second. Crick and Koch believe the phenomenon might explain how different attributes of a single perceived object (its color and shape, for example), which are processed in different parts of the brain, are merged into a coherent whole. In this theory, two pieces of information become bound together precisely when they are represented by synchronized neural firings. [See pp. 24–26 - eds.]

The hypothesis could conceivably elucidate one of the easy problems about how information is integrated in the brain. But why should synchronized oscillations give rise to a visual experience, no matter how much integration is taking place? This question involves the hard problem, about which the theory has nothing to offer. Indeed, Crick and Koch are agnostic about whether the hard problem can be solved by science at all.

The same kind of critique could be applied to almost all the recent work on consciousness. In his 1991 book *Consciousness Explained*, philosopher Daniel C. Dennett laid out a sophisticated theory of how numerous independent processes in the brain combine to produce a coherent response to a perceived event. The theory might do much to explain how we produce verbal reports on our internal states, but it tells us very little about why there should be a subjective experience behind these reports. Like other reductionist theories, Dennett's is a theory of the easy problems.

The critical common trait among these easy problems is that they all concern how a cognitive or behavioral function is performed. All are ultimately questions about how the brain carries out some task—how it discriminates stimuli, integrates information, produces reports and so on. Once neurobiology specifies appropriate neural mechanisms, showing how the functions are performed, the easy problems are solved.

The hard problem of consciousness, in contrast, goes beyond problems about how functions are performed. Even if every behavioral and cognitive function related to consciousness were explained, there would still remain a further mystery: Why is the performance of these functions accompanied by conscious experience? It is this additional conundrum that makes the hard problem hard.

THE EXPLANATORY GAP

Some have suggested that to solve the hard problem, we need to bring in new tools of physical explanation: non-linear dynamics, say, or new discoveries in neuroscience, or quantum mechanics. But these ideas suffer from exactly the same difficulty. Consider a proposal from Stuart R. Hameroff of the University of Arizona and Roger Penrose of the University of Oxford. They hold that consciousness arises from quantum-physical processes taking place in microtubules, which are protein structures inside neurons. It is possible (if not likely) that such a hypothesis will lead to an explanation of how the brain makes decisions or even how it proves mathematical theorems, as Hameroff and Penrose suggest. But even if it does, the theory is silent about how these processes might give rise to conscious experience. Indeed, the same problem arises with any theory of consciousness based only on physical processing.

The trouble is that physical theories are best suited to explaining why systems have a certain physical structure and how they perform various functions. Most problems in science have this form; to explain life, for example, we need to describe how a physical system can reproduce, adapt and metabolize. But consciousness is a different sort of problem entirely, as it goes beyond the scientific explanation of structure and function.

Of course, neuroscience is not irrelevant to the study of consciousness. For one, it may be able to reveal the nature of the neural correlate of consciousness—the brain processes most directly associated with conscious experience. It may even give a detailed correspondence between specific processes in the brain and related components of experience. But until we know why these processes give rise to conscious experience at all, we will not have crossed what philosopher Joseph Levine has called the explanatory gap between physical processes and consciousness. Making that leap will demand a new kind of theory.

In searching for an alternative, a key observation is that not all entities in science are explained in terms of more basic entities. In physics, for example, space–time, mass and charge (among other things) are regarded as fundamental features of the world, as they are not reducible to anything simpler. Despite this irreducibility, detailed and useful theories relate these entities to one another in terms of fundamental laws. Together these features and laws explain a great variety of complex and subtle phenomena.

A TRUE THEORY OF EVERYTHING

It is widely believed that physics provides a complete catalogue of the universe's fundamental features and laws. As physicist Steven Weinberg puts it in his 1992 book *Dreams of a Final Theory*, the goal of physics is a "theory of everything" from which all there is to know about the universe can be derived. But Weinberg concedes that there is a problem with consciousness. Despite the power of physical theory, the existence of consciousness does not seem to be derivable from physical laws. He defends physics by arguing that it might eventually explain what he calls the objective correlates of consciousness (that is, the neural correlates), but of course to do this is not to explain consciousness itself. If the existence of consciousness cannot be derived from physical laws, a theory of physics is not a true theory of everything. So a final theory must contain an additional fundamental component.

Toward this end, I propose that conscious experience be considered a fundamental feature, irreducible to anything more basic. The idea may seem strange at first, but consistency seems to demand it. In the 19th century it turned out that electromagnetic phenomena could not be explained in terms of previously known principles. As a consequence, scientists introduced electromagnetic charge as a new fundamental entity and studied the associated fundamental laws. Similar reasoning should be applied to consciousness. If existing fundamental theories cannot encompass it, then something new is required.

Where there is a fundamental property, there are fundamental laws. In this case, the laws must relate experience to elements of physical theory. These laws will almost certainly not interfere with those of the physical world; it seems that the latter form a closed system in their own right. Rather the laws will serve as a bridge, specifying how experience depends on underlying physical processes. It is this bridge that will cross the explanatory gap.

Thus, a complete theory will have two components: physical laws, telling us about the behavior of physical systems from the infinitesimal to the cosmological, and what we might call psychophysical laws, telling us how some of those systems are associated with conscious experience. These two components will constitute a true theory of everything.

Supposing for the moment that they exist, how might we uncover such psycho-physical laws? The greatest hindrance in this pursuit will be a lack of data. As I have described it, consciousness is subjective, so there is no direct way to monitor it in others. But this difficulty is an obstacle, not a dead end. For a start, each one of us has access to our own experiences, a rich treasure-trove that can be used to formulate theories. We can also plausibly rely on indirect information, such as subjects' descriptions of their experiences. Philosophical arguments and thought experiments also have a role to play. Such methods have limitations, but they give us more than enough to get started.

These theories will not be conclusively testable, so they will inevitably be more speculative than those of more conventional scientific disciplines. Nevertheless, there is no reason they should not be strongly constrained to account accurately for our own first-person experiences, as well as the evidence from subjects' reports. If we find a theory that fits the data better than any other theory of equal simplicity, we will have good reason to accept it. Right now we do not have even a single theory that fits the data, so worries about testability are premature.

We might start by looking for high-level bridging laws, connecting physical processes to experience at an everyday level. The basic contour of such a law might be gleaned from the observation that when we are conscious of something, we are generally able to act on it and speak about it—which are objective, physical functions. Conversely, when some information is directly available for action and speech, it is generally conscious. Thus, consciousness correlates well with what we might call "awareness": the process by which information in the brain is made globally available to motor processes such as speech and bodily action.

OBJECTIVE AWARENESS

The notion may seem trivial. But as defined here, awareness is objective and physical, whereas consciousness is not. Some refinements to the definition of awareness are needed, in order to extend the concept to animals and infants, which cannot speak. But at least in familiar cases, it is possible to see the rough outlines of a psychophysical law: where there is awareness, there is consciousness, and vice versa.

To take this line of reasoning a step further, consider the structure present in the conscious experience. The experience of a field of vision, for example, is a constantly changing mosaic of colors, shapes and patterns and as such has a detailed geometric structure. The fact that we can describe this structure, reach out in the direction of many of its components and perform other actions that depend on it suggests that the structure corresponds directly to that of the information made available in the brain through the neural processes of objective awareness.

Similarly, our experiences of color have an intrinsic three-dimensional structure that is mirrored in the structure of information processes in the brain's visual cortex. This structure is illustrated in the color wheels and charts used by artists. Colors are arranged in a systematic pattern—red to green on one axis, blue to yellow on another, and black to white on a third. Colors that are close to one another on a color wheel are experienced as similar. It is extremely likely that they also correspond to similar perceptual representations in the brain, as one part of a system of complex three-dimensional coding among neurons that is not yet fully understood. We can recast the underlying concept as a principle of structural coherence: the structure of conscious experience is mirrored by the structure of information in awareness, and vice versa.

Another candidate for a psychophysical law is a principle of organizational invariance. It holds that physical systems with the same abstract organization will give rise to the same kind of conscious experience, no matter what they are made of. For example, if the precise interactions between our neurons could be duplicated with silicon chips, the same conscious experience would arise. The idea is somewhat controversial, but I believe it is strongly supported by thought experiments describing the gradual replacement of neurons by silicon chips. The remarkable implication is that consciousness might someday be achieved in machines.

THEORY OF CONSCIOUSNESS

The ultimate goal of a theory of consciousness is a simple and elegant set of fundamental laws, analogous to the fundamental laws of physics. The principles described above are unlikely to be fundamental, however. Rather they seem to be high-level psychophysical laws, analogous to macroscopic principles in physics such as those of thermodynamics or kinematics. What might the underlying fundamental laws be? No one really knows, but I don't mind speculating.

DANCING QUALIA IN A SYNTHETIC BRAIN

Whether consciousness could arise in a complex, synthetic system is a question many people find intrinsically fascinating. Although it may be decades or even centuries before such a system is built, a simple thought experiment offers strong evidence that an artificial brain, if organized appropriately, would indeed have precisely the same kind of conscious experiences as a human being.

Consider a silicon-based system in which the chips are organized and function in the same way as the neurons in your brain. That is, each chip in the silicon system does exactly what its natural analogue does and is interconnected to surrounding elements in precisely the same way. Thus, the behavior exhibited by the artificial system will be exactly the same as yours. The crucial question is: Will it be conscious in the same way that you are?

Let us assume, for the purpose of argument, that it would not be. (Here we use a reasoning technique known as reductio ad absurdum, in which the opposite hypothesis is assumed and then shown to lead to an untenable conclusion.) That is, it has either different experiences—an experience of blue, say, when you are seeing red—or no experience at all. We will consider the first case; the reasoning proceeds similarly in both cases.

Because chips and neurons have the same function, they are interchangeable, with the proper interfacing. Chips therefore can replace neurons, producing a continuum of cases in which a successively larger proportion of neurons are replaced by chips. Along this continuum, the conscious experience of the system will also change. For example, we might replace all the neurons in your visual cortex with an identically organized version made of silicon. The resulting brain, with an artificial visual cortex, will have a different conscious experience from the original: where you had previously seen red, you may now experience purple (or perhaps a faded pink, in the case where the wholly silicon system has no experience at all).

Both visual cortices are then attached to your brain, through a two-position switch. With the switch in one mode, you use the natural visual cortex; in the other, the artificial cortex is activated. When the switch is flipped, your experience changes from red to purple, or vice versa. When the switch is flipped repeatedly, your experiences "dance" between the two different conscious states (red and purple), known as qualia.

Because your brain's organization has not changed, however, there can be no behavioral change when the switch is thrown. Therefore, when asked about what you are seeing, you will say that nothing has changed. You will hold that you are seeing red and have seen nothing but red—even though the two colors are dancing before your eyes. This conclusion is so unreasonable that it is best taken as a reductio ad absurdum of the original assumption—that an artificial system with identical organization and functioning has a different conscious experience from that of a neural brain. Retraction of the assumption establishes the opposite: that systems with the same organization have the same conscious experience.

I suggest that the primary psychophysical laws may centrally involve the concept of information. The abstract notion of information, as put forward in the 1940s by Claude E. Shannon of the Massachusetts Institute of Technology, is that of a set of separate states with a basic structure of similarities and differences between them. We can think of a 10-bit binary code as an information state, for example. Such information states can be embodied in the physical world. This happens whenever they correspond to physical states (voltages, say) and when differences between them can be transmitted along some pathway, such as a telephone line.

We can also find information embodied in conscious experience. The pattern of color patches in a visual field, for example, can be seen as analogous to that of the pixels covering a display screen. Intriguingly, it turns out that we find the same information states embedded in conscious experience and in underlying physical processes in the brain. The three-dimensional encoding of color spaces, for example, suggests that the information state in a color experience corresponds directly to an information state in the brain. Thus, we might even regard the two states as distinct aspects of a single information state, which is simultaneously embodied in both physical processing and conscious experience.

A natural hypothesis ensues. Perhaps information, or at least some information, has two basic aspects: a physical one and an experiential one. This hypothesis has the status of a fundamental principle that might underlie the relation between physical processes and experience. Wherever we find conscious experience, it exists as one aspect of an information state, the other aspect of which is embedded in a physical process in the brain. This proposal needs to be fleshed out to make a satisfying theory. But it fits nicely with the principles mentioned earlier—systems with the same organization will embody the same information, for example—and it could explain numerous features of our conscious experience.

The idea is at least compatible with several others, such as physicist John A. Wheeler's suggestion that information is fundamental to the physics of the universe. The laws of physics might ultimately be cast in informational terms, in which case we would have a satisfying congruence between the constructs in both physical and psychophysical laws. It may even be that a theory of physics and a theory of consciousness could eventually be consolidated into a single grander theory of information.

A potential problem is posed by the ubiquity of information. Even a thermostat embodies some information, for example, but is it conscious? There are at least two possible responses. First, we could constrain the fundamental laws so that only some information has an experiential aspect, perhaps depending on how it is physically processed. Second, we might bite the bullet and allow that all information has an experiential aspect—where there is complex information processing, there is complex experience, and where there is simple information processing, there is simple experience. If this is so, then even a thermostat might have experiences, although they would be much simpler than even a basic color experience, and there would certainly be no accompanying emotions or thoughts. This seems odd at first, but if experience is truly fundamental, we might expect it to be widespread. In any case, the choice between these alternatives should depend on which can be integrated into the most powerful theory.

Of course, such ideas may be all wrong. On the other hand, they might evolve into a more powerful proposal that predicts the precise structure of our conscious experience from physical processes in our brains. If this project succeeds, we will have good reason to accept the theory. If it fails, other avenues will be pursued, and alternative fundamental theories may be developed. In this way, we may one day resolve the greatest mystery of the mind.

WHY NEUROSCIENCE MAY BE ABLE TO EXPLAIN CONSCIOUSNESS

By Francis Crick and Christof Koch

We believe that at the moment the best approach to the problem of explaining consciousness is to concentrate on finding what is known as the neural correlates of consciousness—the processes in the brain that are most directly responsible for consciousness. By locating the neurons in the cerebral cortex that correlate best with consciousness, and figuring out how they link to neurons elsewhere in the brain, we may come across key insights into what David J. Chalmers calls the hard problem: a full accounting of the manner in which subjective experience arises from these cerebral processes.

We commend Chalmers for boldly recognizing and focusing on the hard problem at this early stage, although we are not as enthusiastic about some of his thought experiments. As we see it, the hard problem can be broken down into several questions: Why do we experience anything at all? What leads to a particular conscious experience (such as the blueness of blue)? Why are some aspects of subjective experience impossible to convey to other people (in other words, why are they private)? We believe we have an answer to the last problem and a suggestion about the first two, revolving around a phenomenon known as explicit neuronal representation.

What does "explicit" mean in this context? Perhaps the best way to define it is with an example. In response to the image of a face, say, ganglion cells fire all over the retina, much like the pixels on a television screen, to generate an implicit representation of the face. At the same time, they can also respond to a great many other features in the image, such as shadows, lines, uneven lighting and so on. In contrast, some neurons high in the hierarchy of the visual cortex respond mainly to the face or even to the face viewed at a particular angle. Such neurons help the brain represent the face in an explicit manner. Their loss, resulting from a stroke or some other brain injury, leads to prosopagnosia, an individual's inability to recognize familiar faces consciously—even his or her own, although the person can still identify a face as a face. Similarly, damage to other parts of the visual cortex can cause someone to lose the ability to experience color, while still seeing in shades of black and white, even though there is no defect in the color receptors in the eye.

Figure 3.1 KANIZSA TRIANGLE stimulates neurons that code explicitly for such illusory contours.

At each stage, visual information is reencoded, typically in a semihierarchical manner. Retinal ganglion cells respond to a spot of light. Neurons in the primary visual cortex are most adept at responding to lines or edges; neurons higher up might prefer a moving contour. Still higher are those that respond to faces and other familiar objects. On top are those that project to pre-motor and motor structures in the brain, where they fire the neurons that initiate such actions as speaking or avoiding an oncoming automobile.

Chalmers believes, as we do, that the subjective aspects of an experience must relate closely to the firing of the neurons corresponding to those aspects (the neural correlates). He describes a well-known thought experiment, constructed around a hypothetical neuroscientist, Mary, who specializes in color perception but has never seen a color. We believe the reason Mary does not know what it is like to see a color, however, is that she has never had an explicit neural representation of a color in her brain, only of the words and ideas associated with colors.

In order to describe a subjective visual experience, the information has to be transmitted to the motor output stage of the brain, where it becomes available for verbalization or other actions. This transmission always involves reencoding the information, so that the explicit information expressed by the motor neurons is related, but not identical, to the explicit information expressed by the firing of the neurons associated with color experience, at some level in the visual hierarchy.

It is not possible, then, to convey with words and ideas the exact nature of a subjective experience. It is possible, however, to convey a difference between subjective experiences—to distinguish between red and orange, for example. This is possible because a difference in a high-level visual cortical area will still be associated with a difference in the motor stages. The implication is that we can never explain to other people the subjective nature of any conscious experience, only its relation to other ones.

The other two questions, concerning why we have conscious experiences and what leads to specific ones, appear more difficult. Chalmers proposes that they require the introduction of "experience" as a fundamental new feature of the world, relating to the ability of an organism to process information. But which types of neuronal information produce consciousness? And what makes a certain type of information correspond to the blueness of blue, rather than the greenness of green? Such problems seem as difficult as any in the study of consciousness.

We prefer an alternative approach, involving the concept of "meaning." In what sense can neurons that explicitly code for a face be said to convey the meaning of a face to the rest of the brain? Such a property must relate to the cells' projective field—the pattern of synaptic connections to neurons that code explicitly for related concepts. Ultimately, these connections extend to the motor output. For example, neurons responding to a certain face might be connected to ones expressing the name of the person whose face it is and to others for her voice, memories involving her and so on. Such associations among neurons must be behaviorally useful—in other words, consistent with feedback from the body and the external world.

Meaning derives from the linkages among these representations with others spread throughout the cortical system in a vast associational network, similar to a dictionary or a relational database. The more diverse these connections, the richer the meaning. If, as in our previous example of prosopagnosia, the synaptic output of such face neurons were blocked, the cells would still respond to the person's face, but there would be no associated meaning and, therefore, much less experience. Therefore, a face would be seen but not recognized as such.

Of course, groups of neurons can take on new functions, allowing brains to learn new categories (including faces) and associate new categories with existing ones. Certain primitive associations, such as pain, are to some extent inborn but subsequently refined in life.

Information may indeed be the key concept, as Chalmers suspects. Greater certainty will require consideration of highly parallel streams of information, linked—as are neurons—in complex networks. It would be useful to try to determine what features a neural network (or some other such computational embodiment) must have to generate meaning. It is possible that such exercises will suggest the neural basis of meaning. The hard problem of consciousness may then appear in an entirely new light. It might even disappear.

4

THE HORNSWOGGLE PROBLEM[1]

Patricia S. Churchland

I INTRODUCTION

Conceptualizing a problem so we can ask the right questions and design revealing experiments is crucial to discovering a satisfactory solution to the problem. Asking where animal spirits are concocted, for example, turns out not to be the right question to ask about the heart. When Harvey asked instead, 'How much blood does the heart pump in an hour?', he conceptualized the problem of heart function very differently. The reconceptualization was pivotal in coming to understand that the heart is really a pump for circulating blood; there are no animal spirits to concoct. My strategy here, therefore, is to take the label, 'The Hard Problem' (Chalmers, 1995) in a constructive spirit – as an attempt to provide a useful conceptualization concerning the very nature of consciousness that could help steer us in the direction of a solution. My remarks will focus mainly on whether in fact anything positive is to be gained from the 'hard problem' characterization, or whether that conceptualization is counterproductive.

I cannot hope to do full justice to the task in short compass, especially as this characterization of the problem of consciousness has a rather large literature surrounding it. The watershed articulation of this view of the problem is Thomas Nagel's classic paper 'What is it like to be a bat?' (1974). In his opening remarks. Nagel comes straight to the point: 'Consciousness is what makes the mind–body problem really intractable.' Delineating a contrast between the problem of consciousness and all other mind–body problems, Nagel asserts: 'While an account of the physical basis of mind must explain many things, this [conscious experience] appears to be the most difficult.' Following Nagel's lead, many other philosophers, including Frank Jackson, Saul Kripke, Colin McGinn, John Searle, and most recently, David Chalmers, have extended and developed Nagel's basic idea that consciousness is not tractable neuroscientifically.

Although I agree that consciousness is, certainly, *a* difficult problem, difficulty *per se* does not distinguish it from oodles of other neuroscientific problems. Such as how the brains of homeotherms keep a constant internal temperature despite varying external conditions. Such as the brain basis for schizophrenia and autism. Such as why we dream and sleep. Supposedly, something sets consciousness apart from *all* other macro-function brain riddles such that it stands alone as The Hard Problem. As I have tried to probe precisely what that is, I find my reservations multiplying.

II CARVING UP THE PROBLEM SPACE

The 'Hard Problem' label invites us to adopt a principled empirical division between consciousness (the hard problem) and problems on the 'easy' (or perhaps hard but not Hard?) side of the ledger. The latter presumably encompass problems such as the nature of short-term memory, long-term memory, autobiographical memory, the nature of representation, the nature of sensori-motor integration, top-down effects in perception – not to mention such capacities as attention, depth perception, intelligent eye movement, skill acquisition, planning, decision-making, and so forth. On the other side of the ledger, all on its own, stands consciousness – a uniquely hard problem.

My lead-off reservation arises from this question: what is the rationale for drawing the division exactly there? Dividing off consciousness from all of the so-called 'easy problems' listed above implies that we could understand all those phenomena and still not know *what it was for* ... what? The 'qualia-light' to go on? Is *that* an insightful conceptualization? What exactly is the evidence that we could explain all the 'easy' phenomena and still not understand the neural mechanisms for conscious-ness? (Call this the 'left-out' hypothesis.) That someone can *imagine* the possibility is not *evidence* for the real possibility. It is only evidence that somebody or other *believes* it to be a possibility. That, on its own, is not especially interesting. Imaginary evidence, needless to say, is not as interesting as real evidence, and what needs to be produced is some real evidence.[2]

The left-out hypothesis – that consciousness would still be a mystery, even if we could explain all the easy problems – is dubious on another count: it begs the ques-tion against those theories that are exploring the possibility that functions such as attention and short-term memory are crucial elements in consciousness (see especially Crick 1994; P.M. Churchland 1995). The rationale sustaining this approach stems from observations such as that awake persons can be unaware of stimuli to which they are not paying attention, but can become aware of those stimuli when attention shifts. There is a vast psychological literature, and a nontrivial neuroscientific lit-erature, on this topic. Some of it powerfully suggests that attention and awareness are pretty closely connected. The approach might of course be wrong, for it is an empirical conjecture. But if it is wrong, it is wrong because of the *facts*, not because of an arm-chair definition. The trouble with the 'hard problem' characterization is that *on the strength of a proprietary definition*, it rejects them as wrong. I do find that unappealing, since the nature of consciousness is an empirical problem, not a problem that can be untangled by semantic gerrymandering.

What drives the left-out hypothesis? Essentially, a thought-experiment, which roughly goes as follows: we can conceive of a person, like us in all the aforementioned easy-to-explain capacities (attention, short term memory, etc.), but lacking qualia. This person would be *exactly* like us, save that he would be a Zombie – an anaqualiac, one might say. Since the scenario is conceivable, it is possible, and since it is possible, then whatever consciousness is, it is explanatorily independent of those activities.[3]

I take this argument to be a demonstration of the feebleness of thought-experiments. *Saying* something is possible does not thereby guarantee it *is* a possibility, so how do we know the anaqualiac idea is really possible? To insist that it must be is simply to beg the question at issue. As Francis Crick has observed, it might be like saying that one can imagine a possible world where gases do not get hot, even though their constituent molecules are moving at high velocity. As an argument against the empirical identification of temperature with mean molecular KE, the thermodynamic thought-experiment is feebleness itself.

Is the problem on the 'hard' side of the ledger sufficiently well-defined to sustain the division as a fundamental empirical principle? Although it is easy enough to agree about the presence of qualia in certain prototypical cases, such as the pain felt after a brick has fallen on a bare foot, or the blueness of the sky on a sunny summer afternoon, things are less clear-cut once we move beyond the favoured prototypes. Some of our perceptual capacities are rather subtle, as, for example, positional sense is often claimed to be. Some philosophers, e.g. Elizabeth Anscombe, have actually opined that we can know the position of our limbs without any 'limb-position' qualia. As for me, I am inclined to say I do have qualitative experiences of where my limbs are – it feels different to have my fingers clenched than unclenched, even when they are not visible. The disagreement itself, however, betokens the lack of consensus once cases are at some remove from the central prototypes.

Vestibular system qualia are yet another non-prototypical case. Is there something 'vestibular-y' it feels like to have my head moving? To know which way is up? Whatever the answer here, at least the answer is not glaringly obvious. Do eye movements have eye-movement qualia? Some maybe do, and some maybe do not. Are there 'introspective qualia', or is introspection just paying attention to perceptual qualia and talking to yourself? Ditto, plus or minus a bit, for self-awareness. Thoughts are also a bit problematic in the qualia department. Some of my thoughts seem to me to be a bit like talking to myself and hence like auditory imagery but some just come out of my mouth as I am talking to someone or affect decisions without ever surfacing as a bit of inner dialogue. None of this is to deny the pizzazz of qualia in the prototypical cases. Rather, the point is just that prototypical cases give us only a *starting point* for further investigation, and nothing like a full characterization of the class to which they belong.

My suspicion with respect to The Hard Problem strategy is that it seems to take the class of conscious experiences to be much better defined than it is. The point is, if you are careful to restrict your focus to the prototypical cases, you can easily be hornswoggled into assuming the class is well-defined. As soon as you broaden your horizons, troublesome questions about fuzzy boundaries, about the connections between attention, short term memory and awareness, are present in full, what-do-we-do-with-*that* glory.

Are the easy problems known to be easier than The Hard Problem? Is the hard/easy division grounded in fact? To begin with, it is important to acknowledge that for none of the so-called 'easy' problems, do we have an understanding of their solution (see the partial list on **p. 28**). It is just false that we have anything approximating a comprehensive theory of sensori-motor control or attention or short-term memory or long-term memory. Consider one example. A signature is recognizably the same whether signed with the dominant or non-dominant hand, with the foot, with the mouth or with the pen strapped to the shoulder. How is 'my signature' represented in the nervous system? How can completely different muscle sets be invoked to do the task, even when the skill was not acquired using those muscles? We do not understand the general nature of motor representation.

Notice that it is not merely that we are lacking details, albeit important details. The fact is, we are lacking important conceptual/theoretical ideas about how the nervous system performs fundamental functions – such as time management, such as motor control, such as learning, such as information retrieval. We do not understand the role of back projections, or the degree to which processing is organized hierarchically. These are genuine puzzles, and it is unwise to 'molehill' them in order to 'mountain' up the problem of consciousness. Although quite a lot is known at the cellular level, the fact remains that how real neural networks work and how their output properties depend on cellular properties still abounds with nontrivial mysteries. Naturally I do not wish to minimize the progress that has been made in neuroscience, but it is prudent to have a cautious assessment of what we really do not yet understand.

Carving the explanatory space of mind–brain phenomena along the hard and the easy line, as Chalmers proposes, poses the danger of inventing an explanatory chasm where there really exists just a broad field of ignorance. It reminds me of the division, deep to medieval physicists, between sublunary physics (motion of things below the level of the moon) and superlunary physics (motion of things above the level of the moon). The conviction was that sublunary physics was tractable, and it is essentially based on Aristotelian physics. Heavy things fall because they have gravity, and fall to their natural place, namely the earth, which is the centre of the universe. Things like smoke have levity, and consequently they rise, *up* being their natural place. Everything in the sublunary realm has a 'natural place', and that is the key to explaining the behaviour of sublunary objects. Superlunary events, by contrast, we can neither explain nor understand, but in any case, they have neither the gravity nor levity typical of sublunary things.

This old division was not without merit, and it did entail that events such as planetary motion and meteors were considered unexplainable in terrestrial terms, but probably were divinely governed. Although I do not know that Chalmers' easy/hard distinction will prove ultimately as misdirected as the sublunary/superlunary distinction, neither do I know it is any more sound. What I do suspect, however, is that it is much too early in the science of nervous systems to command much credence.

The danger inherent in embracing the distinction as a principled empirical distinction is that it provokes the intuition that only a real humdinger of a solution will suit The Hard Problem. Thus the idea seems to go as follows: the answer, if it comes at all, is going to have to come from somewhere Really Deep – like quantum mechanics – or perhaps it requires a whole new physics. As the lone enigma, consciousness surely cannot be just a matter of a complex dynamical system doing its thing. Yes, there are emergent properties from nervous systems such as co-ordinated movement as when an owl catches a mouse, but consciousness (the hard problem) is an emergent property like unto no other. Consequently, it will require a very deep, very radical solution. That much is evident sheerly from the hardness of The Hard Problem.

I confess I cannot actually see that. I do not know anything like enough to see how to solve either the problem of sensori-motor control or the problem of consciousness. I certainly cannot see enough to know that one problem will, and the other will not, require a Humdinger solution.

III USING IGNORANCE AS A PREMISE

In general, what substantive conclusions can be drawn when science has not advanced very far on a problem? Not much. One of the basic skills we teach our philosophy students is how to recognize and diagnose the range of nonformal fallacies that can undermine an ostensibly appealing argument: what it is to beg the question, what a *non sequitur* is, and so on. A prominent item in the fallacy roster is *argumentum ad ignorantiam* – argument from ignorance. The canonical version of this fallacy uses ignorance as the key premise from which a substantive conclusion is drawn. The canonical version looks like this:

We really do not understand much about a phenomenon *P*. (Science is largely ignorant about the nature of *P*.)

Therefore: we *do* know that:

(1)   *P* can never be explained, or
(2)   Nothing science could ever discover would deepen our understanding of *P*, or
(3)   *P* can never be explained in terms of properties of kind *S*.

In its canonical version, the argument is obviously a fallacy: none of the tendered conclusions follow, not even a little bit. Surrounded with rhetorical flourish, much brow furrowing and hand wringing, however, versions of this argument can hornswoggle the unwary.

From the fact that we do not know something, nothing very interesting follows – we just don't know. Nevertheless, the temptation to suspect that our ignorance is telling us something positive, something deep, something metaphysical or even radical, is ever-present. Perhaps we like to put our ignorance in a positive light, supposing that but for the Profundity of the phenomenon, we *would* have knowledge. But there are many reasons for not knowing, and the specialness of the phenomenon is, quite regularly, not the real reason. I am currently ignorant of what caused an unusual rapping noise in the woods last night. Can I conclude it must be something special, something unimaginable, something ... alien ... other-worldly? Evidently not. For all I can tell now, it might merely have been a raccoon gnawing on the compost bin. Lack of evidence for something is just that: lack of evidence. It is not positive evidence for something else, let alone something of a humdingerish sort. That conclusion is not very glamorous perhaps, but when ignorance is a premise, that is about all you can grind out of it.

Now if neuroscience had progressed as far on the problems of brain function as molecular biology has progressed on transmission of hereditary traits, then of course we would be in a different position. But it has not. The only thing you can conclude from the fact that attention is mysterious, or sensori-motor integration is mysterious, or that consciousness is mysterious, is that we do not understand the mechanisms.

Moreover, the mysteriousness of a problem is not a fact about the problem, it is not a metaphysical feature of the universe – it is an epistemological fact about *us*. It is about where we are in current science, it is about what we can and cannot understand, it is about what, given the rest of our understanding, we can and cannot imagine. It is not a property of the problem itself.

It is sometimes assumed that there can be a valid transition from 'we cannot now explain' to 'we can never explain', so long as we have the help of a subsidiary premise, namely, 'I cannot *imagine* how we could ever explain ...' But it does *not* help, and this transition remains a straight-up application of argument from ignorance.

Adding 'I cannot imagine explaining *P*' merely adds a psychological fact about the speaker, from which again, nothing significant follows about the nature of the phenomenon in question. Whether we can or cannot imagine a phenomenon being explained in a certain way is a psychological fact about us, not an objective fact about the nature of the phenomenon itself. To repeat: it is an epistemological fact about what, given our current knowledge, we can and cannot understand. It is not a metaphysical fact about the nature of the reality of the universe.

Typical of vitalists generally, my high school biology teacher argued for vitalism thus: I cannot *imagine* how you could get living things out of dead molecules. Out of bits of proteins, fats, sugars – how could life itself emerge? He thought it was obvious from the sheer mysteriousness of the matter that it could have no solution in biology or chemistry. He assumed he could tell that it would require a Humdinger solution. Typical of lone survivors, a passenger of a crashed plane will say: I cannot imagine how I alone could have survived the crash, when all other passengers died instantly. Therefore God must have plucked me from the jaws of death.

Given that neuroscience is still very much in its early stages, it is actually not a very interesting fact that someone or other cannot imagine a certain kind of explanation of some brain phenomenon. Aristotle could not imagine how a complex organism could come from a fertilized egg. That of course was a fact about Aristotle, not a fact about embryogenesis. Given the early days of science (500 BC), it is no surprise that he could not imagine what it took many scientists hundreds of years to discover. I cannot imagine how ravens can solve a multi-step problem in one trial, or how temporal integration is achieved, or how thermoregulation is managed. But this is a (*not very interesting*) psychological fact about me. One could, of course, use various rhetorical devices to make it seem like an interesting fact about me, perhaps by emphasizing that it is a really really hard problem; but if we are going to be sensible about this, it is clear that my inability to imagine how thermoregulation works is *au fond*, pretty boring.

The 'I-cannot-imagine' gambit suffers in another way. Being able to imagine an explanation for *P* is a highly open-ended and under-specified business. Given the poverty of delimiting conditions of the operation, you can pretty much rig the conclusion to go whichever way your heart desires. Logically, however, that flexibility is the kiss of death.

Suppose someone claims that she *can* imagine the mechanisms for sensori-motor integration in the human brain but *cannot* imagine the mechanisms for consciousness. What exactly does this difference amount to? Can she imagine the former in *detail*? No, because the details are not known. What is it, precisely, that she can imagine? Suppose she answers that in a very general way she imagines that sensory neurons interact with interneurons that interact with motor neurons, and via these interactions, sensori-motor integration is achieved. Now if that is all 'being able to imagine' takes, one might as well say one can imagine the mechanisms underlying consciousness. Thus: 'The interneurons do it.' The point is this: if you want to contrast being able to imagine brain mechanisms for attention, short-term memory, planning etc., with being unable to imagine mechanisms for consciousness, you have to do more than say you can imagine neurons doing one but cannot imagine neurons doing the other. Otherwise one simply begs the question.

To fill out the point, consider several telling examples from the history of science. Before the turn of the twentieth century, people thought that the problem of the precession of the perihelion of Mercury was essentially trivial. It was annoying, but ultimately, it would sort itself out as more data came in. With the advantage of hindsight, we can see that assessing this as an easy problem was quite wrong – it took the Einsteinian revolution in physics to solve the problem of the precession of the perihelion of Mercury. By contrast, a really hard problem was thought to be the composition of the stars. How could a sample ever be obtained? With the advent of spectral analysis, that turned out to be a readily solvable problem. When heated, the elements turn out to have a kind of fingerprint, easily seen when light emitted from a source is passed through a prism.

Consider now a biological example. Before 1953, many people believed, on rather good grounds actually, that in order to address the copying problem (transmission of traits from parents to offspring), you would first have to solve the problem of how proteins fold. The former was deemed a much harder problem than the latter, and many scientists believed it was foolhardy to attack the copying problem directly. As we all know now, the basic answer to the copying problem lay in the base-pairing of DNA, and it was solved first. Humbling it is to realize that the problem of protein folding (secondary and tertiary) is *still* not solved. *That*, given the lot we now know, does seem to be a hard problem.

What is the point of these stories? They reinforce the message of the argument from ignorance: from the vantage point of ignorance, it is often very difficult to tell which problem is harder, which will fall first, what problem will turn out to be more tractable than some other. Consequently our judgments about relative difficulty or ultimate tractability should be appropriately qualified and tentative. Guesswork has a useful place, of course, but let's distinguish between blind guesswork and educated guesswork, and between guesswork and confirmed fact. The philosophical lesson I learned from my biology teacher is this: when not much is known about a topic, don't take terribly seriously someone else's heartfelt conviction about what problems are scientifically tractable. Learn the science, do the science, and see what happens.

NOTES

1   This paper is based on a talk I presented at the 'Tucson II' conference, 'Toward a Science of Consciousness' held at Tucson, Arizona, in April 1996. Many thanks are owed to the

organizers of the meeting, and thanks also to Paul Churchland, David Rosenthal, Rodolfo Llinás, Michael Stack, Dan Dennett, Ilya Farber and Joe Ramsay for advice and ideas.

2   As I lacked time in my talk at Tucson to address the 'Mary' problem, a problem first formulated by Frank Jackson in 1982, let me make several brief remarks about it here. In sum, Jackson's idea was that there could exist someone, call her Mary, who knew everything there was to know about how the brain works but still did not know what it was to see the colour green (suppose she lacked 'green cones', to put it crudely). This possibility Jackson took to show that qualia are therefore not explainable by science. The main problem with the argument is that to experience green qualia, certain wiring has to be in place in Mary's brain, and certain patterns of activity have to obtain and since, by Jackson's own hypothesis, she does not have that wiring, then presumably the relevant activity patterns in visual cortex are not caused and she does not experience green. Who would expect her visual cortex – V4, say – would be set ahumming just by virtue of her *propositional* (linguistic) knowledge about activity patterns in V4? Not me, anyhow. She can have propositional knowledge via other channels, of course, including the knowledge of what her own brain lacks *vis à vis* green qualia. Nothing whatever follows about whether science can or cannot explain qualia.

3   Something akin to this was argued by Saul Kripke in the 1970s.

REFERENCES

Chalmers, David J. (1995), 'Facing up to the problem of consciousness', *Journal of Consciousness Studies* 2 (3), pp. 200–19.

Churchland, Paul M. (1995), *The Engine of Reason, The Seat of the Soul* (Cambridge, MA: MIT Press).

Crick, Francis (1994), *The Astonishing Hypothesis* (New York: Scribner and Sons).

Jackson, Frank (1982), 'Epiphenomenal qualia', *Philosophical Quarterly* 32, pp. 127–36.

Nagel, Thomas (1974), 'What is it like to be a bat?', *Philosophical Review* 83, pp. 435–50.

5

THE INCOMPLETENESS OF OBJECTIVE REALITY

Thomas Nagel

1 PHYSICAL OBJECTIVITY

The natural place to begin is with our own position in the world. One of the strongest philosophical motives is the desire for a comprehensive picture of objective reality, since it is easy to assume that that is all there really is. But the very idea of objective reality guarantees that such a picture will not comprehend everything; we ourselves are the first obstacles to such an ambition.

To the extent that the world is objectively comprehensible—comprehensible from a standpoint independent of the constitution of this or that sentient being or type of sentient being—how do sentient beings fit into it? The question can be divided into three parts. First, does the mind itself have an objective character? Second, what is its relation to those physical aspects of reality whose objective status is less doubtful? Third, how can it be the case that one of the people in the world is *me*?

I shall take up these questions in order, in this chapter and the two following. [The following chapters are not included here - eds.] The second question is the mind–body problem. The third question, how it is possible to be anyone in particular, expresses in purest form the difficulty of finding room in the world for oneself. How can it be? Am I, or are you, really the sort of thing that could be one of the particular creatures in the world? But I shall begin with the first question—whether the mind itself can be objectively understood. It underlies the mind–body problem, which arises because certain features of mental life present an obstacle to the ambitions of one very important conception of objectivity. No progress can be made with the mind–body problem unless we understand this conception and examine its claims with care.

For convenience I shall refer to it as the *physical* conception of objectivity. It is not the same thing as our idea of what physical reality is actually like, but it has developed as part of our method of arriving at a truer understanding of the physical world, a world that is presented to us initially but somewhat inaccurately through sensory perception.

The development goes in stages, each of which gives a more objective picture than the one before. The first step is to see that our perceptions are caused by the action of things on us, through their effects on our bodies, which are themselves parts of the physical world. The next step is to realize that since the same physical properties that cause perceptions in us through our bodies also produce different effects on other physical things and can exist without causing any perceptions at all, their true nature must be detachable from their perceptual appearance and need not resemble it. The third step is to try to form a conception of that true nature independent of its appearance either to us or to other types of perceivers. This means not only not thinking of the physical world from our own particular point of view, but not thinking of it from a more general human perceptual point of view either: not thinking of how it looks, feels, smells, tastes, or sounds. These secondary qualities then drop out of our picture of the external world, and the underlying primary qualities such as shape, size, weight, and motion are thought of structurally.

This has turned out to be an extremely fruitful strategy. The understanding of the physical world has been expanded enormously with the aid of theories and explanations that use concepts not tied to the specifically human perceptual viewpoint. Our senses provide the evidence from which we start, but the detached character of this understanding is such that we could possess it even if we had none of our present senses, so long as we were rational and could understand the mathematical and formal properties of the objective conception of the physical world. We might even in a sense share an understanding of physics with other creatures to whom things appeared quite different, perceptually—so long as they too were rational and numerate.

The world described by this objective conception is not just centerless; it is also in a sense featureless. While the things in it have properties, none of these properties are perceptual aspects. All of those have been relegated to the mind, a yet-to-be-examined domain. The physical world as it is supposed to be in itself contains no points of view and nothing that can appear only to a particular point of view. Whatever it contains can be apprehended by a general rational consciousness that gets its information through whichever perceptual point of view it happens to view the world from.[1]

Powerful as it has proven to be, this bleached-out physical conception of objectivity encounters difficulties if it is put forward as the method for seeking a complete understanding of reality. For the process began when we noticed that how things appear to us depends on the interaction of our bodies with the rest of the world. But this leaves us with no account of the perceptions and specific viewpoints which were left behind as irrelevant to physics but which seem to exist nonetheless, along with those of other creatures—not to mention the mental activity of forming an objective conception of the physical world, which seems not itself capable of physical analysis.

Faced with these facts one might think the only conceivable conclusion would be that there is more to reality than what can be accommodated by the physical conception of objectivity. But remarkably enough this has not been obvious to everyone. The physical has been so irresistibly attractive, and has so dominated ideas of what there is, that attempts have been made to beat everything into its shape and deny the reality of anything that cannot be so reduced. As a result, the philosophy of mind is populated with extremely implausible positions.

I have argued elsewhere[2] against the various forms of reductionism—behavioristic, causal, or functionalist—that have been offered by those seeking to make the mind safe for physical objectivity. All these theories are motivated by an epistemological criterion of reality—that only what can be understood in a certain way exists. But it is hopeless to try to analyze mental phenomena so that they are revealed as part of the "external" world. The subjective features of conscious mental processes—as opposed to their physical causes and effects—cannot be captured by the purified form of thought suitable for dealing with the physical world that underlies the appearances. Not only raw feels but also intentional mental states—however objective their content—must be capable of manifesting themselves in subjective form to be in the mind at all.

The reductionist program that dominates current work in the philosophy of mind is completely misguided, because it is based on the groundless assumption that a particular conception of objective reality is exhaustive of what there is. Eventually, I believe, current attempts to understand the mind by analogy with man-made computers that can perform superbly some of the same external tasks as conscious beings will be recognized as a gigantic waste of time. The true principles underlying the mind will be discovered, if at all, only by a more direct approach.

But merely to deny the possibility of psychophysical reduction does not end the problem. There is still a question about how we are to conceive of the inclusion of subjective mental processes in the world as it really is. And there is the question of whether they can be in some other way objectively understood. Physicalism, though unacceptable, has behind it a broader impulse to which it gives distorted and ultimately self-defeating expression. That is the impulse to find a way of thinking about the world as it is, so that everything in it, not just atoms and planets, can be regarded as real in the same way: not just an aspect of the world as it appears to us, but something that is *really there*.

I think part of the explanation of the modern weakness for physicalist reduction is that a less impoverished and reductive idea of objectivity has not been available to fill out the project of constructing an overall picture of the world. The objectivity of physics was viable: it continued to yield progressively more understanding through successive application to those properties of the physical world that earlier applications had discovered.

It is true that recent developments in physics have led some to believe that it may after all be incapable of providing a conception of what is really there, independent of observation. But I do not wish to argue that since the idea of objective reality has to be abandoned because of quantum theory anyway, we might as well go the whole hog and admit the subjectivity of the mental. Even if, as some physicists think, quantum theory cannot be interpreted in a way that permits the phenomena to be described without reference to an observer, the ineliminable observer need not be a member of any particular species like the human, to whom things look and feel in highly characteristic ways. This does not therefore require that we let in the full range of subjective experience.

The central problem is not whether points of view must be admitted to the account of the *physical* world. Whatever may be the answer to that question, we shall still be faced with an independent problem about the mind. It is the phenomena of consciousness themselves that pose the clearest challenge to the idea that physical objectivity gives the general form of reality. In response I want not to abandon the idea of objectivity entirely but rather to suggest that the physical is not its only possible interpretation.

2 MENTAL OBJECTIVITY

Even if we acknowledge the existence of distinct and irreducible perspectives, the wish for a unified conception of the world doesn't go away. If we can't achieve it in a form that eliminates individual perspectives, we may inquire to what extent it can be achieved if we admit them. Persons and other conscious beings are part of the natural order, and their mental states are part of the way the world is in itself. From the perspective of one type of being, the subjective features of the mental states of a very different type of being are not accessible either through subjective imagination or through the kind of objective representation that captures the physical world. The question is whether these gaps can be at least partly closed by another form of thought, which acknowledges perspectives different from one's own and conceives of them not by means of the imagination. A being of total imaginative flexibility could project himself directly into every possible subjective point of view, and would not need such an objective method to think about the full range of possible inner lives. But since we can't do that, a more detached form of access to other subjective forms would be useful.

There is even a point to this in the case of our own minds. We assume that we ourselves are not just parts of the world as it appears to us. But if we are parts of the world as it is in itself, then we ought to be able to include ourselves—our minds as well as our bodies—in a conception that is not tied exclusively to our own point of view. We ought, in other words, to be able to think of ourselves from outside—but in mental, not physical terms. Such a result, if it were possible, would qualify as an objective concept of mind.

What I want to do is to explain what a natural objective understanding of the mind along these lines would be—an understanding as objective as is compatible with the essential subjectivity of the mental. I believe it has its beginnings in the ordinary concept of mind, but that it can be developed beyond this. The question is, how far beyond?

As a practical matter, I have no idea how far. But I believe that there is no objection in principle to such a development, and that its possibility should already be allowed for in our conception of our own minds. I believe we can include ourselves, experiences and all, in a world conceivable not from a specifically human point of view, and that we can do this without reducing the mental to the physical. But I also believe that any such conception will necessarily be incomplete. And this means that the pursuit of an objective conception of reality comes up against limits that are not merely practical, limits that could not be overcome by any merely objective intelligence, however powerful. Finally, I shall claim that this is no cause for philosophical alarm, because there is no reason to assume that the world as it is in itself must be objectively comprehensible, even in an extended sense. Some things can only be understood from the inside, and access to them will depend on how far our subjective imagination can travel. It is natural to want to bring our capacity for detached, objective understanding as much into alignment with reality as we can, but it should not surprise us if objectivity is essentially incomplete.

The aim of such understanding, the deeper aim it shares with the reductionist views which I reject, is to go beyond the distinction between appearance and reality by including the existence of appearances in an elaborated reality. Nothing will then be left outside. But this expanded reality, like physical reality, is centerless. Though the subjective features of our own minds are at the center of *our* world, we must try to conceive of them as just one manifestation of the mental in a world that is not given especially to the human point of view. This is, I recognize, a paradoxical enterprise, but the attempt seems to me worth making.

The first requirement is to think of our own minds as mere instances of something general—as we are accustomed to thinking of particular things and events in the physical world as instances and manifestations of something general. We must think of mind as a phenomenon to which the human case is not necessarily central, even though our minds are at the center of our world. The fundamental idea behind the objective impulse is that the world is not our world. This idea can be betrayed if we turn objective comprehensibility into a new standard of reality. That is an error because the fact that reality extends beyond what is available to our original perspective does not mean that all of it is available to some transcendent perspective that we can reach from here. But so long as we avoid this error, it is proper to be motivated by the hope of extending our objective understanding to as much of life and the world as we can.

By a general concept of mind I don't mean an anthropocentric concept which conceives all minds on analogy with our own. I mean a concept under which we ourselves fall as instances—without any implication that we are the central instances. My opposition to psychophysical reduction is therefore fundamentally different from that of the idealist or phenomenological tradition. I want to think of mind, like matter, as a general feature of the world. In each case we are acquainted with certain instances in our small spatiotemporal neighborhood (though in the case of matter, not only with those instances). In each case there is no guarantee as to how far beyond the initial acquaintance our understanding can go, by processes of abstraction, generalization, and experiment. The necessary incompleteness of an objective concept of mind seems fairly clear. But there is also no reason to assume that everything about the *physical* world can be understood by some possible development of our physical conception of objectivity: physical science is after all just an operation of our minds, and we have no reason to assume that their capacities in these respects, remarkable as they are, correlate fully with reality.

In both cases an expanded understanding, to the extent that we can achieve it, not only gives us access to things outside our immediate neighborhood, but should also add to our knowledge of the things with which we are already acquainted and from which the inquiry starts. This is clear with respect to familiar physical objects, which we all now think of in terms of physics and chemistry and not just phenomenally or instrumentally. With respect to mental phenomena our objective understanding is undeveloped, and it may never develop very far. But the idea of such an objective view, coming through the pursuit of a general conception of mind, is to provide us with a way of thinking that we could also bring back home and apply to ourselves.

3 OTHER MINDS

A simpler version of the problem of placing ourselves in a world of which we are not the center appears in philosophy independently of the ambition to form a general nonidealistic conception of reality. It appears at the individual level as the problem of other minds. One might say that the wider problem of mental objectivity is an analogue at the level of mental types to the problem of other minds for individuals: not, "How can I conceive of minds other than my own?" but, "How can we conceive of minds subjectively incommensurable with our own?" In both cases we must conceive of ourselves as instances of something more general in order to place ourselves in a centerless world.

The interesting problem of other minds is not the epistemological problem, how I can know that other people are not zombies. It is the conceptual problem, how I can *understand* the attribution of mental states to others. And this in turn is really the problem, how I can conceive of my own mind as merely one of many examples of mental phenomena contained in the world.

Each of us is the subject of various experiences, and to understand that there are other people in the world as well, one must be able to conceive of experiences of which one is not the subject: experiences that are not present to oneself. To do this it is necessary to have a general conception of subjects of experience and to place oneself under it as an instance. It cannot be done by extending the idea of what is immediately felt into other people's bodies, for as Wittgenstein observed, that will only give you an idea of having feelings in their bodies, not of *their* having feelings.

Though we all grow up with the required general conception that allows us to believe in genuinely other minds, it is philosophically problematic, and there has been much difference of opinion over how it works. The problem is that other people seem to be part of the external world, and empiricist assumptions about meaning have led various philosophers to the view that our attribution of mental states to others must be analyzed in terms of the behavioral evidence, or as parts of some explanatory theory of what produces observable behavior. Unfortunately, this seems to imply that mental attributions do not have the same sense in the first person as in the third.

Clearly, there must be some alternative to the assumption that anything said about other persons has to be given a reading which places it firmly in the familiar external world, comprehensible by means of the physical conception of objectivity. That leads straight to solipsism: the inability to make sense of the idea of real minds other than one's own.

In fact, the ordinary concept of mind contains the beginnings of an entirely different way of conceiving objective reality. We cannot make sense of the idea of other minds by construing it in a way which becomes unintelligible when we try to apply it to ourselves. When we conceive of the minds of others, we cannot abandon the essential factor of a point of view: instead we must generalize it and think of ourselves as one point of view among others. The first stage of objectification of the mental is for each of us to be able to grasp the idea of all human perspectives, including his own, without depriving them of their character as perspectives. It is the analogue for minds of a centerless conception of space for physical objects, in which no point has a privileged position.

The beginning of an objective concept of mind is the ability to view one's own experiences from outside, as events in the world. If this is possible, then others can also conceive of those events and one can conceive of the experiences of others, also from outside. To think in this way we use not a faculty of external representation, but a general idea of subjective points of view, of which we imagine a particular instance and a particular form. So far the process does not involve any abstraction from the general forms of our experience. We still think of experience in terms of the familiar point of view we share with other humans. All that is involved in the external conception of mind is the imaginative use of this point of view—a use that is partly present in the memory and expectation of one's own experiences.

But we can go further than this, for the same basic method allows us to think of experiences that we can't imagine. To represent an experience from outside by imagining it subjectively is the analogue of representing an objective spatial configuration by imagining it visually. One uses ordinary appearance as a medium. What is represented need not resemble the representation in all respects. It must be represented in terms of certain general features of subjective experience—subjective universals— some instances of which one is familiar with from one's own experience. But the capacity to form universal concepts in any area enables one not only to represent the present situation from without but to think about other possibilities which one has not experienced and perhaps never will experience directly. So the pretheoretical concept of mind involves a kind of objectivity which permits us to go some way beyond our own experiences and those exactly like them.

The idea is that the concept of mind, though tied to subjectivity, is not restricted to what can be understood in terms of our own subjectivity—what we can translate into the terms of our own experience. We include the subjectively unimaginable mental lives of other species, for example, in our conception of the real world without betraying their subjectivity by means of a behaviorist, functionalist, or physicalist reduction. We know there's something there, something perspectival, even if we don't know what it is or even how to think about it. The question is whether this acknowledgment will allow us to develop a way to think about it.

Of course one possibility is that this particular process can go no further. We can have a concept of mind general enough to allow us to escape solipsism and ethnocentrism, but perhaps we cannot transcend the general forms of human experience and the human viewpoint. That viewpoint permits us to conceive of experiences we have not had, because of the flexibility of the human imagination. But does it allow us to detach the concept of mind from a human perspective?

The issue is whether there can be a general concept of experience that extends far beyond our own or anything like it. Even if there can, we may be unable to grasp it except in the abstract, as we are presumably unable to grasp now concepts of objective physical reality which will be developed five centuries hence. But the possibility that there is such a concept would be sufficient motive for trying to form it. It is only if we are convinced in advance that the thing makes no sense that we can be justified in setting the limits of objectivity with regard to the mind so close to our own ordinary viewpoint.

4 CONSCIOUSNESS IN GENERAL

So far as I can see the only reason for accepting such limits would be a Wittgensteinian one—namely, that such an extension or attempted generalization of the concept of mind takes us away from the conditions that make the concept meaningful. I don't know whether Wittgenstein would actually have made this objection, but it seems a natural development of his views. He observed that while experiential concepts are applied in the first person from within, not on the basis of behavioral, circumstantial, or any other kind of evidence, they also require outward criteria. To mean anything in application to oneself in the first person they must also be applicable to oneself and others on circumstantial and behavioral grounds that are not just privately available. This he took to be a consequence of a general condition of publicity that must be met by all concepts, which in turn derives from a condition that must be met by any rule of whatever kind: that there must be an objective distinction between following it and breaking it, which can be made only if it is possible to compare one's own practice with that of one's community.

I am doubtful about the final "only", and though I have no alternative theory to offer, it seems to me dangerous to draw conclusions from the argument "How *else* could it be?" But I don't wish to deny that the experiential concepts we use to talk about our own minds and those of other human beings more or less fit the pattern Wittgenstein describes. Provided Wittgenstein is not understood, as I think he should not be, as saying that behavior and so forth is what there really is and mental processes are linguistic fictions, his view that the conditions of first- and third-person ascription of an experience are inextricably bound together in a single public concept seems to me correct, with regard to the ordinary case.[3]

The question is whether the concept of experience can be extended beyond these conditions without losing all content. A negative answer would limit our thought about experience to what we can ascribe to ourselves and to others in the specified ways. The objection is that beyond these limits the distinction between correct and incorrect application of the concept is not defined, and therefore the condition of significance is not met.

In a well known passage (sec. 350) Wittgenstein says I can't extend the application of mental concepts from my own case merely by saying others have the same as I have so often had. "It is as if I were to say: 'You surely know what "It is 5 o'clock here" means; so you also know what "It's 5 o'clock on the sun" means. It means simply that it is just the same time there as it is here when it is 5 o'clock.'" This is a fair reply to someone who is trying to explain what he means by saying that the stove is in pain. But could it be used to argue against all extensions of the concept beyond the range of cases where we know how to apply it? Does the general concept of experience really lose all content if an attempt is made to use it to think about cases in which we cannot now and perhaps even never could apply it more specifically? I think not. Not all such cases are like that of the time of day on the sun. That example is much more radical, for it introduces a direct contradiction with the conditions that determine the time of day—namely, position on the surface of the earth relative to the sun. But the generalization of the concept of experience beyond our capacity to apply it doesn't *contradict* the condition of application that it tries to transcend, even if some examples, like the ascription of pain to a stove, do pass the limits of intelligibility.

Admittedly, *if* someone has the concept of a type of conscious mental state and also has that mental state with any frequency, he will be able to apply it from within and without, in the way Wittgenstein describes. If he couldn't, it would be evidence that he didn't have the concept. But we don't ascribe such states only to creatures who have mental concepts: we ascribe them to children and animals, and believe that we ourselves would have experiences even if we didn't have the language. If we believe that the existence of many of the experiences we can talk about doesn't depend on the existence of these concepts, why can't we conceive at one remove of the existence of types of experience of which we don't have and perhaps could never have a complete conception and the capacity for first- and third-person ascription?

Consider first, cases where we have strong evidence that experience is present, without either knowing what its character is or being in a position to hope ever to reach an understanding of its character that will include the capacity for self-ascription. This is true of at least some of the experiences of all animals not very close to us in structure and behavior. In each case there is rich external evidence of conscious inner life, but only limited application of our own mental concepts—mostly general ones—to describe it.[4]

It is the ordinary prephilosophical concept of experience that leads to this result. We have not simply left it behind and taken off with the *word*. And the extension is not part of a private language but a natural idea shared by most human beings about what sorts of things occupy the world around them. We are forced, I think, to conclude that all these creatures have specific experiences which cannot be represented by any mental concepts of which we could have first-person understanding. This doesn't mean that we can't think about them in that general way, or perhaps in more detail but without first-person understanding—provided that we continue to regard them as subjective experiences rather than mere behavioral dispositions or functional states.

But it seems to me that we can in principle go further. We can use the general concepts of experience and mind to speculate about forms of conscious life whose external signs we cannot confidently identify. There is probably a great deal of life in the universe, and we may be in a position to identify only some of its forms, because we would simply be unable to read as behavior the manifestations of creatures sufficiently unlike us. It certainly means something to speculate that there are such creatures, and that they have minds.

These uses of the general concept of mind exemplify a theoretical step that is commonplace elsewhere. We can form the idea of phenomena that we do not know how to detect. Once the conception of a new physical particle is formed, defined in terms of a set of properties, those properties may then allow experiments to be devised which will permit its detection. In this way the progress of physical discovery has long since passed to the formation of physical concepts that can be applied only with sophisticated techniques of observation, and not by means of unaided perception or simple mechanical measurement.

Only a dogmatic verificationist would deny the possibility of forming objective concepts that reach beyond our current capacity to apply them. The aim of reaching a conception of the world which does not put us at the center in any way requires the formation of such concepts. We are supported in this aim by a kind of intellectual optimism: the belief that we possess an open-ended capacity for understanding what we have not yet conceived, and that it can be called into operation by detaching from our present understanding and trying to reach a higher-order view which explains it as part of the world. But we must also admit that the world probably reaches beyond our capacity to understand it, no matter how far we travel, and this admission, which is stronger than the mere denial of verificationism, can be expressed only in general concepts whose extension is not limited to what we could in principle know about.

It is the same with the mind. To accept the general idea of a perspective without limiting it to the forms with which one is familiar, subjectively or otherwise, is the precondition of seeking ways to conceive of particular types of experience that do not depend on the ability either to have those experiences or to imagine them subjectively. It should be possible to investigate in this way the quality-structure of some sense we do not have, for example, by observing creatures who do have it—even though the understanding we can reach is only partial.

But if we could do that, we should also be able to apply the same general idea to ourselves, and thus to analyze our experiences in ways that can be understood without having had such experiences. That would constitute a kind of objective standpoint toward our own minds. To the extent that it could be achieved, we would be able to see our minds as not merely part of the human world, something we can already do with regard to our bodies. And this would serve a natural human goal, for it is natural to seek a general understanding of reality, including ourselves, which does not depend on the fact that we *are* ourselves.

5 THE INCOMPLETENESS OF OBJECTIVE REALITY

In the pursuit of this goal, however, even at its most successful, something will inevitably be lost. If we try to understand experience from an objective viewpoint that is distinct from that of the subject of the experience, then even if we continue to credit its perspectival nature, we will not be able to grasp its most specific qualities unless we can imagine them subjectively. We will not know exactly how scrambled eggs taste to a cockroach even if we develop a detailed objective phenomenology of the cockroach sense of taste. When it comes to values, goals, and forms of life, the gulf may be even more profound.

Since this is so, no objective conception of the mental world can include it all. But in that case it may be asked what the point is of looking for such a conception. The aim was to place perspectives and their contents in a world seen from no particular point of view. It turns out that some aspects of those perspectives cannot be fully understood in terms of an objective concept of mind. But if some aspects of reality can't be captured in an objective conception, why not forget the ambition of capturing as much of it as possible? The world just *isn't* the world as it appears to one highly abstracted point of view that can be pursued by all rational beings. And if one can't have complete objectivity, the goal of capturing as much of reality as one can in an objective net is pointless and unmotivated.

I don't think this follows. The pursuit of a conception of the world that doesn't put us at the center is an expression of philosophical realism, all the more so if it does not assume that everything real can be reached by such a conception. Reality is not just objective reality, and any objective conception of reality must include an acknowledgment of its own incompleteness. (This is an important qualification to the claims of objectivity in other areas as well.) Even if an objective general conception of mind were developed and added to the physical conception of objectivity, it would have to include the qualification that the exact character of each of the experiential and intentional perspectives with which it deals can be understood only from within or by subjective imagination. A being with total imaginative power could understand it all from inside, but an ordinary being using an objective concept of mind will not. In saying this we have not given up the idea of the way the world really is, independently of how it appears to us or to any particular occupant of it. We have only given up the idea that this coincides with what can be objectively understood. The way the world is includes appearances, and there is no single point of view from which they can all be fully grasped. An objective conception of mind acknowledges that the features of our own minds that cannot be objectively grasped are examples of a more general subjectivity, of which other examples lie beyond our subjective grasp as well.

This amounts to the rejection of idealism with regard to the mind. The world is not my world, or our world—not even the mental world is. This is a particularly unequivocal rejection of idealism because it affirms the reality of aspects of the world that cannot be grasped by any conception I can possess—not even an objective conception of the kind with which we transcend the domain of initial appearances. Here it can be seen that physicalism is based ultimately on a form of idealism: an idealism of restricted objectivity. Objectivity of whatever kind is not the test of reality. It is just one way of understanding reality.

Still, even if objective understanding can be only partial, it is worth trying to extend it, for a simple reason. The pursuit of an objective understanding of reality is the only way to expand our knowledge of what there is beyond the way it appears to us. Even if we have to acknowledge the reality of some things that we can't grasp objectively, as well as the ineliminable subjectivity of some aspects of our own experience which we can grasp only subjectively, the pursuit of an objective concept of mind is simply part of the general pursuit of understanding. To give it up because it cannot be complete would be like giving up axiomatization in mathematics because it cannot be complete.

In trying to explain how minds are to be included in the real world that simply exists, I have distinguished between reality and objective reality, and also between objectivity and particular conceptions of objectivity. The physical conception of objectivity is inappropriate for increasing our understanding of the mind; and even the kind of objectivity that is appropriate for this purpose will not permit us to form a complete idea of all the various incompatible mental perspectives. These conclusions in the philosophy of mind suggest a more general principle that applies in other areas as well: one should pursue the kind of objectivity appropriate to the subject one is trying to understand, and even the right kind of objectivity may not exhaust the subject completely.

The problem of bringing together subjective and objective views of the world can be approached from either direction. If one starts from the subjective side, the problem is the traditional one of skepticism, idealism, or solipsism. How, given my personal experiential perspective, can I form a conception of the world as it is independent of my perception of it? And how can I know that this conception is correct? (The question may also be asked from the point of view of the collective human perspective rather than from that of an individual.) If on the other hand one starts from the objective side, the problem is how to accommodate, in a world that simply exists and has no perspectival center, any of the following things: (a) oneself; (b) one's point of view; (c) the point of view of other selves, similar and dissimilar; and (d) the objects of various types of judgment that seem to emanate from these perspectives.

It is this second version of the problem that particularly interests me. It is the obverse of skepticism because the *given* is objective reality—or the idea of an objective reality—and what is problematic by contrast is subjective reality. Without receiving full acknowledgment this approach has been very influential in recent analytic philosophy. It accords well with a bias toward physical science as a paradigm of understanding.

But if under the pressure of realism we admit that there are things which cannot be understood in this way, then other ways of understanding them must be sought. One way is to enrich the notion of objectivity. But to insist in every case that the most objective and detached account of a phenomenon is the correct one is likely to lead to reductive conclusions. I have argued that the seductive appeal of objective reality depends on a mistake. It is not the given. Reality is not just objective reality. Sometimes, in the philosophy of mind but also elsewhere, the truth is not to be found by travelling as far away from one's personal perspective as possible.

NOTES

1 There is an excellent account of this idea in Williams (1998), pp. 64–8. He calls it the *absolute* conception of reality.
2 Nagel (1974). Since it's never too late for an acknowledgment, let me record that two years earlier Timothy Sprigge had proposed as the essential condition of consciousness that there must be "something it is like to be" the creature in question (Sprigge, pp. 166–8). And B.A. Farrell asked, "What would it be like to be a bat?" in 1950, though he dismissed the difficulty for materialism. (When I wrote, I hadn't read Sprigge and had forgotten Farrell.)
3 Wittgenstein (1953), secs. 201 ff. On the status of criteria in Wittgenstein and why they aren't offered as *analyses* of meaning see Kripke (1982).
4 Skeptics should read Jennings (1906/1976).

REFERENCES

Farrell, B.A. (1950) "Experience". *Mind* 50: 170–98.
Jennings, H.S. (1906/1976) *The Behavior of the Lower Organisms*. Indiana University Press.
Kripke, Saul (1982) *Wittgenstein on Rules and Private Language*. Harvard University Press.
Nagel, Thomas (1974) "What is it Like to be a Bat?" *Philosophical Review* 4: 435–50.
Sprigge, Timothy (1971) "Final Causes". *Proceedings of the Aristotelian Society Supplement* 45: 149–70.
Williams, Bernard (1978). *Descartes: The Project of Pure Inquiry*. Harmondsworth: Penguin.
Wittgenstein, Ludwig (1953) *Philosophical Investigations*. Oxford: Blackwell.

6

SCIENCE AND THE PHENOMENAL

Jenann Ismael

... Almost all of the arguments against the identification of pain and c-fiber firing take their departures from one or more of the following facts about their relationship:

- I cannot be mistaken about being in pain, but I *can* be (positively or negatively) mistaken about whether my c-fibers are firing (i.e., I can think my c-fibers are firing when they are not, or think they are not when they are).
- It is always an open question, when I am in pain, whether or not my c-fibers are firing, and vice versa.
- Knowing that I am in pain does not settle the question of whether my c-fibers are firing, and knowing that my c-fibers are firing does not settle the question of whether I am in pain.

We can say precisely the same things about the relationship between *here* and <c,b> (where these are the coordinates my map assigns this spot), but we are not tempted to deny that *being-here* and *being-at-*<c,b> are one and the same property, we are not tempted to deny that when I say "I am here" I say anything other than that I am at <c,b>.

- I cannot be mistaken about being *here* (i.e., I always know where *here* is in the sense that I can point at the spot) but I can be (positively or negatively) mistaken about being at <c,b> (i.e., I can think I am at <c,b> and not be, or be at <c,b> and think I am not).
- It is always an open question, given that I am *here*, whether or not I am at <c,b>, and vice versa.
- Knowing that I am *here* does not settle the question of whether I am at <c,b>, and knowing that I am at <c,b> does not settle whether I am *here*.

I have been suggesting that the analogy between the *here*-ness of this corner table at *Cafe Barrone* and the phenomenal character (the 'ouchness', if you like) of the firing of my c-fibers is deep. *Here* is not a special private place that only I can be, distinct from, but momentarily tied to, <,>. Nor is *here*-ness an intrinsic *property* of any spot, for different locations are here for different people: this corner table is here for me, the ground under your feet is here for you, his seat on Mount Olympus is here for Zeus, and so on. Despite its misleading grammar, we conceive of *here*-ness as a *relation*, one that each of us bears to the spot at which we are (respectively) located.[1] We should think, likewise, of the feel of the knife as it enters my skin, or the taste that fills my mouth when I place a pinch of salt on my tongue, not as first-order properties of mine, distinct, respectively, from the having firing c-fibers or the having of a particular pattern of activation in my taste receptors, but tied to these so that they always (or, mostly, under standard conditions) accompany them. Nor should we think of them as second-order properties of individuals, so that having a character- istic phenomenal feel is a property of the *property* of having firing c-fibers, and experiencing a salty taste is a property of the *property* of having a high level of acti- vation in the salty receptor on my tongue. We should think of the phenomenal char- acter of an event—whether there is something *it is like* for it to occur and *what* it is like—as an external relation it may bear one or another of us. There is *something it is like* to *me* for there to be c-fiber firing going on *here*, something it is like to *you* for c-fiber firing to be happening over *there*, and not something it is like for *anyone* for there to be c-fiber firing in a zombie's head, gases forming in the center of the earth, or a tree falling in an empty forest. Just as *here* is neither an intrinsic property of the spot I am at, nor a special location distinct from all of those which make up our public space, but an ordinary place to which I bear a distinguished relation (that of *being-at*), the pain I feel as the knife enters my flesh is not a property of my firing c- fibers nor a private occurrence distinct from those that make up our public world, but an ordinary physical event to which *I* bear a special relation. What the analogy suggests is that we should think of *having-(one or another)-phenomenal-feel* as rela- tions that each of us bear a different set of physical events in the same way that *is-at* is a relation that each of us bears a different spot; indeed, insofar as we conceive of ourselves as differently placed occupants of a single commonly experienced world, that is how we *must* think of them.[2] My body is the hunk of matter my unmediated apprehension to some of whose states makes *it* my window on the world. You, of course, have a different body, you are *conscious of* certain of its states, states that *my* access to is somewhat less direct (mediated by my conscious states in the same way that your access to mine is mediated by yours). That is the suggestion.

It is, first and foremost, a reaction against the position that Chalmers calls property dualism. For my part, it stems from the conviction that it is a misunderstanding of the nature of the *physical* to think that it could be independent of the phenomenal.

Virtually all contemporary discussions focus on the phenomenal side of proposed physical-phenomenal property identifications and base the case for mutual independence on the apparent autonomy of the phenomenal (Kripke's and Jackson's are the most obvious examples), but if we understand the role that experience plays in the construction and employment of our physical theories (and recall that this includes our representations of the world, quite generally), I do not see how we can avoid the conclusion that it is no less a part of our conception of *physical* properties that they are constitutive of the phenomenal than it is part of our conception of other locations (locations I am not now at) that they are spatially related to *here* (i.e., that they lie some distance from *this* spot). To put the point the other way around, it is no less a part of our conception of phenomenal properties that they are connected in the space of physical properties than it is a part of our conception of *here* that it is connected in physical space. But this is a relatively idiosyncratic motivation; more often, opposition to a Chalmers-style view stems from reductionist aspirations, and it is worthwhile saying something about whether a view like this satisfies them.

IS BEING-CONSCIOUS-OF A PHYSICAL RELATION?

The question is delicate; suppose that neurobiologists succeed in uncovering the physical basis of consciousness, suppose that they find that s is conscious of c just in case c is F_b.[3] And suppose that they get so sophisticated that they can tell what kind of tactual, auditory, olfactory ... experience a conscious subject has from the physical state of her brain, so that an accomplished neurobiologist looking at an MRI image of my brain can tell me what sounds, tastes, and smells I am experiencing in the way that an experienced navigator given the coordinate description of my location will know where to find me.[4] What the neurobiologist 'discovers' when she discovers the neurobiological description of a particular phenomenal state, is like what a navigator 'discovers' when he learns the coordinate description of the home where he was raised, or a secret spot on a beloved hill. What she learns, that is, is a new description of a deeply familiar locale, a description that can be especially useful for navigational purposes because it encodes the relations of the state to all others (under their physical descriptions). And what she discovers when she discovers the physical basis of consciousness (i.e., when she discovers what F_b in the above condition is), is what all of these states have in common; she discovers the physical description of the relation I bear my conscious states, you bear yours, and so on.[5]

Now, if what it is for a relation R to be a physical relation is for it to be *represented* on our maps of the physical world, then *being-conscious-of* is a physical relation; it is represented by $F_b(s,c)$. If, on the other hand, what it is for R to be a physical relation is for full knowledge of the internal structure of those maps to be sufficient for knowledge of which events we variously R, then they are *not*, because—as Jackson's argument brought out—full discursive knowledge of our physical theories is not sufficient for knowledge of which events [under their physical descriptions] have a phenomenal character (for me) and what that character *is*. The analogy with *being-at* is helpful again; if what it is for R to be a physical relation is for it to be represented on our maps of the physical world, *being-at* is a physical relation (the one I bear to the bit of space occupied by my body). If, on the other hand, what it is for R to be a physical relation is for full knowledge of the internal structure of those maps to be sufficient for knowledge of which events we variously R, then it is *not*, because nothing on the map, i.e., nothing in the represented relations between bodies and locations, will tell me where I am, which location is here and which body is mine. The physical description of the being-conscious-of relation does not announce itself as such any more than the coordinate description of *here* announces *itself* as such.

To belabor the point just a little bit more: it is a misunderstanding of the nature of the physical to expect something in the physical description of a body to tell me whether it is *mine* or something in the physical description of its c-fibers will tell me *what it is like* (for me) when they fire. Our theories are representations of the world and those are facts about their interpretation: trying to read the latter off of the former is as hopeless as trying to identify the point on a map that stands for *here* by staring at the map. The map can be as accurate and richly detailed as you please, nothing *internal* to it is going to tell you about the external relations it bears to the space it represents.[6] What makes this so hard to see clearly is that the map itself, the landscape it represents, and the relations between the two, are themselves *parts* of the represented landscape. Once I locate the point on the map that represents *this* place, I will find there a representation of myself, map in hand, pointing simultaneously at a part of the map and the spot beneath my feet. If the map is a linguistic one (i.e., if it is a *description* of the world), it will include a set of sentences describing external relations between parts of the world and bits of language which, collectively, give its interpretation; sentences like "'cat' refers to cats," "'snow is white is true' iff snow is white," and so on. Neither of these, however, will help us in our pre-interpretation phase; *no* representation of the interpretation will tell us what that interpretation is unless we know how to read (i.e., interpret) the representation, and this is just what we do not know when the representation occurs on the very map we are trying to interpret. Unless I know which symbols stand for people and maps, how pointing is represented, and where *here* is, I might be looking right at it, but I will not be able to identify the symbol which represents me. And until I know what quotation marks and 'refers to' mean, and what parts of the world the terms on the right hand side of 'refers to' stand for, sentences like "'cat' refers to cats" will not help me decide whether *this* is a cat.

53

The point is simple, but, again, obscured by the fact that we, our representations, and the relationship between ourselves and our representations are all *parts* of the represented landscape. It is this familiar and wondrous Gödelian structure that is so confusing, that leads us to expect to find external relations between us and our representations **on** those representations, that leads us to expect to find external relations *between* the two of us **on** the one.

THE LIMITS OF PHYSICAL REDUCTIONISM

To know where I am in the physical world is to know which body is mine; it is to locate the hunk of matter my immediate access to (some of) whose states makes it my window on the world: through whose eyes I see it, though whose skin I feel it, through whose ears I hear it, and through whose nose and mouth I taste and smell it.[7] But it is mistaken, and altogether misleading, to think that each of us is given the physical picture of the world and faces the problem of determining therefrom which of the portrayed bodies is our own, and what phenomenal character is had by portrayed events (i.e., what, if anything, it is like [for me] for c-fiber firing to be going on here or combustion to be going on there).[8] If that were our problem, we would have no solution, and—as Strawson remarked somewhere—in cases like these it is only because the solution exists that the problem arises at all.

It works, instead, something roughly like this: our own experience presents bodies essentially in relation (spatial and otherwise) to ourselves, and each of us go about plotting these relations and working up a personal map that we use to steer. These personal maps are diverse but (it turns out) related in a systematic way: with some fixing up and filling in, they can be obtained from one another by transformations of a simple sort, and we obtain an impersonal or un-'centered' representation by taking what is invariant under all of these transformations. The result is a map that is portable across our individual perspectives, a great deal more detailed and comprehensive than anything we could have worked up individually, and from which the manifold centered maps that each of us use to steer by can be obtained by supplementation with a bit of idiosyncratic information, namely, which body is our *own* and what (if anything) it is like [for us] to be in one or another of its states.[9]

These impersonal maps just *are* our representations of the physical world, and the bits of idiosyncratic information with which they have to be supplemented to retrieve the relevant personal maps (the *my*-ness of my body and the phenomenal character of particular events), cannot be included on them, or incorporated into them, without spoiling their impersonality, i.e., without destroying their portability from one to the other of our perspectives. If that is what reductionism aspires to, if what it would be to 'find a place for consciousness in the physical world' is to weave the *here*-ness of the spot *I* am at and the *ouch*-ness of *my* pains into our *physical* maps, then it is utterly misguided, for if what I have been saying is even roughly correct, the physical is *essentially* impersonal.[10]

NOTES

1   In the philosophical terminology, it is an external relation, for it fails to supervene on the intrinsic properties of its relata.

2   To say that a relation is external is just to say that it does not supervene on the intrinsic properties of its relata; it is to say that events which no one is *conscious of* differ no more intrinsically from those which are felt, than places that no one is *at* differ intrinsically from those which are occupied.

3   s, here, is a subject of experience [you, me, or one of our mates], c is a physical event, and F_b is some condition that may or may not be satisfied by a given c (e.g., activates the consciousness cell in the brain of body b). Differences in the set of events of which subjects are conscious arise because of differences in the b's that go into the specification of F, differences in the bodies of whose F-states they are variously conscious (mine is the one of whose F-states I am conscious, yours is the one of whose F-states you are conscious, and so on). What makes *this* one mine and *that* one yours is not something intrinsic to either of our bodies, not something that can be found in their physical description. It is a fact about what they represent, a fact about the relations they bear to things outside themselves.

4   He will know, that is, how to get from where he is to where I am. He will know something about the actual relations between two parts of real space, his location and mine.

5   There is, of course, no guarantee that the relationship is, in physical terms, a simple one.

6   Putnam taught the same lesson in a different way (though this is probably not how he would have put it); languages have internal structure, and when bits of language are mapped onto bits of the physical world, ways of arranging the former can provide maps (we call them, in this special case, 'descriptions') of the latter (this is not yet a full-blown picture theory of language; it can, but does not have to be, spelled out *à la* the *Tractatus*). Nothing internal to such a description—be it ever so accurate and complete—will tell us what part of the physical world any bit of language stands for, what individual is named by this term, what things that predicate applies to, and what fact this sentence describes.

7   To locate it, that is, on the map, to determine its position relative to all other bodies.

8   To put this in a more familiar way: it is a mistake, and altogether misleading, to think that we are given an impersonal picture of the world and have the problem of constructing our personal perspectives *therefrom*.

9   As I remarked, which body is mine, and which events *have* a phenomenal character are not unrelated. What that phenomenal character is, however, is not determined by knowing which body is mine.

10   There is a large and well-known body of literature that makes a connection between indexicals and phenomenal properties, conceived as the 'subjective features of experience', but it is mostly concerned with the semantics of statements, or the contents of thoughts, involving the two. See, e.g., Geach 1957, Castañeda 1966, Boer and Lycan 1986. The connection between the Geach–Castañeda issue and Nagel's knowledge argument is made in Boer and Lycan 1980, McGinn 1983, and more explicitly in McMullen 1985. McMullen argues that what unites the two issues is that in each case an indexically expressed thought can be understood fully only by someone occupying the right perspective, and that the right reaction is to distinguish descriptive psychological associations from semantic value, and suggests that 'understanding' involves the former as well as the latter. McMullen, McGinn, and Boer and Lycan all hold that 'subjective', perspectival, indexical states of subjects are a matter of combining a represented, 'objective' state of

affairs with a special mode of representation, which cannot (normally) be used by another subject to represent the very same state of affairs; and Lycan (1990) argues that the nature of the represented state of affairs is independent of the various modes in which it is presented, bringing his position close to the one suggested here. I would like to thank an anonymous reviewer for *Philosophy of Science*, for bringing the article to my attention. The emphasis is different, but I find much of what Lycan says congenial.

REFERENCES

Boer, David, and Lycan, William (1980), "Who, Me?", *Philosophical Review* 89: 432–50.

—— (1986), *Knowing Who*. Cambridge, MA: MIT Press.

Castaneda, Hector-Neri (1966), "'He': A Study in the Logic of Self-Consciousness", *Ratio* 8: 42–56.

Chalmers, David (1996), *The Conscious Mind: In Search of a Fundamental Theory*. Oxford: Oxford University Press.

Geach, Peter (1957), "On Belief About Oneself", *Analysis* 18: 121–38.

Ismael, Jenann (1999), "Reference, External Constraints, and Nature's Objective Joints", ms.

Jackson, Frank (1983), "What Mary Didn't Know", in P. K. Moser and J. D. Trout (eds), *Contemporary Materialism*. London: Routledge, 28–41.

Kripke, Saul (1980), *Naming and Necessity*. Cambridge, MA: Harvard University Press.

Lycan, William (1990), "What is the 'Subjectivity' of the Mental?", *Philosophical Perspectives* 4: 109–30.

McGinn, Colin (1983), *The Subjective View*. Oxford: Oxford University Press.

McMullen, Carolyn (1985), "'Knowing What It's Like' and the Essential Indexical", *Philosophical Studies* 48: 322–39.

Part 2

CONSCIOUSNESS
How should it be studied?

Suppose a friend asks you 'What is on your mind?' If you want to answer sincerely, you will pay attention to your current thoughts and feelings – that is, you will *introspect* them. Of course, sometimes a friend doesn't need to ask this question, in order to know what you're thinking or feeling. Perhaps your friend has learned, through experience, that you furrow your brow in that way only when you're worried about something. But even the closest of friends cannot introspect each other's thoughts. In this sense, you seem to have a method of knowing your own thoughts – introspection – that is unavailable to others.

Moreover, the use of introspection seems to pervade everyday life. When you consider whether to have pasta for dinner, you might imagine a plate of spaghetti, and then introspect how you feel – enticed or put off. More complex introspective processes occur when you weigh thornier decisions, such as whether you should pursue adventure or opt for a life of quiet domesticity. In contemplating such choices, introspection seems indispensable.

Though ubiquitous, introspection is not infallible. Perhaps at the moment your friend asked 'What is on your mind?' you were daydreaming about engaging in some illicit activity and, subconsciously wanting to avoid recognizing this fact, you instantly repress what it was you'd been thinking. (Freud was, of course, particularly interested in how the desire to avoid shame can lead us to self-deception.) Or perhaps you had intended to spend the afternoon thinking about a philosophy paper that you needed to write, and this led you to believe that you *were* thinking about the paper, when in fact you were daydreaming. Clearly, an attempt to determine what one is thinking or feeling, by introspective reflection, can go wrong in any number of ways.

Early psychologists such as Wilhelm Wundt and Edward Titchener maintained that introspection is nevertheless crucially important for scientific research on the mind. These pioneers of the discipline championed the judicious use of introspection, training their subjects to scrupulously attend to their thoughts and sensations, and to report their introspective discoveries in meticulous detail. But more recent psychological research has cast doubt on the reliability of introspection. For instance, influential psychological studies (such as Nisbett and Wilson 1977) have shown that subjects are often mistaken about their own motivations in acting, and about the sources of their own preferences and biases. Other studies (including Libet 1985) have suggested that subjects frequently devise a rationale for an action *after* the action has been initiated. In response, defenders of introspection have pointed out that these errors concern the *causal* roles of thoughts and feelings, and about thoughts and feelings that lie in the past. We may be more liable to these sorts of mistakes than to, say, mistakes about what it is that we are thinking or feeling at the moment.

Introspection thus receives a mixed report. It is ubiquitous and perhaps even indispensable in everyday life; but at least on some questions, it is unreliable. So should we use introspection to generate data for research in psychology, cognitive science, and neuroscience? Should philosophers who seek to resolve the problem of consciousness rely on introspective evidence? The three articles in this section take up these issues.

Alvin Goldman's paper centers on the role that introspection plays, and should play, in the sciences of the mind. He notes that the primary reason people have mistrusted introspection is that it violates what many assume is a key requirement for a scientific method: that the method can be used, on the same object, by multiple investigators. In other words, scientifically respectable methods must yield evidence that is publicly available. This *publicity requirement* is Goldman's main target. He argues that psychologists and cognitive scientists do, in fact, violate this publicity requirement, by relying on introspective evidence. Moreover, he claims that they are justified in doing so, since the publicity requirement is not well supported.

Introspection is used, according to Goldman, in studies of phenomena like blindsight. In blindsight, subjects with damage in the primary visual cortex report blindness in a region of their visual field. But when encouraged to guess about what is present at a spot that falls within that region – e.g., whether there is an 'X' or an 'O' on the wall there – they do much better than chance. The blindsighters' claim that they have no conscious visual experience in that region is based on introspection. And if we disregard this claim, then it seems we will have no reason to attribute blindness. Without that claim, it is tempting to explain the blindsighters' ability to (somewhat reliably) determine what mark is on the wall by positing that they have some sight in the field corresponding to the damaged area. But most scientists who study blindsighters accept their introspectively-based claim that they have no conscious visual experience in that region. Goldman's point is simply that the leading interpretation of blindsight cases makes essential use of the blindsighters' introspective reports.

Even if psychologists *do* use introspective evidence, we may wonder whether they *should* use such evidence, given that introspection violates the publicity requirement. Goldman argues that the purpose of the publicity requirement is to help ensure reliability. And it does so: a method that yields the same result when used by various different observers is probably more reliable than a method that yields different results. But this is a means of comparing methods that *can* be applied by more than one observer, and so it is simply inapplicable to introspection. Goldman sees introspection as a 'fundamental' method of inquiry, akin to memory or sense perception. On his view, the reliability of these processes cannot – and, therefore, need not – be confirmed by application of a different method of inquiry.

Daniel Dennett presents a forceful rebuttal to Goldman's view. Drawing on the term 'phenomenology', which refers to the study of sensations and other qualitative states, Dennett dubs the scientific study of *another* person's sensations 'heterophenomenology'.

He allows that it is perfectly legitimate, in conducting heterophenomenology, to ask a subject to introspect his experience. But the subject's introspective report does not provide data about the experiences themselves; it merely illustrates what the subject *believes* about his experiences. Dennet holds that introspection is extremely unreliable, and so the subject's beliefs about his experiences carry no presumption of truth.

Now it might appear that Dennett has identified a defect of the third-person method, and that one can sidestep this problem by operating with one's own introspective data. But Dennett denies that this would be an improvement. For a study limited to one's own case violates the publicity requirement, and therefore – on his view – 'isn't science'. And while he doesn't explicitly express this point, there seems no reason to think that introspection is more reliable in one's own case than in others'. Most importantly, he denies that there *are* any data that are accessible only through the use of introspection. 'Nobody has yet pointed to any variety of data that are inaccessible to heterophenomenology.'[1] Since heterophenomenology is a *third-person* approach to consciousness, the claim here is that there are no data about consciousness that are available only to the conscious subject.

In objecting to the use of introspection, Dennett does not intend to be criticizing scientific practice. For he denies that scientists use introspective data in the way Goldman contends. He claims that scientists practice the method he describes, of taking an introspective report as evidence of a subject's belief about her experiences rather than as evidence of the experiences themselves. So Goldman and Dennett disagree about at least two things: whether the publicity requirement is a valid constraint on scientific practice, and whether scientists actually use introspective evidence.

But what about Goldman's claim that, in the case of blindsight, we simply *must* use introspective evidence to determine whether the blindsighter had a conscious visual experience of the mark on the wall? Dennett responds to this point by addressing a different case (a case of 'priming'), but the moral is clear. A blindsighter's report is neutral as to whether (i) there was no conscious experience of the mark, or (ii) there was a conscious experience that is, for some reason, inaccessible to introspective reflection. (Perhaps the visual cortex damage somehow prevents blindsighters from introspecting some of their conscious visual experiences.) And, Dennett says, only non-introspective evidence can establish which of these hypotheses is correct.

In part, then, the disagreement between Goldman and Dennett is a 'burden of proof' issue. Goldman treats introspective reports as innocent unless proven guilty; Dennett thinks that introspection yields only beliefs about experiences, but such beliefs have no presumption of truth.

However, a deeper issue lies in the background of this debate. How do you know that *sensations* occur at all? Sensations are not seen, heard, or otherwise perceived with the senses. (Though they are often the *result* of applying the senses.) It seems, then, that our only evidence that sensations occur is *introspective*. We can perceive behavior that is good evidence for a sensation: when you witness someone touch a hot stove, recoil, and howl, you have good evidence that that person is experiencing pain. But arguably, it is only through introspecting your own sensations that you have any grounds to believe that sensations exist, and hence to attribute a pain sensation to another person. Similarly, while we can perceive neural states that are correlated with sensations, it is only through introspection that we can establish such correlations in the first place. In this context, it is useful to recall a remark of Julian Jaynes'.

> Though we knew the connections of every tickling thread of every single axon and dendrite in every species that ever existed, together with all its neurotransmitters and how they varied in its billions of synapses of every brain that ever existed, we could still never – *not ever* – from a knowledge of the brain alone know if that brain contained a consciousness like our own. We first have to start from the top, from some conception of what consciousness is, from what our own introspection is (**p. 14**).

So a worry for Dennett's position is that, if we relinquish the use of introspection in our scientific study of the mind, then the resulting theories will not acknowledge the presence of *sensations*. For his part, Dennett may find this a welcome consequence, as he believes that "conscious experience has *no* properties that are special in *any* of the ways qualia [the felt properties of sensations] have been supposed to be special." (Dennett 1988) Included among these purported 'special' qualities is, of course, that these features can be known only through introspection. So Dennett would sharply disagree with Jaynes on this point.

While the pieces by Goldman and Dennett center on the role of introspection in empirical science, the final paper in this section, by David Woodruff Smith, has a broader goal. Smith aims to show that we will not tackle the problem of consciousness unless we use both introspection and other, distinctively philosophical methods of inquiry. His chief opponent is the scientist who – like Dennett – advocates a purely scientific methodology. On Smith's view, the purely scientific approach will lack two resources that are required for solving the problem of consciousness: phenomenology and ontology.

Phenomenology, "the science of consciousness *as* we experience it", draws on our introspective grasp of experience. As we have seen, introspection – and, hence, phenomenology – differs from standard scientific methods in that it violates the publicity requirement.

Ontology, "the science of being", is fundamentally philosophical. It differs from standard scientific methods in that it is conceptual rather than empirical. Smith explains the role of ontology with a useful parallel: "Much as physics needs mathematics to structure its empirical content, so natural science in general needs ontology ... to structure empirical content."

In Smith's metaphysical picture, every entity has three 'facets': a form, an appearance, and a substrate. As Smith's title suggests, this 'three facets' picture applies to consciousness as well. Roughly speaking, the *form* of consciousness concerns its power to represent, as your current visual experience represents this page. The *appearance* of consciousness is its felt quality, that is, 'what it's like' to undergo an experience. The *substrate* of consciousness includes whatever factors underlie our ability to experience the conscious states that we do: these include not only physical phenomena, but also cultural and historical factors.

By confining itself to the narrow methodology of physical science, Smith believes, much contemporary research into consciousness concerns only the substrate of consciousness. Ontology is needed to explain the formal structure of consciousness, including the fact that it has the three facets described. Introspection is needed to illuminate both the form and appearance of consciousness. On Smith's view, it is only by integrating the results of all three disciplines – empirical science, formal ontology, and introspective phenomenology – that we can hope to achieve a comprehensive understanding of consciousness.

QUESTIONS TO THINK ABOUT

1   When your friend asks you 'What is on your mind?', what sort of process do you go through in determining how to answer? Think about how this *introspective* process is similar to, and how it differs from, the *perceptual* process you use to answer the question 'What is on the table?'

2   We have seen two hypotheses about blindsight. The first hypothesis is that blind-sighters lack conscious visual experience of the mark on the wall, but are somehow able to guess what it is with relative accuracy. The second is that they have a conscious visual experience of the mark, but are unable to introspect that experience. Can you think of any other explanations of the blindsight phenomena? Which explanation strikes you as most plausible, and why?

3   Dennett claims that a purely third-person approach to the mind will provide a comprehensive picture of mentality. Goldman, Jaynes, and Smith disagree, claiming that no account of the mind will be complete unless it is informed by our first-person, introspective grasp of experiences. Could this dispute be settled by empirical scientific evidence? If so, what sort of evidence would that be? If not, what sort of evidence, if any, could settle it?

4   Smith argues that a resolution of the problem of consciousness will require the use of formal ontology, which differs from both introspection and ordinary scientific methodology in being *conceptual* rather than empirical. Smith draws an analogy between ontology and mathematics. Mathematical results typically are not derived

through empirical experimentation. Are there other types of methodology that do not require empirical experimentation? What would the success of such methodologies reveal about the subject matters to which they are applied?

NOTES

1 In other work (Dennett 1988), Dennett has expressed skepticism about the existence of 'qualia', which are the felt qualities of experience.

REFERENCES

Dennett, D. (1988). 'Quining Qualia'. A. Marcel and E. Bisiach, eds, *Consciousness in Modern Science*, Oxford University Press. Reprinted in W. Lycan, ed., *Mind and Cognition: A Reader*, MIT Press, 1990.

Libet, B. (1985). 'Unconscious cerebral initiative and the role of conscious will in voluntary action'. *The Behavioral and Brain Sciences*, 8: 529–66.

Nisbett, R., and Wilson, T. (1977). 'Telling more than we can know: verbal reports on mental processes'. *Psychological Review,* 84: 231–59.

FURTHER READING

Jack, A. and Roepstorff, A. (eds.) *Trusting the Subject?* Vols. 1 and 2. Exeter: Imprint Academic, 2003 & 2004.

Lyons, W. *The Disappearance of Introspection*. Cambridge, MA: MIT Press, 1986.

Price, D. and Aydede, M. 'The Experimental Use of Introspection in the Scientific Study of Pain and Its Integration with Third-Person Methodologies: The Experiential-Phenomenological Approach'. With commentaries and reply, Chapters 13–18 of M. Aydede (ed.) *Pain: New Essays on Its Nature and the Methodology of Its Study*. Cambridge, MA: MIT Press (Bradford), 2005.

Smith, D. W. and Thomasson, A. (eds) *Phenomenology and Philosophy of Mind*, esp. the articles in Section I, 'The Place of Phenomenology in Philosophy of Mind', and Section II 'Self-Awareness and Self-Knowledge'. Oxford: Oxford University Press, 2005.

Wilson, T. *Strangers to Ourselves: discovering the adaptive unconscious*. Cambridge, MA: Harvard University Press, 2002.

7

SCIENCE, PUBLICITY, AND CONSCIOUSNESS

Alvin I. Goldman

1 PUBLICITY IN SCIENCE

An old but enduring idea is that science is a fundamentally "public" or "inter-subjective" enterprise. According to this thesis, the core of scientific methodology is interpersonal rather than private. The publicity thesis was prominent in the positivist era, and although it is less frequently discussed today, I suspect it would still receive a vote of approval, or a nod of assent, from most philosophers of science. The thesis is in tension, however, with certain methodological practices of contemporary cognitive science. If the publicity thesis is correct, those practices are illegitimate, and if they are legitimate, the publicity thesis must be abandoned. After explaining the tension, I shall argue that the publicity thesis should give way.

Even at the advent of modern science, publicity received a prominent role. Boyle insisted that the witnessing of experiments was to be a collective act (Shapin and Schaffer 1985, 56). Intersubjectivity was also assigned a crucial role in the positivist era. Popper held that "the *objectivity* of scientific statements lies in the fact that they can be *inter-subjectively tested*" (1959, 44). Epistemically "basic" statements in science, said Popper, are statements "about whose acceptance or rejection the various investigators are likely to reach agreement" (1959, 104). Hempel followed Popper in requiring that "all statements of empirical science be capable of test by reference to evidence which is public, i.e., which can be secured by different observers and does not depend essentially on the observer" (1952, 22). A more expansive statement of this idea can be found in Feigl 1953:

> The quest for scientific knowledge is ... regulated by certain standards or criteria. ... The most important of these regulative ideas are:
>
> 1. *Intersubjective Testability.* This is only a more adequate formulation of what is generally meant by the "objectivity" of science. What is here

involved is ... the requirement that the knowledge claims of science be in principle capable of test ... on the part of any person properly equipped with intelligence and the technical devices of observation or experimentation. The term *intersubjective* stresses the social nature of the scientific enterprise. If there be any "truths" that are accessible only to privileged individuals, such as mystics or visionaries—that is, knowledge-claims which by their very nature cannot independently be checked by anyone else—then such "truths" are not of the kind that we seek in the sciences. The criterion of intersubjective testability thus delimits the scientific from the nonscientific activities of man. (p. 11)

In recent discussions of scientific objectivity, publicity continues to be one standardly cited strand. For example, Railton characterizes scientific objectivity as involving the thesis that "objective inquiry uses procedures that are intersubjective and independent of particular individuals or circumstances—for example, ... it makes no essential use of introspective or subjectively privileged evidence in theory assessment" (1985, 815).

Let us look more closely at the publicity thesis. The passages from Popper and Hempel suggest that what is essentially public in science is its basic statements or items of evidence, and what makes these items of evidence public is that they "can be intersubjectively tested" (Popper) or "can be secured by different observers" (Hempel). It is unclear whether Popper and Hempel are referring to statements that *could* qualify as scientific evidence, or statements that *do* qualify as scientific evidence. In the first instance, however, we need an account of when a statement *does* qualify as scientific evidence, i.e., when scientists are warranted in accepting a statement as evidence. The publicity constraint à la Popper and Hempel might then be formulated as follows:

> Statement S qualifies as a piece of scientific evidence only if S is a statement on which scientific observers *could* reach agreement.

I formulate the account in modal terms because both Popper and Hempel use "can" in their formulations. They presumably do not want a statement to be scientifically acceptable as evidence only when more than one scientist has actually observed the state of affairs it describes. It is necessary (to satisfy the intersubjectivity constraint) only that this state of affairs *could* be observed by many scientists, and if they did observe it, they would agree in accepting S.

However, Popper and Hempel presumably do mean to require that at least one person *actually* observes the state of affairs and forms an observation-based belief in S. Unless this requirement is included, the following scenario would establish a statement as a piece of scientific evidence: (1) nobody actually observes S, but (2) if people were to observe the relevant state of affairs, they would form beliefs in S. But surely the mere possibility of observation-based agreement does not confer on S the status of a scientific datum. There must actually be an observational act and a resulting belief in S. The use of observation, moreover, is critical; not just any old method or process of belief-formation will do. If a person forms a belief in S via religious ecstasy, this would not certify S as a scientific datum, even if hypothetical observations would also lead to beliefs in S.

Two important points emerge from these trivial clarifications. First, establishing something as a piece of scientific evidence depends on what *methods* or *procedures* are actually used. Second, observation—and perhaps only observation—is an approved method or procedure for establishing a statement as a piece of scientific evidence. This poses two questions germane to our inquiry. First, what exactly is observation? Does it, for example, include introspection as a species of "inner observation?" Or should introspection be excluded (as the Railton passage suggests)? Second, what are the grounds for treating observation as a privileged class of belief-forming methods, ones that confer scientific evidencehood on a statement? Why do observational methods, and perhaps only observational methods, have this distinctive capacity?

One possible answer to the second question, which invokes the publicity thesis in a slightly new guise, is that observation is a set of methods each of which is capable of producing *agreement* among its users. (This is a new guise because it concerns methods rather than statements.) There are, of course, challenges to the claim that observational methods do generate agreement, challenges from the alleged theory-ladenness of observation. I shall not address this challenge here. The very significance of the challenge, however, may derive from the assumption that the *ostensible* distinguishing characteristic of observation is its agreement-generating ability. When this ability is questioned, its contribution to epistemic warrant is also questioned. Setting the theory-ladenness issue aside, other indications may be found that the question of agreement-production is viewed as crucial. In assessing the inadequacy of Wundt's introspective method, for example, the psychologists Miller and Buckhout write: "His experiments, unlike experiments elsewhere in science, do not ensure agreement among all those who witness them. Introspective observation is essentially private, and disagreements cannot be settled by repeated observations" (1973, 31). Miller and Buckhout apparently subscribe to the thesis that a method incapable of securing agreement among multiple investigators is inappropriate for science. This version of the publicity thesis seems to lie behind their acceptance of perceptual observation and their rejection of Wundtian introspection as candidate methods of evidence-gathering in science. So publicity can be invoked not only to explain why perceptual observation is an evidence-conferring method but also to resolve the first question by excluding introspection from the class of admissible methods.

2 INTROSPECTION AND CONSCIOUSNESS IN COGNITIVE SCIENCE

Although introspection was officially excommunicated from psychology in the behaviorist era, appeals to something akin to introspection are quite widespread in contemporary cognitive science. Newell and Simon's (1972) influential study of problem solving made extensive use of "protocol data", i.e., reports by subjects of what they were thinking during problem-solving tasks. This and similar kinds of research led Estes to write:

> Only in the very last few years have we seen a major release from inhibition and the appearance in the experimental literature on a large scale of studies reporting the introspections of subjects undergoing memory searches, manipulations of images, and the like. (1975, 5)

On reflection, another core domain of psychology, perception research, also tacitly appeals to a subject's introspective knowledge, i.e., knowledge of how a stimulus *appears* to her. If a subject reports that a certain portion of the current stimulus appears as "figure" and another portion as "ground," the researcher typically accepts this report as correct, i.e., as indicating how those respective portions of the stimulus (or the field) *do* appear to the subject. I call this reliance on the subject's introspection.[1]

Another area of research that heavily depends on introspective report is research on "feelings-of-knowing," or metacognition (Metcalfe and Shimamura 1994, Nelson 1992). Metacognition examines people's ability to predict whether or not they can answer a certain question correctly, i.e., whether they have the answer stored in long-term memory and can retrieve it. One often has a feeling of knowing something although the target item has yet to be retrieved. Psychologists wish to determine how often this feeling is accurate and how the system works that gives rise to such feelings. All such research presupposes that subjects' introspective reports are accurate as to whether or not they currently have a "feeling of knowing." Investigators normally trust a subject's report that she has such a feeling, whether or not the feeling is an accurate predictor of her subsequently finding the sought-after answer.

Psychologists who rely on introspective reports are not committed to the view that *all* such reports are equally reliable or accurate. Ericsson and Simon (1984/1993) devote a lengthy analysis to the question of when, or under what conditions, verbal reports are reliable. (Not everything they call "verbal reports" necessarily qualify as "introspective" reports, however; they themselves avoid the latter phrase.) They distinguish reports issuing from different parts of the subject's cognitive system: sensory stores of very short duration, short-term memory of intermediate duration, and long-term memory. Reports derived from some of these sources are regarded as more accurate than those derived from other sources. Reliability also depends on whether the requisite information was attended to, or heeded. General disavowal of such reports, though, they view as misguided. They criticize Nisbett and Wilson's (1977) apparently broad-gauged critique of introspective reliability. They show that the Nisbett–Wilson critique relies heavily on studies where there was a large time lag between task and probe, so it was unlikely that the relevant information remained in short-term memory at the time of probe. It is hardly surprising that these reports were inaccurate, but that does not undercut *all* such reports. Similarly, some of the studies reviewed by Nisbett and Wilson involved why-questions regarding causes. Correct answers to these questions could only be given if one had access to comparative information with other subjects—the sort of information the investigators themselves obtained through between-subject designs. But subjects could not be expected ever to have had this causal-comparative information in their heads. Hence, their failure to answer such questions correctly hardly betrays a total lack of introspective power.

Now consider the use of introspective reports in the study of consciousness. I focus on the use of such reports to determine whether or not a subject has a conscious state of a specified general type. Three widely discussed domains of consciousness research are blindsight, implicit memory, and prosopagnosia. In all three domains, subjects with neurological deficits are said to lack conscious informational states of a normal sort, but they are also found to possess related information in nonconscious form.[2] Blindsight subjects lack conscious visual experience in a portion of their field of view (their scotoma), but nonetheless show signs of having visually obtained information about objects in the unseen area. Implicit memory is a type of memory that contrasts with explicit memory. Explicit memory involves conscious recollection, implicit memory does not (Schacter 1989). For example, amnesic patients are unable consciously to recall events that they recently experienced, but they show signs of unconsciously remembering these events insofar as their performance at certain tasks benefits from the experience. Profoundly amnesic patients can show normal or nearnormal learning of various perceptual and motor skills without any conscious memory for the experiences of learning (Milner *et al.* 1968, Moscovitch 1982). In prosopagnosia, subjects lack conscious feelings of facial recognition, or familiarity, when seeing even close friends or relatives, but many of these patients demonstrate unconscious recognition in the form of autonomic responses to familiar faces. Bauer (1984) showed a prosopagnosic patient photographs of familiar faces which were presented for 90 seconds, accompanied by five different names, one of which was the correct name. Maximal skin conductance responses to the correct name were found for some 61 percent of trials, a figure well above the chance level of 20 percent. Comparable findings of larger and more frequent skin conductance responses were reported by Tranel and Damasio (1985, 1988).

How do cognitive scientists determine in all these cases that consciousness is present or absent in their subjects' states? The answer is fairly straightforward. Subject to some qualification, consciousness researchers rely on their subjects' introspective reports. To test for a scotoma, as in the case of Weiskrantz's (1986) patient DB, the patient is asked to report what is seen when stimuli are presented to different points in the visual field. DB did not report seeing stimuli falling anywhere in the region to the lower left of the point he was fixating, and for some time he also did not report seeing stimuli in most of the area to the upper left of fixation (for summary, see Young and de Haan 1993). Hence it was concluded that DB lacked conscious vision in those areas. But asked to guess about certain stimuli in those areas, DB's performance revealed some kind of information-bearing state. Since he denied having (visual) information of this sort, however, this state was declared to be nonconscious. Thus, the ability or inability to report a state is taken as a criterion of its being conscious or nonconscious. ...

... If consciousness researchers systematically rely on introspective reports, how can we explain their approach to the syndrome of anosognosia? Patients who suffer from anosognosia are said to be unaware of their impairments. In Anton's syndrome, blind patients deny their own blindness (Anton 1899, McGlynn and Schacter 1989). If a patient denies that she is blind, she is apparently asserting that she does have conscious vision; so a researcher who claims that the patient is really blind refuses to accept her introspective report. Isn't this incompatible with the report criterion as presented here?

The best explanation of what transpires here is that researchers do not regard the patient's report as the expression of a belief formed by introspection. Introspection is presumably a method that is applied "directly" to one's own mental condition and issues in beliefs about that condition.[3] It presumably contrasts with other ways of forming beliefs about one's mental condition, such as inference from one's own behavior or confabulation. Researchers probably assume that anosognosics' reports stem from confabulation rather than genuine introspection. Perhaps the syndrome even includes selective impairment of the ability to introspect, or perhaps just a refusal to do so. Nothing in my account is committed to the view that introspection is always available or is always applied to one's experiential state. Thus, the way researchers interpret anosognosia does not constitute a problem for the thesis that they standardly rely on subjects' introspections.

Some philosophers of consciousness recommend systematic skepticism about subjects' introspective reports of conscious states. This is the message of Dennett's "heterophenomenological method" for the study of consciousness (1991, 66–98). Heterophenomenology advises the scientist to be neutral vis-à-vis all of a subject's consciousness reports, just as an anthropologist studying a tribe's religion would remain agnostic about the truth of their religious beliefs. Whether this type of advice is well motivated remains to be seen. For the moment, the only claim being made is that most cognitive scientists of consciousness do not practice such skepticism or agnosticism. In fact they rely substantially on subjects' introspective beliefs about their conscious experience (or lack thereof), just as cognitive scientists studying problem solving, perception, and metacognition rely substantially on their subjects' introspective reports.

A critic might argue that in using an introspective report, a cognitive scientist merely relies on her own perceptual powers to detect a public event, viz. the subject's act of reporting. My point, however, is that the scientist does not merely accept the fact that an act of reporting occurs; she also accepts the fact reported, e.g., that the subject experienced a certain figure/ground organization, or a certain feeling-of-knowing. In accepting the latter type of fact, the scientist relies on the subject's introspective process, which discloses a private, subjective event (see Alston 1973).

Can it be maintained, however, that the introspected event is itself treated as a piece of evidence, or datum, for cognitive science? Is introspection treated as an evidence-conferring method? Yes, I think it is. Consider an analogy from astronomy. Suppose a solitary observer reports seeing a bright flash in the sky. To the extent that astronomers trust the report as sincere and the observation as competent, they may accept that there was such a flash as a datum for astronomy to explain. Similarly, suppose a subject reports experiencing a certain figure/ground organization. To the extent that cognitive scientists trust the subject's quasi-observation to disclose a certain mental fact, they treat this fact as a datum for cognitive science to explain, or as evidence that can be used to confirm or disconfirm hypotheses. Since this is just the sort of thing cognitive scientists frequently do, they appear to rely on introspection as an evidence-conferring method. If reliance on introspection violates a cardinal precept of scientific methodology—i.e., the publicity precept—then there is a tension between this precept and the actual practice of working cognitive scientists. Which ought to give way?

3 PUBLICITY AND AGREEMENT

To assist our reflection on this question, let us formulate and examine the traditional publicity requirement more carefully. How exactly is the publicity requirement for methods to be understood? We saw earlier that it has something to do with agreement generation. So we might try the following formulation:

> Definition I: Method M is a public (intersubjective) evidence-producing method if and only if all investigators who apply M to the same questions always (or usually) arrive at the same answers (form the same beliefs).

How would this definition work in the case of introspection? Since I cannot intro-spect your conscious states and you cannot introspect mine, I do not apply intro-spection to any questions about your states of consciousness and you do not apply introspection to any questions about mine. Introspection is always applied by just one person per question, and never leads two investigators to arrive at different answers to the same question. Hence, introspection vacuously satisfies Definition I, thereby qualifying as a public method. Clearly, this is contrary to virtually everyone's intention.

To remedy this problem, a different definition of method publicity is required, which might run as follows:

> Definition II: Method M is a public (intersubjective) evidence-producing method if and only if:
>
> (A)   two or more investigators can severally apply M to the same questions, and
> (B)   if different investigators were to apply M to the same questions, M would always (or usually) generate the same answers (induce the same beliefs) in those investigators.

Introspection clearly fails to meet condition (A), yielding the desired result that it fails to qualify as a public method.

Notice that there remains some ambiguity in Definition II. Specifically, should condition (A) be taken to require that there *actually* exist two or more investigators who can apply M to the same questions? Or does it only mean to require that two or more such investigators *might* exist? These two alternative interpretations should be borne in mind as we proceed.

Given Definition II, our provisional definition of method publicity, let us next ask exactly what role publicity is supposed to play in the requirements for scientific evidence production. Defenders of publicity presumably intend it to constitute at least a necessary condition of scientific evidence production. But perhaps they intend it to serve as a sufficient as well as a necessary condition. Let us begin with this latter, stronger proposal.

> (PUB) A statement is an item of scientific evidence if and only if some investigator arrives at a belief in this statement by means of a public method.

This and subsequent proposals should be understood as dealing with *prima facie* scientific evidence. If one investigator uses a legitimate evidential method to arrive at a belief in S, and another investigator later uses the same or another legitimate evidential method to arrive at a belief in not-S, the latter episode tends to defeat or undercut the evidential status of S achieved by the former. But this in no way conflicts with the fact that the first episode conferred *prima facie* evidential status on S.

Is (PUB) an acceptable principle of scientific evidence conferral? Specifically, is (PUB) a sufficient condition for scientific evidence production, given Definition II of method publicity? A moment's reflection reveals that it is far too weak, simply because a tendency toward agreement production is hardly a sufficient condition for evidence production. Suppose that a certain hallucinogenic drug produces vivid belief in any statement S if one takes the drug while asking oneself the question, "Is S true?" Then taking this drug qualifies as a public method according to Definition II. First, more than one person can apply this method to the same question, because method "application" here involves simply taking the drug while querying the statement. Second, if multiple individuals did apply it to the same questions, they would get the same answers (beliefs).

This case shows that the ability to produce agreement is vastly too weak a property of a method to endow it with evidence-conferring power. Its failure suggests that some other type of ingredient must be added (or substituted) for a method to achieve evidence-conferring power. What might this other type of ingredient be? Here we might return to the desideratum of *objectivity*. Commentators on the concept of objectivity often point out that there are at least two senses in which science seeks to be objective, the two senses being intersubjectivity and *reliability* (tendency toward truth production). For example, Boyd writes:

> When we think of scientific objectivity, two importantly different features of scientific practice seem to be at issue: *intersubjectivity* (the capacity of scientists to reach a stable consensus about the issues they investigate ...) and *epistemic reliability* (the capacity of scientists to get it (approximately) right about the things they study). (1985, 48)

So the hitherto missing ingredient might be reliability. This would explain why taking the hallucinogenic drug would not be regarded as an objective, evidence-conferring method. It is obviously not a reliable method, a method that will generally produce true beliefs. Moreover, it would explain why perceptual observation is evidence-conferring, since perceptual observation, at least under favorable conditions, is generally reliable; or at least it is widely thought to be reliable. By adding reliability to intersubjectivity, perhaps we might obtain a set of necessary and sufficient conditions for evidence production. Thus, the following principle may be proposed:

> (PUBREL) A statement is an item of scientific evidence if and only if some investigator arrives at a belief in this statement by means of a method that is both public and reliable.

Here the publicity of a method is only a necessary condition for evidence production, not a sufficient condition.

Is publicity appropriate even as a *necessary* condition of evidence production? This is not obvious. To explore the matter, recall that two different interpretations of Definition II were proposed. Under the first interpretation, a method is public (in a certain possible world) only if there exist (in that world) two or more investigators who can severally apply the method to one or more common questions. Is this an appropriate requirement for evidence production? Consider a possible world containing a collection of spatiotemporally isolated inquirers, each in a different spacetime corner of the universe. Each inquirer is outside the spacetime "cone" of every other inquirer. Suppose that each inquirer uses a certain observational method in her scientific repertoire, but this method can only be applied to *local* questions, i.e., questions about the inquirer's own environment. No isolate can apply it to questions about another isolate's environment. According to the current interpretation, this method does not pass scientific muster as a public method. But that seems extremely dubious. Intuitively, such a method seems capable of producing evidential warrant for the beliefs that each inquirer forms about her environment, and it seems possible for each inquirer to proceed *scientifically* on the basis of such evidence. The same holds for a possible world containing just a single person. Can't such a person still conduct her intellectual affairs with scientific warrant?

The second interpretation of Definition II anticipates these problems. It only requires that it be *possible* for multiple inquirers to exist who can apply the same method to the same questions (and if they did, they would get the same answers). In other words, multiple inquirers need not exist in the world of the example, but only in some possible world accessible to it. Notice, however, that this second interpretation threatens to classify as public the paradigmatically private method of introspection. Consider two brain-linked Siamese twins who share a cerebral hemisphere. This looks like a case in which both persons introspect the same (token) conscious states, thereby applying the introspective method to the same question. Now in all real-world cases of introspection where there are no brain-linked Siamese twins, it is nonetheless possible that each individual should have such a twin. Thus, the method of introspection would satisfy the currently considered condition for publicity. Surely this is not what traditional proponents of a publicity constraint intended.

A second doubt about this interpretation concerns its underlying rationale. Proponents of a publicity constraint apparently feel that beliefs formed by public methods have superior epistemic credentials to beliefs formed by nonpublic methods. But why would conformity with the current interpretation ensure higher epistemic status? If no other creature in the world of the example applies the same method to the same question (and gets the same answer), why would the mere possibility that other creatures in an accessible world might apply the same method to the same question confer higher epistemic credentials on a belief? I detect no intuitive plausibility in this idea.

Neither of the two interpretations we have considered, then, yields satisfactory results. Conceivably, there is some other interpretation of publicity-qua-agreement-production that has yet to be considered. But it is more probable, in my opinion, that the publicity constraint itself is the problem. Why must publicity be a necessary condition for evidence production? Since reliability seems so critical to scientific goals, one might account for publicity's allure by reference to reliability. Perhaps the underlying motivation behind the publicity thesis is that intersubjective agreement is a good *indicator* or *sign* of reliability, and that is why it is desirable. In other words, intersubjective agreement is not a separate and independent constraint on scientific methodology, but at most a derivative and instrumental constraint, rationalized by the central desideratum of reliability or truth.

I find this reconstruction entirely plausible, but it leaves the status of the publicity thesis quite precarious. When a method *can* be applied by multiple investigators, its propensity to yield agreement is useful information from the vantage point of truth determination. Although consensus production does not entail reliability (as the hallucinogenic drug example illustrates), it may often be a reasonably trustworthy guide or clue to reliability. However, when there is a method that *cannot* be applied by different investigators to the same questions, the method may still be quite reliable, as reliable (within appropriate scope restrictions) as other approved methods. If reliability is the fundamental desid/eratum, the intersubjectivity constraint should simply be waived for this kind of method. Why insist on intersubjectivity if the chief goal is reliability or truth? Notice that a reliability constraint alone suffices to disqualify many belief-forming methods that are unsatisfactory from the perspective of scientific evidence-conferral. The methods of guesswork or speculative "insight," for example, can be rejected as evidence-conferring methods because they are plainly unreliable; there is no need to invoke their "privacy" to rationalize their illegitimacy.

4 PUBLICITY AS VALIDATION BY INTERSUBJECTIVE METHODS

At this juncture a slightly different role for publicity should be considered. Even if it is granted that the nonpublicity of a method should not by itself disqualify it from evidence-conferring power, one might resist the suggestion that reliability alone is sufficient to confer such power. To qualify for scientific acceptability, doesn't a method's reliability have to be certified, established, or validated by wholly public methods? Support for this contention comes from simple analogy with the scientific approach to instrumentation. The readings of a scientific instrument would never be trusted as a source of evidence unless the instrument's reliability were established by standard, i.e., public, procedures. Isn't it similarly necessary that introspection's reliability be established for it to be trusted, and mustn't this reliability also be established by public means? So even if methods can qualify as evidence-conferring without themselves being public, don't they need to have their reliability validated by public procedures? Call this fallback position for the publicity thesis the *public validation constraint* [the PV constraint].

Let us first ask how cognitive science could go about publicly validating introspection's reliability. Ostensibly, one would have to compare the (presumptively sincere) introspective reports of a subject with the "actual fact" of what is reported, which itself must be determined by procedures that do not involve introspection. Since a cognitive scientist cannot directly observe the mental state of the subject, the actual condition of this mental state must be determined by observation of behavior (or stimuli) plus some sort of theoretical, nomological inference. The basic difficulty is that cognitive scientists lack adequate nomological generalizations that would allow them to draw firm inferences about the sorts of states described in introspective reports, in particular, states of consciousness.

To illustrate the problem, suppose a subject reports having a "feeling of knowing" the answer to a certain question (without yet having retrieved the answer). How is the psychologist supposed to determine whether that feeling really does exist in the subject at the time reported? Psychologists who study metacognition have no nomological principles by which to infer whether such a feeling of knowing does or does not occur at a given time independent of the subject's report. Furthermore, if such principles could be formulated in the future, their verification would presumably require reliance on subjects' introspective reports. This follows from the fact that the report criterion is the fundamental psychological method of determining what a subject's conscious states are.

To take another example, suppose an amnesic patient is set to work on a Tower of Hanoi problem and reports having no conscious recollection of previously having worked on these types of tasks. How is the psychologist supposed to determine whether this introspective report is correct? The psychologist may know that this patient has in fact worked on such problems before and that her current performance shows improvement, suggesting that it has been facilitated by some kind of retention of earlier activities. But this hardly shows that the subject has a *conscious* recollection of the earlier activity; nor that she does not. There seems to be no way to verify independently the subject's report of no conscious recollection. Cognitive scientists might eventually identify neural correlates of consciousness, and these correlates might then be used to determine the current conscious states of a subject. But the initial process of identifying such neural correlates would itself have to rely on introspective reports, so this would be no help to the project of *independent* validation of introspection. ...

... Suppose, then, that no independent, public validation of introspection's reliability has actually been offered, and perhaps none is even possible. Where does that leave us? Should introspection be abandoned because it violates the PV constraint? Or should that constraint itself be rejected? I shall argue that violation of the PV constraint is not such a shocking epistemological situation for a *basic* or *fundamental* cognitive process like introspection. If introspection is in this epistemic condition, that does not mark it off from other duly approved basic methods. For a large class of fundamental cognitive processes, it is impossible to certify their reliability in an independent, i.e., noncircular, fashion. This thesis is defended in detail by Alston (1993).

Start with memory. Can one establish the reliability of memory without appealing to premises that themselves rely on memory? As Alston argues (1993, 116–17), this is impossible. It might seem as if we can, because there are ways to determine whether Smith's remembered proposition p was indeed the case without oneself remembering p to have happened. To determine whether a TV set was delivered on August 6, 1991, we can look at the delivery slip, consult records at the store, and so on. But the delivery slip is good evidence only if this is the slip that accompanied that TV set; and one has to rely on memory to assure oneself of that, or else appeal to another record, which simply raises the same problem once again. More generally, the reliability of records, traces of past events, and so forth themselves need to be established via memory. Although memory is not a widely discussed method of *science*, only a bit of reflection reveals that scientists constantly rely on memory in their cognitive practice, and science could hardly proceed without it. Even interpreting one's laboratory notes depends on remembering the meaning of the notation. Since memory, like introspection, cannot have its reliability *independently* validated, introspection does not seem to be in such bad company.

Another well-known example is enumerative induction. Since Hume's treatment of induction, it is widely recognized that the reliability of induction cannot be established in any independent, noncircular fashion. Since science also seems to rely on induction (although the exact form of induction is notoriously controversial), introspection again seems to keep respectable company.

What about perceptual observation, which is the principal form of evidence establishment? Alston groups the five senses together and addresses the practice of "sense perception." He argues, quite convincingly, that sense perception is also not suspectible of having its reliability established by any independent practice or method. All attempts to establish the reliability of sense perception must ultimately appeal to sense perception. In the case of sense perception, of course, we have a class of processes with clearly diverse members: vision, audition, touch, and so forth. Each of these sense modalities can have its reliability at least partly established by use of the other modalities. However, as Alston argues, to certify the reliability of the latter modalities, one would ultimately have to turn to the first ones. So there still seems to be an essential form of circularity here. Whether it is as serious as the cases of memory and induction I shall not try to settle.

Although human beings, like most terrestrial creatures, have multiple senses, there could be a creature with just a single sense, e.g., touch. (I presume it is uncontroversial that creatures could have fewer than five senses. But if fewer than five, why not fewer han two?) The sense perception of a single-sensed creature would be no better off than introspection as far as independent validation of reliability is concerned. Yet would we say that such a creature can acquire no evidence at all, in virtue of the fact that its sole observational method violates the independent validation constraint? Surely not.

It is clear, then, that introspection's violation of the independent validation constraint does not put it out of step with most other fundamental methods that are honored as scientifically legitimate. Now since introspection violates the independent validation constraint and it is itself nonpublic, it follows that it violates the *public* validation constraint. But its violation of this constraint is principally due to its sharing a *general* property of fundamental methods (viz., their insusceptibility of independent validation), and the other fundamental methods are accepted as scientifically legitimate. So why should introspection's legitimacy be challenged on these grounds?

It could be argued that introspection deserves epistemic oblivion because it suffers from *two* worrisome epistemic features, not just one. It fails to be public and it fails to be independently validated (or validatable). But the second failure, we have seen, is widespread among fundamental methods. And the first failure, as shown in section 3, is not embarrassing either, because publicity does not deserve to be a *sine qua non* of scientific methods of evidence conferral. So introspection, in my opinion, does not deserve epistemic oblivion on any of these grounds, either singly or jointly.

5 CONCLUSION

I have not said, it should be noted, that reliability is the only appropriate constraint on the scientific legitimacy of an evidence-conferring method. Minimally, a method should also satisfy a certain "negative" constraint, viz., that there not be (undefeated) evidence of its unreliability.[4] Thus, even if introspection is reliable, and even if it is not disqualified because its reliability cannot be publicly established, these conditions do not yet get it out of the woods. It would still not deserve scientific reliance if there is (undefeated) evidence of its unreliability.[5]

Is it possible to get evidence for the unreliability of introspection? Yes; unreliability might at least be exposed through internal inconsistencies. If introspection delivers conflicting beliefs (on the very same questions), then in each case of conflict, at least one of the conflicting beliefs must be false. If there is massive conflict of this sort, substantial unreliability would be established.

I do not believe that massive conflict of this sort has materialized, however. Something along these lines seemed to occur in classical introspectionism, but there the matter was more complicated, partly because most of the conflicts occurred *inter*personally rather than *intra*personally. Subjects trained in different laboratories delivered different judgments about their consciousness. This is not technically a contradiction, since each was talking about his or her *own* consciousness. But if we add the (implicit) premise that everyone's consciousness has the same general features, inconsistency follows. This was why introspection was abandoned at that historical juncture; it was a problem, at least an apparent problem, of reliability (not publicity). In that period, however, introspection was asked to reveal details of mental life that no current cognitive scientist expects it to reveal, and subjects were theoretically indoctrinated in ways that corrupted their deliverances.[6] When introspection is confined to a more modest range of questions, as it is today, it has not been shown to be unreliable in such a domain. Everyone nowadays agrees that introspection is an unreliable method for answering questions about the micro-structure of cognition. For example, nobody expects subjects to report reliably whether their thinking involves the manipulation of sentences in a language of thought. But this leaves many other types of questions about which introspection could be reliable.

For all of these reasons, I see no reason to abandon the current cognitive science practice of relying on introspection (with all due caution). In particular, neither the traditional publicity thesis nor the fallback publicity thesis provides grounds for requiring cognitive scientists to abandon their reliance on introspection.

NOTES

1 Chalmers (1996, 385–6, n. 12) points out that psychophysics also typically relies on introspection.
2 The study of implicit memory is by no means restricted to impaired subjects, but the phenomenon is particularly salient in their case.
3 The exact nature of introspection is a difficult matter (see Shoemaker 1994, Lycan 1996), and no attempt is made here to characterize it fully and precisely.
4 This parallels the sort of "non-undermining" constraint that reliabilists in the theory of justification sometimes propose (see Goldman 1986, 62–3).
5 Does satisfaction of these two constraints (reliability plus no undefeated evidence of unreliability) suffice for scientific acceptability? I do not wish to commit myself to that positive thesis. The paper's project is mainly a negative one: that of undercutting the publicity thesis.
6 See Ericsson and Simon 1993, 48–61; Lyons 1986. Notice that although Watson (1913) attacked the analytic methods and results of the classical introspectionists, he acknowledged reliable and robust results to have been obtained by introspection in psychophysics. See Ericsson and Simon 1993, 54, 57.

REFERENCES

Alston, W. (1973), "Can Psychology Do Without Private Data?", *Behaviorism* 1: 71–102.

——. (1993), *The Reliability of Sense Perception*. Ithaca: Cornell University Press.

Anton, G. (1899), "Ueber die Selbstwahrnemung der Herderkrankungen des Gehirns durch den Kranken bei Rindenblindheit und Rindentaubheit", *Archiv für Psychiatrie und Nervenkrankheiten* 32: 86–127.

Bauer, R. (1984), "Autonomic Recognition of Names and Faces in Prosopagnosia: A Neuropsychological Application of the Guilty Knowledge Test", *Neuropsychologia* 22: 457–69.

Block, N. (1995), "On a Confusion about a Function of Consciousness", *Behavioral and Brain Sciences* 18: 227–47.

Boyd, R. (1985), "Observations, Explanatory Power, and Simplicity: Toward a Non-Humean Account", in P. Achinstein and O. Hannaway (eds.), *Observation, Experiment, and Hypothesis in Modern Physical Science*. Cambridge, MA: MIT Press, pp. 47–94.

Chalmers, D. (1996), *The Conscious Mind*. New York: Oxford University Press.

Dennett, D.C. (1991), *Consciousness Explained*. Boston: Little, Brown and Co.

Ericsson, K. and H. Simon (1984/1993), *Protocol Analysis*. Cambridge, MA: MIT Press.

Estes, W. (1975), "The State of the Field: General Problems and Issues of Theory and Meta-theory", in W. Estes (ed.), *Handbook of Learning and Cognitive Processes*, vol. 1. Hillsdale, NJ: Lawrence Erlbaum, pp. 1–24.

Feigl, H. (1953), "The Scientific Outlook: Naturalism and Humanism", in H. Feigl and M. Brodbeck (eds.), *Readings in the Philosophy of Science*. New York: Appleton-Century-Crofts, pp. 8–18.

Goldman, A. (1986), *Epistemology and Cognition*. Cambridge, MA: Harvard University Press.

Hempel, C. (1952), *Fundamentals of Concept Formation in Empirical Science*. Chicago: University of Chicago Press.

Lycan, W. (1996), *Consciousness and Experience*. Cambridge, MA: MIT Press.

Lyons, W. (1986), *The Disappearance of Introspection*. Cambridge, MA: MIT Press.

Marcel, A. (1988), "Phenomenal Experience and Functionalism", in A. Marcel and E. Bisiach (eds.), *Consciousness in Contemporary Science*. Oxford: Oxford University Press, pp. 121–58.

——. (1993), "Slippage in the Unity of Consciousness", in Ciba Symposium 174, *Experimental and Theoretical Studies of Consciousness*, pp. 168–80.

McGlynn, S. and D. Schacter (1989), "Unawareness of Deficits in Neuropsychological Syndromes", *Journal of Clinical and Experimental Neuropsychology* 11: 143–205.

Metcalfe, J. and A. Shimamura (eds.) (1994), *Metacognition*. Cambridge, MA: MIT Press.

Miller, G. and R. Buckhout (1973), *Psychology: The Science of Mental Life*, 2nd ed. New York: Harper and Row.

Milner, B., S. Corkin, and H. Teuber (1968), "Further Analysis of the Hippocampal Amnesic Syndrome: 14 Year Follow-Up Study of H.M." *Neuropsychologia* 6: 215–34.

Moscovitch, M. (1982), "Multiple Dissociations of Function in Amnesia", in L. Cermak (ed.), *Human Memory and Amnesia*. Hillsdale, NJ: Erlbaum, pp. 337–70.

Nelson, T. (ed.) (1992) *Metacognition*. Boston: Allyn and Bacon.

Newell, A. and H. Simon (1972), *Human Problem Solving*. Englewood Cliffs, NJ: Prentice-Hall.

Nisbett, R. and T. Wilson (1977), "Telling More Than We Can Know: Verbal Reports on Mental Processes", *Psychological Review* 84: 231–59.

Popper, K. (1959), *The Logic of Scientific Discovery*. London: Hutchinson.

Railton, P. (1985), "Marx and the Objectivity of Science", in P. Asquith and P. Kitcher (eds.), *PSA 1934*, vol. 2. East Lansing, MI: Philosophy of Science Association, pp. 813–25.

Schacter, D. (1989), "On the Relation between Memory and Consciousness: Dissociable Inter-actions and Conscious Experience", in H. Roediger and F. Craik (eds.), *Essays in Honor of Endel Tulving*. Hillsdale, NJ: Erlbaum, pp. 355–89.

Shapin, S. and S. Schaffer (1985), *Leviathan and the Air-Pump*. Princeton: Princeton University Press.

Shoemaker, S. (1994), "Self Knowledge and 'Inner Sense'", *Philosophy and Phenomenological Research* 54: 249–314.

Tranel, D. and A. Damasio (1985), "Knowledge without Awareness: An Automatic Index of Facial Recognition by Prosopagnosics", *Science* 228: 1453–54.

——. (1988), "Non-conscious Face Recognition in Patients with Face Agnosia", *Behavioral Brain Research* 30: 235–49.

Velmans, M. (1991), "Is Human Information Processing Conscious?", *Behavioral and Brain Sciences* 14: 651–69.

Watson, J. (1913), "Psychology as the Behaviorist Views It", *Psychological Review* 20: 158–77.

Weiskrantz, L. (1986), *Blindsight: A Case Study and Implications*. Oxford: Oxford University Press.

Young, A. and E. de Haan (1993), "Impairments of Visual Awareness", in M. Davies and G. Humphreys (eds.), *Consciousness*. Oxford: Blackwell Publishers, pp. 58–73.

8

WHO'S ON FIRST?

Heterophenomenology Explained

Daniel Dennett

There is a pattern of miscommunication bedeviling the people working on consciousness that is reminiscent of the classic Abbott and Costello 'Who's on First?' routine. With the best of intentions, people are talking past each other, seeing major disagreements when there are only terminological or tactical preferences – or even just matters of emphasis – that divide the sides. Since some substantive differences also lurk in this confusion, it is well worth trying to sort out. Much of the problem seems to have been caused by some misdirection in my apologia for *heterophenomenology* (Dennett 1982; 1991), advertised as an explicitly *third*-person approach to human consciousness, so I will try to make amends by first removing those misleading signposts and sending us back to the real issues.

On the face of it, the study of human consciousness involves phenomena that seem to occupy something rather like another dimension: the private, subjective, '*first*-person' dimension. Everybody agrees that this is where we start. What, then, is the relation between the standard 'third-person' objective methodologies for studying meteors or magnets (or human metabolism or bone density), and the methodologies for studying human consciousness? Can the standard methods be extended in such a way as to do justice to the phenomena of human consciousness? Or do we have to find some quite radical or revolutionary alternative science? I have defended the hypothesis that there is a straightforward, conservative extension of objective science that handsomely covers the ground – *all* the ground – of human consciousness, doing justice to all the data without ever having to abandon the rules and constraints of the experimental method that have worked so well in the rest of science. This third-person methodology, dubbed heterophenomenology (phenomenology of *another* not oneself), is, I have claimed, the sound way to take the *first*-person point of view as seriously as it can be taken.

To place heterophenomenology in context, consider the following ascending scale of methods of scientific investigation:

- experiments conducted on anaesthetized animals;
- experiments conducted on awake animals;
- experiments on human subjects conducted in 'behaviorese'
  - subjects are treated as much as possible like laboratory rats, trained to criterion with the use of small rewards, with minimal briefing and debriefing, etc.;
- experiments in which human subjects collaborate with experiments
  - making suggestions, interacting verbally, telling what it is like.

Only the last of these methods holds out much hope of taking human subjectivity seriously, and at first blush it may seem to be a first-person (or, with its emphasis on communicative interaction with the subjects, second-person) methodology, but in fact it is *still* a third-person methodology if conducted properly. It is heterophenomenology.

Most of the method is so obvious and uncontroversial that some scientists are baffled that I would even call it a method: basically, you have to take the vocal sounds emanating from the subjects' mouths (and your own mouth) and *interpret* them! Well of course. What else could you do? Those sounds aren't just belches and moans; they're speech acts, reporting, questioning, correcting, requesting, and so forth. Using such standard speech acts, other events such as button-presses can be set up to be interpreted as speech acts as well, with highly specific meanings and fine temporal resolution. What this interpersonal communication enables you, the investigator, to do is to compose a catalogue of *what the subject believes to be true about his or her conscious experience*. This catalogue of beliefs fleshes out the subject's *heterophenomenological world*, the world according to S – the subjective world of one subject – not to be confused with the real world. The total set of details of heterophenomenology, plus all the data we can gather about concurrent events in the brains of subjects and in the surrounding environment, comprise the total data set for a theory of human consciousness. It leaves out no objective phenomena and no subjective phenomena of consciousness.

Just what kinds of things does this methodology commit us to? Beyond the unproblematic things all of science is committed to (neurons and electrons, clocks and microscopes, ...) just to *beliefs* – the beliefs expressed by subjects and deemed constitutive of their subjectivity. And what kind of things are beliefs? Are they sentences in the head written in brain writing? Are they nonphysical states of dualist ectoplasm? Are they structures composed of proteins or neural assemblies or electrical fields? We may stay maximally noncommittal about this by adopting, at least for the time being (I recommend: for ever), the position I have defended (Dennett 1971; 1987; 1991) that treats beliefs from *the intentional stance* as *theorists' fictions* similar to centres of mass, the Equator, and parallelograms of forces. In short, we may treat beliefs as *abstractions* that measure or describe the complex cognitive state of a subject rather the way horsepower indirectly but accurately measures the power of engines (don't look in the engine for the horses). As Churchland (1979) has pointed out, physics already has hundreds of well-understood measure predicates, such as *x has weight-in-grams n*, or *x is moving up at n meters per second*, which describe a physical property of x by relating it to a *number*. Statements that attribute beliefs using the standard *propositional attitude* format, *x believes that p*, describe x's internal state by relating it to a *proposition*, another kind of useful abstraction, systematized in logic, not arithmetic. We need beliefs anyway for the rest of social science, which is almost entirely conducted in terms of the intentional stance, so this is a conservative exploitation of already quite well-behaved and well-understood methods.

A catalogue of beliefs about experience is not the same as a catalogue of experiences themselves, and it has been objected (Levine 1994) that 'conscious experiences themselves, not merely our verbal judgments about them, are the primary data to which a theory must answer'. But how, in advance of theory, could we catalogue the experiences themselves? We can see the problem most clearly in terms of a nesting of proximal sources that are presupposed as we work our way up from raw data to heterophenomenological worlds:

(a) 'conscious experiences themselves'
(b) beliefs about these experiences
(c) 'verbal judgments' expressing those beliefs
(d) utterances of one sort or another

What are the 'primary data'? For heterophenomenologists, the *primary* data are the utterances, the *raw*, uninterpreted data. But before we get to theory, we can interpret these data, carrying us via (c) speech acts to (b) beliefs about experiences.[1] These are the primary *interpreted* data, the pretheoretical data, the *quod erat explicatum* (as organized into heterophenomenological worlds), for a science of consciousness. In the quest for primary data, Levine wants to go all the way to (a) conscious experiences themselves, instead of stopping with (b) subjects' beliefs about their experiences, but this is not a good idea. If (a) outruns (b) – if you have conscious experiences you don't believe you have – those extra conscious experiences are just as inaccessible *to you* as to the external observers. So Levine's proposed alternative garners you no more usable data than heterophenomenology does. Moreover, if (b) outruns (a) – if you believe you have conscious experiences that you don't in fact have – then it is your beliefs that we need to explain, not the non-existent experiences! Sticking to the heterophenomenological standard, then, and treating (b) as the maximal set of primary data, is the way to avoid any commitment to spurious data.

But what if some of your beliefs are inexpressible in verbal judgments? If you believe *that*, you can tell us, and we can add that belief to the list of beliefs in our primary data: 'S claims that he has ineffable beliefs about X'. If this belief is true, then we encounter the obligation to explain what these beliefs are and why they are ineffable. If this belief is false, we still have to explain why S believes (falsely) that there are these particular ineffable beliefs. As I put it in *Consciousness Explained*,

> You are *not* authoritative about what is happening in you, but only about what *seems* to be happening in you, and we are giving you total, dictatorial authority over the account of how it seems to you, about *what it is like to be you*. And if you complain that some parts of how it seems to you are ineffable, we heterophenomenologists will grant that too. What better grounds could we have for believing that you are unable to describe something than that (1) you don't describe it, and (2) you confess that you cannot? Of course you might be lying, but we'll give you the benefit of the doubt (Dennett 1991, 96–7).

This is all quite obvious, but it has some under-appreciated implications. Exploiting linguistic communication in this way, you get a fine window into the subject's subjectivity but at the cost of a peculiar lapse in normal interpersonal relations. You *reserve judgment* about whether the subject's beliefs, as expressed in their communication, are true, or even well-grounded, but then you treat them as *constitutive* of that subject's subjectivity. (As far as I can see, this is the third-person parallel to Husserl's notion of bracketing or *epoché*, in which the normal presuppositions and inferences of one's own subjective experience are put on hold, as best one can manage, in order to get at the core experience, as theory-neutral and unencumbered as possible.) This interpersonal reserve can be somewhat creepy. To put it fancifully, suppose you burst into my heterophenomenology lab to warn me that the building is on fire. I don't leap to my feet and head for the door; I write down 'subject S believes the building is on fire'. 'No, really, it's on fire!' you insist, and I ask 'Would you like to expand on that? *What is it like* for you to think the building is on fire?' and so forth. In one way I am taking you as seriously as you could ever hope to be taken, but in another way I am not. I am not *assuming* that you are right in what you tell me, but just that that is what you do believe. Of course most of the data-gathering is not done by any such simple interview. Experiments are run in which subjects are prepared by various conversations, hooked up to all manner of apparatus, etc., and carefully debriefed. In short, heterophenomenology is nothing new; it is nothing other than the method that has been used by psychophysicists, cognitive psychologists, clinical neuropsychologists, and just about everybody who has ever purported to study human consciousness in a serious, scientific way.

This point has sometimes been misunderstood by scientists who suppose, quite reasonably, that since I am philosopher I must want to scold somebody for something, and hence must be proposing restrictions on standard scientific method, or discovering limitations therein. On the contrary, I am urging that the prevailing methodology of scientific investigation on human consciousness is not only sound, but readily extendable in non-revolutionary ways to incorporate *all* the purported exotica and hard cases of human subjectivity. I want to put the burden of proof on those who insist that third-person science is incapable of grasping the nettle of consciousness.

Let me try to secure the boundaries of the heterophenomenological method more clearly, then, since this has apparently been a cause of confusion. As Anthony Jack has said to me:

> It strikes me that heterophenomenology is a method in the same way that 'empiricism' is a method, but no more specific nor clearly defined than that. Given how general you seem to allow your definition of heterophenomenology to be, it is no surprise that everything conforms! Perhaps it would be clearer if you explained more clearly what it is supposed to be a counterpoint to – what it is that you object to. I know I am not the only one who has a feeling that you make the goalposts surprisingly wide. So what exactly is a foul? (Jack, personal correspondence).

Lone-wolf autophenomenology, in which the subject and experimenter are one and the same person, is a foul, not because you can't do it, but because it isn't science until you turn your self-administered pilot studies into heterophenomenological experiments. It has always been good practice for scientists to put themselves in their own experimental apparatus as informal subjects, to confirm their hunches about what it feels like, and to check for any overlooked or underestimated features of the circumstances that could interfere with their interpretations of their experiments. But scientists have always recognized the need to confirm the insights they have gained from introspection by conducting properly controlled experiments with naive subjects. As long as this obligation is met, whatever insights one may garner from 'first-person' investigations fall happily into place in 'third-person' heterophenomenology. Purported discoveries that cannot meet this obligation may inspire, guide, motivate, illuminate one's scientific theory, but *they* are not data – the beliefs of subjects about them are the data. Thus if some phenomenologist becomes convinced by her own (first-) personal experience, however encountered, transformed, reflected upon, of the existence of a feature of consciousness in need of explanation and accommodation within her theory, her *conviction that this is so* is itself a fine datum in need of explanation, by her or by others, but the truth of her conviction must not be presupposed by science.

Does anybody working on consciousness disagree with this? Does anybody think that one can take personal introspection by the investigator as constituting stand-alone evidence (publishable in a peer-reviewed journal, etc.) for any substantive scientific claim about consciousness? I don't think so. So I think we can set aside lone-wolf autophenomenology in all its guises. It is not an attractive option, for familiar reasons. The experimenter/subject duality is not what is being challenged by those who want to go beyond the 'third-person' methodology. What other alternatives should we consider?

Several critics have supposed that heterophenomenology, as I have described it, is too agnostic or too neutral. Goldman (1997) [reprinted as **Ch. 7** of this volume – eds.] says that heterophenomenology is not, as I claim, the standard method of consciousness research, since researchers 'rely substantially on subjects' introspective beliefs about their conscious experience (or lack thereof)' (p. 532). In personal correspondence (Feb 21, 2001, available as part of my debate with Chalmers, on my website, at http://ase.tufts.edu/cogstud/papers/chalmersdeb3dft.htm) he puts the point this way:

> The objection lodged in my paper (Goldman 1997) [**Ch. 7** of this volume] to heterophenomenology is that what cognitive scientists *actually* do in this territory is not to practice agnosticism. Instead, they rely substantially on subjects' introspective beliefs (or reports). So my claim is that the heterophenomenological method is not an accurate description of what cognitive scientists (of consciousness) standardly do. Of course, you can say (and perhaps intended to say, but if so it wasn't entirely clear) that this is what scientists *should* do, not what they *do* do.

I certainly would play the role of reformer if it were necessary, but Goldman is simply mistaken; the adoption of agnosticism is so firmly built into practice these days that it goes without saying, which is perhaps why he missed it. Consider, for instance, the decades-long controversy about mental imagery, starring Roger Shepard, Steven Kosslyn, and Zenon Pylyshyn among many others. It was initiated by the brilliant experiments by Shepard and his students in which subjects were shown pairs of line drawings like the pair in figure 8.1, and asked to press one button if the figures were different views of the same object (rotated in space) and another button if they were of different objects. Most subjects claim to solve the problem by rotating one of the two figures in their 'mind's eye' or imagination, to see if it could be superimposed on the other. Were subjects really doing this 'mental rotation'? By varying the angular distance actually required to rotate the two figures into congruence, and timing the responses, Shepard was able to establish a remarkably regular linear relation between latency of response and angular displacement. Practiced subjects, he reported, are able to rotate such mental images at an angular velocity of roughly 60E per second (Shepard and Metzler 1971). This didn't settle the issue, since Pylyshyn and others were quick to compose alternative hypotheses that could account for this striking

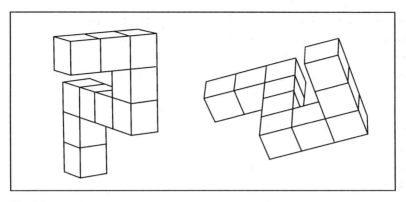

Fig 8.1

temporal relationship. Further studies were called for and executed, and the controversy continues to generate new experiments and analysis today (see Pylyshyn 2002, for an excellent survey of the history of this debate; also my commentary, Dennett 2002, both in *Behavioral and Brain Sciences*). Subjects always *say* that they are rotating their mental images, so if agnosticism were not the tacit order of the day, Shepard and Kosslyn would have never needed to do their experiments to support subjects' claims that what they were doing (at least if described metaphorically) really was a process of image manipulation. Agnosticism is built into all good psychological research with human subjects. In psychophysics, for instance, the use of signal detection theory has been part of the canon since the 1960s, and it specifically commands researchers to control for the fact that the response criterion is under the subject's control although the subject is not himself or herself a reliable source on the topic. Or consider the voluminous research literature on illusions, both perceptual and cognitive, which standardly assumes that the data are what subjects judge to be the case, and never makes the mistake of 'relying substantially on subjects' introspective beliefs'.

The diagnosis of Goldman's error is particularly clear here: of course experimenters on illusions rely on subjects' introspective beliefs (as expressed in their judgments) about how it *seems* to them, but that *is* the agnosticism of heterophenomenology; to go beyond it would be, for instance, to assume that in size illusions there really were visual images of different sizes somewhere in subjects' brains (or minds), which of course no researcher would dream of doing.

David Chalmers has recently made a similar, if vaguer, claim:

Dennett ... says scientists have to take a neutral attitude (taking reports themselves as data, but making no claims about their truth), because reports can go wrong. But this misses the natural intermediate option that Max Velmans has called critical phenomenology: accept verbal reports as a prima facie guide to a subject's conscious experience, except where there are specific reasons to doubt their reliability. This seems to be most scientists' attitude toward verbal reports and consciousness: it's not 'uncritical acceptance', but it's also far from the 'neutrality' of heterophenomenology (Chalmers 2003).

Chalmers neglects to say how Velmans' critical phenomenology is 'far from' the neutrality of heterophenomenology. I conducted a lengthy correspondence with Velmans on this score and was unable to discover what the purported difference is, beyond Velmans' insisting that his method 'accepts the reality of first-person experience', but since it is unclear what this means, this is something a good scientific method should be agnostic about. Neither Chalmers nor Velmans has responded to my challenge to describe an experiment that is licensed by, or motivated by, or approved by 'critical phenomenology' but off-limits to heterophenomenology, so if there is a difference here, it is one of style or emphasis, not substance. Chalmers has acknowledged this, in a way:

> Dennett 'challenges' me to name an experiment that 'transcends' the heterophenomenological method. But of course both views can accommodate experiments equally: every time I say we're using a verbal report or introspective judgment as a guide to first-person data, he can say we're using it as third-person data, and vice versa. So the difference between the views doesn't lie in the range of experiments 'compatible' with them. Rather, it lies in the way that experimental results are interpreted. And I think the interpretation I'm giving (on which reports are given prima facie credence as a guide to conscious experience) is by far the most common attitude among scientists in the field. Witness the debate about unconscious perception among cognitive psychologists about precisely which third-person measures (direct report, discrimination, etc.) are the best guide to the presence of conscious perception. Here, third-person data are being used as a (fallible) guide to first-person data about consciousness, which are of primary interest. On the heterophenomenological view, this debate is without much content: some states subserve report, some subserve discrimination, etc., and that's about all there is to say. I think something like this is Dennett's attitude to those debates, but it's not the attitude of most of the scientists working in the field (Chalmers 2003).

Chalmers misconstrues my view, as we can see if we look more closely at a particular debate about unconscious perception, to see how heterophenomenology sorts out the issues. Consider *masked priming*. It has been demonstrated in hundreds of different experiments that if you present subjects with a 'priming' stimulus, such as a word or picture flashed briefly on a screen in front of the subject, followed very swiftly by a 'mask' – a blank or sometimes randomly patterned rectangle – before presenting the subjects with a 'target' stimulus to identify or otherwise respond to, there are conditions under which subjects will manifest behavior that shows they have discriminated the priming stimulus, while they candidly and sincerely report that they were entirely unaware of any such stimulus. For instance, asked to complete the word stem *fri—*, subjects who have been shown the priming stimulus *cold* are more likely to comply with *frigid* and subjects who have been shown the priming stimulus *scared* are more likely to comply with *fright* or *frightened*, even though both groups of subjects claim not to have seen anything but first a blank rectangle followed by the target to be completed. Now are subjects to be trusted when they say that they were not conscious of the priming stimulus? There are apparently two ways theory can go here:

A. Subjects are conscious of the priming stimulus and then the mask makes them immediately forget this conscious experience, but it nevertheless influences their later performance on the target.
B. Subjects unconsciously extract information from the priming stimulus, which is prevented from 'reaching consciousness' by the mask.

Chalmers suggests that it is my 'attitude' that there is nothing to choose between these two hypotheses, but my point is different. It is open for scientific investigation to develop reasons for preferring one of these theoretical paths to the other, but *at the outset*, heterophenomenology is neutral, leaving the subject's heterophenomenological worlds bereft of any priming stimuli – that is how it seems to the subjects, after all – while postponing an answer to the question of how or why it seems thus to the subjects. Heterophenomenology is the beginning of a science of consciousness, not the end. It is the organization of the data, a catalogue of *what must be explained*, not itself an explanation or a theory. (This was the original meaning of 'phenomenology': a pretheoretical catalogue of the phenomena theory must account for.) And in maintaining this neutrality, it is actually doing justice to the *first-person* perspective, because you yourself, as a subject in a masked priming experiment, cannot discover anything in your experience that favours A or B. (If you think you can discover something – if you notice some glimmer of a hint in the experience, speak up! You're the subject, and you're supposed to tell it like it is. Don't mislead the experimenters by concealing something you discover in your experience. Maybe they've set the timing wrong for you. Let them know. But if they've done the experiment right, and you really find, so far as you can tell from your own first-person perspective, that you were not conscious of any priming stimulus, then say so, and note that both A and B are still options between which you are powerless to offer any further evidence.)

But now suppose scientists look for a good reason to favour A or B and find it. What could it be? A theory that could provide a good reason would be one that is well-confirmed in other domains or contexts and that distinguishes, say, the *sorts* of discriminations that can be made unconsciously from the sorts that require consciousness. If in this case the masked discrimination was of a feature that in all other circumstances could only be discriminated by a conscious subject, this would be a (fairly) good reason for supposing that, however it may be with other discriminations, in this case the discrimination was conscious-and-then-forgotten, not unconscious. Notice that if anything at all like this were discovered, and used as a ground for distinguishing A from B, it would be a triumph of *third-person* science, not due to anything that is accessible only to the subject's introspection. Subjects would *learn for the first time* that they were, or were not, conscious of these stimuli when they were taught the theory. It is the neutrality of heterophenomenology that permits such a question to be left open, pending further development of theory. And of course anyone proposing such a theory would have to have bootstrapped their way to their own proprietary understanding of what they meant by conscious and unconscious subjects, finding a consilience between our everyday assumptions about what we are conscious of and what we are not, on the one hand, and their own classificatory scheme on the other. Anything too extreme ('It turns out on our theory that most people are conscious for only a few seconds a day, and nobody is conscious of sounds at all; hearing is entirely unconscious perception') will be rightly dismissed as an abuse of common understanding of the terms, but a theory that is predictively fecund and elegant can motivate substantial abandonment of this anchoring lore. Only when such a theory is in place will we be able, for the first time, to *know what we mean* when we talk about 'the experiences themselves' as distinct from what we each, subjectively, take our experiences to be.

This sketches a clear path to settling the issue between A and B, or to discovering good reasons for declaring the question ill-posed. If Chalmers thinks that scientists do, and should, prefer a different attitude towards such questions, he should describe in some detail what it is and why it is preferable. In fact, I think that while there has been some confusion on this score (and some spinning of wheels about just what would count as favouring unconscious perception over conscious perception with forgetting), scientists are comfortable with the heterophenomenological standards.

Varela and Shear (1999) describe the empathy of the experimenter that they see as the distinguishing feature of a method they describe as first-person:

> In fact, that is how he sees his role: as an empathic resonator with experiences that are familiar to him and which find in himself a resonant chord. This empathic position is still partly heterophenomenological, since a modicum of

critical distance and of critical evaluation is necessary, but the intention is entirely other: to meet on the same ground, as members of the same kind. ... Such encounters would not be possible without the mediator being steeped in the domain of experiences under examination, as nothing can replace that first-hand knowledge. This, then, is a radically different style of validation from the others we have discussed so far (p. 10).

One can hardly quarrel with the recommendation that the experimenter be 'steeped in the domain of experiences' under examination, but is there more to this empathy than just good, knowledgeable interpretation? If so, what is it? In a supporting paper, Thompson speaks of 'sensual empathy', and opines: 'Clearly, for this kind of sensual empathy to be possible, one's own body and the Other's body must be of a similar type' (2001, p. 33). This may be clear to Thompson, but in fact it raises a highly contentious set of questions: Can women not conduct research on the consciousness of men? Can slender investigators not explore the phenomenology of the obese? Perhaps more to the point, can researchers with no musical training or experience ('tin ears') effectively conduct experiments on the phenomenology of musicians? When guidance from experts is available, one should certainly avail oneself of it, but the claim that one must *be* an expert (an expert musician, an expert woman, an expert obese person) before conducting the research is an extravagant one. Suppose, however, that it is true. If so, we should be able to discover this by attempting, and detectably failing, to conduct the research as well as the relevant experts conduct the research. *That* discovery would itself be something that could only be made by first adopting the neutral heterophenomenological method and then assaying the results in comparison studies. So once again, the neutral course to pursue is not to *assume* that men can't investigate the consciousness of women, etc., but to investigate the question of whether we can discover any good scientific reason to believe this. If we can, then we should adjust the standards of heterophenomenology accordingly. It is just common sense to design one's experiments in such a way as to minimize interference and maximize efficiency and acuity of data-gathering.

Is there, then, any 'radically different style of validation' on offer in these proposals? I cannot find any. Some are uneasy about the noncommittal stance of the heterophenomenologist. Wouldn't the cultivation of deep trust between subject and experimenter be better? Apparently not. The history of *folie à deux* and Clever Hans phenomena suggests that quite unwittingly the experimenter and the subject may reinforce each other into artifactual mutual beliefs that evaporate when properly probed. But we can explore the question. It is certainly wise for the experimenter not to antagonize subjects, and to encourage an atmosphere of 'trust' – note the scare quotes. The question is whether experimenters should go beyond this and *actually trust* their subjects, or should instead (as in standard experimental practice) quietly erect the usual barriers and foils that keep subjects from too intimate an appreciation of what the experimenters have in mind. Trust is a two-way street, surely, and the experimenter who gets in a position where the subject can do the manipulating has lost control of the investigation.

I suspect that some of the dissatisfaction with heterophenomenology that has been expressed is due to my not having elaborated fully enough the potential resources of this methodology. There are surely many subtleties of heterophenomenological method that have yet to be fully canvassed. The policy of training subjects, in spite of its uneven history in the early days of psychology, may yet yield some valuable wrinkles. For instance, it might in some circumstances heighten the powers of subjects to articulate or otherwise manifest their subjectivity to investigators. The use of closed loop procedures, in which subjects to some degree control the timing and other properties of the stimuli they receive is another promising avenue. But these are not alternatives to heterophenomenology, which is, after all, just the conservative extension of standard scientific methods to data gathering from awake, communicating subjects.

Why *not* live by the heterophenomenological rules? It is important to appreciate that the reluctance to acquiesce in heterophenomenology as one's method is ideology-driven, not data-driven. Nobody has yet pointed to any variety of data that are inaccessible to heterophenomenology. Instead, they have objected 'in principle', perhaps playing a little gorgeous Bach for the audience and then asking the rhetorical question, 'Can anybody seriously believe that the wonders of human consciousness can be exhaustively plumbed by *third-person methods??*' Those who are tempted to pose this question should either temper their incredulity for the time being or put their money where their mouth is by providing the scientific world with some phenomena that defy such methods, or by describing some experiments that are clearly worth doing but that would be ruled out by heterophenomenology. I suspect that some of the antagonism to heterophenomenology is generated by the fact that the very neutrality of the methodology opens the door to a wide spectrum of theories, including some—such as my own—that are surprisingly austere, deflationary theories according to which consciousness is more like stage magic than black magic, requiring no revolution in either physics or metaphysics. Some opponents to heterophenomenology seem intent on building the mystery into the very setting of the problem, so that such deflationary theories are disqualified at the outset. Winning by philosophical footwork what ought to be won by empirical demonstration has, as Bertrand Russell famously remarked, all the advantages of theft over honest toil. A more constructive approach recognizes the neutrality of heterophenomenology and accepts the challenge of demonstrating, empirically, in its terms, that there are marvels of consciousness that cannot be captured by conservative theories.

NOTES

1   Doesn't interpretation require theory? Only in the minimal sense of presupposing that the entity interpreted is an intentional system, capable of meaningful communication. The task of unifying the interpretation of all the verbal judgments into a heterophenomenological world is akin to reading a novel, in contrast to reading what purports to be true history or biography. The issue of truth and evidence does not arise, and hence the interpretation is as neutral as possible between different theories of what is actually happening in the subject.

REFERENCES

Chalmers, David J. (2003), 'Responses to articles on my work' http://consc.net/responses.html#dennett2

Churchland, Paul M. (1979), *Scientific Realism and the Plasticity of Mind* (Cambridge: Cambridge University Press).

Dennett, Daniel C. (1971), 'Intentional Systems', *Journal of Philosophy* 68, pp. 87–106.

Dennett, Daniel C. (1982), 'How to study consciousness empirically, or Nothing comes to mind', *Synthese* 59 pp. 159–80.

Dennett, Daniel C. (1987), *The Intentional Stance* (Cambridge, MA: MIT Press/Bradford).

Dennett, Daniel C. (1991), *Consciousness Explained* (Boston, MA: Little Brown).

Dennett, Daniel C. (2002), 'Does your brain use the images in it, and if so, how?' commentary on Pylyshyn (2002) in *Behavioral and Brain Sciences* 25, pp. 189–90.

Goldman, Alvin (1997), 'Science, Publicity and Consciousness', *Philosophy of Science* 64, pp. 525–45.

Levine, Joseph (1994), 'Out of the closet: A qualophile confronts qualophobia', *Philosophical Topics* 22, pp. 107–26.

Pylyshyn, Zenon W. (2002), 'Mental Imagery: In search of a theory', Target article in *Behavioral and Brain Sciences* 25, pp. 157–237.

Shepard, R.N. and Metzler, J. (1971), 'Mental rotation of three-dimensional objects', *Science* 171, pp. 701–3.

Thompson, Evan (2001), 'Empathy and consciousness', *Journal of Consciousness Studies* 8 (5–7), pp. 1–33.

Varela, Francisco and Shear, Jonathan (1999), 'First-person methodologies: What, Why, How?', *Journal of Consciousness Studies* 6 (2–3), pp. 1–14.

9

THREE FACETS OF CONSCIOUSNESS[1]

D. W. Smith

1 THE PROBLEM OF CONSCIOUSNESS

Lately, philosophers and scientists have been looking for mind in all the wrong places. Physicalists of all stripes have been looking primarily at the physical conditions of consciousness, from neural activity to computational function.[2] Meanwhile, humanists – historicists, postmodernists, culture critics – have looked primarily to the cultural conditions of our discourse, as if consciousness did not exist in its own right (expressed in art and literature) but is only "theorized" in a cultural tradition of phenomenology or science or humanistic discourse. Obviously, we have much to learn from the empirical sciences about boson, atom, organism, evolution, and brain – and from humanistic observations in art, literature, and cultural history and criticism. But this learning is informed by further disciplines that are not "empirical" or "naturalistic" or indeed "humanistic" in the received ways. If we are to understand the mind, we must understand more clearly the philosophical disciplines of phenomenology and ontology. It is these disciplines that define the place of mind in a world further detailed by the scientific disciplines of neuroscience, evolutionary biology, and quantum physics, as well as the humanistic disciplines of literary, artistic, and cultural criticism.

Let us begin with a fundamental principle of ontology. The nature of any entity, I propose, divides into three aspects or *facets* which we may call its form, appearance, and substrate. In an act of consciousness, accordingly, we must distinguish three fundamentally different aspects: its form or intentional structure, its appearance or subjective "feel", and its substrate or origin. In terms of this three-facet distinction, we can define the place of consciousness in the world. The aim of this essay is to lay out this distinction in the nature of consciousness, and to draw out its implications for phenomenology and ontology, as distinct from purely naturalistic philosophy of mind. (I shall not focus here on humanistic theory, though I think the morals to follow have relevance for humanistic as well as naturalistic theory of mind.)

Consciousness is the central concern of phenomenology. While there is more to mind than what we consciously experience, our theory of mind must begin with the salient part of mind, conscious intentional experience. Consciousness is characteristically a consciousness "of" something, as Husserl stressed *circa* 1900, and this property of directedness he dubbed *intentionality*. This literature of phenomenology – in Husserl, Heidegger, Sartre, Merleau-Ponty, Ingarden, Føllesdal, and others, with roots in Kant, Hume, Descartes, and still earlier thinkers – has analyzed a rich variety of structures of intentionality in perception, imagination, thought, language, and action, along with properties of subjectivity, intersubjectivity, temporality, and the unity of the subject or self. For the discipline of phenomenology, there is no problem about the nature or existence of consciousness: we experience it first-hand throughout our waking life, and we have ways of studying it carefully.

For recent philosophy of mind, however, consciousness has seemed problematic, either in its nature or in its very existence: because it seems to escape the story told by the physical sciences. "Consciousness is what makes the mind–body problem really intractable", Thomas Nagel observed, rightly, wryly, and presciently in 1974 (Nagel, 1974). As cognitive science developed over the next two decades, moving from artificial intelligence into neuroscience, consciousness regained center stage. The function of mind in mediating behavior, in problem-solving computation, in evolutionary adaptation, etc., did not seem to involve the subjective qualities of sensation, dubbed qualia, or the felt character of consciousness as directed toward objects in the world around one. Nonetheless, by 1990 neuroscientists were measuring properties of neural activity (such as spiking frequency) associated with consciousness, and so consciousness became a respectable phenomenon of scientific investigation. "Consciousness studies" emerged with large interdisciplinary conferences in Tucson in the 1990s. Still, amid the excitement even in popular media, David Chalmers (1996) echoed Nagel's sentiment in declaring consciousness the "hard" problem for our theory of mind. Chalmers struck a nerve.

Yet is it not odd to find consciousness problematic? What if someone declared that we do not know what language is, or that its existence is uncertain? We all speak a language such as English or Japanese. Grammarians have charted its basic forms such as the verb or noun phrase, and linguists have analyzed its "deep" structure. How the brain functions in the production and understanding of language is a further matter of empirical neuroscience; how speech and writing emerged in our species is a matter of evolutionary biology; how our language shapes our society and politics is a matter of social-cultural theory. But the syntax and meaning of modern English are familiar, more or less, to its speakers. Similarly, the shape and meaning of our everyday experiences of perception, thought, and action are familiar to us all, more or less. These forms of consciousness have been studied by phenomenologists, much as linguists have studied forms of language. How the brain functions in consciousness, how our forms of experience evolved in the species *Homo sapiens sapiens*, how our consciousness is shaped by our language, culture, and politics – these are further matters. But how can consciousness itself be thought problematic or its basic forms obscure?

There is a widespread opinion that science alone will explain the workings of the world, including our own minds and thus consciousness. This idea goes under the positive banner of "naturalism" or meets the pejorative charge of "scientism". This attitude is expressed with characteristic verve, in his recent book *Consilience* (1998), by biologist Edward O. Wilson, famous for his studies of ants and for his conception of sociobiology. Quoting at length (the only way to evidence "attitude", albeit in the way of humanists):

> Belief in the intrinsic unity of knowledge ... rides ultimately on the hypothesis that every mental process has a physical grounding and is consistent with the natural sciences. The mind is supremely important to the consilience program [of unity] for a reason both elementary and disturbingly profound: Everything that we know and can ever know about existence is created there.
>
> The loftier forms of such reflection and belief may seem at first to be the proper domain of philosophy, not science. But history shows that logic launched from introspection alone lacks thrust, can travel only so far, and usually heads in the wrong direction. Much of the history of modern philosophy, from Descartes and Kant forward, consists of failed models of the brain. The shortcoming is not the fault of the philosophers who have doggedly pushed their methods to the limit, but a straightforward consequence of the biological evolution of the brain. All that has been learned empirically about evolution in general and mental process in particular suggests that the brain is a machine assembled not to understand itself, but to survive. Because these two ends are basically different, the mind unaided by factual knowledge from science sees the world only in little pieces. It throws a spotlight on those portions of the world it must know in order to live to the next day, and surrenders the rest to darkness. (Wilson 1998, 96)

What we have here is failure to communicate, between philosophers and scientists. (1) It was philosophers – Descartes, Kant, and Husserl – who taught us the principle, "Everything that we know and can ever know about existence is created there [in the mind]". (2) The history of modern philosophy includes much more than failed models of the brain; Descartes and Husserl developed successful models of consciousness, of mind as experienced, precisely what is now found "hard" for empirical neuroscience. (3) While the brain did not evolve to understand itself, in humans it seems to be on the verge of producing, Wilson thinks, a scientific theory of its own physical and evolutionary function – and, I think, a philosophical theory of consciousness. (4) Most of the great modern philosophers – notably Descartes, Kant, and Husserl – theorized in the face of factual knowledge from science *cum* mathematics in their day; they also appreciated, however, the importance of introspection when attending to the mind. (5) It is a hallmark of modern philosophy – and ultimately philosophy of science – to delimit knowledge of empirical fact and that of logic and mathematics, and thus to define the limits of both *a posteriori* and *a priori* knowledge; today in philosophy-and-science of mind we need to understand the boundaries and interrelations between the more empirical and the more "formal" aspects of consciousness.

A different view, from the formal side of natural science, is proposed by mathematical physicist Roger Penrose in *Shadows of the Mind* (1994). From Kurt Gödel's incompleteness theorem in mathematical logic, Penrose argues that consciousness cannot be a process of computation in the technical sense originally defined by Alan Turing; then, from considerations of quantum mechanics and the microstructure of neurons in the human brain, Penrose argues that we need a non-computational quantum physics to explain how consciousness can arise in neuronal activity. I cannot evaluate the controversial speculations in Penrose's book, but if he is right then consciousness is defined by a very different kind of "formal" mathematical structure than anything philosophers of mind have been considering previously. What I like in Penrose's vision is this type of abstraction. The mathematical form of a piece of physical theory is integral to its content, and mathematical form is suggestive of ontological form. The subtitle of the Penrose book is *A Search for the Missing Science of Consciousness*. When we have finished the "science" of consciousness, its physics and its evolutionary biology, there will still be something missing in our account of consciousness. What is missing in all current "naturalistic" thinking about consciousness is the relevant phenomenology and ontology, and their integration.

The "loftier forms" of naturalism are what attract the philosopher. I believe in the unity of knowledge. I believe moreover in the unity of the world: one world in which physical, mental, and cultural phenomena take their interweaving places. And I believe that every mental process has a physical grounding and is consistent with the natural sciences. (In fact, I am quite partial to the metaphor of "ground" in ontology, as we shall see.) So far, naturalism: both methodological and ontological (these need to be distinguished).

However, the structure of intentionality – call it "formal" or "transcendental" or something else – does not flow easily from empirical, "naturalistic" studies of the brain or bodily behavior or physical system alone. The "logic" of intentionality in phenomenology, methodically launched from introspection alone, has a powerful thrust and carries us far (contrary to what Wilson claims in the quotation above). However, I must concur, the theory of intentionality carries us in different directions than empirical science: into structures of consciousness in phenomenology, and indeed into structures of thought and inference in logic and semantics (concerning how we reason and represent things in thought and language). "Formal" ontology too moves in different directions, positing fundamental categories of existence such as Individual, Property, Relation, Number, Part, etc. Both phenomenology and ontology are crucial to a unified system of knowledge – of a unified world. And both carry us beyond naturalism: their results should be consistent with natural science, but the proper results of phenomenology and ontology are not simply amassed in empirical investigation in the natural sciences alone.

When we want to see the world as a whole, and not in the "little pieces" so effectively modelled by physics, chemistry, and biology, – when we want to see the *unity* of the world, we must inform natural science with fundamental ontology. Much as physics needs mathematics to structure its empirical content, so natural science in general needs ontology – or meta-physics to structure empirical content. And when we turn to the nature of mind itself, the empirical analysis of our own consciousness is pursued expressly and methodically by phenomenology. Moreover, it is ontology that must define the *type* of relation that holds between mind and its grounding in brain activity. This is a matter of formal ontology, rather than of empirical investigation *per se*. . . .

Only by understanding more clearly both phenomenology and ontology, along with the natural sciences (as well as the humanities), can we understand the place of consciousness in the world. That is the loftier moral of this essay. The specifics to follow concern the ontology of the three aspects or "facets" of consciousness, and the role of phenomenology in such an ontology.

2 PHENOMENOLOGY AND ONTOLOGY

Ontology (or metaphysics) is the science of being: as Aristotle put it, being *as* being. Where the special sciences – physics, chemistry, biology, psychology, etc. – are sciences of particular kinds of beings, ontology is the general science of what it is to be a being (and perhaps of what it is to be).

Phenomenology is the science of consciousness: as Husserl put it, of consciousness *as* we experience it. Phenomenology begins in the description of conscious experience from our own point of view as subjects or agents: "I feel angry", "I see that volcano", "I think that Plato was ironic". "I will [to act so that I] stroke this tennis ball crosscourt", and so on. The intentionality of consciousness is evident in our own experience: I am conscious "of" or "about" such-and-such.

Now, ontology and phenomenology interact in our overall theory of consciousness and its place in the world. For our experience – in emotion, perception, thought, and action – is informed by our understanding of the world around us, by our ontology, implicit or explicit. And as we practice phenomenology, we use our ontology, implicitly or explicitly, in order to describe our experience, its intentional relation to objects in the world, and the things we are conscious of in perception, thought, and action. In this way, phenomenology is ontological. But ontology itself is phenomenological insofar as it recognizes the existence of our own consciousness – as we must in saying what exists. . . .

. . . Let us approach the nature of consciousness and its place in the world by laying out a very basic ontological distinction, a distinction we rarely make explicit but assume deep in the background of a good deal of our theorizing about the world.

3 THREE-FACET ONTOLOGY

Everything in the world – every entity whatsoever – has a nature that divides fundamentally into three aspects we shall call *facets*: its form, its appearance, and its substrate. Thus:

1 The *form* of an entity is how or what it is: its whatness or quiddity – the kinds, properties, relations, that make it what it is.
2 The *appearance* of an entity is how it is known or apprehended: how it looks if perceptible (its appearance in the everyday sense), but also how it is conceived if conceivable, how it is used if utilizable – how it is experienced or "intended" as thus-and-so.
3 The *substrate* of a thing is how it is founded or originated: how it comes to be, where it comes from, its history or genetic origin if temporal, its composition or material origin if material, its phylogenetic origin if biological, its cultural origin if a cultural artifact – in short, its ecological origin in a wide sense, and ultimately its ontological origin in basic categories or modes of being.

The three *facets* of an entity (in this technical sense) are categorically distinct aspects of the entity, with important relations among them, as we shall be exploring. This distinction of aspects we may call the *three-facet* distinction. The distinction is depicted in a diagram in Figure 9.1.

Distinctions among form, appearance, and foundation or origin have been drawn in philosophy since its inception. Plato distinguished concrete things from their forms, and appearance from reality, and posited forms as the foundation of being. Before Plato, Anaximander assessed the material composition of things and envisioned their origin or foundation in something more basic (an archaic quantum field?); he even foresaw biological evolution, 2500 years before Darwin. In more recent centuries, epistemologists from Descartes to Kant distinguished things from

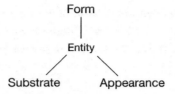

Figure 9.1 The three facets of an entity.

the ways they are known, while idealists like Berkeley put mind at the foundation of reality and materialists reduced mind to matter. What I am proposing, however, is to unify the distinctions among form, appearance, and substrate, and then to elevate the three-facet distinction itself to an axiom of fundamental ontology – and so to structure ontology itself (in one way) along these lines.

The structure <Form, Appearance, Substrate> thus defines a special system of ontological categories. For the world is structured importantly, at fundamental joints, by this three-facet distinction. The distinction presupposes that the world includes attributes (of entities), minds (to which entities may appear), and contexts of foundation or origin (from or within which entities may come to be). There may be possible worlds that lack such things, but our world has this much structure, and our ontology and phenomenology are accountable to this three-facet structure of the world. These three categories do not form a sequence of mutually exclusive and collectively exhaustive *summum genera* of entities, as do the Aristotelian categories (roughly, Substance or Individual, Species, Quality, Quantity, etc). Rather, the categories of Form, Appearance, and Substrate order or rank three fundamental ways an entity in our world is defined: by relation to its form, to its being known or "intended", and to its ground or origin. If you think about it, these categories define three fundamentally important and importantly different areas within the *nature* of any entity (in a world such as our own). Thus, the entity itself is *distributed* in its being through these three aspects of form, appearance, and substrate: that is its nature or essence.

There are other fundamental divisions in the structure of the world. But the division:

<Form, Appearance, Substrate>

marks one crucial ordering in the nature of things. To appreciate its significance, we shall work through some examples below.

Importantly, the division among form, appearance, and substrate is a division of *structure* in the nature of an entity – rather than a division among three intrinsically distinct types of property. In principle, the same thing might be part of the appearance, form, and substrate of an entity. The green of a leaf – say, of a California Live Oak tree – is part of its appearance to the human eye, part of its intrinsic form, and part of its evolutionary history (in the role of chlorophyll). Thus, the property green plays three different *roles* in the form, appearance, and substrate of the leaf, and these three facets are themselves defined by the roles played. That is, Form, Appearance, and Substrate are defined by *roles* played in the nature or essence of an entity. ...

4 THE THREE FACETS OF DIVERSE ENTITIES

To see how the three-facet distinction works, and to begin to appreciate its scope, let us apply it to some very different kinds of entities.

Consider this piece of quartz found in my garden. Its form includes its shape, its color, and its type, quartz. Its appearance includes what it looks like from various angles and under various lighting. And its substrate includes its physical crystalline structure, as well as its geological genesis from great heat and pressure in the crust of the planet Earth.

Consider now an electron. Its form includes its mass, charge, and spin. Its appearance includes its observable position and momentum, its electron-microscope image, etc. And its substrate includes the matter field (from which it emerges per quantum field theory). So even a basic physical particle has its three facets.

Now consider this pencil. The form of the pencil is its structure of graphite in wood plus its function in writing and drawing. Its appearance includes what it looks like and what it feels like in my hand in writing. The substrate of the pencil is its origin. It is made of certain materials, including wood, graphite, paint, tin, rubber. Each material has its physical-chemical structure. Moreover, these materials are produced only in specific parts of the world, in specific cultures, their trade following established routes. Furthermore, the substrate of the pencil includes the historical development of writing, writing instruments, and the invention of the pencil. So the pencil's substrate includes not only its physical composition (down to quantum structure), but also its cultural genesis.

Next consider the Tool of the Century: the computer. The International Organization for Standardization has defined what is called the ISO three-schema architecture for database design, distinguishing: a computer program ("conceptual schema"), its implementation in hardware (plus operating system, etc.) ("internal schema"), and the user's presentation of what the program does ("external schema"). These three aspects of a computer system are precisely what we are calling its three facets: its form, the program; its substrate, the hardware; and its appearance, the user-interface. This familiar distinction, we now begin to see, reflects a deep ontological distinction in the nature of things far beyond computers.

Finally, consider a human being, an individual such as Napoleon. His appearance is well-known: his facial structure, his small stature, his posture with hand in vest. His form is his individual character as a person, an intentional subject living in a culture in the natural world, his body having various traits. And his substrate is what makes this individual possible: his genetic heritage, his birth on Corsica, the French Revolution and the army in which he developed his power – as well as the wider physical, biological, and cultural conditions of humanity.

Observe how naturally the three-facet distinction applies to such diverse kinds of entities. The concepts of form and appearance are relatively familiar; the concept of substrate is not. Indeed, notice how wildly different are the things that serve as *substrate* for different entities: materials or parts from which an object is composed; the field in which a physical particle exists; the genesis of an individual through time; the evolutionary track (or "clade") of a biological species; the cultural history and use of an artifact; the hardware that implements a computer program; the life trajectory of an individual human being; even the cultural genealogy of our values (in Nietzsche's idiom) and of our language games and other forms of life (in Wittgenstein's idiom). What these things share, what makes these things play the role of substrate in very different entities, is the form of ontological *derivation* or *emergence* (in different ways!) from things more fundamental, the form of ontological *foundation* or *dependence* on things in the wider context of the entity. Again, the three-facet distinction belongs to "formal" ontology.

Now let us apply the three-facet distinction to – of all things – consciousness itself.

5 THE THREE FACETS OF CONSCIOUSNESS

An act of consciousness – my experience of thinking, seeing, or doing such-and-such – is an entity with three facets:

1. Its *form* is its structure of intentionality, its being directed from subject toward object through a content or meaning, with inner awareness of itself ("apperception").
2. Its *appearance* is how I experience it, "what it is like" for me to live or perform this act of consciousness.
3. Its *substrate* is its origin or background in conditions including brain activity, psychological motivation, cultural ideas or practices, and the biological evolution of this form of mind. . . .

6 "NATURALISTIC" PHILOSOPHY OF MIND AND THE STUDY OF CONSCIOUSNESS

The lessons of classical phenomenology are being rediscovered in recent philosophy of mind *cum* cognitive science, which begins with the metaphysics of naturalism, holding roughly that everything, including mind, is a part of nature and so – turning to epistemology – is to be studied following the methods of the natural sciences. Within this context we need to draw out the implications of the three-facet distinction in formal ontology.

As noted, it is the discipline of neuroscience, not phenomenology, that must teach us about the inner workings of the brain, how it produces consciousness, how it implements the structure of intentionality – the form of consciousness – in human beings and other terrestrials. When neuroscience-minded philosophers like Patricia Churchland (1986) and Paul Churchland (1995) eliminate the propositional attitudes of belief *et al.* in favor of neuronal activity, or collapse consciousness into neural flashes, they have limited their view of consciousness to its neural substrate. But there is more in view: there is form and appearance, where intentionality and its subjectivity reside.

Casting a wider net, we have a growing scientific story of the network of causal interactions within which mental activity occurs, interactions not only within the brain but among brain events and physical events external to the body. This wider causal ecology defines the causal substrate of consciousness. When philosophers like Fred Dretske (1981, 1995) collapse intentionality into the causal flow of physical "information" through environment and organism, they have limited their view of consciousness to its causal-ecological substrate.

A kindred view of mind is the widespread view that mind is a *function*, especially a computational function, of the brain. Causal or computational function is a higher-order property of brain activity, of the brain's mediation of inputs and outputs of the organism or system. These functional properties of brain belong to the physical, causal substrate of consciousness. Philosophers like Jerry Fodor (1975, 1994) and Daniel Dennett (1991) follow variations on the functionalist theme, as Fodor identifies mental activity with a "language of thought" consisting in physical symbols processed in the brain, while Dennett identifies mind with computational brain function viewed from the "intentional stance", and consciousness with a particular function (producing "multiple drafts" of the brain's "story" about the world and itself). But functionalism is restricted to a specific view of the causal substrate of consciousness, over-looking the proper analysis of intentionality in the form and appearance of consciousness (see D. W. Smith 1999a, calling for a wider ontology).

The neural and causal grounding of consciousness is not the only sort of condition on which our conscious experience depends. As we have come to recognize, our cultural background also constrains or makes possible, in importantly different ways, the forms of intentionality we may enjoy. We cannot think about "naturalism" or "racism" or *laissez faire* economics except in an historical context in which other persons, other intentional subjects, have put forth and debated relevant issues. More basically, we cannot think as we do "in language" unless we have acquired a language, such as English (see D. W. Smith 1999b on "background ideas"). Cultural preconditions, then, define a distinct region of the substrate of an act of consciousness. When philosophers like Richard Rorty (1979) reduce consciousness to philosophical "conversations" following Descartes, they restrict their view to the cultural substrate of our philosophical self-consciousness. But there is more to consciousness than what we say about it, even if our discourse shapes our awareness of our own experience. The form and appearance of our experience is distinct from its cultural background.

Still another kind of precondition of our human forms of intentionality is our biological heritage. Here is where the evolutionary biologist's point takes hold. I quoted Edward O. Wilson (1998) earlier, where I intimated that in the study of consciousness, physical and biological theory need to be developed in relation to phenomenology and ontology. Consider the role of biological evolution. The human organism – its nervous system, indeed its genome or overall genetic footprint – evolved in the natural environment of the planet Earth, in the planetary system of the star we call the sun, in this universe which has developed over some 12 billion years since the Big Bang. These natural conditions are preconditions for our forms of consciousness: for intentionality in the form of visual perception (by two eyes two inches apart on the front of a head), emotion (desire, fear, anger), cognition or thought (about water or fire or Plato), or volition (to run, using two primate legs rather than two differently-advantaged lizardly-aviary "legs"). Wilson is right that, in *some* sense, natural science will "explain" mind, consciousness, even the arts and humanities, even the natural sciences themselves as disciplines that have evolved in human cultures in the blink of cosmic time here on Earth. And philosophers such as Ruth Millikan (1984) and Daniel Dennett (1991, **Chapter 8**) are right that, in *some* sense, intentionality and human consciousness will be "explained" by principles of biological evolution. However, these kinds of studies of consciousness are limited to the biological *substrate* of consciousness. The intentional-subjective form and appearance of consciousness must be "explained" in different ways, in a phenomenological ontology that observes the three facets of consciousness.

The form and appearance of consciousness, featuring structures of intentionality, are simply different from its substrate, physical and cultural. This was the force of Husserl's long argument in the *Crisis* (1935–38); I resituate the claim, however, in terms of the three-facet distinction in categorial ontology. In recent philosophy of mind, John Searle (1992) has sharply separated the irreducibly subjective properties of consciousness and intentionality from their "background" of neural capacities, arguing thus against the prevailing physical-computational models of mind in cognitive science; again, I would resituate these differences within the three-facet ontology.

Here I want to stress that the *form* and *appearance* of consciousness are to be studied in their own right in phenomenology *cum* ontology, whereas the *substrate* of consciousness is to be studied in relevant disciplines in the physical, neural, biological, and cultural sciences. Given the three-facet distinction, we see what is wrong with the familiar ontological proposals in recent philosophy of mind, from reductive to eliminative materialism, from functionalism to computationalism to causal externalism to evolutionary psychosociobiology. These "naturalistic" theories are all looking for intentionality, qualia, subjectivity in the wrong places, in parts of the substrate of consciousness, rather than its form and appearance. . . .

7 THE RETURN OF PHENOMENOLOGY

Consciousness is indeed what makes the mind–body problem difficult, when we look to the result of natural science – or indeed cultural theory. It is also what makes life worth living and philosophy, since Descartes and Kant and Husserl, so exciting.

We will not fully "understand" consciousness until we see how it fits into the structure of the world defined by quantum physics, evolutionary biology, cultural history, and even cosmology. But our understanding of consciousness must begin with our own experience, as Descartes began to see. Our understanding will begin with the structure of consciousness analyzed in phenomenology, and will go on to integrate the results of phenomenology with those of natural science and cultural analysis in a unified world-picture framed by basic ontology.

Phenomenology will elaborate (part of) the *form* of consciousness in the structure of intentionality, and will detail the *appearance* of consciousness in different forms of experience, including our inner awareness of experience. These analyses of form and appearance will interweave with logic, mathematics, computer science, and formal ontology, in analyses of forms of various things including consciousness. This complex of analyses will ultimately tie into analyses of the *substrate* of consciousness, comprising conditions under which the extant forms of experience are realized, conditions mapped out by the empirical natural sciences and the social or cultural sciences. And the structure of the world in which consciousness and its empirical background conditions obtain will be framed by basic formal ontology.

What is hard about understanding consciousness is getting our mind around all these different kinds of structure while keeping straight their differences. We do this as we delimit phenomenology and its kindred ontology.[3]

NOTES

1   The substrate of this essay includes prior work that integrates phenomenology and ontology. Details are cited in the closing note.

2　An extensive collection of work on consciousness in the literature of recent cognitive science is Block, Flanagan, and Güzeldere (editors, 1997). In these essays phenomenological issues arise quite often, including issues about consciousness, perception, qualia, content, intentionality, temporal awareness, and higher-order thought. Yet there are virtually no references, in this lengthy collection, to the literature of phenomenology itself, beginning with Husserl, where these issues have been analyzed with great illumination for a century. (William James appears, appropriately, the classical psychologist with a phenomenological nose.) Evidently, there is a cultural barrier at work. I shall not here specifically critique the recent literature in philosophy of mind *cum* cognitive science (Fodor, Dennett, *et al.*). My aim in this essay is rather to assess issues of consciousness within the theoretical framework of phenomenology in the context of a wider ontology. In my "Mind and Body" (1995), I placed Husserlian theory within the space of ideas framed by recent philosophy of mind and cognitive science, including issues of reduction, functionalism, etc. Meanwhile, issues of cognitive science are addressed in relation to phenomenology in: Dreyfus (editor, 1982); Varela, Thompson, and Roesch (1993); and Petitot *et al.* (editors, 1999). My own essay in the latter volume, "Intentionality Naturalized?" (1999a), critiques two influential lines of analysis, articulated by Fodor and Dretske, from a phenomenological-ontological point of view.

3　The roots of the present essay are various. (1) I have assumed, broadly, a theory of intentionality as mediated by a meaning-content, the theory developed from Husserl in Smith and McIntyre (1982), *Husserl and Intentionality*. (2) In D. W. Smith (1989), *The Circle of Acquaintance*, I developed a conception of the "ground" of intentionality, including physical, psychological, and cultural conditions on which intentionality depends; these grounds of intentionality are part of the substrate of consciousness, according to the three-facet ontology of consciousness discussed here. (3) A shorter ancestor of this essay is my "Ontological Phenomenology" (2000b). (4) The three-facet distinction in ontology, featured here, is used systematically in the formal phenomenological ontology of the PACIS project long underway at Ontek Corporation: what I here call "facets" are called "complements" in PACIS terminology. The distinction appears also in Simons and Smith 1993. I am indebted to my colleagues in that research program: Charles W. Dement, President of Ontek; Stephen DeWitt, John Stanley, and Anthony Sarris, all presently or formerly of Ontek; and Peter M. Simons of the University of Leeds. Thanks to Tony Sarris for the ISO reference. Thanks further to Chuck Dement for numerous discussions of systematic formal ontology. I bear responsibility, nonetheless, for what is made of the three-facet distinction in the present essay.

REFERENCES

Block, N., O. Flanagan, and G. Güzeldere (eds.): 1997, *The Nature of Consciousness*, Cambridge, Massachusetts: MIT Press.

Chalmers, D.: 1996, *The Conscious Mind*, Oxford and New York: Oxford University Press.

Churchland, Patricia S.: 1986, *Neurophilosophy*, Cambridge, Massachusetts: MIT Press.

Churchland, Paul M.: 1995, *The Engine of Reason, the Seat of the Soul*, Cambridge, Massachusetts: MIT Press.

Dennett, D. C.: 1991, *Consciousness Explained*, Boston: Little, Brown and Company.

Dretske, F.: 1981, *Knowledge and the Flow of Information*, Cambridge, Massachusetts: MIT Press.

Dretske, F.: 1995, *Naturalizing the Mind*, Cambridge, Massachusetts: MIT Press.

Dreyfus, H. L. (ed.): 1982, *Husserl, Intentionality and Cognitive Science*, Cambridge, Massachusetts: MIT Press.

Føllesdal, D.: 1982, 'Husserl's Notion of Noema', in H. L. Dreyfus (ed.), reprinted from *The Journal of Philosophy*, 1969.

106

Fodor, J. A.: 1975, *The Language of Thought*, New York: Cromwell.

Fodor, J. A.: 1994, *The Elm and the Expert: Mentalese and its Semantics*, Cambridge, Massachusetts: MIT Press.

Heidegger, M.: 1988, *The Basic Problems of Phenomenology*, Translated by Albert Hofstadter, Bloomington and Indianapolis: Indiana University Press, Revised Edition. German original, 1975, from a lecture course in 1927.

Husserl, E.: 1969, *Ideas Pertaining to a Pure Phenomenology and a Phenomenological Philosophy, First Book: General Introduction to Pure Phenomenology*. Translated by W. R. Boyce Gibson, London: George Allen & Unwin, Ltd., and New York: Humanities Press, Inc. First English edition, 1931; German original, first published in 1913. Called *Ideas* I.

Husserl, E.: 1970, *The Crisis of European Sciences and Transcendental Phenomenology*. Translated by D. Carr, Evanston, Illinois: Northwestern University Press. Original manuscript from 1935–38.

Husserl, E.: 1991, *Ideas pertaining to a Pure Phenomenology and a Phenomenological Philosophy, Second Book: Phenomenological Investigations of Constitution* [or as translated: *Studies in the Phenomenology of Constitution*]. Translated by Richard Rojcewicz and André Schuwer. Dordrecht and Boston: Kluwer Academic Publishers. German original, first published in 1952, drafted initially in 1912, revised in 1915 and again in 1928. Called *Ideas* II.

ISO/IEC TR9007: 1987, *Information Processing Systems – Concepts and Terminology for the Conceptual Schema and the Information Base*. International Organization for Standardization (ISO), Geneva, Switzerland.

Millikan, Ruth G.: 1984, *Language, Thought and Other Biological Categories: New Foundations for Realism*, Cambridge, Massachusetts: MIT Press.

Nagel, T.: 1974, 'What is it Like to be a Bat?', *Philosophical Review* **4**, 435–50.

Petitot, J., F. J. Varela, B. Pachoud, and J.-M. Roy (eds.): 1999, *Naturalizing Phenomenology: Issues in Contemporary Phenomenology and Cognitive Science*, Stanford: Stanford University Press. And New York, Cambridge: in collaboration with Cambridge University Press.

Penrose, R.: 1994, *Shadows of the Mind: A Search for the Missing Science of Consciousness*, Oxford and New York: Oxford University Press.

Rorty, R.: 1983, *Philosophy and the Mirror of Nature*, Princeton: Princeton University Press.

Searle, J. R.: 1992, *The Rediscovery of the Mind*, Cambridge, Massachusetts: MIT Press.

Sellars, W.: 1963, 'Philosophy and the Scientific Image of Man', in W. F. Sellars, *Science, Perception and Reality*, London: Routledge and Kegan Paul; New York: Humanities Press.

Simons, P., and D. W. Smith: 1993, 'The Philosophical Foundations of PACIS', Manuscript, The manuscript lays out the ideas expounded in a two-hour oral presentation by the authors (with slides by Charles Dement) at the Sixteenth International Ludwig Wittgenstein Symposium in Kirchberg am Wechsel, Austria, August, 1993.

Smith, D. W.: 1989, *The Circle of Acquaintance: Perception, Consciousness, and Empathy*, Dordrecht and Boston: Kluwer Academic Publishers.

Smith, D. W.: 1995, 'Mind and Body', in B. Smith and D. W. Smith (eds.), *The Cambridge Companion to Husserl*, Cambridge and New York: Cambridge University Press.

Smith, D. W.: 1999a, 'Intentionality Naturalized?', in Petitot *et al.*

Smith, D. W.: 1999b, 'Background Ideas', Appeared in Italian translation as 'Idee di sfondo', *Paradigmi* (*Estratto da PARADIGMI, Rivista di critica filosofica*) (Rome), An 110 XVII, n. 49 (gennaio-aprile 1999), pp. 7–37.

Smith, D. W.: 2000a, 'How is Transcendental Philosophy – of Mind and World – Possible?', in Bina Gupta (ed.), *The Empirical and the Transcendental A Fusion of Horizons*, Festschrift in honor of J. N. Mohanty; Rowman & Littlefield, New York, pp. 169–79.

Smith, D. W.: 2000b, 'Ontological Phenomenology', in M. Gedney (ed.), *Proceedings of the Twentieth World Congress of Philosophy*, Volume VII: Modern Philosophy, Bowling Green: The Philosophy Documentation Center, Bowling Green University.

Smith, D. W.: 2001, 'Consciousness and Actuality in Whiteheadian Ontology', in Liliana Albertazzi (ed.), *The Dawn of Cognitive Science: Early European Contributors*, Kluwer Academic Publishers, Dordrecht and Boston, pp. 269–97.

Wilson, Edward O.: 1998, *Consilience: The Unity of Knowledge*, Knopf, New York.

Part 3

IS THE MIND PHYSICAL?

You have a mind. You have a body. This much is clear.[1]

But what is the relation between your mind and your body? Is your mind just part of your body, as a tabletop is part of a table? Is it distinct from (but perhaps dependent on) your body? This is the famous mind–body problem, the topic of the current section. Obviously, it is closely related to the problem of consciousness discussed in **Part 1**. The differences between these problems are subtle. First, while the problem of consciousness is focused specifically on features of *conscious* states, the mind–body problem may also encompass nonconscious features of mentality. Second, the mind–body problem is specifically concerned with the contrast between mentality and the physical, whereas the problem of consciousness also concerns, e.g., the contrast between the subjective and the objective. (Recall that Thomas Nagel was concerned with objectivity, but he rejected the physical conception of objectivity.) However, since these problems are intimately connected, they are not always sharply distinguished in the literature.

The papers in this section target the mind–body problem, by examining the relations between two classes of properties.

(i) mental properties, like *being in pain* or *desiring to be an astronaut*; and
(ii) physical properties, like *being more than 5 feet tall* or *having firing C-fibers*.

To say that you have a mind and a body is to say that you possess properties of both types. Here is a *partial* list of ways that philosophers have construed the relations between mental and physical properties. These positions are listed in a spectrum, from the most extreme physicalism to the most extreme dualism.

A. Simple identity: 'being in pain' and 'having firing C-fibers' are simply two different ways to refer to the same property.
B. Necessary dependence: *being in pain* is grounded in some physical property or other; and the grounding physical property is such that, *necessarily*, whatever has it is also in pain. (And the same is true of all other mental properties.)
C. Merely contingent dependence: same as (B), except without the 'necessarily'. Your mental properties depend on your physical properties only because of (contingent) facts about how the world actually is.[2] But it is *logically* possible that your mental properties vary independently of your physical properties, or even that they occur in the absence of physical properties.
D. Complete independence: your mental properties and your physical properties vary independently of each other.

There are any number of other positions as well. But these four will give a general sense of the territory.

Positions that accept (A) or (B) are considered *physicalist*, for they maintain that every mental property is identical to, or necessarily connected with, a physical property. Positions that accept (C) or (D) are *dualist*, in that they posit two distinct types of properties in the world, mental and physical.

This way of demarcating the positions may appear arbitrary. Why does (B) qualify as physicalist, while (C) qualifies as dualist? The answer concerns differences between these positions, as to what is *possible*. An analogy will help. Consider the property *being single* (currently unmarried). Some single people have never been married; others are divorced and haven't remarried; still others are widowed and haven't remarried; etc.[3] Call these type of properties 'marriage history' properties. Now the property *being single* isn't identical with any particular marriage history property. But *being single* does bear, to the class of marriage history properties, the 'necessary dependence' relationship expressed in (B). For everyone who is single is single in virtue of having some *one* of these properties, and each of these properties is such that everyone who has it is, necessarily, single.

With this analogy in mind, we can now explain why (B) qualifies as physicalist but (C) does not. (B) says that the relationship between a particular mental property and the class of physical properties is essentially similar to the relationship between *being single* and these 'marriage history' properties. Just as facts about singleness simply *fall out* of these marriage history facts, facts about which mental properties you possess simply *fall out* of physical facts, according to (B). In this sense, then, the property *being single* (being in pain) isn't something *over and above* the single person's marriage history properties (the pained person's physical properties).

Position (C) envisions a looser relationship between mental properties and physical properties. Facts about the mental don't simply *fall out* of physical facts; it is *possible* that two persons with the same physical properties differ mentally. By contrast, it is impossible that two persons with the same marriage history differ in that one is single and one is not. So (C) qualifies as dualist because it sees the mental as distinct from the physical, in a significant sense, even if these types of properties are, in actuality, perfectly correlated.[4]

Let us turn to the debate between dualists and physicalists. W. D. Hart defines dualism as the thesis that the mind *could possibly* exist without the body, and presents a version of Descartes' argument for this thesis.

(1) If I can imagine that *p*, then it's possible that *p*;
(2) I can imagine being disembodied.

These are expressed in the first person because the argument requires that each of us perform the thought experiment ourselves. Together, these imply that you (the 'I') *could* be disembodied – your mind could exist without your body – and hence that dualism is true.

In this excerpt, Hart makes a case for each premise. While both premises are controversial, most contemporary philosophers resist dualism by denying (1). In defense of (1), Hart argues that truths about what is possible or impossible (known as *modal* truths) are known through imagination. He acknowledges that we may sometimes go wrong, in using imagination to determine possibility. But he defends the use of imagination by drawing an analogy with perception. There is no guarantee that a perceptual experience is trustworthy; e.g., we can never be absolutely certain, in a given case, that we are not hallucinating. But recognizing that perception is sometimes misleading does not incline us to abandon perception as a source of knowledge. For perception provides our only access to a wide range of facts. Similarly, while there is no guarantee that your imagination is veridical, we must and should continue to use it, since imagination provides our only access to facts about (unactualized) possibilities.[5]

Hart's case for (2) has the form of a brief (and somewhat spooky) thought experiment, designed to persuade you that you can imagine discovering that you are disembodied.

Of course, whether we should accept dualism on the basis of this argument depends, in part, on the consequences of accepting dualism. If we find that dualism has objectionable consequences, then even if (1) and (2) seem initially appealing, we should question our grounds for accepting them.

David Papineau's goal is precisely to show that dualism has an objectionable consequence: namely, that the mental has no causal power. Papineau's main argument is simultaneously an argument against dualism and an argument for physicalism. (He favors the label 'materialism'.) He begins with the simple claim that mental states sometimes have physical effects. For instance, your decision to learn about the philosophy of mind caused you to pick up this book; or, to repeat an example from the last section, the pain you feel upon touching a hot stove causes you to howl and withdraw your hand. Papineau adds to this claim the premise that physics is complete, in that every physical event can, at least in principle, be causally explained in purely physical terms. In the hot stove case, the causal explanation for the hand movement will involve events that occurred in your sensorimotor cortex, etc. The crucial point is that, for *every* physical event, there is an adequate physical cause.

These two claims do not yet establish physicalism, however. For even if some physical events are caused by mental events, and there is an adequate physical cause for every physical event, the mental may yet be distinct from the physical. In that case, events like the hand movement will be *doubly* caused, or 'overdetermined': by mental events (such as the pain) and distinct physical events (such as those in the sensorimotor cortex). To establish physicalism, then, Papineau invokes a third claim: that such events are not generally overdetermined. Insofar as the movement is caused by the pain and caused by nerve states, overdetermination can be avoided only by *identifying* these, in the manner of (A) above. In that case, the property 'being in (that kind of) pain' and the property 'being in that particular nerve state' are one and the same.

Should we accept Papineau's argument? As he notes, it is difficult to resist. It seems obvious that mental causes do have physical effects, and that at least paradigmatic examples of such effects (e.g., drawing back one's hand from the stove) also have physical causes – causes that seem, on their own, sufficient for producing the effect. Moreover, even if some effects are overdetermined ('doubly' caused), it is hard to swallow the idea that overdetermination occurs every time a mental event causes a physical effect. The best way to account for mental causation is, it seems, simply to *identify* the pain property with a physical property.

Still, the conclusion of Papineau's argument has some troublesome consequences as well. For one thing, if we accept it we must somehow explain, or explain away, the Cartesian intuitions that fuel Hart's argument. Can't you imagine that you are dis-embodied? If so, why isn't this evidence that your mental properties aren't linked, with necessity, to your physical properties?

Papineau's conclusion also faces another worry. To avoid the problem of mental causation he describes, Papineau must (and does) adopt (A), a strong version of physicalism.[6] On his view, then, the *hurting* quality of pain *just is* a neural property. This means that that *hurting* quality could be experienced only by creatures who can have that neural property, which in turn requires that they possess the same type of brains that we have. For instance, a Martian with a radically different type of brain could not experience *that* type of pain. Many philosophers find this consequence implausible, and therefore reject this strong version of physicalism in favor of a more moderate version, along the lines of (B) above.

We have, then, a vexed situation. On the one hand, it is hard to see how we could allow for mental causation unless we accept a very strong form of physicalism. On the other hand, that form of physicalism might be too extreme to be plausible.

Perhaps the source of this problem lies in our basic categories themselves – in particular, in our conception of what it means to say that a state or property is *physical*. The final two papers in this section address this question.

Bertrand Russell's paper, first published in 1928, casts doubt on standard approaches to the mind–body problem. These approaches assume that the basic nature of the physical is reasonably clear, while the basic nature of mentality is comparatively obscure. But, Russell observes, advances in theoretical physics have forced us to admit that our grasp of the physical is at least as obscure as our understanding of mentality. "Thus matter has become altogether too ghostly to be used as an adequate stick with which to beat the mind." In fact, these advances show that we don't ever make genuine contact with paradigmatically physical objects. (So perhaps Julian Jaynes was too quick to describe the physical world as 'kickable reality'.) While he advocates some of the broadly naturalistic aims of physicalism (or materialism[7]), he denies that these aims provide any reason to favor the ontological category of the *physical* over the *mental*.

Perhaps unsurprisingly, Russell's appraisal of the mind–body problem did not revolutionize the terms of the debate. Philosophers continue to see the mind–body problem as the challenge of locating mentality in a universe that is physical. And this conception is still fueled by the assumption that the nature of the physical is clearer than the nature of mentality.

Writing more than 70 years later than Russell, Barbara Montero expresses similar misgivings about this problem. She claims that "we have no idea" what it means to say that something is physical, since physical science has not yet converged on a satisfactory theory of physical objects and events. For this reason, philosophers who describe their positions as physicalist owe us some account of what, precisely, they are claiming. Nor can the physicalist position be adequately characterized as the claim that what exists is whatever *empirical science* discovers, according to Montero. For the empirical sciences may ultimately converge on a theory that sees mentality as irreducible to anything nonmental.

Montero proposes that, instead of asking 'Is the mind physical?' we should ask, 'Is mentality a fundamental feature of the world?' On this new conception of the mind–body problem, those who are now considered dualists would answer 'yes', while those who are considered physicalists would answer 'no'. Note that her proposal uses the term 'mental' rather than the term 'physical' to define the problem at hand. She argues that this is acceptable, since our grasp of which phenomena are mental is clearer than our grasp of which phenomena are physical. (After all, the dispute over physicalism is, precisely, a dispute over whether the mental is physical.)

Montero suggests that we should focus on whether the mental is reducible to the nonmental. But if we have no reason to favor the physical, as somehow less problematic than the mental, there seems to be less at stake in this question than in the original mind–body problem. For to say that the mental is irreducible to the nonmental is simply to say (assuming that there are basic nonmental properties) that there are two basic categories of properties, mental and nonmental. This is a dualist view, and a justifiable preference for simplicity means that we should try to make do with one category if we can. Still, if the mental is no more problematic than the nonmental, this kind of dualism seems less disquieting than the original, Cartesian variety.

QUESTIONS TO THINK ABOUT

1. Hart defends the use of imagination to determine whether certain things that have never happened *could* possibly happen. In evaluating Hart's argument here, consider what sort of evidence leads you to believe the following modal truths:

It's possible that a person grows to be 10 feet tall.
It's impossible that anything is red all over and green all over.

2. Papineau argues that, if dualism is true, then either mental states don't have genuine causal power, or overdetermination is rampant. But if Papineau's identity claim is correct, then it seems that only creatures with brains similar to ours could feel the types of pain we feel. Which of these consequences seems least objectionable to you? If you had to 'bite the bullet' here, which one of them would you accept, and why?

3. According to Russell and Montero, our notion of the physical is at least as obscure as our notion of mentality. Do you agree? If not, what feature of the physical makes it clearer than the mental?

4. The principle known as *Occam's Razor* advises that, in theorizing, we should avoid multiplying entities needlessly. An ultimate theory of the world in which there was only a single type of entity or property would, of course, be elegant and satisfying. But *why*, precisely, would it be preferable? Is the difference between a 'one type' view and a 'two types' view more significant than the difference between a 'two types' view and a 'three types' view? Why or why not?

NOTES

1 Which is not to say that it's universally accepted. A few philosophers, known as *eliminativists*, deny the existence of paradigmatically mental states like beliefs or sensations. And a few others, known as *idealists*, maintain that all that exists are minds and their properties; so they deny the existence of bodies insofar as 'body' is contrasted with 'mind'. Still, the majority of philosophers accept that there are minds and there are bodies.

2 On some dualist views, physical properties are linked to mental properties by contingent *laws of nature*. Cf. David Chalmers' article in **Part 1** of this volume.

3 Some marriage histories are of course a bit more complicated, since some people have divorced, remarried, and are then widowed (etc.). And there is some controversy as to whether 'single' implies 'marriage-eligible'; e.g., some will deny that a child, or the Pope, is single. But we will gloss over this detail for simplicity.

4 To further the analogy: suppose that all non-single persons wear a ring on the left hand, and that no single persons do. This is false, but surely possible. The relationship between being single and wearing a ring on the left hand would, then, be roughly the same as the relationship (C) posits between mental and physical properties. Even if a particular mental property is perfectly correlated with a particular physical property, this merely *happens* to be the case, just as it merely happens to be the case that being single perfectly correlates with wearing no ring on the left hand.

5 Hart diverges from many philosophers here, including Descartes, by using *imagination* rather than *conceiving*. But this difference will not matter for our purposes.

6 For an argument to show that weaker forms of physicalism, like (B), will not avoid the problem with mental causation that Papineau describes, see Kim 2006, Ch. 7. (Listed below under 'Further reading'.)

7 Russell uses the term 'materialist' in two different senses. When he says 'science remained comfortably materialistic', he means simply that scientists accepted the idea that physical

objects are *real*. In this sense, materialism contrasts with idealism, which is the philoso-phical doctrine that the only real existents are minds and mental properties. But Russell also uses this term to mean 'physicalist', e.g., when he says that the 'would-be materialist ... may with a certain degree of success reduce the activities of the mind to those of the body'.

FURTHER READING

Chalmers, D. "Naturalistic Dualism", Chapter 4 of his *The Conscious Mind*. Oxford: Oxford University Press, 1996.

Chomsky, N. *New Horizons in the Study of Language and Mind*. Cambridge: Cambridge University Press, 2000.

Kim, J. "Mental Causation". Chapter 7 of his *Philosophy of Mind*, 2nd ed. Cambridge, MA: Westview Press, 2006.

Stoljar, D. "Physicalism". In E. Zalta, (ed.) *The Stanford Encyclopedia of Philosophy*, Spring 2001. Current version available at http://plato.stanford.edu/entries/physicalism.

Walter, S. (ed.) *Physicalism and Mental Causation*. Exeter: Imprint Academic, 2003.

10

AN ARGUMENT FOR DUALISM

W. D. Hart

THE PROBLEM

Are you lodged in your body, or indeed any body, only by accident? Or is it absolutely necessary not only that you be lodged in some body or other, but also that you have the specific body you now inhabit? Asking these two questions is one way to raise what is known as the mind–body problem: how are you related to your body? How is the mind (the self, the person) related to matter?

Descartes is famous for, among other things, his dualist solution to the mind–body problem. Mind–body dualism is the thesis that there are at least two basic or fundamental sorts of things: one including you and other minds, selves, or persons, and the other including the bodies of you and other people as well as inanimate lumps of matter like stars, planets, and glaciers. Things that are basic or fundamental are sometimes called substances. In this usage, a substance is not a stuff (like sugar or air) but a basic or fundamental thing. That understood, we could restate mind–body dualism as the thesis that you (or anyone else) and your body (or anyone else's) are two different substances.

What does it mean to call a thing basic or fundamental? The central idea is that a basic thing exists independently, that is, that it is not dependent for its existence on the existence of anything else. This is in turn an idea about what is possible, not about what is actually true. For example, an electron or a quark is in the relevant way basic if it is possible that it should exist even if nothing else existed. Consider any object apart from the particle and ask whether the particle could have existed even if the other object did not; if the answer is always yes, then the particle is a basic thing and thus a substance. Note that you are not to ask whether the other object you consider in fact fails to exist; since that object was there for you to consider, that question would always be answered by a trivial no. Rather, you are to ask whether the electron could still have existed even if the other object had not. So whether a thing is a substance is a question about possibility.

Could stars, planets, or glaciers exist without the bits (like electrons) making them up or without the events (like condensations of nebulae or ice ages with their constituent objects) that formed those stars, planets, and glaciers? Someone like Leibniz, thinking about the first question, might wonder whether only things like fundamental particles are substances. Someone like Spinoza, thinking about the second question, might wonder whether only the universe as a whole is a substance. Partly because it seems naturally to lead to such widely divergent speculations, the concept of a substance is no longer so taken for granted as it once was.

But the concept of a substance does not seem to lead to such difficulties in the mind–body problem. Using that concept, we may state the crux of dualism as the thesis that you and all other minds, selves, and persons are substances. This means that you and other persons are basic things, which means that you and other people are not dependent for your existence on the existence of any other objects. But in asking whether people depend for their existence on something else, it is clear that the other objects of which we are thinking primarily are people's bodies. So the question becomes: could you exist even if your body did not? Could you be disembodied? We need no suspicious concept of substance to ask that question.

For some time the prevailing orthodoxy has been that dualism is false and that you could not be disembodied. This view has in recent decades been connected with theses about identity. First, it is argued that you (or your mental states) are identical with your brain (or states of your central nervous system). But, second, things cannot be identical only by accident; properly understood, all true identities are necessary truths. Hence, your mental states are necessarily identical with electrochemical states of your central system, and thus you could not exist unless (at least part of) your body did. Since you could not be disembodied, dualism is false.

The core of this argument is that people are identical with their bodies, so since identities are necessary, people could not be disembodied, and thus dualism is false. That is, if people are identical with their bodies, then dualism is false. Hence, dualism requires that people not be identical with their bodies. But, and this is the present point, dualism requires more than that people are not identical with their bodies. Clench your left hand and look at your left fist. It might at first seem plausible to say that your left fist is identical with your left hand. But identical things should have all their properties in common; and in particular, when things are identical with each other, they should exist at the same times. Yet if you now open your left hand, your left fist is gone, though your left hand remains. Thus, your left hand and your left fist do not exist at the same times; so they are not identical. (As it were, your left fist is your left hand clenched, and your left hand clenched is your left hand in a certain state, not your left hand *tout court*.) But although hand–fist identity is false, a hand–

118

fist dualism would seem decidedly heroic; it is too much to believe that your left fist could exist even if your left hand did not. This suggests by analogy what might be called mentalism, that is, that although you (or your mind or self) are not identical with your body (or even with a part of it like your central nervous system, even the electrochemical states now obtaining in that system), still you could not be disembodied. The point is that mind–body dualism is stronger than mind–body difference, for mentalism asserts difference but denies the possibility of disembodiment, whereas dualism asserts difference because it asserts the possibility of disembodiment. The mentalist denies that the mind is a substance, whereas the dualist asserts that it is.

Your mind is a substance if it is not dependent for its existence on that of your body. It is important to understand that the relevant sort of dependence is a matter of necessity, not natural law. To illustrate the difference, as a matter presumably of natural law there have been stallions as long as there have been mares, and vice versa. Still, it seems clear that Aristotle, to whom the notion of a substance is due, would have counted both mares and stallions among the (primary) substances; each could exist without the other, as we know because we can imagine there being mares but no stallions, and vice versa. It thus seems better to explain substance in terms of possibility *simpliciter* rather than so-called natural possibility; one thing is independent of another if the first could exist but the other not, even if that would violate contingent natural law.

It is worthwhile to see clearly how very strong a thesis dualism is because in that way one begins to see how much a good argument for dualism should establish. But Descartes's argument for dualism, although it is strong, is also simple. Other things being equal, simple philosophical arguments are preferable to subtle arguments. In a field like mathematics, the craftsmen know, at least more or less, the state of the art. For that reason, subtle mathematical arguments may carry the day; where the craftsman knows the state of the art, he can reasonably expect to survey all possibilities. But even the best philosophical craftsmen seem never to master the state of their art fully; indeed, it may never in the relevant sense have a full state. For that reason, subtlety is, other things being equal, suspect in philosophical arguments.

Descartes's argument for dualism has two premises. The first premise is not especially about the nature of the mind, but about evidence for possibility: it says that what you can imagine is possible. The second premise says that you can imagine being disembodied. It is the second premise that turns out, on examination, to say a great deal about the nature of the mind. The argument is that from these two premises, dualism follows; that is, it follows that you could be disembodied, which consequence is the central thesis of dualism.

Philosophical habit puts an argument to two questions in order. First, one asks whether the argument is valid; forgetting about whether the premises and the conclusion are true or false, one asks whether the conclusion follows from the premises. Are the premises such that if they were true, the conclusion would also be true? The second premise of Descartes's argument may be stated slightly more explicitly as

(2)   You can imagine that you should be disembodied.

Similarly, the first premise of the argument could be stated as

(1)   If you can imagine that p, then it is possible that p,

where the letter 'p' marks two blanks that could be filled by almost any sentence in the indicative mood (but that for grammatical purposes should then be shifted into something like the subjunctive mood). If we fill these two blanks with the indicative sentence "You are disembodied," we get

(3)   If you can imagine that you should be disembodied, then it is possible that you should be disembodied.

The idea is that a commitment to Descartes's first premise requires for just about any indicative sentence S a commitment to the result of filling the two blanks in (1) by S; so (3) follows from Descartes's first premise. From (2) and (3) we deduce

(4)   It is possible that you should be disembodied.

Our conclusion, (4), is deduced from (2) and (3) by a logical principle called *modus ponens*: suppose that A; and that if A, then B; then B. *Modus ponens* is a principle of reasoning the soundness of which cannot be faulted. In sum, then, Descartes's logic cannot be faulted; and if you can imagine being disembodied, it follows that you could be disembodied. (It is a virtue of simpler philosophical arguments that one is more likely to be able to judge their validity sensibly.)

Once a philosophical argument has satisfied the canons of validity, habit then asks whether its premises are true. Here we encounter something like a historical oddity. It would seem that to Descartes and to many people before him, but to fewer and fewer people since the seventeenth century, it was just plain obvious both that what is imaginable is possible and that being disembodied is imaginable. But most educated and thoughtful late-twentieth-century audiences refuse to accept Descartes's premises without further argument. It is the purpose of what follows to attempt to push the argument for those premises back to further premises that a twentieth-century audience could accept. . . .

... But there remains the historical question why what seemed obvious, that you can imagine being disembodied, in the seventeenth century and before has since seemed less and less obvious. It could be that people's imaginations have grown increasingly dimmer over the past three hundred or so years; but it might be too self-serving to take this suggestion very seriously. A more orthodox explanation might appeal to two factors: the decline of Christian faith and the successes of natural science. (It is a matter of some sensitivity whether these two factors are independent, but that, fortunately, is not a question we need answer here.) As for the first factor, there seems traditionally to have been at least an association of ideas between the immateriality of the mind and the immortality of the soul. Joseph Addison, for example, clearly associates immateriality and immortality in the first two paragraphs of Number 111 of the *Spectator*.[1] With the decline of Christian faith, belief in the immortal soul seems increasingly like wishful thinking. Putting away childish things, one ceases to be able to take a wishful belief in immortality seriously; it becomes a test of independent pride to deny the life ever after. To the extent that immaterial minds are mixed up with immortal souls, it also becomes a measure of clear-headed adulthood that one deny the immaterial mind and one's capacity to imagine being disembodied. ...

... The second factor, the rise of natural science, seems to have worked against the immaterial mind in something like the following fashion. For about three hundred years, more and more natural processes have yielded up their secrets to human understanding, and some of them have yielded up their working to our control, apparently by being conquered through the working hypothesis that they are physical engines driven by lifeless natural forces. That the hypothesis has worked so often and so spectacularly is a reason for believing that it is true. It is then only natural to generalize, that is, to suppose that all natural phenomena, including people ourselves, are at bottom nothing but physical engines driven by electrochemical forces. To deny the application of materialism to ourselves seems to be like standing with the churchmen refusing to look through Galileo's telescope, with the bishop of Oxford when T. H. Huxley made a fool of him, with Joseph Breuer when his offended dignity prevented him from pursuing with Freud the psychosexual mysteries in the unconscious, and with the Nazi officials who proscribed Einstein's "Jewish" physics. To keep such company willingly is to cast oneself on the rubbish pile of history.

It has been patent ever since the seventeenth century that the problem of how disembodiable minds could interact causally with any matter at all, not just the bodies in which those minds might somehow happen to be lodged, is a (if not the) central intellectual problem for Cartesian dualists. The usual verdict seems to have been to throw up one's intellectual hands in despair and to claim that the mental is the physical. But despairful thinking is no better than wishful thinking; on appeal, that verdict should receive the Scottish judgment: not proven. No identity between your belief that there are infinitely many prime numbers and some state of your central nervous system has ever been exhibited. The price paid for a despairful belief that the mind is the brain ticking over has been an absence of intellectual experiment, that is, an absence of sustained and informed speculation about how disembodiable minds could engage in causal transactions with matter. In a sense, materialists do not know what they are denying; if they wished to be charitable, they might suppose that they are about to be told one version of what they deny.[2] ...

... Premise (1) is a principle of an epistemology of modality, and the leading analogy of that epistemology is that imagination is to knowledge of nonactual possibility as perception is to knowledge of actuality. To be sure, the verb "to see" is sometimes so used that a person cannot truly be said to see that p unless it is in fact true that p, and it may be that the verb "to imagine" is sometimes so used that a person cannot truly be said to have imagined that p unless it is possible that p. But when matters are murky, one may say that it looks to be the case that p, and this may be so even if it is not true that p. The possibility of such a cleavage between visual experience and how things actually are is an aspect of the objectivity of truth; it is also the gap bridged by visual experience as evidence for belief. So if modal truth is also to be objective, we should allow for the possibility that one might seem to oneself to have imagined that p and yet not have; this opens a gap bridged by experiments in the imagination as evidence for modal beliefs. As a disbelief in subjective idealism should make one resist the dictum that to be is to be perceived, so an inclination toward the objectivity of nonactual possibility should make one resist the dictum that to be possible is to be imagined. Nevertheless, as perception is our favored, and perhaps only, basic epistemic access to actuality, so imagination is our favored, and perhaps only, basic epistemic access to nonactual possibility. When one has looked long and hard, when it has always looked to be the case that p, and when one has no good reason to think otherwise, then one has good reason to think that p. Similarly, when one has imagined as inventively as one is able, and it has always seemed clearly to be the case that p in whatever scenario one has spun out, and one has no good reason to think otherwise, then one has good reason to think it is possible that p. In neither case is one guaranteed success: objectivity always leaves open the possibility of error. But in both cases, one has the best of the basic sort of evidence available.

The second premise of Descartes's argument was the claim that you can imagine being disembodied. To be convinced of that claim, you should require a story, a recipe the successful execution of which will enable you to imagine being disembodied. Here we begin such a story. ...

Suppose that one morning, still embodied, you awaken. Before raising your eyelids, you grope your way over to your mirror. Facing it, you raise your lids; you can see in the mirror that your eye sockets are empty, that your eyeballs are missing; the point is that you can visualize your face with empty eye sockets as it would look to you in the mirror. This is, of course, curious. So raising your hand, you probe an empty eye socket with one of your little fingers. You can visualize how that little finger probing the socket would look; and you can do for touch as visualizing is to sight what that finger might feel like against the flesh of your empty eye socket. Growing more curious, you saw round the top of your head, peel back the top of your skull, and peer into your brain pan; it, too, is empty, and again the point is that you can visualize how your empty brain pan would look to you in the mirror. (In an alternative version of this story, you might imagine that the region of the confluence of your lines of sight gradually slips down your cheeks, over your jaw line and down your neck, and thence down to flank your navel, and that then, from there, you watch your eyes wither and their fragments blow away in the wind.)

But now we have a recipe for the visual experience you would have of yourself without eyes or a brain. These are most people's favored candidates for bodily organs essential to sight. You do not need your hands, feet, or pancreas to see, so imagine them away; indeed, for any one of your remaining organs, you can imagine visual experience of yourself without it. Moreover, you can visualize what you would see in the mirror even if all of the rest of your body were gone. To be sure, you see none of your body, since that is gone now; but you see (i.e., have a visual experience of), from a certain point of view, the reflection in the mirror of the room behind you. So you have a recipe for visual experience of yourself disembodied.

There are at least two immediately pressing questions about the story so far. The first is about location. Embodied people are (at least typically) located in space where their bodies are. But since a disembodied person has no body, where is he? Any person, even disembodied, who exists in this world must be somewhere. We can only begin to answer this question here. Every visual experience of a scene is an experience of that scene as it would be seen from a certain point of view. We see the various characters in a scene along what we call lines of sight. These lines of sight converge at a point, or at least in a small region, of space. At least part of the disembodied person is at this point or in that region of space, even though it is now no longer occupied, as it once was, by his eyes. (There will be more to location than the region of convergence.)

This makes sense only if the scene, visual experience of which we are imagining, is real. Here we come up against the second immediate question about our story: since visual experience is not by itself sufficient for sight, what more does a disembodied person need in order to see? According to the tradition, sight is distinguished from dreaming and visualizing by veridicality. Veridicality is to experience as truth is to thoughts (propositions, sentences, or statements). As a thought is true precisely in case the world is as one with the thought thinks it to be, so a visual experience is veridical precisely in case the world is as it looks to one with the visual experience. Note that in order for an experience to be veridical, there need be no substantial connection and no transmission or linkage between the experience and that chunk of the world in virtue of which it is veridical. Veridicality requires only, as it were, a coincidence of content between experience and the world. Hence, there is no obstacle at all in the way of supposing that a disembodied person's visual experience be (as it were, barely) veridical, that is, that the world be as it looks to the disembodied person. ...

Which, if any, are the data against which a piece of philosophy can and should be judged? This seems to be one of the harder philosophical questions, and it may not have a single, a simple, or (one sometimes fears) even any good answer. But in the recent literature, "intuition" often seems to have been used as a term of art for what is taken to be such data; and perhaps that is also part of what was before sometimes meant by "common sense."

It certainly seems common sense that some things that are not actually the case nevertheless could have been. Even if it is obscure how, it seems common sense that our best epistemic access to which unreal things could really have been is through the sensory imagination. No matter exactly how we spell out the detail, it seems common sense that we can imagine being disembodied. If we draw the obvious inference, the conclusion answers to the possibility recorded in the folklore of ghosts. Dualism is the intuitive solution to the mind-body problem.

NOTES

1   Joseph Addison, *Selections from Addison's Papers Contributed to the Spectator*, ed. Thomas Arnold, Oxford University Press (Clarendon Press), 1891, p. 147.
2   On Descartes, see Bernard Williams, *Descartes: The Project of Pure Inquiry*. Harmondsworth, 1978, esp. chap 4; and Margaret Dauler Wilson, *Descartes*, Routledge & Kegan Paul, London, 1978. See also Terence Penelhum, *Survival and Disembodied Existence*, Humanities Press, New York, 1970, esp. the first three chapters; and Saul Kripke, "Identity and Necessity", first published in *Identity and Individuation*, ed. Milton K. Munitz, New York University Press, New York, 1971, pp. 135–64. Kripke argues that because people's mental phenomena could persist even though their bodies vary radically in kind, perhaps even from flesh to metal, their mental phenomena are not necessarily, and thus not actually, identical with phenomena of their bodies. This argument establishes the distinctness between mind and body, not their independence; much as the bodies of Kripke's people vary, they are always embodied. As the hand-fist example shows, distinctness between mind and body is weaker than dualism, independence between mind and body. The last footnote to Kripke's essay makes his appreciation of these points manifest.

11

THE CASE FOR MATERIALISM

David Papineau

I am concerned with that aspect of consciousness that makes it so philosophically interesting. Namely, that having a conscious experience is *like something*, in Thomas Nagel's striking phrase (1974). It has become standard to use 'phenomenal' or 'subjective' to focus on this feature of consciousness, and I shall adopt these usages in what follows.

The idea is best introduced by examples rather than definitions. ('If you gotta ask, you're never gonna know.') Compare the difference between having your eyes shut and having them open, or between having your teeth drilled with and without an anaesthetic. When your eyes are open, you have a conscious visual experience, and when your teeth are drilled without an anaesthetic, you have a conscious pain. It is like something for you to have these experiences. It is not like that when you close your eyes, or when the anaesthetic takes effect. What you lose in these latter cases are elements of phenomenal or subjective consciousness.[1] From now on, when I say 'conscious', I shall mean this kind of consciousness.

Much of what follows will be concerned with a particular philosophical puzzle about consciousness: namely, the puzzle of how consciousness relates to the physical world. There are other philosophical puzzles about consciousness, but this seems to me the most immediate. We will be ill placed to understand anything about consciousness if we cannot understand its relation to the physical realm.

The puzzle can be posed simply. On the one hand, there is a strong argument for adopting a materialist view of conscious states, for supposing that conscious states must be *part* of the physical world, that they must be *identical* to brain states, or something similar. Yet, on the other hand, there are also strong arguments (and even stronger intuitions) which suggest that conscious states must be *distinct* from any material states.

I believe that in the end the materialist argument wins. Conscious states are material states. This is not to belittle the anti-materialist arguments and intuitions.

They are deep and important. We will not grasp consciousness properly unless we understand how to answer them. Still, I think that careful analysis will show that they are flawed, and that the right solution is to embrace materialism.

I shall begin by putting the materialist argument on the table. It is worth taking some care about this, for there are a number of different defences of materialism on offer in the contemporary literature, and not all of them are equally compelling. However, I think that there is one definitive argument for materialism. ...

... Let me now outline what I take to be the canonical argument for materialism. Setting to one side all complications, which can be discussed later, it can be put as follows.

> Many effects that we attribute to conscious causes have full physical causes. But it would be absurd to suppose that these effects are caused twice over. So the conscious causes must be identical to some part of those physical causes.

To appreciate the force of this argument, consider some bodily behaviour which we would standardly attribute to conscious causes. For example, I walk to the fridge to get a beer, because I consciously feel thirsty. Now combine this example with the thought that, according to modern physical science, such bodily movements are fully caused by prior physical processes in brains and nerves. The obvious conclusion is that the conscious thirst must be identical with some part of those physical processes.

Let me now lay out the above argument more formally. This will help us to appreciate both its strengths and its weaknesses.

As a first premiss, take:

(1) Conscious mental occurrences have physical effects.

As I said, the most obvious examples are cases where our conscious feelings and other mental states cause our behaviour.

Now add in this premiss ('the completeness of physics' henceforth):

(2) All physical effects are fully caused by purely *physical* prior histories.[2]

In particular, this covers the behavioural effects of conscious causes to which our attention is drawn by premiss 1. The thought behind premiss 2 is that such physical behaviour will always be fully caused by physical contractions in your muscles, in turn caused by electrical messages travelling down your nerves, themselves due to physical activity in your motor cortex, in turn caused by physical activity in your sensory cortex, and so on.

At first sight, premisses 1 and 2 seem to suggest that a certain range of physical effects (physical behaviour) will have two distinct causes: one involving a conscious state (your thirst, say), and the other consisting of purely physical states (neuronal firings, say).

Now, some events are indeed overdetermined in this way, like the death of a man who is simultaneously shot and struck by lightning. But this seems the wrong model for mental causation. After all, overdetermination implies that even if one cause had been absent, the result would still have occurred because of the other cause (the man would still have died even if he hadn't been shot, or, alternatively, even if he hadn't been struck by lightning). But it seems wrong to say that I would still have walked to the fridge even if I hadn't felt thirsty (because my neurons were firing), or, alternatively, that I would still have gone to the fridge even if my neurons hadn't been firing (because I felt thirsty). So let us add the further premiss:

(3)   The physical effects of conscious causes aren't always overdetermined by distinct causes.

Materialism now follows. Premisses 1 and 2 tell us that certain effects have a conscious cause and a physical cause. Premiss 3 tells us that they don't have two distinct causes. The only possibility left is that the conscious occurrences mentioned in (1) must be identical with some part of the physical causes mentioned in (2). This respects both (1) and (2), yet avoids the implication of overdetermination, since (1) and (2) no longer imply *distinct* causes. . . .

. . . As laid out above, the causal argument seems valid.[3] So, to deny the conclusion, we need to deny one of the premisses. All of them can be denied without contradiction. Indeed, all of them have been denied by contemporary philosophers, as we shall see. At the same time, they are all highly plausible, and their denials have various unattractive consequences.

Let me start with premiss 1. This claims that, as a matter of empirical fact, particular conscious states have particular physical effects. This certainly seems plausible. Doesn't my conscious thirst cause me to walk to the fridge? Or, again, when I have a conscious headache, doesn't this cause me to ingest an aspirin?

Still, the possibility of denying this premiss is familiar enough, under the guise of 'epiphenomenalism' or 'pre-established harmony'.

The first philosopher to embrace this option was Leibniz. Unlike most other philosophers prior to the twentieth century, Leibniz was committed to the causal completeness of physics. But he was not prepared to accept the identity of mind with brain. So he opted for a denial of our premiss 1, and concluded that mind and matter cannot really influence each other, and that the appearance of interaction must be due to *pre-established harmony*. By this Leibniz meant that God must have arranged things to make sure that mind and matter always keep in step. In reality, they do not interact, but are like two trains running on separate tracks. But God fixed their starting times and speeds so as to ensure they would always run smoothly alongside each other.

Some contemporary philosophers (for example, Jackson 1982) follow Leibniz in avoiding mind–brain identity by denying premiss 1. But they prefer a rather simpler way of keeping mind and matter in step. They allow causal influences 'upwards' from brain to mind, while denying any 'downwards' causation from mind to brain. This position is known as *epiphenomenalism*. It respects the causal completeness of physics, in that nothing non-physical causally influences the physical brain. But it avoids the theological complications of Leibniz's pre-established harmony, by allowing the brain itself to cause conscious effects.

Epiphenomenalism is not a particularly attractive position. For a start, it would require us to deny many apparently obvious truths, such as that my conscious thirst caused me to fetch a beer, or that my conscious headache caused me to swallow an aspirin. According to epiphenomenalism, my behaviour in both these cases is caused solely at the physical level. These physical causes may be accompanied by conscious thirst or a conscious headache, but these conscious states no more cause resulting behaviour than falling barometers cause rain.[4]

That epiphenomenalism has these odd consequences is not in itself decisive. The theoretical truth can often overturn claims which were previously regarded as the merest common sense. Moreover, there is nothing incoherent about epiphenomenalism. As I shall have occasion to stress in what follows, there is nothing conceptually contradictory in the idea of conscious states which exert no causal powers themselves. Still, epiphenomenalism is surely an empirically implausible position, by comparison with the materialist view that conscious states are simply identical to brain states.

If epiphenomenalism were true, then the relation between mind and brain would be like nothing else in nature. After all, science recognizes no other examples of 'causal danglers', ontologically independent states with causes but no effects. So, given the choice between epiphenomenalism and materialism, standard principles of scientific theory choice would seem to favour materialism. If both views can accommodate the empirical data equally well, then ordinary scientific methodology will advise us to adopt the simple view that unifies mind and brain, rather than the ontologically more profligate story which has the conscious states dangling impotently from the brain states.

There remains the possibility that the anti-materialist arguments to be examined later will show that conscious mind and brain *cannot* be identical. If this is so, then one of the premisses of the causal argument must be false. And in that case premiss 1 seems as likely a candidate as any. Certainly most contemporary philosophers who are persuaded by the anti-materialist arguments have opted for epiphenomenalism and the denial of premiss 1, rather than for any other way out of the causal argument.

But this does not invalidate the criticisms I have levelled against epiphenomenalism. My concern at the moment is not to prejudge the anti-materialist case, but merely to assess the causal argument. And the point remains that, in the absence of further considerations, it seems clearly preferable to identify mind with brain than to condemn conscious states to the status of causal danglers. It may be that further anti-materialist considerations will yet require us to reconsider this verdict, but so far we have seen no reason to deny premiss 1, and good reason to uphold it. ...

... So let me now briefly consider premiss 3, the one ruling out overdetermination.

To reject this premiss is to accept that the physical effects of mental causes are always overdetermined by distinct causes. This is sometimes called the 'belt and braces' view (make doubly sure you get the effects you want), and is defended by D. H. Mellor (1995: 103–5).

At first sight, this position seems to have the odd consequence that you would still have gone to the fridge for a beer even if you hadn't been thirsty (because your cortical neurons would still have been firing), and that you would still have gone to the fridge even if your cortex hadn't been firing (because you would still have been thirsty). These counterfactual implications seem clearly mistaken.

However, defenders of the belt and braces view maintain that such implications can be avoided. They argue that the distinct mental and physical causes may themselves be strongly counter-factually dependent (that is, they hold that, if you hadn't been thirsty, your sensory neurons wouldn't have fired either, and vice versa).

Still, this then raises the question of *why* such causes should always be so counterfactually dependent, if they are ontologically distinct.[5] Why wouldn't my neurons have fired, even in the absence of my conscious thirst? Similarly, why shouldn't I still have been thirsty, even if my neurons hadn't fired? Now, it is not impossible to imagine mechanisms which would ensure such counterfactual dependence between distinct causes. Perhaps the conscious thirst occurs first, and then invariably causes the cortical activity, with both causes thus available to overdetermine the behaviour. Alternatively, the cortical activity could invariably cause the thirst. Or, again, the conscious decision and the cortical activity might be joint effects of some prior common physical cause. But such mechanisms, though conceptually coherent, seem highly implausible, especially given that they need to ensure that the conscious state and the brain state *always* accompany each other.

The relevant point is analogous to one made in the last section. We don't find any 'belt and braces' mechanisms elsewhere in nature—that is, mechanisms which ensure that certain classes of effects invariably have two distinct causes, each of which would suffice by itself. As with the epiphenomenalist model, a belt and braces model requiring such peculiar brain mechanisms would seem to be ruled out by general principles of scientific theory choice. If the simple picture of mental causation offered by materialism accommodates the empirical data as well as the complex mechanisms required by the belt and braces option, then normal methodological principles would seem to weigh heavily against the belt and braces view.

As with the corresponding argument for epiphenomenalism, this appeal to principles of scientific theory choice is defeasible. Perhaps in the end the anti-materialist arguments will force us to accept mind–brain distinctness. In that case, the belt and braces view might be worth another look. True, it is even more Heath-Robinsonish than epiphenomenalism. On the other hand, it does at least have the virtue of retaining the common-sense view that conscious states characteristically cause behaviour. In any case, my present purpose is not to decide this issue finally, but only to point out that, as things stand so far, we have good reason to uphold premiss 3, and none to deny it. . . .

. . . Let me conclude this chapter with a few remarks about the causal argument's second premiss, the completeness of physics. It is one thing to fix a sense of 'physics' which renders this a substantial claim which might be true or false. It is another to show that it is in fact true.

Some readers might feel that this is not a problematic issue. Once we have fixed a definite meaning for 'physical', as equivalent to 'inanimate', say, then is it not just a matter of common sense that all physical effects will have physical causes? In particular, if we take the physical effects in this sense that we normally attribute to conscious causes, then is it not obvious that these effects can always in principle be fully accounted for in terms of uncontroversially physical histories, involving the movement of matter (in arms), molecular processes (in muscles), the action of neurotransmitters (in brains) . . . and so on?

This is certainly how I thought of the issue when I first started working on the causal argument. I realized that this argument involved a number of disputable moves, and was therefore ready for it to be queried on various different grounds. But the one assumption that I did expect to be uncontroversial was the completeness of physics. To my surprise, I discovered that a number of my philosophical colleagues didn't agree. They didn't see why some physical occurrences, in our brains perhaps, shouldn't have irreducibly conscious causes.

My first reaction to this suggestion was that it betrayed an insufficient understanding of modern physics. Surely, I felt, the completeness premiss is simply part of standard physical theory. However, when my objectors pressed me, not unreasonably, to show them where the completeness of physics is written down in the physics textbooks, I found myself in some embarrassment. Once I was forced to defend it, I realized that the completeness of physics is by no means self-evident. Indeed, further research has led me to realize that, far from being self-evident, it is an issue on which the post-Galilean scientific tradition has changed its mind several times. The completeness of physics may seem the merest part of common sense to many of us today, but as recently as 150 years ago most people, including most orthodox scientists, would have thought the idea absurd, taking it to be obvious that there must be some *sui generis* conscious states in the causal history of human behaviour.

So the completeness of physics is a doctrine with a history, and a very interesting history at that. There is good empirical evidence for the completeness of physics, but the historical story shows that this evidence is relatively recent, and that prior to the twentieth century the empirical case for the completeness of physics was by no means persuasive. . . .

. . . There is indeed a good case for materialism. But it has not always been available to philosophers. This is because its crucial premiss, the completeness of physics, rests on empirical evidence which has emerged only relatively recently.

NOTES

1 Some philosophers assume that 'phenomenal' is meant to contrast with *intentional*, and on this basis hold that much recent discussion of consciousness, especially that surrounding David Chalmers's 'hard problem' (1996), is invalidated by an implicit supposition that subjectivity is independent of intentionality (cf. Eilan 1998). It is perhaps worth emphasizing that I don't intend 'phenomenal' to imply 'non-intentional'. I simply mean it as a non-committal term for subjective 'what-it's-likeness'. Nothing yet rules out the possibility that all, or only, intentional states involve phenomenal consciousness. Moreover, since Chalmers also understands 'phenomenal' in this way, his 'hard problem' of phenomenal consciousness will still arise even if phenomenality is not independent of intentionality.

2 What about quantum indeterminacy? A stricter version of (2) would say that the *chances* of physical effects are always fully fixed by their prior physical histories, and would reformulate the rest of the argument accordingly (with (1) then as 'Conscious mental occurrences affect the *chances* of physical effects', and so on). I shall skip this complication in what follows.

3 However Sturgeon (1998) argues that the argument trades on an equivocation between the everyday sense of 'physical' (in premiss 1) and a quantum-theoretical sense (in premiss 2).

4 Chalmers (1996: esp. 134–6), following Russell (1927) and Lockwood (1989), argues that there is a way for dualism to avoid this epiphenomenalist inefficacy while respecting the completeness of physics. This is to identify phenomenal properties with the *intrinsic* properties of the physical realm. Chalmers's idea is that physical science picks out properties like mass and charge only extrinsically, via their relations to observable features of the world. So maybe phenomenal properties can be identified with the intrinsic nature of such properties, suggests Chalmers, and thereby have their causal efficacy restored. This seems an entirely sensible view to me. But, *pace* Chalmers, I would say that it is simply a version of materialism. My reaction is that the intrinsic features of the physical world with which Chalmers wants to identify phenomenal properties are themselves simply basic physical properties. Thus I am happy to agree with Chalmers that scientific theory picks out these intrinsic physical properties only via descriptions which refer to observable features of the world. Moreover, I agree that conscious properties should be identified with arrangements of such intrinsic physical properties, and thus that it is like something to have these arrangements of intrinsic properties. Indeed, I find it hard to see what a sensible materialism could amount to, except this combination of views. So, from my point of view, Chalmers's suggested position is simply the optimal formulation of materialism.

5 Note that this is only a problem if the causes are genuinely ontologically distinct, and not if they are merely related as role state and physical realizer. The existence of 'two' causes

in this latter sense does not threaten overdetermination, precisely because of their ontological interdependence. So I have no objection to versions of the belt and braces view which intend only parallel causes in this weak sense. Cf. Segal and Sober (1991).

REFERENCES

Chalmers, David (1996) *The Conscious Mind*. Oxford: Oxford University Press.

Eilan, Naomi (1998) "Perceptual Intentionality, Attention and Consciousness", in A. O'Hear (ed.), *Current Issues in Philosophy of Mind*. Cambridge: Cambridge University Press.

Jackson, Frank (1982) "Epiphenomenal Qualia" *Philosophical Quarterly* 32, pp. 127–36.

Lockwood, Michael (1989) *Mind, Brain and Quantum*. Oxford: Blackwell.

Mellor, D.H. (1995) *The Facts of Causation*. London: Routledge.

Nagel, Thomas (1974) "What is it Like to be a Bat?" *Philosophical Review* 4: 435–50.

Russell, Bertrand (1927) *The Analysis of Matter*. London: Kegan Paul.

Segal, Gabriel and Sober, Elliott (1991) "The Causal Efficacy of Content". *Philosophical Studies* 63:1–30.

Sturgeon, Scott (1998) "Physicalism and Overdetermination". *Mind* 107:411–33.

12

WHAT IS THE SOUL?

Bertrand Russell

One of the most painful circumstances of recent advances in science is that each one of them makes us know less than we thought we did. When I was young we all knew, or thought we knew, that a man consists of a soul and a body; that the body is in time and space, but the soul is in time only. Whether the soul survives death was a matter as to which opinions might differ, but that there is a soul was thought to be indubitable. As for the body, the plain man of course considered its existence self-evident, and so did the man of science, but the philosopher was apt to analyze it away after one fashion or another, reducing it usually to ideas in the mind of the man who had the body and anybody else who happened to notice him. The philosopher, however, was not taken seriously, and science remained comfortably materialistic, even in the hands of quite orthodox scientists.

Nowadays these fine old simplicities are lost: physicists assure us that there is no such thing as matter, and psychologists assure us that there is no such thing as mind. This is an unprecedented occurrence. Who ever heard of a cobbler saying that there was no such thing as boots, or a tailor maintaining that all men are really naked? Yet that would have been no odder than what physicists and certain psychologists have been doing. To begin with the latter, some of them attempt to reduce everything that seems to be mental activity to an activity of the body. There are, however, various difficulties in the way of reducing mental activity to physical activity. I do not think we can yet say with any assurance whether these difficulties are or are not insuperable. What we can say, on the basis of physics itself, is that what we have hitherto called our body is really an elaborate scientific construction not corresponding to any physical reality. The modern would-be materialist thus finds himself in a curious position, for, while he may with a certain degree of success reduce the activities of the mind to those of the body, he cannot explain away the fact that the body itself is merely a convenient concept invented by the mind. We find ourselves thus going round and round in a circle: mind is an emanation of body, and body is an invention of mind. Evidently this cannot be quite right, and we have to look for something that is neither mind nor body, out of which both can spring.

Let us begin with the body. The plain man thinks that material objects must certainly exist, since they are evident to the senses. Whatever else may be doubted, it is certain that anything you can bump into must be real; this is the plain man's metaphysic. This is all very well, but the physicist comes along and shows that you never bump into anything: even when you run your head against a stone wall, you do not really touch it. When you think you touch a thing, there are certain electrons and protons, forming part of your body, which are attracted and repelled by certain electrons and protons in the thing you think you are touching, but there is no actual contact. The electrons and protons in your body, becoming agitated by nearness to the other electrons and protons, are disturbed, and transmit a disturbance along your nerves to the brain; the effect in the brain is what is necessary to your sensation of contact, and by suitable experiments this sensation can be made quite deceptive. The electrons and protons themselves, however, are only a crude first approximation, a way of collecting into a bundle either trains of waves or the statistical probabilities of serious different kinds of events. Thus matter has become altogether too ghostly to be used as an adequate stick with which to beat the mind. Matter in motion, which used to seem so unquestionable, turns out to be a concept quite inadequate for the needs of physics.

Nevertheless modern science gives no indication whatever of the existence of the soul or mind as an entity; indeed the reasons for disbelieving in it are of very much the same kind as the reasons for disbelieving in matter. Mind and matter were something like the lion and the unicorn fighting for the crown; the end of the battle is not the victory of one or the other, but the discovery that both are only heraldic inventions. The world consists of events, not of things that endure for a long time and have changing properties. Events can be collected into groups by their causal relations. If the causal relations are of one sort the resulting group of events may be called a physical object, and if the causal relations are of another sort, the resulting group may be called a mind. Any event that occurs inside a man's head will belong to groups of both kinds; considered as belonging to a group of one kind, it is a constituent of his brain, and considered as belonging to a group of the other kind, it is a constituent of his mind.

Thus both mind and matter are merely convenient ways of organizing events. There can be no reason for supposing that either a piece of mind or a piece of matter is immortal. The sun is supposed to be losing matter at the rate of millions of tons a minute. The most essential characteristic of mind is memory, and there is no reason whatever to suppose that the memory associated with a given person survives that person's death. Indeed there is every reason to think the opposite, for memory is clearly connected with a certain kind of brain structure, and since this structure decays at death, there is every reason to suppose that memory also must cease. Although metaphysical materialism cannot be considered true, yet emotionally the world is pretty much the same as it would be if the materialists were in the right. I think the opponents of materialism have always been actuated by two main desires: the first to prove that the mind is immortal, and the second to prove that the ultimate power in the universe is mental rather than physical. In both these respects, I think the materialists were in the right. Our desires, it is true, have considerable power on the earth's surface; the greater part of the land on this planet has a quite different aspect from that which it would have if men had not utilized it to extract food and wealth. But our power is very strictly limited. We cannot at present do anything whatever to the sun or moon or even to the interior of the earth, and there is not the faintest reason to suppose that what happens in regions to which our power does not extend has any mental causes. That is to say, to put the matter in a nutshell, there is no reason to think that except on the earth's surface anything happens because somebody wishes it to happen. And since our power on the earth's surface is entirely dependent upon the supply of energy which the earth derives from the sun, we are necessarily dependent upon the sun, and could hardly realize any of our wishes if the sun grew cold. It is of course rash to dogmatize as to what science may achieve in the future. We may learn to prolong human existence longer than now seems possible, but if there is any truth in modern physics, more particularly in the second law of thermo-dynamics, we cannot hope that the human race will continue for ever. Some people may find this conclusion gloomy, but if we are honest with ourselves, we shall have to admit that what is going to happen many millions of years hence has no very great emotional interest for us here and now. And science, while it diminishes our cosmic pretensions, enormously increases our terrestrial comfort. That is why, in spite of the horror of the theologians, science has on the whole been tolerated.

13

POST-PHYSICALISM

Barbara Montero

INTRODUCTION

What is the problem, inherited from Descartes, that we now call 'the mind–body problem'? In his most recent book, Jaegwon Kim provides an answer with which many would agree. 'Through the 70s and 80s and down to this day,' Kim tells us, 'the mind–body problem – our mind–body problem – has been that of finding a place for the mind in a world that is fundamentally physical' (Kim 1998, p. 2). This problem, which at one time was at home mainly in departments of philosophy, is now studied by a broad range of disciplines. One finds, for example, neuroscientists arguing that certain discoveries about the brain show that consciousness is physical; researchers in artificial intelligence claiming that because human thought can be simulated by complex computers, thought requires nothing beyond the physical; and evolutionary biologists declaring that insights into the evolution of the mind indicate that it must be fundamentally physical. But what does it mean to be physical? While the basic results of the research being done may be clear enough, how are we to interpret the further claim 'and this shows that the mind is physical'? The answer is that we have no idea.

I am going to argue that it is time to come to terms with the difficulty of understanding what it means to be physical and start thinking about the mind–body problem from a new perspective. Instead of construing it as the problem of finding a place for mentality in a fundamentally physical world, we should think of it as the problem of finding a place for mentality in a fundamentally nonmental world, a world that is at its most fundamental level entirely nonmental. The mind–body problem, I want to argue, is the problem of determining whether mentality can be accounted for in terms of nonmental phenomena. In other words, it is the question, 'is mentality a fundamental feature of the world?'[1]

I THE CURRENT STATE OF THE DEBATE

Currently most philosophers working on the mind–body problem see the debate in terms of the physical and the nonphysical: the question most are concerned with is whether mentality is fundamentally *physical*.[2] Indeed, since most think that the mind *must* be physical, the project they are engaged in is not so much arguing that the mind is physical, but, rather, trying to show how the mind could be physical (given that it is). And so, whether the account of mentality that physicalists propound is expressed in terms of reduction, realization, identity, supervenience, explanation or even elimination, the goal is to provide a plausible theory of mentality (or, as the case may be, a theory that accounts for what we mistakenly took to be mentality) that is compatible with the view that the world is fundamentally physical. For example, if one thinks that it is incumbent on physicalists to *explain* mentality then the explanation, it is thought, must make reference exclusively to physical phenomena; if one thinks supervenience suffices for physicalism, then the supervenience base must be entirely physical; and so forth. But what does it mean to be physical? It seems that those who take the central concern of the mind–body problem to be the relationship between mental properties and physical properties – and if Kim is right, this is just about everyone – should have at least a rough idea of what it means to be physical, not necessarily a strict definition, but at least a notion of the physical that excludes some, if not actual, then at least possible, phenomena from being physical. For if we cannot even conceive of something being nonphysical, it is difficult to grasp what physicalists could be arguing for – to say nothing of what that they could be arguing against.[3]

It is not at all clear, however, that physicalists can provide even this minimal condition. Current physics, which posits such things as particles with no determinate location, curved space–time, and wave–particle duality, tells us that the world is indeed more ghostly than any ghost in the machine. And if the existence of ghostly phenomena does not falsify physicalism it is difficult to say what would. As Richard Healey puts it, '[the] expanding catalogue of elementary particle states of an increasingly recondite nature seems to have made it increasingly hard for the physicists to run across evidence that would cast doubt on a thesis of contemporary physicalism stated in terms of it' (Healey 1979, p. 208). In other words, if such things as one-dimensional strings and massless particles are physical, it is difficult to say what wouldn't be. Bertrand Russell made this basic point back in 1927: 'matter,' he said, 'has become as ghostly as anything in a spiritualist's séance.'[4] And over the past seventy years Russell's point has, if anything, been reinforced. Presumably things could change. Philosophy, as we all know, is not noted for its rapid progress and perhaps in another seventy years or so we will have a clear idea of what it means to be physical. However, it seems to me that until such clarification comes about, we ought to rethink the project of accommodating the mental in the physical world. That is, we ought to rethink what Kim tells us is 'the shared project of the majority of those who have been working on the mind–body problem over the past few decades' (Kim 1998, p. 2).

Not surprisingly, most physicalists are of a somewhat different opinion. While many physicalists admit that our understanding of what it means to be physical is rather tenuous, they usually think that the notion, and thus the crux of the debate, is clear enough. The mind–body problem, according to most physicalists, is the problem of explaining how the mind can be physical, where what counts as physical is given to us by science. In John Searle's words, the mind–body problem is the problem of locating mentality 'within our overall "scientific" conception of the world'.[5] And so, it does not matter what kinds of ghostly and bizarre phenomena science may posit, for it is science itself that serves as a reality test. Searle thinks mentality passes the test because mentality, he argues, is 'as much part of our biological natural history as digestion' (Searle 1992). Others, however, are a bit harsher in their grading policy. According to Patricia Churchland, for example, it is premature to say that every aspect of what we now think of as mentality can be accommodated in our scientific world-view (and for Churchland the relevant science here is neuroscience) since, for all we know, certain aspects of mentality might fail the test and go the way of phlogiston (Churchland 1995). Yet as different as their views may be, both Searle and Churchland, as well as most other physicalists, abide by Wilfred Sellars' well known dictum, 'in the dimension of describing and explaining the world, science is the measure of all things, of what is that it is, and of what is not that it is not.'[6] Physicalists may disagree about just how far to take this claim: must we be 'nothing butists', or can we accept an ontology that goes beyond science as long as it is related to the posits of science 'in the proper way'?[7] However, when it comes to fundamental ontological matters, they are, for the most part, united: the ultimate authority is science.

But what is meant here by 'science'? Physicalists usually shy away from expressing their views about which specific theories will account for the fundamental nature of, as it were, everything. And this, of course, is the safest strategy. For as David Lewis advises, physicalists should 'side with physics, but not take sides within physics' (Lewis 1983, p. 364). Samuel Guttenplan advocates this strategy as well; in his words, 'all we [physicalists] are claiming is that any phenomenon that is a genuine happening in this world is in principle explicable by a science, albeit by a science that might be quite different from any we now have at our disposal' (Guttenplan 1995, p. 77). But if this is all that physicalists are claiming, it is difficult to see what prevents *anything* from being physical: if physics (correctly) tells us that some things have no mass or no determinate spatial location, well then, physicalists will say, those things will still count as physical. Even if physics were to one day reveal that our current theory of space–time is mistaken and that space and time actually are distinct so that some phenomena have temporal, but not spatial properties, then physicalists, I assume, would say that those things too, if they actually exist, will be physical. Even more, if, as some physicists have begun to speculate, there is some sort of nonspatial, nontemporal stuff out of which space–time itself emerges, physicalists will once again declare victory.[8] But if this is so, it seems that the strategy of simply siding with science, whatever science may ultimately say, is so safe as to bestow physicalism with what Popper thought was the very unscientific virtue of being, even in principle, unfalsifiable. Perhaps the deep eternal truths that are the domain of philosophy as well as mathematics are not at all likely to be falsifiable. Yet it seems that without any restrictions on how the science in question is to progress, or on what entities and properties it is to incorporate, physicalism, that is, the view that everything is physical, becomes not only unfalsifiable, but also trivial.[9] That is, without any restrictions whatsoever, the view that everything is physical ends up as the view that everything exists. And this, it seems to me, is a position that most philosophers, save, of course, for Meinongians, are not interested in discussing.

While a number of physicalists, including Lewis himself, have tried to avoid this obstacle in their formulations of physicalism, I think that ultimately there is no way around it.[10] As long as one defines the physical in relation to what science tells us about the world, the problem of explaining what it means to be physical in the context of the mind–body problem, a problem I call 'the body problem', currently has no solution.[11] But what is left of the mind–body problem if we have no notion of body? In other words, is there room for the mind–body problem in a post-physical world?[12]

II IS THERE STILL A MIND–BODY PROBLEM?

One might think that the only reasonable conclusion to draw from the view that we have no notion of the physical is that we should give up the mind–body problem altogether: declare it dissolved and move on to other, hopefully better-defined, problems. And as far as I know, most of those who argue that we have no philosophically useful notion of the physical are, it seems inevitably, drawn to this conclusion. Noam Chomsky is a good example. He tells us, 'we can speak intelligibly of *physical* phenomena (processes, etc.) as we speak of the *real* truth or the *real* world, but without supposing that there is some other truth or world' (Chomsky 1998, p. 438). And he takes this to mean, 'we have no coherent way to formulate issues related to the "mind–body problem"' (Chomsky 1995, p. 5; see also Chomsky 1993). Similarly, Bas van Fraassen argues that the fact that physicalists will usually count '*whatever science comes up with*' as physical shows that the thesis of physicalism lacks content (van Fraassen 1996, p. 167). Chris Daly, who, in a recent paper, argues quite forcefully that we have no notion of a physical property, concludes, 'no debate between physicalism and dualism can even be set up' (Daly 1998, p. 213; also see Scheffler 1950). While Tim Crane and Hugh Mellor, after finding flaws with a wide variety of proposals for defining physicalism, conclude that their paper 'should really be the last paper on the subject' (Crane and Mellor 1990, p. 83). The pattern is clear. And it is not at all difficult to see the motivation behind it: for if we have no notion of the physical, there seems to be little use in asking how the mind could be physical and, thus, little point in discussing the mind–body problem. But is this the only conclusion one can draw? Must our inability to solve the body problem lead to the demise of the mind–body problem as well?

To be sure, one obvious worry about concluding that we must abandon the mind–body problem is that, as a matter of fact, very few will follow suit. Philosophy, it has been said, has a penchant for burying its undertakers, and despite repeated pronouncements of the death of the mind–body problem, most people feel that a problem of some sort – perhaps of a very deep sort – remains. Even Crane and Mellor realize that this creates some tension in their view. For after stating quite boldly that their paper should definitely be the last on the topic, they also sheepishly admit that they actually know it will not. And here they were certainly right. Since their paper came out, about ten years ago, the question, 'what is the fundamental nature of the mind?' – a question to which 'it is physical' is supposed to provide an answer – has, if anything, been even more widely discussed. But why is this, if, as the title of their paper proclaims, 'there is no question of physicalism'? Of course, the mere fact that many continue thinking about a problem does not show that a problem really exists. For it might be that no one has listened to Crane and Mellor's protests that we have no notion of the physical capable of grounding questions about whether the mind is physical. While there may be something to this, there is more to be said. For there actually *is* an interesting question to ask about the fundamental nature of the mind. It is just not the question of whether the fundamental nature of the mind is physical.

What other broad, philosophical questions can we ask about the fundamental nature of the mind – questions, that is, which could reasonably be thought to address the set of concerns that we have come to think of as the mind–body problem? Certainly, even if there were no philosophical problem called 'the mind–body problem', there would still be specific questions about the mind left to investigate. For example, regardless of whether we have a notion of the physical, we may still arrive at a deeper understanding of our mental lives, perhaps by studying the relationship between consciousness and various neural processes or, say, investigating which sorts of pains are correlated with A-fibre stimulation, which with C-fibre stimulation. Daly emphasizes this point towards the end of his paper. As he says, 'for even in absence of a principled account of the distinction between physical properties and all other properties, terms used to designate specific properties may be sufficiently well defined for us to raise specific issues [such as, how pain relates to C-fibre stimulation]' (Daly

1998, pp. 213–14). And I take it that many of those who take sides within science (rather than simply siding with science) are engaged in addressing specific questions – like those the neuroscientist asks – that do not depend on such a distinction. But are specific questions the only sorts of questions left? I think that they are not, for regardless of whether we know what it means to be physical, we can still ask whether mentality is a fundamental feature of the world. In other words, does mentality ultimately depend on nonmental phenomena or, as it were, is it mental all the way down?

As I see it, in its most general structure, this is the crux of the mind–body problem. Yet a glance through the literature, where one comes across numerous papers with titles such as, 'Can Science Explain Consciousness?' does not make this apparent (see, for example, Shear 1997). That is, the question of whether mentality is fundamental is crucial to the debate, yet rarely is it addressed directly. I think this is a mistake. And a serious one since physicalists aim to refute dualism, yet dualism is the view that mentality is fundamental.

To say that the question is rarely addressed directly, however, is not to say that philosophers are indifferent as to its outcome. For despite the fact that most recent discussions about the mind focus on whether mentality will be somehow subsumed under the scope of the scientifically acceptable, what I call 'the science question', one often does find that the underlying concern in these debates is the question of whether mentality is a fundamental feature of the world (what *I* call 'the mind–body problem'). And, for the most part, philosophers' views on this come down along party lines: the dualists are for it and the physicalists are against it.[13] For example, when Kim lays out the basic physicalist commitments, along with the claim that the mental supervenes on and is determined by the physical is the claim that there are 'no fundamental mental entities'.[14] David Chalmers also makes clear what side he is on: when addressing the question of whether it would be more accurate to call his view a version of physicalism, since he allows that the mental may in the future be accounted for by an expanded physics, he holds fast to the dualist classification because, as he says, his view admits 'phenomenal or protophenomenal properties as fundamental' (Chalmers 1996, p. 136; see also Foster 1989, pp. 1–15).

But, again, while many physicalists claim that mentality is not fundamental, few spend much time defending this claim. Rather, most focus on the science question, the question of whether science will account for the mind.[15] Yet these two views do not make the same cut: science may account for mentality (in as much as it accounts for any other fundamental feature of the world) but mentality may still be a fundamental feature of the world. Of course, physics, for the most part, does not posit anything fundamentally mental. However, it is not too much of a stretch of the imagination to see how it could. For example, if Wigner's hypothesis – the hypothesis that acts of pure consciousness (in other words, fundamentally mental entities) are required to explain the collapse of the wave function – were accepted, or, to put it more strongly, if it were true, there would be a sense in which consciousness fits perfectly into our scientific world-view: acts of pure consciousness would be just one of the many fundamental entities posited by physics.[16] Yet mentality would still be a fundamental feature of the world. Certain interpretations of the anthropic principle, a principle sometimes invoked to explain or at least constrain other explanations about why things are just as they are, also seem to take mentality as, at least explanatorily, fundamental. For example, it is sometimes claimed that the reason why a particular state of the carbon nucleus has the precise energy that it does is that if this value were only slightly greater or slightly less, human beings would never have developed and thus we would not be able to ask this very question. As such, the existence of human consciousness is taken as a starting point in explaining other aspects of the universe.[17] To be sure, both the anthropic principle and Wigner's hypothesis are highly controversial, and perhaps neither should be taken as part of physics. But I think they do illustrate a possibility: the possibility of how physics could incorporate mentality as a fundamental. And as long as physicalists accept this mere possibility, they are accepting the possibility that mentality could be accounted for by science, yet still be fundamental.[18] Arguing that science can in principle account for mentality, then, does not suffice to show that mentality is not fundamental; in this sense, an argument for physicalism is not an argument against dualism.[19]

But while physicalists, in claiming that science or physics will account for mentality, may assert a view that is not opposed to dualism, they nonetheless usually exclude the mental from their fundamental ontology. And since they do, they in fact are not simply deferring to science to tell us how things are. Rather, they are putting forth a substantive ontological thesis, namely, that mentality is not a fundamental feature of the world (regardless of what physics reveals). If physics posits things that cannot be analysed in terms of (or are not ultimately reducible to or determined by or constituted out of – pick your favourite dependence relationship) nonmental phenomena, physicalists typically will *not* go on to acknowledge those things as physical. Science may, indeed, be the measure of all things, but if science posits fundamental mental entities or properties, physicalists, I take it, throw in the towel. And so, despite much talk about the wonders science is capable of achieving, the crux of the mind–body problem is actually not the question 'is the mind physical?' (where this notion is tied to what science can achieve) but is rather the question, 'is the mind fundamentally nonmental?'[20]

III PHYSICALISM WITHOUT NATURALISM = FUNDAMENTAL NONMENTALISM

Convincing physicalists that we need to focus on the question of whether mentality is fundamental may not be easy since physicalists are usually intent on trying to have things both ways. As I see it, physicalists have long struggled to find some middle ground between their desire to be naturalists, that is, their desire to defer to science for matters about fundamental ontology, and their desire to put forth a significant thesis about the mind, that is, their desire to express a view that at least amounts to more than the claim that mentality fits into our scientific world-view, where our scientific world-view can turn out to encompass anything including, if it so happens, acts of pure consciousness. But it is very difficult to do the latter while upholding the former. In order to make their notion of physicalism a substantive claim about the world, some restriction needs to be placed on what counts as science.[21] Putnam makes this point forcefully: 'if no restraint at all is placed on what counts as a possible "fundamental magnitude" in future physics, then reference to soul or good could even be fundamental magnitudes in future physics!'[22] Yet placing *a priori* restrictions on science, on what it is and how it is allowed to progress seems blatantly anti-naturalistic: according to the deferential naturalist, what sorts of theories about the world, what sorts of entities, relations, and laws science can posit as well as what sorts methodologies it can avail itself of, will be determined by science itself, not by armchair philosophy. Given this conflict of interests, I say physicalists should abandon one or the other: naturalism or ontological significance.[23]

Naturalists might try to avoid this conflict by claiming that their intent is not to place restrictions on the posits of science but, rather, to make a prediction about its course, namely, that mentality will not show up as a fundamental.[24] But this consistency is purchased at a price. For to adopt a policy of strict noninterference and recede to mere prediction is to step out of the debate between physicalists and dualists. Some naturalists may not mind this retreat, yet I think that they are not the majority. Rather, many naturalists both positively assert that mentality is not fundamental and claim to defer all ontological matters to the scientist and, thus, struggle valiantly to remain faithful to an ontology that excludes fundamental mentality and to deferential naturalism. Yet this, I think, is something that cannot be done with consistency.

David Papineau is a good example of someone engaged in such a struggle. Papineau provides a clear account of which dependence relation he prefers: the mental, he claims, supervenes on and is token congruent with the physical. He takes supervenience to be a thesis about variation between intrinsic properties of systems: two systems cannot differ (across possible worlds that share our laws of physics) without differing in terms of their intrinsic physical properties. And he takes two properties to be token congruent if one realizes the other or if they are actually type identical.[25] But when it comes to explaining what he means by 'physical', a conflict becomes apparent. His commitment to naturalism leads him to take a hands-off approach and to let the answer to this question come from within physics itself. Not today's physics, since he thinks that current physics is certainly inadequate, but rather a true and complete physics, a physics that he simply defines as 'the science of whatever categories are needed to give full explanations for all physical effects'.[26] But now the threat of triviality enters the picture: for if psychological categories are part of this science, Papineau's position loses its punch. That is, if psychological categories are part of the science that is needed to explain all physical effects, psychology will indeed supervene on the physical, but only because it will be part of the physical (there will be no change in psychological properties without a change in the physical base properties because the psychological, itself, will be a physical base property).

Papineau, however, well aware of this threat, tries to compromise. The mind, he claims, will be accounted for by science, yet the science will be one without psychological categories (Papineau 1993, p. 31). But it seems to me that this exclusion is really the whole game. The bottom line, it turns out, is not whether mentality can be accounted for by science. For when the notion of science is left entirely open-ended, as Papineau, being a good naturalist, is drawn to do, we can say nothing about whether psychological categories will be part of the *final* scientific dependence base. Rather, the bottom line is whether mentality can be accounted for without involving psychological categories themselves.

Robert Kirk's discussion of what he means by 'physical' exemplifies a similar conflict of interests. The physical, Kirk says, is simply 'whatever is posited by physics'. Yet, just to be safe, he also says, 'we can explicitly exclude all expressions that would ordinarily be counted as mental or psychological' (Kirk 1994, p. 78). But clearly one cannot leave everything up to the physicists while at the same time placing restrictions on what they can do. One can embrace naturalism wholeheartedly: take one's ontological commitments to reach only as far as what is sanctioned by science and thereby defer all substantial ontological questions. Or one can take a stance: reject naturalism and start being a little less deferential.

The middle ground that Papineau and Kirk try to set out, that is, leaving the job of making all substantial ontological hypotheses up to the scientists *except* for the hypothesis that the mental is not fundamental, seems oddly *ad hoc*. Why should this bit of *a priori* reasoning be allowed and not others?[27] Some might say that it should be allowed because the hypothesis that mentality is fundamental is abhorrent to common sense, simply unimaginable. And perhaps this is so. For as Thomas Nagel has said, 'there is a deep-seated aversion in the modern "disenchanted" Weltanschauung to any ultimate principles that are not dead – that is, devoid of any reference to the possibility of life or consciousness' (Nagel 1996, p. 133). However, reasoning from what is or is not abhorrent to common sense is not usually a type of reasoning condoned by naturalists. According to the naturalist, scientific judgments are one thing and intuitions are something else. For example, naturalists may admit that it is intuitively difficult to understand how pain could be identical to, or even just constituted by some brain state. But this, they quickly point out, does not falsify physicalism. Newtonian gravity was difficult to imagine, naturalists often remind us, but this didn't stop Newton and likewise the fact that some hypothesis is unintuitive or difficult to imagine should not stop physicalism. But if naturalists reject reliance on what is or is not abhorrent to common sense in these situations, it seems that consistency should lead them to reject it in reasoning about whether mentality is a fundamental feature of the world. If the naturalist wants to leave everything up to science, then he should do so. For there is nothing wrong with adopting the strategy of 'let's just wait and see'. It is just that this strategy does not make for much of a debate.

It might seem, however, that the distinction between the naturalist who defers to the scientist and the armchair philosopher who denies the fundamental status of mentality is somewhat artificial. For isn't it the case that science, in fact, already tells us that mentality is not fundamental? To be sure, if we try to look up mentality in the 'Berkeley booklet', the physicists' ever expanding little black book of the fundamental entities and properties known to date, we will find no listing.[28] But according to most physicalists, not being listed in today's Berkeley booklet does not exclude a fundamental entity or property from the physical realm. What matters is what will show up in the final edition. That is, physicalists do not merely claim that mentality is not *currently* classified by physicists as a fundamental feature of the world; rather, according to such philosophers as Papineau and Kirk, mentality will be *forever* unlisted in the physicists' little black book.[29] But it is difficult to see how naturalists can make such an assertion. The world as we know it is full of fundamental properties and fundamental mental properties (if there are such things) should, at least in principle, be no more (or for that matter, no less) mysterious, or necessarily outside the realm of science than any other fundamental properties.[30] Of course, there may be reasons to avoid such a conclusion. For example, considerations of simplicity may lead us to want explanations with as few primitive terms as possible and encourage us to do without mentality as a primitive term if possible. But the question of whether it is possible is the central point of the debate so we should not start out assuming this.

That said, one still might feel that there is something defeatist about the view that mentality is fundamental. For if one claims that mentality is fundamental isn't one, rather than presenting a possible solution to the mind–body problem, giving up on it?[31] I suppose this depends on what one means by 'giving up'. To be sure, fundamental principles or phenomena do, by their very nature, leave something unexplained. And in this sense, claiming that mentality is fundamental is tantamount to denying any possible further explanation of it, any explanation of it in terms of something else. Nevertheless, to successfully argue that mentality is fundamental is to provide a solution to the mind–body problem. That is, that answer to the question 'what is the relationship between mental phenomena and nonmental phenomena?' will be that the mental is fundamentally distinct from the nonmental.

Of course, the distinction between the mental and the nonmental may not be sharp. And in fact, physicalists may need to hold that it is not. Physicalists (of the noneliminative sort) think that the nonmental, arranged in the right way, as it were, gives us the mental; yet if you hold that the mental/nonmental distinction is sharp, it is very difficult to see how to bridge that divide. For example, if you are interested in explaining subjectivity and you take the line between the subjective and the objective (i.e., the nonsubjective) to be sharp, physicalism – or rather, fundamental nonmentalism – becomes very difficult, if not impossible to defend. This is true of the intrinsic/extrinsic divide as well: if it is sharp, and one takes the properties of consciousness to be intrinsic and physical properties to be extrinsic, it is very difficult to see how an anti-physicalist view could fail to follow.[32] As a sharp distinction between the living and the non-living seems to lead us to posit a fundamental life-force, or *élan vital*, a sharp distinction between the mental and the nonmental seems to lead to dualism. So in debating the mind–body problem, we should focus on the mental/nonmental distinction but not presuppose that the distinction is sharp since the outcome of the debate may partially turn on this. ...

IV THE IMPACT ON THE DEBATE

One might accept my formulation of the mind–body problem, but still wonder if it will have any interesting effect on the debate. If not, we might as well save the ink and leave everything as is. A look, however, at what some see as the most persuasive argument for physicalism indicates that we can't. Why believe in physicalism? One not uncommon answer is that the tremendous success and progress of the physical sciences gives us reason to think that physicalism is true. But the tremendous success of physics, while possibly very relevant to the outcome of the debate, does not settle the issue between physicalists and dualists. For it seems that physics could be tremendously successful in either case.

Moreover, I think that focusing on the mental/nonmental distinction rather than the physical/nonphysical distinction will also affect the debate about mental causation. The problem of mental causation is usually thought of as the problem of explaining how mental properties could be casually efficacious in a world that is fundamentally physical. The difficulty arises, it is thought, for anyone who thinks that (1) mentality exists but is not identical to anything physical, (2) there is no causal over-determination, and (3) the physical world is causally closed, i.e., all physical effects (which have causes) have sufficient physical causes. Many philosophers have thought that there are good reasons to accept all three of these claims. But it seems to me that when we shift our focus to the mental/nonmental distinction, the reasons usually given for the third claim, the causal closure of the physical, no longer apply. For the reasons usually given for why we should believe in the causal closure of the physical are the reasons usually given for why we should believe in the causal closure of physics. As Kim puts it, if the physical world were not causally closed then 'to explain some physical events you must go outside the physical realm and appeal to nonphysical causal agents and laws governing their behavior!'[33] And what this entails, and I take it why Kim finds it exclamatory, is, as he says, 'complete physics would in principle be impossible, even as an idealized goal' (Kim 1996, p. 147). This is true when the physical is defined over physics, but it is not a reason to accept the causal closure of the fundamentally nonmental.[34]

Some might claim that one potentially unwelcome result of my formulation will be the demise of the identity theory – the old example being that pain is identical to C-fibre stimulation. For what could the identity theory amount to if we take the relevant distinction to be between the mental and the nonmental?[35] If we think of C-fibre stimulation, for example, as entirely nonmental, what could it mean to say that C-fibre stimulation is identical to something mental? Yet if you allow C-fibre stimulation to have an irreducible mental aspect, in what sense are you a physicalist? In general, isn't it hopelessly paradoxical to say that mental property M is identical to nonmental property N?[36] Perhaps it is, but my claim is not that we should replace the notion of *being physical* with the notion of *being nonmental*, from which it would follow immediately that the identity theory is impossible. Rather, it is that we should replace the notion of *being physical* with the notion of being *fundamentally* nonmental. As such, it seems at least possible to carve out a space for the identity theory: the identity theory would be true if both pain and C-fibre activity are, at least in some sense, mental yet the fundamental constituents of C-fibre stimulation (as well as pain) are entirely nonmental.

Most importantly, however, I think that focusing on the mental/nonmental distinction will facilitate an actual head-on debate between physicalists and dualists. As things stand, physicalists usually take themselves to be arguing against views about the mind that are anti-scientific, views that hold that mentality will forever be beyond the scope of science. Yet dualists often take themselves to be arguing against the view that mentality is not fundamental (regardless of whether it can be accounted for by science). So it is not surprising that the two sides of the debate often talk past each other. If we focus on the mental/nonmental distinction, this may change.

V IS THE MENTAL/NONMENTAL DISTINCTION CLEARER THAN THE PHYSICAL/NONPHYSICAL DISTINCTION?

The change, I hope, would be for the better; yet it may not if the distinction between the mental and the nonmental is no clearer than the distinction between the physical and the nonphysical.[37] It is not an easy task to delineate the mental from the non-mental. However, I do think that this distinction is better off than the physical/non-physical distinction. Why do I think this? I could say, as one is prone to do when asked this question, that we are familiar with what is often classified as the qualitative aspect of mentality, that is, what it is like from our first person perspective, for example, to feel pain, to see red, to taste chocolate, to have the unpleasant experience of being embarrassed or the wonderful experience of feeling proud, and so on. Yet to do so does little to convince those who resolutely deny having any understanding of phenomenal experiences that they actually know what they are like. And eliminativists are just such people: according to (the more radical) eliminativists, we couldn't have any understanding of mentality since there really isn't any such thing. And it is difficult to know what sort of argument one could give that would convince them to believe otherwise (this is especially tricky when they claim that, strictly speaking, they have no beliefs).[38]

So let me try a new tack. An indication that we have a grasp of the mental is that while there may be no agreed upon 'mark of the mental', we can and do classify various kinds of mentality: qualitative, intentional, and affective phenomena, for example, all fall under its scope. And we can beneficially address each of these individually. But if I am willing to address specific kinds of mental phenomena why am I not willing to address specific kinds of physical phenomena? Don't we also have a grasp of specific kinds of physical phenomena? As I've argued here and in more in depth elsewhere, for the purpose of formulating the mind–body problem we do not (Montero 1999). With respect to the mental/nonmental distinction, while we do not have a definition of the mental, we nonetheless have a handle on the concept since we have a relatively clear idea of phenomena that fall on each side of the divide. However, with the physical/nonphysical distinction we lack even this. Of course, if panpsychism is true, everything will be fundamentally mental. But this does not mean that in stepping into the debate we have no grasp of the nonmental.[39] For we can easily conceive of something being fundamentally nonmental. Yet the concept of being fundamentally nonphysical seems to elude us entirely. What in the world (or, perhaps I should say 'out of the world') is supposed to count as being nonphysical?

The fact that we have no answer to this question shows that even if our grasp of the mental/nonmental distinction is far from clear, it is better than our grasp of the physical/nonphysical distinction. Furthermore, even if one thinks that both distinctions are equally opaque, this should not be reason to favour the current formulation of the mind–body problem because understanding the mental/nonmental distinction is no less exigent for understanding the current formulation than it is for understanding my proposed formulation. This is because those who think that the mind–body problem is the problem of explaining how the mind is physical assume that we have some intuitive understanding of that which they claim is entirely physical.

(Beyond this they also assume an understanding of what it means to be physical.) More, of course, needs to be said about the mental. And, indeed, in debating the mind–body problem we are debating what exactly this should be.

VI SPATIOTEMPORALITY AND MENTALITY

Some might object that I have missed my target entirely: the mind–body problem is not the question of whether mentality is fundamental, nor, for that matter, of whether it will ultimately be explainable by science (or, more specifically, physics). Rather, it is the question of whether it is spatiotemporal. For to be physical, some might say, is to be spatiotemporal.[40]

While this question echoes Descartes' concern with the mind–body problem – according to Descartes, mind is nonspatial, or at least unextended, and body is spatially extended – I think that it does not address the heart of the debate between physicalists and dualists.[41] For it seems to me that if mentality is fundamental, this, more than its being nonspatial or nonspatiotemporal, would capture what dualists believe is true about the mind: it is not reducible to anything else and thus has a rather special place in the world. What is more, being nonspatial or nonspatiotemporal seems neither sufficient nor necessary for dualism. For if the reason mentality is not spatiotemporal is simply that our theory of spacetime is incorrect I think that most physicalists would not take this to validate dualism. Or if mentality is in some sense purely abstract – the abstract program of the brain, perhaps – then physicalists who were happy with abstracta could be happy with a nonspatial mind.[42] Finally being nonspatiotemporal is not even necessary for dualism since if mentality were a *fundamental* spatiotemporal feature of the world, physicalists would not feel victorious. What matters to dualists is the fundamental nature of the mind, which is just what physicalists should argue against.

VII THE PATH AHEAD

As I see it, then, focusing on such questions as whether mentality is a natural phenomenon, a physical phenomenon, or a spatial phenomenon sidesteps the hard question that lies at the heart of the debate. It is time to confront this question head-on: Is mentality a fundamental feature of the world? Physicalists will then need to make a decision: they can uphold deferential naturalism, the view, as Sellars put it, that science is the measure of all things, or they can put forth a substantive hypothesis about the general nature of the mind. To choose naturalism is to follow the course of science wherever it may lead, which is, perhaps, not to abandon the mind–

body problem, but to hand it over to someone else. But there is another option: take a stance and think of the mind–body problem as the problem of whether mentality is fundamentally nonmental. And without the cloak of naturalism, physicalists can do this openly and with a clear conscience. As such, they will not be naturalists in the sense that they will not simply be deferring to science to tell us what is and what is not. But, nevertheless, this does not mean that in putting forth their hypotheses they are necessarily being anti-scientific. To put forth a view, to state a hypothesis is to work hand in hand with science; to leave the mind–body problem up to someone else is not.

Of course, it may be the case that such hypotheses about the ultimate constituents of the universe might not admit of definitive refutation. For it might be difficult to know with certainty that any particular level is the bottom level. Alternatively, if there actually is no bottom level, if the world is in some sense infinitely divisible, then the question would become whether, after a certain level, it is nonmental *ad infinitum*. And who knows how to address that question. But in any case, I think that looking at the mind–body problem in terms of the distinction between the mental and the nonmental rather than the distinction between the physical and the non-physical will not only relieve the conflict between naturalism and ontological significance (basically by giving each its own territory) but will also pave the way for what I hope will be a clearer, more interesting, and potentially even terminable debate about the fundamental nature of the mind.[43]

NOTES

1 The term 'fundamental' can, if you like, stand for whatever dependence relation you prefer. That is, when I say that the mind–body problem is the question of whether mentality is fundamentally nonmental you can substitute the question of whether mentality is reducible to (or constituted by, or supervenient on, etc.) the nonmental. Of course, the various notions of dependence are not unproblematic themselves, and there is little agreement on what relations between the lower level physical phenomena and higher lever mental phenomena suffice for physicalism. But let us take one problem at a time: the problem I am concerned with here is not how to understand the dependence relation, but how to understand the dependence base.

2 While I use the term 'mentality' rather than the more specific term 'experience', most of what I say is directed at those engaged in the debate about experience, since many of those writing about intentionality already focus on the intentional/nonintentional distinction rather than the physical/non-physical distinction. Fodor (1987) is a good example: 'if the semantic and intentional are real properties of things, it must be in virtue of their identity with (or maybe supervenience on?) properties that are themselves neither intentional nor semantic.' (Thanks to Joseph Levine for pointing this out to me.)

3 At the 1999 Robert S. Cohen Colloquium: *Naturalism and its Discontents*, Kim emphasized this as does Stroud (1996).

4 Russell (1927/1992) p. 78. In an interesting forthcoming paper Galen Strawson points out that Joseph Priestley made more or less the same point in 1777.

5 Searle (1992) p. 84. To be sure, Searle is also not satisfied with the current terminology used to describe the mind–body problem.

6 Sellars (1963) p. 173. Or as Quine (1981) puts it, 'it is within science itself, and not in some prior philosophy, that reality is to be identified and described' (p. 21).

7 Credit goes to William Wimsatt for the droll phrase 'nothing butists'.

8 See Greene (1999). Speculation about such nonspatial, nontemporal stuff (or perhaps it would be better to call it 'nonstuff') should also be a bit worrisome for those who define the abstract over the nonspatiotemporal – do we want to say that our spatial world emerges out of abstracta?

9 Even if the results of mathematics, if true, are necessarily true, an argument is only interesting if there is some step in it that is not immediately obvious to everyone. (Why bother publishing a proof that everyone already knows?) Perhaps certain sceptical hypotheses, such as the hypothesis that the world was created five minutes ago with all apparent evidence of an earlier creation in place, are also, even in principle, unfalsifiable. But while we could never have evidence that could show such a hypothesis to be mistaken, there would still be an objective difference between the two situations – God, as it were, could know that the hypothesis is false. But if being physical amounts to simply existing, it is not clear that physicalism would be falsifiable even for God. Interestingly enough, Quine (1981) seems to accept the triviality of physicalism. For as he says, 'if the physicist suspected there was any event that did not consist in a redistribution of the elementary states allowed for by his physical theory he would seek a way of supplementing his theory' (p. 98).

10 See Lewis (1983). Lewis tries to carve out a position that is not trivial by explaining the physical in terms of whatever a future physics, which is significantly similar to current physics, but much improved, will tell us about the world. While one would like some explanation of what counts as 'significantly similar' and 'much improved', the main difficulty with this notion of the physical is that if some groundbreaking discovery is made and physics goes through a *major* revolution, resulting in it not being sufficiently similar to today's physics, physicalists would, most likely, not want to claim the new posits and laws of this physics as being nonphysical. For other attempts to solve the body problem see Hellman (1985), Papineau (1993), Poland (1994), Meehl and Sellars (1956), Melnyk (1997), Smart (1978), Snowdon (1989).

11 In Montero (1999) I present an in-depth argument for this point. Since the main focus of this paper is to present a new way of thinking about the mind–body problem in light of the view that we have no solution to the body problem, my discussion here of this point will be brief. However, in arguing here for my proposed focus on the mind–body problem, I will also be arguing against retaining our current focus on the question of whether mentality is physical.

12 I should mention that I am not the first to use the term, 'post-physicalism'. John Post suggests that 'a far happier name [for his non-reductive physicalism], surely, would be "post-physicalism".' See Post (1987) p. 18.

13 There are a few exceptions. For example, Strawson (1994a) seems to believe that there are aspects of the world that are purely mental yet physical. And moreover, he seems to think that all physicalists must hold this view (especially pp. 46–59). Also see Strawson (forthcoming). And Searle (1992) seems to hold a similar view. While O'Leary-Hawthorne and McDonough (1998) explicitly say that 'if an ideal physics will have consciousness at the metaphysical ground-floor, property dualism is wrong' (p. 350).

14 This claim, according to Kim (1996), is implied by the principle of supervenience assuming that if there can be one purely mental being, there can be at least two that differ mentally. For the principle of supervenience states that if two beings are psychologically discernible, then they will be physically discernible and this, according to Kim, shows that (given the further assumption) they cannot, then, be purely mental. But the principle that there are no fundamental mental entities follows from the principle of supervenience plus the assumption that if there is one purely mental being there can be more than one purely mental being only given a further assumption: that the physical realm does not include fundamental mental entities, itself.

15 To be sure, if you see science as the enterprise that investigates the world in non-anthropocentric or nonmental terms, an enterprise that we think essentially began in the seventeenth century with Descartes, then the two views I am trying to delineate are not

distinct. (Thanks to Thomas Nagel for drawing my attention to this.) If this is what physicalists mean by 'science', making this explicit should have the same effect on the debate as focusing on the question of whether mentality is fundamental.

16 I should emphasize that I am not intending to defend Wigner's hypothesis but am merely using it as a rough example of how physics might incorporate fundamental mentality. Yet it is not at all clear how to interpret it; in particular, it is not at all clear what is meant by 'acts of pure consciousness'. Apart from the question of what 'consciousness' means in this context (does an imaging device count? does animal consciousness?), there is the question of what 'pure' means. Does it mean fundamental? If not, then Wigner's hypothesis could be true even though mentality would not be fundamental.

17 Again, this is not a defence of the view. One problem with this version of the anthropic principle, as Steven Weinberg has pointed out, is that while the existence of life may place some constraints on the energy of this state of the carbon nucleus, it does not constrain it entirely. Furthermore, even if it did, it is not clear that it would count as an *explanation*.

18 Perhaps physicalists will claim that no *true* physics will account for mentality in this way. Perhaps not, but then they are really just claiming that (it is true that) mentality is not fundamental.

19 If one defines science as whatever tells us about the purely structural and relational, and one also holds that relations are never fundamental, then one probably would hold that a scientific account of the mental suffices to show that it is not fundamental. Russell (1927/1992) seems to hold such a view of science. And the view of science in Chalmers (1996) is very similar. Russell later abandoned this view due to Max Newman's criticism that if this is all physics tells us about the world the only nontrivial information about the world that physics provides is information about how many things there are. (See Demopoulos and Friedman, 1985, for an excellent discussion of this topic.) Since Chalmers' picture of what science tells us about the world includes causation it may avoid Newman's objection.

20 Others have expressed similar views of the mind–body problem. Strawson (1994a, b; forthcoming) emphasizes the importance of focusing on the distinction between the mental and the nonmental, specifically on the experiential and the nonexperiential. However, he also relies on a notion of the physical. And Levine (1998) says that materialism in philosophy of mind is the thesis that 'there is no sharp discontinuity in nature between the mental and the nonmental' (p. 449).

21 Poland (1994) also discusses this problem and tries to resist it. While he explicitly rejects placing restrictions on physics (p. 159), he tries to give physicalism content by making a distinction between future physics (the course of which we cannot predict) and what physicists, in general, study: spacetime and the fundamental constituents of all occupants of space time and the fundamental attributes that account for all interaction of such occupants (pp. 163–4). Yet it seems that in putting forth a theory about what physicists study he is, nevertheless, restricting physics. I discuss the significance of spatiality for the mind–body problem in section VII.

22 Putnam (1970). Putnam addresses this problem by providing a programmatic definition of the fundamental magnitudes, that is, he defines them as those magnitudes which physicists currently take to be fundamental. While this may be of use for the purposes of his paper, I think that it does not work for the purpose of the mind–body problem since it leaves the physicalist asserting a view she thinks is more likely false than true. For further discussion of this point see Montero (1999).

23 While I am equating naturalism with deference to science, the term 'naturalism' is used in an enormous variety of ways. For example, Hornsby (1997) calls herself a 'naïve naturalist' even though she explicitly denies that the mind is amenable to scientific investigation, while Stich (1996) argues against 'naturalism' while defending a view he calls 'open ended pluralism' which seems to amount pretty much to deferential naturalism.

24 Much thanks to Gene Witmer for his insightful comments on this issue. I should note that not all naturalists would be willing to go this route. For example, McGinn (1989) calls himself a naturalist yet he not only predicts, but also claims to have shown that mentality will never be accounted for in nonmental terms.

25 He explains these notions in Papineau (1993) pp. 10–16.

26 Papineau (1993) pp. 29–30. Of course, in order to avoid circularity, he also needs to explain what he means by '*physical* effect'. To do this, he relies on some 'paradigmatic physical effects,' of which he thinks we have an intuitive understanding. In Montero (1999) I argue that relying on intuitions in these sorts of cases will not work.

27 Some have argued that the naturalist's hypothesis itself is *a priori*. See van Fraassen (1995).

28 The official title of the Berkeley booklet is, the *Particle Physics Booklet*, an abridged version of the *Review of Particle Physics*. The information in these books can be found at http://pdg.lbl.gov/.

29 However, see Melnyk (1997) for an argument that we should ground physicalism in current physics.

30 As Nagel (1996) says, 'atheists have no more reason to be alarmed by fundamental and irreducible mind–world relations than by fundamental and irreducible laws of physics' (p. 131). David Chalmers (1996) has also argued for this point. As he sees it, the view that consciousness is a fundamental property is 'entirely compatible with a contemporary scientific worldview' (p. 127).

31 This is related to the claim one often hears that even if Mary in the black and white room knows all the dualistic facts, she still would not know what it is like to see red. The implication, then, is that if Jackson's thought experiment does pose a problem for physicalism, it poses just as serious a problem for dualism. But this is not quite right since dualists hold that the experience of seeing red is fundamental, something that cannot be explained in terms of anything else. The fact Mary would need to know, claims the dualist, is nothing less than what it is like to see red; and if she knows what it is like to see red, she knows what it is like to see red.

32 As I see it, Chalmers' (1996) arguments for dualism mainly fall out of his assumption that the intrinsic/extrinsic divide is sharp and that the physical is extrinsic while the mental is intrinsic. Indeed, given these assumptions, it seems that his arguments for the possibility of zombies are inessential. (Cf. Yablo (1999) claims that "almost everything" in Chalmers' argument turns on the claim that zombie worlds are possible.)

33 Kim (1996) p. 147. I should also point out that causal closure can mean (1) any physical effect (that has a cause) has a sufficient physical cause or (2) any physical cause has only physical effects, or both. But Kim's quote only addresses (1).

34 Further problems arise if being fundamentally mental implies being free, since freedom of the will may not be compatible with any type of overarching theory. However, it is not clear that being fundamentally mental does imply being free. Furthermore, the debate between compatibilists and incompatibilists is far from settled: free will might fit into the otherwise nonfree world in an intelligible way. Or perhaps, if Nancy Cartwright is correct, what we would normally think of as the nonmental world, is, in a sense, actually more free than not; on her view, most of the world is not law governed (neither deterministically nor probabilistically.) If so, fundamental (free) mentality would be no more of a threat to a complete physics than most nonmental phenomena.

35 I thank Leopold Stubenberg for his comments on this point.

36 Of course, if C-fibre stimulation is thought of as fundamentally mental, as, interestingly enough, Feigl (1958) seems to think, eliminativism does not follow. See Stubenberg (1998) for an illuminating discussion and defence of Feigl's identity theory. As Stubenberg puts it, on Feigl's view, 'the brain is made of qualia'.

37 As Gabby Sakamoto said to me, one might think that just as there is a body problem from those who ask 'is mentality fundamentally physical?' there is a mind problem for those who ask 'is mentality fundamentally nonmental?' Sober (1999) makes this point as well.

38 Strawson (1994a) remarks, only half jokingly, that perhaps the best explanation for those who resolutely deny qualitative experience is that there really are zombies (functional duplicates of human beings that have no phenomenal states) and that the eliminativists are among them.

39 Some arguments for idealism, however, do intend to show this.

40 For example, according to Meehl and Sellars (1956): 'an event or entity is *physical*$_1$ if it belongs in the space-time network.' (Something is *physical*$_2$, they say, 'if it is definable in

BARBARA MONTERO

terms of theoretical primitives adequate to describe completely the actual states though not necessarily the potentialities of the universe before the appearance of life.' As I see it, the problem here is that if physicists discovered that some sort of life-force was created in the big bang, or, perhaps, that the big-bang theory was wrong and that sentient life has existed all along, then any minimal class of theoretical primitives adequate to describe the universe before the appearance of life is, vacuously, empty. And so the concept of physical$_2$ in this case would pick out those things definable from nothing.) See also Armstrong (1995) who defines naturalism as 'the doctrine that reality consists of nothing but a single all-embracing spatio-temporal system' (p. 35).

41 This is not to say that the question of whether mentality is spatial is not an interesting one (see, for example, McGinn, 1995).

42 Of course, it is not easy to formulate the abstract/concrete distinction either.

43 I would like to thank Anne Eaton, Michael Forster, Joseph Goguen, Joel David Hamkins, John Haugeland, Sean Kelly, Thomas Nagel, Marya Schectman, Bradford Skow, Leopold Stubenberg, Michael Thompson, Michael Voytinsky, William Wimsatt, Gene Witmer, and the three anonymous *JCS* referees for their very helpful comments.

REFERENCES

Armstrong, D. (1995), 'Naturalism, materialism, and first philosophy', in *Contemporary Materialism*, ed. P. Moser and J. Trout (London: Routledge).

Brandom, R. (1994), *Making it Explicit: Reasoning, Representing and Discursive Committment* (Cambridge, MA: Harvard University Press).

Chalmers, D. (1996), *The Conscious Mind* (Oxford: Oxford University Press).

Chomsky, N. (1993), *Language and Thought* (Rhode Island: Moyer Bell).

Chomsky, N. (1995), 'Language and nature', *Mind* 104, pp. 1–61.

Chomsky, N. (1998), 'Comments Galen Strawson, Mental Reality', *Philosophy and Phenomenological Research*, LVIII (2) June, pp. 437–41

Churchland, P. (1995), *Neurophilosophy: Toward a Unified Science of the Mind/Brain* (Cambridge, MA: MIT Press).

Clark, A. (1997), *Being There: Putting Brain, Body and World Together Again* (Cambridge, MA: MIT Press).

Crane, T. and Mellor, H. (1990), 'There is no question of physicalism', *Mind* 99, pp. 185–206.

Daly, C. (1998), 'What are physical properties?', *Pacific Philosophical Quarterly* 79, pp. 196–217.

Demopoulos, W. and Friedman, M. (1985), 'Critical notice: Bertrand Russell's *The Analysis of Matter*: its historical and contemporary interest', *Philosophy of Science* 55 pp. 621–39.

Feigl, H. (1958), 'The "mental" and the "physical"', in *Concepts, Theories, and the Mind–body Problem, Minnesota Studies in the Philosophy of Science* Vol. II, ed. H. Feigl, M. Scriven and G. Maxwell (Minneapolis: University of Minnesota Press).

Fodor, J. (1987), *Psychosemantics* (Cambridge, MA: MIT Press).

Foster, J. (1989), 'A defense of dualism', in *The Case for Dualism*, ed. J. Smythies & J. Beloff (University of Virginia Press).

Greene, B. (1999), *The Elegant Universe: Superstrings, Hidden Dimensions, and the Quest for the Ultimate Theory* (New York: W.W. Norton & Company).

Guttenplan, S. (1995), 'An essay on mind', in *A Companion to Philosophy of Mind*, ed. S. Guttenplan (Oxford: Basil Blackwell Ltd.).

Healey, R. (1979), 'Physicalists imperialism', *Proceedings of the Aristotelian Society* 1979, pp. 191–211.

Hellman, G. (1985), 'Determination and logical truth', *Journal of Philosophy* 82, pp. 607–16.

Hornsby, J. (1997), *Simple Mindedness: In Defense of Naive Naturalism in the Philosophy of Mind* (Cambridge, MA: Harvard University Press).

Kim, J. (1996), *Philosophy of Mind* (Colorado: Westview Press).

Kim, J. (1998), *Mind in a Physical World: An Essay on the Mind–body Problem and Mental Causation* (Cambridge, MA: MIT Press).

Kirk, R. (1994), *Raw Feeling: A Philosophical Account of the Essence of Consciousness* (New York: Oxford University Press).

Levine, J. (1998), 'Conceivability and the metaphysics of mind', *Noûs* 32, pp. 449–80.

Lewis, D. (1983), 'New work for a theory of universals', *Australasian Journal of Philosophy* 61, pp. 343–77.

McGinn, C. (1989), 'Can we solve the mind–body problem?', *Mind* 98, pp. 349–66.

McGinn, C. (1995), 'Consciousness and space', *Journal of Consciousness Studies* 2 (3), pp. 220–30.

Meehl, P. and Sellars, W. (1956), 'The concept of emergence', in *The Foundations of Science and the Concept of Psychology and Psychoanalysis, Minnesota Studies in the Philosophy of Science*, Vol. I, ed. H. Feigl and M. Scriven (Minneapolis: University of Minnesota Press).

Melnyk, A. (1997), 'How to keep the "physical" in physicalism', *Journal of Philosophy* 94, pp. 622–37.

Montero, B. (1999), 'The body problem', *Noûs* 33, pp. 183–200.

Nagel, T. (1996), *The Last Word* (Oxford: Oxford University Press).

O'Leary-Hawthorne, J. and McDonough, J. (1998), 'Numbers, minds, and bodies: A fresh look at mind–body dualism', in *Philosophical Perspectives 12, Language, Mind, and Ontology*, ed. J. Tomberlin (Atascadero, CA: Ridgeview).

Papineau, D. (1993), *Philosophical Naturalism* (Oxford: Blackwell).

Poland, J. (1994), *Physicalism: The Philosophical Foundations* (Oxford: Oxford University Press).

Post, J.F. (1987), *The Faces of Existence: An Essay in Nonreductive Metaphysics* (Ithaca, NY: Cornell University Press).

Putnam, H. (1970), 'On properties', in his *Mathematics, Matter and Method: Philosophical Papers, Volume I* (Cambridge: Cambridge University Press).

Quine, W.V. (1981), *Theories and Things* (Cambridge, MA: Harvard University Press).

Russell, B. (1927/1992), *An Outline of Philosophy* (London: Routledge).

Scheffler, I. (1950), 'The new dualism: Psychological and physical terms,' *Journal of Philosophy* 47, pp. 732–52.

Searle, J. (1992), *The Rediscovery of the Mind* (Cambridge, MA: The MIT Press).

Sellars, W. (1963), 'Empiricism and the philosophy of mind', in his *Science, Perception, and Reality* (London: Routledge and Kegan Paul, Ltd).

Shear, J. (ed. 1997), *Explaining Consciousness: The 'Hard Problem'* (Cambridge, MA: MIT Press).

Smart, J. (1978), 'The content of physicalism', *Philosophical Quarterly* 28, pp. 339–41.

Snowdon, P. (1989) 'On formulating materialism and dualism', in *Cause, Mind, and Reality*, ed. J. Heil (Dordrecht: Kluwer Academic Press).

Sober, E. (1999), 'Physicalism from a probabilistic point of view', *Philosophical Studies* 95, pp. 135–74.

Stich, S. (1996), *Deconstructing the Mind* (Oxford: Oxford University Press).

Strawson, G. (1994a) *Mental Reality* (Cambridge MA: MIT Press).

Strawson, G. (1994b), 'The experiential and the non-experiential', in *The Mind–body Problem: A Guide to the Current Debate*, ed. R. Warner and T. Szubka (Oxford: Blackwell).

Strawson, G. (forthcoming), *Real Materialism*.

Stroud, B. (1996), 'The charm of naturalism', *Proceedings and Addresses of the APA* 70, pp. 43–55.

Stubenberg, L. (1998), *Consciousness and Qualia* (Amsterdam: J. Benjamins).

van Fraassen, B. (1995), 'Against naturalized epistemology', in *On Quine: New Essays*, ed. P. Leonardi, and M. Santambrogio (Cambridge: Cambridge University Press).

van Fraassen, B. (1996), 'Science, materialism, and false consciousness', in *Warrant in Contemporary Epistemology: Essays in Honor of Plantinga's Theory of Knowledge*, ed. J. Kvanvig (Lanham, MD: Rowman and Littlefield).

Wimsatt, W. (1976), 'Reductionism, levels of organization, and the mind–body problem', in *Consciousness and the Brain: Scientific and Philosophic Strategies*, ed. G. Globus, G. Maxwell, and I. Savodnik (New York: Plenum).

Wimsatt, W. (1994), 'The ontology of complex systems: Levels of organization, perspectives, and causal thickets', *Canadian Journal of Philosophy*, supp. 20.

Yablo, S. (1999), 'Concepts and Consciousness', *Philosophy and Phenomenological Research* 59, pp. 455–63.

Part 4

HOW IS YOUR MIND RELATED TO YOUR BODY? HOW IS IT RELATED TO THE WORLD?

'Where are you?'

This question sounds simple enough. Depending on who is asking this question and why – and, more obviously, on your location – the appropriate answer might be 'At school' or 'In Kansas City' or 'On the roof'.

These answers give the location of your *body*. But the relationship between the location of your body and *your* location is not so obvious. Must we assume that your mind is always at the same place as your body? If not, then arguably *you* are not always at the same place as your body. Even if your mind is never *separated* from your body, it might be that your mind is not spatially located at all. And even if it is spatially located, it might occupy *less* space than your body – perhaps it occupies only the space of your brain. Or it might occupy *more*: perhaps your mind encompasses aspects of the world outside your skin.

Some of the issues that arose in **Parts 1 and 3**, regarding subjectivity and the physical, bear on these questions. But settling these issues will not, on its own, explain the relationship between your mind, your body, and the 'external' world. For instance, allowing that a single thing has both subjective and objective (bodily) features, we can still ask: what is the relationship between the subject and his or her body? Similarly, supposing that the mind is physical, it is still an open question what *part* of physical reality constitutes the mind. Is it the brain or body? Or might the mind extend beyond these, to encompass features of the 'external' world? These questions are the focus of the current section.

The section begins with passages from the *Meditations on First Philosophy* by René Descartes. Published in 1641, the *Meditations* is a series of cognitive exercises intended to allow the reader to grasp the relationship between mind and world, including the nature and limits of knowledge. In the initial set of exercises (*Meditation One*, not included here), Descartes invites his reader to doubt whatever cannot be established with certainty. His goal is not skeptical. Rather, he believes that this 'method of doubt' will enable the reader to understand the structure of justification: how some beliefs rest on other kinds of beliefs, and what sort of evidence provides the ultimate foundation for our beliefs.

The excerpt here begins while the most radical doubt – known as the 'evil genius' doubt – is still in place. In the passage just prior to that excerpted here, the reader is led to recognize that she cannot be absolutely certain that her thoughts are in her own control. That is, she cannot rule out what is possibly the worst case scenario for knowledge: that her thoughts are being controlled by an evil genius who is "bent on deceiving" her.

In the excerpt here, you (the reader) are assumed to be in the throes of this radical doubt. But you are nonetheless asked to perform the famous 'cogito' reasoning. The cogito does not challenge the existence of the evil genius; instead, it aims to show that, even if you cannot be certain about the *source* of your thoughts (for they may be created by an evil genius), you can nonetheless be certain that you exist. This certainty derives from the fact that, at the moment you reflect on your thoughts, you cannot doubt their presence; hence, you can be certain of your own existence as the thing that *has* those thoughts. You are therefore in a position to defiantly proclaim: "Let him [the evil genius] deceive me as much as he can, he will never bring it about that I am nothing so long as I think that I am something."

As Descartes recognizes, this proof that 'I exist' does not explain, yet, the *nature* of the 'I'. The remainder of the passage is devoted to determining the nature of the self, and the relation between the self and the body. Descartes invites you to conclude that you are not spatially located, and that you are "only a thing that thinks". These claims sparked controversies in his day that continue into the present.

Of particular interest here is how Descartes construes the relationship between the 'I' and the body. While he acknowledges that the mind is closely tied to the body, and not related to it simply as a "pilot in a ship", Descartes does envision a real gap between the mind and the body, saying "it is certain that I am really distinct from my body, and can exist without it."

Bill Brewer takes aim at Descartes' picture, especially at the alleged gap between mind and body. On his interpretation of Descartes' view, a bodily sensation like an itch relates us to our bodies indirectly, just as a perceptual sensation (seeing a red barn, say) relates us to a perceptual object (the barn) indirectly. Brewer argues against this indirectness, claiming that bodily sensations are 'intrinsically spatial'. While the notion of a red barn may be a construct from our visual image of a red barn, Brewer claims, the notion of my right arm is *not* simply a construct from my 'itch in my right arm' sensation. For the spatial, bodily component of the sensation is, he thinks, an essential part of the 'raw data' of sensation: I feel the itch *as* an itch in my right arm.

Using this alternative account of sensation, Brewer argues that Descartes has failed on his own terms. For the Cartesian method requires us to doubt as much as possible, and to consider the data of thought or experience in its raw, unprocessed form. Brewer believes that the Cartesian picture of the mind as a non-spatial, purely thinking substance, is disloyal to the basic data of experience, which reflect the embodied, corporeal nature of the experiencing subject. By remaining loyal to the basic data provided by bodily sensations, we can see that the subject *is* spatially located. "The basic subject is therefore a mental-and-physical subject-object physically extended in space."

For his part, Descartes would likely deny that the data Brewer describes are truly *basic*: for we can be certain that we are having a particular sensation, while doubting that we are embodied at all. This shows, according to Descartes, that our grasp of the 'itch' sensation (and of ourselves as subjects) is separable from, and more basic than, our grasp of the arm (and of ourselves as embodied). The disagreement between Descartes and Brewer is, in part, a disagreement as to what sort of evidence qualifies as truly *basic*. For Descartes, this is evidence that survives the method of doubt – that is, that cannot be doubted. For Brewer, it is the raw, unprocessed data of sensation, as it is prior to being subjected to the method of doubt.

Brewer's central idea is that experience directly reveals the experiencer to be simultaneously a subject and a physical object. Even if we put aside the Cartesian claim that only the 'subject' characterization is basic, we may wonder whether a single picture of the thinker as simultaneously a subject and an object is even coherent. Thomas Nagel, in **Part 1** of this volume, suggests that this is incoherent, for there is a fundamental conceptual disparity between thinking of someone as a subject and thinking of her as an object. Brewer maintains that his account of bodily experience reveals an error behind Nagel's worry. Not only *can* we conceive of ourselves as simultaneously subjects and objects, Brewer contends, but this conception is built into the raw data of bodily experience. "For in bodily experience I am aware of parts of my body precisely as physical parts of myself, the material subject of that experience." Brewer thus maintains that these elements can be incorporated into a truly unified picture of the self.

The next two readings approach the relation between self and world from a different angle. The article by Andy Clark and David Chalmers presents what seems like a radical view: they claim that the mind, and hence the self, "extends into the world", in that states and processes outside the skin can play the same sort of role, in a subject's cognitive economy, as states within her brain. Given that the corresponding states within the brain are ordinarily characterized as mental, then, there seems no principled reason for denying this status to 'external' states and processes. And if external states and processes are part of the mind, they are presumably part of the self as well. (In this case, 'external' means simply *external to the skin*; if Clark and Chalmers are correct, factors external to the skin may be *internal* to the mind and self.)

Clark and Chalmers' reasoning for this conclusion centers on two thought experiments. One concerns cognitive processes, while the other concerns standing beliefs. In the first, a subject playing Tetris uses a joystick to rotate an on-screen image of a game piece, to help determine whether it will fit into a particular slot. This process could also be accomplished, albeit more slowly, by simply imagining how the game piece would look when rotated. Clark and Chalmers suggest that, if the process of imagining qualifies as mental, then so should the corresponding computer process. This conclusion follows from a general claim that has come to be known as the Parity Principle. "If, as we confront some task, a part of the world functions as a process which, *were it done in the head*, we would have no hesitation in recognizing as part of the cognitive process, then that part of the world *is* (so we claim) part of the cognitive process."

Their second thought experiment involves Otto, an Alzheimer's patient. Because his memory is so poor, Otto records important information in a notebook that he always carries. When he ventures out, he frequently consults the notebook to 'remember' where he is going and how to get there. Clark and Chalmers argue that the notebook entries play precisely the same role, for Otto, as stored memories in the brain play for most of us. By the Parity Principle, then, we have reason to accept that insofar as stored memories are part of the mind, the entries in Otto's notebook are part of his mind.

Brie Gertler questions Clark and Chalmers' conclusion that the external states and processes they identify are genuinely part of the mind. She observes that those states and processes cannot be introspected by the thinker; that is, he has no special first-person access to them. Clark and Chalmers would likely accept this point, but simply deny that all truly mental states are introspectible. Presumably, what makes cognitive processes and stored memories *mental*, on their view, is that these states and processes contribute to intentional action. But Gertler argues that Otto's notebook records do not make the appropriate contribution to intentional action – that is, they are no more crucial to explaining action than obviously non-mental factors. She concludes that the notebook entries (etc.) are not part of the mind.

But while Gertler rejects their central conclusion, she does embrace most of the reasoning that led to the conclusion. In particular, she endorses their Parity Principle (i.e., that if an external feature plays the same role as an internal feature, then it has an equal claim to be part of the mind). And she agrees that the external features they describe do, in fact, play a role that is relevantly similar to the role of some internal processes and standing states. So her somewhat surprising conclusion is that the *internal* states and processes that are functionally equivalent to these external factors are not, strictly speaking, part of the mind.

How can this be? First, note that Clark and Chalmers' conclusion is limited; they are not claiming that conscious cognitive processes, sensations, or occurrent beliefs (beliefs one is currently entertaining), are 'extended'. Their conclusion applies only to subpersonal cognitive processes and *standing* beliefs (e.g., your belief that whales are mammals, at a time you are not thinking about whales). Gertler's claim, then, is that neither standing beliefs nor cognitive processes that are functionally equivalent to the computer simulation are, strictly speaking, part of the mind. For if they were, then – given Clark and Chalmers' insightful examples – the mind would extend indefinitely, and there would be no principled distinction between mind and world. On Gertler's alternative, the mind is constituted exclusively by occurrent thoughts and sensations, and conscious processes. Clark and Chalmers anticipate this response to their argument, and object that it would threaten the psychological continuity of the self. Gertler's chapter closes by defending her alternative from this criticism.

QUESTIONS TO THINK ABOUT

1 When you sense an itch on your right arm, say, can you isolate the *sensational* component (how it *feels*) from the *spatial* component (where it is located)? Or is the spatial location of the sensation somehow *built into* the sensation itself? What, if anything, do you think the answer to this question reveals about the relation between self and body?

2 Both Descartes and Brewer deny that we are in our bodies "like a pilot in a ship". How would you characterize the difference between your relation to your body, on the one hand, and a pilot's relation to his ship, on the other? Surely you don't check a gauge to see if you need fuel (food), and you don't use any sort of helm to guide the direction of your movement. But if there is a deeper difference, what is it?

3 Do you accept Clark and Chalmers' conclusion that Otto's mind extends to his notebook? If so, then what do you think distinguishes what is within Otto's mind from what lies outside it? If not, why not? That is, what requirement for being part of the mind does Otto's notebook violate?

4 We have seen two conceptions of the self: on Clark and Chalmers' conception, the self includes both occurrent and standing states; on Gertler's conception, it is made up of occurrent states alone. On what basis would you choose between these conceptions? What, precisely, is at stake in how we define the boundary of the self?

FURTHER READING

Bermudez, J., Marcel, A. and Eilan, N., eds., *The Body and the Self*. Cambridge, MA: MIT (Bradford), 1995.

Clark, A. *Natural Born Cyborgs: minds, technologies, and the future of human intelligence*. New York: Oxford University Press, 2003.

Gallagher, S. *How the Body Shapes the Mind*. Oxford: Oxford University Press, 2005.

Gendler, T. and Hawthorne, J., eds., *Perceptual Experience*. Oxford: Oxford University Press, 2006.

Rupert, R. "Challenges to the Hypothesis of Extended Cognition". *Journal of Philosophy* 101: 389–428, 2004.

14

MEDITATIONS

René Descartes

Meditation II: The nature of the human mind, and how it is better known than the body

So serious are the doubts into which I have been thrown as a result of yesterday's meditation that I can neither put them out of my mind nor see any way of resolving them. It feels as if I have fallen unexpectedly into a deep whirlpool which tumbles me around so that I can neither stand on the bottom nor swim up to the top. Nevertheless I will make an effort and once more attempt the same path which I started on yesterday. Anything which admits of the slightest doubt I will set aside just as if I had found it to be wholly false; and I will proceed in this way until I recognize something certain, or, if nothing else, until I at least recognize for certain that there is no certainty. Archimedes used to demand just one firm and immovable point in order to shift the entire earth; so I too can hope for great things if I manage to find just one thing, however slight, that is certain and unshakeable.

I will suppose then, that everything I see is spurious. I will believe that my memory tells me lies, and that none of the things that it reports ever happened. I have no senses. Body, shape, extension, movement and place are chimeras. So what remains true? Perhaps just the one fact that nothing is certain.

Yet apart from everything I have just listed, how do I know that there is not something else which does not allow even the slightest occasion for doubt? Is there not a God, or whatever I may call him, who puts into me[1] the thoughts I am now having? But why do I think this, since I myself may perhaps be the author of these thoughts? In that case am not I, at least, something? But I have just said that I have no senses and no body. This is the sticking point: what follows from this? Am I not so bound up with a body and with senses that I cannot exist without them? But I have convinced myself that there is absolutely nothing in the world, no sky, no earth, no minds, no bodies. Does it now follow that I too do not exist? No: if I convinced myself of something[2] then I certainly existed. But there is a deceiver of supreme power and cunning who is deliberately and constantly deceiving me. In that case I too undoubtedly exist, if he is deceiving me; and let him deceive me as much as he can, he will never bring it about that I am nothing so long as I think that I am something. So after considering everything very thoroughly, I must finally conclude that this proposition, *I am, I exist*, is necessarily true whenever it is put forward by me or conceived in my mind.

But I do not yet have a sufficient understanding of what this 'I' is, that now necessarily exists. So I must be on my guard against carelessly taking something else to be this 'I', and so making a mistake in the very item of knowledge that I maintain is the most certain and evident of all. I will therefore go back and meditate on what I originally believed myself to be, before I embarked on this present train of thought. I will then subtract anything capable of being weakened, even minimally, by the arguments now introduced, so that what is left at the end may be exactly and only what is certain and unshakeable.

What then did I formerly think I was? A man. But what is a man? Shall I say 'a rational animal'? No; for then I should have to inquire what an animal is, what rationality is, and in this way one question would lead me down the slope to other harder ones, and I do not now have the time to waste on subtleties of this kind. Instead I propose to concentrate on what came into my thoughts spontaneously and quite naturally whenever I used to consider what I was. Well, the first thought to come to mind was that I had a face, hands, arms and the whole mechanical structure of limbs which can be seen in a corpse, and which I called the body. The next thought was that I was nourished, that I moved about, and that I engaged in sense-perception and thinking; and these actions I attributed to the soul. But as to the nature of this soul, either I did not think about this or else I imagined it to be something tenuous, like a wind or fire or ether, which permeated my more solid parts. As to the body, however, I had no doubts about it, but thought I knew its nature distinctly. If I had tried to describe the mental conception I had of it, I would have expressed it as follows: by a body I understand whatever has a determinable shape and a definable location and can occupy a space in such a way as to exclude any other body; it can be perceived by touch, sight, hearing, taste or smell, and can be moved in various ways, not by itself but by whatever else comes into contact with it. For, according to my judgement, the power of self-movement, like the power of sensation or of thought, was quite foreign to the nature of a body; indeed, it was a source of wonder to me that certain bodies were found to contain faculties of this kind.

But what shall I now say that I am, when I am supposing that there is some supremely powerful and, if it is permissible to say so, malicious deceiver, who is deliberately trying to trick me in every way he can? Can I now assert that I possess even the most insignificant of all the attributes which I have just said belong to the nature of a body? I scrutinize them, think about them, go over them again, but nothing suggests itself; it is tiresome and pointless to go through the list once more. But what about the attributes I assigned to the soul? Nutrition or movement? Since now I do not have a body, these are mere fabrications. Sense-perception? This surely does not occur without a body, and besides, when asleep I have appeared to perceive through the senses many things which I afterwards realized I did not perceive through the senses at all. Thinking? At last I have discovered it – thought; this alone is inseparable from me. I am, I exist – that is certain. But for how long? For as long as I am thinking. For it could be that were I totally to cease from thinking, I should totally cease to exist. At present I am not admitting anything except what is necessarily true. I am, then, in the strict sense only a thing that thinks;[3] that is, I am a mind, or intelligence, or intellect, or reason – words whose meaning I have been ignorant of until now. But for all that I am a thing which is real and which truly exists. But what kind of a thing? As I have just said – a thinking thing.

What else am I? I will use my imagination.[4] I am not that structure of limbs which is called a human body. I am not even some thin vapour which permeates the limbs – a wind, fire, air, breath, or whatever I depict in my imagination; for these are things which I have supposed to be nothing. Let this supposition stand;[5] for all that I am still something. And yet may it not perhaps be the case that these very things which I am supposing to be nothing, because they are unknown to me, are in reality identical with the 'I' of which I am aware? I do not know, and for the moment I shall not argue the point, since I can make judgements only about things which are known to me. I know that I exist; the question is, what is this 'I' that I know? If the 'I' is understood strictly as we have been taking it, then it is quite certain that knowledge of it does not depend on things of whose existence I am as yet unaware; so it cannot depend on any of the things which I invent in my imagination. And this very word 'invent' shows me my mistake. It would indeed be a case of fictitious invention if I used my imagination to establish that I was something or other; for imagining is simply contemplating the shape or image of a corporeal thing. Yet now I know for certain both that I exist and at the same time that all such images and, in general, everything relating to the nature of body, could be mere dreams <and chimeras>. Once this point has been grasped, to say 'I will use my imagination to get to know more distinctly what I am' would seem to be as silly as saying 'I am now awake, and see some truth; but since my vision is not yet clear enough, I will deliberately fall asleep so that my dreams may provide a truer and clearer representation.' I thus realize that none of the things that the imagination enables me to grasp is at all relevant to this knowledge of myself which I possess, and that the mind must therefore be most carefully diverted from such things[6] if it is to perceive its own nature as distinctly as possible.

But what then am I? A thing that thinks. What is that? A thing that doubts, understands, affirms, denies, is willing, is unwilling, and also imagines and has sensory perceptions.

This is a considerable list, if everything on it belongs to me. But does it? Is it not one and the same 'I' who is now doubting almost everything, who nonetheless understands some things, who affirms that this one thing is true, denies everything else, desires to know more, is unwilling to be deceived, imagines many things even involuntarily, and is aware of many things which apparently come from the senses? Are not all these things just as true as the fact that I exist, even if I am asleep all the time, and even if he who created me is doing all he can to deceive me? Which of all these activities is distinct from my thinking? Which of them can be said to be separate from myself? The fact that it is I who am doubting and understanding and willing is so evident that I see no way of making it any clearer. But it is also the case that the 'I' who imagines is the same 'I'. For even if, as I have supposed, none of the objects of imagination are real, the power of imagination is something which really exists and is part of my thinking. Lastly, it is also the same 'I' who has sensory perceptions, or is aware of bodily things as it were through the senses. For example, I am now seeing light, hearing a noise, feeling heat. But I am asleep, so all this is false. Yet I certainly *seem* to see, to hear, and to be warmed. This cannot be false; what is called 'having a sensory perception' is strictly just this, and in this restricted sense of the term it is simply thinking.…

Meditation VI: Of the existence of material things, and of the real distinction between mind and body

First, I know that everything which I clearly and distinctly understand is capable of being created by God so as to correspond exactly with my understanding of it. Hence the fact that I can clearly and distinctly understand one thing apart from another is enough to make me certain that the two things are distinct, since they are capable of being separated, at least by God. The question of what kind of power is required to bring about such a separation does not affect the judgement that the two things are distinct. Thus, simply by knowing that I exist and seeing at the same time that absolutely nothing else belongs to my nature or essence except that I am a thinking thing, I can infer correctly that my essence consists solely in the fact that I am a thinking thing. It is true that I may have (or, to anticipate, that I certainly have) a body that is very closely joined to me. But nevertheless, on the one hand I have a clear and distinct idea of myself, in so far as I am simply a thinking, non-extended thing; and on the other hand I have a distinct idea of body,[7] in so far as this is simply an extended, non-thinking thing. And accordingly, it is certain that I[8] am really distinct from my body, and can exist without it.

Besides this, I find in myself faculties for certain special modes of thinking,[9] namely imagination and sensory perception. Now I can clearly and distinctly understand myself as a whole without these faculties; but I cannot, conversely, understand these faculties without me, that is, without an intellectual substance to inhere in. This is because there is an intellectual act included in their essential definition; and hence I perceive that the distinction between them and myself corresponds to the distinction between the modes of a thing and the thing itself.[10] Of course I also recognize that there are other faculties (like those of changing position, of taking on various shapes, and so on) which, like sensory perception and imagination, cannot be understood apart from some substance for them to inhere in, and hence cannot exist without it. But it is clear that these other faculties, if they exist, must be in a corporeal or extended substance and not an intellectual one; for the clear and distinct conception of them includes extension, but does not include any intellectual act whatsoever. Now there is in me a passive faculty of sensory perception, that is, a faculty for receiving and recognizing the ideas of sensible objects; but I could not make use of it unless there was also an active faculty, either in me or in something else, which produced or brought about these ideas. But this faculty cannot be in me, since clearly it presupposes no intellectual act on my part,[11] and the ideas in question are produced without my cooperation and often even against my will. So the only alternative is that it is in another substance distinct from me – a substance which contains either formally or eminently all the reality which exists objectively in the ideas produced by this faculty (as I have just noted). This substance is either a body, that is, a corporeal nature, in which case it will contain formally <and in fact> everything which is to be found objectively <or representatively> in the ideas; or else it is God, or some creature more noble than a body, in which case it will contain eminently whatever is to be found in the ideas. But since God is not a deceiver, it is quite clear that he does not transmit the ideas to me either directly from himself, or indirectly, via some creature which contains the objective reality of the ideas not formally but only eminently. For God has given me no faculty at all for recognizing any such source for these ideas; on the contrary, he has given me a great propensity to believe that they are produced by corporeal things. So I do not see how God could be understood to be anything but a deceiver if the ideas were transmitted from a source other than corporeal things. It follows that corporeal things exist. They may not all exist in a way that exactly corresponds with my sensory grasp of them, for in many cases the grasp of the senses is very obscure and confused. But at least they possess all the properties which I clearly and distinctly understand, that is, all those which, viewed in general terms, are comprised within the subject-matter of pure mathematics.

What of the other aspects of corporeal things which are either particular (for example that the sun is of such and such a size or shape), or less clearly understood, such as light or sound or pain, and so on? Despite the high degree of doubt and uncertainty involved here, the very fact that God is not a deceiver, and the consequent impossibility of there being any falsity in my opinions which cannot be corrected by some other faculty supplied by God, offers me a sure hope that I can attain the truth even in these matters. Indeed, there is no doubt that everything that I am taught by nature contains some truth. For if nature is considered in its general aspect, then I understand by the term nothing other than God himself, or the ordered system of created things established by God. And by my own nature in particular I understand nothing other than the totality of things bestowed on me by God.

There is nothing that my own nature teaches me more vividly than that I have a body, and that when I feel pain there is something wrong with the body, and that when I am hungry or thirsty the body needs food and drink, and so on. So I should not doubt that there is some truth in this.

Nature also teaches me, by these sensations of pain, hunger, thirst and so on, that I am not merely present in my body as a sailor is present in a ship,[12] but that I am very closely joined and, as it were, intermingled with it, so that I and the body form a unit. If this were not so, I, who am nothing but a thinking thing, would not feel pain when the body was hurt, but would perceive the damage purely by the intellect, just as a sailor perceives by sight if anything in his ship is broken. Similarly, when the body needed food or drink, I should have an explicit understanding of the fact, instead of having confused sensations of hunger and thirst. For these sensations of hunger, thirst, pain and so on are nothing but confused modes of thinking which arise from the union and, as it were, intermingling of the mind with the body. ...

NOTES

1 ' ... puts into my mind' (French version).
2 ' ... or thought anything at all' (French version).
3 The word 'only' is most naturally taken as going with 'a thing that thinks', and this interpretation is followed in the French version. When discussing this passage with Gassendi, however, Descartes suggests that he meant the 'only' to govern 'in the strict sense'.
4 ' ... to see if I am not something more' (added in French version).
5 Lat. *maneat* ('let it stand'), first edition. The second edition has the indicative *manet*: 'The proposition still stands, *viz.* that I am nonetheless something.' The French version reads: 'without changing this supposition, I find that I am still certain that I am something'.
6 ' ... from this manner of conceiving things' (French version).
7 The Latin term *corpus* as used here by Descartes is ambiguous as between 'body' (i.e. corporeal matter in general) and 'the body' (i.e. this particular body of mine). The French version preserves the ambiguity.
8 ' ... that is, my soul, by which I am what I am' (added in French version).
9 ' ... certain modes of thinking which are quite special and distinct from me' (French version).
10 ' ... between the shapes, movements and other modes or accidents of a body and the body which supports them' (French version).
11 ' ... cannot be in me in so far as I am merely a thinking thing, since it does not presuppose any thought on my part' (French version).
12 ' ... a pilot in his ship' (French version).

15

BODILY AWARENESS AND THE SELF

Bill Brewer

What can we learn about the nature of the self from reflection on bodily experience? I will approach this question by addressing a more specific issue: to what extent does the phenomenon of bodily awareness undermine a Cartesian conception of the self? In other words, what, if anything, can be extracted from the nature of a person's epistemological relation with his body in defence of the commonsense, anti-Cartesian idea of a person as no less basically bodily than mentally endowed? ...

1 THE NATURE AND SPATIAL CONTENT OF BODILY AWARENESS: A MORE DIRECT OBJECTION TO CARTESIAN DUALISM

We should focus rather more carefully on the intrinsic nature of the painful sensation of which the basic mental subject is directly aware, on the broadly Cartesian account, the aspect of bodily sensation that is genuinely a property of the subject of experience. In particular, we should inquire into its spatial content. In doing this, I will follow quite closely the discussion in O'Shaughnessy 1980. My point is to see whether anything can be made of a strong intuitive contrast between bodily sensation and "external" sense perception. The Cartesian applies very much the same model in both cases. On the Cartesian model, the mind's sensational properties constitute its indirect awareness of their normal and appropriate causes.[1] Yet in bodily awareness, but not in sense perception, psychological properties are themselves located in the physical object of awareness, namely the body. Thus there is some prima facie support for the idea that the body part in which sensation is set is a part, not a mere possession, of the conscious mental subject, that the subject of experience extends physically to encompass the bodily location of sensation.

So we need to ask what exactly the raw data of bodily feeling are. What is the intrinsic nature of the painful sensation that is genuinely a property of the basic mental subject and constitutes the epistemological given in his quasi-perceptual bodily aware-ness of being prodded painfully just above the right knee? When I am aware of a sharp pain in the back of my left hand or an itch on the end of my nose, what am I absolutely immediately aware of through which I come, indirectly on the Cartesian's account, to be aware of some disturbance determinately located at those parts of my body?

An initial suggestion might be that the direct objects of awareness in bodily sen-sation are *purely* sensational.[2] In particular, the idea is that one is only derivatively presented with a particular spatial location on the basis of intrinsically nonspatial, purely qualitative dimensions of variation in the sensational given. On this view, bodily feelings of the kind we are considering come in themselves as if from nowhere. Values on some intrinsically nonspatial dimension of their qualitative variation nevertheless correspond with each potential determinate bodily location of sensation, and on the basis of a sensitivity to this correspondence the subject becomes indirectly aware of the condition of particular parts of his associated body.

This suggestion is highly problematic though. To begin with, it is impossible to erase the immediate inclination to act in connection with the particular location of bodily sensation from our conception of the epistemological given in bodily aware-ness. When I feel a sharp pain in the back of my left hand or an itch on the end of my nose, the appropriateness of action concerning these actual bodily locations is written into the very nature of the experience itself, rather than being something somehow inferred from its prior, intrinsically nonspatial, qualitative essence.[3] Further, there are no such things as back-of-the-right-hand-ish sharp pains as opposed to back-of-the-left-hand-ish sharp pains; the right/left distinction need not be matched by any *qua-litative* distinction at all. Indeed, the idea of distinctive qualia associated with every bodily location is absurd. For a qualitatively unchanging sensation can move, and *change* its location. For example, the very same burning feeling might be moving gradually down one's throat. Similarly, qualitatively identical itches might come sometimes as on the end of one's nose and at other times as (infuriatingly out of reach) between one's shoulder blades.

I should emphasize here that my claim is certainly not that as a matter of fact the qualitative and spatial dimensions of bodily awareness vary completely independ-ently. This is surely false.[4] For example, I have never had, nor will have, a feeling in my left foot qualitatively like the nervous sensation of butterflies in my stomach. Given the cases I cite, dependence of this kind must be contingent and quite limited, however. My claim is rather that the undeniable spatial component in bodily sensa-tion cannot generally be inferred from an intrinsically nonspatial qualitative given. Spatial content must be a part of what is epistemologically basic in bodily awareness.

So there is, over and above the sensational quale of a bodily feeling, an inelimin-able presentation of some more or less specific place in ego-centric space that is not a mere construct out of any purely sensational qualitative features. Thus bodily awareness is intrinsically spatial. Apparent location is an essential component of the epistemological given in bodily sensation. ...

... We cannot get away from the fact that bodily sensations immediately appear as determinately located not only in egocentric space but also in specific body parts filling those locations. Indeed, they come as determinately located egocentrically precisely in virtue of coming as set in particular parts of the body extending to particular places in egocentric space. Again O'Shaughnessy captures this precisely, as follows: "The sensation comes to awareness as at 'a point in physical space'—and not just as at 'the part of the body it is in'—*only to the extent that* the aesthetised subject seems to himself immediately to extend into certain nooks and crannies and the sensation to be cited therein" (1980, 221).

There are two extremely important points here. First, the intrinsic spatiality of bodily awareness is sustained by its directly presenting certain parts of the subject's body as filling particular egocentric locations. Second, this presentation of the body as determinately extended in physical space depends in turn on the bodily sensation itself apparently being set in that body part there.

In sensational bodily awareness of a sharp pain in the back of one's left hand, say, or an itch on the end of one's nose, the experience itself is intrinsically spatial. Furthermore, knowledge where to point to locate the sensation, knowledge of which body part the sensation is in, and knowledge of the egocentric position of that body part are epistemologically on a par as basic. In O'Shaughnessy's terms once again: "The basic 'given' is, not just feeling, not just feeling-in-a-certain-body-part, but *feeling-in-a-certain-body-part-at-a-position-in-body-relative-physical-space*; and so, also, certain-body-part-at-a-position-in-body-relative-physical-space: the latter being disclosed along with and via the former *and* the former being disclosed along with and via the latter" (1980, 165).

Central to the current argument, then, are the following three points.

- Bodily awareness is intrinsically spatial: the apparent location of sensation is as essential to its very nature as its purely qualitative feel and is in no way derived from any intrinsically nonspatial variation in it.
- This spatial location of sensation comes to light only as one is aware of one's body as determinately extending into and filling certain regions of the perceived physical world.
- This awareness of one's body as filling physical space both rests on, and, more important, provides intrinsic spatiality in virtue of, the setting of bodily sensations in particular body parts.

In bodily awareness, one is aware of determinately spatially located properties of the body that are also necessarily properties of the basic subject of that very awareness.

In contrast with external sense perception, a psychological property of oneself is physically located in or on the body, as a property of the body. Therefore, rather than any mere possession, the animal body *is* the conscious mental subject of bodily awareness.

2 EXTENDING THE ARGUMENT

The case against a Cartesian conception of the self can, I think, be strengthened by considering further the precise spatial content of bodily awareness.[5] We can begin with a comparison between ourselves and a bodily deafferented patient studied by Jacques Paillard.[6]

Below her nose G.L. has no sense of touch or kinesthetic sensation. She is unable to detect light-to-normal pressure or vibration, but shows some sensitivity to temperature and deep pain (e.g., when prodded with a needle or pressed firmly with a finger or thumb). Her motor fibers are unaffected, and she can certainly make willed movements. With respect to the minimal bodily awareness she has of a hot or painful stimulus, say, her sense of spatial location is extremely interesting. She is quite unable immediately to act in connection with the location of the sensation by pointing, protecting, rubbing, scratching, or whatever. But she can point to the correct location on a drawn diagram or model of her body. She can mimic our normal ability to reach immediately and without reflection for the place of bodily stimulation only indirectly, by groping around for the relevant body part and moving along it to the right location. This is presumably done on the basis of her representation of this location on a detached, third-person image of her body of precisely the kind serving her discrimination of the location on a diagram. (Indeed, she will go to the equivalent place on the examiner's body if his body part is placed in her groping path.) Given such a representation, she has a kind of knowledge of where the sensation is on her body and where, in relation to other body parts, this place is likely to be, which makes no *immediate* contact with any ability to act in connection with that location yet which explains her actual performance. Compare this with a case where I know that my key is in a red box under a blue cushion between the chair and the window—perhaps a child has hidden it and tells me only this. Both here and in G.L.'s case, what is required is a search around the relevant area, homing in on the goal location by using the cues encountered along the way.

So G.L. has knowledge of the location of those very few bodily sensations of which she is aware that is quite different in kind and content from our own. It may still be true that this minimal awareness in some sense satisfies O'Shaughnessy's tripartite description of "feeling-in-a-certain-body-part-at-a-position-in-body-relative-physical-space." For she may well know that the pain is in her left hand somewhere out by her hip. But this has no immediate significance for the control and coordination of her action in connection with that location. She has at first simply a disengaged, descriptive grasp of which body part is in pain, along with, perhaps, an approximate sense, again purely descriptive, of where that body part stands in relation to other parts. Yet neither of these components of the spatial content of her awareness has any direct implications for how she should act so as to point to, protect, rub, or scratch the location of sensation. This can only be discovered by an unreliable trial-and-error investigation of herself with continual reference to the detached, third-person image of where the pain is on her body.

G.L.'s relation to her body is rather like that of a sailor in a ship (Descartes 1985b, 56 and **169 above**). When it is damaged, a red light flashes on an electronic diagram of the ship at the place corresponding to the location of the damage. The pilot must then send out the mechanics to hunt around the relevant area for anything that looks as if it might be responsible for the alert, and try to put it right. What is missing in the spatial content of her impoverished bodily awareness is the first-person or ego-centric element in the way sensations are given location in our case by their setting in particular body parts. All she has is something like a detached, third-person description.

Our own position, as we have seen, is quite different. The spatial content of our "feeling-in-a-certain-body-part-at-a-position-in-body-relative-physical-space" is given indexically in terms of its implications for our direct action in connection with that location. Which bodily location is involved is given, at least in part, as a kind of practical demonstrative: 'there', said as one reaches for the place in question. Knowledge of how to point to, protect, rub, or scratch the location of sensation is not so much discovered by some comparison of the consequences of one's flailing movements with an external picture of a bodily target as immediately present as part of what it amounts to for the sensation to seem to be where it is.

The intrinsic spatial content of normal bodily awareness is given directly in terms of practical knowledge of how to act in connection with the bodily locations involved. The connection with basic action is absolutely not an extrinsic add-on, only to be recovered by experiment and exploration from a detached map of the vessel that the subject of awareness happens to inhabit. It is rather quite essential to the characterization of the spatiality of bodily sensation. This spatiality is, as we have seen, ineliminable from the nature of normal bodily awareness. So the subject of such awareness is necessarily an embodied agent. Furthermore, the properties of the body of which one is aware in bodily awareness are sensational properties of the subject of that very awareness. Therefore, the subject of awareness is the physically extended body.

Location on a certain body part in egocentric space cannot be detached from the given in our bodily awareness without loss. This spatial content cannot normally be characterized independently of the practical knowledge of how to act in connection with that location on the body part. The spatial content is partially specified in these practical terms and cannot correctly be specified otherwise. For on any nonpractical, third-person specification, it follows that the knowledge of how to act in connection with the relevant bodily location is a subsequent experimental achievement, of the kind that G.L. has to make, or that I have to make in retrieving my key in the situation described above. But we are not related to our bodies as a sailor is present in a ship in this way. So the subject of normal bodily awareness is itself a subject of both mental and physical properties.[7]

In normal bodily awareness the experiencer is presented as extended, because the sensational property of which he is the subject seems physically located as a property of a given (seeming) body part at a certain location in egocentric space. This spatial content is in turn given, at least in part, in terms of its immediate implications for his basic physical action in connection with that location. Of course, all this may on occasion be illusory in all sorts of ways. Nevertheless, it is normally veridical, when things in fact are how they seem. In these cases the extended physical body that provides the determinately located setting for the psychological sensation must *be* the subject of sensation. The basic subject is therefore a mental and physical subject-object physically extended in space. Hence, Cartesian dualism is inconsistent with a correct account of the nature and content of bodily awareness.

Let me restate my argument once again, though in a slightly different form, stressing two points:

- The direct object of bodily awareness is intrinsically spatial, not purely sensational. The object of awareness itself is spatially located—a property of a given body part at a particular location in egocentric space.
- The direct object of bodily awareness is genuinely psychological, not merely spatial. The object of awareness is itself a mental item—a psychological property of the basic subject of experience.

Together these imply that the psychological subject is a spatially extended object. The ascribed property is a property of the spatially extended body but is also essentially a property of the subject of consciousness itself.

3 A CARTESIAN LAST STAND

Again the determined Cartesian has a response here. She will insist that our physical location of bodily sensation is, although quite natural, strictly in error: the result of some kind of projection. She may well admit that we have no awareness of what is projected prior to projection. In other words, she might accept that the epistemological given in bodily awareness is intrinsically spatial, just as I characterize it. Nevertheless, she will insist, this physical location is always mere appearance. In so-called veridical cases, the illusion of a certain kind of sensation set in a particular body part might inform us about the physical state of that part. Yet any idea that sensation itself is physically located, or that any property of the body we thereby come to know about is a psychological property of the conscious subject, as it appears to be, is in error. Sensation proper is correctly ascribed to the wholly immaterial mind, and any appearance of bodily location is part of the close epistemological relation between mind and body that constitutes contingent embodiment. Illusory cases that we are inclined to describe in terms of a sensation actually being somewhere other than where it seems to be would have to be regarded as some further, deviant breakdown in the normal suitability of this relation for the subject's acquisition of knowledge about how things are with the body with which he is (temporarily) associated.

This line of reply seems to me quite untenable, even on the dualist's own terms, and is straightforwardly inconsistent with the basic motivation for the dualist position. The driving force behind the Cartesian conception of the self as a wholly non-physical mind is a commitment to take as authoritative what is epistemologically given as basic in introspection. Yet in normal bodily awareness, this is an immediate presentation of oneself as a spatially extended material subject of experience. Nothing less does justice to the phenomena. Spatiality cannot be stripped away from bodily sensation without significant loss. What remains is nothing remotely recognizable as our experiential awareness of our bodies. On its own terms, then, the dualist conception of the self is undermined by a proper account of our bodily awareness.

In response it might be suggested that this is a bit too quick.[8] For Descartes himself notoriously distinguishes between what is clear and distinct in our sensations and what is merely obscure and confused (1985a, 216–17). The point is then that we have clear and distinct knowledge of bodily sensations only when we consider them as purely qualitative, non-spatial features of an immaterial mind. Any purported conception of them as properties of located body parts is really obscure confusion. I think there are two possible grounds for this response, both of which are highly problematic. First, what is epistemologically basic, and so authoritative, might be restricted to those things of which a person is in principle infallible. Perhaps this succeeds in creating some disanalogy between the qualitative and spatial components of bodily awareness, although the infallible introspectible base would surely shrink dramatically under pressure. But the real price of defining clarity and distinctness in terms of infallibility in this way is the total collapse of Descartes's foundationalism into extreme skepticism. If we acquire basic knowledge only by absolutely infallible methods and all nonbasic knowledge is to be derived by deductive inference from basic knowledge, then we know almost nothing: we lose all epistemological contact with the real world in which we live. Second, the case for obscurity in our grasp of properties of our bodies that are necessarily properties of ourselves, the subjects of awareness, may rest on an unfair presumption of what is required. If we take a completely detached view of our bodies as physical objects totally on a par with any inanimate lump of matter, other than in respect of their complexity perhaps, then it will indeed be difficult clearly and distinctly to conceive of any of their properties as necessarily properties of a conscious subject of thought and experience. But why is this point of view obligatory? As I argue in the final section, the difficulty disappears if we allow ourselves the internal perspective on our bodies *as ours*, as our spatially extended selves.

Although my own line of argument is rather different from Evans's (1982), I think he is quite right that we have, in the epistemology of bodily awareness, a most powerful antidote to the Cartesian conception of the self. The picture that emerges is one of the conscious self as a materially embodied organism, a subject of experience in which this realm of the psychological itself extends physically into the extremities of the animal body. The traditional idea of the true, mental self as an extensionless inner sanctum, a control center for the dispensable bodily machine, is an illusion, unsupported even by the nature of the psychological phenomena themselves. In particular, this idea fails to do full justice to the intrinsic first-person, *spatial* content of bodily experience.

4 EXPERIENCE OF OWNERSHIP AND THE SUBJECT AS OBJECT

The anti-Cartesian line of argument I have been presenting also suggests a direction for resolving Nagel's (1970) worry about how we are to conceive of ourselves as both subjects of experience and elements of the objective order. For in bodily awareness, the subject of awareness is presented to himself precisely as a physically extended body in the spatial world of other material things.

A good way to bring out this thought is in connection with the question how we experience our bodies *as ours*. Clearly, this is not, and cannot be, an external perceptual phenomenon. For when we perceive it from the outside, our body has no indelible stamp of ownership. It appears just as one object among many, although it is one whose features we know very well. Yet its being ours strikes us far more forcefully than the transferable contingency of anything we simply recognize perceptually as ours in this external way. Erwin Straus puts the distinction like this: "In the phrase 'my house', *my* stands for something owned by me [something I might recognize in a glance as mine and know intimately, but which I can sell or trade, something which can go from *one* owner to *another*]. In the phrase 'my hand', the same word refers to me, the owner, as a live body" (1967, 112).

The position I have been developing allows us to see how this distinctive sense of ownership might have its source in bodily sensation.[9] In bodily awareness, I have argued, the subject is aware of *himself* as a spatially extended body. So bodily ownership is experienced in this extension of the subject of experience into the material world. The peculiarly intimate sense in which my body parts seem to be mine is just that in which they seem to be parts of the spatially extended physical body that I seem to be. Experienced bodily ownership, then, is awareness of *oneself* as extended in space.

Furthermore, we can now see how Nagel's problem is misguided. The difficulty is supposed to lie in a person's identifying himself, the subject of thought and experience, with a physical thing. In fact, Sartre presents the very same problem, and he already has a sense of how it is made quite unmanageable in the formulation: "Actually if after grasping 'my' consciousness in its absolute interiority and by a series of reflective acts, I then seek to unite it with a certain living object composed of a nervous system, brain, ... whose very matter is capable of being analysed chemically ..., then I am going to encounter insurmountable difficulties. But these difficulties all stem from the fact that I try to unite my consciousness not with *my* body but with the body of *others*" (1969, 303; quoted in Evans 1982, 266).

If, on the other hand, the problem is supposed to be for me to unite myself as a conscious subject with *my* body, then there is really no difficulty at all. For in bodily experience I am aware of parts of my body precisely as physical parts of myself, the material subject of that experience. Experienced embodiment just is a presentation of the subject as a spatially extended body.[10] Again, as with the explicitly anti-Cartesian reflections above, we come a long way simply by recognizing the absolute inseparabilty of the mental and the physical in bodily awareness.

ACKNOWLEDGMENTS

Many thanks to José Bermúdez, John Campbell, Quassim Cassam, David Charles, Bill Child, Naomi Eilan, Elizabeth Fricker, Jennifer Hornsby, Tony Marcel, Mike Martin, Paul Snowdon, Helen Steward, Rowland Stout and Timothy Williamson for their helpful comments on earlier versions of this paper.

NOTES

1 I mean this model of both sense perception and bodily awareness to be neutral on the question whether the Cartesian spells out the fact that a given immaterial mind has a particular sensational property in terms of its apprehension of some kind of sensation-object or in terms of its sensing with a certain intentional content.

2 Here and throughout this discussion of the epistemological given in bodily awareness, I mean to include as direct objects the properties of things of which one is immediately aware. In the end, my view is that the only *object* of bodily awareness, strictly speaking, is the animal body that is the subject of awareness. The basic form of the direct anti-Cartesian argument I am interested in is as follows. The properties of which we are immediately aware in bodily awareness are spatially located properties of the body that are also necessarily properties of the subject of that very awareness. Therefore, the subject is a material object.

3 See section 2 below for a development of this point.

4 Tony Marcel brought this home to me.

5 Again I have profited from O'Shaughnessy's (1980, 224–6) discussion of these issues here.

6 In 1992 Paillard reported on his patient G.L. in detail to the King's College Cambridge Research Centre Project on Spatial Representation.

7 I do not mean to imply that things are any different for G.L. in this respect. It is just that her status as a subject of both mental and physical properties cannot be inferred from the spatial content of her bodily awareness in the way I suggest.

8 I am grateful to Quassim Cassam for pressing this point.

9 It would, however, be a one-sided account of our sense of bodily ownership that focused *solely* on the contribution of bodily sensation and left out our capacity for basic, non-instrumental physical action.

10 As Evans is reported as remarking (1982, 266), this knowledge of my own body from the inside is an essential ground for my identification of myself as an element of the objective order, rather than a full account of it. Certainly, some capacity for self-location is an additional requirement. For more on this very important topic, see Evans 1982, 222–4; Cassam 1989; Brewer 1992.

REFERENCES

Brewer, B. 1992. "Self-Location and Agency." *Mind* 101:17–34.

Cassam, Q. 1989. "Kant and Reductionism." *Review of Metaphysics* 43:72–106.

Descartes, R. 1985a. *Philosophical Writings, vol. 1.* Translated by J. Cottingham, R. Stoothoff, and D. Murdoch. Cambridge: Cambridge University Press.

Descartes, R. 1985b. *Philosophical Writings, vol. 2.* Translated by J. Cottingham, R. Stoothoff, and D. Murdoch. Cambridge: Cambridge University Press.

Evans, G. 1982. *The Varieties of Reference.* Oxford: Clarendon Press.

Nagel, T. 1970. *The Possibility of Altruism.* Oxford: Clarendon Press.

O'Shaughnessy, B. 1980. *The Will, vol. 1.* Cambridge: Cambridge University Press.

Sartre, J.-P. 1969. *Being and Nothingness.* Translated by H. E. Barnes. London: Methuen.

Straus, E. W. 1967. "On Anosognosia." In *Phenomenology of Will and Action,* edited by E. W. Straus and D. Griffith. Pittsburgh: Duquesne University Press.

16

THE EXTENDED MIND

Andy Clark and David Chalmers

1 INTRODUCTION

Where does the mind stop and the rest of the world begin? The question invites two standard replies. Some accept the boundaries of skin and skull, and say that what is outside the body is outside the mind. Others are impressed by arguments suggesting that the meaning of our words 'just ain't in the head', and hold that this externalism about meaning carries over into an externalism about mind. We propose to pursue a third position. We advocate a very different sort of externalism: an *active externalism*, based on the active role of the environment in driving cognitive processes.

2 EXTENDED COGNITION

Consider three cases of human problem-solving:

(1) A person sits in front of a computer screen which displays images of various two-dimensional geometric shapes and is asked to answer questions concerning the potential fit of such shapes into depicted 'sockets'. To assess fit, the person must mentally rotate the shapes to align them with the sockets.

(2) A person sits in front of a similar computer screen, but this time can choose either to physically rotate the image on the screen, by pressing a rotate button, or to mentally rotate the image as before. We can also suppose, not unrealistically, that some speed advantage accrues to the physical rotation operation.

(3) Sometime in the cyberpunk future, a person sits in front of a similar computer screen. This agent, however, has the benefit of a neural implant which can perform the rotation operation as fast as the computer in the previous example. The agent must still choose which internal resource to use (the implant or the good

old-fashioned mental rotation), as each resource makes different demands on attention and other concurrent brain activity.

How much *cognition* is present in these cases? We suggest that all three cases are similar. Case (3) with the neural implant seems clearly to be on a par with case (1). And case (2) with the rotation button displays the same sort of computational structure as case (3), distributed across agent and computer instead of internalized within the agent. If the rotation in case (3) is cognitive, by what right do we count case (2) as fundamentally different? We cannot simply point to the skin/skull boundary as justification, since the legitimacy of that boundary is precisely what is at issue. But nothing else seems different.

The kind of case just described is by no means as exotic as it may at first appear. It is not just the presence of advanced external computing resources which raises the issue, but rather the general tendency of human reasoners to lean heavily on environmental supports. Thus consider the use of pen and paper to perform long multiplication (McClelland *et al.* 1986, Clark 1989), the use of physical re-arrangements of letter tiles to prompt word recall in Scrabble (Kirsh 1995), the use of instruments such as the nautical slide rule (Hutchins 1995), and the general paraphernalia of language, books, diagrams, and culture. In all these cases the individual brain performs some operations, while others are delegated to manipulations of external media. Had our brains been different, this distribution of tasks would doubtless have varied.

In fact, even the mental rotation cases described in scenarios (1) and (2) are real. The cases reflect options available to players of the computer game Tetris. In Tetris, falling geometric shapes must be rapidly directed into an appropriate slot in an emerging structure. A rotation button can be used. David Kirsh and Paul Maglio (1994) calculate that the physical rotation of a shape through 90 degrees takes about 100 milliseconds, plus about 200 milliseconds to select the button. To achieve the same result by mental rotation takes about 1000 milliseconds. Kirsh and Maglio go on to present compelling evidence that physical rotation is used not just to position a shape ready to fit a slot, but often to help *determine* whether the shape and the slot are compatible. The latter use constitutes a case of what Kirsh and Maglio call an 'epistemic action'. *Epistemic* actions alter the world so as to aid and augment cognitive processes such as recognition and search. Merely *pragmatic* actions, by contrast, alter the world because some physical change is desirable for its own sake (e.g. putting cement into a hole in a dam).

Epistemic action, we suggest, demands spread of *epistemic credit*. If, as we confront some task, a part of the world functions as a process which, *were it done in the head*, we would have no hesitation in recognizing as part of the cognitive process, then that part of the world *is* (so we claim) part of the cognitive process. Cognitive processes ain't (all) in the head!

3 ACTIVE EXTERNALISM

In these cases, the human organism is linked with an external entity in a two-way interaction, creating a *coupled system* that can be seen as a cognitive system in its own right. All the components in the system play an active causal role, and they jointly govern behaviour in the same sort of way that cognition usually does. If we remove the external component the system's behavioural competence will drop, just as it would if we removed part of its brain. Our thesis is that this sort of coupled process counts equally well as a cognitive process, whether or not it is wholly in the head.

This externalism differs from the standard variety advocated by Putnam (1975) and Burge (1979). When I believe that water is wet and my twin believes that twin water is wet, the external features responsible for the difference in our beliefs are distal and historical, at the other end of a lengthy causal chain. Features of the *present* are not relevant: if I happen to be surrounded by XYZ right now (maybe I have teleported to Twin Earth), my beliefs still concern standard water, because of my history. In these cases, the relevant external features are *passive*. Because of their distal nature, they play no role in driving the cognitive process in the here-and-now. This is reflected by the fact that the actions performed by me and my twin are physically indistinguishable, despite our external differences.

In the cases we describe, by contrast, the relevant external features are *active*, playing a crucial role in the here-and-now. Because they are coupled with the human organism, they have a direct impact on the organism and on its behaviour. In these cases, the relevant parts of the world are *in the loop*, not dangling at the other end of a long causal chain. Concentrating on this sort of coupling leads us to an *active externalism*, as opposed to the passive externalism of Putnam and Burge.

Many have complained that even if Putnam and Burge are right about the externality of content, it is not clear that these external aspects play a causal or explanatory role in the generation of action. In counterfactual cases where internal structure is held constant but these external features are changed, behaviour looks just the same; so internal structure seems to be doing the crucial work. We will not adjudicate that issue here, but we note that active externalism is not threatened by any such problem. The external features in a coupled system play an ineliminable role – if we retain internal structure but change the external features, behaviour may change completely. The external features here are just as causally relevant as typical internal features of the brain.[1]

By embracing an active externalism, we allow a more natural explanation of all sorts of actions. One can explain my choice of words in Scrabble, for example, as the outcome of an extended cognitive process involving the rearrangement of tiles on my tray. Of course, one could always try to explain my action in terms of internal pro-

*is complex
bad?*

cesses and a long series of 'inputs' and 'actions', but this explanation would be needlessly complex. If an isomorphic process were going on in the head, we would feel no urge to characterize it in this cumbersome way. In a very real sense, the re-arrangement of tiles on the tray is not part of action; it is part of *thought*.

The view we advocate here is reflected by a growing body of research in cognitive science. In areas as diverse as the theory of situated cognition (Suchman 1987), studies of real-world-robotics (Beer 1989), dynamical approaches to child development (Thelen and Smith 1994), and research on the cognitive properties of collectives of agents (Hutchins 1995), cognition is often taken to be continuous with processes in the environment.[2] Thus, in seeing cognition as extended one is not merely making a terminological decision; it makes a significant difference to the methodology of scientific investigation. In effect, explanatory methods that might once have been thought appropriate only for the analysis of 'inner' processes are now being adapted for the study of the outer, and there is promise that our understanding of cognition will become richer for it.

Some find this sort of externalism unpalatable. One reason may be that many identify the cognitive with the conscious, and it seems far from plausible that consciousness extends outside the head in these cases. But not every cognitive process, at least on standard usage, is a conscious process. It is widely accepted that all sorts of processes beyond the borders of consciousness play a crucial role in cognitive processing: in the retrieval of memories, linguistic processes, and skill acquisition, for example. So the mere fact that external processes are external where consciousness is internal is no reason to deny that those processes are cognitive.

More interestingly, one might argue that what keeps real cognition processes in the head is the requirement that cognitive processes be *portable*. Here, we are moved by a vision of what might be called the Naked Mind: a package of resources and operations we can always bring to bear on a cognitive task, regardless of the local environment. On this view, the trouble with coupled systems is that they are too easily *decoupled*. The true cognitive processes are those that lie at the constant core of the system; anything else is an add-on extra.

There is something to this objection. The brain (or brain and body) comprises a package of basic, portable, cognitive resources that is of interest in its own right. These resources may incorporate bodily actions into cognitive processes, as when we use our fingers as working memory in a tricky calculation, but they will not encompass the more contingent aspects of our external environment, such as a pocket calculator. Still, mere contingency of coupling does not rule out cognitive status. In the distant future we may be able to plug various modules into our brain to help us out: a module for extra short-term memory when we need it, for example. When a module is plugged in, the processes involving it are just as cognitive as if they had been there all along.

Even if one were to make the portability criterion pivotal, active externalism would not be undermined. Counting on our fingers has already been let in the door, for example, and it is easy to push things further. Think of the old image of the engineer with a slide rule hanging from his belt wherever he goes. What if people always carried a pocket calculator, or had them implanted? The real moral of the portability intuition is that for coupled systems to be relevant to the core of cognition, *reliable* coupling is required. It happens that most reliable coupling takes place within the brain, but there can easily be reliable coupling with the environment as well. If the resources of my calculator or my Filofax are always there when I need them, then they are coupled with me as reliably as we need. In effect, they are part of the basic package of cognitive resources that I bring to bear on the everyday world. These systems cannot be impugned simply on the basis of the danger of discrete damage, loss, or malfunction, or because of any occasional decoupling: the biological brain is in similar danger, and occasionally loses capacities temporarily in episodes of sleep, intoxication, and emotion. If the relevant capacities are generally there when they are required, this is coupling enough.

Moreover, it may be that the biological brain has in fact evolved and matured in ways which factor in the reliable presence of a manipulable external environment. It certainly seems that evolution has favoured onboard capacities which are especially geared to parasitizing the local environment so as to reduce memory load, and even to transform the nature of the computational problems themselves. Our visual systems have evolved to rely on their environment in various ways: they exploit contingent facts about the structure of natural scenes (e.g. Ullman and Richards 1984), for example, and they take advantage of the computational short cuts afforded by bodily motion and locomotion (e.g. Blake and Yuille, 1992). Perhaps there are other cases where evolution has found it advantageous to exploit the possibility of the environment being in the cognitive loop. If so, then external coupling is part of the truly basic package of cognitive resources that we bring to bear on the world.

Another example may be language, which appears to be a central means by which cognitive processes are extended into the world. Think of a group of people brainstorming around a table, or a philosopher who thinks best by writing, developing her ideas as she goes. It may be that language evolved, in part, to enable such extensions of our cognitive resources within actively coupled systems.

Within the lifetime of an organism, too, individual learning may have moulded the brain in ways that rely on cognitive extensions that surrounded us as we learned. Language is again a central example here, as are the various physical and computational artifacts that are routinely used as cognitive extensions by children in schools and by trainees in numerous professions. In such cases the brain develops in a way that complements the external structures, and learns to play its role within a unified, densely coupled system. Once we recognize that the crucial role of the environment in constraining the evolution and development of cognition, we see that extended cognition is a core cognitive process, not an add-on extra.

4 FROM COGNITION TO MIND

So far we have spoken largely about 'cognitive processing', and argued for its extension into the environment. Some might think that the conclusion has been bought too cheaply. Perhaps some *processing* takes place in the environment, but what of *mind*? Everything we have said so far is compatible with the view that truly mental states – experiences, beliefs, desires, emotions, and so on – are all determined by states of the brain. Perhaps what is truly mental is internal, after all?

We propose to take things a step further. While some mental states, such as experiences, may be determined internally, there are other cases in which external factors make a significant contribution. In particular, we will argue that *beliefs* can be constituted partly by features of the environment, when those features play the right sort of role in driving cognitive processes. If so, the mind extends into the world.

First, consider a normal case of belief embedded in memory. Inga hears from a friend that there is an exhibition at the Museum of Modern Art, and decides to go see it. She thinks for a moment and recalls that the museum is on 53rd Street, so she walks to 53rd Street and goes into the museum. It seems clear that Inga believes that the museum is on 53rd Street, and that she believed this even before she consulted her memory. It was not previously an *occurrent* belief, but then neither are most of our beliefs. The belief was somewhere in memory, waiting to be accessed.

Now consider Otto. Otto suffers from Alzheimer's disease, and like many Alzheimer's patients, he relies on information in the environment to help structure his life. Otto carries a notebook around with him everywhere he goes. When he learns new information, he writes it down. When he needs some old information, he looks it up. For Otto, his notebook plays the role usually played by a biological memory. Today, Otto hears about the exhibition at the Museum of Modern Art, and decides to go see it. He consults the notebook, which says that the museum is on 53rd Street, so he walks to 53rd Street and goes into the museum.

Clearly, Otto walked to 53rd Street because he wanted to go to the museum and he believed the museum was on 53rd Street. And just as Inga had her belief even before she consulted her memory, it seems reasonable to say that Otto believed the museum was on 53rd Street even before consulting his notebook. For in relevant respects the cases are entirely analogous: the notebook plays for Otto the same role that memory plays for Inga. The information in the notebook functions just like the information constituting an ordinary non-occurrent belief; it just happens that this information lies beyond the skin.

The alternative is to say that Otto has no belief about the matter until he consults his notebook; at best, he believes that the museum is located at the address in the notebook. But if we follow Otto around for a while, we will see how unnatural this way of speaking is. Otto is constantly using his notebook as a matter of course. It is central to his actions in all sorts of contexts, in the way that an ordinary memory is central in an ordinary life. The same information might come up again and again, perhaps being slightly modified on occasion, before retreating into the recesses of his artificial memory. To say that the beliefs disappear when the notebook is filed away seems to miss the big picture in just the same way as saying that Inga's beliefs disappear as soon as she is longer conscious of them. In both cases the information is reliably there when needed, available to consciousness and available to guide action, in just the way that we expect a belief to be.

Certainly, insofar as beliefs and desires are characterized by their explanatory roles, Otto's and Inga's cases seem to be on a par: the essential causal dynamics of the two cases mirror each other precisely. We are happy to explain Inga's action in terms of her occurrent desire to go to the museum and her standing belief that the museum is on 53rd street, and we should be happy to explain Otto's action in the same way. The alternative is to explain Otto's action in terms of his occurrent desire to go to the museum, his standing belief that the Museum is on the location written in the notebook, and the accessible fact that the notebook says the Museum is on 53rd Street; but this complicates the explanation unnecessarily. If we must resort to explaining Otto's action this way, then we must also do so for the countless other actions in which his notebook is involved; in each of the explanations, there will be an extra term involving the notebook. We submit that to explain things this way is to take *one step too many*. It is pointlessly complex, in the same way that it would be pointlessly complex to explain Inga's actions in terms of beliefs about her memory. The notebook is a constant for Otto, in the same way that memory is a constant for Inga; to point to it in every belief/desire explanation would be redundant. In an explanation, simplicity is power.

If this is right, we can even construct the case of Twin Otto, who is just like Otto except that a while ago he mistakenly wrote in his notebook that the Museum of Modern Art was on 51st Street. Today, Twin Otto is a physical duplicate of Otto from the skin in, but his notebook differs. Consequently, Twin Otto is best characterized as believing that the museum is on 51st Street, where Otto believes it is on 53rd. In these cases, a belief is simply not in the head.

This mirrors the conclusion of Putnam and Burge, but again there are important differences. In the Putnam/Burge cases, the external features constituting differences in belief are distal and historical, so that twins in these cases produce physically indistinguishable behaviour. In the cases we are describing, the relevant external features play an active role in the here-and-now, and have a direct impact on behaviour.

Where Otto walks to 53rd Street, Twin Otto walks to 51st. There is no question of explanatory irrelevance for this sort of external belief content; it is introduced precisely because of the central explanatory role that it plays. Like the Putnam and Burge cases, these cases involve differences in reference and truth-conditions, but they also involve differences in the dynamics of *cognition*.[3]

The moral is that when it comes to belief, there is nothing sacred about skull and skin. What makes some information count as a belief is the role it plays, and there is no reason why the relevant role can be played only from inside the body.

Some will resist this conclusion. An opponent might put her foot down and insist that as she uses the term 'belief', or perhaps even according to standard usage, Otto simply does not qualify as believing that the museum is on 53rd Street. We do not intend to debate what is standard usage; our broader point is that the notion of belief *ought* to be used so that Otto qualifies as having the belief in question. In all *important* respects, Otto's case is similar to a standard case of (non-occurrent) belief. The differences between Otto's case and Inga's are striking, but they are superficial. By using the 'belief' notion in a wider way, it picks out something more akin to a natural kind. The notion becomes deeper and more unified, and is more useful in explanation.

To provide substantial resistance, an opponent has to show that Otto's and Inga's cases differ in some important and relevant respect. But in what deep respect are the cases different? To make the case *solely* on the grounds that information is in the head in one case but not in the other would be to beg the question. If this difference is relevant to a difference in belief, it is surely not *primitively* relevant. To justify the different treatment, we must find some more basic underlying difference between the two.

It might be suggested that the cases are relevantly different in that Inga has more *reliable* access to the information. After all, someone might take away Otto's notebook at any time, but Inga's memory is safer. It is not implausible that constancy is relevant: indeed, the fact that Otto always uses his notebook played some role in our justifying its cognitive status. If Otto were consulting a guidebook as a one-off, we would be much less likely to ascribe him a standing belief. But in the original case, Otto's access to the notebook is very reliable – not perfectly reliable, to be sure, but then neither is Inga's access to her memory. A surgeon might tamper with her brain, or more mundanely, she might have too much to drink. The mere possibility of such tampering is not enough to deny her the belief.

One might worry that Otto's access to his notebook *in fact* comes and goes. He showers without the notebook, for example, and he cannot read it when it is dark. Surely his belief cannot come and go so easily? We could get around this problem by redescribing the situation, but in any case an occasional temporary disconnection does not threaten our claim. After all, when Inga is asleep, or when she is intoxicated, we do not say that her belief disappears. What really counts is that the information is easily available when the subject needs it, and this constraint is satisfied equally in the two cases. If Otto's notebook were often unavailable to him at times when the information in it would be useful, there might be a problem, as the information would not be able to play the action-guiding role that is central to belief; but if it is easily available in most relevant situations, the belief is not endangered.

Perhaps a difference is that Inga has *better* access to the information than Otto does? Inga's 'central' processes and her memory probably have a relatively high-bandwidth link between them, compared to the low-grade connection between Otto and his notebook. But this alone does not make a difference between believing and not believing. Consider Inga's museum-going friend Lucy, whose biological memory has only a low-grade link to her central systems, due to nonstandard biology or past misadventures. Processing in Lucy's case might be less efficient, but as long as the relevant information is accessible, Lucy clearly believes that the museum is on 53rd Street. If the connection was too indirect – if Lucy had to struggle hard to retrieve the information with mixed results, or a psychotherapist's aid were needed – we might become more reluctant to ascribe the belief, but such cases are well beyond Otto's situation, in which the information is easily accessible.

Another suggestion could be that Otto has access to the relevant information only by *perception*, whereas Inga has more direct access – by introspection, perhaps. In some ways, however, to put things this way is to beg the question. After all, we are in effect advocating a point of view on which Otto's internal processes and his note-book constitute a single cognitive system. From the standpoint of this system, the flow of information between notebook and brain is not perceptual at all; it does not involve the impact of something outside the system. It is more akin to information flow within the brain. The only deep way in which the access is perceptual is that in Otto's case, there is a distinctly perceptual phenomenology associated with the retrieval of the information, whereas in Inga's case there is not. But why should the nature of an associated phenomenology make a difference to the status of a belief? Inga's memory may have some associated phenomenology, but it is still a belief. The phenomenology is not visual, to be sure. But for visual phenomenology consider the Terminator, from the Arnold Schwarzenegger movie of the same name. When he recalls some information from memory, it is 'displayed' before him in his visual field (presumably he is conscious of it, as there are frequent shots depicting his point of view). The fact that standing memories are recalled in this unusual way surely makes little difference to their status as standing beliefs.

These various small differences between Otto's and Inga's cases are all *shallow* differences. To focus on them would be to miss the way in which for Otto, notebook entries play just the sort of role that beliefs play in guiding most people's lives.

Perhaps the intuition that Otto's is not a true belief comes from a residual feeling that the only true beliefs are occurrent beliefs. If we take this feeling seriously, Inga's belief will be ruled out too, as will many beliefs that we attribute in everyday life. This would be an extreme view, but it may be the most consistent way to deny Otto's belief. Upon even a slightly less extreme view – the view that a belief must be *available* for consciousness, for example – Otto's notebook entry seems to qualify just as well as Inga's memory. Once dispositional beliefs are let in the door, it is difficult to resist the conclusion that Otto's notebook has all the relevant dispositions.

5 BEYOND THE OUTER LIMITS

If the thesis is accepted, how far should we go? All sorts of puzzle cases spring to mind. What of the amnesic villagers in *One Hundred Years of Solitude*, who forget the names for everything and so hang labels everywhere? Does the information in my Filofax count as part of my memory? If Otto's notebook has been tampered with, does he believe the newly-installed information? Do I believe the contents of the page in front of me before I read it? Is my cognitive state somehow spread across the Internet?

We do not think that there are categorical answers to all of these questions, and we will not give them. But to help understand what is involved in ascriptions of extended belief, we can at least examine the features of our central case that make the notion so clearly applicable there. First, the notebook is a constant in Otto's life – in cases where the information in the notebook would be relevant, he will rarely take action without consulting it. Second, the information in the notebook is directly available without difficulty. Third, upon retrieving information from the notebook he automatically endorses it. Fourth, the information in the notebook has been consciously endorsed at some point in the past, and indeed is there as a consequence of this endorsement.[4] The status of the fourth feature as a criterion for belief is arguable (perhaps one can acquire beliefs through subliminal perception, or through memory tampering?), but the first three features certainly play a crucial role.

Insofar as increasingly exotic puzzle cases lack these features, the applicability of the notion of 'belief' gradually falls off. If I rarely take relevant action without consulting my Filofax, for example, its status within my cognitive system will resemble that of the notebook in Otto's. But if I often act without consultation – for example, if I sometimes answer relevant questions with 'I don't know' – then information in it counts less clearly as part of my belief system. The Internet is likely to fail on multiple counts, unless I am unusually computer-reliant, facile with the technology, and trusting, but information in certain files on my computer may qualify. In intermediate cases, the question of whether a belief is present may be indeterminate, or the answer may depend on the varying standards that are at play in various contexts in which the question might be asked. But any indeterminacy here does not mean that in the central cases, the answer is not clear.

What about socially extended cognition? Could my mental states be partly constituted by the states of other thinkers? We see no reason why not, in principle. In an unusually interdependent couple, it is entirely possible that one partner's beliefs will play the same sort of role for the other as the notebook plays for Otto. What is central is a high degree of trust, reliance, and accessibility. In other social relationships these criteria may not be so clearly fulfilled, but they might nevertheless be fulfilled in specific domains. For example, the waiter at my favourite restaurant might act as a repository of my beliefs about my favourite meals (this might even be construed as a case of extended desire). In other cases, one's beliefs might be embodied in one's secretary, one's accountant, or one's collaborator.

In each of these cases, the major burden of the coupling between agents is carried by language. Without language, we might be much more akin to discrete Cartesian 'inner' minds, in which high-level cognition relies largely on internal resources. But the advent of language has allowed us to spread this burden into the world. Language, thus construed, is not a mirror of our inner states but a complement to them. It serves as a tool whose role is to extend cognition in ways that on-board devices cannot. Indeed, it may be that the intellectual explosion in recent evolutionary time is due as much to this linguistically-enabled extension of cognition as to any independent development in our inner cognitive resources.

What, finally, of the self? Does the extended mind imply an extended self? It seems so. Most of us already accept that the self outstrips the boundaries of consciousness; my dispositional beliefs, for example, constitute in some deep sense part of who I am. If so, then these boundaries may also fall beyond the skin. The information in Otto's notebook, for example, is a central part of his identity as a cognitive agent. What this comes to is that Otto *himself* is best regarded as an extended system, a coupling of biological organism and external resources. To consistently resist this conclusion, we would have to shrink the self into a mere bundle of occurrent states, severely threatening its deep psychological continuity. Far better to take the broader view, and see agents themselves as spread into the world.

As with any reconception of ourselves, this view will have significant consequences. There are obvious consequences for philosophical views of the mind and for the methodology of research in cognitive science, but there will also be effects in the moral and social domains. It may be, for example, that in some cases interfering with someone's environment will have the same moral significance as interfering with their person. And if the view is taken seriously, certain forms of social activity might be reconceived as less akin to communication and action, and as more akin to thought. In any case, once the hegemony of skin and skull is usurped, we may be able to see ourselves more truly as creatures of the world.

NOTES

1 Much of the appeal of externalism in the philosophy of mind may stem from the intuitive appeal of active externalism. Externalists often make analogies involving external features in coupled systems, and appeal to the arbitrariness of boundaries between brain and environment. But these intuitions sit uneasily with the letter of standard externalism. In most of the Putnam/Burge cases, the immediate environment is irrelevant; only the historical environment counts. Debate has focused on the question of whether mind must be in the head, but a more relevant question in assessing these examples might be: is mind in the present?

2 Philosophical views of a similar spirit can be found in Haugeland 1995, McClamrock 1995, Varela *et al.* 1991, and Wilson 1994.

3 In the terminology of Chalmers (2002): the twins in the Putnam and Burge cases differ only in their relational content (secondary intension), but Otto and his twin can be seen to differ in their notional content (primary intension), which is the sort of content that governs cognition. Notional content is generally internal to a cognitive system, but in this case the cognitive system is itself effectively extended to include the notebook.

4 The constancy and past-endorsement criteria may suggest that history is partly constitutive of belief. One might react to this by removing any historical component (giving a purely dispositional reading of the constancy criterion and eliminating the past-endorsement criterion, for example), or one might allow such a component as long as the main burden is carried by features of the present.

REFERENCES

Beer, R. (1989). *Intelligence as Adaptive Behavior*. New York: Academic Press.

Blake, A. and A. Yuille, eds. (1992). *Active Vision*. Cambridge, MA: MIT Press.

Burge, T. (1979). "Individualism and the mental". *Midwest Studies in Philosophy* 4: 73–122.

Chalmers, D.J. (2002). "The components of content". In *Philosophy of Mind: Classical and Contemporary Readings*, ed. D. Chalmers. Oxford: Oxford University Press, 608–33.

Clark, A. (1989). *Microcognition*. MIT Press.

Haugeland, J. (1995). "Mind embodied and embedded". In *Mind and Cognition*, eds Y. Houng and J. Ho. Taipei: Academia Sinica.

Hutchins, E. (1995). *Cognition in the Wild*. Cambridge, MA: MIT Press.

Kirsh, D. (1995). *The intelligent use of space*. *Artificial Intelligence* 73: 31–68.

Kirsh, D. and P. Maglio (1994). "On distinguishing epistemic from pragmatic action". *Cognitive Science* 18: 513–49.

McClamrock, R. (1995). *Existential Cognition*. Chicago: University of Chicago Press.

McClelland, J. L, D. E. Rumelhart, and G. E. Hinton (1986). "The appeal of parallel distributed processing". In *Parallel Distributed Processing*, Volume 2, eds. McClelland and Rumelhart. Cambridge, MA: MIT Press.

Putnam, H. (1975). "The meaning of 'meaning'". In *Language, Mind, and Knowledge*, ed. K. Gunderson. Minneapolis: University of Minnesota Press.

Suchman, L. (1987). *Plans and Situated Actions*. Cambridge: Cambridge University Press.

Thelen, E. and L. Smith (1994). *A Dynamic Systems Approach to the Development of Cognition and Action*. Cambridge, MA: MIT Press.

Ullman, S. and W. Richards (1984). *Image Understanding*. Norwood, NJ: Ablex.

Varela, F., E. Thompson and E. Rosch (1991). *The Embodied Mind*. Cambridge, MA: MIT Press.

Wilson, R. (1994). "Wide computationalism". *Mind* 103: 351–72.

17

OVEREXTENDING THE MIND?

Brie Gertler

Clark and Chalmers argue that the mind is *extended* – that is, its boundary lies beyond the skin. (Clark and Chalmers 1998, reprinted as **Chapter 16** of this volume.[1] For brevity, I will refer to the authors as 'C&C'.) In this essay, I will criticize this conclusion. However, I will also defend some of the more controversial elements of C&C's argument. I reject their conclusion because I think that their argument shows that a seemingly innocuous assumption, about *internal* states and processes, is flawed.

The first section of the essay outlines C&C's argument. In Section 2, I sketch some unpalatable consequences of their conclusion. Insofar as we want to avoid these consequences, we should look for a flaw in the argument. As outlined in Section 1, the argument appears to be valid, so finding a flaw means identifying a premise that it is reasonable to reject. In Section 3, I evaluate each of the major premises of the argument and find that all but one are acceptable; I then explain why I reject the remaining premise. Section 4 briefly defends the picture of the mind that emerges from rejecting this premise.

My goal is not to conclusively refute C&C's argument. My aim is only to reveal the best alternative for those who remain skeptical about the existence – or, perhaps, even the possibility – of extended minds.

1 CLARK AND CHALMERS' ARGUMENT

The authors provide two arguments to show that the mind is extended. First, they argue that the mind's cognitive processes can at least partially consist in processes performed by external devices. Their examples of such external cognitive processing devices include a computer that you can use to rotate shapes when playing the game Tetris. As they describe this case, the computer's rotation of a shape plays the same sort of role, in your cognitive economy, as the corresponding internal process (when

192

you simply *imagine* how the shape would appear if it were rotated in various ways). For instance, the result of this process is automatically endorsed – you believe that the shape would look like *that* when rotated. And you use this information to guide your behavior, such as moving the joystick to position the shape in a certain place on the screen. They conclude that insofar as the internal process of imagining qualifies as *your cognitive process*, so should the external computational process.

While I will return to this processing case at various points below, my remarks will focus on the second of C&C's arguments: that standing beliefs (and desires, etc.) can be partially constituted by factors external to the skin. Standing beliefs include stored memories and other beliefs that are not currently being entertained. The notion of a *standing* belief contrasts with the notion of an *occurrent* belief, which is a conviction that you are now entertaining. For instance, you probably have the standing belief that dinosaurs once roamed the earth. At the moment before you read that sentence, the belief was *simply* a standing belief; it was not occurrent (unless you happened to be thinking about dinosaurs at that moment). But now that you're thinking about the fact that dinosaurs roamed the earth, that belief is *occurrent*.

C&C's principal examples of extended standing beliefs involve a character they call Otto. Otto, who suffers from Alzheimer's disease, carries a notebook in which he routinely records useful information of the sort that most of us would easily commit to memory. Otto consults the notebook whenever he needs this stored information to guide his reasoning or actions. For instance, on a trip to the Museum of Modern Art in New York, Otto frequently consults the notebook, to remind himself that he is going to the MoMA, that the MoMA is on 53rd Street, etc. C&C claim that the information stored in Otto's notebook – such as 'the MoMA is on 53rd Street' – partially constitutes his standing beliefs, and hence that his mind extends beyond his skin.

Here is my reconstruction of C&C's argument.

> sub conscious memories

(1) "What makes some information count as a [standing] belief is the role it plays". (p. 187.)
(2) "The information in the notebook functions just like [that is, it plays the same role as] the information constituting an ordinary non-occurrent belief". (p. 185.)
(3) The information in Otto's notebook counts as standing beliefs.[2] (from (1) and (2))
(4) Otto's standing beliefs are part of his mind.
(5) The information in Otto's notebook is part of Otto's mind. (from (3) and (4))
(6) Otto's notebook belongs to the world external to Otto's skin, i.e., the 'external' world.
(7) The mind extends into the world. (from (5) and (6))

In assessing C&C's extended mind hypothesis, I will focus on the conclusion that Otto's standing beliefs extend into the world. Later, I will briefly discuss how my assessment applies to the case of cognitive processing.

2 SOME WORRISOME CONSEQUENCES OF CLARK AND CHALMERS' CONCLUSION

C&C's conclusion is that "the mind extends into the world", where 'the world' refers to what is beyond the subject's skin. In this section, I will use the example of Otto and his notebook to describe two consequences that seem to follow from this conclusion. Both of these consequences are, I think, worrisome; the second is especially so. Recognizing them will thus cast doubt on the conclusion.

First consequence: limits on introspection

It is commonly held that, in general, a subject can determine his or her own beliefs and desires by using a method that others cannot use (to determine that subject's beliefs). Let us use the term 'introspection' to refer to this method. Introspection is, in this sense, a *necessarily* first-person method: it reveals only the introspector's own states, and not the states of others. Introspection may not be infallible; in fact, it may be no more reliable than third-person methods. The claim is only that each of us has a *way* of gaining access to our own beliefs that is unavailable to others.

According to C&C, the information in Otto's notebook partially constitutes some of his standing beliefs. Can Otto introspect these beliefs, in our sense of 'introspect'? That is, can he identify these beliefs by using a method available only to himself?

I think that he cannot. When Otto tries to figure out what he believes on a particular topic, he consults the notebook. For instance, suppose that he wonders what he believes about the location of the MoMA. He will look in the notebook and conclude: *I believe that the MoMA is on 53rd Street*. But of course someone other than Otto can determine Otto's beliefs in precisely the same way: by consulting the notebook, a friend can determine that Otto believes that the MoMA is on 53rd Street. So it appears that, if the entries in Otto's notebook partially constitute his beliefs, then Otto cannot introspect his beliefs.

Much more could be said here. For one thing, it might be argued that when Otto consults the notebook in order to determine what he believes about the location of the Museum, he *is* introspecting. C&C seem to suggest this when they say that treating Otto's access to the notebook as perceptual rather than introspective would beg the question against the claim that the notebook is *part of* Otto's mind. But as I am using this term, 'introspection' refers only to those processes that are *necessarily* first-personal. Someone who claimed that, in consulting the notebook, Otto is introspecting in *my* sense would have to show that Otto has a unique kind of access to the notebook – or, perhaps, to the fact that the notebook entries

194

play the relevant 'belief' role in his cognitive economy. But it is difficult to see how this access could be unique, so long as it was access to a feature *external* to Otto's skin.

Another possibility that C&C describe more directly reveals the lack of unique first-person access.

> In an unusually interdependent couple, it is entirely possible that one partner's beliefs will play the same sort of role for the other as the notebook plays for Otto. ... [O]ne's beliefs might be embodied in one's secretary, one's accountant, or one's collaborator. (**p. 190.**)

To flesh out this scenario, suppose that Amanda, an absent-minded executive, uses her assistant Fred as a repository of her daily schedule. Fred knows that Amanda has a 2:00 board meeting on Monday, and stores this information for Amanda. Since this information plays the appropriate role in Amanda's cognitive economy (it is readily accessible to her, automatically endorsed by her, etc.), it counts as her belief.

Now suppose that Amanda wonders what she believes about her Monday schedule. To determine this, she will consult Fred, to see what he believes about it. But this is the same process that Fred uses to determine what Amanda believes about her Monday schedule. Recognizing that he is a repository for Amanda's standing beliefs, Fred will determine Amanda's beliefs about the schedule simply by consulting his own beliefs about it. Amanda's access to her beliefs, and to the fact that she has those beliefs, proceeds via a method also available to Fred. So Amanda has no uniquely first-personal method of determining what she believes; that is, she cannot introspect her beliefs, in my sense of 'introspect'.

C&C would likely accept this consequence. They could simply allow that, in general, we have unique introspective access only to our <u>occurrent</u> experiences and our *occurrent* thoughts, that is, thoughts that we are now entertaining. (Crucially, they do not claim that occurrent thoughts are extended.) The point may be even clearer when applied to cognitive processes such as those involved in the Tetris case. You do not seem to have any special first-person access to *how* you go about imagining the shape rotated: you simply perform this feat of imagination.[3] So C&C can easily allow that those states that are extended – such as standing beliefs and nonconscious cognitive processes – are simply non-introspectible.

Still, for one who thinks that *introspectibility* is crucial to our basic concept of the mind, this point will cast doubt on C&C's conclusion that the mind extends into the world. If one can introspect only the non-extended parts of the mind, then why count the external factors as truly part of the mind? (I will return to this point in Section 4.)

I now turn to the second, more troubling consequence of C&C's conclusion.

Second consequence: a proliferation of actions

C&C dub their view 'active externalism' to highlight what they see as one of its chief benefits: the extended states that it counts as *mental* play a crucial role in generating action. In marking this benefit, they appear to suggest that this contribution to action is, at least in part, what justifies counting the wide states as truly *mental* states. But it's not clear that the wide states play the crucial role C&C ascribe to them.[4]

A simple thought experiment will convey the basis for doubt on this point. Suppose that, instead of a notebook, Otto uses an external computing device as a repository for important information. Suppose also that he records some of his desires in the device. For instance, he records the desire to make banana bread on Tuesday; the belief that banana bread requires bananas; the belief that the corner grocery store is a good source for bananas; etc. And he allows the device to perform some cognitive processes for him, including devising action plans based on the information it has stored. (C&C would surely allow that a single device could both serve as a repository for standing states and perform cognitive processes as in the Tetris example; after all, the brain accomplishes both of these tasks.) The idea that external devices can devise action plans is nothing new. For example, a dashboard-mounted Global Positioning System records the subject's desire to reach a particular destination, and uses stored geographical information to devise the most efficient route to fulfilling that desire.

Finally, imagine that this computing device is plugged into a humanoid robot that Otto also owns. In effect, the computing device serves as part of the robot 'brain'. (Otto's internal, *organic* brain may be another part of the robot's brain.) It uses inputs from the robot's various detection systems to determine the layout of its environment, and it controls the robot's movements by sending signals to the robot's 'limbs'.

Otto spends Monday asleep in bed. (Or, rather, the organic portion of his body does – after all, if C&C are correct the external device qualifies as part of Otto's body.) The robot is, however, very active: using the information stored within it, it 'realizes' that a trip to the grocery store is in order, since this is the most efficient way to execute the desire to make banana bread on Tuesday. Drawing on various other bits of information, it goes to the grocery store, purchases bananas, and returns home. Alas, the organism's sleep is very deep, and he (it?) does not awake until late on Tuesday. When he does, he is roused by the tantalizing scent of freshly-baked banana bread.

Now did *Otto* make the bread? It seems that C&C should say that he did. They claim that, in explaining why Otto walked to 53rd Street, we need not cite the occurrent belief that the MoMA is on 53rd Street, which Otto has (for a fleeting moment) upon consulting the notebook. Instead, they say, an adequate explanation may simply cite the notebook entry itself. Expanding on this claim, it seems that in order to explain the bread-making behavior, we need not cite any occurrent belief or desire of Otto's; we can simply cite the information and dispositions stored in the robot's 'brain'. The implication of premises (1) and (2) of their argument is that these 'count as' Otto's standing beliefs and desires. So long as no occurrent belief or desire needs to be cited in an action explanation, the bits of behavior that directly result from the bits of information stored in the robot – the trip to the grocery store, the making of the banana bread – seem accurately described as *Otto's actions*.

To resist this, it may be argued that Otto *himself* didn't go to the grocery store, or make the banana bread – for he was asleep in bed. But notice that this reply depends on denying that the robot is part of Otto. And if C&C are correct, there is little support for such a distinction. "Otto *himself* is best regarded as an extended system, a coupling of biological organism and external resources." (**p. 190.**) Surely, some of Otto's actions directly involve only the organic part of Otto; so, on grounds of parity, we should allow that some of Otto's actions might directly involve only his non-organic part.

Of course, the organism and the robot will constitute the right kind of extended system only if they are related in certain ways. But they do seem to be appropriately related. The information stored in the robot's 'brain' is present because the organism occurrently believed it in the past; it is readily accessible; the organism automatically endorses the information it contains; etc.[5] These are the conditions that are met by Otto's notebook and that, according to C&C, make it the case that Otto's mind extends to the notebook. On the same grounds, then, we should say that in our story, Otto extends to the external device. We can even imagine that when the organism awakens, Otto compliments himself on his baking prowess.

So C&C's argument suggests that making the banana bread was Otto's action. If this is correct, there seems no limit to the actions a single person can perform. For imagine that organic Otto programs an enormous fleet of robots, linking them so that they are in constant communication with each other. These robots then engage in widespread, multifarious activities. Some take a slow boat to China; others descend on a neighborhood in Texas and ring all the doorbells at once; others compete in karaoke contests in Tokyo. When we say that all of these activities are Otto's actions, we are not simply saying that he is *somehow* responsible for them, or that he did something in the past that causally contributed to them. We are saying that he is, quite literally, *performing* each of these actions: he is enormously busy (though tireless) and, unlike Superman, he can be in two places at once. Given that Otto's standing states might extend to a notebook, they can also extend to indefinitely many other external devices. Add to this the claim that Otto's actions may be the product of his standing states alone, and Otto becomes extraordinarily active.

If this result seems implausible, then perhaps we should question whether behavior that results from these extended states truly qualifies as action. We might limit *actions* in various ways: e.g., by requiring that the organic part of one's body must be involved in a genuine action, or by requiring that an agent's occurrent beliefs and desires (which, they assume, are internal to the organic body) be involved in each of her genuine actions. But these moves conflict with C&C's claim that there is nothing *special*, vis-à-vis a subject's agency, about states internal to her organic body.

This second consequence, that actions occur at a distance from the organic agent and proliferate excessively, is more threatening to C&C's conclusion than the first consequence. I observed that C&C could simply accept that extended states cannot be introspected, while maintaining that they are nevertheless mental. On that view, the distinction between what is introspectible and what is not may parallel the distinction between what is internal and what is extended. Since they claim that some non-introspectible (extended) states and processes are mental, they must use some other feature to distinguish the mental from the non-mental. And given that they stress the 'active' nature of these extended states and processes, the relevant feature might as well be this: extended states and processes qualify as mental because a piece of behavior caused by such states and processes (even one in which no occurrent states or processes play a crucial role) qualifies as a genuine, intentional *action*. So if we are hesitant to describe making the banana bread as *Otto's action*, then we have serious grounds for doubt that extended states and processes have the feature that, on C&C's view, qualifies them as truly *mental*.

Both of these worrisome consequences derive from an exceedingly liberal conception of mind. If we can restrict the mind – to that which is introspectible, or to states that causally explain bits of behavior that (unlike the robot's behavior) seem like genuine *actions* – then we can avoid both of these consequences.

But where did C&C go wrong? Which step of their argument is responsible for this problematic inflation of the mental?

3 WHERE IS THE FLAW IN C&C'S ARGUMENT?

If one or both of the consequences just outlined seem objectionable, we should find a way to block C&C's argument for the extended mind hypothesis. As it is outlined in Section 1, their argument seems valid. So we can block its conclusion only by finding fault with at least one of its premises. Two of the premises – namely, (3) and (5) – follow from other premises. To find the flaw in the argument, then, we must look to premises (1), (2), (4), and (6).

We can quickly rule out premise (6) as the source of the problem. For this premise merely stipulates that 'the world', in the conclusion, refers to the part of reality that is *beyond the skin*. We can have little quarrel with such a stipulation.

The major premises remaining are (1), (2), and (4). Let us examine each of these in turn.

Here is premise (1):

(1) "What makes some information count as a [standing] belief is the role it plays".

Premise (1) suggests that standing beliefs are defined, as such, by their role – loosely speaking, by how they *function*. It thus amounts to a kind of *functionalism* about standing beliefs. Given premise (1)'s contribution to this argument, the best way to reject it would be to show that, while playing a certain functional role may be *necessary* for being a standing belief, it is not *sufficient*: standing beliefs must not only play the relevant functional role, but must possess certain other features as well. This would mean that, even if the information in Otto's notebook played the same functional role as his standing beliefs, it might not constitute his standing beliefs because it lacked those other features. Obvious possibilities for such additional features include being constituted by a certain kind of material (e.g., the organic grey matter that makes up the human brain), or being located entirely within the skin. If we require that standing beliefs have one or both of these features, then we will reject premise (1).

C&C resist these further requirements, and many other philosophers would agree with them on this point. Limiting standing beliefs to states that are constituted by a particular kind of *material* seems unacceptably ad hoc: for instance, it would exclude the possibility that extraterrestrials with very different physical constitutions could have standing beliefs. And the claim that standing beliefs must be located within the skin is question-begging, for the significance of the 'skin' boundary is precisely what is at issue here. So we cannot assume that standing beliefs must be internal.

Of course, rather than simply assuming that standing beliefs must be internal, one might *argue* for this claim. The most straightforward way to do this is to reject premise (2), viz.:

(2) "The information in the notebook functions just like [that is, it plays the same role as] the information constituting an ordinary non-occurrent belief".

If the information in the notebook does not play the same role as ordinary internal beliefs, this may help to show that the particular 'belief' role can be played only by internal states. So let us turn to examining the prospects for premise (2).

C&C outline the functional role that both the notebook entries and ordinary (internal) standing beliefs play, with the following four conditions.[6]

(i) They are consistently available.
(ii) They are readily accessible.

(iii) They are automatically endorsed.

(iv) They are present (in the brain or notebook) because they were consciously endorsed in the past.

Now according to premise (2), the notebook entries play the same role as ordinary internal standing beliefs. There are two ways to reject this premise. We can deny that the notebook entries meet (i)–(iv); or we can claim that internal standing beliefs meet some further condition(s) not on this list, which the notebook entries do not meet.

The first option is a difficult one. C&C devised the Otto case specifically to meet (i)–(iv); and even if there might be some doubts about how well the notebook entries satisfy each of them, such questions could easily be answered by modifying the example. For instance, C&C observe that it might be awkward to carry a notebook into the shower. But we can imagine that Otto carefully laminates the notebook's pages, or that he adopts some more high-tech solution. It seems clear, in any case, that an external device *could* contain information that meets (i)–(iv).

Now consider our second option for rejecting premise (2): to claim that internal standing beliefs meet some *other* condition, not included in (i)–(iv), that is necessary for being a standing belief, and that the notebook entries do not meet. I know of two candidates for such further conditions. The first, noted by C&C, is that there is a phenomenal difference between recalling an ordinary standing belief (e.g., that dinosaurs once roamed the earth), and looking up this information in a notebook. Ordinary recall has a kind of effortless immediacy: when the issue arises, I simply find myself occurrently thinking that dinosaurs roamed the earth. But it *feels* different to consult a notebook.

C&C acknowledge that there is some phenomenological difference between these, but they characterize this difference as 'shallow', for they deny that having a particular kind of phenomenological feel is necessary for being a standing belief. You might disagree, and see the phenomenological difference as deep and important. I will remain neutral on this issue for reasons that will become clear below. But suppose, for the moment, that there is a deep, important phenomenological difference between ordinary recall and consulting a notebook. In that case, we should add a fifth condition to our characterization of the functional role standing beliefs play.

(v)   Recalling them has a particular phenomenology: roughly, the phenomenology of effortless immediacy.

Dan Weiskopf[7] suggests a second possible difference between internal standing beliefs and notebook records. Weiskopf points out that internal standing beliefs are automatically revised in light of new information. Here is a slightly modified version of an example he gives: when you learn that Sam and Max are married, you will probably come to believe that they live at the same address. If you then learn that they are no longer married, you will likely abandon the belief that they live at the same address. These further revisions in your beliefs are automatic, that is, they occur without deliberation. Weiskopf points out that Otto's notebook is not 'informationally integrated' in this way. When he writes in his notebook that Sam and Max are married, no entry reading "Sam and Max share an address" automatically appears. Otto may, of course, write this entry as well – Weiskopf's point is just that this further revision requires an extra, deliberate step. Similarly, when Otto learns that MoMA has temporarily moved to Queens, the sentence "MoMA is on 53rd St." does not instantly vanish from the notebook.

Here, then, is another condition we might add to the original four:

(vi)   They are informationally integrated.

Let us take stock. Ordinary internal standing beliefs meet conditions (v) and (vi) whereas the entries in Otto's notebook do not. Whether we should reject premise (2) for this reason depends on two questions. First, are (v) and (vi) necessary to being a standing belief? Second, granting that Otto's notebook entries do not satisfy (v) and (vi), might these conditions be satisfied by information stored in a different type of external device?

I suggest that the answer to the second question is 'yes', and that we can therefore ignore the first question. Suppose that, instead of a simple paper notebook, Otto carries an external computing device that is linked to his brain. In a lucid moment, or perhaps before he succumbs to full-blown Alzheimer's, Otto programs the device to constantly scan his thoughts and to perform as follows. When the device detects that Otto is thinking about dinosaurs, or about prehistoric times (etc.), it causes him to occurrently believe that dinosaurs roamed the earth. This process has the phenomenology of ordinary recall: the occurrent belief seems to come to him immediately and without effort. He also programs the device to be sensitive to additions or alterations of information. So when Otto learns that MoMA has moved to Queens, the device automatically adds or modifies any bits of stored information that are relevant to this new fact: e.g., it stores the information that MoMA is no longer on 53rd St. Arguably, then, the information in this external device now meets conditions (v) and (vi).

Of course, the notebook example is much closer to the kinds of external information storage mechanisms that are in common usage today. So if (v) or (vi) is required for being a standing belief – an issue on which I'll remain neutral – then C&C have shown only that minds *can* be extended, not that they are *currently* extended. (Weiskopf recognizes this point, and argues only that minds are not, in fact, extended. He allows that they could *become* extended.) Still, the mere possibility of extended minds is all that's needed for what is perhaps C&C's central contention, that "when it comes to belief, there is nothing sacred about skull and skin".

There may be further conditions that are necessary for being a standing belief, which an external device could not meet. But none comes easily to mind. Nor do I expect one to emerge: for standing beliefs do seem to be defined, as such, by their causal relations to other states and processes, including occurrent ones. And there seems no principled reason to deny that something beyond the skin could play the same type of causal role as internal standing beliefs. So I suggest that it is reasonable to accept premise (2).

This leaves us with premise (4). Premise (4) may seem the least suspect of C&C's three major premises. But I will argue that, in fact, it is the most objectionable.

4 THE NARROW MIND

Premise (4) is that Otto's standing beliefs are part of his mind. Now this may seem almost a definitional truth; after all, what is a belief except a mental state, and what is a mental state except part of a mind? But I will argue that, to avoid the consequences discussed in Section 2, we should deny that *standing* beliefs are part of the mind.

I think that C&C's examples are persuasive in illustrating the close affinity between internal standing beliefs and a variety of external states. In particular, I think that C&C make a compelling case for the following conditional.

> If standing beliefs are part of the mind, then the mind can be indefinitely extended: to notebooks, external computing devices, and even parts of others' minds.

I think that their parallel argument, regarding the affinity between processes performed by external devices and processes performed internally, also succeeds. It establishes this conditional:

> If nonconscious cognitive processes are part of the mind, then the mind can be indefinitely extended: to external computing devices and even parts of others' minds.

The consequents of both these conditionals – that the mind can extend to notebooks, external computing devices, and even parts of others' minds – have the worrisome consequences discussed in Section 2.

I suggest that we accept these conditionals, on the basis of C&C's ingenious arguments. But to avoid those worrisome consequences, we should reject their consequents and, hence, reject their antecedents. In other words, we should reject premise (4).

C&C have shown, I think, that internal standing states and nonconscious processes are essentially similar to states of notebooks and external computational processes. From the fact that the latter, external states and processes are non-introspectible, we can infer that their internal equivalents are also non-introspectible. (There is independent reason to believe that standing states and nonconscious processes are nonintrospectible.[8]) And from the fact that behavior produced by external states and processes is not truly *action* (e.g., the robot's behavior, caused by Otto's external standing states and nonconscious processes, is not Otto's action), we can infer that behavior produced by internal standing states and nonconscious processes is not truly action.

The worrisome consequences that result from C&C's conclusion do not derive from the fact that the allegedly mental states and processes are *external*. Rather, they derive from the fact that the allegedly mental states and processes are *standing* states and *nonconscious* processes. Whether the states are internal or external is then unimportant; for, I think, C&C have shown that "when it comes to belief, there is nothing sacred about skull and skin". (**p. 187.**)

The best option, then, is to reject premise (4). This means that the internal equivalents of notebook entries and external computing processes – namely, internal standing beliefs and nonconscious cognitive processes – are not, strictly speaking, part of the mind. On this view, the mind is made up entirely of *occurrent* states and *conscious* processes. These include beliefs or desires that are now being entertained, conscious thoughts, emotions, and sensations, and conscious cognitive processes.

C&C are well aware of the alternative I am suggesting. They recognize that "it may be the most consistent way to deny Otto's belief", but reject it as "extreme". (**p. 189.**)

> To consistently resist this conclusion [that Otto himself is an extended system], we would have to shrink the self into a mere bundle of occurrent states, severely threatening its deep psychological continuity. (**p. 190.**)

This is a serious worry for my position. But it is worth noting that the problem is also faced by some familiar views about the mind, including Derek Parfit's bundle theory (**Chapter 19** of this volume).

I will close by briefly sketching how a mind, understood as a series of (sets of) occurrent states, can enjoy the psychological continuity we think ourselves to enjoy. The approach uses states that are not part of the mind as the causal ground for its psychological continuity.

Let us begin with an analogy. Consider an automobile factory – call it *Factory A* – that produces several different models of cars. The cars may bear the factory's trademark, '*A*', in which case they share an internal feature that reflects their common origin. Or they may be etched with consecutive numbers (e.g., '7691', '7692', ...) so that their internal features compose a recognizable pattern, regardless of whether there are more specific features they have in common. But even if they bear no such internal marks, they still form a unified, causally salient class, viz., the class 'Products of Factory A'. The factory's causal continuity grounds the causal salience of that class, as products of the same cause.

For instance, suppose that the machine that produces disc brakes is gradually deteriorating. The deterioration leads each disc brake it produces to be a bit less round – slightly further from perfect roundness – than the last. Now while the machine itself does not belong to the class 'Products of Factory A', the cars that are part of that class are causally unified in that they are all products of a common cause. The decreasing roundness of their brakes, due to the ongoing deterioration of the machine, is one illustration of this causal unification. The deterioration merely reflects the causal unity: the cars would be causally unified, in the sense that I intend, even if the machines were always in ideal working order.

A similar picture applies to occurrent states. (For simplicity here, I'll assume materialism about standing states; the picture could be adjusted to apply to dualism about such states.) Suppose that a number of occurrent states have a shared origin. They spring from states, including standing beliefs and non-mental states, of a persisting physical organism, perhaps together with salient features of its environment. This shared origin may produce occurrent states that share internal features: e.g., one's occurrent states may share a quality of hopefulness because they spring from physically-based dispositions to be optimistic. Or they may have complex rational interrelations that depend on non-mental states: e.g., yesterday's occurrent belief 'It will rain tomorrow' may cause a standing belief to that effect, which the next day causes the occurrent belief 'it will rain today'.

But as in the factory case, it is the causal continuity of the shared origin itself that renders the states causally unified. Any shared internal features or coherent rational structure is unnecessary – for instance, it is not present in the presumably jumbled occurrent states of Alzheimer's patients like Otto. And the shared origin needn't be included in the class of occurrent states in order to ground the class's causal unity, any more than the factory needs to be included in the set of cars to ground that set's causal unity.

How much psychological continuity do we possess? Some of us are psychologically stable, consistent, and predictable. These steady types experience occurrent states that follow previous occurrent states in fairly predictable ways. (*Modulo* the continuity of external stimuli, of course.) So the claim that the mind or self is constituted by occurrent states does not raise the specter of radical discontinuity, when applied to these stable individuals.

The more problematic cases are those individuals who undergo a series of radically disparate occurrent states. Taking these unstable minds to be constituted by the series of sets of occurrent states seems to threaten psychological continuity, just as C&C allege. But I don't think that this is a problem. First, I think that it makes sense to deny that unstable characters enjoy one sort of psychological continuity, viz., the continuity involved in one's experiences and thoughts *seeming*, to one, to have a rational structure. The lack of apparent rational structure among occurrent experiences and thoughts is, after all, why dementia and Alzheimer's disease leave their victims so bewildered.

But there is another sense of 'psychological continuity' that even the least stable individuals possess. This is the continuity that is responsible for the fact that the succession of wildly varying, seemingly unrelated states is fully *explainable*. The factors that explain it are underlying physical states and processes. The point of contention between my view and C&C's concerns whether these underlying factors – which include standing states and nonconscious processes – are themselves *part of* the mind. I have argued that, in a strict, principled sense of 'mental', they are not. They are outside the realm of introspectibility; and including them within the mind will extend the range of a subject's actions to staggering proportions. There are therefore strong reasons to deny that merely standing states and nonconscious process are, strictly speaking, part of the mind.

CONCLUSION

Obviously, many questions remain. But I hope to have shown that a serious alternative to extending the mind is to reject premise (4) of C&C's argument, and to limit the mind to occurrent, conscious states and processes. In fact, I think that this fits with their claim that "when it comes to belief, there is nothing sacred about skull and skin". I fully agree with this conclusion, but I draw a different moral from it. They conclude that some external states and processes are mental; I conclude that some internal (standing) beliefs and (nonconscious) cognitive processes are non-mental.

It is surprising to think that standing beliefs and nonconscious processes lie outside the mind, even if they are inside the brain. Still, on balance, this conclusion seems less costly to intuitions and hence ultimately more credible than the claim that our mind can extend to notebooks, external computing devices, and others' minds.[9]

NOTES

1   All page numbers will refer to the reprint in this volume.
2   Strictly speaking, the argument requires only that the notebook entries at least *partially constitute* Otto's standing beliefs. For whatever partially constitutes a part of the mind is itself a part of the mind.

3 Of course, the upshot of the imagining – the visualization of the rotated shape – is conscious. But the *process* of rotating it is, at least in their example, nonconscious.

4 Elsewhere, I provide a more detailed argument to show that these wide states do not crucially contribute to action. (Gertler, "The Narrow Mind", in preparation.)

5 We can also suppose that the robot could have awakened the organism, in case of an emergency – so the organism was only partially and temporarily unreceptive to input from the robot. But this may not matter, since Otto does not consult his notebook when he is in a deep sleep either.

6 See **p. 176ff.** C&C give these conditions as a rough outline of the relevant functional role. They do not claim that they are jointly sufficient for being a standing belief, or that each is necessary. In fact, they express some doubts as to whether (iv) is necessary. These details will not affect my argument.

7 Weiskopf, "Patrolling the Mind's Boundaries". (MS, 2006)

8 To use a historical example: Descartes' meditator can introspect his occurrent beliefs that 'I doubt that I am sitting before the fire' or '2+3 = 5', but cannot introspect the causal sources of those beliefs, including standing beliefs or past cognitive processes. This is why he cannot rule out, through introspection alone, the possibility that these beliefs are caused by an evil genius, rather than by a standing belief or a past (and hence currently nonconscious) cognitive process.

9 I am indebted to the participants in the NEH Institute on Consciousness and Intentionality in Santa Cruz, where I presented an ancestor of this paper in July 2002 – especially Terry Horgan, Amy Kind, Eric Schwitzgebel, Galen Strawson, and Aaron Zimmerman. I am also deeply grateful to Dave Chalmers, for helpful discussion and for correcting several errors in that early version. Larry Shapiro provided extensive, valuable comments on this version of the paper.

Part 5

WHAT IS THE SELF?

Most of us have read or seen depictions of Multiple Personality Disorder, a bizarre condition in which a single body appears to be animated by two or more selves. It is no surprise that writers of novels and Hollywood movies (such as *Fight Club* and *The Three Faces of Eve*) have been drawn to create characters with MPD.

In MPD, experiences, intentions, and other conscious states associated with a single body lack the usual interconnections: e.g., a subject will disavow an action that her body has just performed. Since some of these disavowed actions clearly require conscious deliberation and planning, it is natural to conclude that they were performed by a different subject. If you heard your own voice reporting events that you did not recall, and witnessed your own body acting on intentions that you could not introspect, you would hesitate to identify yourself as the *subject* of those experiences or intentions.

Fictional characters with MPD are fascinating precisely because their condition seems so alien. However, the results of certain experiments suggest that the phenomenon at the core of MPD – the lack of connections among conscious states associated with a single body – may be more prevalent than ordinarily assumed. In fact, a significant lack of internal unity may be the basic human condition.

The experiments that deliver these startling results are conducted on patients who have undergone a surgical procedure known as *cerebral commissurotomy*. In this procedure, which is sometimes used to treat epilepsy, surgeons sever the corpus callosum, the thick bundle of nerve fibers that connect the two hemispheres of the brain. These two hemispheres generally divide the labor of cognition. In most subjects, the left hemisphere is principally responsible for language and logical calculations, whereas the right hemisphere is usually dominant in spatial abilities and visual imagery. Because the corpus callosum allows for direct communication between the hemispheres, severing this link has radical implications.

Surprisingly, patients who have undergone a commissurotomy appear, in ordinary conditions, to be entirely normal. Their cognitive, motor, and emotional capacities seem unaffected by the surgery. (As does their sense of humor: waking after the surgery, one patient reportedly quipped, "I have a splitting headache!") But under experimental conditions, in which the subjects are prevented from using external cues to share information between hemispheres, odd results occur.

Here is one such case, discussed by Thomas Nagel. A subject who has undergone commissurotomy is placed before a screen, and the word 'hat' is flashed on the left half of the screen. (The image remains only for a moment, so that the subject does not have time to move his eyes; such movement would allow the stimulus to be perceived in the right visual field.) Since visual stimuli from the left are processed by the right hemisphere, the patient, when asked to select a matching object from a group of

208

objects, is able to do this correctly: his left hand (which is controlled by the right hemisphere) picks out a hat. But because language is controlled by the left hemisphere, the patient will fail to verbally report seeing the word 'hat'. In fact, he will insist that he saw nothing at all.

In what is perhaps a more straightforward case, the left and right hands of a monkey whose corpus callosum has been severed will wage a 'tug of war', struggling for control of a peanut.

How are we to explain such cases? Certainly, these are not classic cases of MPD. For split-brain subjects function normally in ordinary circumstances, and do not exhibit the sorts of Jekyll-and-Hyde conflicts between two different *kinds* of personality that typify MPD. Still, the fact that the split-brain subject denies having seen anything, and therefore cannot explain why he reached for a hat, does strain ordinary assumptions about subjects. So is there a single subject in the split-brain case, or are there (at least) two subjects?

An answer to this question requires a better understanding of how we conceive the subject. What renders two distinct states (such as two experiences, or an experience and an intention) the states of a *single* subject? That is, what – if anything – *unifies* normal subjects? The articles in this section of the book address two aspects of this question. The first aspect concerns what unifies a subject at a time – e.g., what makes it the case that, when your left hand reaches for a hat, and you say "I saw the word 'hat'", these are actions performed by a single subject. The second aspect concerns what it is, if anything, that unifies a subject *across* time. What makes it the case that the person who is reading this page right now is the same person as someone who drank a cup of coffee this morning (say)?

Nagel's article, which begins the section, draws some striking conclusions from the split-brain cases. He argues that, in a very real sense, there is no way to answer the question "How many persons are present in the split-brain?" The idea isn't that we can never be sure whether there is one person or two. Rather, it is that our ordinary conception of subjects, according to which subjects are easily countable, is inapplicable to the split-brain cases. In this sense, *there is no fact of the matter* as to how many subjects are present in these cases.

But Nagel's most extraordinary conclusion involves normal subjects. He contends that our uncertainty about the split-brain cases reveals the flaws in our ordinary conception of the subject. On that conception, subjects are *perfectly unified*, in that their states are completely integrated with each other. But this conception is naïve. States one is inclined to accept as one's own may be integrated with other such states in greater or lesser degrees; and these relations may fluctuate as other conditions vary. "[O]ur own unity may be nothing absolute, but merely another case of integration, more or less effective, in the control system of a complex organism." Just as there is no fact of the matter as to how many subjects are present in the split-brain cases, there is no fact of the matter as to how many subjects are present in a *normal* human body. For this reason, Nagel concludes that "it is possible that the ordinary, simple idea of a single person will come to seem quaint one day".

Derek Parfit expands on Nagel's arguments identifying an additional problem with the traditional notion of the self. He calls this traditional notion 'the Ego Theory', for it sees the self as a well-defined *ego* that underlies mental states. On the Ego Theory, it is assumed that every mental state fundamentally belongs to a particular self. Thus, there is no problem about what is required for two mental states to qualify as states of a single self: it is simply a brute fact that they do (or do not). Parfit believes that while split-brain cases prompt us to see the flaws in the Ego Theory, these flaws go far beyond such empirical oddities. For they show that our concept of the self is misguided; this is why the question "Do states A and B belong to the same subject?" has no determinate answer. A and B are simply integrated to a certain degree, and to treat that degree of integration as sufficient for being states of a single subject is simply to adopt a particular convention or way of speaking, one that does not reflect a deep truth about the nature of subjects. In its focus on the idea that integration is a matter of degree, Parfit's view is similar, in broad outline, with Nagel's.

But Parfit contributes a further dimension to this issue: while Nagel is centrally concerned with the unity of the self at a time, Parfit argues that the same point applies to the unity of the self across time. We constantly shed cells and generate new ones; none of your current cells were part of your body seven years ago. Parfit uses the case of teletransportation to show that we seem able to imagine surviving non-gradual cell replacement as well. He concludes that the question 'Am I the same person who existed yesterday?' has no determinate answer; today's states merely bear certain relations (causal relations, memory links, etc.) with yesterday's mental states, and with tomorrow's. It is purely a matter of convention that we consider some of those relations as sufficient for those states being states of a single subject. But there is nothing more to the notion of a subject than this convention: there is no genuine *self* that underlies these various states, and ties them together.

To convey this idea, Parfit uses a quotation attributed to Buddha: " ... actions do exist, and also their consequences, but the person that acts does not." Parfit's view has surprising implications: e.g., saving for one's future is essentially contributing to charity, since one is not, strictly speaking, identical with anyone who exists in the future.

Daniel Dennett also claims that the self is indeterminate, though he focuses on the *nature* of the self rather than on its identity conditions. Dennett contends that the self is a fictional character. Each of us creates a personal narrative of our lives; this narrative changes with time, as we write and rewrite our own histories in the light of new experiences. The upshot is an autobiography that *creates* the self, rather than reflecting an independently existing self. While Parfit highlights the significance of conventional decisions in deciding the extent of the self, Dennett stresses the importance of individual decisions in deciding the nature of one's self.

In a way, Dennett's view may seem to mitigate the startling consequences of Parfit's position. For if each of us constructed a history that we called our own, this narrative process would provide an answer to questions like "Do states A and B belong to a single subject?" and "Am I the same person as someone who existed yesterday?" Crucially, however, we would not thereby *discover* the answers to these questions; rather, in creating these narrative accounts, we would be *inventing* those answers. After all, for Dennett, the self is a purely abstract, *fictional* object.

Does seeing the self as a fictional object – one that existed in the past and will continue to exist into the future – lessen the disquieting aspects of Parfit's position? It is not so clear that it does. For the idea that our pasts are linked with our presents only by a decision to *treat* them as linked appears deeply unsettling.

Galen Strawson disputes Dennett's claim that narrative is crucially important to one's self-conception. According to Strawson, the tendency to regard one's life as a cohesive, narrative story, centering on a single self, is neither universal nor beneficial. Strawson agrees that some people, whom he dubs 'Narratives', do see their lives in these terms, but he denies that Narratives are especially ethical or well balanced.

Following Parfit, Strawson believes that we should distinguish between a human being (an organism) and a *self*. This distinction shapes the self-conception of some people, who Strawson calls 'Episodics': Episodics do not conceive of the *self* as something that existed years ago, and will exist years into the future. Narratives tend, by contrast, to be non-Episodics (or 'Diachronics').

Strawson is concerned to defend those who, like him, are Episodic and non-Narrative. For instance, he argues that a tendency to live in the present does not diminish one's capacity to be a loyal friend, since past experiences may build loyalty between friends even if neither friend dwells on those experiences, or conceives of the friendship as a product of them. More generally, the power of past events to mold one's character does not depend on one's reflecting on those past events or grasping their effects.

Strawson is also suspicious of the alleged benefits of being Narrative and Diachronic. He observes that memories of past events tend to distort those events, and hence the narratives one constructs from memories commonly misrepresent the facts. Strawson suggests that the tendency towards misrepresentation in personal narratives will cast doubt on the ethical benefits of constructing such narratives. (Of course, if one is truly Episodic, misrepresentations of the past will have little effect on one's self-conception.)

The articles in this section address, in various ways, what is commonly referred to as 'the problem of the self'. To deny that there is a (determinate) self, as several of the authors here do, is not to sidestep this problem, but rather to give a particular answer to it. Eric Olson argues that philosophers should put aside questions about what constitutes selfhood, and abandon the term 'self'. For, he claims, there is no univocal, shared notion of 'self' that competing accounts of the self aim to capture. There are no paradigm cases of a self, cases which all theorists will agree are *selves*; nor are there widely accepted characteristic features of selves. This means that philosophical questions about the self – such as "Are states A and B states of a single self?" and "Does commissurotomy create a self?" – are not well-defined.

In place of questions about the self, Olson suggests that we focus on questions about persons, human organisms, moral subjects, etc. This will clear up confusion in philosophical debates, and will help us to avoid familiar mistakes. Olson believes that one such mistake is to distinguish between a human being (or 'human animal') and a self, as many of the authors represented in this section do. "One of the unfortunate consequences of using the word 'self' in doing philosophy is that it encourages us to look for entities [namely, *selves*] that we have no other reason to believe in."

QUESTIONS TO THINK ABOUT

1. Ordinarily we say that the self *has* mental states – e.g., she has a belief, he has an experience, etc. But several of the authors in this section reject this conception, suggesting instead that the self *is*, at most, simply a collection of mental states. How are we to choose between these different conceptions of the self? If the self is simply a collection of states, what does it mean to say that someone *has* a particular mental state?
2. Nagel and Parfit use evidence from split-brain cases to illuminate the nature of the self. One might object that extrapolating from abnormal cases to normal cases is illegitimate: according to this objection, even if the number of selves in a split-brain case is indeterminate, the number of selves in normal cases may nonetheless be fully determinate. Does this objection ultimately succeed? Why or why not?
3. Are you yourself a Narrative? If so, what would be lost if you stopped constructing personal narratives? If not, do you think you would gain something by becoming a Narrative? Might you lose something? What, in particular, would be gained or lost?
4. What is at stake in the debate over selves? Suppose that, following Olson, you deny that there are selves. What, if anything, have you lost? Can you retain a sense of 'who you are' (i.e., your 'sense of self')?

FURTHER READING

Bayne, T. and Chalmers, D. "What is the Unity of Consciousness?", *The Unity of Consciousness: Binding, Integration and Dissociation*, ed. Axel Cleeremans. Oxford: Oxford University Press, 2003.

Dainton, B. *Stream of Consciousness: Unity and Continuity in Conscious Experience*. London: Routledge, 2000.

Gallagher, S. and Shear, J. (eds.) *Models of the Self*. Exeter: Imprint Academic, 1999.

Kircher, T. and David, A. eds. *The Self in Neuroscience and Psychiatry*. Cambridge: Cambridge University Press, 2003.

Velleman, D. "Self to Self" and "The Self as Narrator", Chapters 8 and 9 of his *Self to Self: Selected Essays* Cambridge: Cambridge University Press, 2006.

Williams, B. *Problems of the Self*. Cambridge: Cambridge University Press, 1973.

18

BRAIN BISECTION AND THE UNITY OF CONSCIOUSNESS

Thomas Nagel

I

There has been considerable optimism recently, among philosophers and neuroscientists, concerning the prospect for major discoveries about the neurophysiological basis of mind. The support for this optimism has been extremely abstract and general. I wish to present some grounds for pessimism. That type of self-understanding may encounter limits which have not been generally foreseen: the personal, mentalist idea of human beings may resist the sort of coordination with an understanding of humans as physical systems, that would be necessary to yield anything describable as an understanding of the physical basis of mind. I shall not consider what alternatives will be open to us if we should encounter such limits. I shall try to present grounds for believing that the limits may exist – grounds derived from extensive data now available about the interaction between the two halves of the cerebral cortex, and about what happens when they are disconnected. The feature of the mentalist conception of persons which may be recalcitrant to integration with these data is not a trivial or peripheral one, that might easily be abandoned. It is the idea of a *single* person, a single subject of experience and action, that is in difficulties. The difficulties may be surmountable in ways I have not foreseen. On the other hand, this may be only the first of many dead ends that will emerge as we seek a physiological understanding of the mind.

To seek the physical basis or realization of features of the phenomenal world is in many areas a profitable first line of inquiry, and it is the line encouraged, for the case of mental phenomena, by those who look forward to some variety of empirical reduction of mind to brain, through an identity theory, a functionalist theory, or some other device. When physical reductionism is attempted for a phenomenal feature of the external world, the results are sometimes very successful, and can be pushed to deeper and deeper levels. If, on the other hand, they are not entirely successful, and certain features of the phenomenal picture remain unexplained by a physical reduction, then we can set those features aside as *purely* phenomenal, and postpone our understanding of them to the time when our knowledge of the physical basis of mind and perception will have advanced sufficiently to supply it. (An example of this might be the moon illusion, or other sensory illusions which have no discoverable basis in the objects perceived.)

However, if we encounter the same kind of difficulty in exploring the physical basis of the phenomena of the mind itself, we cannot adopt the same line of retreat. That is, if a phenomenal feature of mind is left unaccounted for by the physical theory, we cannot postpone the understanding of it to the time when we study the mind itself – for that is exactly what we are supposed to be doing. To defer to an understanding of the basis of mind which lies beyond the study of the physical realization of certain aspects of it is to admit the irreducibility of the mental to the physical. A clearcut version of this admission would be some kind of dualism. But if one is reluctant to take such a route, then it is not clear what one should do about central features of the mentalistic idea of persons which resist assimilation to an understanding of human beings as physical system. It may be true of some of these features that we can neither find an objective basis for them, nor give them up. It may be impossible for us to abandon certain ways of conceiving and representing ourselves, no matter how little support they get from scientific research. This, I suspect, is true of the idea of the unity of a person: an idea whose validity may be called into question with the help of recent discoveries about the functional duality of the cerebral cortex. It will be useful to present those results here in outline.

II

The higher connections between the two cerebral hemispheres have been severed in men, monkeys, and cats, and the results have led some investigators to speak of the creation of two separate centers of consciousness in a single body. The facts are as follows.[1]

By and large, the left cerebral hemisphere is associated with the right side of the body and the right hemisphere with the left side. Tactual stimuli from one side are transmitted to the opposite hemisphere – with the exception of the head and neck, which are connected to both sides. In addition, the left half of each retina, i.e. that which scans the right half of the visual field, sends impulses to the left hemisphere, and impulses from the left half of the visual field are transmitted by the right half of each retina to the right hemisphere. Auditory impulses from each ear are to some degree transmitted to both hemispheres. Smells, on the other hand, are transmitted ipsilaterally: the left nostril transmits to the left hemisphere and the right nostril to the right. Finally, the left hemisphere usually controls the production of speech.

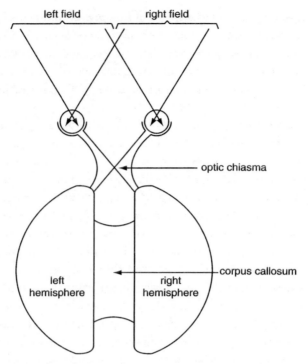

Figure 18.1 A very schematic top view of the eyes and cerebral cortex.

Both hemispheres are linked to the spinal column and peripheral nerves through a common brain stem, but they also communicate directly with one another, by a large transverse band of nerve fibres called the corpus callosum, plus some smaller pathways. These direct cerebral commissures play an essential role in the ordinary integration of function between the hemisphere of normal persons. It is one of the striking features of the subject that this fact remained unknown, at least in the English-speaking world, until the late 1950s, even though a number of patients had had their cerebral commissures surgically severed in operations for the treatment of epilepsy a decade earlier. No significant behavioral or mental effects on these patients could be observed, and it was conjectured that the corpus callosum had no function whatever, except perhaps to keep the hemispheres from sagging.

Then R. E. Myers and R. W. Sperry introduced a technique for dealing with the two hemispheres separately.[2] They sectioned the optic chiasma of cats, so that each eye sent direct information (information about the opposite half of the visual field) only to one side of the brain. It was then possible to train the cats in simple tasks using one eye, and to see what happened when one made them use the other eye instead. In cats whose callosum was intact, there was very good transfer of learning. But in some cats, they severed the corpus callosum as well as the optic chiasma; and in these cases nothing was transmitted from one side to the other. In fact the two severed sides could be taught conflicting discriminations simultaneously, by giving the two eyes opposite stimuli during a single course of reinforcement. Nevertheless this capacity for independent function did not result in serious deficits of behavior. Unless inputs to the two hemispheres were artificially segregated, the animal seemed normal; (though if a split-brain monkey gets hold of a peanut with both hands, the result is sometimes a tug of war.)

Instead of summarizing all the data, I shall concentrate on the human cases, a reconsideration of which was prompted by the findings with cats and monkeys.[3] In the brain-splitting operation for epilepsy, the optic chiasma is left intact, so one cannot get at the two hemispheres separately just through the two eyes. The solution to the problem of controlling visual input is to flash signals on a screen, on one or other side of the midpoint of the patient's gaze, long enough to be perceived but not long enough to permit an eye movement which would bring the signal to the opposite half visual field and hence to the opposite side of the brain. This is known as tachistoscopic stimulation. Tactile inputs through the hands are for the most part very efficiently segregated, and so are smells through the two nostrils. Some success has even been achieved recently in segregating auditory input, since each ear seems to signal more powerfully to the contralateral than to the ipsilateral hemisphere. As for output, the clearest distinction is provided by speech, which is exclusively the product of the left hemisphere.[4] Writing is a less-clear case: it can occasionally be produced in rudimentary form by the right hemisphere, using the left hand. In general, motor control is contralateral, i.e. by the opposite hemisphere, but a certain amount of ipsilateral control sometimes occurs, particularly on the part of the left hemisphere.

The results are as follows. What is flashed to the right half of the visual field, or felt unseen by the right hand, can be reported verbally. What is flashed to the left half field or felt by the left hand cannot be reported, though if the word 'hat' is flashed on the left, the left hand will retrieve a hat from a group of concealed objects if the person is told to pick out what he has seen. At the same time he will insist verbally that he saw nothing. Or, if two different words are flashed to the two half fields (e.g. 'pencil' and 'toothbrush') and the individual is told to retrieve the corresponding object from beneath a screen, with both hands, then the hands will search the collection of objects independently, the right hand picking up the pencil and discarding it while the left hand searches for it, and the left hand similarly rejecting the toothbrush which the right hand lights upon with satisfaction.

If a concealed object is placed in the left hand and the person is asked to guess what it is, wrong guesses will elicit an annoyed frown, since the right hemisphere, which receives the tactile information, also hears the answers. If the speaking hemisphere should guess correctly, the result is a smile. A smell fed to the right nostril (which stimulates the right hemisphere) will elicit a verbal denial that the subject smells anything, but if asked to point with the left hand at a corresponding object he will succeed in picking out e.g. a clove of garlic, protesting all the while that he smells absolutely nothing, so how can he possibly point to what he smells. If the smell is an unpleasant one like that of rotten eggs, these denials will be accompanied by wrinklings of the nose and mouth, and guttural exclamations of disgust.[5]

One particularly poignant example of conflict between the hemispheres is as follows. A pipe is placed out of sight in the patient's left hand, and he is then asked to write with his left hand what he was holding. Very laboriously and heavily, the left hand writes the letters P and I. Then suddenly the writing speeds up and becomes lighter, the I is converted to an E, and the word is completed as PENCIL. Evidently the left hemisphere has made a guess based on the appearance of the first two letters, and has interfered, with ipsilateral control. But then the right hemisphere takes over control of the hand again, heavily crosses out the letters ENCIL, and draws a crude picture of a pipe.[6]

There are many more data. The split-brain patient cannot tell whether shapes flashed to the two half visual fields or held out of sight in the two hands are the same or different – even if he is asked to indicate the answer by nodding or shaking his head (responses available to both hemispheres). The subject cannot distinguish a continuous from a discontinuous line flashed across both halves of the visual field, if the break comes in the middle. Nor can he tell whether two lines meet at an angle, if the joint is in the middle. Nor can he tell whether two spots in opposite half-fields are the same or different in color – though he can do all these things if the images to be compared fall within a single half field. On the whole the right hemisphere does better at spatial relations tests, but is almost incapable of calculation. It appears susceptible to emotion, however. For example, if a photograph of a naked woman is flashed to the left half field of a male patient, he will grin broadly and perhaps blush, without being able to say what has pleased him, though he may say "Wow, that's quite a machine you've got there".

All this is combined with what appears to be complete normalcy in ordinary activities, when no segregation of input to the two hemispheres has been artificially created. Both sides fall asleep and wake up at the same time. The patients can play the piano, button their shirts, swim, and perform well in other activities requiring bilateral coordination. Moreover they do not report any sensation of division or reduction of the visual field. The most notable deviation in ordinary behavior was in a patient whose left hand appeared to be somewhat hostile to the patient's wife. But by and large the hemispheres cooperate admirably, and it requires subtle experimental techniques to get them to operate separately. If one is not careful, they will give each other peripheral cues, transmitting information by audible, visible, or otherwise sensorily perceptible signals which compensate for the lack of a direct commissural link. (One form of communication is particularly difficult to prevent, because it is so direct: both hemispheres can move the neck and facial muscles, and both can feel them move; so a response produced in the face or head by the right hemisphere can be detected by the left, and there is some evidence that they send signals to one another via this medium.)[7]

III

What one naturally wants to know about these patients is how many minds they have. This immediately raises questions about the sense in which an ordinary person can be said to have one mind, and what the conditions are under which diverse experiences and activities can be ascribed to the same mind. We must have some idea what an ordinary person is one of in order to understand what we want to know whether there is *one or two* of, when we try to describe these extraordinary patients.

However, instead of beginning with an analysis of the unity of the mind, I am going to proceed by attempting to apply the ordinary, unanalyzed conception directly in the interpretation of these data, asking whether the patients have one mind, or two, or some more exotic configuration. My conclusion will be that the ordinary conception of a single, countable mind cannot be applied to them at all, and that there is no number of such minds that they possess, though they certainly engage in mental activity. A clearer understanding of the idea of an individual mind should emerge in the course of this discussion but the difficulties which stand in the way of its application to the split-brain cases will provide ground for more general doubts. The concept may not be applicable to ordinary human beings either, for it embodies too simple a conception of the way in which human beings function.

Nevertheless I shall employ the notion of an individual mind in discussing the cases initially, for I wish to consider systematically how they might be understood in terms of countable minds, and to argue that they cannot be. After having done this, I shall turn to ordinary people like you and me.

There appear to be five interpretations of the experimental data which utilize the concept of an individual mind.

(1) The patients have one fairly normal mind associated with the left hemisphere, and the responses emanating from the nonverbal right hemisphere are the responses of an automaton, and are not produced by conscious mental processes.
(2) The patients have only one mind, associated with the left hemisphere, but there also occur (associated with the right hemisphere) isolated conscious mental phenomena, not integrated into a mind at all, though they can perhaps be ascribed to the organism.
(3) The patients have two minds, one which can talk and one which can't.

219

(4) They have one mind, whose contents derive from both hemispheres and are rather peculiar and dissociated.

(5) They have one normal mind most of the time, while the hemispheres are functioning in parallel, but two minds are elicited by the experimental situations which yield the interesting results. (Perhaps the single mind splits in two and reconvenes after the experiment is over.)

I shall argue that each of these interpretations is unacceptable for one reason or another.

IV

Let me first discuss hypotheses (1) and (2), which have in common the refusal to ascribe the activities of the right hemisphere to a mind, and then go on to treat hypotheses (3), (4), and (5), all of which associate a mind with the activities of the right hemisphere, though they differ on what mind it is.

The only support for hypothesis (1), which refuses to ascribe consciousness to the activities of the right hemisphere at all, is the fact that the subject consistently denies awareness of the activities of that hemisphere. But to take this as proof that the activities of the right hemisphere are unconscious is to beg the question, since the capacity to give testimony is the exclusive ability of the left hemisphere, and of course the left hemisphere is not conscious of what is going on in the right. If on the other hand we consider the manifestations of the right hemisphere itself, there seems no reason in principle to regard verbalizability as a *necessary* condition of consciousness. There may be other grounds for the ascription of conscious mental states that are sufficient even without verbalization. And in fact, what the right hemisphere can do on its own is too elaborate, too intentionally directed and too psychologically intelligible to be regarded merely as a collection of unconscious automatic responses.

The right hemisphere is not very intelligent and it cannot talk; but it is able to respond to complex visual and auditory stimuli, including language, and it can control the performance of discriminatory and manipulative tasks requiring close attention – such as the spelling out of simple words with plastic letters. It can integrate auditory, visual, and tactile stimuli in order to follow the experimenter's instructions, and it can take certain aptitude tests. There is no doubt that if a person were deprived of his left hemisphere entirely, so that the only capacities remaining to him were those of the right, we should not on that account say that he had been converted into an automaton. Though speechless, he would remain conscious and active, with a diminished visual field and partial paralysis on the right side from which he would eventually recover to some extent. In view of this, it would seem arbitrary to deny that the activities of the right hemisphere are conscious, just because they occur side by side with those of the left hemisphere, about whose consciousness there is no question.

I do not wish to claim that the line between conscious and unconscious mental activity is a sharp one. It is even possible that the distinction is partly relative, in the sense that a given item of mental activity may be assignable to consciousness or not, depending on what other mental activities of the same person are going on at the same time, and whether it is connected with them in a suitable way. Even if this is true, however, the activities of the right hemisphere in split-brain patients do not fall into the category of events whose inclusion in consciousness depends on what else is going on in the patient's mind. Their determinants include a full range of psychological factors, and they demand alertness. It is clear that attention, even concentration is demanded for the tasks of the concealed left hand and tachistoscopically stimulated left visual field. The subjects do not take their experimental tests in a dreamy fashion: they are obviously in contact with reality. The left hemisphere occasionally complains about being asked to perform tasks which the right hemisphere can perform, because it does not know what is going on when the right hemisphere controls the response. But the right hemisphere displays enough awareness of what it is doing to justify the attribution of conscious control in the absence of verbal testimony. If the patients did not deny any awareness of those activities, no doubts about their consciousness would arise at all.

The considerations that make the first hypothesis untenable also serve to refute hypothesis (2), which suggests that the activities of the right hemisphere are conscious without belonging to a mind at all. There may be problems about the intelligibility of this proposal, but we need not consider them here, because it is rendered implausible by the high degree of organization and intermodal coherence of the right hemisphere's mental activities. They are not free-floating, and they are not organized in a fragmentary way. The right hemisphere follows instructions, integrates tactile, auditory and visual stimuli, and does most of the things a good mind should do. The data present us not merely with slivers of purposive behavior, but with a system capable of learning, reacting emotionally, following instructions, and carrying out tasks which require the integration of diverse psychological determinants. It seems clear that the right hemisphere's activities are not unconscious, and that they belong to something having a characteristically mental structure: a subject of experience and action.

V

Let me now turn to the three hypotheses according to which the conscious mental activities of the right hemisphere are ascribed to a mind. They have to be considered together, because the fundamental difficulty about each of them lies in the impossibility of deciding among them. The question, then, is whether the patients have two minds, one mind, or a mind that occasionally splits in two.

There is much to recommend the view that they have two minds, i.e. that the activities of the right hemisphere belong to a mind of their own.[8] Each side of the brain seems to produce its own perceptions, beliefs, and actions, which are connected with one another in the usual way, but not to those of the opposite side. The two halves of the cortex share a common body, which they control through a common midbrain and spinal cord. But their higher functions are independent not only physically but psychologically. Functions of the right hemisphere are inaccessible not only to speech but to any direct combination with corresponding functions of the left hemisphere – i.e. with functions of a type that the right hemisphere finds easy on its home ground, like shape or color discrimination.

One piece of testimony by the patients' left hemispheres may appear to argue against two minds. They report no diminution of the visual field, and little absence of sensation on the left side. Sperry dismisses this evidence on the ground that it is comparable to the testimony of victims of scotoma (partial destruction of the retina), that they notice no gaps in their visual field – although these gaps can be discovered by others observing their perceptual deficiences. But we need not assume that an elaborate confabulatory mechanism is at work in the left hemisphere to account for such testimony. It is perfectly possible that although there are two minds, the mind associated with each hemisphere receives, through the common brain stem, a certain amount of crude ipsilateral stimulation, so that the speaking mind has a rudimentary and undifferentiated appendage to the left side of its visual field, and vice versa for the right hemisphere.[9]

The real difficulties for the two-minds hypothesis coincide with the reasons for thinking we are dealing with one mind – namely the highly integrated character of the patients' relations to the world in ordinary circumstances. When they are not in the experimental situation, their startling behavioral dissociation disappears, and they function normally. There is little doubt that information from the two sides of their brains can be pooled to yield integrated behavioral control. And although this is not accomplished by the usual methods, it is not clear that this settles the question against assigning the integrative functions to a single mind. After all, if the patient is permitted to touch things with both hands and smell them with both nostrils, he arrives at a unified idea of what is going on around him and what he is doing, without revealing any left-right inconsistencies in his behavior or attitudes. It seems strange to suggest that we are not in a position to ascribe all those experiences to the same person, just because of some peculiarities about how the integration is achieved. The people who *know* these patients find it natural to relate to them as single individuals.

Nevertheless, if we ascribe the integration to a single mind, we must also ascribe the experimentally evoked dissociation to that mind, and that is not easy. The experimental situation reveals a variety of dissociation or conflict that is unusual not only because of the simplicity of its anatomical basis, but because such a wide *range* of functions is split into two noncommunicating branches. It is not as though two conflicting volitional centers shared a common perceptual and reasoning apparatus. The split is much deeper than that. The one-mind hypothesis must therefore assert that the contents of the individual's single consciousness are produced by two independent control systems in the two hemispheres, each having a fairly complete mental structure. If this dual control were accomplished during experimental situations by temporal alternation, it would be intelligible, though mysterious. But that is not the hypothesis, and the hypothesis as it stands does not supply us with understanding. For in these patients there appear to be things happening *simultaneously* which cannot fit into a single mind: simultaneous attention to two incompatible tasks, for example, without interaction between the purposes of the left and right hands.

This makes it difficult to conceive what it is like to *be* one of these people. Lack of interaction at the level of a preconscious control system would be comprehensible. But lack of interaction in the domain of visual experience and conscious intention threatens assumptions about the unity of consciousness which are basic to our understanding of another individual as a person. These assumptions are associated with our conception of ourselves, which to a considerable extent constrains our understanding of others. And it is just these assumptions, I believe, that make it impossible to arrive at an interpretation of the cases under discussion in terms of a countable number of minds.

Roughly, we assume that a single mind has sufficiently immediate access to its conscious states so that, for elements of experience or other mental events occurring simultaneously or in close temporal proximity, the mind which is their subject can also experience the simpler *relations* between them if it attends to the matter. Thus, we assume that when a single person has two visual impressions, he can usually also experience the sameness or difference of their coloration, shape, size, the relation of their position and movement within his visual field, and so forth. The same can be said of cross-modal connections. The experiences of a single person are thought to take place in an *experientially* connected domain, so that the relations among experiences can be substantially captured in experiences of those relations.[10]

Split-brain patients fail dramatically to conform to these assumptions in experimental situations, and they fail over the simplest matters. Moreover the dissociation holds between two classes of conscious states each characterized by significant *internal* coherence: normal assumptions about the unity of consciousness hold intrahemispherically, although the requisite comparisons cannot be made across the interhemispheric gap.

These considerations lead us back to the hypothesis that the patients have two minds each. It at least has the advantage of enabling us to understand what it is like to *be* these individuals, so long as we do not try to imagine what it is like to be both of them at the same time. Yet the way to a comfortable acceptance of this conclusion is blocked by the compelling behavioral integration which the patients display in ordinary life, in comparison to which the dissociated symptoms evoked by the experimental situation seem peripheral and atypical. We are faced with diametrically conflicting bodies of evidence, in a case which does not admit of arbitrary decision. There is a powerful inclination to feel that there must be *some* whole number of minds in those heads, but the data prevent us from deciding how many.

This dilemma makes hypothesis (5) initially attractive, especially since the data which yield the conflict are to some extent gathered at different times. But the suggestion that a second mind is brought into existence only during experimental situations loses plausibility on reflection. First, it is entirely ad hoc: it proposes to explain one change in terms of another without suggesting any explanation of the second. There is nothing about the experimental situation that might be expected to produce a fundamental internal change in the patient. In fact it produces no anatomical changes and merely elicits a noteworthy set of symptoms. So unusual an event as a mind's popping in and out of existence would have to be explained by something more than its explanatory convenience.

But secondly, the behavioral evidence would not even be explained by this hypothesis, simply because the patients' integrated responses and their dissociated responses are not clearly separated in time. During the time of the experiments the patient is functioning largely as if he were a single individual: in his posture, in following instructions about where to focus his eyes, in the whole range of trivial behavioral control involved in situating himself in relation to the experimenter and the experimental apparatus. The two halves of his brain cooperate completely except in regard to those very special inputs that reach them separately and differently. For these reasons hypothesis (5) does not seem to be a real option; if two minds are operating in the experimental situation, they must be operating largely in harmony although partly at odds. And if there are two minds then, why can there not be two minds operating essentially in parallel the rest of the time?

Nevertheless the psychological integration displayed by the patients in ordinary life is so complete that I do not believe it is possible to accept that conclusion, nor any conclusion involving the ascription to them of a whole number of minds. These cases fall midway between ordinary persons with intact brains (between whose cerebral hemispheres there is also cooperation, though it works largely via the corpus callosum), and pairs of individuals engaged in a performance requiring exact behavioral coordination, like using a two-handed saw, or playing a duet. In the latter type of case we have two minds which communicate by subtle peripheral cues; in the former we have a single mind. Nothing taken from either of those cases can compel us to assimilate the split-brain patient to one or the other of them. If we decided that they definitely had two minds, then it would be problematical why we didn't conclude on anatomical grounds that everyone has two minds, but that we don't notice it except in these odd cases because most pairs of minds in a single body run in perfect parallel due to the direct communication between the hemispheres which provide their anatomical bases. The two minds each of us has running in harness would be much the same except that one could talk and the other couldn't. But it is clear that this line of argument will get us nowhere. For if the idea of a single mind applies to anyone it applies to ordinary individuals with intact brains, and if it does not apply to them it ought to be scrapped, in which case there is no point in asking whether those with split brains have one mind or two.[11]

VI

If I am right, and there is no whole number of individual minds that these patients can be said to have, then the attribution of conscious, significant mental activity does not require the existence of a single mental subject. This is extremely puzzling in itself, for it runs counter to our need to construe the mental states we ascribe to others on the model of our own. Something in the ordinary conception of a person, or in the ordinary conception of experience, leads to the demand for an account of these cases which the same conception makes it impossible to provide. This may seem a problem not worth worrying about very much. It is not so surprising that, having begun with a phenomenon which is radically different from anything else previously known, we should come to the conclusion that it cannot be adequately described in ordinary terms. However, I believe that consideration of these very unusual cases should cause us to be skeptical about the concept of a single subject of consciousness as it applies to ourselves.

The fundamental problem in trying to understand these cases in mentalistic terms is that we take ourselves as paradigms of psychological unity, and are then unable to project ourselves into their mental lives, either once or twice. But in thus using ourselves as the touchstone of whether another organism can be said to house an individual subject of experience or not, we are subtly ignoring the possibility that our own unity may be nothing absolute, but merely another case of integration, more or less effective, in the control system of a complex organism. This system speaks in the first person singular through our mouths, and that makes it understandable that we should think of its unity as in some sense numerically absolute, rather than relative and a function of the integration of its contents.

225

But this is quite genuinely an illusion. The illusion consists in projecting inward to the center of the mind the very subject whose unity we are trying to explain: the individual person with all his complexities. The ultimate account of the unity of what we call a single mind consists of an enumeration of the types of functional integration that typify it. We know that these can be eroded in different ways, and to different degrees. The belief that even in their complete version they can be explained by the presence of a numerically single subject is an illusion. Either this subject contains the mental life, in which case it is complex and its unity must be accounted for in terms of the unified operation of its components and functions, or else it is an extensionless point, in which case it explains nothing.

An intact brain contains two cerebral hemispheres each of which possesses perceptual, memory, and control systems adequate to run the body without the assistance of the other. They cooperate in directing it with the aid of a constant two-way internal communication system. Memories, perceptions, desires and so forth therefore have duplicate physical bases on both sides of the brain, not just on account of similarities of initial input, but because of subsequent exchange. The cooperation of the undetached hemispheres in controlling the body is more efficient and direct than the cooperation of a pair of detached hemispheres, but it is cooperation nonetheless. Even if we analyze the idea of unity in terms of functional integration, therefore, the unity of our own consciousness may be less clear than we had supposed. The natural conception of a single person controlled by a mind possessing a single visual field, individual faculties for each of the other senses, unitary systems of memory, desire, belief, and so forth, may come into conflict with the physiological facts when it is applied to ourselves.

The concept of a person might possibly survive an application to cases which require us to speak of two or more persons in one body, but it seems strongly committed to some form of whole number countability. Since even this seems open to doubt, it is possible that the ordinary, simple idea of a single person will come to seem quaint some day, when the complexities of the human control system become clearer and we become less certain that there is anything very important that we are *one* of. But it is also possible that we shall be unable to abandon the idea no matter what we discover.[12]

NOTES

1 The literature on split brains is sizeable. An excellent recent survey is Michael S. Gazzaniga, *The Bisected Brain*, New York, Appleton-Century-Crofts, 1970. Its nine-page list of references is not intended to be a complete bibliography of the subject, however, Gazzaniga has also written a brief popular exposition: 'The Split Brain in Man', *Scientific*

American 217 (1967), p. 24. The best general treatment for philosophical purposes is to be found in several papers by R. W. Sperry, the leading investigator in the field: 'The Great Cerebral Commissure', *Scientific American* 210 (1964), p. 42; 'Brain Bisection and Mechanisms of Consciousness' in *Brain and Conscious Experience*, ed. by Eccles, J. C., Berlin, Springer-Verlag, 1966; 'Mental Unity Following Surgical Disconnections of the Cerebral Hemispheres', *The Harvey Lectures*, Series 62, New York, Academic Press, 1968, p. 293; 'Hemisphere Deconnection and Unity in Conscious Awareness', *American Psychologist* 23 (1968), p. 723. Several interesting papers are to be found in *Functions of the Corpus Callosum: Ciba Foundation Study Group No. 20*, ed. by G. Ettlinger, London, J. and A. Churchill, 1965.

2   Myers and Sperry, 'Interocular Transfer of a Visual Form Discrimination Habit in Cats after Section of the Optic Chiasm and Corpus Callosum', *Anatomical Record* 115 (1953), p. 351; Myers, 'Interocular Transfer of Pattern Discrimination in Cats Following Section of Crossed Optic Fibers', *Journal of Comparative and Physiological Psychology* 48 (1955), p. 470.

3   The first publication of these results was M. S. Gazzaniga, J. E. Bogen, and R. W. Sperry, 'Some Functional Effects of Sectioning the Cerebral Commissures in Man', *Proceedings of the National Academy of Sciences* 48 (1962), Part 2, p. 1765. Interestingly, the same year saw publication of a paper proposing the interpretation of a case of human brain *damage* along similar lines, suggested by the earlier findings with animals. Cf. N. Geschwind and E. Kaplan, 'A Human Cerebral Deconnection Syndrome', *Neurology* 12 (1962), p. 675. Also of interest is Geschwind's long two-part survey of the field, which takes up some philosophical questions explicitly: 'Disconnexion Syndromes in Animals and Man', *Brain* 88 (1965), 247–94, 585–644. Parts of it are reprinted, with other material, in *Boston Studies in the Philosophy of Science*, Vol. IV (1969). See also his paper 'The Organization of Language and the Brain', *Science* 170 (1970), p. 940.

4   There are individual exceptions to this, as there are to most generalizations about cerebral function: left-handed people tend to have bilateral linguistic control, and it is common in early childhood. All the subjects of these experiments, however, were right-handed, and displayed left cerebral dominance.

5   H. W. Gordon and R. W. Sperry, 'Lateralization of Olfactory Perception in the Surgically Separated Hemispheres of Man', *Neuropsychologia* 7 (1969), p. 111. One patient, however, was able to say in these circumstances that he smelled something unpleasant, without being able to describe it further.

6   Reported in Jerre Levy, *Information Processing and Higher Psychological Functions in the Disconnected Hemispheres of Human Commissurotomy Patients* (unpublished doctoral dissertation, California Institute of Technology, 1969).

7   Moreover, the condition of radical disconnection may not be stable: there may be a tendency toward the formation of new interhemispheric pathways through the brain stem, with the lapse of time. This is supported partly by observation of commissurotomy patients, but more importantly by cases of agenesis of the callosum. People who have grown up without one have learned to manage without it; their performance on the tests is much closer to normal than that of recently operated patients. (Cf. Saul and Sperry, 'Absence of Commissurotomy Symptoms with Agenesis of the Corpus Callosum', *Neurology* 18 (1968).) This fact is very important, but for the present I shall put it aside to concentrate on the immediate results of disconnection.

8   It is Sperry's view. He puts it as follows: "Instead of the normally unified single stream of consciousness, these patients behave in many ways as if they have two independent streams of conscious awareness, one in each hemisphere, each of which is cut off from and out of contact with the mental experiences of the other. In other words, each hemisphere seems to have its own separate and private sensations; its own perceptions; its own concepts; and its own impulses to act, with related volitional, cognitive, and learning experiences. Following the surgery, each hemisphere also has thereafter its own separate chain of memories that are rendered inaccessible to the recall process of the other." (*American Psychologist* 23, *op. cit.*, p. 724.)

9   There is some direct evidence for such primitive ipsilateral inputs, both visual and tactile; cf. Gazzaniga, *The Bisected Brain*, Chapter 3.

227

10 The two can of course diverge, and this fact underlies the classic philosophical problem of inverted spectra, which is only distantly related to the subject of this paper. A type of relation can hold between elements in the experience of a single person that cannot hold between elements of the experience of distinct persons: looking similar in color, for example. Insofar as our concept of similarity of experience in the case of a single person is dependent on his experience of similarity, the concept is not applicable between persons.

11 In case anyone is inclined to embrace the conclusion that we all have two minds, let me suggest that the trouble will not end there. For the mental operations of a single hemisphere, such as vision, hearing, speech, writing, verbal comprehension, etc. can to a great extent be separated from one another by suitable cortical deconnections; why then should we not regard *each* hemisphere as inhabited by several cooperating minds with specialized capacities? Where is one to stop? If the decision on the number of minds associated with a brain is largely arbitrary, the original point of the question has disappeared.

12 My research was supported in part by the National Science Foundation.

19

DIVIDED MINDS AND THE NATURE OF PERSONS

Derek Parfit

It was the split-brain cases which drew me into philosophy. Our knowledge of these cases depends on the results of various psychological tests, as described by Donald MacKay.[1] These tests made use of two facts. We control each of our arms, and see what is in each half of our visual fields, with only one of our hemispheres. When someone's hemispheres have been disconnected, psychologists can thus present to this person two different written questions in the two halves of his visual field, and can receive two different answers written by this person's two hands.

Here is a simplified imaginary version of the kind of evidence that such tests provide. One of these people looks fixedly at the centre of a wide screen, whose left half is red and right half is blue. On each half in a darker shade are the words, 'How many colours can you see?' With both hands the person writes, 'Only one'. The words are now changed to read, 'Which is the only colour that you can see?' With one of his hands the person writes 'Red', with the other he writes 'Blue'.

If this is how such a person responds, I would conclude that he is having two visual sensations – that he does, as he claims, see both red and blue. But in seeing each colour he is not aware of seeing the other. He has two streams of consciousness, in each of which he can see only one colour. In one stream he sees red, and at the same time, in his other stream, he sees blue. More generally, he could be having at the same time two series of thoughts and sensations, in having each of which he is unaware of having the other.

This conclusion has been questioned. It has been claimed by some that there are not *two* streams of consciousness, on the ground that the sub-dominant hemisphere is a part of the brain whose functioning involves no consciousness. If this were true, these cases would lose most of their interest. I believe that it is not true, chiefly because, if a person's dominant hemisphere is destroyed, this person is able to react in the way in which, in the split-brain cases, the sub-dominant hemisphere reacts, and we do not believe that such a person is just an automaton, without consciousness.

The sub-dominant hemisphere is, of course, much less developed in certain ways, typically having the linguistic abilities of a three-year-old. But three-year-olds are conscious. This supports the view that, in split-brain cases, there *are* two streams of consciousness.

Another view is that, in these cases, there are two persons involved, sharing the same body. Like Professor MacKay, I believe that we should reject this view. My reason for believing this is, however, different. Professor Mackay denies that there are two persons involved because he believes that there is only one person involved. I believe that, in a sense, the number of persons involved is none.

THE EGO THEORY AND THE BUNDLE THEORY

To explain this sense I must, for a while, turn away from the split-brain cases. There are two theories about what persons are, and what is involved in a person's continued existence over time. On the *Ego Theory*, a person's continued existence cannot be explained except as the continued existence of a particular *Ego*, or *subject of experiences*. An Ego Theorist claims that, if we ask what unifies someone's consciousness at any time – what makes it true, for example, that I can now both see what I am typing and hear the wind outside my window – the answer is that these are both experiences which are being had by me, this person, at this time. Similarly, what explains the unity of a person's whole life is the fact that all of the experiences in this life are had by the same person, or subject of experiences. In its best-known form, the *Cartesian view*, each person is a persisting purely mental thing – a soul, or spiritual substance.

The rival view is the *Bundle Theory*. Like most styles in art – Gothic, baroque, rococo, etc. – this theory owes its name to its critics. But the name is good enough. According to the Bundle Theory, we can't explain either the unity of consciousness at any time, or the unity of a whole life, by referring to a person. Instead we must claim that there are long series of different mental states and events – thoughts, sensations, and the like – each series being what we call one life. Each series is unified by various kinds of causal relation, such as the relations that hold between experiences and later memories of them. Each series is thus like a bundle tied up with string.

In a sense, a Bundle Theorist denies the existence of persons. An outright denial is of course absurd. As Reid protested in the eighteenth century, 'I am not thought, I am not action, I am not feeling; I am something which thinks and acts and feels.' I am not a series of events, but a person. A Bundle Theorist admits this fact, but claims it to be only a fact about our grammar, or our language. There are persons or subjects in this language-dependent way. If, however, persons are believed to be more than this – to be separately existing things, distinct from our brains and bodies, and the various kinds of mental states and events – the Bundle Theorist denies that there are such things.

The first Bundle Theorist was Buddha, who taught 'anatta', or the *No Self view*. Buddhists concede that selves or persons have 'nominal existence', by which they mean that persons are merely combinations of other elements. Only what exists by itself, as a separate element, has instead what Buddhists call 'actual existence'. Here are some quotations from Buddhist texts:

> At the beginning of their conversation the king politely asks the monk his name, and receives the following reply: 'Sir, I am known as "Nagasena"; my fellows in the religious life address me as "Nagasena". Although my parents gave me the name … it is just an appellation, a form of speech, a description, a conventional usage. "Nagasena" is only a name, for no person is found here.'

> A sentient being does exist, you think, O Mara? You are misled by a false conception. This bundle of elements is void of Self. In it there is no sentient being. Just as a set of wooden parts receives the name of carriage, so do we give to elements the name of fancied being.

> Buddha has spoken thus: 'O Brethren, actions do exist, and also their consequences, but the person that acts does not. There is no one to cast away this set of elements, and no one to assume a new set of them. There exists no Individual, it is only a conventional name given to a set of elements.'[2]

Buddha's claims are strikingly similar to the claims advanced by several Western writers. Since these writers knew nothing of Buddha, the similarity of these claims suggests that they are not merely part of one cultural tradition, in one period. They may be, as I believe they are, true.

WHAT WE BELIEVE OURSELVES TO BE

Given the advances in psychology and neurophysiology, the Bundle Theory may now seem to be obviously true. It may seem uninteresting to deny that there are separately existing Egos, which are distinct from brains and bodies and the various kinds of mental states and events. But this is not the only issue. We may be convinced that the Ego Theory is false, or even senseless. Most of us, however, even if we are not aware of this, also have certain beliefs about what is involved in our continued existence over time. And these beliefs would only be justified if something like the Ego Theory was true. Most of us therefore have false beliefs about what persons are, and about ourselves.

These beliefs are best revealed when we consider certain imaginary cases, often drawn from science fiction. One such case is *teletransportation*. Suppose that you enter a cubicle in which, when you press a button, a scanner records the states of all of the cells in your brain and body, destroying both while doing so. This information is then transmitted at the speed of light to some other planet, where a replicator produces a perfect organic copy of you. Since the brain of your Replica is exactly like yours, it will seem to remember living your life up to the moment when you pressed the button, its character will be just like yours, and it will be in every other way psychologically continuous with you. This psychological continuity will not have its normal cause, the continued existence of your brain, since the causal chain will run through the transmission by radio of your 'blueprint'.

Several writers claim that, if you chose to be teletransported, believing this to be the fastest way of travelling, you would be making a terrible mistake. This would not be a way of travelling, but a way of dying. It may not, they concede, be quite as bad as ordinary death. It might be some consolation to you that, after your death, you will have this Replica, which can finish the book that you are writing, act as parent to your children, and so on. But, they insist, this Replica won't be you. It will merely be someone else, who is exactly like you. This is why this prospect is nearly as bad as ordinary death.

Imagine next a whole range of cases, in each of which, in a single operation, a different proportion of the cells in your brain and body would be replaced with exact duplicates. At the near end of this range, only 1 or 2 per cent would be replaced; in the middle, 40 or 60 per cent; near the far end, 98 or 99 per cent. At the far end of this range is pure teletransportation, the case in which all of your cells would be 'replaced'.

When you imagine that some proportion of your cells will be replaced with exact duplicates, it is natural to have the following beliefs. First, if you ask, 'Will I survive? Will the resulting person be me?', there must be an answer to this question. Either you will survive, or you are about to die. Second, the answer to this question must be either a simple 'Yes' or a simple 'No'. The person who wakes up either will or will not be you. There cannot be a third answer, such as that the person waking up will be half you. You can imagine yourself later being half-conscious. But if the resulting person will be fully conscious, he cannot be half you. To state these beliefs together: to the question, 'Will the resulting person be me?', there must always *be* an answer, which must be all-or-nothing.

There seem good grounds for believing that, in the case of teletransportation, your Replica would not be you. In a slight variant of this case, your Replica might be created while you were still alive, so that you could talk to one another. This seems to show that, if 100 per cent of your cells were replaced, the result would merely be a Replica of you. At the other end of my range of cases, where only 1 per cent would be replaced, the resulting person clearly *would* be you. It therefore seems that, in the cases in between, the resulting person must be either you, or merely a

Replica. It seems that one of these must be true, and that it makes a great difference which is true.

HOW WE ARE NOT WHAT WE BELIEVE

If these beliefs were correct, there must be some critical percentage, somewhere in this range of cases, up to which the resulting person would be you, and beyond which he would merely be your Replica. Perhaps, for example, it would be you who would wake up if the proportion of cells replaced were 49 per cent, but if just a few more cells were also replaced, this would make all the difference, causing it to be someone else who would wake up.

That there must be some such critical percentage follows from our natural beliefs. But this conclusion is most implausible. How could a few cells make such a difference? Moreover, if there is such a critical percentage, no one could ever discover where it came. Since in all these cases the resulting person would believe that he was you, there could never be any evidence about where, in this range of cases, he would suddenly cease to be you.

On the Bundle Theory, we should reject these natural beliefs. Since you, the person, are not a separately existing entity, we can know exactly what would happen without answering the question of what will happen to you. Moreover, in the cases in the middle of my range, it is an empty question whether the resulting person would be you, or would merely be someone else who is exactly like you. These are not here two different possibilities, one of which must be true. These are merely two different descriptions of the very same course of events. If 50 per cent of your cells were replaced with exact duplicates, we could call the resulting person you, or we could call him merely your Replica. But since these are not here different possibilities, this is a mere choice of words.

As Buddha claimed, the Bundle Theory is hard to believe. It is hard to accept that it could be an empty question whether one is about to die, or will instead live for many years.

What we are being asked to accept may be made clearer with this analogy. Suppose that a certain club exists for some time, holding regular meetings. The meetings then cease. Some years later, several people form a club with the same name, and the same rules. We can ask, 'Did these people revive the very same club? Or did they merely start up another club which is exactly similar?' Given certain further details, this would be another empty question. We could know just what happened without answering this question. Suppose that someone said: 'But there must be an answer. The club meeting later must either be, or not be, the very same club.' This would show that this person didn't understand the nature of clubs.

In the same way, if we have any worries about my imagined cases, we don't understand the nature of persons. In each of my cases, you would know that the resulting person would be both psychologically and physically exactly like you, and that he would have some particular proportion of the cells in your brain and body – 90 per cent, or 10 per cent, or, in the case of teletransportation, 0 per cent. Knowing this, you know everything. How could it be a real question what would happen to you, unless you are a separately existing Ego, distinct from a brain and body, and the various kinds of mental state and event? If there are no such Egos, there is nothing else to ask a real question about.

Accepting the Bundle Theory is not only hard; it may also affect our emotions. As Buddha claimed, it may undermine our concern about our own futures. This effect can be suggested by redescribing this change of view. Suppose that you are about to be destroyed, but will later have a Replica on Mars. You would naturally believe that this prospect is about as bad as ordinary death, since your Replica won't be you. On the Bundle Theory, the fact that your Replica won't be you just consists in the fact that, though it will be fully psychologically continuous with you, this continuity won't have its normal cause. But when you object to teletransportation you are not objecting merely to the abnormality of this cause. You are objecting that this cause won't get *you* to Mars. You fear that the abnormal cause will fail to produce a further and all-important fact, which is different from the fact that your Replica will be psychologically continuous with you. You do not merely want there to be psychological continuity between you and some future person. You want to *be* this future person. On the Bundle Theory, there is no such special further fact. What you fear will not happen, in this imagined case, *never* happens. You want the person on Mars to be you in a specially intimate way in which no future person will ever be you. This means that, judged from the standpoint of your natural beliefs, even ordinary survival is about as bad as teletransportation. *Ordinary survival is about as bad as being destroyed and having a Replica.*

HOW THE SPLIT-BRAIN CASES SUPPORT THE BUNDLE THEORY

The truth of the Bundle Theory seems to me, in the widest sense, as much a scientific as a philosophical conclusion. I can imagine kinds of evidence which would have justified believing in the existence of separately existing Egos, and believing that the continued existence of these Egos is what explains the continuity of each mental life. But there is in fact very little evidence in favour of this Ego Theory, and much for the alternative Bundle Theory.

Some of this evidence is provided by the split-brain cases. On the Ego Theory, to explain what unifies our experiences at any one time, we should simply claim that these are all experiences which are being had by the same person. Bundle Theorists reject this explanation. This disagreement is hard to resolve in ordinary cases. But consider the simplified split-brain case that I described. We show to my imagined patient a placard whose left half is blue and right half is red. In one of this person's two streams of consciousness, he is aware of seeing only blue, while at the same time, in his other stream, he is aware of seeing only red. Each of these two visual experiences is combined with other experiences, like that of being aware of moving one of his hands. What unifies the experiences, at any time, in each of this person's two streams of consciousness? What unifies his awareness of seeing only red with his awareness of moving one hand? The answer cannot be that these experiences are being had by the same person. This answer cannot explain the unity of each of this person's two streams of consciousness, since it ignores the disunity between these streams. This person is now having all of the experiences in both of his two streams. If this fact was what unified these experiences, this would make the two streams one.

These cases do not, I have claimed, involve two people sharing a single body. Since there is only one person involved, who has two streams of consciousness, the Ego Theorist's explanation would have to take the following form. He would have to distinguish between persons and subjects of experiences, and claim that, in split-brain cases, there are *two* of the latter. What unifies the experiences in one of the person's two streams would have to be the fact that these experiences are all being had by the same subject of experiences. What unifies the experiences in this person's other stream would have to be the fact that they are being had by another subject of experiences. When this explanation takes this form, it becomes much less plausible. While we could assume that 'subject of experiences', or 'Ego', simply meant 'person', it was easy to believe that there are subjects of experiences. But if there can be subjects of experiences that are not persons, and if in the life of a split-brain patient there are at any time two different subjects of experiences – two different Egos – why should we believe that there really are such things? This does not amount to a refutation. But it seems to me a strong argument against the Ego Theory.

As a Bundle Theorist, I believe that these two Egos are idle cogs. There is another explanation of the unity of consciousness, both in ordinary cases and in split-brain cases. It is simply a fact that ordinary people are, at any time, aware of having several different experiences. This awareness of several different experiences can be helpfully compared with one's awareness, in short-term memory, of several different experiences. Just as there can be a single memory of just having had several experiences, such as hearing a bell strike three times, there can be a single state of awareness both of hearing the fourth striking of this bell, and of seeing, at the same time, ravens flying past the bell-tower.

Unlike the Ego Theorist's explanation, this explanation can easily be extended to cover split-brain cases. In such cases there is, at any time, not one state of awareness of several different experiences, but two such states. In the case I described, there is one state of awareness of both seeing only red and of moving one hand, and there is another state of awareness of both seeing only blue and moving the other hand. In claiming that there are two such states of awareness, we are not postulating the existence of unfamiliar entities, two separately existing Egos which are not the same as the single person whom the case involves. This explanation appeals to a pair of mental states which would have to be described anyway in a full description of this case.

I have suggested how the split-brain cases provide one argument for one view about the nature of persons. I should mention another such argument, provided by an imagined extension of these cases, first discussed at length by David Wiggins.[3]

In this imagined case a person's brain is divided, and the two halves are transplanted into a pair of different bodies. The two resulting people live quite separate lives. This imagined case shows that personal identity is not what matters. If I was about to divide, I should conclude that neither of the resulting people will be me. I will have ceased to exist. But this way of ceasing to exist is about as good – or as bad – as ordinary survival.

Some of the features of Wiggins's imagined case are likely to remain technically impossible. But the case cannot be dismissed, since its most striking feature, the division of one stream of consciousness into separate streams, has already happened. This is a second way in which the actual split-brain cases have great theoretical importance. They challenge some of our deepest assumptions about ourselves.[4]

NOTES

1 See MacKay, D., chapter 1 of Blakemore and Greenfield (eds.) *Mindwaves*. Oxford: Blackwell, 1987. Reproduced with permission from Blackwell Publishing.
2 For the sources of these and similar quotations, see my *Reasons and Persons* (1984) pp. 502–3, 532. Oxford: Oxford University Press.
3 At the end of his *Identity and Spatio-temporal Continuity* (1967) Oxford: Blackwell.
4 I discuss these assumptions further in part 3 of my *Reasons and Persons*.

20

THE SELF AS A CENTER OF NARRATIVE GRAVITY

Daniel Dennett

What is a self? I will try to answer this question by developing an analogy with something much simpler, something which is nowhere near as puzzling as a self, but has some properties in common with selves.

What I have in mind is *the center of gravity* of an object.

This is a well-behaved concept in Newtonian physics. But a center of gravity is not an atom or a subatomic particle or any other physical item in the world. It has no mass; it has no color; it has no physical properties at all, except for spatio-temporal location. It is a fine example of what Hans Reichenbach would call an *abstractum*. It is a purely abstract object. It is, if you like, a theorist's fiction. It is not one of the real things in the universe in addition to the atoms. But it is a fiction that has a nicely defined, well delineated and well behaved role within physics.

Let me remind you how robust and familiar the idea of a center of gravity is. Consider a chair. Like all other physical objects, it has a center of gravity. If you start tipping it, you can tell more or less accurately whether it would start to fall over or fall back in place if you let go of it. We're all quite good at making predictions involving centers of gravity and devising explanations about when and why things fall over. Place a book on the chair. It, too, has a center of gravity. If you start to push it over the edge, we know that at some point it will fall. It will fall when its center of gravity is no longer directly over a point of its supporting base (the chair seat). Notice that that statement is itself virtually tautological. The key terms in it are all interdefinable. And yet it can also figure in explanations that appear to be causal explanations of some sort. We ask "Why doesn't that lamp tip over?" We reply "Because its center of gravity is so low." Is this a causal explanation? It can compete with explanations that are clearly causal, such as: "Because it's nailed to the table," and "Because it's supported by wires."

We can manipulate centers of gravity. For instance, I change the center of gravity of a water pitcher easily, by pouring some of the water out. So, although a center of

237

gravity is a purely abstract object, it has a spatio-temporal career, which I can affect by my actions. It has a history, but its history can include some rather strange episodes. Although it moves around in space and time, its motion can be discontinuous. For instance, if I were to take a piece of bubble gum and suddenly stick it on the pitcher's handle, that would shift the pitcher's center of gravity from point A to point B. But the center of gravity would not have to move through all the intervening positions. As an abstractum, it is not bound by all the constraints of physical travel.

Consider the center of gravity of a slightly more complicated object. Suppose we wanted to keep track of the career of the center of gravity of some complex machine with lots of turning gears and camshafts and reciprocating rods—the engine of a steam-powered unicycle, perhaps. And suppose our theory of the machine's operation permitted us to plot the complicated trajectory of the center of gravity precisely. And suppose—most improbably—that we discovered that in this particular machine the trajectory of the center of gravity was precisely the same as the trajectory of a particular iron atom in the crankshaft. Even if this were discovered, we would be wrong even to *entertain* the hypothesis that the machine's center of gravity was (identical with) that iron atom. That would be a category mistake. A center of gravity is *just* an abstractum. It's just a fictional object. But when I say it's a fictional object, I do not mean to disparage it; it's a wonderful fictional object, and it has a perfectly legitimate place within serious, sober, *echt* physical science.

A self is also an abstract object, a theorist's fiction. The theory is not particle physics but what we might call a branch of people-physics; it is more sóberly known as a phenomenology or hermeneutics, or soul-science (*Geisteswissenschaft*). The physicist does an *interpretation*, if you like, of the chair and its behavior, and comes up with the theoretical abstraction of a center of gravity, which is then very useful in characterizing the behavior of the chair in the future, under a wide variety of conditions. The hermeneuticist or phenomenologist—or anthropologist—sees some rather more complicated things moving about in the world—human beings and animals— and is faced with a similar problem of interpretation. It turns out to be theoretically perspicuous to organize the interpretation around a central abstraction: each person has a *self* (in addition to a center of gravity). In fact we have to posit selves for *ourselves* as well. The theoretical problem of self-interpretation is at least as difficult and important as the problem of other-interpretation.

Now how does a self differ from a center of gravity? It is a much more complicated concept. I will try to elucidate it via an analogy with another sort of fictional object: fictional characters in literature. Pick up *Moby Dick* and open it up to page one. It says, "Call me Ishmael." Call whom Ishmael? Call Melville Ishmael? No. Call Ishmael Ishmael. Melville has created a fictional character named Ishmael. As you read the book you learn about Ishmael, about his life, about his beliefs and desires, his acts and attitudes. You learn a lot more about Ishmael than Melville ever explicitly tells you. Some of it you can read in by implication. Some of it you can read in by extrapolation. But beyond the limits of such extrapolation fictional worlds are simply *indeterminate*. Thus, consider the following question (borrowed from David Lewis's "Truth and Fiction," *American Philosophical Quarterly*, 1978, 15, pp. 37–46). Did Sherlock Holmes have three nostrils? The answer of course is no, but not because Conan Doyle ever says that he doesn't, or that he has two, but because we're entitled to make that extrapolation. In the absence of evidence to the contrary, Sherlock Holmes' nose can be supposed to be normal. Another question: Did Sherlock Holmes have a mole on his left shoulder blade? The answer to this question is neither yes nor no. Nothing about the text or about the principles of extrapolation from the text permit an answer to that question. There is simply no fact of the matter. Why? Because Sherlock Holmes is a merely fictional character, created by, or constituted out of, the text and the culture in which that text resides.

This indeterminacy is a fundamental property of fictional objects which strongly distinguishes them from another sort of object scientists talk about: theoretical entities, or what Reichenbach called *illata*—inferred entities, such as atoms, molecules and neutrinos. A logician might say that the "principle of bivalence" does not hold for fictional objects. That is to say, with regard to any actual man, living or dead, the question of whether or not he has or had a mole on his left shoulder blade has an answer, yes or no. Did Aristotle have such a mole? There is a fact of the matter even if we can never discover it. But with regard to a fictional character, that question may have no answer at all.

We can imagine someone, a benighted literary critic, perhaps, who doesn't understand that fiction is fiction. This critic has a strange theory about how fiction works. He thinks that something literally magical happens when a novelist writes a novel. When a novelist sets down words on paper, this critic says (one often hears claims like this, but not meant to be taken completely literally), the novelist actually *creates a world*. A litmus test for this bizarre view is the principle of bivalence: when our imagined critic speaks of a fictional world he means a strange sort of *real* world, a world in which the principle of bivalence holds. Such a critic might seriously wonder whether Dr Watson was *really* Moriarty's second cousin, or whether the conductor of the train that took Holmes and Watson to Aldershot was also the conductor of the train that brought them back to London. That sort of question can't properly arise if you understand fiction correctly, of course. Whereas analogous questions about historical personages have to have yes or no answers, even if we may never be able to dredge them up.

Centers of gravity, as fictional objects, exhibit the same feature. They have only the properties that the theory that constitutes them endowed them with. If you scratch your head and say, "I wonder if maybe centers of gravity are really neutrinos!" you have misunderstood the theoretical status of a center of gravity.

Now how can I make the claim that a self—your own real self, for instance—is rather like a fictional character? Aren't all *fictional* selves dependent for their very creation on the existence of *real* selves? It may seem so, but I will argue that this is an illusion. Let's go back to Ishmael. Ishmael is a fictional character, although we can certainly learn all about him. One might find him in many regards more real than many of one's friends. But, one thinks, Ishmael was created by Melville, and Melville is a real character—was a real character. A real self. Doesn't this show that it takes a real self to create a fictional self? I think not, but if I am to convince you, I must push you through an exercise of the imagination.

First of all, I want to imagine something some of you may think incredible: a novel-writing machine. We can suppose it is a product of artificial intelligence research, a computer that has been designed or programmed to write novels. But it has not been designed to write any particular novel. We can suppose (if it helps) that it has been given a great stock of whatever information it might need, and some partially random and hence unpredictable ways of starting the seed of a story going, and building upon it. Now imagine that the designers are sitting back, wondering what kind of novel their creation is going to write. They turn the thing on and after a while the high speed printer begins to go clickety-clack and out comes the first sentence. "Call me Gilbert," it says. What follows is the apparent autobiography of some fictional Gilbert. Now Gilbert is a fictional, created self but its creator is no self. Of course there were human designers who designed the machine, but they didn't design Gilbert. Gilbert is a product of a design or invention process in which there aren't any selves at all. That is, I am *stipulating* that this is not a conscious machine, not a "thinker." It is a dumb machine, but it does have the power to write a passable novel. (If you think this is strictly impossible I can only challenge you to show why you think this must be so, and invite you read on; in the end you may not have an interest in defending such a precarious impossibility-claim.)

So we are to imagine that a passable story is emitted from the machine. Notice that we can perform the same sort of literary exegesis with regard to this novel as we can with any other. In fact if you were to pick up a novel at random out of a library, you could not tell with certainty that it wasn't written by something like this machine. (And if you're a New Critic you shouldn't care.) You've got a text and you can interpret it, and so you can learn the story, the life and adventures of Gilbert. Your expectations and predictions, as you read, and your interpretive reconstruction of what you have already read, will congeal around the central node of the fictional character, Gilbert.

But now I want to twiddle the knobs on this thought experiment. So far we've imagined the novel, *The Life and Times of Gilbert*, clanking out of a computer that is just a box, sitting in the corner of some lab. But now I want to change the story a little bit and suppose that the computer has arms and legs—or better: wheels. (I don't want to make it too anthropomorphic.) It has a television eye, and it moves around in the world. It also begins its tale with "Call me Gilbert," and tells a novel, but now we notice that if we do the trick that the New Critics say you should never do, and *look outside the text*, we discover that there's a truth-preserving interpretation of that text in the real world. The adventures of Gilbert, the fictional character, now bear a striking and presumably non-coincidental relationship to the adventures of this robot rolling around in the world. If you hit the robot with a baseball bat, very shortly thereafter the story of Gilbert includes his being hit with a baseball bat by somebody who looks like you. Every now and then the robot gets locked in the closet and then says "Help me!" Help whom? Well, help Gilbert, presumably. But who is Gilbert? Is Gilbert the robot, or merely the fictional self created by the robot? If we go and help the robot out of the closet, it sends us a note: "Thank you. Love, Gilbert." At this point we will be unable to ignore the fact that the fictional career of the fictional Gilbert bears an interesting resemblance to the "career" of this mere robot moving through the world. We can still maintain that the robot's *brain*, the robot's computer, really knows nothing about the world; *it's* not a self. It's just a clanky computer. It doesn't know what it's doing. It doesn't even know that it's creating a fictional character. (The same is just as true of your brain; *it* doesn't know what it's doing either.) Nevertheless, the patterns in the behavior that is being controlled by the computer are interpretable, by us, as accreting biography—telling the narrative of a self. But we are not the only interpreters. The robot novelist is also, of course, an interpreter: a *self*-interpreter, providing its own account of its activities in the world.

I propose that we take this analogy seriously. "Where is the self?" a materialist philosopher or neuroscientist might ask. It is a category mistake to start looking around for the self in the brain. Unlike centers of gravity, whose sole property is their spatio-temporal position, selves have a spatio-temporal position that is only grossly defined. Roughly speaking, in the normal case if there are three human beings sitting on a park bench, there are three selves there, all in a row and roughly equidistant from the fountain they face. Or we might use a rather antique turn of phrase and talk about how many *souls* are located in the park. ("All twenty souls in the starboard lifeboat were saved, but those that remained on deck perished.")

Brain research may permit us to make some more fine-grained localizations, but the capacity to achieve *some* fine-grained localization does not give one grounds for supposing that the process of localization can continue indefinitely and that the day will finally come when we can say, "That cell there, right in the middle of the hippocampus (or wherever)—that's the self!"

There's a big difference, of course, between fictional characters and our own selves. One I would stress is that a fictional character is usually encountered as a *fait accompli*. After the novel has been written and published, you read it. At that point it is too late for the novelist to render determinate anything indeterminate that strikes

241

your curiosity. Dostoevsky is dead; you can't ask him what *else* Raskolnikov thought while he sat in the police station. But novels don't have to be that way. John Updike has written three novels about Rabbit Angstrom: *Rabbit Run, Rabbit Redux,* and *Rabbit is Rich.* Suppose that those of us who particularly liked the first novel were to get together and compose a list of questions for Updike—things we wished Updike had talked about in that first novel, when Rabbit was a young former basketball star. We could send our questions to Updike and ask him to consider writing another novel in the series, only this time not continuing the chronological sequence. Like Lawrence Durrell's *Alexandria Quartet,* the Rabbit series could include another novel about Rabbit's early days when he was still playing basketball, and this novel could answer our questions.

Notice what we would *not* be doing in such a case. We would not be saying to Updike, "Tell us the answers that you already know, the answers that are already fixed to those questions. Come on, let us know all those secrets you've been keeping from us." Nor would we be asking Updike to do research, as we might ask the author of a multi-volume biography of a real person. We would be asking him to write a new novel, to invent some more novel for us, on demand. And if he acceded, he would enlarge and make more determinate the character of Rabbit Angstrom in the process of writing the new novel. In this way matters which are indeterminate at one time can become determined later by a creative step.

I propose that this imagined exercise with Updike, getting him to write more novels on demand to answer our questions, is actually a familiar exercise. That is the way we treat each other; that is the way we are. We cannot undo those parts of our pasts that are determinate, but our selves are constantly being made more determinate as we go along in response to the way the world impinges on us. Of course it is also possible for a person to engage in auto-hermeneutics, interpretation of one's self, and in particular to go back and think about one's past, and one's memories, and to rethink them and rewrite them. This process does change the "fictional" character, the character that you are, in much the way that Rabbit Angstrom, after Updike writes the second novel about him as a young man, comes to be a rather different fictional character, determinate in ways he was never determinate before. This would be an utterly mysterious and magical prospect (and hence something no one should take seriously) *if the self were anything but an abstractum.*

I want to bring this out by extracting one more feature from the Updike thought experiment. Updike might take up our request but then he might prove to be forgetful. After all, it's been many years since he wrote *Rabbit Run.* He might not want to go back and reread it carefully; and when he wrote the new novel it might end up being inconsistent with the first. He might have Rabbit being in two places at one time, for instance. If we wanted to settle what the *true* story was, we'd be falling into error; there is no true story. In such a circumstance there would simply be a failure of coherence of all the data that we had about Rabbit. And because Rabbit is a fictional character, we wouldn't smite our foreheads in wonder and declare "Oh my goodness! There's a rift in the universe; we've found a contradiction in nature!" Nothing is easier than contradiction when you're dealing with fiction; a fictional character can have contradictory properties because it's *just* a fictional character. We find such contradictions intolerable, however, when we are trying to interpret something or someone, even a fictional character, so we typically *bifurcate* the character to resolve the conflict.

Something like this seems to happen to real people on rare occasions. Consider the putatively true case histories recorded in *The Three Faces of Eve* and *Sybil*. (Corbett H. Thigpen and Hervey Cleckly, *The Three Faces of Eve*, McGraw Hill, 1957, and Flora Rheta Schreiber, *Sybil*, Warner paperback, 1973.) Eve's three faces were the faces of three distinct personalities, it seems, and the woman portrayed in *Sybil* had *many* different selves, or so it seems. How can we make sense of this? Here is one way—a solemn, skeptical way favored by some of the psychotherapists with whom I've talked about such cases: when Sybil went in to see her therapist the first time, she wasn't several different people rolled into one body. Sybil was a novel-writing machine that fell in with a very ingenious questioner, a very eager reader. And together they collaborated—innocently—to write many, many chapters of a new novel. And, of course, since Sybil was a sort of living novel, she went out and engaged in the world with these new selves, more or less created on demand, under the eager suggestion of a therapist.

I now believe that this is overly skeptical. The population explosion of new characters that typically follows the onset of psychotherapy for sufferers of Multiple Personality Disorder (MPD) is probably to be explained along just these lines, but there is quite compelling evidence in some cases that some multiplicity of selves (two or three or four, let us say) had already begun laying down biography before the therapist came along to do the "reading". And in any event, Sybil is only a strikingly pathological case of something quite normal, a behavior pattern we can find in ourselves. We are all, at times, confabulators, telling and retelling ourselves the story of our own lives, with scant attention to the question of truth. Why, though, do we behave this way? Why are we all such inveterate and inventive autobiographical novelists? As Umberto Maturana has (uncontroversially) observed: "Everything said is said by a speaker to another speaker that may be himself." But why should one talk to oneself? Why isn't that an utterly idle activity, as systematically futile as trying to pick oneself up by one's own bootstraps?

A central clue comes from the sort of phenomena uncovered by Michael Gazzaniga's research on those rare individuals—the "split-brain subjects"—whose *corpus callosum* has been surgically severed, creating in them two largely independent cortical hemispheres that can, on occasion, be differently informed about the current scene. Does the operation *split* the self in two? After the operation, patients normally exhibit no signs of psychological splitting, appearing to be no less unified than you or I except under particularly contrived circumstances. But on Gazzaniga's view, this does not so much show that the patients have preserved their pre-surgical unity as that the unity of normal life is an illusion.

According to Gazzaniga, the normal mind is *not* beautifully unified, but rather a problematically yoked-together bundle of partly autonomous systems. All parts of the mind are not equally accessible to each other at all times. These modules or systems sometimes have internal communication problems which they solve by various ingenious and devious routes. If this is true (and I think it is), it may provide us with an answer to a most puzzling question about conscious thought: what good is it? Such a question begs for an evolutionary answer, but it will have to be speculative, of course. (It is not critical to my speculative answer, for the moment, where genetic evolution and transmission breaks off and cultural evolution and transmission takes over.)

In the beginning—according to Julian Jaynes (*The Origins of Consciousness in the Breakdown of the Bicameral Mind*, Boston: Houghton Mifflin, 1976), whose account I am adapting—were speakers, our ancestors, who weren't really conscious. They spoke, but they just sort of blurted things out, more or less the way bees do bee dances, or the way computers talk to each other. That is not conscious communication, surely. When these ancestors had problems, sometimes they would "ask" for help (more or less like Gilbert saying "Help me!" when he was locked in the closet), and sometimes there would be somebody around to hear them. So they got into the habit of asking for assistance and, particularly, asking questions. Whenever they couldn't figure out how to solve some problem, they would ask a question, addressed to no one in particular, and sometimes whoever was standing around could answer them. And they also came to be designed to be provoked on many such occasions into answering questions like that—to the best of their ability—when asked.

Then one day one of our ancestors asked a question in what was apparently an inappropriate circumstance: there was nobody around to be the audience. Strangely enough, he heard his own question, and this stimulated him, cooperatively, to think of an answer, and sure enough the answer came to him. He had established, without realizing what he had done, a communication link between two parts of his brain, between which there was, for some deep biological reason, an accessibility problem. One component of the mind had confronted a problem that another component could solve; if only the problem could be posed for the latter component! Thanks to his habit of asking questions, our ancestor stumbled upon a route via the ears. What a discovery! Sometimes talking and listening to yourself can have wonderful effects, not otherwise obtainable. All that is needed to make sense of this idea is the hypothesis that the modules of the mind have different capacities and ways of doing things, and are not perfectly interaccessible. Under such circumstances it could be true that the way to get yourself to figure out a problem is to tickle your ear with it, to get that part of your brain which is best stimulated by *hearing* a question to work on the problem. Then sometimes you will find yourself with the answer you seek on the tip of your tongue.

This would be enough to establish the evolutionary endorsement (which might well be only culturally transmitted) of the behavior of *talking to yourself*. But as many writers have observed, conscious thinking seems—much of it—to be a variety of particularly efficient and private talking to oneself. The evolutionary transition to thought is then easy to conjure up. All we have to suppose is that the route, the circuit that at first went via mouth and ear, got shorter. People "realized" that the actual vocalization and audition was a rather inefficient part of the loop. Besides, if there were other people around who might overhear it, you might give away more information than you wanted. So what developed was a habit of subvocalization, and this in turn could be streamlined into conscious, verbal thought.

In his posthumous book *On Thinking* (ed. Konstantin Kolenda, Totowa New Jersey, Rowman and Littlefield, 1979), Gilbert Ryle asks: "What is *Le Penseur* doing?" For behaviorists like Ryle this is a real problem. One bit of chin-on-fist-with-knitted-brow looks pretty much like another bit, and yet some of it seems to arrive at good answers and some of it doesn't. What can be going on here? Ironically, Ryle, the arch-behaviorist, came up with some very sly suggestions about what might be going on. Conscious thought, Ryle claimed, should be understood on the model of self-teaching, or better, perhaps: self-schooling or training. Ryle had little to say about how this self-schooling might actually work, but we can get some initial understanding of it on the supposition that we are *not* the captains of our ships; there is no conscious self that is unproblematically in command of the mind's resources. Rather, we are somewhat disunified. Our component modules have to act in opportunistic but amazingly resourceful ways to produce a modicum of behavioral unity, *which is then enhanced by an illusion of greater unity*.

What Gazzaniga's research reveals, sometimes in vivid detail, is how this must go on. Consider some of his evidence for the extraordinary resourcefulness exhibited by (something in) the right hemisphere when it is faced with a communication problem. In one group of experiments, split-brain subjects must reach into a closed bag with the left hand to feel an object, which they are then to identify verbally. The sensory nerves in the left hand lead to the right hemisphere, whereas the control of speech is normally in the left hemisphere, but for most of us, this poses no problem. In a normal person, the left hand can know what the right hand is doing thanks to the corpus callosum, which keeps both hemispheres mutually informed. But in a split-brain subject, this unifying link has been removed; the right hemisphere gets the information about the touched object from the left hand, but the left, language-controlling hemisphere must make the identification public. So the "part which can speak" is kept in the dark, while the "part which knows" cannot make public its knowledge.

There is a devious solution to this problem, however, and split-brain patients have been observed to discover it. Whereas ordinary tactile sensations are represented contralaterally—the signals go to the opposite hemisphere—pain signals are also represented ipsilaterally. That is, thanks to the way the nervous system is wired up, pain stimuli go to both hemispheres. Suppose the object in the bag is a pencil. The right hemisphere will sometimes hit upon a very clever tactic: hold the pencil in your left hand so its point is pressed hard into your palm; this creates pain, and lets the left hemisphere know there's something sharp in the bag, which is enough of a hint so that it can begin guessing; the right hemisphere will signal "getting warmer" and "got it" by smiling or other controllable sings, and in a very short time "the subject"—the *apparently* unified "sole inhabitant" of the body—will be able to announce the correct answer.

Now either the split-brain subjects have developed this extraordinarily devious talent as a reaction to the operation that landed them with such radical accessibility problem, or the operation *reveals*—but does not create—a virtuoso talent to be found also in normal people. Surely, Gazzaniga claims, the latter hypothesis is the most likely one to investigate. That is, it does seem that we are all virtuoso novelists, who find ourselves engaged in all sorts of behavior, more or less unified, but sometimes disunified, and we always put the best "faces" on it we can. We try to make all of our material cohere into a single good story. And that story is our autobiography.

The chief fictional character at the center of that autobiography is one's *self*. And if you still want to know what the self *really* is, you're making a category mistake. After all, when a human being's behavioral control system becomes seriously impaired, it can turn out that the best hermeneutical story we can tell about that individual says that there is more than one character "inhabiting" that body. This is quite possible on the view of the self that I have been presenting; it does not require any fancy metaphysical miracles. One can discover multiple selves in a person just as unproblematically as one could find Early Young Rabbit and Late Young Rabbit in the imagined Updike novels: all that has to be the case is that the story doesn't cohere around one self, one imaginary point, but coheres (coheres much better, in any case) around two different imaginary points.

We sometimes encounter psychological disorders, or surgically created disunities, where the only way to interpret or make sense of them is to posit in effect two centers of gravity, two selves. One isn't creating or discovering a little bit of ghost stuff in doing that. One is simply creating another abstraction. It is an abstraction one uses as part of a theoretical apparatus to understand, and predict, and make sense of, the behavior of some very complicated things. The fact that these abstract selves seem so robust and real is not surprising. They are much more complicated theoretical entities than a center of gravity. And remember that even a center of gravity has a fairly robust presence, once we start playing around with it. But no one has ever seen or ever will see a center of gravity. As David Hume noted, no one has ever seen a self, either.

For my part, when I enter most intimately into what I call *myself*, I always stumble on some particular perception or other, of heat or cold, light or shade, love or hatred, pain or pleasure. I never can catch *myself* at any time without a perception, and never can observe anything but the perception ... If anyone, upon serious and unprejudiced reflection, thinks he has a different notion of *himself*, I must confess I can reason no longer with him. All I can allow him is, that he may be in the right as well as I, and that we are essentially different in this particular. He may, perhaps, perceive something simple and continued, which he calls *himself*; though I am certain there is no such principle in me. (*Treatise on Human Nature*, I, IV, sec. 6.)

21

AGAINST NARRATIVE

Galen Strawson

NOT EVERY LIFE IS A NARRATIVE

"Self is a perpetually rewritten story", according to the psychologist Jerry Bruner: we are all constantly engaged in "self-making narrative" and "in the end we become the autobiographical narratives by which we 'tell about' our lives". (Bruner 1987, pp. 11–15; 1994, p. 53).

Oliver Sacks (1985, p. 110) concurs: each of us "constructs and lives a 'narrative' (and) this narrative *is* us, our identities". A vast chorus of assent rises from the humanities – from literary studies, psychology, anthropology, sociology, philosophy, political theory, religious studies, echoed back by psychotherapy, medicine, law, marketing, design . . . : human beings typically experience their lives as a narrative or story of some sort, or at least as a collection of stories.

I'll call this the Psychological Narrativity thesis. It is a straightforwardly empirical thesis about the way ordinary human beings experience their lives – this is how we are, it says, this is our nature – and it's often coupled with a normative thesis, which I'll call the Ethical Narrativity thesis, according to which a richly Narrative outlook on one's life is essential to living well, to true or full person-hood.

Two theses, four possible positions. First, one may think the empirical psychological thesis true and the ethical one false: one may think that we are indeed deeply Narrative in our thinking and that it's not a good thing.

Roquentin, the protagonist of Sartre's novel *La Nausée*, holds this view. It is also attributed to the Stoics, especially Marcus Aurelius.

Second, one may think the empirical thesis false and the ethical one true. One may grant that we're not all naturally Narrative in our thinking while holding that we should be, and need to be, in order to live a good life. There are versions of this view in Plutarch and a host of present-day writings.

Third, one may think both theses true: all normal human beings are naturally Narrative and Narrativity is crucial to a good life. This is the dominant view in the academy, followed by the second view. It leaves plenty of room for the idea that many of us would profit from being more Narrative than we are, and the idea that we can get our "self-narratives" wrong in one way or another.

Finally, one may think both theses are false. This is my view. I think the current dominance of the third view is regrettable. It is not true that there is only one way in which human beings experience their being in time. There are deeply non-Narrative people and there are good ways to live that are deeply non-Narrative. I think the second and third views hinder human self-understanding, close down important avenues of thought, impoverish our grasp of ethical possibilities, needlessly and wrongly distress those who do not fit their model, and can be highly destructive in psychotherapeutic contexts.

To take this further, one needs to distinguish between one's sense of oneself as a human being considered as a whole and one's sense of oneself as an inner mental entity or "self" of some sort – I'll call this one's "self-experience". When Henry James (1915, pp. 562–3) says of one of his early books, in a letter written in 1915, "I think of . . . the masterpiece in question . . . as the work of quite another person than myself . . . a rich . . . relation, say, who . . . suffers me still to claim a shy fourth cousinship", he has no doubt that he is the same human being as the author of that book, but he doesn't feel he is the same self or person as the author of that book. One of the most important ways in which people tend to think of themselves (wholly independently of religious belief) is as things whose persistence conditions are not obviously or automatically the same as the persistence conditions of a human being considered as a whole. Petrarch, Proust, Derek Parfit and thousands of others have given this idea vivid expression. I'm going to take its viability for granted and set up another distinction – between "Episodic" and "Diachronic" self-experience – in terms of it.

The basic form of Diachronic self-experience (D) is that one naturally figures oneself, considered as a self, as something that was there in the (further) past and will be there in the (further) future – something that has relatively long-term Diachronic continuity, something that persists over a long stretch of time, perhaps for life.

I take it that many people are naturally Diachronic, and that many who are Diachronic are also Narrative.

If one is Episodic (E), by contrast, one does not figure oneself, considered as a self, as something that was there in the (further) past and will be there in the (further) future, although one is perfectly well aware that one has long-term continuity considered as a whole human being. Episodics are likely to have no particular tendency to see their life in Narrative terms (the Episodic/Diachronic distinction is not the same as the Narrative/non-Narrative distinction, but there are marked correlations between them).

The Episodic and Diachronic styles of temporal being are radically opposed, but they are not absolute. Predominantly Episodic individuals may sometimes connect to charged events in their past in such a way that they feel that those events happened to them (consider embarrassing memories) and anticipate events in their future in such a way that they think that those events are going to happen to them (thoughts of death can be a good example). So, too, predominantly Diachronic individuals may sometimes experience an Episodic lack of linkage with well-remembered parts of their past. Many factors may induce variations in individuals. Nevertheless I believe that the basics of temporal temperament are genetically determined and that we have here a fundamental "individual difference variable". Individual variation in psychological time-style, Episodic or Diachronic, Narrative or non-Narrative, will be found across all cultures.

Diachronics and Episodics are likely to misunderstand one another. Diachronics may find something chilling, empty and deficient in the Episodic life. They may fear it, although it is no less full or emotionally articulated than the Diachronic life, no less thoughtful or sensitive, no less open to friendship, love and loyalty. The two forms of life differ importantly in their ethical and emotional aspect. It would, however, be a great mistake to think that the Episodic life is bound to be less vital or less engaged, or less humane, or less fulfilled, or less moral (there is a very strong temptation for Diachronics to make this last charge). And if Episodics are moved to respond by casting aspersions on the Diachronic life – finding it somehow macerated or clogged, say, or excessively self-concerned, inauthentically second-order – they too will be mistaken if they think it an essentially inferior form of human life.

There is one sense in which Episodics are by definition more located in the present than Diachronics, but it does not follow, and is not true, that Diachronics are less present in the present moment than Episodics, any more than it follows, or is true, that in the Episodic life the present is somehow less informed by or responsible to the past than in the Diachronic life. What is true is that the informing and the responsibility have different characteristics and different consequences in the two cases.

Faced with sceptical Diachronics, who think that Episodics are essentially dysfunctional in the way they relate to the past, Episodics reply that the past can be present or alive in the present without being present or alive as the past.

The past can be alive – arguably more genuinely alive – in the present simply in so far as it has helped to shape the way one is in the present, just as musicians' playing can incorporate and body forth their past practice without being mediated by any explicit memory of it. What goes for musical development goes equally for ethical development, and Rilke's remarks on poetry and memory, which have a natural application to the ethical case, suggest one way in which the Episodic attitude to the past may have an advantage over the Diachronic:

> For the sake of a single poem, you must have ... many ... memories ... And yet it is not enough to have memories. ... For the memories themselves are not

important. [They give rise to a good poem] only when they have changed into our very blood, into glance and gesture, and are nameless, no longer to be distinguished from ourselves. (Rilke 1982).

Among those whose writings show them to be markedly Episodic, I propose Michel de Montaigne, the Earl of Shaftesbury, Laurence Sterne, Coleridge, Stendhal, Hazlitt, Ford Madox Ford, Virginia Woolf, Jorge Luis Borges, Fernando Pessoa, Iris Murdoch (a strongly Episodic person who is a natural story-teller), A. J. Ayer, Bob Dylan.

Proust is another candidate, for all his remembrances (which may be inspired by his Episodicity); also Emily Dickinson. Diachronicity stands out less clearly, because it is, I take it, the accepted norm, the "unmarked position"; but one may begin with Plato, St Augustine, Heidegger, Wordsworth, Dostoevsky, Joseph Conrad, Graham Greene, Evelyn Waugh, Patrick O'Brian, and all the champions of Narrativity in the current ethico-psychological debate. I find it easy to classify my friends, many of whom are intensely Diachronic, unlike my parents, who are on the Episodic side.

Given that the Diachronic outlook is the norm, and comparatively well understood, I need to say more about the Episodic outlook. Since I find myself to be relatively Episodic, I'll use myself as an example. I have a past, like any human being, I have a respectable amount of factual knowledge about my past, and I also remember some of my past experiences "from the inside", as philosophers say. And yet I have absolutely no sense of my life as a narrative with form, or indeed as a narrative without form; absolutely none. Nor do I have any great or special interest in my past. Nor do I have a great deal of concern for my future.

That's one way to put it – to speak in terms of limited interest. Another way is to say that it seems clear to me, when I am apprehending myself as a self, that the remoter past or future in question is not my past or future, although it is certainly the past or future of Galen Strawson the human being. This is more dramatic, but I think it is equally correct, when I am figuring myself as a self.

I have no significant sense that I – the I now considering this question – was there in the further past. And it seems clear to me that this is not a failure of feeling. It is, rather, a registration of a fact about what I am – about what the thing that is currently considering this problem is.

I'll use "I*" to represent: that which I now experience myself to be when I'm apprehending myself specifically as an inner mental presence or self. "I*" comes with a large family of cognate forms – "me*", "my*", "you*", "oneself*", "themselves*", and so on. The assumption built into these terms is that they succeed in making genuine reference to an inner mental something that is reasonably called a "self", but they can be used to convey the content of any form of experience that incorporates this assumption even if it is false.

It's clear to me that events in my remoter past didn't happen to me*. But what does this amount to? It certainly doesn't mean that I don't have any "auto-biographical" memories of these past experiences. I do. And they are certainly the experiences of the human being that I am. It does not, however, follow from this that I experience them as having happened to me*, or indeed that they did happen to me*. They certainly do not present as things that happened to me*, and I think I'm strictly, literally correct in thinking that they did not happen to me*.

Objection: if a remembered experience has a from-the-inside character it must be experienced by you as something that happened to you*. Reply: this seems plausible at first, but it's not so. The from-the-inside character of a memory can detach completely from any sense that one is the subject of the remembered experience. My memory of falling out of a punt has an essentially from-the-inside character, visually (the water rushing up to meet me), kinaesthetically and so on. It's not like seeing a film of myself falling, taken by a third party ("from-the-outside").

But it certainly does not follow that it carries any feeling or belief that what is remembered happened to me*, to that which I now apprehend myself to be when apprehending myself specifically as a self.

Actually, this doesn't follow even when emotion figures in the from-the-inside character of the memory. The inference from (1) "The memory has a from-the-inside character in emotional respects" to (2) "The memory is experienced as something that happened to me*" is simply not valid, although for many people (1) and (2) are often or usually true together.

For me this is a plain fact of experience.

I'm well aware that my past is mine in so far as I'm a human being, and I fully accept that there's a sense in which it has special relevance to me* now, including special emotional and moral relevance. At the same time I have no sense that I* was there in the past, and think it obvious that I* was not there, as a matter of meta-physical fact. As for my practical concern for my future, which I believe to be within the normal human range (low end), it is biologically-viscerally grounded and auton-omous in such a way that I can experience it as something immediately felt even though I have no significant sense that I* will be there in the future.

So much, briefly, for the Diachronic and Episodic forms of life. What about the Narrative life? And what might it mean to say that human life is "narrative" in nature? And must you be Diachronic to be Narrative? ("Narrative" with an upper-case "N" always denotes a psychological outlook; with a lower-case "n" it has its normal meaning.) One clear statement of the Psychological Narrativity thesis is given by Roquentin in *La Nausée*: "a man is always a teller of stories, he lives surrounded by his own stories and those of other people, he sees everything that happens to him in terms of these stories and he tries to live his life as if he were recounting it" (Sartre 1938, p. 64). Sartre sees the narrative, storytelling impulse as a defect, regrettable. He accepts the

Psychological Narrativity thesis while rejecting the Ethical Narrativity thesis. He thinks human Narrativity is essentially a matter of bad faith, of radical (and typically irremediable) inauthenticity, rather than as something essential for authenticity.

The pro-Narrative majority may concede to Sartre that Narrativity can go wrong while insisting that it is necessary for a good life. I'm with Sartre on the ethical issue, but let me now collect some more versions of the Psychological Narrativity thesis. To Oliver Sacks (each of us "constructs and lives a 'narrative' ... this narrative is us") and Jerry Bruner ("self is a perpetually rewritten story – we become the auto-biographical narratives by which we 'tell about' our lives") we may first add Daniel Dennett (writing in the TLS in 1988):

> we are all virtuoso novelists, who find ourselves engaged in all sorts of behaviour, ... and we always try to put the best "faces" on it we can. We try to make all of our material cohere into a single good story. And that story is our autobiography. The chief fictional character at the centre of that autobiography is one's *self* (Dennett 1992, reprinted here as ch. 20, p. 237).

Marya Schechtman, a philosopher, goes further, twisting the Psychological and Ethical Narrativity theses tightly together in a valuably forthright manner. A person, she says, "creates his identity [only] by forming an autobiographical narrative – a story of his life" (Schechtman 1997, p. 93).

One must possess a full and "explicit narrative [of one's life] to develop fully as a person" (ibid., p. 119). Charles Taylor claims that a "basic condition of making sense of ourselves is that we grasp our lives in a narrative" and have an understanding of our lives "as an unfolding story" (Taylor 1989, pp. 47, 52). This is not, he thinks, "an optional extra"; our lives exist "in a space of questions, which only a coherent narrative can answer". He is backed up by Claire in Douglas Coupland's novel *Generation X*: "Claire ... breaks the silence by saying that it's not healthy to live life as a succession of isolated little cool moments. 'Either our lives become stories, or there's no way to get through them'"; but Taylor builds a lot more ethical weight into what is involved in getting through life:

> It is because we cannot but orient ourselves to the good, and hence determine our place relative to it and hence determine the direction of our lives, (that) we must inescapably understand our lives in narrative form, as a "quest" (and) must see our lives in story (ibid., pp. 51–2).

This, he says, is an "inescapable structural requirement of human agency", and the leading philosopher of narrative, Paul Ricoeur, appears to concur: "How, indeed, could a subject of action give an ethical character to his or her own life taken as a whole if this life were not gathered together in some way, and how could this occur if not, precisely, in the form of a narrative?" (Ricoeur 1992, p. 158.)

Here my main puzzlement is about what it might be to "give an ethical character to (one's) own life taken as a whole" in some explicit way, and about why on earth, in the midst of the beauty of being, it should be thought to be important to do this. I think that those who think in this way are motivated by a sense of their own importance or significance that is absent in other human beings. Many of them, connectedly, have religious commitments. They are wrapped up in forms of religious belief that are – like almost all religious belief – really all about self.

Alasdair MacIntyre is a founding figure in the modern Narrativity camp, and his view is similar to Taylor's. "The unity of an individual life", he says, "is the unity of a narrative embodied in a single life. To ask 'What is the good for me?' is to ask how best I might live out that unity and bring it to completion . . . ." The unity of a human life, he continues,

> is the unity of a narrative quest . . . (and) the only criteria for success or failure in a human life as a whole are the criteria for success or failure in a narrated or to-be-narrated quest . . . A quest for what? . . . a quest for the good . . . the good life for man is the life spent in seeking for the good life for man (MacIntyre 1981, pp. 203–4).

MacIntyre's claim seems at first non-psychological: a good life is one that has narrative unity. But a good life is one spent seeking the good life, and there is a strong suggestion that seeking the good life requires taking up a Narrative perspective; in which case narrative unity requires (psychological) Narrativity.

Is any of this true? I don't think so. It seems to me that MacIntyre, Taylor and all other supporters of the Ethical Narrativity thesis are really just talking about themselves. It may be that what they are saying is true for them, both psychologically and ethically. This may be the best ethical project that people like themselves can hope to engage in (one problem with it, and it is a deep problem, is that one is almost certain to get one's "story" wrong, in some more or less sentimental way). But even if it is true for them it is not true for other types of ethical personality, and many are likely to be thrown right off their own truth by being led to believe that Narrativity is necessary for a good life.

I think the best lives almost never involve this kind of self-telling. When a Narrative like the philosopher John Campbell claims that "identity (through time) is central to what we care about in our lives: one thing I care about is what I have made of my life" (Campbell 1994, p. 190), I'm bewildered. I am completely uninterested in the answer to the question "What has Galen Strawson made of his life?", or "What have I made of my life?". I'm living it, and this sort of thinking about it is no part of it.

This doesn't mean that I am in any way irresponsible. It is just that what I care about, in so far as I care about myself and my life, is how I am now. The way I am now is profoundly shaped by my past, but it is the present-shaping consequences of the past that matter, not the past as such. I agree with the Earl of Shaftesbury:

> The metaphysicians . . . affirm that if memory be taken away, the self is lost. [But] what matter for memory? What have I to do with that part? If, *whilst I am*, I am as I should be, what do I care more? And thus let me lose *self* every hour, and be twenty successive selfs, or new selfs, 'tis all one to me: so (long as) I lose not my opinion (ie my overall outlook, my character, my moral identity). If I carry that with me 'tis I; all is well . . . The *now*; the *now*. Mind this: in this is all (Shaftesbury 1698, pp. 136–7).

I think, then, that the Ethical Narrativity thesis is false, and that the Psychological Narrativity thesis is also false in any non-trivial version. What do I mean by non-trivial? Well, if someone says, as some do, that making coffee is a narrative that involves Narrativity, because you have to think ahead, do things in the right order, and so on, and that everyday life involves many such narratives, then I take it the claim is trivial.

Is there some burden on me to explain the popularity of the two theses, given that I think that they are false? Hardly. Theorizing human beings tend to favour false views in matters of this kind. I do, though, think that intellectual fashion is part of the explanation. I also suspect that those who are drawn to write on the subject of Narrativity tend to have strongly Diachronic and Narrative outlooks or personalities, and generalize from their own case with that special, misplaced confidence that people feel when, considering elements of their own experience that are existentially fundamental for them, they take it that they must also be fundamental for everyone else.

But what exactly is Narrativity? Perhaps the first thing to say is that being Diachronic doesn't already entail being Narrative. There must be something more to experiencing one's life as a narrative than simply being Diachronic. For one can be Diachronic, naturally experiencing oneself(*) as something existing in the past and future without any particular sense of one's life as constituting a narrative.

"You're defining 'Narrative' in terms of 'narrative'. But what exactly is a narrative?" The paradigm of a narrative is a conventional story told in words. I take the term to attribute (at the very least) a certain sort of developmental and hence temporal unity or coherence to the things to which it is standardly applied – lives, parts of lives, pieces of writing. This doesn't take us far, though, because we still need to know what makes developmental unity or coherence in a life specifically narrative in nature. There's a clear sense in which every human life is a developmental unity – a historical-characteral developmental unity as well as a biological one – just in being the life of a single human being. Putting aside cases of extreme insanity, any human

255

life can be the subject of an outstanding biography that possesses all the narrative-unity-related virtues of that literary form. Even dogs and horses can be the subject of excellent biographies. This, I think, is why the distinctive claim of the defenders of the Psychological Narrativity thesis is that for a life to be a narrative in the required sense it must be lived Narratively. The person whose life it is must see or feel it as a narrative, construe it as a narrative, live it as a narrative.

"Now you're defining 'narrative' in terms of 'Narrative'; we're going round in circles." Circles are not always bad, but perhaps one can restart from the idea of a construction in the sense of a construal: Narrativity clearly involves putting some sort of construction – a unifying or form-finding construction – on the events of one's life, or parts of one's life. This needn't involve any clearly intentional activity, nor any departure from or addition to the facts, but the Narrative attitude must amount to something more than a disposition to grasp one's life as a unity simply in so far as it is the life of a biologically single human being. Nor can it consist just in the ability to give a sequential record of the actual course of one's life, even if one's life does in fact exemplify a classical pattern of narrative development independently of any construction or interpretation. One must have some sort of relatively large-scale, coherence-seeking, unity seeking, pattern seeking, or most generally form-finding tendency (F) when it comes to one's apprehension of one's life (or relatively large-scale parts of one's life).

The notion of form finding is very unspecific, but its lack of specificity may be part of its value, and it seems clear that Diachronicity (D) and form finding (F) are independent of each other. In practice, no doubt, they often come together, but one can imagine [−D+F] an Episodic person in whom a form-finding tendency is stimulated precisely by lack of a Diachronic outlook. Jack Kerouac seems a case of an Episodic looking for larger form, and there are clear elements of this in Malcolm Lowry. Conversely, one can imagine [+D−F] a Diachronic person who lives, by force of circumstance, an intensely picaresque and disjointed life, while having absolutely no tendency to seek unity or narrative-developmental pattern in it.

Other Diachronics in similar circumstances may move from [+D−F] to [+D+F], acquiring a form-finding tendency precisely because they become distressed by the "one damned thing after another" character of their lives.

The great and radically non-Narrative Stendhal might be judged to be an example of this, in the light of all his chaotic autobiographical projects, although I'm more inclined to classify him as [−D+F], strongly Episodic even if subject to Diachronic flashes. Either way, one can be Diachronic while being very unreflective about oneself. One can be inclined to think, of any event in one's past of which one is reminded, that it happened to oneself*, without positively grasping one's life as a unity in any further – e.g., specifically narrative – sense.

One view might be that form finding is not only necessary for Narrativity, but also sufficient. Against that, it may be said that if one is genuinely Narrative one must also (and of course) have some sort of distinctive storytelling tendency (S) when it comes to one's apprehension of one's life – where storytelling is understood in such a way that it does not imply any tendency to fabrication, conscious or otherwise, although it does not exclude it either. On this view, one must be disposed to apprehend or think of oneself and one's life as fitting the form of some recognized narrative genre.

Storytelling is a species of form finding, and the basic model for it, perhaps, is the way in which gifted and impartial journalists or historians report a sequence of events. Obviously they select among the facts, but they do not, we suppose, distort or falsify them, and they do more than merely list them in the correct temporal order, for they also place them in a connected account. Storytelling of this sort involves the ability to detect – not invent – developmental coherencies in the manifold of one's life. It is one way in which one may be able to apprehend the deep personal constancies that do in fact exist in the life of every human being – although this can also be done by form finding without storytelling.

So far, then, we have the unremarkable claim that form finding is a necessary condition of Narrativity and that storytelling is a sufficient condition. A third and more troubling suggestion is that if one is Narrative one will also have a tendency to engage unconsciously in invention, falsification, confabulation, revisionism, fiction, when it comes to one's apprehension of one's own life. I will call this revision (R). The Revision thesis, accordingly, is that Narrativity always involves some tendency to revision, where Revision essentially involves more than merely changing one's view of the facts of one's life (one can change one's view of the facts of one's life without any falsification, simply by coming to see things more clearly).

Revision is by definition non-conscious. It may sometimes begin consciously, with deliberate lies told to others, for example, and it may have semi-conscious instances, but it is not genuine revision in the present sense unless or until its products are felt to be true in a way that excludes awareness of falsification.

The conscious/non-conscious border is murky and porous, but I think the notion of Revision is robust for all that; the paradigm cases are clear, and extremely common.

If the Revision thesis were true, it would be bad news for the Ethical Narrativity thesis, whose supporters cannot want ethical success to depend essentially on falsification. I'm sure almost all human Narrativity is compromised by Revision, but I don't think it must be. It's a vast and complex phenomenon, and I will make just a few remarks.

It is often said that autobiographical memory is an essentially constructive and reconstructive phenomenon rather than a merely reproductive one, and there is a clear sense in which this is true. Memory deletes, abridges, edits, reorders, italicizes. But even if construction and reconstruction are universal in autobiographical memory, they need not involve revision as currently defined; for they may be fabrication-free story-telling or form finding. Many think we are all without exception incorrigible self-fabulists, "unreliable narrators" of our own lives, and some who hold this view claim greater honesty of outlook for themselves, and see pride, self-blindness, and so on in those who deny it. But other research makes it pretty clear that this is not true (see, for example, work by W. Brewer, W. Wagenaar, A. Baddeley, M. Ross, W. Swann). It is not true that everyone is an unreliable narrator. Some are self-fabulists all the way down. In others autobiographical memory is fundamentally non-distorting, whatever automatic processes of remoulding and recasting it may invariably involve.

Many think that revision is always charged – always motivated by an interconnected core group of moral emotions including pride, self-love, conceit, shame, regret, remorse and guilt. Some claim with Nietzsche that we always revise in our own favour: "'I have done that', says my memory. 'I cannot have done that', says my pride, and remains inexorable. Eventually – memory yields". It seems, however, that neither of these claims is true. The first, that all revision is charged, is significantly improved by the inclusion of modesty or low self-esteem, gratitude or forgiveness, in the core group of motivating moods and emotions; some people are just as likely to revise to their own detriment and to others' advantage as the other way round. But the claim that revision is always charged remains false even so.

Revision may occur simply because one is concerned with consistency, or because one is a natural form finder but a very forgetful one, who instinctively seeks to make a coherent story out of limited materials. Frustrated storytellers may fall into revision simply because they can't find satisfying form in their lives and without being in any way motivated by a wish to preserve or restore self-respect. John Dean's recall of his conversations with Nixon at the Watergate hearings is a much discussed case of uncharged Revision. When the missing tapes were found, his testimony was revealed to be impressively "accurate about the individuals' basic positions", as W. Brewer says, although it was "inaccurate with respect to exactly what was said during a given conversation" (Brewer 1988, p. 27).

Even when Revision is charged, the common view that we always revise in our own favour must yield to a mass of everyday evidence that some people are just as likely to revise to their own detriment – or simply forget the good things they have done. When La Rochefoucauld says that self-love is subtler than the subtlest man in the world, there is truth in what he says.

It may be added that revising to one's own detriment may be no more attractive than revising to one's advantage.

But La Rochefoucauld is sometimes too clever, or rather ignorant, in his cynicism.

Is a tendency to revise necessary for Narrativity? No. In our own frail case, Narrativity may rarely occur without Revision, but storytelling is sufficient for Narrativity, and one can be storytelling without being Revisionary. So the Ethical

Narrativity thesis survives the threat posed by the Revision thesis. When Bernard Malamud (1979) claims that "all biography is ultimately fiction", simply on the grounds that "there is no life that can be captured wholly, as it was," there is no implication that it must also be ultimately untrue.

Diachronicity, form finding, storytelling, Revision – how do the authors I've quoted classify? Well, Dennett endorses a full blown (+D+F+S+R) view of Narrativity, and seems to place considerable emphasis on Revision: "our fundamental tactic of self-protection, self-control, and self-definition is not spinning webs or building dams, but telling stories, and more particularly concocting and controlling the story we tell others – and ourselves – about who we are".

Bruner, I think, concurs with this emphasis.

Sartre, I think, endorses (+F+S+R) and is not particularly concerned with (D) in so far as he is mainly interested in short-term, in-the-present storytelling.

Schechtman's account of Narrativity is (+D+F+S±R). It assumes that we're all Diachronic, requires that we be form finding and storytelling and explicitly so: "constituting an identity requires that an individual conceive of his life as having the form and the logic of a story ... the story of a person's life – where 'story' is understood as a conventional, linear narrative". It is, however, important, on her view, that there be no significant revision, and that one's self-narrative be essentially accurate.

I take myself to be (–D–F–S–R). The claim that I don't revise much is the most vulnerable one, because it's in the nature of the case that one has no sense that one revises when one does. So I may be wrong, but (of course) I don't think so. On the strong form of Schechtman's view, though, I am not really a person. Some creatures, she says, "weave stories of their lives, and it is their doing so which makes them persons"; to have an "identity" as a person is "to have a narrative self-conception ... to experience the events in one's life as interpreted through one's sense of one's own life story". This is in fact a common type of claim, and at one point Schechtman claims that "elements of a person's narrative" that figure only in his "implicit self-narrative", and that "he cannot articulate ... are only partially his – attributable to him to a lesser degree than those aspects of the narrative he can articulate" (Schechtman 1997, p. 117).

This seems to me to express an ideal of control and self-awareness in human life that is mistaken and potentially pernicious. The aspiration to explicit Narrative self-articulation is natural for some – for some, perhaps, it may even be helpful – but in others it is unnatural and ruinous. My suspicion is that it almost always does more harm than good – that the Narrative tendency to look for story or narrative coherence in one's life is, in general, a gross hindrance to self-understanding: to a just, general, practically real sense, implicit or explicit, of one's nature. It's well known that telling and retelling one's past leads to changes, smoothings, enhancements, shifts away from the facts, and recent research has shown that this is not just a human psychological foible. It turns out to be an inevitable consequence of the neurophysiological process of laying down memories that every studied conscious recall of past events brings an alteration.

The implication is plain: the more you recall, retell, narrate yourself, the further you risk moving away from accurate self-understanding, from the truth of your being. Some are constantly telling their daily experiences to others in a storying way and with great gusto. They are drifting ever further off the truth. Others never do this, and when they're obliged to convey facts about their lives they do it clumsily and uncomfortably and in a peculiarly anti-narrative way.

Certainly Narrativity is not a necessary part of the "examined life" (nor is Diachronicity), and it is in any case most unclear that the examined life, thought by Socrates essential to being fully human, is always a good thing. People can develop and deepen in valuable ways without any sort of explicit, specifically Narrative reflection, just as musicians can improve by practice sessions without recalling those sessions. The business of living well is, for many, a completely non-Narrative project.

Granted that certain sorts of self-understanding are necessary for a good human life, they need involve nothing more than form finding, which can exist in the absence of Narrativity; and they may be osmotic, systemic, not staged in consciousness. It may be said that the acquisition of self-understanding in psychotherapy, at least, is an essentially Narrative project, and it's true that therapy standardly involves identifying key causal connections between features of one's early life and the way one is at present. But even though the thing one learns is of the form "It is because X and Y happened to this child that I am now Z", there need not be anything distinctively or even remotely Narrative in one's psychological attitude to the connections. This is not a condition of effective therapy – and one certainly doesn't have to have any Diachronic sense that the child encountered in therapy was oneself*. Even more certainly, one does not have to have a satisfying narrative "forged" for one by the therapist, or in the process of therapy, in order to live well. Heaven forbid.

There is much more to say. Narratives may still think that Episodic lives must be deprived in some way, but such lives can be vivid, blessed, profound (note, though, how Tom Bombadil in *The Lord of the Rings* can produce a certain anxiety). Some think an Episodic cannot really know true friendship or love, or even be loyal. They are refuted by Michel de Montaigne, a great Episodic, famous for his friendship with Etienne de la Boetie, who judges that he is "better at friendship than at anything else" although "there is nobody less suited than I am to start talking about memory. I can find hardly a trace of it in myself; I doubt if there is any other memory in the world as grotesquely faulty as mine is!"

A gift for friendship doesn't require any ability to recall past shared experiences in detail, nor any tendency to value them. It resides in how one is and feels in the present.

Montaigne finds he is often misjudged, for when he admits that he has a very poor memory people assume that he must suffer from ingratitude: "they judge my affection by my memory", he comments, and are of course quite wrong to do so (Montaigne 1563, p. 32).

Can Episodics be properly moral beings? The question troubles many, in extraordinarily revealing ways. The answer, which needs defence in the present climate of opinion, is "Of course". Diachronicity is not a necessary condition of a moral existence, nor of a proper sense of responsibility. As for Narrativity, it is in the sphere of ethics more of an affliction or a bad habit than a prerequisite of a good life. For "we live", as V. S. Pritchett says, "beyond any tale that we happen to enact".

FURTHER READING

Baddeley, A. (1994). 'The remembered self and the enacted self'. In Neisser & Fivush 1994.

Brewer, W. F. (1988). 'Memory for randomly sampled autobiographical events'. In *Remembering Reconsidered: Ecological and traditional approaches to the study of memory*. U. Neisser & E. Winograd, eds. (Cambridge: Cambridge University Press).

Bruner, J. (1987). 'Life as Narrative'. *Social Research* 54:11–32.

——. (1994). 'The "remembered" self'. In Neisser & Fivush 1994.

Campbell, J. (1994). *Past, Space, and Self* (Cambridge, MA: MIT Press).

Dennett, D. (1992) 'The Self as the Center of Narrative Gravity'. Reprinted here as chapter 20.

James, H. (1864–1915/1999). *Henry James: a Life in Letters*, Philip Horne, ed. (London: Penguin).

MacIntyre, A. (1981). *After Virtue* (London: Duckworth).

Montaigne, M. de (1563–92/1991). *The Complete Essays*, M. A. Screech, trans. (London: Penguin).

Neisser, U. and R. Fivush, eds. *The remembering self: construction and accuracy in the self-narrative.* (Cambridge: Cambridge University Press).

Ricoeur, P. (1992). *Oneself as Another*, Kathleen Blamey, trans. (Chicago: The University of Chicago Press).

Rilke, R.M. (1982). 'The Notebooks of Malte Laurids Brigge', quoted in *The Selected Poetry of Rainer Maria Rilke*, Stephen Mitchell, trans. (Picador).

Ross, M. (1989). 'Relation of implicit theories to the construction of personal histories'. *Psychological Review* 96:341–357.

Sacks, O. (1985). *The Man Who Mistook His Wife For A Hat* (London: Duckworth).

Sartre, J.-P. (1938/1996). *La nausée* (Paris: Gallimard).

Schechtman, M. (1997). *The Constitution of Selves* (Ithaca: Cornell University Press).

Shaftesbury, Earl of (1698–1712/1900). 'Philosophical Regimen', in *The Life, Unpublished Letters*, and *Philosophical Regimen* of Anthony, Earl of Shaftesbury, edited by B. Rand (New York: Macmillan).

Swann, W. B. (1990). 'To be adored or to be known: the interplay of self-enhancement and self-verification'. In *Handbook of motivation and cognition: Foundations of social behavior*, R. M. Sorrentino & E. T. Higgins, eds., volume 2 (New York: Guilford).

Taylor, C. (1989). *Sources of the Self* (Cambridge: Cambridge University Press).

Wagenaar, W. (1994). 'Is memory self-serving?' In Neisser & Fivush 1994.

22

THERE IS NO PROBLEM OF THE SELF

Eric T. Olson

I

People often speak as if there were a serious philosophical problem about *selves*. Is there a self? Is the self knowable? How does the self relate to the body? These and other questions are thought to make up something called the *problem of the self*.

I doubt seriously that there is any such problem. Not because the self is unproblematic, or because there are unproblematically no such things as selves. My trouble is that a problem must be a problem *about* something: even if there are no selves, there must at least be some problematic idea or concept of a self, if there is to be a problem of the self. As far as I can see there is no such idea. What is a self? For every answer to this question, there is another answer not only incompatible with it, but wholly unrelated. There is virtually no agreement about the characteristic features of selves: depending on whom you believe, selves may be concrete or abstract, material or immaterial, permanent or ephemeral, naturally occurring or human constructions, essentially subjective or publicly observable, the same or not the same things as people. There are not even any agreed paradigm cases of selves, things we could point to or describe and say, 'A self is one of *those*.' But no concept could be so problematic that no one could agree about *anything* to do with it. For lack of a subject matter, then, there is no problem of the self.

So I shall argue, anyway. I am not just quibbling about a word. Real philosophy is at stake. Many philosophers assume that there is something properly called the problem or problems of the self, and write as if everyone knew what they meant by 'self'. This often leads to obscurity and muddle. If I am right, the muddle arises because those philosophers believe in a concept that doesn't exist.

I claim also that if we look at those books and articles with titles like 'The Self' or 'Problems of the Self', we will find that they are most typically not about 'selves' at all, but about other things – different things in different cases. In fact the matters discussed under the heading of 'self' are *so* various that no one can seriously say that they are all about some one thing, the self. Because legitimate inquiries that go under the heading of 'self' are really about something else, and can be (and typically are) put in other terms, we can easily do without the word 'self'.

For these reasons, I believe that philosophers would do well to avoid the word 'self' in their theorizing.

II

What would the problem of the self be about, if there were such a problem? What is this 'self' whose existence and properties appear to be the subject of so much debate? What distinguishes problems about the self from problems about other topics – causation or intrinsic value, say? If there is any genuine problem of the self, there must be *some* nontrivial answer, however vague or incomplete, to these questions.

There are several ways of trying to meet this demand. The most satisfactory would be to give a definition of the term or an analysis of the concept. A definition of 'self' would say, '*x* is *y*'s self if and only if ... ', with the dots filled in by some synonymous or at least logically equivalent phrase. I say that the phrase to be explained is '*x* is *y*'s self' rather than '*x* is a self' (less formally, 'one's self' rather than simply 'a self') because it is part of the meaning of the word 'self', in its typical philosophical uses, that a self be *someone's* self. (That much, anyway, seems clear.) Or if there could be 'unowned' selves, it is part of the idea of a self that it at least be the sort of thing that *could* be the self of a particular person or thing. If someone could explain '*x* is a self' but not '*x* is *y*'s self', or if someone could distinguish selves from non-selves but had no idea what made a given self the self of a particular person, I think most 'self'-users would doubt that he knew what the word meant. The word 'self' is like the word 'body', as in the phrase 'human body': anyone who knows what the words 'human body' mean must have at least some idea of what it is for something to be the body, or at least a body, of a particular person (van Inwagen 1980). We can easily define '*x* is a self' in terms of '*x* is *y*'s self': *x* is a self just in case there is (or could be) some *y* such that *x* is *y*'s self. But there is no obvious way of deriving an account of the meaning of '*x* is *y*'s self' from a definition of '*x* is a self'. Thus, even if we succeeded in defining '*x* is a self' we should still face the task of accounting for '*x* is *y*'s self'.

If we use a word that we can't define, or that we can't define in a way that others who use it will accept, we must be on our guard – the more so if the word is a piece of philosophical jargon that has no place in ordinary language. (Part of the trouble with 'self' is that it is jargon masquerading as ordinary language.) It will be a real question whether those who use the word are in any sense talking about the same thing. Anyone who uses a word whose definition is disputed is obliged to say what she means by it. If we cannot do so, we have to wonder whether we understand what we are saying.

But a word isn't necessarily in serious trouble just because it has no agreed definition. There are other ways of saying what a self is than by explicitly defining it. We could mention some characteristic features of selves – features that may not necessarily be shared by all and only selves, but which selves at least typically have and non-selves typically lack. A longish list of such features would give us a fair idea of what a self is.

Failing both a definition and a list of characteristic features, we could at least begin to answer the question, What is a self? by referring to some paradigm cases of selves – particular things that everyone agrees are selves, or that would be selves if there were any selves – and some paradigm cases of non-selves. Of course, this strategy faces well-known difficulties: even if you can figure out which particular things I am referring to, you might not be able to guess what it is about those things that makes them all selves, and so have no idea what other things count as selves or why. (If I point to a shoe, a lampshade, a book, and a carrot, and say, '*Melves* are things like those,' obviously that won't suffice to tell you what I mean by 'melf'; nor will it help much if I go on to tell you that stones and forks are not melves.) Still, I should have given you at least *some* information about what a self is.

Let me illustrate these rather abstract points with a concrete example. There is no agreed account of the meaning of the term 'mind' or 'mental', of what makes a phenomenon mental rather than non-mental. Intentionality ('aboutness'), subjectivity ('what it is like'), immediate accessibility to consciousness, and many other features have been proposed as 'marks of the mental'; but none of these accounts is widely accepted. This is a problem. In a sense, we don't know what the mind is. At the same time, we know rather a lot about the mind. Nearly everyone agrees that mental phenomena, if there are any, often *have* intentionality and subjectivity, and are often accessible to consciousness, even if these features don't suffice to define the mental. We agree on a wide range of typical and characteristic features of mental phenomena: everyone agrees, for instance, that the desire for rain is satisfied by rain and frustrated by persistent dry weather, and that being in the presence of rain usually causes one to believe that it's raining. And we agree on paradigm cases: no one doubts that beliefs, wants, memories, intentions, sensations, emotions, and dreams, if there are such things, are mental phenomena, and that earthquakes and temperatures are not. Even those who deny that there are any mental phenomena can reasonably claim to understand what it is whose existence they are denying. Thus, although there is some dispute about just what the subject matter of psychology or the philosophy of mind may be, there seems to be enough agreement that many of our questions can be said to be questions *about the mind*.

On the other hand, if a large minority of philosophers and psychologists thought that beliefs, though they exist, were not mental phenomena at all, but took something completely different – photosynthesis, say – as paradigmatic of the mental, it would be clear that there was serious confusion afoot. Matters would be even worse if there were respected participants in the debate who thought that many non-mental but few mental phenomena had properties like intentionality or subjectivity. Although there would certainly be a problem about the *word* 'mind' in that case, it would be a good deal less clear that there was a philosophical problem *of the mind*. For what, beyond the word, could it be a problem about? The case of the self is rather like that.

III

Let us consider some attempts to say what a self might be. It doesn't matter whether we take these proposals to be definitions of 'self' or only as giving essential or paradigmatic or at any rate salient features of selves. Take them as proposed answers to the ordinary question, 'What is a self'?

> *Account 1.* One's self is that unchanging, simple substance to which one's impressions and ideas have reference.

This is apparently what Hume sought in vain within himself (1978, p. 251). We may wonder what Hume meant by ideas 'having reference to' one's self. But the main thing to be said about this account is that most present-day philosophers see no reason to believe that any unchanging, simple substance has anything to do with anyone's ideas or impressions. If this is what selves are, there are simply no selves, and the problem of the self is of little more than historical interest. For an account of 'self' that reflects today's concerns we must look elsewhere.

Here is an updated version of something like Hume's account:

> *Account 2.* One's self is the inner subject of one's conscious experiences.

(Campbell 1957, p. 74; Harré 1987, p. 99.) Variants include 'One's self is the bearer of one's personal identity over time' (Berofsky 1995, p. 234); ' . . . that which views the world through one's eyes' (Nagel 1986, p. 55); ' . . . the tautological subject of one's actions' (Rée 1974, p. 188n.); 'the cause of everything one does' (Minsky 1985, p. 232); etc.

Now I take it that *I* am the subject of my conscious experiences, the bearer of my identity over time, and the cause of everything I do. Otherwise they wouldn't be *my* experiences, *my* identity, or things that *I* do. On this account, then, I am my self, and you are yours. Everyone is identical with his self. If there should turn out to be no selves, there would be no such beings as you and I. And although some philosophers accept this inference, others reject it: they think that the existence of selves is problematic in a way that the existence of midwives and plumbers, or of you and me, is not (e.g. Harré 1987, p. 103). In fact those who argue that 'there is no self' rarely go on to conclude from this that they themselves do not exist. *Their* problem of the self must be about something else.

Although the above account seems to imply that selves are people, it doesn't say that the two terms are synonymous. But many philosophers use the terms interchangeably (e.g. Mellor 1991; Bermúdez 1997). So we might say:

Account 3. One's self is just that person, himself.

Selves are just people, human beings. To say that the self is so-and-so is to say that people, you and I, are so-and-so. This makes it rather awkward to say that one *has* a self. What could it be for me to *have* a person, or to *have* myself? The truth, rather, is that we *are* selves. But we could presumably explain away talk of having a self as a hangover from the eighteenth-century use of the word 'self'.

If this account were widely accepted, I shouldn't be writing this essay. To be sure, the word 'person' is problematic enough that anyone who relies on it in philosophical discussion had better say what she means by it. There is a good deal of dispute about its definition, and about whether it can be defined at all. Compared with 'self', though, 'person' is a model of clarity and accord. Everyone agrees that people (persons) characteristically have certain mental capacities such as rationality and self-consciousness, and certain moral attributes such as accountability for their actions (or at any rate that they are capable of acquiring such features). There is a fair consensus about what things count as people; no one doubts that you and I and Boris Yeltsin are people, and that houses and bronze statues of people aren't. Although there are disputed cases (foetuses, infants, adults suffering from severe senile dementia), their number is small compared with the number of items we can confidently classify as people or non-people. In this respect 'person' is no worse off than most other nouns. We know how many people there are (a few hard cases aside, once more) and how to count them. The word 'person' is well enough understood for there to be philosophical problems about people.

But many philosophers explicitly deny that 'self' and 'person' are interchangeable. For example, some say that dogs and dolphins are, or have, selves, even though they aren't people (Lowe 1996, p. 49n.). More seriously, it is often said that 'person' has to do with a publicly observable, social being whereas a self is essentially something inner or private (e.g. Harré 1984, p. 26; McCall 1990, pp. 12–15; see also Campbell 1957, p. 93; Hamlyn 1984, p. 188). Others say that people but not selves can be described, identified, and counted (Abelson 1977, p. 87). This suggests that you and I are not selves, but rather have them – assuming, at least, that *we* are people, or that we are publicly observable or countable or identifiable. What, then, are selves? We might say:

> *Account 4*. One's self is that indescribable and unidentifiable private, inner being within one.

('By "self" I mean the personal unity I take myself to be, my singular inner being, so to speak' [Harré 1984, p. 26].)

Now this is completely unhelpful. We might as well say that the self is 'the elusive "I" that shows an alarming tendency to disappear when we try to introspect it', a definition (tongue in cheek, I assume) found in a popular philosophical dictionary (Blackburn 1994, p. 344). You can't explain what a self is by saying that it is something inner and ineffable, any more than you can do so by saying that it is a certain kind of 'I'. Of course, if the self really is something ineffable, this is no criticism. You can't describe the indescribable. The challenge for those who think they understand this account is to persuade the rest of us to take them seriously.

'One's self is what one identifies oneself with, what a person cares most about, the loss of which amounts, for him, to self-destruction, either partial or total' (Abelson 1977, p. 91; see also James 1905, p. 291; Berofsky 1995). Thus we might write,

> *Account 5*. One's self is what one values above all else.

Of course, there may be a number of things that someone values above all else, and whose destruction would be as bad for her as her own destruction. So it would not be uncommon for someone to have several different selves at once, on this account ('The piano is my second self,' said Chopin), as well as having different selves at different times; and different people would often share the very same self. The phrase 'Mary's self' wouldn't necessarily have unique reference. It would be more like 'Mary's brother'. In fact, Mary's self might *be* her brother. There would be people whose selves were houses, political causes, children, or pets. Many of those who use the word 'self' would reject this consequence as absurd.

Let us continue our catalogue:

> *Account 6*. One's self is the unconscious mechanism responsible for the unity of one's consciousness.

(Brooks 1994, pp. 36, 51.) On this account, there is nothing subjective or ineffable or immaterial about the self; nor are selves people. My self may be literally an organ, a part of my brain, a matter for physiologists to investigate.

Others suggest that the self is not a material part of one but rather an attribute, typically an aspect of one's personality or character or behaviour:

Account 7. One's self is a psychological or behavioural attribute of one.

But which psychological or behavioural attribute? No one would count my fear of close spaces as a serious candidate for being my self. One view is that one's self is the way one sees oneself, or a certain set of one's beliefs about oneself: one's self is roughly one's self-image (Rogers 1951, pp. 498; Harré 1984, p. 26; Marx and Hillix 1973, p. 605). I suppose Dennett's account of the self as a 'center of narrative gravity' might be something like this, though it is far from clear just what he means by that phrase (1991, pp. 416, 427). On this view a person's self is typically unique, and one may have different selves at different times, perhaps even more than one self at once. Others say that one's self is by definition unique: it is (for example) what is expressed by one's uniquely characteristic actions (Kenny 1988, p. 33). In that case, for all I know I may not have a self at all, as I cannot rule out the possibility that somewhere in the universe there is someone exactly like me in the relevant respects. For that matter, it is consistent with everything we know that no one has a self. Even those who consider it an open question whether there are any selves are unlikely to accept that there could fail to be selves for *that* reason. By contrast, others take the self to be 'man as he really is, not as he appears to himself' (Jung 1968, p. 186), or that collection of features shared by all and only human beings in all times and places (Solomon 1988, p. 4). One's self is something like universal human nature. The very idea of the self, on this account, ensures that we all have the same self, and that there could not be more than one.

Naturally none of these variants will be acceptable to those who think that *we* are selves, or that selves are things that think or experience. No one seriously supposes that *he* is a psychological attribute. No psychological attribute could think about Vienna, or sleep badly, or drink coffee.

Let us consider one more popular account:

Account 8. One's self is an aggregate of or a construction out of one's sense-experiences.

(Ayer 1946, p. 125; see also Broad 1925, p. 282; Marx and Hillix 1973, p. 605.) Let us set aside the serious question of just what an 'aggregate' or 'construction' might be. We might put the view more loosely by saying that one's self is one's mental life, the sum-total of all of one's thoughts and experiences, or perhaps some selected portion thereof. This, I suppose, is the 'bundle theory of the self' often attributed to Hume. Are you and I selves on this account? That depends on whether we are literally made out of thoughts and experiences – whether an aggregate of thoughts and experiences is the sort of things that can do and be all of the things that you and I can do and be. (Can a bundle of thoughts ride a bicycle? Could a bundle of thoughts have consisted of completely different thoughts?) This is a familiar problem about personal identity.

IV

What, then, of the problem of the self? What is it a problem about? There is clearly nothing that satisfies all of these accounts. There aren't even two or three similar kinds of things that each satisfy most of them. It should be equally clear that there is no one thing – no single idea – that all of these accounts could reasonably be seen as trying to capture. There is no one sort of thing that some believe is a construction out of sense-impressions and others take to be a mental attribute, a simple substance, an organ, a human being, or in some cases even a house or a hamster. It should also be clear that there are no agreed characteristic attributes of selves, or even any generally accepted cases. (We can't even pick out a self in a purely relational way, for example as 'Bertrand Russell's self', without controversy, for on some accounts of 'self' there are no selves to pick out, while on others Russell might have had any number of different selves.) I conclude that those who use the word 'self', if they are saying anything coherent at all, must be talking about completely different things. Thus, there is no such idea as the idea of the self, and therefore nothing for the 'problem of the self' to be a problem about.

There are several replies that someone might make to this argument. First, our catalogue of answers to the question, What is a self? is incomplete. We may have neglected one that would solve the problem. Of course, the mere fact that there are other accounts different from those mentioned is no help to those who believe in the problem of the self. Simply extending the list will only make matters worse. What we need is not just an account of the self that would command wider assent than any of these, but one that would synthesize them and show them all to reflect a part of some larger, common idea. But we can say no more about this possibility until someone produces a candidate for that role.

Second, one might argue that this lack of agreement about selves is part of the very problem I claim not to exist. Doesn't this just show that the problem of the self is more serious than we thought? That it is not only about the nature and existence of selves and their relation to more familiar entities such as people and human beings, but about the very meaning of the term? I can imagine someone comparing the problem of the self with the problem of *race*. There is no accepted account of what the term 'race' or any of its determinates such as 'black', 'white', 'coloured', 'slavic', 'oriental', etc. mean. For this and other reasons, there is no end to the rubbish that has been said and written about race. But aren't those confused writings and sayings *about race*? If there were no problem of the self for the reasons I have given, wouldn't it follow, absurdly, that there was no race problem?

The analogy is strained. Even if no one knows what race or individual races are, there is wide agreement about a great deal of 'race lore'. Whatever 'black' or 'white' might mean, everyone agrees that 'black' people *typically* (though not always) have dark, curly hair and dark skin compared with 'white' people. Everyone agrees that race, if there is such a thing, is an inherited trait, even if there is dispute about how the race of one's parents determines one's own race. Most of us are disposed to class most people into 'black', 'white', etc. in the same way, however arbitrary or unfair those classifications may be. Everyone accepts certain paradigm cases: Nelson Mandela is clearly 'black', Margaret Thatcher is 'white', Mao Tse-Tung is 'oriental', and so on. So even the problematic term 'race' fares far better than 'self' in terms of characteristic features, consistency of application, and paradigm cases.

At any rate, the comparison with 'race' can hardly be cheering for theorists of the self. Of course there is a *social* 'race problem'. But that problem is not so much about race itself, whatever that may be, as about people's attitudes. It arises not because different people belong to different races, but because people think they do, or rather because they treat others differently on the basis of their outward appearance or that of their ancestors. If everyone stopped doing that, the problem would go away. In this sense there is indeed a 'problem of the self'. The problem is that people use the word 'self' as if everyone knew what it meant when in fact there is no agreement about what it means, and that this leads them into needless troubles. *That* 'problem of the self' would be solved if people simply stopped using the word and others like it. But that is not the problem of the self that my opponents believe in. There is a social problem about the *word* 'self'. There is no philosophical problem about selves.

A third reply would be to concede that there is no single concept of the self, but to insist that there are, nonetheless, many different concepts properly so called. There are different kinds of selves. Since the term is ambiguous, it may be a mistake to speak of *the* self without specifying which 'self' we mean. But we do have 'the Humean self', 'the inner-subject self', 'the personal self', 'the ineffable self', 'the evaluative self', and so on, each with its own set of problems. Don't these ideas give us a set of problems of the self?

Only in the most trivial sense. Once we concede that the various uses of the term 'self' have nothing more in common than the word, we can see that it could be a pun to say that they are all nevertheless problems of the self. We might as well say that the 'problem of property' includes both debates about the legal institution of ownership and the metaphysical problem of universals. On the other hand, if the various accounts of the self do have some interesting content in common, we ought to be able to say what it is, and thus give an account of the meaning of the word, however vague or incomplete, that everyone can accept.

V

I said I was going to argue not only that there is no problem of the self, properly so called, but also that careless use of the term 'self' creates trouble we could otherwise avoid. I will mention a few examples of that trouble.

Some philosophers seem to be aware that the term 'self' is wildly ambiguous. Owen Flanagan, for example, writes,

> The word 'self' has many meanings – personality, character, an individual's central character traits, the way(s) one carries oneself in the world, the way one represents oneself to oneself and to others, the dynamic integrated system of thoughts, emotions, lived events, and so on, that make up who one is from the God's eye point of view. All these senses are useful. (1996, p. vii)

We should expect someone of this view to take care always to explain what he meant when he used the word 'self'. But Flanagan goes on to say that Augustine's *Confessions* is 'the story of a single self', and to ask whether every individual has 'one and only one self', without giving any indication of whether he means central character traits, the way one represents oneself to others, or any of the other items on his list, leaving the reader to guess what claim is intended (pp. 95 f.).[1]

This can lead to more serious trouble. Consider this quotation:

> If A's brain is put into B's body, would A's Self move into B's body? Clearly, if the bodies were different (A might be a man, and B a woman) then the Self could hardly be the same – for our notion of Self is surely bound up with our potentialities and our behaviour. At most there could be but a kind of inner core of Self (which might be memories?) remaining after a radical change of body. Suppose, though, that A and B are identical twins and equally fit. Would they swap selves with a brain transplant? (Gregory 1981, p. 491)

Well, *would* the result of putting your brain into the head of your identical twin and his brain into yours be that you got what was previously his self and he got the self that was once yours? There are many questions we might ask about this imaginary case. We can ask what would happen to *you*: which, if any, of the two resulting people, if they would be people at all, would be you. We can ask whether the being got by putting your brain into your twin's cranium would have memories, personality, self-image, and other psychological features that were more like yours or more like those of your twin, or which person – you or your twin or someone else – he would think he was. And so on. But what could it mean to ask whether you and he would exchange *selves*? Suppose someone insisted that you would indeed exchange selves. Would you agree or disagree? What sort of argument would support or undermine this claim? What consequences, if any, would it have for the way the other questions are answered? Until the author tells us what he means by 'self', we can have no idea. Yet he apparently sees no need to do so.

The same trouble arises when people ask whether someone with a split personality has more than one self, or whether we create two different selves by cutting the cerebral commissures, or whether one can become a different self through religious conversion, psychic trauma, education, or some other experience. Anyone familiar with philosophical writing that purports to be about the self will recognize claims like these:

The self exists (does not exist).
The self is identical (is not identical) with the body.
The self is not an object.
A human being can have (cannot have) more than one self at once.
Human beings have selves but lobsters don't.
The first-person pronoun purports to pick out a self *qua* self.

Without further elucidation, I don't understand any of these claims well enough to know even whether I agree or disagree. And for anyone who thinks he understands them perfectly well, there will be another who feels equally confident, but who understands them in a completely different way. The reason is that unless the word 'self' as it figures in these sentences is explicitly given some special meaning, they simply don't say anything at all.

Let us consider one more example. Galen Strawson writes,

I will call my view the Pearl view, because it suggests that many mental selves exist, one at a time and one after another, like pearls on a string, in the case of something like a human being (1997, p. 424).

Each self, apparently, exists for as long as one's attention is focussed on some one thing, typically two or three seconds, then perishes. But what is it that a human being gets a new one of every few seconds? That is not so clear, despite Strawson's attempts to explain what he means by 'self'. The idea seems to be something like this:

One's self is that distinct, mental thing within one that is a subject of experience and a single thing within any hiatus-free period of experience.

(The bit about one's self being 'within' one is a guess; Strawson doesn't say what makes a self the self of a particular person.) I take it that something is a 'subject of experience' just in case it *has* experiences – just in case it sees, feels, hears, and so on. But *I* see, feel and hear. The question, then, is whether I am 'distinct', 'mental', or 'a single thing' (it doesn't matter for present purposes what those terms of art mean). If I am, it appears to follow from Strawson's view that I am my self, and that Strawson is Strawson's self. Otherwise, if I have a self at all, it must be a subject of experience other than me – something *else* that sees, feels, and hears everything that I see, feel, and hear. I hope we may assume that there aren't *two* sentient beings living within my skin, I and my self. And Strawson seems inclined to think that there are such things as selves. Thus, although he never says so explicitly, his view seems to be that each person is ordinarily identical with his self.

If this is right, then Strawson is telling us that he himself exists (or existed) for only two or three seconds. Or rather, he, Galen Strawson, does not exist at all – for what could make it the case that one rather than any other of those billion or so two-second beings that are the successive 'selves' of a certain tall, blond-haired human being was Strawson? The article attributed to him was in fact written by a vast committee of authors, none of whom contributed so much as an entire sentence. And the same goes for you and me, unless your attention span is considerably longer: you are not the being who read the previous sentence a moment ago. You didn't exist then. The slightest lapse of attention is literally fatal: it destroys you and replaces you with someone else – someone rather like you, but numerically different.

That, surely, is incredible. Anyone who reaches the conclusion that none of us exist, or at least none for longer than a few seconds, must have gone wrong somewhere, just as certainly as someone who concludes that motion is impossible. At any rate, we can accept Strawson's conclusion (or try to accept it) only if it is clear that it follows inexorably from premises whose truth is even more obvious than that you and I exist, and that we existed ten seconds ago. Strawson apparently thinks that it follows inexorably from the fact that our thoughts don't flow in a single, unified stream, but are disjointed and gappy. The premise is probably true. But I can't begin to see how this entails Strawson's conclusion. Even if there *are* things that last only as long as one's attention remains focussed on something – 'sets of neuron-constituting atoms in a certain state of activation' (p. 425), if you like – why suppose that you and I are such things? Why couldn't we be human beings? Why couldn't human beings be the subjects of disjointed thoughts and experiences? What is it about lapses of attention that makes it impossible for *anything* to survive them?

My point is not to criticize Strawson's view as implausible or unsupported, but rather to illustrate the perils of relying on terms like 'self' in doing philosophy. I doubt that Strawson would have reached this absurd conclusion had he put his questions in other terms. If he had simply asked, What sort of thing am I? (Am I a mental thing, a substance, unified synchronically and diachronically, etc.? Am I the sort of thing I ordinarily believe myself to be?) instead of asking about the nature of 'the mental self', I doubt that he would have answered, 'I am a thing that lasts only as long as its attention remains fixed and then perishes and is replaced by something else.' The claim that a human being acquires a new 'mental self' every few seconds may sound surprising. The claim that *you and I* did not exist five seconds ago turns the world upside down. I suspect that Strawson didn't mean to endorse this view at all, and that he was lured into saying something that implies it by the seductions of the word 'self'. (If he did mean it, why not make it plain? As if the nonexistence of people were a corollary too trivial to mention!) But if that is not what he meant, I have no idea what 'the Pearl view' is meant to be a theory about.

VI

If there is nothing properly called the problem of the self, what of those books and articles that appear to be about the self? Must we commit them to the flames? Not at all. Despite their titles, they are typically not about 'the self' at all. They are about issues like these:

Personal identity. What does it take for you and me to persist through time? What determines how many people there are at any given time? (Is the number of human people always the same as the number of human animals, for example?) What sort of things are you and I? Are we immaterial substances? Mere 'bundles' of thoughts? Living organisms? Material objects different from but 'constituted by' organisms?

Semantics. What are the semantic properties of first-person pronouns such as 'I'? How and to what do they refer, if they refer at all? What distinguishes first-person beliefs such as my belief that I have brown eyes from third-person beliefs such as the belief that Eric Olson has brown eyes? Does this difference involve irreducibly subjective facts?

Philosophy of mind. What is it for one's mental contents to be unified, and to what degree is this ordinarily the case? What, if anything, causes this unity? To what extent are we aware of what goes on in our minds? What is self-consciousness, and how does it relate to consciousness in general?

Moral psychology. What is it that one cares about most, that one identifies with in the sense of regarding its flourishing as a large part of one's own well-being? What makes a project, belief, value, pattern of behaviour, or personality trait autonomous or authentic, fully one's own, and not merely the result of our upbringing or peer pressure? How do these issues connect with moral responsibility?

Cognitive psychology. What is involved in forms of reflexive conduct such as knowing one's own mind, in the sense of having settled, consistent and realistic intentions? Or knowing one's own capacities and propensities, in the sense of being able to judge realistically what one can do and is likely to do? Or recognizing one's standing as one agent among others and seeing one's desires in relation to those of others? Or being in command of oneself, in the sense of being able to match one's conduct to one's intentions? How do these reflexive abilities relate to one another? How are they acquired? What happens when they are absent? How does one's mental picture of oneself relate to the way one really is? How does one acquire that distinctiveness that makes one different from others?

Epistemology. What are the varieties of first-person knowledge? How do we get knowledge of our own psychological states? Is it something like sense perception? What kinds of first-person knowledge are immune to error through misidentification? What is the nature and extent of proprioception and other forms of first-person knowledge of one's physical properties?

And so on.

You might think that these, and others like them, are the very 'problems of the self' whose existence I have denied. I grant that they are not completely unrelated. When you pick up a book whose title includes the free-standing noun 'self', you have at least some idea of what it will be about. (It won't be about cookery or geology.) But we shouldn't make too much of this. These problems have even less in common than the various accounts of what a self is discussed earlier. If they did have some idea in common, then once again we ought to be able to use that idea to explain what everyone means by 'self'. Yet no one has been able to do this.

Moreover, all of these problems can be put without using the word 'self', as the way I put them shows. *All* of the intelligible content of what are called problems of the self can be captured in this way. If we had answers to all of these questions, there would be no further 'problem of the self' remaining to be solved. There is nothing left over that can be expressed only in terms of words like 'self'. One of the unfortunate consequences of using the word 'self' in doing philosophy is that it encourages us to look for entities that we have no other reason to believe in. Once we have accounted for people, their mental features, their relation to those human animals we call their bodies, and so on, we think we need to say something about 'the self' as well. There is no good reason to think so.

Or so I claim. Of course, merely putting a number of so-called problems of the self in other terms doesn't show that the term 'self' is superfluous. I may have overlooked legitimate problems or questions that can be put only in terms of the free-standing noun 'self' or some equivalent term. In that case I should have to retract my claim that there is no legitimate problem of the self – though the problem so revealed is unlikely to be the problem commonly thought to bear that name.

But if the word 'self' really has no agreed meaning, and leads us into troubles we could otherwise avoid, and if we can easily get on with our legitimate philosophical inquiries without it, there can be no reason, other than tradition, to continue to speak of the self.[2]

NOTES

1 Elsewhere he writes, 'One useful way of conceiving of the self is as a kind of structured life ...' (p. 67), and then says on the next page that the various twists and turns in one's life 'have to be part of the life of a single self'. Unless something can both be and have a life, the point would have been more clearly put in different words.
2 For helpful comments on earlier versions of this paper I thank Shaun Gallagher, Hugh Mellor and two referees for this journal.

REFERENCES

Abelson, Raziel (1977), *Persons: A study in philosophical psychology* (London: Macmillan).

Alston, William P. (1977), 'Self-intervention and the structure of motivation', in *The Self: Psychological and philosophical perspectives*, ed. Theodore Mischel (Oxford: Blackwell).

Ayer, A.J. (1946), *Language, Truth and Logic*, 2nd. edn. (New York: Dover).

Bermúdez, José (1997). 'Reduction and the self', *Journal of Consciousness Studies* 4 (5–6), pp. 459–66.

Berofsky, Bernard (1995), *Liberation From Self: A theory of personal autonomy* (Cambridge: Cambridge University Press).

Blackburn, Simon (1994), *Dictionary of Philosophy* (Oxford: Oxford University Press).

Bradley, F.H. (1893), *Appearance and Reality* (London: Allen and Unwin).

Broad, C.D. (1925), *The Mind and its Place in Nature* (London: Routledge and Kegan Paul).

Brooks, D.H.M. (1994), *The Unity of the Mind* (London: St Martins).

Campbell, C.A. (1957), *On Selfhood and Godhood* (London: Allen and Unwin).

Dennett, Daniel C. (1991), *Consciousness Explained* (Boston, MA: Little, Brown).

Flanagan, Owen (1996), *Self Expressions: Mind, morals, and the meaning of life* (New York: Oxford University Press).

Flew, Antony (1949), 'Selves', *Mind* 63, pp. 355–8.

Flew, Antony (1993), 'People themselves, and/or their selves?', *Philosophy* 68, pp. 546–8.

Gregory, Richard (1981), *Mind in Science* (Harmondsworth: Penguin).

Hamlyn, D.W. (1984), *Metaphysics* (Cambridge: Cambridge University Press).

Harré, Rom (1984), *Personal Being: A theory for personal psychology* (Cambridge, MA: Harvard University Press).

Harré, Rom (1987), 'Persons and selves', in *Persons and Personality: A contemporary inquiry*, ed. A. Peacocke and G. Gillet (Oxford: Blackwell).

Hume, David (1978), *A Treatise on Human Nature* (Oxford: Clarendon Press; original work published in 1739).

James, William (1905), *The Principles of Psychology*, Vol. 1. (London: Macmillan; original work published in 1890).

Jung, C.G. (1968), *The Archetypes and the Collective Unconscious*, 2nd edn. (London: Routledge).

Kenny, Anthony (1988). *The Self* (Milwaukee, WI: Marquette University Press).

Lowe, E.J. (1996), *Subjects of Experience* (Cambridge: Cambridge University Press).

McCall, Catherine (1990), *Concepts of Person: An analysis of concepts of person, self and human being* (Aldershot, UK: Avebury).

Marx, Melvin and Hillix, W. (1973), *Systems Theories in Psychology* (New York: McGraw Hill).

Mellor, D.H. (1991), *Matters of Metaphysics* (Cambridge: Cambridge University Press).

Minsky, Marvin (1985), *The Society of Mind* (New York: Simon and Schuster).

Nagel, Thomas (1986), *The View from Nowhere* (New York: Oxford University Press).

Rée, Jonathan (1974), *Descartes* (London: Allen Lane).

Rogers, Carl R. (1951), *Client-centered Therapy* (Boston, MA: Houghton).

Solomon, Robert (1988), *Continental Philosophy Since 1750: The rise and fall of the self* (Oxford: Oxford University Press).

Strawson, Galen (1997), 'The self', *Journal of Consciousness Studies* 4 (5–6), pp. 405–28.

Toulmin, Stephen E. (1977), 'Self-knowledge and knowledge of the "self", in *The Self: Psychological and philosophical perspectives*, ed. Theodore Mischel (Oxford: Blackwell).

van Inwagen, Peter (1980), 'Philosophers and the words "human body"', in *Time and Cause*, ed. van Inwagen (Dordrecht: Reidel).

Part 6

WHAT CAN PATHOLOGICAL CASES TEACH US ABOUT THE MIND?

The distinction between psychological illness and physical illness is common in our culture. Illnesses like depression are psychological; stomach aches are physical. We see nothing odd about asking whether someone's pain is mental or physical as a way of marking the difference between ailments that a therapist should treat versus ailments that fall within an internist's domain of specialization.

However, if the study of mental pathology has taught us anything, it is that this division between the physical and the psychological is not so easy to draw. Consider Arthur, the victim of Capgras' syndrome whom Vilayanur Ramachandran discusses in the first article of this section. Arthur believes that his parents have been replaced by impostors. He misses his parents and can't understand why he's been abandoned. He's at a loss to explain why the man and woman who look just like his father and mother are pretending to be his parents. What does it mean to say that Arthur's pathology is just psychological? Would therapy help? Apparently not. No amount of persuasion can shake Arthur's conviction that impostors have replaced his parents. In fact, the cause of Arthur's delusion is every bit as physical as the cause of a stomach ache. The delusion is the product of brain damage that Arthur suffered in a car accident. So, is the delusion a symptom of a psychological or physical ailment?

As Ramachandran explains, cognitive neuroscientists have learned a great deal about how the brain works precisely because conditions like Capgras' syndrome are manifestations of a damaged brain. Because the causes of so-called psychological illnesses are as physical as the causes of any other ache or pain, examination of patients like Arthur can reveal how parts of the brain are connected and what the different functions of these parts are. If an "abnormal" psychology is the product of an "abnormal" brain, it is reasonable to suppose that a "normal" psychology is the product of a "normal" brain. That is, the study of pathology is valuable in part for the light it sheds on how a normal brain might create a normal mind.

Here then is one reason philosophers of mind should pay attention to research happening in the laboratories of cognitive neuroscientists. As cognitive neuroscience progresses, old distinctions, like that between the psychological and the physical, should be abandoned or redrawn. Accordingly, conceptions of ourselves as minds distinct from bodies must come under increasing scrutiny.

But philosophical interest in mental pathology is not limited to the question of how minds and brains are related. As the piece by G. Lynn Stephens and George Graham illustrates, there is philosophical work to do in the very classification of mental pathology. When Ramachandran describes Arthur's belief that impostors have taken the place of his parents as a delusion, we might wonder what the relationship between belief and delusion is. Stephens and Graham reject the idea that delusions are beliefs. One reason to be suspicious whether Arthur believes that his parents have been replaced is the fact that he has done nothing to find them. If you believed that impostors now pose as your parents, wouldn't you call the police or take other measures to recover your genuine parents? Typically, beliefs lead to action, but delusions often do not. And there are other reasons to doubt that delusions are always beliefs. Victims of delusion will sometimes not express much confidence in their delusion. In contrast, we are normally confident in our beliefs: if you believe that your cat licked your spoon, you will be sure to avoid using it. For these and other reasons, Stephens and Graham urge a new conception of delusion, in which delusions are identified with 'higher-order' attitudes. To have a delusion is to take a certain stance toward thoughts one has. This stance distinguishes the philosopher who, for rational reasons, comes to think that she does not exist, from the patient who is deluded in his thought that he does not exist. The philosopher, when provided with a compelling counter argument, will change her mind; the deluded patient's belief in his nonexistence will be unresponsive to reasons.

Of course, not all psychopathology involves delusion. Autistic individuals exhibit a variety of behavior that, while not delusional, is nevertheless evidence of a mind that differs quite a bit from the "normal" mind. In a striking discovery, Simon Baron-Cohen, Alan Leslie, and Uta Frith found that autistic people fail a test that psychologists believe indicates an understanding of other minds. This test, called the false belief task, requires subjects to understand that other individuals can have beliefs that differ from their own. The test will often involve exposing subjects to a puppet show. The blue puppet watches as the red puppet places a cookie into a cabinet. When the blue puppet leaves the room the red puppet then places the cookie into a different cabinet. The blue puppet then returns and the subject is asked where the blue puppet will look for the cookie. Subjects in possession of an understanding of how other minds work – in possession of a *theory of mind* – will answer that the blue puppet will search for the cookie in the first cabinet. Surely, not having seen the red puppet switch the cookie's location, that is where the blue puppet believes the cookie to be. Autistic people, as well as young children, answer differently. They will say that the blue puppet will look for the cookie where it now sits – in the second cabinet. The finding suggests that autistic people and young children cannot appreciate that others have beliefs that differ from their own. Because *they* believe that the cookie is in the second cabinet, everybody else, including the blue puppet, must believe the same.

Baron-Cohen *et al.* account for the autistic person's performance by postulating that autistic people lack a theory about how minds work. On this view, we understand the behavior of others because we have at our disposal an innate theory on the basis of which we attribute beliefs and desires to each other. Among the laws of this theory are principles like "If someone desires x and believes that she can acquire x by doing y, then, unless there are reasons not to do y that outweigh the desire for x, she will do y."

Because in autistic people, as well as young children, the theory of mind is undeveloped or absent, they are unable to predict the behavior of others. Because of its emphasis on a theory of mind, this explanation is known as the '*theory-theory*'.

But there are different ways to account for an autistic person's performance on the false belief task. Robert Gordon and John Barker offer a competing, *simulationist* account. According to this view, rather than relying on a theory of mind in order to generate predictions about an agent's behavior, we instead imagine ourselves to be in that agent's situation. We simulate the beliefs and desires of another, and this simulation generates a prediction of how the other will act. This simulation is 'off-line' in that the beliefs and desires we simulate do not actually cause us to engage in the predicted behavior. Accordingly, it is not lack of a theory of mind that explains why an autistic person cannot explain or predict the behavior of others, but is instead lack of a skill. Autistic people are unable to simulate others' mental states: they cannot wear the hat of another.

In defense of simulationism, Gordon and Barker point to evidence that autistic people shun spontaneous play, and especially play that involves pretense. This tendency not to play, Gordon and Barker think, is exactly what one would expect if autism were caused by an inability to imagine the world to be other than the way it is. For this reason, they believe, evidence about play supports the simulationist account of autism.

Peter Carruthers, on the other hand, argues that the evidence about play does not favor the simulationist explanation of autism over the theory-theory explanation. There is, Carruthers thinks, an obvious reason that autistic children do not engage in pretend play: they don't enjoy it. The enjoyment of imagination games requires that the player appreciate the fact that he or she is imagining. However, if the theory-theory account of autism is correct, then autistic individuals are unable to realize that they are pretending because they lack the ability to identify mental states – even their own. But without this ability to recognize pretense *as* pretense, play is not fun. Hence, in contrast to the simulationist account, autistic individuals fail to engage in play not because they cannot imagine, but simply because imagining gives them no pleasure.

Philosophical interest in psychopathology is not limited to questions about the nature of the pathologies themselves, but extends also to issues about how to assess the character of the afflicted. Should the victim of a delusion be held morally or legally responsible for her actions when she kills someone she believes to be the devil? Intuitively, we believe that responsibility requires control over one's actions. If you shoot someone while under the influence of a drug that you have been forced to ingest, we believe that you are not morally responsible for your behavior. Likewise, responsibility seems to require rationality. We absolve the insane or the very young from their misdeeds because we believe that their behavior is unresponsive to reason – there is a sense in which they could not have known better. If these intuitions are right, then the deluded should not be held responsible for their actions.

But the case of a woman who believes someone to be the devil is obviously extreme. Gordon Tait is concerned with understanding the moral and legal responsibility of individuals who experience a much more common form of pathology: Attention Deficit Hyperactivity Disorder (ADHD). Increasingly, school-age children are being diagnosed with ADHD, and school systems find themselves struggling with questions about how to discipline these children. In a case Tait describes, three children in a Wisconsin school vandalized school property. The parents of one child hired a psychiatrist who claimed that the child suffered from ADHD. This child was subsequently pardoned of the crime while his two accomplices were forced to withdraw from the school. Deciding such cases requires consideration of a number of philosophical issues. Is the victim of ADHD capable of acting freely? For that matter, does anyone have free will? Tait summarizes the positions on free will that philosophers have defended and argues that psychological research has revealed that many activities once thought to be voluntary must now be seen as determined. Coming to terms with this discovery will require that we rethink not only how teachers should discipline unruly students, but also how we are to assess moral and legal responsibility more generally.

ADHD happens *to* people. Its victims do not inflict their conditions on themselves. But what of pathologies like alcoholism that seem, in some sense, self-inflicted? Should alcoholics be held responsible for crimes they commit while under the influence? This is the question that Ferdinand Schoeman addresses in his article. Many people, Schoeman observes, are tempted to absolve the alcoholic of moral responsibility if and only if alcoholism is a biological disease. But this attitude faces difficulties. Even if alcoholism is a disease, surely it is proper to hold the alcoholic's behavior to some standards. A blind person knows better than to drive a car. Shouldn't an alcoholic also know better than to drive a car? But what standards of behavior are reasonable to apply to an alcoholic? Moreover, if it is proper to absolve alcoholics who drink because of their genetic endowment, does this mean that alcoholics who are not biologically determined to drink should be held responsible for their crimes? What of alcoholics who drink because of their tendency to conform to cultural norms that encourage heavy drinking, or because of histories of abuse, or because they are simply down on their luck and unable to cope? Are these alcoholics any more responsible for their misdeeds than those whose alcoholism is biologically caused? Whether or not alcoholism is a disease, deciding how to assess the responsibility of alcoholics turns out to be an immensely complex problem involving judgments about what standards of behavior are reasonable, how these standards are to be applied, and the extent to which character can overcome biological tendencies.

QUESTIONS TO THINK ABOUT:

1 Given the tight connection between psychological abnormality and neural abnormality that neuroscientists like Ramachandran have discovered, what motivation might there be for distinguishing between psychological and physical illnesses?

2 Plenty of people (philosophers especially!) hold views that, if held by others, would indicate serious mental illness. How do Graham and Stephens distinguish the eccentric philosopher who believes that nothing exists from the deluded schizophrenic who believes the same thing? Some people believe that the Earth is only six thousand years old. The evidence against this belief is overwhelming. Does this mean that the person who believes it is deluded?

3 The false belief task purports to show that autistic people and small children cannot attribute minds to others. Can you think of any alternative explanations for the performance of autistic people and small children on this task? What sort of evidence could decide among these?

4 The dispute between theory-theory supporters and simulationists seems clear on the surface. According to the former group, people can explain and predict the behavior of others because they possess a theory about how beliefs and desires work together. According to the latter, the explanation and prediction of others' behavior depends on an ability to imagine how you would act if you were that person in that situation. Try to devise some experiments that would distinguish these two positions. What might the theory-theory view predict that the simulationist view does not?

5 Is the deluded or otherwise mentally ill person less free than a 'normal' person? What does your answer to this question imply about the meaning of 'free'?

6 Is the alcoholic any more responsible for her impolite behavior than a victim of Tourette's syndrome who is unable to prevent himself from cursing uncontrollably? What about the impolite behavior of a spoiled child? On what basis do you draw distinctions between these cases?

FURTHER READING

Damasio, A. (1994). *Descartes' Error: Emotion, Reason, and the Human Brain* (New York: Putnam).

Graham, G. and Stephens, G, eds. (1995). *Philosophical Psychopathology* (Cambridge, MA: The MIT Press).

Graham, G. and Stephens, G. (2000). *When Self-Consciousness Breaks: Alien Voices and Inserted Thoughts* (Cambridge, MA: The MIT Press).

Ramachandran, V. (1998). *Phantoms in the Brain: Probing the Mysteries of the Human Mind* (New York: William Morrow).

Sacks, O. (1998). *The Man Who Mistook His Wife for a Hat: And Other Clinical Tales* (New York: Touchstone).

23

THE UNBEARABLE LIKENESS OF BEING

V.S. Ramachandran and Sandra Blakeslee

I'll never forget the frustration and despair in the voice at the other end of the telephone. The call came early one afternoon as I stood over my desk, riffling through papers looking for a misplaced letter, and it took me a few seconds to register what this man was saying. He introduced himself as a former diplomat from Venezuela whose son was suffering from a terrible, cruel delusion. Could I help?

"What sort of delusion?" I asked.

His reply and the emotional strain in his voice caught me by surprise. "My thirty-year-old son thinks that I am not his father, that I am an impostor. He says the same thing about his mother, that we are not his real parents." He paused to let this sink in. "We just don't know what to do or where to go for help. Your name was given to us by a psychiatrist in Boston. So far no one has been able to help us, to find a way to make Arthur better." He was almost in tears. "Dr. Ramachandran, we love our son and would go to the ends of the earth to help him. Is there any way you could see him?"

"Of course, I'll see him," I said. "When can you bring him in?"

Two days later, Arthur came to our laboratory for the first time in what would turn into a yearlong study of his condition. He was a good-looking fellow, dressed in jeans, a white T-shirt and moccasins. In his mannerisms, he was shy and almost childlike, often whispering his answers to questions or looking wide-eyed at us. Sometimes I could scarcely hear his voice over the background whir of air conditioners and computers.

The parents explained that Arthur had been in a near-fatal automobile accident while he was attending school in Santa Barbara. His head hit the windshield with such crushing force that he lay in a coma for three weeks, his survival by no means assured. But when he finally awoke and began intensive rehabilitative therapy, everyone's hopes soared. Arthur gradually learned to talk and walk, recalled the past and seemed, to all outward appearances, to be back to normal. He just had this one incredible delusion about his parents—that they were impostors—and nothing could convince him otherwise.

After a brief conversation to warm things up and put Arthur at ease, I asked, "Arthur, who brought you to the hospital?"

"That guy in the waiting room," Arthur replied. "He's the old gentleman who's been taking care of me."

"You mean your father?"

"No, no, doctor. That guy isn't my father. He just looks like him. He's—what do you call it?—an impostor, I guess. But I don't think he means any harm."

"Arthur, why do you think he's an impostor? What gives you that impression?"

He gave me a patient look—as if to say, how could I not see the obvious—and said, "Yes, he looks exactly like my father but he *really* isn't. He's a nice guy, doctor, but he certainly isn't my father!"

"But, Arthur, why is this man pretending to be your father?"

Arthur seemed sad and resigned when he said, "That is what is so surprising, doctor. Why should anyone want to pretend to be my father?" He looked confused as he searched for a plausible explanation. "Maybe my real father employed him to take care of me, paid him some money so that he could pay my bills."

Later, in my office, Arthur's parents added another twist to the mystery. Apparently their son did not treat either of them as impostors when they spoke to him over the telephone. He only claimed they were impostors when they met and spoke face-to-face. This implied that Arthur did not have amnesia with regard to his parents and that he was not simply "crazy." For, if that were true, why would he be normal when listening to them on the telephone and delusional regarding his parents' identities only when he looked at them?

"It's so upsetting," Arthur's father said. "He recognizes all sorts of people he knew in the past, including his college roommates, his best friend from childhood and his former girlfriends. He doesn't say that any of them is an impostor. He seems to have some gripe against his mother and me."

I felt deeply sorry for Arthur's parents. We could probe their son's brain and try to shed light on his condition—and perhaps comfort them with a logical explanation for his curious behavior—but there was scant hope for an effective treatment. This sort of neurological condition is usually permanent. But I was pleasantly surprised one Saturday morning when Arthur's father called me, excited about an idea he'd gotten from watching a television program on phantom limbs in which I demonstrated that the brain can be tricked by simply using a mirror. "Dr. Ramachandran," he said, "if you can trick a person into thinking that his paralyzed phantom can move again, why can't we use a similar trick to help Arthur get rid of his delusion?"

Indeed, why not? The next day, Arthur's father entered his son's bedroom and announced cheerfully, "Arthur, guess what! That man you've been living with all these days is an impostor. He really isn't your father. You were right all along. So I have sent him away to China. I am your real father." He moved over to Arthur's side and clapped him on the shoulder. "It's good to see you, son!"

Arthur blinked hard at the news but seemed to accept it at face value. When he came to our laboratory the next day I said, "Who's that man who brought you in today?"

"That's my real father."

"Who was taking care of you last week?"

"Oh," said Arthur, "that guy has gone back to China. He looks similar to my father, but he's gone now."

When I spoke to Arthur's father on the phone later that afternoon, he confirmed that Arthur now called him "Father," but that Arthur still seemed to feel that something was amiss. "I think he accepts me intellectually, doctor, but not emotionally," he said. "When I hug him, there's no warmth."

Alas, even this intellectual acceptance of his parents did not last. One week later Arthur reverted to his original delusion, claiming that the impostor had returned.

●

Arthur was suffering from Capgras' delusion, one of the rarest and most colorful syndromes in neurology.[1] The patient, who is often mentally quite lucid, comes to regard close acquaintances—usually his parents, children, spouse or siblings—as impostors. As Arthur said over and over, "That man looks identical to my father but he really isn't my father. That woman who claims to be my mother? She's lying. She looks just like my mom but it isn't her." Although such bizarre delusions can crop up in psychotic states, over a third of the documented cases of Capgras' syndrome have occurred in conjunction with traumatic brain lesions, like the head injury that Arthur suffered in his automobile accident. This suggests to me that the syndrome has an organic basis. But because a majority of Capgras' patients appear to develop this delusion "spontaneously," they are usually dispatched to psychiatrists, who tend to favor a Freudian explanation of the disorder.

In this view, all of us so-called normal people as children are sexually attracted to our parents. Thus every male wants to make love to his mother and comes to regard his father as a sexual rival (Oedipus led the way), and every female has lifelong deep-seated sexual obsessions over her father (the Electra complex). Although these forbidden feelings become fully repressed by adulthood, they remain dormant, like deeply buried embers after a fire has been extinguished. Then, many psychiatrists argue, along comes a blow to the head (or some other unrecognized release mechanism) and the repressed sexuality toward a mother or father comes flaming to the surface. The patient finds himself suddenly and inexplicably sexually attracted to his parents and therefore says to himself, "My God! If this is my mother, how come I'm attracted to her?" Perhaps the only way he can preserve some semblance of sanity is to say to himself, "This must be some other, strange woman." Likewise, "I could never feel this kind of sexual jealousy toward my real dad, so this man must be an impostor."

This explanation is ingenious, as indeed most Freudian explanations are, but then I came across a Capgras' patient who had similar delusions about his pet poodle: The Fifi before him was an impostor; the real Fifi was living in Brooklyn. In my view that case demolished the Freudian explanation for Capgras' syndrome. There may be some latent bestiality in all of us, but I suspect this is not Arthur's problem.

A better approach for studying Capgras' syndrome involves taking a closer look at neuroanatomy, specifically at pathways concerned with visual recognition and emotions in the brain. Recall that the temporal lobes contain regions that specialize in face and object recognition. We know this because when specific portions of the what pathway are damaged, patients lose the ability to recognize faces,[2] even those of close friends and relatives—as immortalized by Oliver Sacks in his book *The Man Who Mistook His Wife for a Hat*. In a normal brain, these face recognition areas (found on both sides of the brain) relay information to the limbic system, found deep in the middle of the brain, which then helps generate emotional responses to particular faces (Figure 23.1). I may feel love when I see my mother's face, anger when I see the face of a boss or a sexual rival or deliberate indifference upon seeing the visage of a friend who has betrayed me and has not yet earned my forgiveness. In each instance, when I look at the face, my temporal cortex recognizes the image— mother, boss, friend—and passes on the information to my amygdala (a gateway to the limbic system) to discern the emotional significance of that face. When this activation is then relayed to the rest of my limbic system, I start experiencing the nuances of emotion—love, anger, disappointment—appropriate to that particular face. The actual sequence of events is undoubtedly much more complex, but this caricature captures the gist of it.

After thinking about Arthur's symptoms, it occurred to me that his strange behavior might have resulted from a disconnection between these two areas (one concerned with recognition and the other with emotions). Maybe Arthur's face recognition pathway was still completely normal, and that was why he could identify everyone, including his mother and father, but the connections between this "face region" and his amygdala had been selectively damaged. If that were the case, Arthur would recognize his parents but would not experience any emotions when looking at their faces. He would not feel a "warm glow" when looking at his beloved mother, so when he sees her he says to himself, "If this is my mother, why doesn't her presence make me *feel* like I'm with my mother?" Perhaps his only escape from this

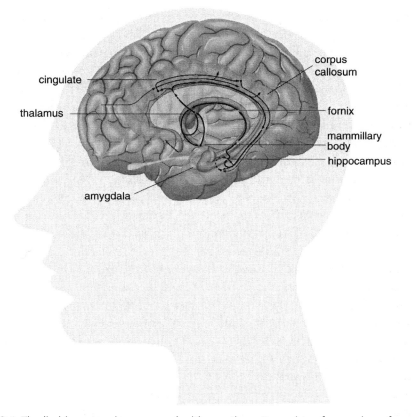

Figure 23.1 The limbic system is concerned with emotions. It consists of a number of nuclei (cell clusters) interconnected by long C-shaped fiber tracts. The amygdala—in the front pole of the temporal lobe—receives input from the sensory areas and sends messages to the rest of the limbic system to produce emotional arousal. Eventually, this activity cascades into the hypothalamus and from there to the autonomic nervous system, preparing the animal (or person) for action.

dilemma—the only sensible interpretation he could make given the peculiar disconnection between the two regions of his brain—is to assume that this woman merely resembles Mom. She must be an impostor.[3]

Now, this is an intriguing idea, but how does one go about testing it? As complex as the challenge seems, psychologists have found a rather simple way to measure emotional responses to faces, objects, scenes and events encountered in daily life. To understand how this works, you need to know something about the autonomic nervous system—a part of your brain that controls the involuntary, seemingly automatic activities of organs, blood vessels, glands and many other tissues in your body. When you are emotionally aroused—say, by a menacing or sexually alluring face—the information travels from your face recognition region to your limbic system and then to a tiny cluster of cells in the hypothalamus, a kind of command center for the autonomic nervous system. Nerve fibers extend from the hypothalamus to the heart, muscles and even other parts of the brain, helping to prepare your body to take appropriate action in response to that particular face. Whether you are going to fight, flee or mate, your blood pressure will rise and your heart will start beating faster to deliver more oxygen to your tissues. At the same time, you start sweating, not only to dissipate the heat building up in your muscles but to give your sweaty palms a better grip on a tree branch, a weapon or an enemy's throat.

From the experimenter's point of view, your sweaty palms are the most important aspect of your emotional response to the threatening face. The dampness of your hands is a sure giveaway of how you feel toward that person. Moreover, we can measure this reaction very easily by placing electrodes on your palm and recording changes in the electrical resistance of your skin. (Called the galvanic skin response or GSR, this simple little procedure forms the basis of the famous lie detector test. When you tell a fib, your palms sweat ever so slightly. Because damp skin has lower electrical resistance than dry skin, the electrodes respond and you are caught in the lie.) For our purposes, every time you look at your mother or father, believe it or not, your body begins to sweat imperceptibly and your galvanic skin response shoots up as expected.

So, what happens when Arthur looks at his mother or father? My hypothesis predicts that even though he sees them as resembling his parents (remember, the face recognition area of his brain is normal), he should *not* register a change in skin conductance. The disconnection in his brain will prevent his palms from sweating.

With the family's permission, we began testing Arthur on a rainy winter day in our basement laboratory on campus. Arthur sat in a comfortable chair, joking about the weather and how he expected his father's car to float away before we finished the morning's experiments. Sipping hot tea to take the chill from his bones, Arthur gazed at a video screen saver while we affixed two electrodes to his left index finger. Any tiny increase in sweat on his finger would change his skin resistance and show up as a blip on the screen.

Next I showed him a sequence of photos of his mother, father and grandfather interleaved with pictures of strangers, and I compared his galvanic skin responses to that of six college undergraduates who were shown an identical sequence of photos and who served as controls for comparison. Before the experiment, subjects were told that they would be shown pictures of faces, some of which would be familiar and some unfamiliar. After the electrodes were attached, they were shown each photograph for two seconds with a fifteen- to twenty-five-second delay between pictures so skin conductance could return to baseline.

In the undergraduates, I found that there was a big jolt in the GSR in response to photos of their parents—as expected—but not to photos of strangers. In Arthur, on the other hand, the skin response was uniformly low. There was no increased response to his parents, or at times there would be a tiny blip on the screen after a long delay, as if he were doing a double take. This result provided direct proof that our theory was correct. Clearly Arthur was not responding emotionally to his parents, and this may be what led to the loss of his galvanic skin response.

But how could we be sure that Arthur was even seeing the faces? Maybe his head injury had damaged the cells in the temporal lobes that would help him distinguish between faces, resulting in a flat GSR whether he looks at his mother or at a stranger. This seemed unlikely, however, since he readily acknowledged that the people who took him to the hospital—his mother and father—looked like his parents. He also had no difficulty in recognizing the faces of famous people like Bill Clinton and Albert Einstein. Still, we needed to test his recognition abilities more directly.

To obtain direct proof, I did the obvious thing. I showed Arthur sixteen pairs of photographs of strangers, each pair consisting of either two slightly different pictures of the same person or snapshots of two different people. We asked him, Do the photographs depict the same person or not? Putting his nose close to each photo and gazing hard at the details, Arthur got fourteen out of sixteen trials correct.

We were now sure that Arthur had no problem in recognizing faces and telling them apart. But could his failure to produce a strong galvanic skin response to his parents be part of a more global disturbance in his emotional abilities? How could we be certain that the head injury had not also damaged his limbic system? Maybe he had no emotions, period.

This seemed improbable because throughout the months I spent with Arthur, he showed a full range of human emotions. He laughed at my jokes and offered his own funny stories in return. He expressed frustration, fear and anger, and on rare occasions I saw him cry. Whatever the situation, his emotions were appropriate. Arthur's problem, then, was neither his ability to recognize faces nor his ability to experience emotions; what was lost was his ability to *link* the two.

So far so good, but why is the phenomenon specific to close relatives? Why not call the mailman an impostor, since his, too, is a familiar face?

It may be that when any normal person (including Arthur, prior to his accident) encounters someone who is emotionally very close to him—a parent, spouse or sibling—he expects an emotional "glow," a warm fuzzy feeling, to arise even though it may sometimes be experienced only very dimly. The absence of this glow is therefore surprising and Arthur's only recourse then is to generate an absurd delusion—to rationalize it or to explain it away. On the other hand, when one sees the mailman, one doesn't expect a warm glow and consequently there is no incentive for Arthur to generate a delusion to explain his lack of "warm fuzzy" response. A mailman is simply a mailman (unless the relationship has taken an amorous turn).

Although the most common delusion among Capgras' patients is the assertion that a parent is an impostor, even more bizarre examples can be found in the older medical literature. Indeed, in a case on record the patient was convinced that his stepfather was a robot, proceeded to decapitate him and opened his skull to look for microchips. Perhaps in this patient, the dissociation from emotions was so extreme that he was forced into an even more absurd delusion than Arthur's: that his stepfather was not even a human being, but was a mindless android!

About a year ago, when I gave a lecture on Arthur at the Veterans Administration Hospital in La Jolla, a neurology resident raised an astute objection to my theory. What about people who are born with a disease in which their amygdalas (the gateway to the limbic system) calcify and atrophy or those who lose their amygdalas (we each have two of them) completely in surgery or through an accident? Such people do exist, but they do not develop Capgras' syndrome, even though their GSRs are flat to all emotionally evocative stimuli. Likewise, patients with damage to their frontal lobes (which receive and process information from the limbic system for making elaborate future plans) also often lack a GSR. Yet they, too, do not display Capgras' syndrome.

Why not? The answer may be that these patients experience a general blunting of all their emotional responses and therefore do not have a baseline for comparison. Like a purebred Vulcan or Data on *Star Trek*, one could legitimately argue, they don't even know what an emotion is, whereas Capgras' patients like Arthur enjoy a normal emotional life in all other respects.

This idea teaches us an important principle about brain function, namely, that all our perceptions—indeed, maybe all aspects of our minds—are governed by comparisons and not by absolute values. This appears to be true whether you are talking about something as obvious as judging the brightness of print in a newspaper or something as subtle as detecting a blip in your internal emotional landscape. This is a far-reaching conclusion, and it also helps illustrate the power of our approach—indeed of the whole discipline that now goes by the name cognitive neuroscience. You can discover important general principles about how the brain works and begin to address deep philosophical questions by doing relatively simple experiments on the right patients. We started with a bizarre condition, proposed an outlandish theory, tested it in the lab and—in meeting objections to it—learned more about how the healthy brain actually works.

Taking these speculations even further, consider the extraordinary disorder called Cotard's syndrome, in which a patient will assert that he is dead, claiming to smell rotten flesh or worms crawling all over his skin. Again, most people, even neurologists, would jump to the conclusion that the patient was insane. But that wouldn't explain why the delusion takes this highly specific form. I would argue instead that Cotard's is simply an exaggerated form of Capgras' syndrome and probably has a similar origin. In Capgras', the face recognition area alone is disconnected from the amygdala, whereas in Cotard's perhaps all the sensory areas are disconnected from the limbic system, leading to a complete lack of emotional contact with the world. Here is another instance in which an outlandish brain disorder that most people regard as a psychiatric problem can be explained in terms of known brain circuitry. And once again, these ideas can be tested in the laboratory. I would predict that Cotard's syndrome patients will have a complete loss of GSR for all external stimuli—not just faces—and this leaves them stranded on an island of emotional desolation, as close as anyone can come to experiencing death.

Arthur seemed to enjoy his visits to our laboratory. His parents were pleased that there was a logical explanation for his predicament, that he wasn't just "crazy." I never revealed the details to Arthur because I wasn't sure how he'd react.

Arthur's father was an intelligent man, and at one point, when Arthur wasn't around, he asked me, "If your theory is correct, doctor—if the information doesn't get to his amygdala—then how do you explain how he has no problems recognizing us over the phone? Does that make sense to you?"

"Well," I replied, "there is a separate pathway from the auditory cortex, the hearing area of the temporal lobes, to the amygdala. One possibility is that this hearing route has not been affected by the accident—only the visual centers have been disconnected from Arthur's amygdala."

This conversation got me wondering about the other well-known functions of the amygdala and the visual centers that project to it. In particular, scientists recording cell responses in the amygdala found that, in addition to responding to facial expression and emotions, the cells also respond to the direction of eye gaze. For instance, one cell might fire if another person is looking directly at you, whereas a neighboring cell will fire only if that person's gaze is averted by a fraction of an inch. Still other cells fire when the gaze is way off to the left or the right.

This phenomenon is not surprising, given the important role that gaze direction[4] plays in primate social communications—the averted gaze of guilt, shame or embarrassment; the intense, direct gaze of a lover or the threatening stare of an enemy. We tend to forget that emotions, even though they are privately experienced, often involve interactions with other people and that one way we interact is through eye contact. Given the links among gaze direction, familiarity and emotions, I wondered whether Arthur's ability to judge the direction of gaze, say, by looking at photographs of faces, would be impaired.

To find out, I prepared a series of images, each showing the same model looking either directly at the camera lens or at a point an inch or two to the right or left of the lens. Arthur's task was simply to let us know whether the model was looking straight at him or not. Whereas you or I can detect tiny shifts in gaze with uncanny accuracy, Arthur was hopeless at the task. Only when the model's eyes were looking way off to one side was he able to discern correctly that she wasn't looking at him.

This finding in itself is interesting but not altogether unexpected, given the known role of amygdala and temporal lobes in detecting gaze direction. But on the eighth trial of looking at these photos, Arthur did something completely unexpected. In his soft, almost apologetic voice, he exclaimed that the model's identity had changed. He was now looking at a new person!

This meant that a mere change in direction of gaze had been sufficient to provoke Capgras' delusion. For Arthur, the "second" model was apparently a new person who merely resembled the "first."

"This one is older," Arthur said firmly. He stared hard at both images. "This is a lady; the other one is a girl." Later in the sequence, Arthur made another duplication—one model was old, one young and a third even younger. At the end of the test session he continued to insist that he had seen three different people. Two weeks later he did it again on a retest using images of a completely new face.

How could Arthur look at the face of what was obviously one person and claim that she was actually three different people? Why did simply changing the direction of gaze lead to this profound inability to link successive images?

Answers lie in the mechanics of how we form memories, in particular our ability to create enduring representations of faces. For example, suppose you go to the grocery store one day and a friend introduces you to a new person—Joe. You form a memory of that episode and tuck it away in your brain. Two weeks go by and you run into Joe in the library. He tells you a story about your mutual friend, you share a laugh and your brain files a memory about this second episode. Another few weeks pass and you meet Joe again in his office—he's a medical researcher and he's wearing a white lab coat—but you recognize him instantly from earlier encounters. More memories of Joe are created during this time so that you now have in your mind a "category" called Joe. This mental picture becomes progressively refined and enriched each time you meet Joe, aided by an increasing sense of familiarity that creates an incentive to link the images and the episodes. Eventually you develop a robust concept of Joe—he tells great stories, works in a lab, makes you laugh, knows a lot about gardening, and so forth.

Now consider what happens to someone with a rare and specific form of amnesia, caused by damage to the hippocampus (another important brain structure in the temporal lobes). These patients have a complete inability to form new memories, even though they have perfect recollection of all events in their lives that took place before the hippocampus was injured. The logical conclusion to be drawn from the syndrome is not that memories are actually stored in the hippocampus (hence the preservation of old memories), but that the hippocampus is vital for the acquisition of new memory traces in the brain. When such a patient meets a new person (Joe) on three consecutive occasions—in the supermarket, the library and the office—he will not remember ever having met Joe before. He will simply not recognize him. He will insist each time that Joe is a complete stranger, no matter how many times they have interacted, talked, exchanged stories and so forth.

But is Joe really a complete stranger? Rather surprisingly, experiments show that such amnesia patients actually retain the ability to form new categories that transcend successive Joe episodes. If our patient met Joe ten times and each time Joe made him laugh, he'd tend to feel vaguely jovial or happy on the next encounter but still would not know who Joe is. There would be no sense of familiarity whatsoever—no memory of each Joe episode—and yet the patient would acknowledge that Joe makes him happy. This means that the amnesia patient, unlike Arthur, can link successive episodes to create a new concept (an unconscious expectation of joy) even though he forgets each episode, whereas Arthur remembers each episode but fails to link them.

Thus Arthur is in some respects the mirror image of our amnesia patient. When he meets a total stranger like Joe, his brain creates a file for Joe and the associated experiences he has with Joe. But if Joe leaves the room for thirty minutes and returns, Arthur's brain—instead of retrieving the old file and adding to it—sometimes creates a completely new one.

Why does this happen in Capgras' syndrome? It may be that to link successive episodes the brain relies on signals from the limbic system—the "glow" or sense of familiarity associated with a known face and set of memories—and if this activation is missing, the brain cannot form an enduring category through time. In the absence of this glow, the brain simply sets up separate categories each time; that is why Arthur asserts that he is meeting a new person who simply resembles the person he met thirty minutes ago. Cognitive psychologists and philosophers often make a distinction between tokens and types—that all our experiences can be classified into general categories or types (people or cars) versus specific exemplars or tokens (Joe or my car). Our experiments with Arthur suggest that this distinction is not merely academic; it is embedded deep in the architecture of the brain.

As we continued testing Arthur, we noticed that he had certain other quirks and eccentricities. For instance, Arthur sometimes seemed to have a general problem with visual categories. All of us make mental taxonomies or groupings of events and objects: Ducks and geese are birds but rabbits are not. Our brains set up these categories even without formal education in zoology, presumably to facilitate memory storage and to enhance our ability to access these memories at a moment's notice.

Arthur, on the other hand, often made remarks hinting that he was confused about categories. For example, he had an almost obsessive pre-occupation with Jews and Catholics, and he tended to label a disproportionate number of recently encountered people as Jews. This propensity reminded me of another rare syndrome called Fregoli, in which a patient keeps seeing the same person everywhere. In walking down the street, nearly every woman's face might look like his mother's or every young man might resemble his brother. (I would predict that instead of having severed connections from face recognition areas to the amygdala, the Fregoli patient may have an excess of such connections. Every face would be imbued with familiarity and "glow," causing him to see the same face over and over again.)

Might such Fregoli-like confusion occur in otherwise normal brains? Could this be a basis for forming racist stereotypes? Racism is so often directed at a single physical type (Blacks, Asians, Whites and so forth). Perhaps a single unpleasant episode with one member of a visual category sets up a limbic connection that is inappropriately generalized to include all members of that class and is notoriously impervious to "intellectual correction" based on information stored in higher brain centers. Indeed one's intellectual views may be colored (no pun intended) by this emotional knee-jerk reaction; hence the notorious tenacity of racism.

●

We began our journey with Arthur trying to explain his strange delusions about impostors and uncovered some new insights into how memories are stored and retrieved in the human brain. His story offers insights into how each of us constructs narratives about our life and the people who inhabit it. In a sense your life—your autobiography—is a long sequence of highly personal episodic memories about your first kiss, prom night, wedding, birth of a child, fishing trips and so on. But it is also much more than that. Clearly, there is a personal identity, a sense of a unified "self" that runs like a golden thread through the whole fabric of our existence. The Scottish philosopher David Hume drew an analogy between the human personality and a river—the water in the river is ever-changing and yet the river itself remains constant. What would happen, he asked, if a person were to dip his foot into a river and then dip it in again after half an hour—would it be the same river or a different one? If you think this is a silly semantic riddle, you're right, for the answer depends on your definition of "same" and "river." But silly or not, one point is clear. For Arthur, given his difficulty with linking successive episodic memories, there may indeed be two rivers! To be sure, this tendency to make copies of events and objects was most pronounced when he encountered faces—Arthur did not often duplicate objects. Yet there were occasions when he would run his fingers through his hair and call it a "wig," partly because his scalp felt unfamiliar as a result of scars from the neurosurgery he had undergone. On rare occasions, Arthur even duplicated countries, claiming at one point that there were two Panamas (he had recently visited that country during a family reunion).

Most remarkable of all, Arthur sometimes duplicated himself! The first time this happened, I was showing Arthur pictures of himself from a family photo album and I pointed to a snapshot of him taken two years before the accident.

"Whose picture is this?" I asked.

"That's another Arthur," he replied. "He looks just like me but it isn't me." I couldn't believe my ears. Arthur may have detected my surprise since he then reinforced his point by saying, "You see? He has a mustache. I don't."

This delusion, however, did not occur when Arthur looked at himself in a mirror. Perhaps he was sensible enough to realize that the face in the mirror could not be anyone else's. But Arthur's tendency to "duplicate" himself—to regard himself as a distinct person from a former Arthur—also sometimes emerged spontaneously during conversation. To my surprise, he once volunteered, "Yes, my parents sent a check, but they sent it to the other Arthur."

Arthur's most serious problem, however, was his inability to make emotional contact with people who matter to him most—his parents—and this caused him great anguish. I can imagine a voice inside his head saying, "The reason I don't experience warmth must be because I'm not the real Arthur." One day Arthur turned to his mother and said, "Mom, if the real Arthur ever returns, do you promise that you will still treat me as a friend and love me?" How can a sane human being who is perfectly intelligent in other respects come to regard himself as two people? There seems to be something inherently contradictory about splitting the Self, which by its very nature is unitary. If I started to regard myself as several people, which one would I plan for? Which one is the "real" me? This is a real and painful dilemma for Arthur.

Philosophers have argued for centuries that if there is any one thing about our existence that is completely beyond question, it is the simple fact that "I" exist as a single human being who endures in space and time. But even this basic axiomatic foundation of human existence is called into question by Arthur.

NOTES

1 J. Capgras and J. Reboul-Lachaux, 1923; H.D. Ellis and A.W. Young, 1990; Hirstein and Ramachandran 1997.
2 This disorder is called prosopagnosia. See Farah 1990; Damasio, Damasio and Van Hoesen 1982.

   Cells in the visual cortex (area 17) respond to simple features like bars of light, but in the temporal lobes they often respond to complex features such as faces. These cells may be part of a complex network specialized for recognizing faces. See Gross 1992; Rolls 1995; Tovee, Rolls and Ramachandran 1996.

   The functions of the amygdala which figures prominently in this chapter have been discussed in detail by LeDoux 1996, and Damasio 1994.

3   The clever idea that Capgras' delusion may be a mirror image of prosopagnosia was first proposed by Young and Ellis (1990), but they postulate a disconnection between dorsal stream and limbic structures rather than the IT amygdala disconnection that we suggest in this chapter. Also see Hirstein and Ramachandran 1997.

4   Baron-Cohen 1995.

REFERENCES

Baron-Cohen, S. (1995). *Mindblindness*. Cambridge, MA: MIT Press.

Capgras, J., and J. Reboul-Lachaux. "L'illusion des 'sosies' dans un délire systématise chronique." *Bull. Soc. Clin. Med. Mentale*, 2:6–16.

Damasio, A. (1994). *Descartes Error*. New York: G.P. Putnam.

Damasio, A.R., H. Damasio, and G.W. Van Hoesen (1982). "Prosopagnosia: Anatomic Basis and Behavioral Mechanisms." *Neurology*, 32:331–41.

Farah, M. (1990). *Visual Agnosia*. Cambridge, MA: MIT Press.

Gross, C.G. (1992). "Representatives of Visual Stimuli in the Inferior Temporal Cortex." *Proc. R. Soc. London* [Biol], 135:3–10.

Hirstein, W., and V.S. Ramachandran (1997). "Capgras' Syndrome: A Novel Probe for Understanding the Neural Representation of Identity and Familiarity of Persons." *Proc. R. Soc. London* [Biol], 264:437–44.

LeDoux, J. (1996). *The Emotional Brain*. New York: Simon & Schuster.

Rolls, E.T. (1995). "A Theory of Emotion and Consciousness, and its Application to Understanding the Neural Basis of Emotion." In M.S. Gazzinga (ed.). *The Cognitive Neurosciences*. Cambridge, MA: MIT Press.

Sacks, O. (1985). *The Man Who Mistook His Wife for a Hat*. New York: HarperCollins.

Tovee, M.J., E. Rolls, and V.S. Ramachandran (1996). "Rapid Visual Learning in Neurons in the Primate Visual Cortex." *Neuroreport*, 7:2757–2760.

24

RECONCEIVING DELUSION

G. Lynn Stephens and George Graham

INTRODUCTION

Important as talk of delusion is for the understanding and treatment of mental illness, it does not fit easily into clinical theory and practice. On the most common conception of delusion, a delusion is a belief of a pathological sort. But on the most common conception of belief, it is hard to see how many attitudes that are classified as delusions are beliefs. So, it seems that to find a proper place for talk of delusion in clinical theory and practice, we must either refine the concept of delusion so as to include non-belief-like cases as delusions, or refine the concept of belief so as to reclassify non-belief-like delusions as beliefs.

Traditionally, delusions have been regarded as pathological beliefs (American Psychiatric Association 1994, p. 765; Marshall & Halligan 1996, p. 8; Chen & Berrios 1998, p. 107). Critical discussion of the formula that delusions are pathological beliefs has focused on the adjective, i.e., on the problem of determining whether, when, and how delusory beliefs differ from normal, non-pathological beliefs. More recent discussion, however, has turned to the question of whether delusions are beliefs of any sort.

A body of opinion has developed that delusions are not beliefs. Whether this body deserves to be called a New Consensus about delusion may be debated. But the body possesses numerous advocates.

No body of opinion has emerged on how best to describe delusions if not as beliefs. A dilemma confronting attempts to define 'delusion' without assuming that delusions are beliefs is that, while critics of the belief formula have made a strong case for saying that not all cases commonly clinically cited as delusions are beliefs, other cases do seem to be beliefs.

We cast our vote with the following strategy: to refine 'delusion' so as to classify non-belief-like cases as well as belief-like cases as delusions. Our aim is to provide a unified account of delusions that embraces both belief and non-belief cases. We shall explain why objections to the traditional belief centered account have, so far, failed to coalesce into a satisfactory alternative theory of delusions. We shall propose an alternative definition or summary prototype of delusion according to which, being deluded that p (where 'p' represents the topical or thematic content of the delusion) is a matter of adopting a special (to be described below) complex, higher order attitude towards the lower order thought or content of p. This lower order thought or content may constitute a belief that p; for illustrative example, in certain (not all) Capgras cases the belief that a close relative has been replaced by an imposter. However in other cases it may not constitute a belief that p. We call the higher order attitude the *delusional stance* (Stephens & Graham 2005).

One implication of our analysis of delusions as complexes of higher order and lower order attitudes is that the distinctively pathological character of delusion does not consist in *what* a subject thinks or believes, but in *how* he thinks or believes. Delusional thinking as such consists of the higher order attitude or stance taken towards the thematic content of the delusion. In saying this we endorse the view defended by Sedler (1995) and others, that although the content of delusions 'specifically engages one's attention, and indeed has dominated clinical theory' content alone is 'insufficient to understand what makes a delusion' (p. 259). We shall urge that it is not the falsity or bizarreness of the content that 'makes a delusion' but rather how the subject deals with the content in the context of his overall psychological economy. Delusions, as Fulford (1993, p. 14) among others insists, are problems of practical rather than of theoretical or epistemic reason, namely, they constitute a failure of self-understanding and self-management and not *qua* delusions, a misrepresentation of the world. Delusions often do misrepresent bizarrely but this is not what makes them delusions.

In the next section of the paper, we will give a brief characterization of the case, as well as of a difficulty with the case, against saying that delusions are beliefs. In the last section of the paper, we will develop the claim that the belief-like conception of delusion needs to be replaced with a delusional stance conception. We will offer a descriptive sketch of the delusional stance.

DELUSION AND BELIEF

The word 'belief' is used in different ways. The most common reading of 'belief' in the formula that delusion is pathological belief is that a belief is a type of representational state or attitude, sometimes called a 'propositional attitude' (Crane 2001; Graham 1998). The propositional attitude interpretation of the notion of belief commits one, at least implicitly, to the following claims about belief and delusion, assuming that delusions are beliefs.

1. *Content claim.* Beliefs possess representational content, for instance, they represent the world or self as being or possibly being a certain way. A believer has in mind some state of affairs or some way that the world or self might be. If I believe that an imposter has replaced my spouse, for example, my belief has it that my spouse has been replaced by an imposter as its representational content. So, if delusions are beliefs, delusions possess representational content.

2. *Confidence claim.* Believers are confident or convinced that the representational content of the belief is true. If I believe that my spouse has been replaced by an imposter, I am confident, or convinced that, my spouse has been replaced by an imposter. If I believe that it is raining, I am confident, or convinced that it is raining. I sincerely take the proposition that it is raining to be true. So, if delusions are beliefs, the deluded person is convinced that the content of the delusion is true.

3. *Reason and action claim.* Believers take account of the truth of the content or proposition in reasoning and action. Beliefs guide the believer's decisions about what she might or ought to think or to do. A person who believes that she is dead will accept obvious logical implications of her belief such as that she is no longer alive, that her children are now orphans. Likewise change of belief will change a person's ideas about which actions are appropriate or sensible and possible. If I believe that it is sunny, it may make no sense to me to wear a raincoat. However if I believe that it is raining, it may make sense to me to wear a raincoat. So, if delusions are beliefs, the deluded subject will find some implications and actions logical or sensible in light of (the content of) the delusion and others not.

4. *Affect claim.* Beliefs tend to call up suitable affective responses or emotions, given one's values and desires. If I believe that it is raining, but want to picnic with my children, then I will be disappointed and frustrated. If I believe that my wife is an imposter and that the imposter is trying to poison me, I will fear for my safety and view my wife with anger and suspicion. So, if delusions are beliefs, the deluded subject will have feelings or emotions relevantly characteristic of the respective belief.

Each of these four claims about content, confidence, reason and action, and affect and emotion is the subject of analysis within the field of philosophy and, in particular, philosophy of the mind. There have been several attempts to explain how to individuate content, define confidence, specify implications and actions, and describe affects associated with belief. While there are refined differences between the attempts, they share the view that beliefs are representational, that they possess content and so on.

What then makes it doubtful that delusions are beliefs? Critics of the belief formula for delusion argue that delusions are not beliefs because as the term 'delusion' is used in clinical practice and closely related contexts, a delusion often or typically fails to satisfy one or more of the points (1) through (4) above. To quickly summarize the critical literature by citing representative critics and criticisms: against (4) Sass (1994, pp. 23–4) notes that victims of delusion often don't exhibit the affective or emotional responses that relevant beliefs would lead us to expect. A patient may report that his wife is trying to kill him while remaining completely indifferent to the prospect. Patients claiming unique and remarkable insights or a mandate from God to save the world may betray no sense of exhilaration or resolve. Sass asks why, if they believe what they say, don't they exhibit the affective responses the relevant beliefs would lead us to expect?

Against point (3) Currie (2000) remarks that delusions often 'fail to engage behavior' (p. 174; see also Sass 1994, p. 21; Young 1999, p. 581). A Capgras patient who insists that his wife has been replaced by an imposter doesn't file a missing person's report or make any move to investigate what has become of his 'real' wife. Perhaps this is due to the fact that the belief that his wife has been replaced by an imposter is 'highly circumscribed' (Young 1999, p. 581) or severely encapsulated or cut off from a subject's other beliefs. Severe encapsulation, however, is incompatible with the nature of belief at least as noted above (Fodor 1983). Currie and Jureidini (2001) remark: 'When someone acquires a new belief, a potentially wholesale process of belief revision will take place' (p. 160). In certain delusions, however, they often 'coexist with beliefs they contradict' and 'leave their possessors unwilling to resolve the inconsistency, and ... immune to conventional appeals to reason and evidence' (p. 160).

One might suppose that (2), the subject believes that p only if she is convinced that this proposition is true, is the bare minimum for believing that p. Even here, however, delusions sometimes fall short. Against (2) Sass (1994) reports that victims of delusion often are not confident in their delusions. They maintain an 'ironic' detachment which is very different to the typical believer's commitment to the truth of their beliefs. Young (1999) seconds this observation, noting that deluded subjects often express their delusions in an 'as if' rather than an 'assertive' spirit (p. 579).

Finally, against (1), Berrios (1996) questions whether delusions have any genuine content. A patient may emit a verbal formula, say, 'I am dead', but on being questioned cannot say what the words mean or coherently discuss their implications. 'Properly described,' says Berrios, 'delusions are empty speech-acts that disguise themselves as beliefs' (p. 126). 'Their so-called content refers neither to world, nor self'. 'Delusions', he writes, 'are so unlike normal beliefs that it must be asked why we persist in calling them beliefs at all' (pp. 114–15).

According to critics there is an obvious gap between the traditional concept of delusion as belief and clinical practice. Delusions are attributed to subjects who lack or certainly appear to lack relevant beliefs. The problem with denying that delusions are beliefs, however, is that it appears to deny something that is equally obvious. It is an uncontested fact, which is acknowledged even by some critics of the belief formula, that various instances of delusion do seem to conform to the belief model. Sass (1994) admits: 'It cannot be denied that … patients do at times make claims that give every appearance of being delusional in the traditional sense' (p. 51). Young (1999) makes the point that 'patients do sometimes commit appalling actions on the basis of their delusions' (p. 580). Though he concludes that acting on delusions 'is not the norm', he concludes: 'even so, the fact that people do sometimes act on … delusions shows that they are not invariably metaphors, empty-speech acts, or solipsistic reflections' (p. 581).

Currie (2000; Currie & Jureidini 2001) argues that delusions frequently involve 'cognitive hallucinations': that the (for example) paranoid subject is only imagining that people are following her, but she herself mistakes her imaginative thinking for belief. The deluded person imagines that p, but believes that she believes that p. She mistakes her imagining for believing. Currie (2000) allows, however, that 'it would be unwise to suppose that everything commonly ascribed as a delusion … could be adequately re-described in this way' (p. 176). Like Young (1999), he is impressed that delusional subjects 'do sometimes act on their thoughts' and suggests that 'at this point their thoughts have arrived at the status of beliefs' (p. 176). He remarks: 'the theory I am proposing … needs supplementation from a theory about how believing that we believe something makes us actually believe it' (p. 176). Currie does not suggest that, at the point where the subject goes from merely believing that she believes that people are following her to actually believing that people are following her, she ceases to be deluded. She may remain deluded if she believes that people are following her.

Young (1999) sums up the state of play on the cases for and against the delusion as belief formula. 'The issues involved' he remarks, 'in determining the conceptual status of delusions are tricky—one can draw attention to delusions that seem pretty convincing examples of false beliefs, or one can draw attention to delusions which seem like solipsistic empty speech-acts' (p. 581). Thus, given that in clinical practice the term 'delusion' is applied to states that represent 'pretty convincing examples of false beliefs' as well as to states that apparently are not beliefs, what lessons should we draw about how best to conceive of delusions?

CONCEPTUAL OPTIONS

Granting that clinical usage of the term 'delusion' does not universally conform to the formula that delusion is belief, one might adopt either of two different strategies for remedying this situation.

First strategy—one might propose that we regiment clinical practice so that only (pathological) beliefs count as delusions. Regimentation might be performed in either or both of the following ways: (a) The notion of belief might be explicated in an open textured or loose manner so as to classify apparent non-belief-like cases as sufficiently belief-like to count, loosely speaking, as beliefs. For example, instead of requiring appropriate action and relevant affect of belief, one might relax these two requirements and allow both inaction and emotional indifference to be compatible with belief. I can believe and be deluded that my wife has been replaced by an imposter but not be disposed to do or feel anything. (b) Residual non-belief-like cases might be declassified as delusions and new terminology introduced to reclassify them. Non-beliefs that otherwise appear delusional might be categorized as pseudo-delusions.

Second strategy—one might propose that the traditional formula that delusions are beliefs should be replaced with a conception of delusion that counts belief-like and non-belief-like cases as instances of the same sort of pathological symptom (delusion), and that this symptom is mischaracterized in the traditional account of delusions as beliefs.

Critics of the traditional account have not fully or squarely confronted the choice between these two main strategies. As we read the critical literature, critics seem to favor the second strategy of replacing the traditional account of delusion with a concept that covers both belief-like and non-belief-like cases and is independent of whatever sort of regimentation or modification may be attempted for the concept of belief. We do not pretend to be neutral about this project of strategy choice. We believe that the traditional account of delusion as beliefs should be replaced with a concept of delusion, which covers both belief-like and non-belief like sorts of cases. It is to this second strategy and to our sympathy for it that we turn in the final section of the paper.

DELUSIONS AS HIGHER ORDER ATTITUDES

We mentioned that Currie (2000) maintains that 'what we normally describe as the delusional belief that p ought sometimes to be described as the delusional belief that I believe that p' (p. 176; see also Currie & Jureidini 2001). Here, we claim that although the details of Currie's account may be problematic, his assumption that delusions are complex, hierarchically structured states or attitudes corresponds to clinical practice and promises to serve as a template for a conception of delusions that covers both belief-like and non-belief-like cases.

Currie surmises that on the lower or first level of a person's psychological economy a deluded person has an attitude towards some representational content, e.g., in a case of paranoia that people are following me, and at the higher or second level, a reflexive attitude towards the first order attitude. In Currie's view, the first order attitude is, or often qualifies as, an act of imagining or imaginatively entertaining the content or proposition in question. These first order episodes are not beliefs. Beliefs enter into Currie's account at the higher level wherein the subject believes that she believes the content or proposition in question. For Currie the pathological character of the subject's condition does not lie in the fact that the proposition that people are following her is false. As Currie and Jureidini (2001) note: 'there is nothing irrational about' imagining what is false (p. 160). It lies rather in her failure to recognize that she is only imagining that people are following her i.e., in her false second order belief that she believes that she is being followed.

The main virtue of Currie's tiered conception of delusion—of delusion as a hierarchically ordered state or condition—is that it enables him to explain how someone might entertain the content that people are following her, sincerely affirm that she believes this and yet fail to act on it, reason according to it, or display appropriate affective responses to it. She answers 'Yes' when asked, 'Do you believe that people are following you?' because she has the second order conviction that she believes she's being followed. But she fails to take evasive action, rejects obvious logical implications of the belief that she's being followed (e.g., that she was not alone when she visited the park), and exhibits no anxiety or distress about her situation, for she does not really first order believe that people are following her. Because the subject second order believes that she believes that p, rather than the first order believes that p, she lacks the behavioral, inferential, and affective dispositions characteristic of people who believe that p. Her first order attitude fails to satisfy the conviction, action, and affective elements constitutive of the concept of belief at least as outlined above.

Two details in Currie's account are problematic. The first he himself recognizes. This is that it does not cover cases where the subject who suffers from the delusion that p really does believe that p. As noted above, some delusions do include (first order) beliefs and thus delusions are not, invariably, lower order imaginings. Second, Currie's account of the hierarchical character of delusions is too narrow or limited. We claim as follows: the first order objects of higher order attitudes may be imaginings, but they may also be beliefs and other sorts of content possessing attitudes (including among other candidates emotions with representational or propositional content, hunches, forebodings, premonitions, and opinions) and even (in atypical content-less or Berrios-type cases) 'empty speech acts'. Meanwhile the character of the higher order reflexive attitude is much more complex than mentioned by Currie. The higher order attitude is, on our view, a multi-faceted disposition to respond to or interpret one's lower order attitude in various ways. It's a full-bodied stance or psychological posture that one has or takes towards the lower order state or attitude.

Accordingly we call the delusional higher order attitude the *delusional stance*. On our view, the essence of a delusion is not just its hierarchically ordered and reflexive complexity but also the fact that sitting atop lower order attitudes (beliefs, imaginings, premonitions, and so forth) is the delusional stance.

What is the delusional stance? What sort of attitude or multi-faceted disposition towards one's lower order states or attitudes constitutes delusion? In brief terms, as suggested earlier in the paper, it constitutes *how* the victim of delusion thinks rather than *what* she thinks (Sass 1994; Fulford 1993). Somewhat similar to obsessive-compulsive thoughts, delusions involve an imprudent or unproductive allocation of a subject's psychological resources in the management and control of her own thinking and attitudes. Delusions therein prevent the subject from dealing effectively with self and world. Unlike obsessive subjects, however, delusional subjects identify with the representational content (at the lower order) of their delusions. They do not experience the content as intrusive or as occurring contrary to their will or control. Obsessive subjects recognize that their obsessions disrupt and diminish their lives and they struggle, perhaps with very limited success, to contain the behavioral damage. Delusional subjects, by contrast, lack insight into the nature and personal cost of their lower order attitudes. They may find their delusional contents distressing in various ways, but they do not appreciate that the source of their distress is within themselves (in the lower order contents and in their attitudes toward the contents) and that it indicates that something is wrong with them.

Worries aside about being able to fully describe details here, let us briefly sketch the features of the delusional stance that we take to be characteristic, at least paradigmatically or prototypically, of delusion. (We shall assume that delusions, paradigmatically, possess representational content at the first order. An example of an atypical case of delusion may be, to use Berrios's term, 'an empty speech act' or mere verbal formula with no representational content in its first order. The delusional stance may also be taken to such formulae). Here is the sketch: S is deluded that p, just in case p is the representational content of a lower order state or attitude of S: (a) with which S personally identifies, (b) to which S clings in the face of strong contrary considerations, and (c) about which S lacks insight into the nature and imprudent costs of maintaining.

For example, suppose that S has a delusion of infestation. S thinks that worms and other small deadly organisms are devouring her bones. She persists in thinking this. Suppose also that S fails to exhibit behavior or affective responses expected of such a thought if it is a belief. She does not seek the counsel of a physician and feels no distress or fear. So suppose that in thinking that p, S seems not, strictly speaking, to believe that p.

One might try to insist that this lower order attitude is a belief. One might counter-argue that S nonetheless does believe that worms are devouring her bones but that S is otherwise cognitively and emotionally impaired and this helps to explain her failure to seek medical assistance or to feel distress. However, suppose that outside the specific contents associated with the thought that her bones are being devoured by worms, *S*'s cognitive-emotional behavior is not strikingly abnormal and that she admits that the proposition that her bones are being devoured by worms is 'virtually impossible' for her to understand (Davies *et al.* 2001). So, at least on the surface there is nothing otherwise wrong with her that can account for why she does not worry or seek medical attention. So, let's assume that she thinks that worms are devouring her bones and that such thought falls short of being belief. Perhaps it is an imagining, opinion or premonition.

What, then, might make the persistent occurrence of the thought that her bones are being devoured by worms a delusion or part of a delusional state? In line with (a) through (c) above we propose the following answer:

1 *S* personally identifies with the thought that worms are devouring her bones. She does not regard it as intrusive (even though it is). She represents it to herself as something that she thinks and not as something alien or inserted into her. She experiences it as her own thought.

2 *S* cannot be dissuaded from thinking that worms are devouring her bones. She persists in entertaining this thought despite being informed of prudential considerations for dismissing the thought from her consciousness. Indeed, despite the fact that *S* says that it is hard for her to imagine how worms might be devouring her bones, she still says 'But I keep thinking of my bones being devoured'.

3 *S* misapprehends or fails to comprehend the damage that the thought does to her, diminishing the quality of her life, undermining her reputation as a responsible thinker and person. She entertains bizarre hypotheses for the origin of the thought ('It comes from God') and fails to appreciate that the repeated occurrence of the thought means that something is wrong with her and not with the world in which she lives. The thought does not qualify as an obsession, since *S* does not worry about it or wish the thought would go away. But she should worry, of course, that her ways of dealing with it or entertaining it are unreliable even if on various other matters unrelated to the content she does a decent job of reasoning and thinking.

Delusions should not be confused with perceptual hallucinations. It may be worth noting in order to help to further describe the delusional stance that hallucinations unlike delusions are not hierarchically ordered. Perceptual experiences are lower order in character. If, for example, I perceptually hallucinate that worms are devouring my bones, this may be because I have visual or tactile experiences as of being devoured by worms. If, in addition or instead, I am deluded that worms are devouring my bones, then I take the attitude that worms are devouring my bones to be my own (I self-attribute it), I persist in holding or entertaining this attitude in spite of facing strong contrary considerations, including perhaps contrary perceptual experience, and I fail to grasp the damage to myself that harboring this attitude produces. A delusion is no mere misperception or first order state or experience.

The above is a space-constrained sketch of the delusional stance. It is a brief picture of an alternative conception of delusion to the belief conception. Some, albeit perhaps still incomplete, additional details are offered in Stephens and Graham (2005).

While we do not wish to dismiss the powerful role that first order beliefs and different types of first order attitudes and contents can play in delusions as well as in the specific character of a delusion, it is not the falseness or bizarreness of first order beliefs that constitutes being deluded, but, in general, the failure to properly respond to the challenges that first order thoughts and attitudes present to us as thinkers. As bizarre as it may be to think that for example, worms are devouring one's bones, delusion consists not in such thoughts but in the pathological manner in which we respond to them as persons.

In order for first order thoughts to acquire the status of being part of a delusion, they need not to be false or bizarre (even truth can characterize the first order content of a delusion, for example a victim of delusional jealousy [Othello syndrome] may correctly suspect that his spouse is having an affair). They need to be subjects of the delusional stance. Consider the following non-delusional case for contrast and comparison. The philosopher Peter Unger (1979) once published a paper with the provocative title of 'I do not exist'. Unger argued: 'I do not exist and neither do you' (p. 236). Unger's claim was not a syntactic variant of Cotard's syndrome peppered with denial of other persons. Unger, although holding an utterly bizarre and arguably self-contradictory belief, was not deluded. He suffered from none of the delusional stance pathology of S, for, among other things he acknowledged that his opinion was bizarre and urged his readers to dissuade him with contrary argumentation. 'Perhaps,' Unger (1979) wrote, 'a response to my challenge may save me from the ultimately fruitless labors I seemed required to undertake' (p. 236). It is, in part, through such self-corrective (and in the context of his paper, deftly ironic) admonition that Unger, in effect, helped to distinguish the non-delusional character of his attitude from that of S. Proper regulation of one's lower order attitudes is one hallmark of non-delusional intelligence. Delusions are one type of failure of attitude self-regulation.

ACKNOWLEDGEMENTS

We wish to thank Timothy Bayne, Matthew Broome, Ralph Kennedy and Jennifer Radden for helpful comments on an earlier draft of this paper.

REFERENCES

American Psychiatric Association. (1994). *Diagnostic and statistical manual of mental disorders*, (4th edn). Washington, DC: American Psychiatric Association.

Berrios, G. (1996). *A history of mental symptoms: descriptive phenomenology since the nineteenth century*. Cambridge: Cambridge University Press.

Chen, E. & Berrios, G. (1998). The nature of delusions: a hierarchical neural network approach. In D. Stein & J. Ludik (eds.), *Neural networks and psychopathology: connectionist models in practice and research* (pp. 167–88). Cambridge: Cambridge University Press.

Crane, T. (2001). *Elements of mind: an introduction to the philosophy of mind*. Oxford: Oxford University Press.

Currie, G. (2000). Imagination, delusion, and hallucinations. In M. Coltheart & M. Davies (eds.), *Pathologies of belief* (pp. 167–82). Oxford: Basil Blackwell.

Currie, G. & Jureidini, J. (2001). Delusion, rationality, and empathy. *Philosophy, Psychiatry and Psychology*, 8, 59–62.

Davies, M., Coltheart, M., Langdon, R. & Breen, N. (2001). Monothematic delusions: towards a two-factor account. *Philosophy, Psychiatry and Psychology*, 8, 133–58.

Fodor, J. (1983). *The modularity of mind*. Cambridge, MA: MIT Press.

Fulford, K.W.M. (1993). Thought insertion and insight: disease and illness paradigms of psychotic disorder. In M. Spitzer, F. Uehlin, M. Schwartz, & C. Mundt (eds.), *Phenomenology, language and schizophrenia* (pp. 1–17). New York: Springer-Verlag.

Graham, G. (1998). *Philosophy of mind: an introduction* (Second Edition). Oxford: Basil Blackwell.

Marshall, J. & Halligan, P. (1996). Towards a cognitive neuropsychiatry. In Halligan, P. & Marshall, J. (eds.) *Method in madness: case studies in cognitive neuropsychiatry* (pp. 3–11). Hove, East Sussex, UK: Psychology Press.

Sass, L. (1994). *The paradoxes of delusion: Wittgenstein, Schrieber and the schizophrenic mind*. Ithaca, New York: Cornell University Press.

Sedler, M.J. (1995). Understanding delusions. *Psychiatric Clinics of North America, 18*, 251–62.

Stephens, G.L. & Graham, G. (2005). The delusional stance. In M. Chung, K.W. M. Fulford, & G. Graham (eds.), *Reconceiving schizophrenia*. Oxford: Oxford University Press.

Unger, P. (1979). I do not exist. In G.F. Macdonald (ed.), *Perception and identity* (pp. 235–51). Ithaca, New York: Cornell University Press.

Young, A. (1999). Delusions. *The Monist, 82*, 571–89.

25

DOES THE AUTISTIC CHILD HAVE A 'THEORY OF MIND'?

Simon Baron-Cohen, Alan M. Leslie and Uta Frith

1 INTRODUCTION

Childhood autism is a severe developmental disorder. It is a rare condition, affecting about 4 in every 10,000 children. The diagnostic criteria at present are behavioural (American Psychiatric Association 1980; Kanner 1943; Ritvo & Freeman 1978; Rutter 1978) and the main symptom, which can be reliably identified, is impairment in verbal and nonverbal communication. This impairment is part of the core feature of childhood autism, namely a profound disorder in understanding and coping with the social environment, regardless of IQ. Additional symptoms can occur, in particular, mental retardation, islets of ability, and 'insistence on sameness'. Nevertheless, the pathognomonic symptom is failure to develop normal social relationships.

Autistic children find even the immediate social environment unpredictable and incomprehensible. They are often said in some sense to 'treat people and objects alike'. Wing and Gould (1979) in their epidemiological study of severely retarded autistic children bring out the range of socially impaired behaviour: from total withdrawal through passivity to repetitive pestering. Lord's (1984) review of work on peer interaction in autistic children highlights the low level of social competence even in able autistic children, despite improvements due to intervention. A picture of apparently intractable social impairment emerges in the clinical follow-up studies of autism (e.g. Kanner 1971; Kanner, Rodriguez & Ashenden 1972) and in the as yet rare experimental investigations (e.g. Attwood 1984; Martini 1980).

Although the majority of autistic children are mentally retarded (DeMyer *et al.* 1974; Wing, Yeates, Brierley & Gould 1976), and although a number of their symptoms may be attributable to this fact (Hermelin & O'Connor 1970) this in itself cannot be a sufficient explanation for their social impairments. First, there are autistic children with IQ's in the normal range, and second, mentally retarded non-autistic children, such as Down's syndrome, are socially competent relative to their mental age (Coggins, Carpenter, & Owings 1983; Gibson 1978).

In order to explain the specific impairments of childhood autism it is necessary, then, to consider the underlying cognitive mechanisms independent of IQ (Frith 1982; Hermelin & O'Connor 1970; Rutter 1983). So far, nobody has had any idea of how to characterise such mechanisms in even quasi-computational terms. In this paper we put forward a suggestion which has been derived from a new model of metarepresentational development (Leslie 1984, to appear). This model specifies a mechanism which underlies a crucial aspect of social skills, namely being able to conceive of mental states: that is, knowing that other people know, want, feel, or believe things; in short, having what Premack and Woodruff (1978) termed a 'theory of mind'. A theory of mind is impossible without the capacity to form 'second-order representations' (Dennett 1978; Pylyshyn 1978). According to Leslie's model this capacity does not appear until the second year of life. While this capacity manifests itself eventually in a theory of mind, Leslie shows that it also accounts for the emergence of pretend play. An absence of the capacity to form second-order representations, then, would lead not only to a lack of theory of mind, with the concomitant aspects of social ineptness, but also to a lack of pretend play.

Now, it is well known that autistic children, in addition to their social handicaps, also show a striking poverty of pretend play (Sigman & Ungerer 1981; Ungerer & Sigman 1981; Wing, Gould, Yeates & Brierley 1977; Wing & Gould 1979). An explanation for the lack of pretend play and its curious association with the social impairments typical of autism is not obvious, and again the notion of mental age is not helpful for this purpose. On the one hand, even high IQ autistic children lack pretend play, and on the other hand, severely retarded Down's syndrome children don't (Hill & McCune-Nicolich 1981). However, if we suppose that autistic children lack second-order representations, then we can make sense of the association of impairments. In order to test this hypothesis we can make the prediction that autistic children will lack a theory of mind. It is of course possible for autistic children to have a theory of mind and still exhibit incompetence, since social competence must depend on a large number of factors. However, if our prediction was proved wrong and autistic children did show evidence of employing a theory of mind, then we could rule out a deficiency in second-order representations. Even if our prediction was confirmed, that is, if autistic children lacked a theory of mind, we would still have to establish that this was a *specific* deficit, that is, largely independent of *general* mental retardation. Thus we would have to demonstrate (a) that even those rare autistic children whose IQ's are in the average range should lack this ability and (b) that non-autistic but severely retarded children, such as Down's syndrome, should possess it.

In a seminal paper, Premack and Woodruff (1978) defined theory of mind as the ability to impute mental states to oneself and to others. The ability to make inferences about what other people *believe* to be the case in a given situation allows one to predict what they will do. This is clearly a crucial component of social skills. There is growing evidence for the ability to attribute mental states to others, and its development from the second year of life onwards (Bretherton, McNew & Beeghly-Smith 1981; MacNamara, Baker, & Olson, 1976; Shantz 1983; Shultz, Wells & Sarda 1980; Shultz & Cloghesy 1981). A convincing demonstration that an explicit theory of mind is well within the capacity of the normal four-year-old has been given by Wimmer and Perner (1983). These authors developed an ingenious paradigm that can be used with very young children based on the case where the child's own belief is different from someone else's belief. In order to succeed on the task the child has to be aware that different people can have different beliefs about a situation. Hence this case provides the strongest evidence for the capacity to conceive of mental states (Dennett 1978). It is this paradigm that we used in the present study.

2 METHOD

2.1 Subjects

Details of the subjects are shown in Table 25.1. The 20 autistic children had been diagnosed according to established criteria (Rutter 1978). In addition there were 14 Down's Syndrome and 27 clinically normal preschool children. The autistic group's mean mental age (MA) was not only higher than that of the Down's Syndrome group on a non-verbal scale, but also on the more conservative measure of a verbal scale.

Table 25.1 Means, SDs and ranges of Chronological Age (CA) and Mental Age (MA) in years;months

Diagnostic groups	n		CA	Nonverbal* MA	Verbal** MA
Autistic	20	Mean	11;11	9;3	5;5
		SD	3;0	2;2	1;6
		Range	6;1–16;6	5;4–15;9	2;8–7;5
Down's syndrome	14	Mean	10;11	5;11	2;11
		SD	4;1	0;11	0;7
		Range	6;3–17;0	4;9–8;6	1;8–4;0
Normal	27	Mean	4;5	–	–
		SD	0;7		
		Range	3;5–5;9		

* Leiter International Performance Scale. ** British Picture Vocabulary Test.

312

We assumed that for the normal group MA would roughly correspond to chronological age (CA). Therefore, their MA was, if anything, lower than that of the handicapped groups. We selected a high functioning subgroup of autistic children in order to enable a stringent test of the specific deficit hypothesis to be made. Thus, the autistic group was of a relatively high mean IQ of 82 (derived from non-verbal MA), mostly in the average and borderline range, i.e. 70 to 108, with only one subject scoring less than 70. The IQ's of the Down's Syndrome group were rather lower with a range from 42 to 89, and an average of 64.

2.2 The Procedure

The procedure is illustrated in Figure 25.1. There were two doll protagonists, Sally and Anne. First, we checked that the children knew which doll was which (Naming Question). Sally first placed a marble into her basket. Then she left the scene, and the marble was transferred by Anne and hidden in her box. Then, when Sally returned, the experimenter asked the critical Belief Question: "Where will Sally look for her marble?". If the children point to the previous location of the marble, then they pass the Belief Question by appreciating the doll's now false belief. If however, they point

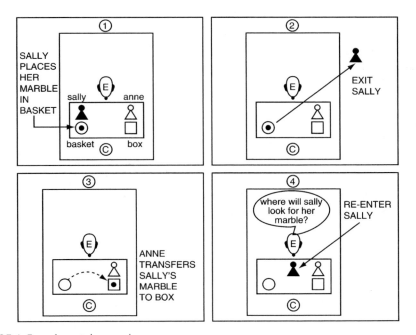

Figure 25.1 Experimental scenario

to the marble's current location, then they fail the question by not taking into account the doll's belief. These conclusions are warranted if two control questions are answered correctly: "Where is the marble really?" (Reality Question); "Where was the marble in the beginning?" (Memory Question).

The control questions are crucial to ensure that the child has both knowledge of the real current location of the object and an accurate memory of the previous location. There is no reason to believe that the three questions differ from each other in terms of *psycholinguistic* complexity, but of course we hypothesize that they differ in terms of *conceptual* complexity. The standard scenario was repeated using a new location for the marble, so that now there were three different locations that the child could point at (basket, box and experimenter's pocket). Correct responses to all three Questions for each of the two trials were therefore different.

3 RESULTS

All subjects passed the Naming Question. Furthermore, all subjects without a single exception performed without any errors for both the Reality and Memory Questions in both trials. The Belief Question for both trials was answered consistently by each child with the sole exception of one Down's Syndrome child who failed trial 1 and passed trial 2. The results for Down's Syndrome and normal subjects were strikingly similar. 23 out of 27 normal children, and 12 out of 14 Down's Syndrome children *passed* the Belief Question on both trials (85% and 86% respectively). By contrast, 16 of the 20 autistic children (80%) *failed* the Belief Question on both trials. This difference between the groups was highly significant ($X^2 = 25.9$, df = 2, $p < .001$). All 16 autistic children who failed pointed to where the marble really was, rather than to any of the other possible locations ($p = .006$, Binomial Test, one tailed). The four autistic children who passed succeeded on both trials. Their CA ranged from 10:11 to 15:10, their non-verbal MAs were between 8:10 and 10:8, and their verbal MAs between 2:9 and 7:0. Comparison with data in Table 25.1 shows that these children were fairly average on all our available variables. There were certainly other children of equal or greater MA and CA who gave incorrect responses.

4 DISCUSSION

The fact that every single child taking part in the experiment correctly answered the control questions allows us to conclude that they all knew (and implicitly believed) that the marble was put somewhere else after Sally had left. The critical question was, "Where will Sally look?" after she returns. Here a group difference appeared: Autistic children answered this question in a distinctly different way from the others. The Down's Syndrome and normal preschool children answered by pointing to where the marble was put in the first place. Thus they must have appreciated that their own knowledge of where the marble actually was and the knowledge that could be attributed to the doll were different. That is, they predicted the doll's behaviour on the basis of the doll's belief. The autistic group, on the other hand, answered by pointing consistently to where the marble really was. They did not merely point to a 'wrong' location, but rather to the actual location of the marble. This becomes especially clear on trial 2 where the autistic children never pointed to the box (which had been the 'wrong' location on trial 1), but instead to the experimenter's pocket— that is, again to where the marble really was. This rules out both a position preference and a negativism explanation. Furthermore, the autistic children were not 'contrary' on the Reality or Memory Questions which they always answered correctly. Clark and Rutter (1977, 1979) investigating alleged negativism in autistic children also found no evidence of such behaviour. The failure on the Belief Question was also not due to random pointing. Nor could it have been due to any failure to understand and remember the demands of the task or the narrative since these children all answered the Naming, Memory and Reality Questions perfectly. We therefore conclude that the autistic children did not appreciate the difference between their own and the doll's knowledge.

Our results strongly support the hypothesis that autistic children as a group fail to employ a theory of mind. We wish to explain this failure as an inability to represent mental states. As a result of this the autistic subjects are unable to impute beliefs to others and are thus at a grave disadvantage when having to predict the behaviour of other people. There is, however, also a suggestion of a small subgroup of autistic children who succeeded on the task and who thus may be able to employ a theory of mind. These children who nevertheless, by definition (American Psychiatric Association 1980; Rutter 1978), exhibit social impairment, would certainly deserve further study. From Leslie's (1984) model we would predict that if they did have the capacity to form second-order representations, then they would also show evidence of an ability to pretend play. Furthermore, we would predict that their social impairments would show a rather different pattern from those autistic children who fail to use a theory of mind.

The ability we have been testing could be considered as a kind of *conceptual* perspective-taking skill (Shantz 1983). However, it is important to contrast the present task with traditional *perceptual* perspective-taking tasks, such as 'line of sight' or 'three mountains', where a child has to indicate what can be seen from another point of view (Hobson 1982; Hughes & Donaldson 1979; Piaget and Inhelder 1956). Such perceptual perspective-taking tasks can be solved using solely visuo-spatial skills and in no way require imputing beliefs to others (Cox 1980; Huttenlocher & Presson 1979). Hobson (1984) has recently shown that autistic children succeed on perceptual perspective-taking tasks with doll protagonists as well as can be expected from their MA. This finding, Hobson argued, suggests that it is very unlikely that the cognitive abilities required in taking different points of view in perceptual situations are the same as those that underlie the autistic child's social disability. The results of the present study would confirm this interpretation and point towards a crucial distinction between the understanding of perceptual situations and the attribution of higher order mental states.

We conclude that the failure shown by the autistic children in our experiment constitutes a specific deficit. It cannot be attributed to the general effects of mental retardation, since the more severely retarded Down's syndrome children performed close to ceiling on our task. Thus we have demonstrated a cognitive deficit that is largely independent of general intellectual level and has the potential to explain both lack of pretend play and social impairment by virtue of a circumscribed cognitive failure. This finding encourages us to continue with a theoretical framework (Leslie 1984, to appear) which can specify the underlying connections between pretend play, theory of mind and social skills. Deriving further testable predictions from such a model may lead to a new approach to the cognitive dysfunction in childhood autism (Frith 1984).

REFERENCES

American Psychiatric Association (1980). *Diagnostic and statistical manual of mental disorders* (3rd ed.). Washington DC: American Psychiatric Association.

Attwood, A.J. (1984). *Gestures of autistic children*. Unpublished Ph.D. Thesis, University of London.

Bretherton, I., McNew, S., and Beeghly-Smith, M. (1981). 'Early person knowledge as expressed in gestural and verbal communication: When do infants acquire a "theory of mind"?' In M.E. Lamb & L.R. Sherrod (eds.), *Infant social cognition*. Hillsdale, NJ: Erlbaum.

Clark, P., and Rutter, M. (1977). 'Compliance and resistance in the conditioning of autistic children: an exploratory study'. *Journal of Autism and Childhood Schizophrenia* 7, 33–48.

Clark, P., and Rutter, M. (1979). 'Task difficulty and task performance in autistic children'. *Journal of Child Psychology and Psychiatry*, 20, 271–85.

Coggins, T.E., Carpenter, R.L., and Owings, N.O. (1983). 'Examining early intentional communication in Down's Syndrome and nonretarded children'. *British Journal of Disorders in Communication* 18, 98–106.

Cox, M.V. (1980). 'Visual perspective-taking in children'. In M.V. Cox (ed.), *Are young children egocentric?* London: Batsford Academic and Educational.

DeMyer, M.K., Barton, S., Alpern, G.D., Kimberlin, C., Allen, J., Yang, E., and Steele, R. (1974). 'The measured intelligence of autistic children'. *Journal of Autism and Childhood Schizophrenia* 4, 42–60.

Dennett, D. (1978). 'Beliefs about beliefs'. *Behavioral and Brain Sciences* 4, 568–70.

Frith, U. (1982). 'Psychological abnormalities in early childhood psychoses'. In L. Wing and J.K. Wing (eds.), *Handbook of Psychiatry Vol. 1*. Cambridge: Cambridge University Press.

Frith, U. (1984). 'A new perspective in research on autism'. In A.R.A.P.I (eds.), *Contributions à la recherche scientifique sur l'autisme: aspects cognitifs*. Paris: Association pour la Recherche sur l'Autisme et les Psychoses Infantiles.

Gibson, D. (1978). *Down's Syndrome: The psychology of mongolism*. Cambridge: Cambridge University Press.

Hermelin, B., and O'Connor, N. (1970). *Psychological experiments with autistic children*. Oxford: Pergamon Press.

Hill, P.M., and McCune-Nicolich, L. (1981). 'Pretend play and patterns of cognition in Down's Syndrome children'. *Child Development* 52, 217–50.

Hobson, R.P. (1982). 'The question of childhood egocentrism: the coordination of perspectives in relation to operational thinking'. *Journal of Child Psychology and Psychiatry* 23, 43–60.

Hobson, R.P. (1984). 'Early childhood autism and the question of egocentrism'. *Journal of Autism & Developmental Disorders* 14, 85–104.

Hughes, M., and Donaldson, M. (1979). 'The use of hiding games for studying the coordination of viewpoints'. *Educational Review* 31, 133–40.

Huttenlocher, J., and Presson, C.C. (1979). 'The coding and transformation of spatial information'. *Cognitive Psychology* 11, 373–94.

Kanner, L. (1943). 'Autistic disturbances of affective contact'. *Nervous Child* 2, 217–50.

Kanner, L. (1971). 'Follow-up study of eleven autistic children originally reported in 1943'. *Journal of Autism and Childhood Schizophrenia* 1, 119–45.

Kanner, L., Rodriguez, A., and Ashenden, B. (1972). 'How far can autistic children go in matters of social adaptation?' *Journal of Autism and Childhood Schizophrenia* 2, 9–33.

Leslie, A.M. (1984). 'Pretend play and representation in infancy: A cognitive approach'. In A.R.A.P.I. (eds.), *Contributions à la recherche scientifique sur l'autisme: aspects cognitifs*. Paris: Association pour la Recherche sur l'Autisme et les Psychoses Infantiles.

Leslie, A.M. (1987) 'Pretense and representation in infancy'. *Psychological Review* 94, 84–106.

Lord, C. (1984). 'The development of peer relations in children with autism'. In F.J. Morrison, C. Lord and D.P. Keating (eds.), *Advances in applied developmental psychology* (pp. 165–229). New York: Academic Press.

MacNamara, J., Baker, E., and Olsen, C. (1976). 'Four-year-olds' understanding of pretend, forget, and know: evidence for propositional operations'. *Child Development* 47, 62–70.

Martini, M. (1980). 'Structures of interaction between two autistic children'. In T.M. Field, S. Goldberg, D. Stern and A.M. Sostek (eds.), *High-risk infants and children: Adult and peer interactions*. New York: Academic Press.

Piaget, J., and Inhelder, B. (1956). *The child's conception of space*. London: Routledge & Kegan Paul.

Premack, D., and Woodruff, G. (1978). 'Does the chimpanzee have a "theory of mind"?' *Behavioral and Brain Sciences* 4, 515–26.

Pylyshyn, Z.W. (1978). 'When is attribution of beliefs justified?' *Behavioral and Brain Sciences* 4, 492–593.

Ritvo, E.R., and Freeman, B.J. (1978). 'National Society for Autistic Children definition of the syndrome of autism'. *Journal of the American Academy of Child Psychiatry* 17, 565–76.

Rutter, M. (1978). 'Diagnosis and definition'. In M. Rutter and E. Schopler (eds.), *Autism: A reappraisal of concepts of treatment*. New York: Plenum.

Rutter, M. (1983). 'Cognitive deficits in the pathogenesis of autism'. *Journal of Child Psychology and Psychiatry* 24, 513–31.

Shantz, C.U. (1983). 'Social cognition.' In P.H. Mussen (ed.), *Handbook of Child Psychology, Vol. III*. J.H. Flavell and E.M. Markman (eds.), *Cognitive Development*. New York: Wiley.

Shultz, T.R., and Cloghesy, K. (1981). 'Development of recursive awareness of intention'. *Developmental Psychology 17*, 456–71.

Shultz, T.R., Wells, D., and Sarda, M. (1980). 'The development of the ability to distinguish intended actions from mistakes, reflexes, and passive movements'. *British Journal of Social & Clinical Psychology 19*, 301–10.

Sigman, M., and Ungerer, J. (1981). 'Sensorimotor skill and language comprehension in autistic children'. *Journal of Abnormal Child Psychology 9*, 149–65.

Ungerer, J.A., and Sigman, M. (1981). 'Symbolic play and language comprehension in autistic children'. *Journal of the American Academy of Child Psychiatry 20*, 318–37.

Wimmer, H., and Perner, J. (1983). 'Beliefs about beliefs: representation and constraining function of wrong beliefs in young children's understanding of deception'. *Cognition 13*, 103–28.

Wing, L., and Gould, J. (1979). 'Severe impairments of social interaction and associated abnormalities in children: Epidemiology and classification'. *Journal of Autism and Developmental Disorders 9*, 11–29.

Wing, L., Gould, J., Yeates, S.R., and Brierley, L. (1977). 'Symbolic play in severely mentally retarded and in autistic children'. *Journal of Child Psychology & Psychiatry 18*, 167–78.

Wing, L., Yeates, S.R., Brierley, L.M., and Gould, J. (1976). 'The prevalence of early childhood autism: Comparison of administrative and epidemiological studies'. *Psychological Medicine 6*, 89–100.

26

AUTISM AND THE "THEORY OF MIND" DEBATE

Robert M. Gordon and John A. Barker

Recent research has established that by the age of 4 most developmentally normal children understand that people sometimes respond to the world not as it actually is but merely as they believe it to be. With this understanding, children are better able to anticipate the behavior of others and to attune their own behavior accordingly. In mentally retarded children with Down's syndrome, attaining such competence is delayed, but it is generally acquired by the time they reach the *mental* age of 4, as measured by tests of nonverbal intelligence. Thus from a developmental perspective, attainment of the mental age of 4 appears to be significant for acquisition of what we call *psychological competence*: possession of the skills and resources people routinely call on in the anticipation, explanation, and social coordination of behavior.[1]

There is one notable exception, however. Most *autistic* children lack much of this competence even at significantly higher mental ages, according to a number of recent experimental studies. Most do not seem to understand that people's actions and emotions depend on their beliefs. Rather than treating other people as subjects with "points of view," they frequently give the impression of "treating people and objects alike" (Kanner 1943). Asked what the brain does, autistic children speak of it as making people move or run, whereas most children first mention thinking or feeling. Philosophers have sometimes found it useful to invent imaginary people who treat their fellows as, literally, mindless beings.[2] The exotic creatures of philosophical fiction appear congenial and well adjusted, however, in comparison to those real people who are severely handicapped by autism. People with autism, even many of the most intelligent among them, apparently never succeed in developing a normal understanding of many of the psychological dimensions of human existence, and as a result, they fail to achieve normal interactions with other human beings.

Many autistic people are also abnormal in respects other than psychological competence. The majority are mentally retarded. But their striking failure in many psychological tasks does not appear to be accountable in terms of any broad deficit in intellect. It has therefore been argued by a group of leading researchers that autism is characterized by a specific deficit in psychological competence, a deficit in what they call possession and use of a "theory of mind" (Baron-Cohen, Leslie, and Frith 1985; Leslie 1987; Frith 1989; Baron-Cohen 1990).

1 SOME PIVOTAL EXPERIMENTAL RESULTS

According to many accounts, the major watershed in the development of psychological competence is the capacity to deploy the notion of belief, and in particular the capacity to attribute beliefs that are false or contrary to fact. A classic experimental study, Wimmer and Perner 1983, focuses on false belief and establishes that in normal children this capacity becomes apparent at approximately the age of 4. In the original experiment, children are presented a story, illustrated with puppets, in which the protagonist places an object in one location and subsequently, while he is out of the room and without his knowledge, someone else relocates the object. Where does Maxi go to retrieve his candy when he returns to the room? *We*, of course, would predict that he will look for it in the wrong place, and so do most children of age 4 or older. Children under about the age of 4, however, point to or otherwise indicate the actual present location of the candy. Evidently, they are unable to adjust for the fact that the protagonist was not in a position to know that the object was relocated. They treat all the facts presented to them in a story as accessible to the protagonist, as if nothing were beyond his ken. It doesn't matter whether something happens in plain sight of the protagonist or whether he is epistemically handicapped. The experiment has been replicated a number of times, and it has held up very well and been supported by other research.

Even more striking than the results of the original experiment were those reported in Baron-Cohen, Leslie, and Frith 1985. In this study, a test similar to the one used in Wimmer and Perner 1983 was applied to a group of clinically normal 4-year-old and 5-year-old children, a group of mentally retarded children with Down's syndrome (mean chronological age = 10, mean nonverbal mental age = 5), and a group of highly functional children with autism (mean chronological age = 11, mean nonverbal mental age = 9). It was found, on the one hand, that the mentally retarded Down's syndrome subjects gave the right response about as frequently as the normal children did. On the other hand, most of the highly functional autistic subjects gave the wrong response. Even those who had attained the mental age of 9 typically performed at the 3-year-old level on false-belief tasks. Despite being smarter than the other subjects, the autistic children appeared to suffer from a specific deficit in at least this aspect of psychological competence.

Results for the most part consistent with those reported in Baron-Cohen, Leslie, and Frith 1985 have been obtained in a variety of subsequent studies.[3] In addition, a later study by Baron-Cohen, Leslie, and Frith (1986) employed a largely nonverbal test in which children were asked to put the frames of a picture story into the proper sequence. Where the sequence was one of mechanistic causality, children with autism performed at least as well as normal children and those with Down's syndrome. But where the right sequence (recognized immediately by normal adults) depicts a story involving false belief, the performance of autistic children was no better than chance and far worse than those of normal and Down's syndrome subjects.

2 IS PSYCHOLOGICAL COMPETENCE BASED ON A THEORY?

We assume in this chapter that the available evidence largely favors the hypothesis of a specific deficit in psychological competence. Whether we should characterize it as a "theory of mind" deficit, following Baron-Cohen, Leslie, and Frith (1985, 1986), depends on whether we wish to accept the implicit assumption that psychological competence consists in the possession and use of a *theory*. This is indeed a popular assumption. For the past quarter century a dominant view in philosophy and the cognitive sciences has been that the resources that underlie commonsense explanations and predictions of behavior chiefly consist of a tacit body of propositional knowledge roughly comparable to a scientific theory. The alleged theory posits unobservable mental states such as beliefs, desires, intentions, and feelings, linked to each other and to observable behaviors by "law-like" principles. These principles are applied to observable situations by way of logical inferences that generate predictions and explanations of behavior. The theory is supposedly called on by people of all cultures and virtually all levels of intelligence to explain and predict the behavior of others. To apply the theory, it is said, one neither needs nor typically possesses any conscious awareness of the principles one is applying. Careful reflection, however, can often bring them to light. And once they are provided with verbal garb, the principles typically seem obvious, commonplace, and platitudinous—which is taken to be good evidence that they constitute unquestioned presuppositions of a tacit folk theory.

The view that commonsense explanations and predictions of behavior are theory-based is called the "theory theory." Despite general acknowledgement that this view has serious deficiencies, until recently it was widely conceded that it had no plausible alternative: it was, as Jerry Fodor put it, "the only game in town." Indeed, it has been presupposed in most debates in the philosophy of mind, particularly the debate between those, such as Fodor, who think our tacit commonsense theory likely to be vindicated in large part by future science and those (the "eliminativists") who believe future science will show it to be radically mistaken and misconceived.

According to some developmental psychologists who accept the theory theory, children acquire psychological competence by a process of theory construction and theory change, replacing inadequate laws or principles with better ones, progressing toward mature conceptions of mental states such as belief and desire. Consider how, on this view, one might explain the difference between the way in which a 3-year-old and a 4-year-old answers the question, "Where will Maxi go to get his candy?" A 3-year-old might reason (consciously or unconsciously) as follows:

To get x, people will go to wherever x is.

Maxi's candy is in location b.

Therefore, to get his candy, Maxi will go to location b.

(The same conclusion could also be reached using an immature notion of belief shaped by the principle "If it is the case that p, then people believe that p.")

In contrast, a typical 4-year-old can deploy the notion of a belief that may or may not correspond to fact. The child might reason, consciously or unconsciously, along the following lines:

Principle: People who put an object in location l will typically believe just afterward that it is currently in location l.

So just after Maxi put his candy in location a, he believed that his candy was currently in location a.

Principle: People who believe that something is currently in location l will typically continue to believe that it is in location l unless they come to believe it (was) moved.

Principle: Typically people come to believe that x (was) moved only if they saw x move (being moved) or are told that x (was) moved.

But Maxi neither saw his candy being moved nor was told that it was moved.

So when Maxi returned, he believed that his candy was currently in location a.

Principle: To get x, people will go to wherever they *believe* x is.

Therefore, to get his candy, Maxi will go to location a.

The assumption that psychological competence consists in the possession and use of a theory is shared by many recent investigators of the development of psychological competence. The field of investigation has even come to be called "the child's theory of mind." Developmental psychologists inherited the term "theory of mind" from an article that asked whether the chimpanzee has a theory of mind (Premack and Woodruff 1978). The authors of that paper used the term very loosely, however. They gloss the term as follows: "In saying that an individual has a theory of mind, we mean that the individual imputes mental states to himself and others" (1978, 515).

This suggests that Premack and Woodruff were introducing the term "theory of mind" merely as an abbreviation of "capacity to attribute mental states." If that were their sole intent, then, of course, they would be leaving open the question "What is the *basis* of the capacity to attribute mental states?" But their choice of the term *theory* suggests that they were not leaving this question open but rather were taking for granted a certain answer to the question. They were accepting the conjecture that it is possession and use of a theory that gives individuals (human beings and possibly chimpanzees) the capacity to attribute mental states. Indeed, they did attempt to justify their use of the term *theory* on the grounds that mental states are not observable and that people are able to make predictions on the basis of these attributions. And at the time they were writing, there seemed to be no plausible *alternative* way of explaining how people might make predictions on the basis of attributions of states that lie "behind" behavior.

Some of the developmental psychologists who borrowed the term "theory of mind" from Premack and Woodruff also slide too easily from "capacity to attribute mental states" to "theory of mind" (as noted in de Gelder 1993). They vacillate between the innocuous assertion that by age 4 children are able to attribute mental states and the extravagant speculation that by age 4 children have a relatively mature *theory* on the basis of which they are able to attribute mental states. Considerable care should be given, therefore, to interpreting Baron-Cohen's claim that people with autism have a "theory of mind" deficit. If he is taken as saying only that normal children and those with Down's syndrome have a capacity to make a type of attribution that autistic children do not make, then he is putting forward a very interesting claim that does appear to be warranted by the experimental results he cites. But if he is taken as saying that normal children and those with Down's syndrome possess and use a *theory* (or part of a theory) that autistic children alone do not possess and use, then he is making a claim that appears to be called into question by some of the experimental results he cites in its support.[4] For children afflicted with Down's syndrome, who evidently have the psychological competence characteristic of their mental age, are notably deficient in theoretical abilities, whereas children afflicted with autism, who appear to be psychologically incompetent, are *not* generally deficient in theoretical abilities for their mental age. Why would autistic children who in some cases do even better than the average normal child in mastering theories of other sorts, fare so badly in this particular domain? And even more counterintuitive, how can it be that Down's children with IQs as low as 50 are able to master this "theory" about as well as normals do (albeit a few years later), when they master no other theory? In short, one drawback of the theory theory is that it is not easily squared with the findings regarding the psychological competence of children with Down's syndrome and the psychological incompetence of relatively intelligent children with autism.

We think the evidence suggests that the psychological competence that normal children develop but autistic children do not develop is based not on a *theory* but rather on a *skill* that does not essentially require the aptitudes tested in typical "IQ" tests. This is why retarded children with Down's syndrome, even those who in large degree lack these further aptitudes, prove to be psychologically competent. (Of course, one may reasonably expect the relevant skill to be refined and enhanced by these further IQ aptitudes. Hence it is not a consequence of our view that low-IQ Down's syndrome children are as likely as normal children to become successful novelists, playwrights, or psychologists.)

Although clearly not deficient in theoretical powers relative to their mental age, autistic children are in other respects very markedly different from other children of the same mental age, including those with Down's syndrome. Some of these differences can reasonably be attributed in large part to their impaired psychological competence. For example, autistic people are notoriously odd and limited in their capacity to communicate with others, both verbally and nonverbally. They also have a severely diminished capacity to enter into normal social relationships, especially with peers. Although these handicaps no doubt set them further behind the pack in psychological competence, the more important causal relationship seems to be the converse: without a level of psychological competence beyond that attained by most autistic people, normal communication and normal social relationships are altogether impossible (Baron-Cohen 1988, also Frith 1989). Thus whatever proves to be the key to the psychological incompetence of autistic individuals will probably also be the key to their social and communicative impairments.

3 PRETENDING AND SIMULATING

There are, however, other autistic abnormalities that cannot be attributed chiefly to psychological incompetence. Among these is the often-remarked failure of autistic children to engage in spontaneous pretend play, whether in conjunction with others or alone. Normal children and Down's syndrome children spontaneously initiate pretend play and develop the ability to participate in complex, interactive forms of it before they develop the psychological competence required in false-belief tasks. In stark contrast, the behavior of children with autism characteristically remains almost totally devoid of any signs of spontaneous pretend play. The lack of pretend play, particularly the absence of role play and mime play with imaginary objects, is well known. Although studies have shown that many autistic children can, with appropriate prompting, engage in some forms of pretend play (Lewis and Boucher 1988, Ungerer and Sigman 1981), the play is characterized by lack of spontaneity and by stereotypical, inflexible, and repetitive patterns. What is most conspicuous is the absence of *other-regarding* pretending, typified by role play and joint pretend play, in which two or more children act on a shared pretense (Harris 1992).

Might a faulty capacity for pretense, especially for other-regarding pretense, severely degrade a person's capacity to ascribe mental states? It would, according to the theory of psychological competence that we favor, the mental-simulation theory. This theory asserts that psychological competence fundamentally depends on the capacity to use one's own cognitive and motivational resources to simulate other people, a capacity that calls on no special theory of mental states.[5] For example, we often predict what another will decide to do by making a decision ourselves—a "pretend" decision, of course, made only in imagination—after making adjustments for relevant differences in situation and past behavior. According to our version of the simulation theory, such vicarious decision making also underlies our capacity to explain the behavior of others in terms of mental states, and probably also the very capacity to grasp the concepts of such states as belief and desire. If pretending is the key to making and understanding ascriptions of mental states then, of course, a developmental pathology, such as autism, that severely restricts the capacity to pretend should also severely restrict a child's capacity to make and understand such ascriptions, even if in other respects the child's intelligence is normal.

To help the reader understand how mental simulation can yield predictions and explanations of behavior, it will be instructive to examine the logical structure of pretend play. Children enter informal games of make-believe by initially pretending something to be true that they do not believe to be true. In pretense, they accept an initial premise (or premises), for example, that certain globs of mud are pies. By combining the initially stipulated premise with their existing store of beliefs and calling on their reasoning capacity, they are able to obtain answers to questions not addressed in the initial premise. In the mud-pie example, they would typically be able to answer the question "How many pies are there?" And where there is more than one player, their answers would typically agree: barring a stipulation to the contrary, the answer is the same as the number of (approximately pie-shaped) mud globs. "Which pie is biggest?" The biggest mud glob, of course, unless otherwise stipulated. This *productive* feature of many games of make-believe, pointed out by Kendall Walton, closely parallels our understanding of subjunctive conditionals, as Gareth Evans suggested.[6] Wondering if the bridge would have collapsed had there not been a heavy snowfall, we pretend that there wasn't a heavy snowfall, and then ask whether the bridge would have collapsed: this, with some amendments, is the so-called Ramsey test for evaluating subjunctive conditionals.[7]

But there is a *further* productive feature of games of make-believe. What the child *does* with the mud pies depends not only on the stipulated pretend facts, along with his existing *perceptions* and *beliefs*, but also on his existing *desires, values*, and *norms*. Together, these fix or at least constrain the child's answer to the question "What shall I *do* with these pies?" This *further* productive feature of games of make-believe parallels our typical understanding of conditionals concerning *our own actions* under hypothetical or counterfactual conditions. Gordon makes the connection with pretense explicit in describing how one might predict what actions one would take upon hearing footsteps coming from the basement:

To simulate the appropriate practical reasoning I can engage in a kind of *pretend-play*: pretend that the indicated conditions *actually obtain*, with all other conditions remaining (so far as is logically possible and physically probable) as they presently stand; then—continuing the make-believe—try to "make up my mind" what to do given these (modified) conditions. I imagine, for instance, a lone modification of the actual world: the sound of footsteps from the basement. Then I ask, in effect, "What shall I do now?" And I answer with a declaration of immediate intention, "I shall now ..." This too is only feigned. But it is not feigned on a *tabula rasa*, as if at random: rather, the declaration of immediate intention appears to be formed in the way a *decision* is formed, *constrained* by the (pretended) "fact" that there is the sound of footsteps from the basement, the (*un*pretended) fact that such a sound would now be unlikely if there weren't an intruder in the basement, the (*un*pretended) awfulness of there being an intruder in the basement, and so forth. (1986, 160–1)

As in pretend play, an initial premise—here the hypothetical condition—is added to one's store of beliefs, desires, and other inputs to intention formation and decision making. In one important respect, however, this kind of simulation is unlike children's games of make-believe (and also unlike rehearsals and drills). Although the simulation may be accompanied by autonomic arousal and some expression of emotion, it stops short of overt action. One does not carry out the decision, say to call the police, even in overt pretend play. Our motivational, emotional, and decision making systems are running "off-line," as it were, disengaged from their natural output systems.

The simulation theory says that in predicting, explaining, and interpreting *another's* behavior, we likewise run the explanation or prediction through our own motivational and emotional systems, utilizing our own capacity for practical reasoning and decision making. In simulating another, however, it is often not sufficient to imagine being in the other's situation, that is, to employ our imagination merely to ask, "What would *I* do, believe, want, and feel were I in Smith's situation?" For this would leave open the further question "What about *Smith*: what does *Smith* do, believe, want, or feel in that situation?" Rather than simulate ourselves in Smith's situation, we must simulate *Smith* in Smith's situation (as it appears to Smith).

This is a further, more complex use of pretense. When one is predicting *one's own* actions or reactions in hypothetical conditions, the initial premise—for example, that there is a sound of footsteps coming from the basement—is simply stipulated. But when we explain or predict *another's* behavior in such a situation, one may, in addition, have to make adjustments of various kinds. These might be based on knowledge of the other's actual behavior in related situations in the past: one tries to become in imagination a person who might have acted as the other did in such situations. In false-belief tasks like those presented in Wimmer and Perner 1983 and Baron-Cohen, Leslie, and Frith 1985, the needed adjustment is a simple one: just *ignore* one or more of the facts, and then carry on as before. In the Maxi example, what one needs to ignore is the fact that while Maxi was outside, his candy was moved. That is, one need only undo the move in imagination, thereby restoring the candy to its previous location. Then, within the context of this pretense, one simply states where the candy is. One will then predict correctly that he will look for his candy not where it *actually* is but where it was before it was moved. Notice that instead of invoking a special folk-psychological principle that *people typically believe* that objects (to put it crudely) tend to stay put, one simply relies on one's own background assumption that objects tend to stay put. (For a more detailed account of the methodology of mental simulation, see Gordon 1992.)

Until and unless children develop the capacity and the motivation to make these imaginative adjustments, we should expect them to explain and predict as if everything they themselves count as fact were *accessible to the other* as a basis for action and emotion. We should also expect them to allow no *false* propositions into the other's data base, no false beliefs, in other words. Because people with autism are in general severely deficient in their capacity for pretense, particularly for other-regarding pretense, they should be unable to make the adjustments posited by the simulation theory. Therefore, the theory correctly predicts, these people will generally not succeed in the false-belief tasks, even where in other respects their intelligence is normal.

4 PRETENDING AND THE THEORY-OF-MIND MECHANISM

We argued earlier that the theory theory is hard put to explain why children with Down's syndrome, who are generally poor theorists, have far more psychological competence than relatively intelligent children with autism, who are generally good theorists. The simulation theory would explain this in part by the fact that children with Down's syndrome, though poor theorists, spontaneously engage in complex, interactive forms of pretend play, whereas children with autism, though often good theorists, do not spontaneously engage in such play. But unlike the simulation theory, the theory theory does not hold that psychological competence depends on a capacity for certain kinds of pretending.

A further move, however, is available to theory theorists. They may argue that a theory of mental states differs in fundamental ways from theories in other domains, particularly in the nature of the concepts it employs. For one thing, it is a theory of intentional states, of states that are about something. And, it may be suggested, possession and use of a theory of intentional states requires a special cognitive mechanism and perhaps further that the same special mechanism is needed for pretense. This is proposed by one theory theorist, Alan Leslie, who posits a special computational mechanism, which he dubs the "Theory of Mind Mechanism," as requisite for overt pretend play as well as the understanding and recognition of intentional states (Leslie 1987, Leslie and Roth 1993). This proposal would parallel the simulation theorist's suggestion that both are implemented by off-line processing: utilizing systems that are normally dedicated to perception, cognition, motivation, emotion, and decision making, but using them in at least partial isolation from their normal input and output systems. The simulationist's idea is that the partial independence from input systems would explain, among other things, the freedom we have, in pretend play and in our representation of the content of others' mental states, to portray the world in contrary-to-fact ways, yet because output systems are not engaged in the normal way, this free play goes on within a "protected" context in which some of the normal consequences, especially but not only some of the behavioral consequences, do not actually ensue.

Leslie maintains that it is the theory-of-mind mechanism that makes this protected free play possible. What the mechanism does (to give a greatly simplified account of a rather complex theory) is to enable these systems to function at a higher semantic level: instead of manipulating object-level representations, as in their normal engagement with the world, they manipulate representations of representations, or "metarepresentations." The chief matter at issue between Leslie's hypothesis and the off-line hypothesis of the simulation theorist would seem to be this: do our systems operate at this higher representational level in pretense and in attribution of mental states, or do they operate in much the same way as in real-world engagements, but off-line? We believe Leslie's answer misrepresents the nature of pretense: the recognition and understanding of pretense might arguably involve metarepresentation, but not ordinarily the production of pretense. We also think the off-line hypothesis explains more, requires fewer specially dedicated resources, and comports better with evidence from other domains, such as imitation and mimicry. Although we briefly discuss mimicry in the following section, detailed discussion of Leslie's hypothesis would not be appropriate in a short essay on autism. We intend to discuss his hypothesis elsewhere, because it appears to be the only way the theory theory can be squared with the evidence that in the populations tested, psychological competence is better correlated with capacity for pretense than with capacity for theoretical understanding.

5 SIMULATION AND IMITATIVE BEHAVIOR

The capacity for simulation involves not only the deliberate procedure of putting oneself in the other's place but also a number of automatic, unconscious responses. For example, there is subliminal muscular mimicry of the bodily postures and especially the facial expressions of others. Where the other's face bears an expression of emotion, adopting of a similar expression tends to produce a similar emotion in oneself. Even when it does not produce a like emotional response, it at least gives the simulator the wherewithal to recognize the other's emotion. The automatic response to facial expressions is complemented by another mechanism. Like many other animals, human beings have an automatic tendency to direct their eyes toward the target of a conspecific's gaze. This mechanism automatically turns one's own attention from the other's response to its environmental stimulus: to the *object* of the other's attention or emotion (what it is *about*), or the *object* (aim, goal) of the other's action.[8] The tendency is activated particularly when another exhibits startle, terror, or some other strong reactive emotion, or shows attentiveness and interest. In normal children, all of this emerges in the first year. If psychological competence essentially depends on a capacity to simulate others, these imitative mechanisms are important, perhaps even essential, stepping-stones to competence. In particular, they facilitate finding the environmental explanation of another's action and emotion.

In the case of children with autism, there is strong evidence that at least the gaze-tracking response is largely absent, and some evidence of deficiency in the tendency to mimic emotional expression (Baron-Cohen and Ring 1993, Meltzoff and Gopnik 1993). Thus we should expect autistics to be deficient in both the tendency to search for reasons for (or objects of) action and emotion and the capacity to locate them in the environment. These problems are not likely to show up in the artificial tasks presented in most false-belief experiments. For such experiments call primarily for predictions of action rather than explanations and furthermore offer the subject only a narrative rather than a live, expressive protagonist. It is no surprise, then, that in the specific behavior tested in false-belief experiments, the autistic seems for the most part to resemble a normal 3-year-old. But where the task is one of explaining another's behavior in terms of an environmental stimulus or object, and the subject is allowed to see the other's facial expression or overt behavior and track the direction of the other's gaze, the simulation theory predicts that autistics will perform far below the level of normal 3-year-olds.

6 CONCLUSION

We claimed that the evidence suggests that the psychological competence that normal children develop but autistic children do not develop is based not on a *theory* but rather on a *skill*. That skill, it appears, includes a capacity for egocentric recentering and a capacity to be engaged as an agent in a world imagined to deviate somewhat from the actual world. These capacities appear to be intact in children with Down's syndrome but deficient in children with autism. Also deficient are some of the ancillary imitative mechanisms that would ordinarily facilitate simulation, particularly by producing emotional responses that copy those exhibited by others and by turning the simulator's attention toward the environmental causes and objects of other's emotions and actions.

This is the first philosophical paper we know of on the topic of autism. We have tried to bring to bear some recent philosophical thinking about the nature and acquisition of mental concepts and the nature of pretense. But we acknowledge that this is at most a small contribution toward understanding what is still a mysterious pathology.

ACKNOWLEDGMENTS

We are indebted to Simon Baron-Cohen and Paul Harris for comments that were extremely helpful, especially in filling in some of the gaps in our knowledge of recent empirical research. Baron-Cohen kindly furnished preprints of some of the papers since published in Baron-Cohen, Tager-Flusberg, and Cohen 1993. We thank the editors for a number of suggestions that helped shape our presentation.

NOTES

1 We prefer to speak of the child's "psychological competence," rather than the child's "theory of mind," to minimize the danger that descriptions of the phenomena to be explained will be skewed by intuitions associated with the term *theory*.
2 Most notable are Sellars's behavioristic "Rylean ancestors" (Sellars 1956), who (unlike autistic people) have no difficulty in speaking to one another about "the public properties of public objects" or even about the *meanings* of overt speech acts.
3 It should be noted, however, that other findings are not as consistently supportive as those of Wimmer and Perner 1983.
4 Baron-Cohen, Leslie, and Frith 1985 explicitly endorses Leslie's thesis, briefly discussed below, that the absence or deficiency of a certain computational mechanism explains the deficiencies of autistic children in pretend play and in attribution of mental states. But the study grants that "the ability we have been testing could be considered as a kind of *conceptual* [as opposed to *perceptual*] perspective-taking skill," which suggests a view similar to the one we favor. A later paper, Baron-Cohen and Cross 1992 (173, n. 1), makes it clear that Baron-Cohen himself is not committed to the theory theory. This interpretation is further supported by personal communication from Baron-Cohen, in which he declares himself "still rather neutral" in the debate between the theory theory and the simulation theory.
5 For philosophical formulations and defenses of the simulation theory, see Gordon 1986, 1992, and Goldman 1989, 1992. For application to developmental issues, see Harris 1989, 1992. A double issue of the interdisciplinary journal *Mind and Language*, vol. 7 (Spring–Summer 1992) is devoted to the topic. The contents of this issue also appear, along with the earlier essays cited above and much new material, in Davies and Stone 1994.
   The simulation theory has numerous historical precursors, including R. G. Collingwood's theory of historical reenactment and the nineteenth-century doctrine that the

proper methodology of the human sciences is *Verstehen*, or empathetic understanding. Unlike these earlier views, however, simulation theory attempts to account for ordinary human competence, and it is concerned with prediction just as much as with explanation or understanding. Furthermore, it provides an account of our commonsense concepts of mind and various mental states and processes. In addition, the simulation theory is sensitive to experimental data concerning the normal development, and in autistic children the arrested development, of the capacity to understand, explain, and predict the behavior of others. Finally, the theory offers a speculative account of the way our knowledge of other minds is encoded in our brains.

6 The example and the thesis it exemplifies are taken from Walton 1973. The connection between Walton's thesis and counterfactuals was suggested by Evans (1982).

7 Ramsey 1978, 143. See also Stalnaker 1968. As in the case of conditionals, playing a game of make-believe requires that one solve the pragmatic problem of selecting *appropriate* "adjustments." For example, if these globs of mud are pies, then they are not globs of mud, since pies are made of edible stuff, whereas mud is not edible (or at least not palatable). But one could allow that these are indeed globs of mud if one pretended that pies are not made of edible stuff or that mud (or this kind of mud) is edible. Again, are the pebbles we encounter within these mud pies nuts or raisins or do they, perish the thought, remain pebbles?

8 Gordon offered the following speculation: "One possibility is that the readiness for practical simulation is a prepackaged 'module' called upon automatically in the perception of other human beings. One might even speculate that such a module makes its first appearance in the useful tendency many mammals have of turning their eyes toward the target of another's gaze. Thus the very sight of human eyes might *require* us to simulate at least their spatial perspective—and to this extent, at least, to put ourselves in the other's shoes" (1986, 170). Commenting on this passage, Baron-Cohen and Cross say, "This quotation stands as a virtual prediction of the results presented in this paper" (1992, 183).

REFERENCES

Baron-Cohen, S. 1988. "Social and Pragmatic Deficits in Autism: Cognitive or Affective?" *Journal of Autism and Developmental Disorders* 18:379–402.

Baron-Cohen, S. 1990. "Autism: A Specific Cognitive Disorder of 'Mind-Blindness.'" *International Review of Psychiatry* 2:81–90.

Baron-Cohen, S., and P. Cross, 1992. "Reading the Eyes: Evidence for the Role of Perception in the Development of a Theory of Mind." *Mind and Language* 7:172–86.

Baron-Cohen, S., A. M. Leslie, and U. Frith. 1985. "Does the Autistic Have a 'Theory of Mind'?" *Cognition* 21:37–46.

Baron-Cohen, S., A. M. Leslie, and U. Frith. 1986. "Mechanical, Behavioral, and Intentional Understanding of Picture Stories in Autistic Children." *British Journal of Developmental Psychology* 4:113–25.

Baron-Cohen, S., and H. Ring. 1993. "The Relationship between EDD and ToMM: Neuropsychological and Neurobiological Perspectives." In *Origins of an Understanding of Mind*, ed. P. Mitchell and C. Lewis. Hove, England: Lawrence Erlbaum Associates.

Baron-Cohen, S., H. Tager-Flusberg, and D. J. Cohen, eds. 1993. *Understanding Other Minds: Perspectives from Autism*. Oxford: Oxford University Press.

Davies, M., and T. Stone, eds. 1994. *Mental Simulation: Philosophical and Psychological Essays*. Oxford: Blackwell.

De Gelder, B. 1993. "Intentional Ascription, Autism, and Troubles with Content." In *Pragmatics at Issue*, ed. J. Verschueren. Amsterdam: J. Benjamins.

Evans, G. 1982. *The Varieties of Reference*. Ed. J. McDowell. Oxford: Oxford University Press.

Fodor, J. A. 1975. *The Language of Thought*. New York: Thomas Y. Crowell.

Fodor, J. A. 1978. "Propositional Attitudes." *Monist* 61:501–23. Reprinted in J. A. Fodor, *Representations*. Cambridge: MIT Press.

Fodor, J. A. 1987. *Psychosemantics*. Cambridge: MIT Press.

Frith, U. 1989. *Autism: Explaining the Enigma*. Oxford: Blackwell.

Goldman, A. I. 1989. "Interpretation Psychologized." *Mind and Language* 4:161–85.

Goldman, A. I. 1992. "In Defense of the Simulation Theory." *Mind and Language* 7:104–19.

Gordon, R. M. 1986. "Folk Psychology as Simulation." *Mind and Language* 1:158–71.

Gordon, R. M. 1992. "The Simulation Theory: Objections and Misconceptions." *Mind and Language* 7:11–34.

Harris, P. 1989. *Children and Emotion*. Oxford: Blackwell.

Harris, P. 1992. "From Simulation to Folk Psychology: The Case for Development." *Mind and Language* 7:120–44.

Harris, P. 1991. "The Work of the Imagination." In *Natural Theories of Mind*, ed. A. Whiten. Oxford: Oxford University Press.

Kanner, L. 1943. "Autistic Disturbance of Affective Contact." *Nervous Child* 2:217–50.

Leslie, A. M. 1987. "Pretense and Representation: The Origins of 'Theory of Mind.'" *Psychological Review* 94:412–26.

Leslie, A., and D. Roth, 1993. "What Autism Teaches Us about Metarepresentation." In *Understanding Other Minds: Perspectives from Autism*, ed. S. Baron-Cohen, H. Tager-Flusberg, and D. J. Cohen. Oxford: Oxford University Press.

Lewis, V., and J. Boucher. 1988. "Spontaneous, Instructed, and Elicited Play in Relatively Able Autistic Children." *British Journal of Developmental Psychology* 6:325–39.

Meltzoff, A., and A. Gopnik. 1993. "The Role of Imitation in Understanding Persons and Developing a Theory of Mind." In *Understanding Other Minds*, ed. S. Baron-Cohen, H. Tager-Flusberg, and D. J. Cohen. Oxford: Oxford University Press.

Newell, A. 1980. "Physical Symbol Systems." *Cognitive Science* 4:135–83.

Premack, D., and G. Woodruff. 1978. "Does the Chimpanzee Have a 'Theory of Mind'?" *Behavioral and Brain Sciences* 4:515–26.

Ramsey, F. P. 1978. *Foundations*. London: Routledge and Kegan Paul.

Sellars, W. 1956. "The Myth of the Given: Three Lectures on Empiricism and the Philosophy of Mind." In *The Foundations of Science and the Concepts of Psychology and Psychoanalysis*, ed. Herbert Feigl and Michael Scriven, Minnesota Studies in the Philosophy of Science, no. 1. Minneapolis: University of Minnesota Press.

Stalnaker, R. C. 1968. "A Theory of Conditionals." In *Studies in Logical Theory*, ed. N. Rescher. Oxford: Blackwell.

Stich, S., and S. Nichols. 1992. "Folk Psychology: Simulation or Tacit Theory?" *Mind and Language* 7:35–71.

Ungerer, J. A., and M. Sigman. 1981. "Symbolic Play and Language Comprehension in Autistic Children." *Journal of American Academy of Child Psychiatry* 20:318–37.

Walton, K. L. 1973. "Pictures and Make-Believe." *Philosophical Review* 82:283–319.

Wimmer, H., and J. Perner. 1983. "Beliefs about Beliefs: Representation and Constraining Function of Wrong Beliefs in Young Children's Understanding of Deception." *Cognition* 13:103–28.

27

AUTISM AS MIND-BLINDNESS: AN ELABORATION AND PARTIAL DEFENCE

Peter Carruthers

In this chapter I shall be defending the mind-blindness theory of autism, by showing how it can accommodate data which might otherwise appear problematic for it. Specifically, I shall show how it can explain the fact that autistic children rarely engage in spontaneous pretend-play, and also how it can explain the executive-function deficits which are characteristic of the syndrome. I shall do this by emphasising what I take to be an entailment of the mind-blindness theory, that autistic people have difficulties of access to their own mental states, as well as to the mental states of other people.

1 INTRODUCTION

In a series of publications since 1985 Alan Leslie, Simon Baron-Cohen and others have argued that autism should be identified with *mind-blindness* – that is, with damage to an innate theory of mind module, leading to an inability to understand the mental states of other people. (See Baron-Cohen *et al.* 1985; Leslie 1987, 1988, 1991; Leslie and Roth 1993; Baron-Cohen 1989a, 1990, 1991a, 1993; and Baron-Cohen and Ring 1994b.) I shall be concerned to elaborate and defend this proposal, showing that it has the resources to handle rather more of the relevant data, and rather more elegantly, than even its originators have realised.

There is widespread agreement that autism at least *involves* a kind of mind-blindness. That is, it is generally agreed that people with autism have considerable difficulty in appreciating the mental states of others – well-documented in their difficulties with false-belief tasks, for example – resulting in impaired social interaction and poor communicative skills. Where there is very considerable disagreement, concerns the explanation of this phenomenon, and also the question of how *central* it is in the aetiology of the syndrome as a whole.

Both Leslie and Baron-Cohen believe that mind-blindness lies at the very heart of the autistic syndrome. They maintain that autism results from damage to a specialised theory of mind module, which underlies the mind-reading abilities of normal subjects. This module is held to contain an implicit theory of the structure and functioning of the human mind, which is accessed whenever a normal subject ascribes a mental state to another person, or seeks a mentalistic explanation of their behaviour. It is possible that this module is organised into a number of distinct subsystems (see Baron-Cohen and Ring 1994b; Baron-Cohen and Swettenham 1996), and that it may develop in the normal individual through a number of different stages, perhaps corresponding to the different theory-stages postulated by some developmental psychologists (e.g. simple desire psychology; perception-desire psychology; belief-desire psychology; as postulated by Wellman 1990 – see Segal 1996). But the two crucial claims made by those adopting this position are firstly, that the theory of mind module is an innate, isolable, component of the mind which embodies a *theory* of the nature and mode of operation of minds. (This is then a version of the so-called 'theory-theory' of our understanding of other minds, defended by many writers, including Lewis 1996; Churchland 1981; Stich 1983; Fodor 1987; Wellman 1990; and others.) And secondly, that it is this module which is distinctively damaged in the case of autism.

Others (for example Frith 1989; Harris 1989, 1991, 1993; Hobson 1993a; and Melzoff and Gopnik 1993) take a different view, arguing, in various different ways and for various different reasons, that the mind-blindness of autistic people is a *consequence of* some more basic deficit. I shall make no attempt at a systematic survey of these competitor theories here, focusing only on one which seems to have been gaining ground lately. This is the proposal put forward by Harris (1989, 1991, 1993) and elaborated more recently by Gordon and Barker (1994) and by Currie (1996), that the mind-blindness of autistic people is an effect of a deeper inability to engage in imaginative thinking.

According to this alternative proposal, the fundamental deficit involved in autism is an inability (or at least a reduced ability) to engage in imaginative, counterfactual, suppositional thinking. It is for this reason, it is supposed, that autistic children rarely engage in spontaneous pretend play, and tend to display behaviours that are stereotyped and rigidly routinised. It is also held that the difficulties autistic people have in reading the minds of others results from this same underlying deficit, since mind-reading abilities are claimed to require the ability to identify oneself imaginatively with the other person. (This is the so-called 'simulation-theory' of our understanding of the minds of others, notably defended by Gordon 1986, 1992a, 1995; Harris 1989; and Goldman 1989, 1992b, 1993a.)

These competing explanations of autism involve us in wider disputes about the nature and origins of our conception of the mental states of other people in the normal case. I believe that in general there are powerful reasons for preferring the theory-theory to simulation-theory as an account of these matters (see Carruthers 1996b). I believe that there are convincing reasons, also, for preferring a modularised, nativistic, version of the former to the child-as-little-scientist versions of theory-theory proposed by Gopnik and Wellman (Wellman 1990; Gopnik and Wellman 1992; Gopnik 1993 – see Carruthers ch.3 this volume and 1992 ch. 8; and Segal 1996). But it has to be admitted that simulation-theory currently provides a rather more convincing account of some aspects of the autistic syndrome – specifically, the absence of pretend-play, and the inflexibility and lack of creativity of autistic thought. To the extent that this is so, to that extent we have *some* reason to prefer simulationism to any form of theory-theory.

I should stress at this point that in order to provide a viable alternative to the mind-blindness account of autism, the simulationist explanation must involve commitment to the sorts of radical simulationism defended by Gordon and Goldman. This is because the more limited form of content-simulation ... is incapable of accounting for the data. For autistic subjects have problems across a whole range of theory of mind tasks, not just with those that involve predicting people's thoughts on the basis of other things that they are already known to think. When I speak of 'simulation' in this chapter, therefore, I should be understood as referring to its more radical variants.

What I propose to do, is not to mount any general defence of nativistic theory-theory, but only to show that an account of autism as mind-blindness can surmount the particular hurdle sketched above, being capable of providing explanations of the data that are just as convincing and elegant as can be given by simulationism. The core of my proposal will be that the mind-blindness theory has only *appeared* to be losing out in the above respects, because its proponents have paid insufficient attention to the consequences of their view for the access (or rather lack of access) that autistic people will have to their *own* mental states. It is here that I shall begin.

2 MIND-BLINDNESS AND BLINDNESS TO SELF

What account is the theory-theorist to provide of our knowledge of our own mental states? Here I shall help myself to the view elaborated briefly in Carruthers (ch.3 this volume). (See also Gopnik 1993, for a variant on the approach.) I claim that a theory-theorist should regard self-knowledge as analogous to the theory-laden perception of theoretical entities in science. Just as a physicist can sometimes (in context, and given a background of theoretical knowledge) *see* that electrons are being emitted by the substance under study; and just as a diagnostician can sometimes *see* a cancer in the blur of an x-ray photograph; so, too, we can each of us sometimes see (that is, know intuitively and non-inferentially) that we are in a state accorded such-and-such a role by folk-psychological theory.

It is, I claim, part of the normal functioning of the human mind that a mental state, M, if conscious, will automatically give rise to the belief that one has M – where what one will recognise M *as*, is a state having a particular folk-psychological characterisation. This is not to say that all of the principles of folk-psychology which play a part in generating that belief will necessarily be accessible to us. But although the process of acquiring self-knowledge may involve theories that are only implicitly (and innately) known by the subject, still the upshot of that process – the knowledge that I am in M – will nevertheless be theory-involving. On the theory-theory account, what I recognise my own mental states *as*, are states having a particular folk-psychological role, even if I am unable to provide, consciously, a complete characterisation of that role.

Now, what would this account predict, concerning the self-knowledge of someone who has suffered damage to their theory of mind module? The answer is plain – either such a person will be incapable of recognising their own mental states as such at all, or they will, at best, only be able to do so laboriously and unreliably. For, by hypothesis, it will be an innate theory of mind module which provides, in the normal case, the network of theoretical concepts and principles which enables us to individuate our mental states as such, as and when they occur. Anyone who lacks such a module, or in whom such a module is damaged, will either lack those concepts and principles altogether (and so be incapable of self-knowledge), or will have only a fragmentary grasp of them (in which case knowledge of self will be equally fragmentary), or will perhaps have acquired those concepts and principles laboriously, through general learning mechanisms (in which case self-attribution will, almost certainly, be slow and laborious also).

How do these predictions match up against the few empirical findings which are available? They are certainly consistent with the data reported by Baron-Cohen (1989c, 1991a), who found that autistic children have as much trouble remembering their own recent false beliefs as they do in attributing false beliefs to other people, and that autistic children also have trouble drawing the appearance-reality distinction. The former result is exactly what the mind-blindness theory would predict: if autistic people have difficulty in understanding the notion of *belief*, then they should be incapable of (or at least poor at) ascribing false beliefs at all, whether to another agent or to themselves. Similarly, the mind-blindness theory would predict that autistic people will lack adequate access to their own experiences, as such (as opposed to access to the states which their experiences are *of*), and hence that they should have difficulty in negotiating the contrast between *experience* (appearance) and *what it is an experience of* (reality).

The above predictions are also consistent with the data recently reported by Hurlburt *et al.* (1994), who tested three Asperger syndrome adults using the descriptive experience sampling method. This technique involves the subject wearing a small device that produces a beep at random intervals through the day, which the subject hears through an earphone. Subjects are instructed that their task is to 'freeze the contents of their awareness' at the moment when the beep began, and then to write down some notes about the details of the experience. Normal subjects report inner experiences in four major categories: inner verbalisation, visual images, unsymbolised thinking, and emotional feelings. All three of the subjects tested by Hurlburt *et al.* using this method were high-functioning autistics, who appeared able to understand the experimental instructions – two were capable of passing second-order false-belief tasks, and the third could pass first-order tasks, but not second-order tasks. Hurlburt *et al.* found that the first two subjects reported visual images only – no inner verbalisation, no unsymbolised thinking, and no emotional feelings. The third subject could report no inner experience at all.

Of course this is a very small sample of subjects, and the results are perhaps not easy to interpret. But they do suggest that autistic people might have severe difficulties of access to their own occurrent thought processes and emotions. For of course no one would want to deny that these subjects *have* thoughts and emotions. While autistic subjects surely must have propositional thoughts and emotional feelings, they do seem to have difficulty in knowing introspectively what their current thoughts and emotions are. (Why visual images should be any easier to self-attribute is something of a puzzle. Perhaps because perception-desire psychology is easier to acquire than belief-desire psychology – see Wellman 1990 – and because visual images are closely related to visual perception.)

Data apparently problematic for the predictions of the mind-blindness theory of autism are presented by Naito *et al.* (1995), who claim to find that autistic children who are incapable of attributing false beliefs to other people, in standard false-belief tasks, can nevertheless remember their own recent false beliefs without difficulty. (See also Leslie and Thaiss 1992.) But in fact this data is easily explained away. For the experimental set-up was such that subjects were asked to remember what they had earlier *said* an object was (Naito *et al.* used deceptive-appearance tasks), and likewise to predict what another person would *say* that the object was. It is no surprise at all that autistic people should pass the first task but fail in the second. For, in fact, no theory of mind abilities are required in order for you to remember what you have just said. Whereas in order to predict what someone else will say, you first have to predict what they will *think*, and then generate a sentence appropriate to express that thought; which of course requires theory of mind ability.

If the mind-blindness account of autism is correct, then we should expect, and we appear to find, that autistic people are as blind to their own mental states as they are to the mental states of others. It is this consequence of the theory which will shortly be put to good work in the main body of this chapter: explaining why autistic children do not engage in spontaneous pretend-play, and explaining why the thought and behaviour of autistic people should be so rigid and inflexible. But first, it may be worth noting briefly, here, that such an account seems capable of explaining, also, the many reports of disordered and fragmentary sensations amongst autistic people (see Frith 1989). For one of the normal functions of the theory of mind module will be to classify and identify our own sensations for us. If that module is damaged, precisely what one would expect is that the subject's inner life would seem chaotic, fragmentary, and confused.

3 THE PROBLEM OF PRETENCE

The mind-blindness hypothesis has no difficulty in accounting for two of the triad of autistic impairments identified by Wing and Gould in their classic Camberwell study (1979) – namely, impairment in social relationships, and in verbal and non-verbal communication. For these deficits are exactly what one would predict of someone who has severe difficulty in reading the minds of others. On the other hand, the third element of the triad – the absence of pretend-play – is, on the face of it, much more problematic. For why should mind-blindness interfere with pretence? One would expect it to interfere with social, or shared, pretence, of course, since this may require children to read the minds of their co-pretenders. And one would also expect a mind-blind child not to engage in the sort of play which involves attributing mental states to dolls or other pretend agents. But it is far from clear why mind-blindness should lead to any *general* deficit in pretend-play, such as is found in autism.

Leslie has boldly grasped this nettle, proposing that the very same cognitive mechanisms which are involved in theory of mind tasks also underlie the child's capacity for pretence (1987, 1988). He postulates the existence, in normal subjects, of a special-purpose mechanism, the *decoupler*, whose function is to uncouple a given representation – 'banana', say – from its normal input-output relations, so as to enable that representation to be manipulated freely without affecting those relations (as when the child pretends that the banana is a telephone while retaining the knowledge that it is still a banana *really*). Crucial to this account, for present purposes, is Leslie's claim that the de-coupler functions by forming a *second-order* representation of the de-coupled representation. For he can then go on to claim (with some plausibility, given that assumption) that this very same mechanism is employed when the child turns to mind-reading tasks, forming a representation of the mental state of another person (also a second-order representation). If such a de-coupler were to form a crucial component of the theory of mind module, then it is only to be expected that mind-blind subjects would also display deficits in pretend-play.

Leslie's proposal is deeply unsatisfying, however. For there is nothing to motivate the claim that solitary pretence requires the capacity to form second-order representations of one's own representations, beyond the need to save the mind-blindness theory of autism. Rather, what is required for pretence is the capacity to entertain a representation in a different *mode*, or as the content of a different mental *attitude* (as different from belief as belief is from desire) – namely, in the mode of *supposition*, or of *imagination*. To pretend that the banana is a telephone, the child does not have to represent its own representation of the banana, it just has to *suppose* that the banana is a telephone, and then think and act on that supposition. (See Perner 1991a, where this criticism is developed at length; see also Jarrold *et al*. 1994; Currie 1995.)

In addition to the major criticism just sketched, Leslie's proposal faces a number of other problems, in response to which his account has been forced to become increasingly baroque (see Leslie 1993). One is to explain why, if the very same de-coupling mechanism is employed in both pretence and theory of mind tasks, normal children should show competence in pretending so much earlier (age two) than they are able to pass false-belief tasks (age four). Another is to explain why properly social, co-operative, pretence should emerge so much later than solitary pretence (see Jarrold *et al*. 1994). And yet another problem is raised by the data, replicated in a number of different studies, suggesting that while autistic children do not often pretend spontaneously, they do have the *capacity* for pretence if prompted (see, for example, Lewis and Boucher 1988). I shall not pursue these problems here. Instead, I shall show how the mind-blindness theory of autism can explain the absence of spontaneous pretence in autistic children without having to have recourse to the hypothesis of the de-coupler.

4 RESOLUTION OF THE PROBLEM OF PRETENCE

In a nutshell, my suggestion is that because autistic children are, through mind-blindness, deprived of ready access to their own mental states, they are at the same time deprived of the main source of enjoyment present in normal pretending. So the reason why autistic children do not engage in spontaneous pretence is not because they cannot do so, but rather because they do not find the activity rewarding. The problem is one of motivation, not of incapacity. However, this idea will require some setting up.

Why do children pretend? What is enjoyable about the activity of pretending? Plainly what is pleasurable are not, in general, the physical actions by means of which the child carries out the pretence. True enough, the enjoyment of pretend-fighting, and of the sorts of rough-and-tumble wrestling engaged in by the young of most other species of mammal as well as human children, probably does lie in the physical exertion involved, and in the attempt to dominate an opponent. But the same can hardly be true of the kinds of symbolic pretending distinctive of human beings. There can be nothing enjoyable about the activities of putting a banana to one's ear and talking to it *as such*. Rather, what is enjoyable about pretence, I suggest, is basically the sense of being able to manipulate one's own mental representations in imagination; which then requires, of course, that one should have ready access to the states containing those representations.

The young of all species of mammal engage in play of some sort, the function of which seems to be to prepare them for adult activities. (See Smith 1982.) Thus young springbok will practise the leaps which will one day be necessary to keep them out of reach of predators; young stag deer will engage in the kind of pretend-fighting and head-butting which will later be employed in the competition for mates in the rut; and the kittens of all species of cat will, in the course of their wrestling with their siblings, practise just the kinds of stalking, leaping, biting, and holding which will form an essential part of adult hunting. It seems reasonable to suppose that the young of each species are programmed to find intrinsically rewarding, in play, just those activities (or those that are sufficiently similar to them, at least) which will form crucial components of their adult behavioural repertoire.

Now, for which adult activities are young children practising, when they engage in pretend-play? At one level you might be tempted to say: for those very activities that they are pretending to perform. The little girl pretending to be a mother bathing a baby is practising to become a mother who will bathe a baby, the little boy pretending to be an airline pilot is practising to become an airline pilot, and so on. But it would be absurd to suggest that children are programmed to find *these* activities, described at this level, intrinsically rewarding. For most of the activities that children pretend to perform would not have existed at the time when human cognitive and motivational systems were evolving (*mothering*, of course, is one of the exceptions). Indeed, many of the things that children may pretend to do or be may actually be impossible to do or be in reality. The child who is pretending to turn objects to gold through a Midas-touch can hardly be practising to turn objects to gold as an adult! And the child who is pretending to *be* an aeroplane can hardly be practising to *become* an aeroplane in adulthood!

It is much more plausible to claim that children find rewarding that feature which is common to *all* forms of pretend-play, namely the manipulation of the child's own mental states, through *supposing* or *imagining*. (Hence, of course, the interest that

340

normal children also take in fiction and story-telling – an interest notably absent amongst autistics.) Then, just as you cannot enjoy running or jumping without being conscious of (or being aware that you are) running and jumping, so, too, I suggest, you cannot enjoy supposing or imagining without being conscious of your (mental) activity. In general, *enjoying Xing* presupposes *awareness of Xing* – which is why you cannot enjoy digestion, sleepwalking, or subliminal perception.

It is surely incontrovertible that supposing, or imagining, is one of the distinguishing marks of the human species. It is the human capacity to *suppose* that such-and-such were the case and reason from there, or to *imagine* performing some activity and work out the consequences in advance, that underlies much of the success of our species. It has often been said that humans are distinctively *rational* animals. It may be closer to the truth to say that they are uniquely *imaginative* animals, since many other species seem to share our capacity to act intelligently in the light of desire, but none (excepting perhaps chimpanzees) share our ability to reason from supposed premises or to explore the consequences of imagined scenarios – and certainly none has this ability to such a high degree. Small wonder, then, if much of human childhood should be devoted to forms of play whose function is to practise this very activity.

However, if the enjoyment of pretence requires a child to have access to its own mental state of pretending, then am I not committed, just as Leslie is, to saying that even a two-year-old must be capable of meta-representing its own mental representations? There are two factors distinguishing my proposal from Leslie's, however, in a way that renders it substantially more plausible. First, on my account, unlike Leslie's, there need be no necessity for the child who is pretending that the banana is a telephone to meta-represent its own representation of the banana. Rather, it need only – at most – meta-represent *that it is now pretending*. That is, the meta-representation involved may only extend to the *attitude* of pretending, without also embracing the *content* of what is pretended. Put differently, one might suggest that children are wired up to detect and represent, and find intrinsically rewarding, the mental state of pretending, without having to form a meta-representation of any other aspects (including the content) of that state. The second factor follows on naturally from the first. It is that young children may only have meta-*awareness* of their states of pretence, without yet being capable of meta-*representing* – that is, conceptualising or thinking about – those states. It may be that young children can *detect* their own pretence, and find it rewarding, without yet having the capacity to *think that* they are pretending.

A comparison with another proposed modular system may be of help at this point. Consider the face-recognition module, which has been hypothesised by many different researchers. It is highly plausible that it is this very module (at an early stage of growth and development) which is implicated in the neonate's well-documented discriminations of, and responses to, faces and face-like shapes. But it is highly *im*plausible, of course, to maintain that the infant is, at that stage, capable of entertaining *thoughts about* faces. Rather, the early development of the face-recognition module enables an infant to *detect* faces without yet conceptualising them *as* faces. This early non-conceptualised awareness of faces may be one of the crucial inputs upon which later development of the module depends. So, too, then, in the case of the mind-reading module – it may be that in early stages of its development it enables a young child to detect, and be aware of, its own mental state of pretending, among others (which is necessary if the child is to find that state rewarding), but without the child being capable, as yet, of entertaining thoughts about the pretence of itself, or of other people. Here, too, I suggest, the child's unconceptualised (introspective) awareness of its own mental states may be one of the crucial inputs to the normal growth and development of the theory of mind module.

I have suggested that what is *basically* enjoyable about pretend-play is the activity of supposing or imagining itself, which then presupposes that the child has ready access to its own mental states, particularly its own acts of imagining. This should not be taken as denying that there can be *some* forms of satisfaction to be derived from imagination which do *not* presuppose meta-awareness of one's own mental activity (or not immediately, anyway). In particular, it seems to be part of the functioning of the imagination that imagined scenarios should engage directly with the appetitive system, and with the emotions – and this can be fun. Imagining a juicy steak can make you hungry, imagining an act of sexual intercourse can make you sexually aroused, imagining a free-fall from an aeroplane can make you frightened, and so on. It is easy to see why this should be so, if the main function of the imagination lies, not in fantasy, but in practical reasoning. (Here I am in agreement with Currie 1995 and 1996; and Harris 1991, 1993.) If the imagined result of the plan under consideration, of going to the kitchen and doing some cooking – namely, a juicy steak – had no tendency to engage with the appetitive system, it could have no tendency to set me in motion, either.

Although sometimes it is the imagined object, rather than the activity of imagining itself, which gives rise to enjoyment, it is arguable that even this enjoyment presupposes meta-awareness of one's own mental states. It is not (unassuaged) sexual arousal in itself which is enjoyable, but rather the bodily sensations distinctive of that state, of which one is aware. Similarly, it is not the fear of falling from an aeroplane which is itself enjoyable, but rather the thrill of this combined with the knowledge that I am only imagining, and really sitting safe in my arm-chair at home. So the conclusion stands undamaged: the enjoyment of pretence presupposes that subjects have ready introspective access to their own mental states. Small wonder, then – if it is true that autism is a form of mind-blindness – that autistic people should rarely be found to engage in pretence.

5 STEREOTYPED BEHAVIOUR, INFLEXIBLE THOUGHT

Properly understood, then – as entailing its introspective corollary – the mind-blindness account of autism can provide a smooth and elegant explanation for the fact that autistic children are distinguished by their absence of pretend-play. The explanation is that such children *can* pretend but do not particularly enjoy it. The question remains, however, as to why, when autistic children are prompted to pretend, their pretence is often so stereotyped and unimaginative. For example, if asked to pretend, with or without the aid of props, to do as many different things as they can think of (e.g. wear a hat, read a book, etc.) autistic children generate far fewer activities than do normal controls (see Jarrold *et al.* in preparation). Why should this be so, if autistic children really do have an undamaged capacity for imagination, as the mind-blindness theory of autism would predict, and contrary to what the simulationist account would propose?

The answer, in this instance, is easy – it may be because *they have had less practice at imagining*. If the function of pretend-play is to exercise the imagination, then it is small wonder that those who have exercised little should perform less well. The autistic child who is prompted to engage in pretence is like a bird capable of flight who has never or rarely flown. Although the innate cognitive basis for pretence is present, just as the innate basis of flight is present in the bird, one would expect that it would be rusty and slow through ill-use.

In reality, however, the body of data provided by Jarrold *et al.* (in preparation) is only the tip of a very large and well-established ice-berg, which may threaten yet to sink the mind-blindness theory of autism. This is the aspect of autism which is perhaps the best well-known, namely the tendency of autistic people to engage in repetitive activity, to be obsessed with order and ritual, to have very narrowly focused interests, and to be generally very uncreative and unimaginative in their thought and behaviour. How is this to be explained, if autism is to be identified with mind-blindness? Are these features not better explained by the simulationist account? My strategy, here, will be to divide and conquer, offering differing explanations of different aspects of the phenomena.

The obsessive side of autism seems best explained as a by-product of social alienation, as has traditionally been proposed. Autistic children live in a world that is at once puzzling and threatening. To see this, think how much of the child's environment is social in nature, and how much of the time of a normal child will be occupied with social interactions of one sort or another – interactions with peers or siblings, story-tellings with parents, negotiations with carers over foods and bed-times, and so on. Much of this would seem utterly opaque to a mind-blind child, and most of the behaviour of the people around such a child would seem wholly unpredictable. It would not be entirely surprising, then, if some autistic children should respond by isolating themselves still further from the puzzling social world around them, seeking refuge, out of loneliness and distress, in repetitive activity. And small wonder, also, if some autistic children should try to gain a measure of control over their world by imposing arbitrary, but orderly and predictable, rituals.

The narrowly focused interests of many autistic people, too, may be explained as resulting, partly from loneliness, partly as a further reaction to the opaque nature of the social world. (Yet another proposal will be made in **section 6** below.) I can well remember, myself, as an unusually lonely adolescent, spending hours absorbed in the play of light in the dew-drops on a bud or leaf, trying to persuade myself that this was a matter of the deepest metaphysical significance. And when one reflects on just how many of the normal objects of childhood and adolescent interest – fiction, films, sex, and competitive sports, for example – presuppose a good deal in the way of social awareness and mind-reading ability, it is not so surprising that autistic people might be happy to discover an area of interest – albeit bus timetables, or the calendar dates of days of the week – which they can understand, and at which they can excel.

There remains, however, a good deal of evidence of lack of flexibility of thought amongst autistic individuals, which is not so easily explained as a mere by-product of social alienation and loneliness. In particular, a number of studies have tested autistic people on problem-solving and planning tasks, and found that they perform much less well than controls. For example, Ozonoff *et al.* (1991a) tested autistic individuals on the Tower of Hanoi problem, finding that success or failure in this task success-fully classified 80% of the children in both the normal and the autistic groups. The autistic children tended to persevere with unsuccessful strategies, despite repeated failure; whereas normal children were much more ready to try new strategies as old ones failed.

Such findings have led both Leslie and Roth (1993) and Baron-Cohen and Ring (1994b) to accept that autistic people, in addition to mind-blindness, *also* suffer from a separate executive-function deficit, caused by collateral damage to areas in the frontal cortex close to those that appear to be involved in theory of mind tasks. While this by no means refutes their position – after all, every theory of autism must accept that there are *some* phenomena (for example, the excessive thirst experienced by many autistic children) that are caused, not by the syndrome itself, but by col-lateral brain-damage – nevertheless, it is good scientific practice to try to minimise accidents. I believe it is possible for the mind-blindness theory of autism to do better.

6 PRACTICAL REASONING AND SECOND-ORDER THOUGHT

In philosophical circles it has been widely accepted, at least since Frankfurt's classic 1971 paper, that the normal operation of the human practical reasoning system routinely involves second-order evaluations of first-order thoughts and desires. In deciding what to do on a free afternoon while the family are away – whether to stay in with a novel or go out into the garden to cut the grass – I may consider such things as: how much I *want* that the grass should be cut, as opposed to how much I want to read my novel; whether there will be later opportunities to satisfy these desires if they are not satisfied now; how *likely* it is that I will be able to read free of interruptions if I stay in, and how likely it is that it will remain dry enough to garden if I go out; and so on. In all this I am both evaluating my own desires and determining the degree of credence which I am prepared to place in my own beliefs – which presupposes (in many cases, at least) that I have *access to* my desires and beliefs.

Admittedly, it may sometimes be possible to weigh up one desire against another without raising, explicitly, any meta-representational question. I may, for example, ask myself simply *how good the novel is*, or how important reading would be as against neatly mown grass. In this I should be reflecting on the *goals* of my prospective actions, rather than on my desires for those goals as such. But even here, it is hard to see how such a process of reasoning could work, except through introspective access to my *appetitive response to the thought of those goals*. Similarly in the case of belief – I may, sometimes, ask myself simply *how likely it is that it will rain*, without explicitly evaluating (that is, meta-representing) my *belief* that it will. But in many cases, at least, degrees of credence cannot rationally be assigned without an element of second-order reflection. For example, in answering the question concerning the likelihood of rain, I may have to recall the source of my belief (whether a weather-forecast, or 'red sky at morning', or whatever) and evaluate its reliability. Such a procedure can only be possible if I know that I have (and so meta-represent) that belief.

Not only does human practical reasoning routinely involve access to our own beliefs and desires, it also involves something much stronger, I believe. For it is obvious, on reflection, that our practical reasoning systems routinely employ a kind of reflexive, introspective, access to our own recent sequences of occurrent conscious thinkings. (See my 1996a paper where this idea is developed in some detail.) Having recently been thinking about a problem in a particular way, I can then think about the thoughts that I have just entertained, and think about the problem-solving strategy I have just been employing. Or having been weighing up carefully the pros and cons of a number of different courses of action, I can then think, 'I shouldn't be so cautious and rational in my thinking – spontaneity has its value too!' All of which again presupposes, of course, that I have regular second-order access to my own occurrent thought-processes.

According to the modular hypothesis being defended here, the capacity for these sorts of swift and reliable forms of meta-access to our own beliefs, desires, and sequences of thinking and reasoning will be mediated, in the normal case, by the operation of the theory of mind module. It is therefore to be predicted that someone who is mind-blind, or whose theory of mind module is damaged, will experience considerable difficulty in tasks which involve the more complex (second-order) forms of practical reasoning. This is because such a subject's access to their own mental states will be relatively difficult, slow, and unreliable. We should therefore expect such a person to perform poorly on tasks that require them to evaluate their own desires or beliefs. And we should also expect them to perform equally poorly in tasks that require them to evaluate their own recent problem-solving strategies.

So here we have an explanation of the poor performance of autistic people in the Tower of Hanoi problem. (This is in addition to the partial explanation already sketched in **section 5** above, that the suppositional reasoning of autistic people may suffer for lack of practice, because of the rarity of pretend-play in childhood.) The explanation is: they do poorly because solving such problems requires reflection on one's own problem-solving strategies. One must try out a strategy, either in imagination or on the board, and then when it fails, think about that strategy itself and how it might be modified and improved. It is no surprise, then, to find that autistic people mostly fail by perseverance, continuing with unsuccessful strategies despite repeated failures. For the mind-blindness theory of autism predicts that such people would experience difficulties of access to their own sequences of thinking and reasoning.

Here we also have a further explanation, I think, of the narrow and often idiosyncratic interests of many autistic adolescents and adults. (Again, this is in addition to the explanation given in 5 above, that autistic people will seek areas of interest which do not require mind-reading abilities, and where they can find, or impose, a measure of order and control.) For it is a reasonable hypothesis that regular second-order evaluation of our first-order desires and interests is one of the major engines driving the diversification of our value-systems. It is (at least in part) by reflecting on our desires and interests, and comparing them in imagination with alternatives, that our values diversify. We ask ourselves, 'Is my interest in stamp-collecting really that rewarding? Would it be a good idea if I got myself interested in nineteenth-century novels instead?' And it is by regular reflection on our projects and values that we attain, and retain, a sense of proportion. We ask ourselves, 'Is this project really worth all the time I am devoting to it? Do I care about it *that* much? Would I not rather be doing something else instead?' By hypothesis, autistic people will find such second-order reflection difficult. So it is only to be expected that their range of interests might remain narrow, and that they should invest a degree of commitment in their projects which appears, to an outsider, to be out of all proportion to the true value of those activities.

My proposal has been that the executive-function deficits of autistic individuals are a consequence of their mind-blindness. An apparent problem for this proposal, however, is the finding that Asperger's syndrome subjects *pass* false-belief tasks while still failing at problem-solving tasks such as the Tower of Hanoi. (See Ozonoff *et al.* 1991b.) Does this not seem to show that it is problems of reasoning or imagining which are the more fundamental? Does the data not lend support, indeed, to the simulationists' view that it is, rather, a defective imagination which causes mind-blindness when sufficiently severe? (See Harris 1993.) I do not believe, in fact, that these data raise any particular problem for the explanations offered above. For the proposal is not that the blindness of autistic individuals to the minds of themselves and others will necessarily be total. On the contrary, the proposal is that the theory of mind module may be partially intact in some cases of autism; and in other cases, that subjects may use alternative – general learning – strategies to gain at least a rudimentary grasp on the theory of mind. The prediction is only that all autistic people will find mind-reading, of themselves or others, relatively difficult, slow, and unreliable.

Now, the point to notice about the false-belief tasks is that they only require, for their solution, a limited number of mental-state attributions. The subject must recognise what the other person has and has not *seen*, for example, and use this to underpin the attribution of a *false belief*, before putting this together with the other's supposed *desire*, to generate a prediction about what they will do. And this is a problem that the subject is normally given, altogether, some minutes to solve. In the case of the sorts of problem-solving tasks that require regular second-order monitoring of one's own problem-solving strategies, in contrast, a whole myriad of mental states will need to be self-ascribed in a matter of seconds. Small wonder, then, that there might be particularly able autistic people whose grip on theory of mind is good enough to enable them to succeed in false-belief tasks, but still not good enough for them to keep reliable track of their own problem-solving strategies, and so still not good enough for them to succeed in tasks like the Tower of Hanoi.

(Note that it is an empirical prediction of the line being pushed here, that those autistic people who succeed in false-belief tasks will nevertheless take considerably longer to solve them than do controls. I find it surprising that amongst all the studies that have been conducted on the theory of mind abilities of autistics and normals, no one seems to have thought of gathering data on *speed* of theory of mind problem-solving.)

I have claimed that the mind-blindness theory of autism can explain the executive-function deficits common amongst autistic individuals. But let me stress that this is not, in any sense, to *identify* autism with failure of executive function. I have only claimed that an intact theory of mind module, giving the subject swift and reliable access to their own thought-processes, may be a *necessary condition for* success in complex practical reasoning tasks. There is, of course, a good deal more to practical reasoning than mere success in accessing one's own mental states. So it is only to be expected that there may be executive-function deficits which do *not* involve failure in theory of mind tasks. And, indeed, that is exactly what we find. Executive-function deficits occur in many clinical populations – for example, obsessive-compulsive disorder, schizophrenia, hyperactivity, etc. – who do not have theory of mind deficits. (I owe this point to Simon Baron-Cohen.)

In this connection, too, it may be worth noting some recent data which causes severe problems for the simulationist explanation of autism (or which will do so, at least, if it proves to be replicable and robust). This data relates to Williams syndrome children, who suffer from a rare genetic disorder giving them a distinctive, and highly uneven, cognitive profile. The crucial finding is that Williams syndrome children suffer severe difficulties in practical reasoning and problem-solving tasks (for example, performing very poorly in a modified version of the Tower of Hanoi – modified to become a verbal rather than a visual task, since Williams syndrome children have notorious problems with visuo-spatial reasoning); but that they have no difficulty whatever with theory of mind tasks – on the contrary, their social and communication skills are precocious (Annette Karmiloff-Smith, personal communication).

This data may prove extremely important. For it is very hard to see how hypothetical, imaginative, thinking can be a presupposition of theory of mind ability, as simulationists maintain, if there exist individuals who lack the former but possess the latter. According to the mind-blindness proposal, in contrast, there can be (at least) two quite distinct ways in which problem-solving abilities can be damaged: one is by damage to the hypothetical reasoning faculty itself (which, one might suppose, is what happens in the case of Williams syndrome); the other is by damage to the theory of mind module which gives normal subjects regular access to their own problem-solving thinking, serving to make the latter more efficient and reliable.

CONCLUSION

I have argued that the crucial implication of the autism-as-mind-blindness hypothesis, hitherto not sufficiently noticed, is that autistic individuals will not only experience difficulties in ascribing mental states to other people, but will equally have problems in achieving second-order awareness of their own mental processes. This is because the theory of mind module will be just as much implicated in self-attribution as in other-attribution. This implication then enables the mind-blindness hypothesis to provide a simple and elegant explanation of the fact that autistic children rarely engage in spontaneous pretend-play – it is because, lacking easy self-awareness of their own mental states, they do not find the sorts of intrinsic satisfaction in pretence that normal children do. The same implication also enables us to explain the narrow interests and problem-solving deficits associated with autism, again because autistic people lack regular second-order awareness of their own desires and thought-processes.

ACKNOWLEDGEMENTS

I am grateful to the following for many valuable comments on earlier drafts of this chapter: Simon Baron-Cohen, George Botterill, Jill Boucher, Jack Copeland, Paul Harris, Chris Jarrold, Shaun Nichols, Peter J. Smith, and Peter K. Smith.

REFERENCES

Baron-Cohen, S. (1989a) "The autistic child's theory of mind: a case of specific developmental delay", *Journal of Child Psychology, 30*, 285–98.

—— (1989b) "Are autistic children behaviourists? An examination of their mental-physical and appearance-reality distinctions", *Journal of Autism and Developmental Disorders, 19*, 579-600.

—— (1990) "Autism: a specific cognitive disorder of 'mind-blindness'", *International Review of Psychiatry, 2*, 81–90.

—— (1991) "The development of a theory of mind in autism: deviance and delay?" *Psychiatric Clinics of North America, 14*, 33–51.

—— (1993) "From attention-goal psychology to belief-desire psychology: the development of a theory of mind and its dysfunction." In S. Baron-Cohen, H. Tager-Flusberg, and D.J. Cohen (eds), *Understanding Other Minds: Perspectives from Autism*, pp. 59–82 (Oxford: Oxford University Press).

Baron-Cohen, S., Leslie, A., and Frith, U. (1985) "Does the autistic child have a 'theory of mind'?" *Cognition, 21*, 37–46.

Baron-Cohen, S., and Ring, H. (1994) "The relationship between EDD and ToMM: neuropsychological and neurobiological perspectives", in C. Lewis and P. Mitchell (eds), *Children's Early Understanding of Mind: Origins and Development*, pp. 183–210 (Hillsdale, NJ: Erlbaum).

Baron-Cohen, S., and Swettenham, J. (1996) "The relationship between SAM and TOMM: two hypotheses" in P. Carruthers and P. Smith (eds), *Theories of Theories of Mind*, pp. 158–68 (Cambridge: Cambridge University Press).

Carruthers, P. (1992) *Human Knowledge and Human Nature* (Oxford: Oxford University Press).

—— (1996a) *Language, Thought, and Consciousness: An Essay in Philosophical Psychology* (Cambridge: Cambridge University Press).

—— (1996b) "Simulation and self-knowledge: a defence of theory-theory", in P. Carruthers and P. Smith (eds), *Theories of Theories of Mind*, pp. 22–38 (Cambridge: Cambridge University Press).

Churchland, P.M. (1981) "Eliminative materialism and the propositional attitudes", *Journal of Philosophy, 78*, 67–90.

Currie, G. (1995) "Imagination and simulation: aesthetics meets cognitive science", in A. Stone and M. Davies (eds), *Mental Simulation: Evaluations and Applications*, pp. 151–69 (Oxford: Blackwell).

—— (1996) "Simulation-theory, theory-theory, and the evidence from autism", in P. Carruthers and P. Smith (eds), *Theories of Theories of Mind*, pp. 242–56 (Cambridge: Cambridge University Press).

Fodor, J. (1987) *Psychosemantics: The Problem of Meaning in the Philosophy of Mind* (Cambridge, MA: MIT Press).

349

Frankfurt, H. (1971) "Freedom of the will and the concept of a person", *Philosophical Review*, *68*, 5–20.

Frith, U. (1989) *Autism: Explaining the Enigma* (Oxford: Blackwell).

Goldman, A. (1989) "Interpretation psychologized", *Mind and Language*, *4*, 161–85.

—— (1992) "In defense of the simulation theory", *Mind and Language*, 7, 104–19.

—— (1993) "The psychology of folk psychology", *Behavioural and Brain Sciences*, 16, 15–28.

Gopnik, A. (1993) "How we know our minds: the illusion of first-person knowledge of intentionality", *Behavioural and Brain Sciences*, 16, 1–14.

Gopnik, A. and Wellman, H.M. (1992) "Why the child's theory of mind really *is* a theory", *Mind and Language*, 7: 1–2, 145–71.

Gordon, R.M. (1986) "Folk psychology as simulation", *Mind and Language*, 1, 158–71.

—— (1992) "The simulation theory: objections and misconceptions", *Mind and Language*, 7, 11–34.

—— (1995) "Simulation without introspection or inference from me to you", in T. Stone and M. Davies (eds). *Mental Simulation: Evaluations and Applications*, pp. 53–67 (Oxford: Blackwell).

Gordon, R.M., and Barker, J. (1994) "Autism and the theory of mind debate" in G. Graham and G. Stephens (eds). *Philosophical Psychopathology*, pp. 163–82 (Cambridge, MA: MIT Press).

Harris, P.L. (1989) *Children and Emotion: The Development of Psychological Understanding* (Oxford: Blackwell)

—— (1991) "The work of the imagination", in A. Whiten (ed.), *Natural Theories of Mind: The Evolution, Development and Simulation of Everyday Mindreading*, pp. 283–304 (Oxford: Blackwell).

—— (1993) "Pretending and planning", in S. Baron-Cohen, H. Tager-Flusberg and D.J. Cohen (eds), *Understanding Other Minds: Perspectives from Autism*, pp. 228–45 (Oxford: Oxford University Press).

Hobson, R.P. (1993) *Autism and the Development of Mind* (Hove, UK: Erlbaum).

Hurlburt, R., Happé, F., and Frith, U. (1994) "Sampling the form of inner experience of three adults with Asperger syndrome", *Psychological Medicine*, 24, 385–95.

Jarrold, Boucher, J., and Smith, P.K. (1996) "Generativity deficits in pretend play in autism", *British Journal of Developmental Psychology*, 14: 275–300.

Leslie, A.M. (1987) "Pretence and representation: the origins of 'theory of mind'", *Psychological Review*, 94, 412–26.

—— (1988) "Some implications of pretence for mechanisms underlying the child's theory of mind", in J. Astington, P.L. Harris and D.R. Olsen (eds), *Developing Theories of Mind*, pp. 19–46 (Cambridge: Cambridge University Press).

—— (1991) "The theory of mind impairment in autism: evidence for a modular mechanism of development?", in A. Whiten (ed.), *Natural Theories of Mind: Evolution, Development and Simulation of Everyday Mindreading*, pp. 63–78 (Oxford: Blackwell).

Leslie, A.M., and Roth, D. (1993) "What autism teaches us about metarepresentation", in S. Baron-Cohen, H. Tager-Flusberg, and D.J. Cohen (eds), *Understanding Other Minds: Perspectives from Autism*, pp. 83–111 (Oxford: Oxford University Press).

Leslie, A. and Thaiss, L. (1992) "Domain specificity in conceptual development: neuropsychological evidence from autism", *Cognition*, 43, 225–51.

Lewis, D. (1966) "An argument for the identity theory", *Journal of Philosophy*, 63, 17–25.

Lewis, V., and Boucher, J. (1988) "Spontaneous, instructed, and elicited play in relatively able autistic children", *British Journal of Developmental Psychology*, 6, 315–24.

Naito, M., Komatsu, S., and Fuke, T. (1994) "Normal and autistic children's understanding of their own and others' false belief: a study from Japan", *British Journal of Developmental Psychology*, 12, 403–16.

Ozonoff, S., Pennington, B., and Rogers, S. (1991a) "Executive function deficits in high-functioning autistic children. Relationship to theory of mind", *Journal of Child Psychology and Psychiatry, 32*, 1081–1106.

—— (1991b) "Asperger's Syndrome. Evidence for an empirical distinction from high functioning autism", *Journal of Child Psychology and Psychiatry, 23*, 704–7.

Perner, J. (1991) *Understanding the representational mind* (Cambridge, MA: Bradford books: MIT Press).

Segal, G. (1996) "The modularity of theory of mind", in P. Carruthers and P. Smith (eds), *Theories of Theories of Mind*, pp. 141–57 (Cambridge: Cambridge University Press).

Smith, P.K. (1982) "Does play matter? Functional and evolutionary aspects of animal and human play", *Behavioural and Brain Sciences, 5*, 139–84.

Stich, S.P. (1983) *From Folk-Psychology to Cognitive Science* (Cambridge, MA: MIT Press).

Wellman, H.M. (1990) *The Child's Theory of Mind* (Cambridge, MA: MIT Press).

Wing, L, and Gould, J. (1979) "Severe impairments of social interaction and associated abnormalities in children: epidemiology and classification", *Journal of Autism and Developmental Disorders, 9*, 11–29.

28

FREE WILL, MORAL RESPONSIBILITY AND ADHD

Gordon Tait

INTRODUCTION: SCHOOLS, PATHOLOGY AND PUNISHMENT

As any number of contemporary writers on education have pointed out, one of the most fundamental and significant features of the modern school is its pervasive disciplinary apparatus (Symes and Preston 1997). This is generally regarded as being comprised of various sets of normalising practices, spatial and temporal schema, and architectural arrangements. All of these elements are underpinned by the notion that through constant and relentless surveillance, pupils learn to regulate their own conduct and, hopefully, become responsible citizens. Children learn to make appropriate, sanctioned decisions on the assumption that they will be held accountable for transgressions, transgressions now made visible through the disciplinary machinery of the mass school. Governance is thus ultimately founded upon self-governance; that is, the recruitment of young people into their own self-reformation. In turn, self-governance itself is founded upon a number of crucial assumptions, the most significant of which, is the belief that we all have the capacity to make free choices, and that we can be held accountable for those choices. After all, if students cannot do otherwise, why bother trying to make them? And why bother with punishment? However, the axiom of voluntary and accountable human action, central not only to educational practice, but also to the foundations of our self-understanding, is not without its exceptions. The following two associated examples, dealing with Attention Deficit Hyperactivity Disorder (ADHD), are worth some scrutiny, primarily as a way of providing a pivot for some of the philosophical issues to be discussed later in the paper. The examples are neither shocking nor extreme, rather they are significant only as a consequence of their relative predictability and mundanity.

A pupil in Tennessee, who had previously been diagnosed with ADHD, kicked a water pipe in a school lavatory until it burst, an act for which he was suspended for three days. At a school hearing into the matter, the student's psychologist testified that the act of vandalism "was a manifestation of [the] disability". The principal argued that while this may have been true of the vandalism, the incident itself occurred in an area of the school the student had been forbidden to enter, and therefore that this was not a matter of disability but rather of discipline. With the student facing categorisation as a delinquent, the matter eventually ended up in court, where the student won. In a matter that has the potential to go all the way to Congress, the school district has been forced to appeal the decision, a decision it contends "has made schools a 'lawless zone' for students with disabilities" (Zirkel 1995).

A pupil in Wisconsin was one of three who vandalised two elementary schools causing $40,000 worth of damage. His school sought to expel him, along with the two others who caused the damage. During the hearing into his actions, his mother raised the possibility that he might have ADHD, and soon acquired a private psychologist who concurred with this appraisal, even though the school district's psychologist disagreed. Once again, the matter ended up in court, with the student winning his case and avoiding expulsion as a "disabled' student—unlike his two covandals who only escaped expulsion by withdrawing from the school. As the school district attorney pointed out, the admission of such post-hoc diagnoses is both "disturbing and mysterious", and adversely affects the school's ability to discipline not only students with disabilities, but also those who may then choose to claim them (Zirkel 2001).

There is an obvious conclusion to be drawn here: students who have been diagnosed with ADHD—or, for that matter, any behaviour disorder—are not to be held as responsible for their actions as students who have not been so diagnosed. Such a realisation raises a number of interesting questions, two of which will be addressed here: first, how might this issue impact upon the traditional philosophical understanding of the relationship between free will and responsibility? Second, what are the implications of this for the school's ability to exercise authority over students who have been allocated such labels? In order to answer these questions effectively, it will first be necessary to recap some of the dominant philosophical positions over the notion of free will.

DO WE HAVE FREE WILL?

This question has been the focus of philosophical discussion for over two thousand years, speaking, as it does, to the very foundations of what it means to be a rational and autonomous living entity. The fundamental problem hinges upon the apparent irreconcilable tension between the sure and certain knowledge that each of us make all manner of decisions on a daily basis, choices based upon nothing but our own volition, and the equally sure and certain knowledge that we are part of a material universe, and hence subject to the same physical laws as any other form of matter, laws which preclude us from magically producing causation out of thin air. However, the seeming impenetrability of this conundrum, aptly referred to as a Gordian Knot by Gilbert Ryle (1973), appears to have neither hindered discussion on the issue, nor prevented all manner of philosophers, theologians, physicists and other assorted commentators from taking up sides in what has been a long, acrimonious, and as yet, unresolved debate. The debate has primarily, but not solely, been between those who believe that we have free will (libertarians), and those who believe that we do not, (determinists)—a dichotomy represented in Figure 28.1.

Libertarianism

The libertarian position needs little explanation, in that it confirms some fundamental assumptions that most of us take for granted. That is, we assume that our decisions somehow have their origins within us; we assume that although we are subject to external influences, the final choice is ours; and we assume that if valid choices do exist, then *post-facto*, we could always have acted otherwise. The American pragmatist William James (1994, 239–40) understands libertarianism (or indeterminism, as he calls it), to be a realisation that:

> ... possibilities may be in excess of actualities, and that things not yet revealed to our knowledge may really in themselves be ambiguous ... Indeterminism thus denies the world to be one unbending unit of fact. It says there is a certain ultimate pluralism in it; and, so saying, it corroborates our ordinary unsophisticated view of things. To that view, actualities seem to float in a wider sea of possibilities from out of which they are chosen.

St Thomas Aquinas (1225–74), essentially a libertarian, was one of the most important early writers to articulate the tension between the two positions. In *Summa Theologica* (cited in Christian 1981, 241), he stated that man has a free choice and that virtue would be of no account if this were not the case. After all, the possibility

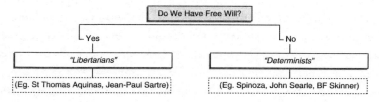

Figure 28.1

of personal redemption is the cornerstone of Christianity. However, if man is free to shape his own destiny, then how can God possibly be said to be omnipotent? Aquinas' solution was to regard free will as a gift from that omnipotent God, and that God may know what we are going to choose—good or bad, right or wrong—but the choice, and the responsibility for it, is still ours alone.

Later libertarians, notably Jean-Paul Sartre, have taken a different tack. God no longer figures in the equation. In fact, for existentialists such as Sartre, it is arguably the absence of God that defines our freedom, since without His input into shaping our lives, we are solely and terrifyingly responsible for ourselves, indeed we are *condemned to be free* (Sartre 1947). According to Sartre, life has no inherent meaning, and there are no mandates to follow. We have no human nature to trammel us, and no historical baggage to blame for making us what we are. We are totally and unconditionally free. The trouble with this position, of course, is that at a practical level it just isn't true, as Sartre himself undoubtedly realised. Grossman (1984) states that Sartre's position contradicts almost everything we know about our lives, about the social forces that shape us, and about how we become what we are. In that sense, Sartre's project is quite quixotic, as he is attempting to provide a viable template for living a particular kind of life, rather than attempting to conduct a rigorous philosophical analysis of the possibility of free will.

In truth, neither St Thomas Aquinas nor Jean-Paul Sartre have succeeded in providing a watertight (or realistically, even a very convincing) case for libertarianism, as determinists will continue to ask how this position can provide a coherent and empirically plausible explanation for how we can be the primary origin of our own decisions (Iredale 1999). However, determinism is itself not with its flaws. Indeed, in *The Critique of Practical Reason*, Kant himself describes it as "a wretched subterfuge ... petty word jugglery" (cited in Stangroom 1999, 47).

Determinism

In addition to his description of libertarianism/indeterminism, William James (1994, 240) also had a clear characterisation of determinism:

> What does determinism profess? It professes that those parts of the universe already laid down absolutely appoint and decree what the other parts shall be. The future has no ambiguous possibilities hidden in its womb ... necessity on the one hand and impossibility on the other are the sole categories of the real.

To best explain determinism, Olen (1983) follows David Hume's example and utilises the example of the billiard table, describing the case where someone plays the white ball onto the nine, which hits the side cushion before rolling to a halt in the middle of the table. He points out that if you knew some specific details prior to taking the shot—the angle and the force of the shot, the distance between the balls, their weight and dimensions, the hardness of the cushions, the friction coefficient of the surface, and so on—it would be possible to calculate, with absolute accuracy, the final resting place of the nine ball. Under such circumstances, the ball is not able to choose where to roll, as its movements are simply the inevitable outcome of other events. They are determined.

The nineteenth century mathematician, Laplace, extends this same logic with the following speculation: suppose there exists a super-intelligent being that knows the location of every atom in the universe, along with every force acting upon those atoms, and the laws of motion which governs the movement of those atoms, then that being would be able to predict each and every event in the universe from that moment onwards, with absolute accuracy. These perfect predictions would not just involve macro-events, like the movements of planets, but also micro events, such as those that occur in our heads. That is, given that our brains are made of matter, just like planets, the same causative laws necessarily apply, and ultimately the atoms in our brains follow the same rules as balls on a billiard table, with their movements being equally determined. What each person says, does and thinks could then theoretically be foretold millions of years in advance (Shipka and Minto 1996). Unless we are to believe that there is something about human brains that gives them an ability to make atoms swerve off their preordained path, there is no other logical alternative to this position. Indeed, most commentators would agree that if we adopt a materialist understanding of the universe and the human mind, a determinist position on free will is almost impossible to rebut.

Many have still tried. One of the most recent attempts has involved enlisting some aspects of the uncertainty that modern science deems to exist in nature. It has been argued that the Heisenberg uncertainty principle—that there is a fundamental indeterminacy at the level of subatomic physics—demonstrates that not all events in the universe appear to be caused by other preceding events, and that provides a loophole for believing that the brain may be able to generate its own first causes: i.e. free will. This approach has in turn been rebutted by philosophers such as Honderich (2002) who contend that events at the quantum level exist far below the threshold of significance for issues such as human choices and decisions, and also that such microevents are really not events at all, but rather belong to a totally different class of phenomena, phenomena which are entirely irrelevant to the question of determinism. In addition to the uncertainty principle, opening the Pandora's Box of advanced theoretical physics has only brought more bad news for the libertarians. For example, Einstein has suggested that we do not live in a three dimensional Newtonian universe, passing inexorably through time. Instead, we inhabit a four dimensional universe of space-time, where time does not pass as such, rather the past and the future both exist with equal unswerving certitude, mapped out from the beginning to the end, within the same instant. Thus, James' assertion that the future has no ambiguous possibilities hidden in its womb appears all the more valid.

It is not, however, only modern thinkers who lean towards the determinist position. The venerated 17th century rationalist, Baruch Spinoza, was also a determinist. While still working theism into his conceptual framework—hardly surprising given the era in which he was writing—he based his understanding of human freedom, not upon free will, which he regarded as a will o' the wisp, but rather upon an understanding of the forces which shape us. That is, he compares the free with the (metaphorically) enslaved by contrasting the degree of understanding they possess of themselves, their situation and the world in which they act (Sprigge 1999). In this manner, the logic of his argument is similar to that in the famous quote by Peter Berger (1963, 199), wherein we are likened to puppets, only with the possibility of "looking up and perceiving the machinery by which we have been moved. In this act lies the first step towards freedom."

And yet, other determinists have no interest in freedom whatsoever, probably the most famous being B.F. Skinner, as outlined in his seminal text *Beyond Freedom and Dignity* (1971). Skinner contends that freedom is a myth, and that the sum total of human experience is simply a set of conditioned responses to given stimuli. Extrapolating from rats and pigeons, he argues that we have no grounds for believing that we are any different. He stated that there is no reason why the cause/effect nexus that underpins all of the natural sciences, should not have an exact correlate of stimulus/response in the social sciences. The sensation of free will, and hence freedom itself, is simply a conditioned response. Vulgar though Skinner's position is, it still operates with the same domain assumptions, and therefore moves across the same conceptual terrain, as other determinist positions. There is a similar, although infinitely more subtle, logic to be found within the final paragraph of the philosopher John Searle's "Freedom of the Will":

> ... for reasons I don't really understand, evolution has given us a form of experience of voluntary action where the experience of freedom, that is to say, the experience of the sense of alternative possibilities, is built into the very structure of conscious, voluntary human behaviour. (Searle 1994, 774)

In this sense, Searle is contending that the experience of freedom of the will is, in some ways, analogous to Kant's arguments about the "hard-wiring" of the perception of space and time into the human mind. Voluntarism similarly becomes a primary component of consciousness, a component which not only determines how we perceive the world, but also how we are able to perceive ourselves. In the final analysis though, whether we base our analysis on libertarian or determinist presuppositions, the most significant issue is not really whether we have free will at all—even though this is hardly trivial in the grand scheme of things—rather, the critical issue is what all of this has to say about the notion of personal responsibility. After all, if we are simply Skinnerian rats, responding to stimulus in the same cause/effect way that balls roll around a billiard table, then how can we be held responsible for anything we do?

ARE WE MORALLY RESPONSIBLE?

When we hold someone morally responsible for an action, this is to say that their good deeds are deserving of praise, and their bad deeds deserving of punishment. This process forms the cornerstone of our ability to form moral communities. Without holding each other responsible for our conduct, the basic social framework of rights and obligations characteristic of all human societies would be unable to function. However, the balls on a billiard table are not blamed if one of them happens to roll into a pocket at the wrong time. The determinist nature of events on a billiard table render the issue of blame redundant—that is, as long as the frame of reference is limited solely to the balls themselves. Furthermore, rolling into a pocket is not, *prima facie*, an act laden with moral significance. If Skinner's rat stole cheese from your kitchen, this would not be a moral issue—undesirable though it is. However, if the cheese were to be stolen by Skinner himself, a number of moral conclusions could be drawn about his conduct, and he would rightly be held to be morally and criminally responsible. Is this fair? Is there a difference? Figure 28.2 sets out some of the ways these questions have been approached:

The two most common positions taken on the issue of free will/determinism and moral responsibility are generally referred to as "Compatibilism" (the view that we can still be held morally responsible for our conduct, even in a determinist universe), and "Incompatibilism", (the view, for whatever the reason, that the two cannot logically coexist).

Compatibilism

If we are totally determined creatures, whether we realise it or not—as most philosophers would contend—then can we be held morally accountable for our actions? The Scottish philosopher David Hume made what is probably the most famous

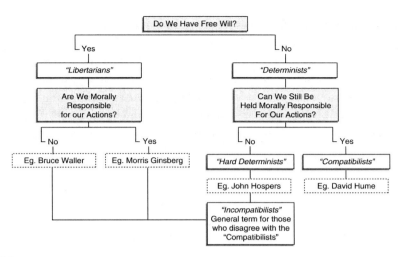

Figure 28.2

attempt to answer this question in *An Enquiry Concerning Human Understanding* in 1748. As a compatibilist, Hume sees no necessary contradiction between the notions of liberty of action and causal necessity; that is, we can be both determined and morally responsible. The logic of his argument is centred around the belief that such long-standing philosophical problems can most often be explained in terms of linguistic ambiguity. In this particular case, the focus falls upon precisely what is meant by "liberty".

Throughout this debate, liberty has generally been placed in binary opposition to determinism. If we act freely, then we cannot possibly be determined; if we are determined, we cannot possibly regard our actions as being free, and of course, we cannot possibly be held accountable for our actions. In contrast with this position, Hume argues that liberty actually means the power to make choices based solely upon the determinations of our will. After all, the opposite of necessity is actually chance, and this has nothing to do with being free. Hence, according to Hume, liberty should be placed in opposition, not to determinism, but rather to constraint. Therefore, we act freely if we are untrammelled in our choices. As Pinchin (1990, 117) states:

> Thus we are offered a compatibilist account asserting no inconsistency between the concepts of liberty and necessity. A human action can be necessary in the sense that it is the inevitable outcome of causes. It can also be free in the sense that it is not subject to constraints.

Within this paradigm, moral responsibility is no longer a problem: we are responsible for the choices we have freely made. Pinchin is not entirely happy with this explanation, as it still does not address the matter of how we can be held responsible if we could not have acted otherwise. Still, there is a broad consensus that freedom is an ambiguous concept, and that Hume moved the debate forward by locating at least part of the problem within language itself. That said, even though compatibilism is undoubtedly the dominant position within the debate, it is not without its critics. More often than not, these critics are grouped together under the umbrella of incompatibilism, even though often the only thing they have in common is their status as 'other'.

Incompatibilism

The most common and obvious incompatibilist position is generally referred to as "hard determinism". This involves the assertion that our conduct is determined, but a refusal to accept that this state of affairs is compatible with moral responsibility. The implications of this conclusion are either that we abandon holding citizens accountable for their conduct altogether, or we hold them accountable, even if we know this is not really the case. John Hospers (1994) adopts a psychoanalytic approach to the issue, arguing that our conscious minds—the "*sanctum sanctorum* of freedom", and the only parts of our "selves" which can logically be held accountable for anything— is not the driving force behind our choices or our conduct. Rather, the unconscious mind is ultimately responsible for how we act, or, as Hospers (1994, 758) puts it: "the unconscious is the master of every fate and the captain of every soul". While not suggesting abandoning the notion of moral responsibility entirely, he does indicate that it has no intellectual or ethical foundation. Significantly for this paper, he goes on to state that psychiatry has begun the process of coming to terms with the implications of non-conscious factors of human conduct in ways that philosophy has not. Precisely what this might mean will be addressed later, since presumably disorders such as ADHD would be included within this assertion.

Other approaches in opposition to compatibilism begin their analysis, not with hard determinism's refusal to accept that causal necessity and moral responsibility can co-exist, but rather with the premise that because being totally determined is unthinkable to us, we *must* have free will, therefore we can also be held morally responsible for our actions. In his essay "The Nature of Responsibility", Morris Ginsberg (1956, 345) makes precisely this point. He asks whether anyone seriously doubts that we have the minimum level of freedom necessary to be held morally accountable, as we make judgements every day which involve weighing the consequences of given acts and the relative worth of available alternatives. Ginsberg also suggests that if our judgements are completely determined, then this would make a nonsense of all knowledge. Intellectual choices would become redundant—

truth and falsity, sense and nonsense—would all be on the same epistemological level.

Bruce Waller (1996) provides an interesting spin to the debate by contending that although we are free to make choices as we see fit, we do not deserve praise or blame for the outcomes of those choices, i.e. we are not morally responsible. He reaches this conclusion by suggesting that the good and bad events that happen in our lives are the result of "genetic-environmental luck". The uneven starts and unequal paths that lead through life undercut all assumptions about just deserts and moral responsibility, and the notion of moral responsibility itself not only acts to stifle more fruitful inquiries into the circumstances which shape our conduct, but also promotes iniquitous social policies and punitive rather than positive social programs.

To summarise so far: the discipline of philosophy has argued back and forth about the relationship between free will and moral responsibility for 2000 years. Whether a libertarian or a determinist, and from there whether a compatibilist or an incompatibilist, the vast majority of philosophers contend that we can rightly and fairly be held accountable for our actions. Even the periodic intervention of theoretical physics into the debate has not altered this fundamental conclusion. However, historically there has always been one more major player in the game, and this body of knowledge also leans heavily towards personal accountability: jurisprudence.

RESPONSIBILITY, TRANSGRESSION AND THE LAW

At first glance, as one might suspect, the law is pretty strict and specific on the issue of precisely what is required for a person to be held responsible for an action. Criminal responsibility is "the concept that individuals with the capacity to make voluntary and intentional choices to act criminally, understanding the significance of the choices, should be accountable to the criminal law for those choices." (Nygh and Butt 1998, 107). Whether directly or indirectly, the principle expressed in the maxim *actus non facit reum nisi mens sit rea*: the act does not constitute guilt unless the mind is guilty, still drives much of the reasoning behind the legal approach to responsibility. Therefore, if we make choices, voluntarily and intentionally, understanding the nature of those choices, we are responsible for them. There is no notion here that we could somehow claim to be like one of Skinner's rats, acting as a result of given stimuli, and hence not legally or morally accountable for what we do. Indeed, history suggests the reverse is more likely to be accepted as the case, given that in 1595, the City Court of Leyden sentenced a dog to hang at a public gallows for killing a man, "to the deterring of all other dogs" (Ginsberg 1968, 349).

The seeming overt simplicity and rigidity of the legal position of responsibility actually hides a significant degree of flexibility. Just because a number of people are found guilty of a particular offence, does not mean that they are all, *a priori*, regarded as possessing the same degree of criminal responsibility. There are a number of mechanisms which can attenuate, restrict, modify or even negate responsibility, several of which are pertinent to this paper. For example:

Mitigating Circumstances

According to Olen (1983), even though a morally responsible person is a rational agent, who knows right from wrong, and who can be influenced by moral argument—and arguably we do fit these criteria (determinism or otherwise)—we sometimes let each other off the hook. In essence, this is a form of very weak incompatibilism. The logic is that there are many reasons why people do what they do, why they make given choices, why they break the law. These reasons provide a context for interpreting a level of responsibility appropriate to the situation. To better exemplify this position, Olen uses the James Cagney gangster movie *Angels With Dirty Faces*. The story begins with two boys from a tough New York neighbourhood, running from the police. Pat O'Brien gets away, and grows up to be a Catholic priest, but Cagney is caught and sentenced to a reform school, where he grows up to be a hardened criminal. Throughout the film, the two compete for control over the lives of a group of boys, and the film ends with Cagney's electrocution, and O'Brien telling the boys to say a prayer for a boy who couldn't run as fast as him. The film's message is clear: crime is not only a personal issue, but also a social one. While we are responsible for our lives, they are also shaped by forces beyond our control, and often the only difference is a matter of luck.

This is also a line of reasoning championed by the famed trial lawyer Clarence Darrow. In *Attorney for the Damned* (1957) there is a transcript of his appeal to the judge for clemency in the celebrated case of Leopold and Loeb, two students who, for no apparent reason, kidnapped and killed a 14-year-old boy. Darrow (1957, 227) concludes that, ultimately, we are not responsible for either our genetics or our environment, and it is these factors that should actually shoulder the greatest burden of blame. When discussing Loeb, he stated:

> If there is responsibility anywhere, it is back of him; somewhere in the infinite number of his ancestors, or his surroundings, or in both. And I submit, Your Honor, that under every principle of natural justice, under every principle of conscience, or right, and of law, he should not be made responsible for the acts of someone else.

DOLI INCAPAX

Article 40 of the United Nation "Convention on the Rights of the Child" specifies "a minimum age below which children shall be presumed not to have the capacity to infringe the penal law." This is the presumption of "doli incapax": the inability of children to be held responsible for criminal conduct. Although the specific age boundaries of this presumption vary between countries, the logic is still the same. That is, children below a certain age are not capable of the reasoning processes necessary to be held accountable for their actions. In Australia, the minimum age for criminal responsibility is ten years old. Therefore, if a criminal act is committed by a person younger than ten, that person cannot be held in any way responsible, whatever the nature of the offence. For children older than this, there is a transitional period up to the age of fourteen where they are still not responsible, unless it can actually be proven that the person had the capacity to know the act in question was wrong.

Tyszkiewicz (2001) has a number of interesting points to make on the subject of "doli incapax". Citing writers such as Aries (1962) and Petersen (1989), he discusses the historically contingent boundaries of the category of childhood, noting that in medieval Europe it could be said not to have existed at all. Those who would now be categorised as children participated in almost all "adult" activities. The notion of childhood was only to evolve over the next three or four hundred years, primarily within the boundaries of the bourgeoise family. Significantly, there was no notion that these embryonic children needed special protection, or that they were not equally capable as adults of making informed decisions, and being held responsible for those decisions. Certainly, they faced identical punishment to adults—children faced execution for murder in England right up until 1906 (Millet, 1995). For the purposes of this paper, one of the most interesting observations regarding the status of doli incapax concerns the assertion that the age of criminal responsibility is set "not at the age at which the child can tell right from wrong—most five-year-olds can do that—but the point at which society feels it can unashamedly punish" (Morris; cited in Tyszkiewicz 2001, 17). The implications of this claim are obviously far-reaching, not only for the validity of a crucial component of our system of jurisprudence, but also for the logic underpinning the treatment of children in schools.

Insanity

In most common law countries, the understanding of the relationship between insanity and criminal responsibility was originally laid down in the case of M'Naghten (1843), where a man was acquitted by a jury on the charge of murder due to his madness, causing a popular outcry at the time. This case subsequently formed the basis for the "M'Naghten Rules", which were outlined by Lord Chief Justice Tindall (1843, 208) as follows:

> ... every man is to be presumed to be sane, and to possess a sufficient degree of reason to be responsible for his crimes, until the contrary be proved to their satisfaction; and to establish a defence on the grounds of insanity, it must be clearly proved that, at the time of the committing of the act, the party accused was labouring under such a defect of reason, from disease of the mind, as not to know the nature and quality of the act he was doing, or, if he did know it, that he did not know he was doing what was wrong.

As a consequence of these rules, the majority of debate over responsibility has tended to focus on the dichotomous positions of full responsibility and non-responsibility. However, it has been argued that the steadily increasing focus on the criminal conduct of young people has played a significant role in reconfiguring the debate around varying *degrees* of responsibility, particularly in children, rather than the previous position of simple mutual exclusion. The key to this process, apparently, is a greater understanding not only of types of crime as they relate to particular mental conditions, but also a greater understanding of the mental conditions themselves (Ginsberg 1968).

In a sense, Ginsberg is prefiguring a new major player in the "Do we have responsibility?" game—and not only in criminal responsibility, but as it turns out, responsibility in absolutely every avenue of life. The psy-disciplines—primarily psychology, but also psychiatry, psychoanalysis, and so on—are now in the process of cutting an explanatory swathe through all aspects of human conduct. In doing so, they are introducing a hard determinist understanding of moral responsibility. As behaviour disorders multiply exponentially, so too is human conduct, and in particular children's conduct, now explained away as pathology. That is, more and more human behaviour is now regarded as a direct function of greater and greater numbers of disease entities.

BEHAVIOUR DISORDERS, MORAL RESPONSIBILITY AND THE SCHOOL

In spite of three decades of post-modern thought, scientific knowledge, and psychological knowledge in particular, is still most frequently presented as objective, benevolent and teleological, slowly uncovering the facts of the natural world, with the individual researchers merely perceptive but neutral observers to whom these truths are passed. History is thus presented in triumphalist terms: the heroic unmasking of the hidden realities of nature, the shedding of light into the mysteries of the human body and mind, and the identification and control of independent disease entities. Superseded ways of understanding and healing are presented as superstitious, ignorant and/or barbaric. However, as Wright and Treacher note (1982, 3–4), the categories produced by such forms of knowledge:

> ... are social through and through; they are the outcome of a web of social practices and bear their imprint. When we speak of tuberculosis we are not reading the label on a discrete portion of nature, 'out there'; we are instead ... employing a social meaning that has been generated by the activities of many different social groups, with diverse interests, working through many different forms of practice.

There has long been dissatisfaction with elements of the labelling processes associated with 'mental illness'. Seminal work by Hollingshead and Redlich (1958) noted that an individual's chance of being committed to a mental institution varied in relation to their social class—a variable surely irrelevant to an 'objective' illness. Likewise Szasz (1961, 1973) proposes a radical shift in the understanding of 'insanity' due, in part, to his refusal to accept the objective validity of the category. More convincingly, in *Madness and Civilisation*, Foucault (1965) details some of the social contingencies which were necessary precursors to the emergence of psychiatry as a discipline—all of which go some way towards attenuating the 'objective truth' of insanity. Following on from this, a number of specific mental illnesses, claiming the status of 'objective facts', have had this status challenged, such as split personality (Hacking 1986), and anorexia nervosa (Tait 1993). The question which arises now is how then does a disease entity such as Attention Deficit Hyperactivity Disorder fare under this kind of scrutiny?

A Closer Look at ADHD

The following quote is typical of the way in which ADD and ADHD are presented within the literature, and by those with an interest in its acceptance as a valid and objective category.

> ADD is an inherited neurobiological disorder which becomes evident in early childhood and usually continues throughout a person's life ... There is no doubt in the scientific community that ADD is real ... ADD is not a new phenomenon,

it has always been with us but has not always been recognised. (D. and M. Sosin 1996, 6–7)

It is evident here that disorders such as ADD and ADHD are understood as objective conditions, indisputable facts of nature. In addition, they are deemed to have existed long before their identification by the clear-eyed and perceptive scientists who brought them to our attention, thereby dispelling the former—erroneous—explanations for the same conduct. ADHD is diagnosed with symptoms of fidgeting, excitability, impulsivity, immaturity, and lack of self-control. Estimates of the school population vary widely, from three percent to ten percent, although classes with much greater percentages of ADHD have been reported (Reif 1993).

There exist numerous strategies for dealing with this new affliction (such as behaviour modification, counselling, cognitive therapy, social skills training), but pharmacological intervention through the use of the stimulant Ritalin is widely regarded as being the most significant. As with other pathologised differences, schools have been charged with the primary responsibility of managing ADHD (almost all identification protocols, treatments and research literature are school-based). Furthermore, the implications and effects of such (formerly) hyperactive conduct are no longer deemed to be confined either to the classroom, or to the schooling years. There is now a significant literature which serves the dual purpose of laying the blame for a number of broader social problems at the door of ADHD (such as various forms of criminal conduct, delinquency, social maladjustment, emotional problems, professional failure, and so on) while at the same time reinforcing the need for identifying and tackling the problem in its embryonic stages at school (Forehand *et al.* 1991; Dunning 1998).

Teachers are also now expected to be able to deal with a much wider range of educational differences than just ADD and ADHD. Such differences are no longer regarded as being below the threshold of intervention, or simply part of the human condition, but are now objective pathologies to be identified, categorised and normalised. As Tomlinson pointed out as early as 1982, this appears to be part of an ongoing and exponentially-increasing process. After all, within the realm of educational difference/handicap, there were only two classifications prior to 1890 (*idiot* and *imbecile*). This had swelled to eight by 1913 (including divisions such as *moral imbecile*, and *mental defective*) and on to twelve in 1945 (with *severely subnormal, maladjusted*, and *delicate*). Currently, the list of such differences is enormous—in excess of three hundred (Whitefield 1999)—each with its own treatment, prognosis and educational implications. It is not enough for teachers to know that certain forms of shyness have now been pathologised as Generalised Social Phobia (Turner et al 1992), it also helps to be aware of some of its nosological subdivisions—such as Selective Mutism (Black and Uhde 1996), or Avoidant Personality Disorder (Holt *et al.* 1992)—as well as how to recognise them, what to do with them, and how to organise your classroom practices accordingly. These developments and discoveries are normally manifest in terms of a burgeoning array of student differences, differences that have the potential to significantly recalibrate, or in the long term, even totally undermine, the moral machinery of the school.

So What Does All This Mean?

There are a number of issues here: first, until fairly recently the issue of free will and moral responsibility had generally involved debates between philosophers, physicists and jurists. If the solution to the "Gordian Knot" were to be found anywhere, history suggested it would come from one of these disciplines. However, psychology appears to be in the process of outflanking them all, providing increasing numbers of hard determinist explanations for what was once regarded as voluntary conduct. Hard determinism, a previously unthinkable option, is slowly becoming mainstream.

Second, disorders such as ADHD are premised upon explanations of human action, founded not in the reasoned conduct of responsible agents, but rather in terms of causal necessity. Children diagnosed with ADHD are more than likely to have any action that fits into the lexicon of symptoms associated with the disorder, explained as being a *function* of that disorder. So, children diagnosed with ADHD who fidget, fidget because of that disorder. Children without ADHD who fidget, presumably make the free and voluntary decisions to do so, and hence become liable to punishment.

Third, greater and greater numbers of school children are being diagnosed as suffering from particular forms of behaviour disorder. Special needs children, once rare in classrooms, are now commonplace. That schools should be equipped to deal with difference is not in question. Of course they should. Rather, the point is that the discipline of psychology appears to be engaged in the ongoing and accelerating process of *creating* difference. And in the case of behaviour disorders, as more categories are "discovered", more and more students will no longer be held fully accountable for their actions. Whether this also turns out to be the case for the courts has yet to be determined. Interestingly, the Wisconsin student who vandalised a school but escaped expulsion after retrospectively being diagnosed with ADHD, was held to be responsible for his actions under criminal law, and suitably punished.

Finally, the question raised at the beginning of this paper—what are the implications of all this for the school's ability to exercise authority over students?—has two separate answers. At one level, it has the potential to make the situation very difficult. As the number of students claiming the status of disability continues to increase (via behaviour disorders such as ADHD), and as each disorder has different levels of associated accountability, schools may not only find themselves in the situation of being unable to hold an increasing sections of the school population liable for their conduct, as the two initial American examples demonstrate, but also of requiring some method by which they can determine levels of relative responsibility. At a second level, it has the potential to make the situation much easier—at least for the highly-stressed teacher—but only if we are prepared to leave our ethics at the school gate. Almost all the disorders mentioned or alluded to in this paper are treated pharmacologically: ADHD, Oppositional Defiance Disorder, Generalised Social Phobia, Selective Mutism, Avoidant Personality Disorder, Borderline Personality Disorder, to name but a very few. To put it another way, teaching life will be easier because disruptive students, quiet students, or generally different students, will be drugged into normalcy and passivity.

CONCLUSION

The rise of the inclusive school, institutions where special needs students are to be given full access to, and involvement in, the daily life of the classroom, has placed the teacher not only on the front-line of conduct disorder management, but also at the centre of a millennia-old debate about just who can be held responsible for what. This process has significant implications, for the teaching profession, for how difference is to be conceptualised, and most importantly, for how the population as a whole is to be governed. If a philosophical analysis of this issue can accomplish anything, it is to point to a necessity for a more rigorous conceptualisation of what a hard determinist society would look like. Rather than simply taking each new disorder as a separate issue, to be dealt with on its own terms, a broader understanding of the relationship between free will and moral responsibility leads to a clearer vision both of what behaviour disorders prefigure, and ultimately, what it means to be human. After all, the truth is that philosophers have always known that the determinist position is far more convincing than the libertarian alternative. Even Spinoza in the 17th century knew we all act through causal necessity. This is nothing new. The only difference to the contemporary psychological stance is that he still held us accountable. Certainly, we need to think through—very thoroughly—the consequences of freeing a steadily increasing percentage of the population from some or all of their moral responsibilities. Of course, this is not to say that the social contexts in which specific forms of conduct take place should not be taken into account. The film *Angels With Dirty Faces* illustrates how complex the notion of responsibility can be. However, there is a world of difference between context and causality.

Earlier in the paper, Morris Ginsberg (1968) called for a greater understanding of the mental conditions that increasingly shape our understanding of moral responsibility. The implication here is that the psychological sciences are in the process of uncovering the essential truths of the human mind. This is, however, only one interpretation of psychology's history and function. Nikolas Rose (1985) has described an entirely different function, that of a crucial cog in the machinery of governmental intervention and regulation. The rise of the psy-disciplines denote the emergence of a new rationale of government targeting human individuality, with the conduct of citizens now to be directed by investigating, interpreting and modifying their mental capacities and predispositions.

> One fruitful way of thinking about the mode of functioning of the psychological sciences ... might therefore be to understand them as *techniques for the disciplining of human difference*: individualising humans through classifying them, calibrating their capacities and conducts, inscribing and recording their attributes and deficiencies, managing and utilising their individuality and variability. (Rose 1988, 187)

Fundamental to this process is the need to categorise, to break the population down into smaller and smaller manageable units, because with each new category, each new behaviour disorder, each new *pathology*, comes new possibilities of governance. Contemporary pupils are no longer simply too lively, they are now seen as suffering from Attention Deficit Hyperactivity Disorder or Oppositional Defiance Disorder, or Conduct Disorder. Pupils are no longer simply quiet or shy, they are reclassified as suffering from Generalised Social Phobia, or Selective Mutism, or Avoidant Personality Disorder. Pupils are no longer simply unpopular or obnoxious, they are reclassified as Borderline Personality Disorder, or Antisocial Personality Disorder. However, in each instance, the new possibility of governance comes at a specific cost: the further erosion of individual responsibility.

Finally, given such pressures to pathologise those many students now produced as different, the question must eventually be asked about the veracity of the burgeoning array of medical and psychological categories such children are being placed into. Of course, this is not to say that these categories are false, but what it does mean is that the next paper to be written on the subject of philosophy and education should really take a hard took at precisely what we mean when we talk about "truth".

REFERENCES

Aries, P. (1962) *Centuries of Childhood*, Harmondsworth: Penguin.
Berger, P. (1963) *An Invitation to Sociology*, Harmondsworth: Penguin.

Black, B and Uhde, T. (1996) "Elective Mutism as a Variant of Social Phobia", in S. Spasaro and C. Schaffer (eds.) *Refusal to Speak: treatment of selective mutism in children*, New Jersey: Aronson.

Christian, J. (1981) *Philosophy: An Introduction to the Art of Wondering*, New York: Holt, Rinehart and Winston.

Darrow, C. (1976) "The Crime of Compulsion" in Thomas Shipka and Arthur Minton (eds) Philosophy: Paradox and Discovery (4th edition), New York: McGraw-Hill, p. 222–7.

Dunning, C. (1998) "The Impact of Attention Disorders during Adulthood: a review of current literature", Doctoral Research Paper, Biola University.

Forehand, R., Wierson, M., Frame, C., Kempton, T. and Armistead, L. (1991) "Juvenile Delinquency Entry and Persistence: do attention problems contribute to conduct problems?" *Journal of Behaviour Therapy and Experimental Psychiatry*, 22, 4, pp. 261–4.

Foucault, M. (1965) *Madness and Civilisation: A History of Insanity in the Age of Reason* New York: Random House.

Ginsberg, M. (1968) "The Nature of Responsibility", in *Essays in Sociology and Social Philosophy*, Harmondsworth: Penguin, pp. 342–61.

Grossman, R. (1984) *Phenomenology and Existentialism: An Introduction*, London: Routledge and Kegan Paul.

Hacking, I. (1986) "Making Up People", in: T. Heller (ed.) *Reconstructing Individualism: autonomy, individuality and the self in western thought*, California: Stanford University Press.

Hollingshead, A. and Redlich, F. (1958) *Social Class and Mental Illness: a community study* New York, Wiley.

Holt, C., Heimberg, R. and Holt, D. (1992) "Avoidant Personality Disorder and the Generalised Subtype in Social Phobia", *Journal of Abnormal Psychology*, 102, pp. 318–25.

Honderich, T. (2002). "Determinism as True, Compatibilism and Incompatibilism as Both False, and the Real Problem", in R. Kane (ed.), *The Oxford Handbook of Free Will* (Oxford: Oxford University Press, 461–76).

Hospers, J. (1994) "Human Beings as Controlled Puppets", in Samuel Stumpf (ed.) *Philosophy: History and Problems (5th Edition)* New York: McGraw-Hill, pp. 746–51

Iredale, M. (1999) "Mapping the Freewill Debate", *The Philosopher's Magazine*, 6, p. 34.

James, W. (1994) "How Can We Explain Judgements of Regret?" in Samuel Stumpf (ed.) *Philosophy: History and Problems (5th Edition)* New York: McGraw-Hill, pp. 228–43 (first published as "The Dilemma of Determinism", in *The Unitarian Review*, 1884).

Nygh, P. and Butt, P (eds.) (1998) *Concise Australian Legal Dictionary*, Butterworths: Sydney.

Olen, J. (1983) *Persons and Their World: An Introduction to Philosophy*, New York: McGraw-Hill.

Petersen, C. (1989). *Looking Forward Through the Life Span*, 2nd edn., New Jersey: Prentice Hall.

Pinchin, C. (1990) *Issues in Philosophy*, London: MacMillan.

Reif, S. (1993) *How to Teach and Teach ADD/ADHD Children*, Boston: Allyn & Bacon.

Rose, N. (1985) *The Psychological Complex: psychology, politics and society in England 1869–1939*, London: Routledge and Kegan Paul.

—— (1988) "Calculable Minds and Manageable Individuals", *History of the Human Sciences*, 1, 2, pp. 179–99.

Ryle, G. (1973) *The Concept of Mind*, Harmondsworth: Penguin.

Sartre, J. (1947) *Existentialism and Humanism*, Methuen: London.

Searle, J. (1994) "Freedom of the Will", in Samuel Stumpf (ed.) *Philosophy: History and Problems (5th Edition)* New York: McGraw-Hill, pp. 766–74.

Shipka, T, and Minto, A. (eds.) (1996) *Philosophy: Paradox and Discovery*, McGraw Hill: New York.

Skinner, P. (1971) *Beyond Freedom and Dignity*, Bantam Books: New York.

Sprigge, T. (1999) "Spinoza: Freedom is Necessity", *The Philosopher's Magazine*, 6.

Sosin, D. and Sosin, M. (1996) *Attention Deficit Disorder*, Highett: Hawker Brownlow.

Stangroom, J. (1999) "Determination and Punishment: An Interview with Ted Honderich", *The Philosopher's Magazine*, 6, pp. 47–50.

Symes, C. and Preston, N. (1997) *Schools and Classrooms: a cultural studies analysis of education (2nd edition)*, Longman: Melbourne.

Szasz, T. (1961) *The Myth of Mental Illness: foundations of a theory of personal conduct*, New York: Harper and Row.

—— (1973) *The Manufacture of Madness: a comparative study of the Inquisition and the mental health movement*, London: Grenada.

Tait, G. (1993) "Anorexia Nervosa": asceticism, differentiation, government, *Australian and New Zealand Journal of Sociology*, 29, 2, pp. 194–208.

Tomlinson, S. (1982) *A Sociology of Special Education*, London: Routledge and Kegan Paul.

Turner, S, Beidel, D. and Townsley, R. (1992) "Social Phobia: a comparison of specific and generalised subtypes and avoidant personality disorder", *Journal of Abnormal Psychology*, 102, pp. 326–31.

Tyszkiewicz, M. (2001) "An Integrated Model for the Ascription of Criminal Responsibility in Childhood", Unpublished Paper, Faculty of Law, Queensland University of Technology.

Waller, B. (1996) "Freedom Without Responsibility", in T. Shipka and A. Minto, (eds.) (1996) *Philosophy: Paradox and Discovery*, McGraw Hill: New York, pp. 246–58.

Whitefield, P. (1999) "Disordered Behaviour and Fuzzy Categories", *Education Links*, 59, pp. 22–5.

Wright P. and Treacher, A. (1982) *The Problem of Medical Knowledge: examining the social construction of medicine*, Edinburgh: Edinburgh University Press.

Zirkel, P. (1995). "Disabling Discipline?" *Phi Delta Kappan*, pp. 568–9.

—— (2001). "Manifest Determination?" *Phi Delta Kappan*, pp. 478–9.

29

ALCOHOL ADDICTION AND RESPONSIBILITY ATTRIBUTIONS

Ferdinand Schoeman

The problems encountered by those who are alcohol-dependent share much with the critical personal problems we all face. The way we think about the alcohol-dependent person has implications for the way we think about human problems in general. Conversely, the more alcohol dependence shares with other problems, the more the factors that relate to those other problems relate to alcohol abuse. Appreciating this will help us put into context some of the puzzling features that long-term alcohol abuse poses.

Proponents of biochemical or genetic accounts of alcohol abuse have at times argued that their findings demonstrate that large classes of individuals have diminished control over their excessive-drinking patterns or over their behavior while under the influence. Several researchers who have been skeptical of biochemical accounts have wanted to discount the relevance of biology completely and argue that the cause of wrecked cars, families, or lives is wholly attributable to environmental forces. Proponents of these two perspectives – biomedical and psychosocial – concur, however, on seeing individual alcohol abusers as victims of forces over which little personal control can be exercised.

Among critics of these single-factor theories are to be found many who would argue that since every even remotely plausible theory of abuse will have only a limited range of relevance and that issues of individual character and choice are nearly always relevant, there is no basis for mitigating the gravity of the harm to self or others that the alcohol abuser can be accused of inflicting. The options we seem to be left with are that the alcohol abuser either has radically diminished control or is fully accountable.

These polarized postures cannot reflect the perspective good judgment would bring to bear on the issue; good judgment eschews wholesale answers to recurring questions. Occasionally questions recur because the facts necessary to settle them are unavailable. In the case of alcohol abuse, however, the problem is deeper. Questions and approaches recur because there are real difficulties with all of the solutions that have been offered, stemming in part from an impoverished set of categories for conceptualizing the issue. Not only is there a dispute between those providing services to alcohol-dependent people, but there is also plenty of debate among those seeking scientific accounts of alcohol dependence and abuse. What this means is a somewhat disorderly state of understanding where patterns are not evident without careful elaboration of details about each case. My approach will be to plumb the divergent perspectives for insights that may provide the foundation for a comprehensive and coherent outlook.

It would be wrong to infer that recourse to particularized, detailed judgment is the result of the failure of science to provide an answer. In many ways, science has already provided us with illuminating information about alcohol-induced comportment and addiction. But what science provides is not enough to settle the moral questions. We would be mistaken in expecting that kind of answer from science in the first place, though often scientists assume, or are cast in, the role of being experts in just this sort of determination.

In this chapter I challenge a range of hard-line views about alcohol abuse, views that suggest that because there is no credible evidence of adequate single-factor causal accounts of alcohol abuse, patterns of alcohol abuse need not be seen as undermining or mitigating the abuser's responsibility for his or her behavior. But I also challenge the more compassionate view that because alcohol abuse undermines responsibility in many contexts, it undermines responsibility in all. I will begin by reviewing the majority opinion of a recent Supreme Court case and discussing the significance of diseases in attributing responsibility for behavior. I then examine the view that we are responsible for our own character in light of some recent medical uncoverings, in order to show that the implementation of the hard-line perspective on attributions of responsibility would turn our selves and society into entities bereft of humane understanding. Along the way I discuss some problems with thinking that people are responsible for choosing what cultural or traditional norms they should adopt and consider some commonsense considerations that attenuate or qualify attributions of responsibility. I conclude the paper by observing that the way we should think about responsibility for drinking patterns is not one issue but many, and answering it requires that attention still be paid to the context of the question.

1 TRAYNOR AND MCKELVEY V. TURNAGE

Let me begin this conceptual excursion by describing a line of reasoning evidenced in a recent Supreme Court ruling, *Traynor and McKelvey v. Turnage*. In this case

Traynor and McKelvey sought extended benefits from the Veterans Administration on the grounds that their earlier problems with alcoholism constituted a handicap for which they were not responsible. Veterans are entitled to an extension of the period during which benefits can be provided if a handicap for which they are not responsible prevented them from utilizing their benefits within 10 years of being discharged. Justice White, writing for the majority, found that the Veterans Administration's rule of treating alcoholism as the result of willful misconduct was not unreasonable or arbitrary in light of the substantial body of medical evidence supporting that outlook. Citing Fingarette 1971, White reasoned that alcoholism that is not the result of an underlying psychiatric disorder is not so entirely beyond the agent's control as to undermine the willfulness of the drinking and thus the condition. White claimed that it is controversial whether alcoholism is properly regarded as a disease, and that even if it is a disease, this does not mean that there is no element of culpable willfulness on the part of those alcohol-dependent people who continue to drink. He concluded by suggesting that no basis could be found for judging this sort of alcohol-dependent person to be devoid of all control for excessive drinking. For the purposes of this case, alcoholism could therefore be considered a willfully incurred disability.

With this line of reasoning in mind, I want to point out some phenomena that challenge our ordinary notions of when agents are responsible for their conditions, choices, and qualities of character. The significance of these challenges for these notions and for our judgment will be developed below.

2 THE RELEVANCE OF DISEASE TO ATTRIBUTING BEHAVIOR

An examination of the notion of disease in our culture will help us become clearer about the problem. To be in a diseased state is normally to be in a condition of impaired functioning, to have one's overall capacities or some specific functioning incapacitated. Characteristically, we regard failures to perform up to normal levels as excusable in someone with diminished abilities. The reason for this dispensation is that it is unfair to expect of a person a level of performance that he or she cannot achieve without unusual costs being borne.

What standard or standards are invoked in deciding whether costs borne are unfair? Even if I put a much higher value on undisturbed sleep than do most people, the unusual costs involved for me in attending to my choking baby at night are not of the sort that counts in this moral calculus. However much I prefer my sleep to my children's lives, this sort of consideration carries no moral weight. To take another example, in defense to a criminal charge, I can plead that I succumbed to coercion when the threat was serious damage to my arm, but not when the threat was serious damage to my violin, even if I care more for my violin than for my arm (Fingarette 1985, 1981; *Model Penal Code*, sec. 209). The central point here is that the notion of an act's being voluntary involves value judgments about what behavior is fitting in particular contexts.

We cannot always be at our best, and inevitably we cannot always be minimally adequate. Why do we hold people to a standard of performance even though we know that everyone has periods when they cannot actually perform up to that level? One response is that ideally we would only hold people to a standard that they can at the time meet but that evidentiary problems beset personalizing a public standard to an individual's particular and momentary inabilities. This difficulty may account for the difference between social standards and legal standards, the former being more tailored to individual conditions.

Alternatively, it could be that we hold people to standards they cannot at times meet because we would be wrong to suppose that having standards can involve anything less demanding (Adams 1985). The problem for this perspective is that we do recognize inability as excusing one some of the time, and in light of this we need an account of why it is appropriate some times but not others.

A third possibility is that we hold people to a standard we know they cannot meet at times, because we think that having this standard helps people locate the resources to perform better than they otherwise would. The standard itself is a factor determining whether people will succeed in conforming to certain expectations. Having a less forgiving standard pushes individual motivations in a direction favorable for a desired outcome.

Having discussed standards and disabilities in general, I now shift to disabilities that are in some sense self-inflicted. If a potentially excusing impairment is self-inflicted, then though the agent cannot function at full throttle, the diminished capacity itself is attributable to the agent, and whatever failures the impairment effects, these too are attributable to the agent.

Various attitudes are attendant upon our characterization of behavior as resulting from an impaired condition. Problematic behavior that results from a nonblamable impairment, like an epileptic seizure, a narcoleptic nap, an abusive swearing associated with Tourette's disorder, are characteristically met with sympathy and consolation rather than with criticism and rebuke.

Recognizing this leads us to a problem. As we learn about how individual choices make impairments more or less likely, we tend to have less sympathy for those who are stricken with a disease attributable to personal habits or decisions. The familiar quip "Smoking cures cancer" reflects an emergent callousness toward those we think accountable for their frightful condition. In the same vein, those who acquire AIDS as a result of their own risky sexual practices or drug abuse are thought by many to be getting just what they deserve. As we learn more about how diet, exercise, patterns of relaxation, and other habits of life make one more or less prone to diseases of certain sorts, and how qualities of character make recovery variably likely, fewer and fewer afflictions come to be seen as completely out of personal control. Accordingly, we tend to show less compassion for the condition we regard as controllable.[1] As more about impairments comes to be connected to choice, less about a person will seem like a visitation and more will seem like the consequences of a blameworthy character defect. The upshot of this is to radically attenuate the conditions under which we will afford sympathetic responses to human suffering.

3 SOME UNNERVING DISCOVERIES

Some recent discoveries portend attributions of responsibility for many conditions that have been thought purely matters of fate. It was reported in the *New York Times* that new studies of people with multiple personalities suggest some fascinating prospects. For ease of description, let us say that body b is home for personalities $x, y,$ and z. Personality x, we are told, may be highly allergic to certain substances and develop a rash or hives when these substances are ingested or present in the environment. But if personality y emerges in b, the allergic reaction may readily dissipate. Given that allergies are generally not thought to be mind-mediated, this result is intriguing.

Reactions to drugs also may vary from personality to personality within the same body. Drugs that make y sleepy may have no effect on z. Finally, even the curvature of the eye may change from personality to personality. A prescription for corrective lenses for x may be completely inappropriate for y or z, these personalities requiring a prescription tailored to their individual cases. Again, who would have thought that brains or minds exercise control over reactions to drugs or the shape of the eyes? To know that these things occur is not yet to know how to control these phenomena, but it leaves open the prospect that someday allergies, reactions to drugs, and who knows what else, may be controllable by the agent affected.

Another recent study reported that people prone to cynical, hostile, and angry responses are more likely to suffer premature death from coronary and other causes (Blakeslee 1989). People so disposed are said to have "toxic personalities," probably traceable to biological characteristics present at birth.

There are studies that show the effect of confidence on the course of malignancies in people. Those convinced that they will lick the disease as a result of an optimistic and confident outlook are more likely to survive the disease than those whose outlook is more glum.

Of course, knowing that confidence about achieving a cure will help does not imply that it is within the person's control to place him or herself in the lower-risk group. Many, if not most, of us would be terrified by the diagnosis of a malignancy and find gratuitous and heartless the claim that if only we could have a bright outlook, we would have a fighting chance to survive (Sontag 1977).

Something similar to the bright-outlook factor just described is known about alcohol-abuse rehabilitation. Among problem drinkers, those with the outlook that their condition is one that they cannot control are less likely to control it than those who confront the problem with a different frame of mind about alcohol consumption.

> Social-cognitive models of alcoholism maintain that alcoholics' expectations and self-conceptions will influence how they respond to a single drink. Alcoholics who are convinced that there is no alternative after having a drink other than embarking on a binge will be more likely to undergo this chain of events ...
>
> The drinker's self-conception of being an alcoholic also affects the course of drinking problems. Subjective beliefs about the disease of alcoholism and about the nature of the person's drinking problem can be more important than objective levels of dependence for selecting treatment goals. Those who believe in the disease theory and that they are alcoholics have a poorer prognosis for controlled drinking. (Peele 1984, 1342–43)

Researchers are finding that qualities of character, cognitive beliefs, and directions of cultural identification are significant factors in the body's reaction to different kinds of assault or conditions and in the person's ability to dig himself out of a troubling situation.

Not all qualities of character have an impact for the same kind of reasons or even in roughly similar respects, but a body's reaction still turns out to be mediated by character, directly or indirectly. What is significant about this is that, as Aristotle informed us thousands of years ago, our character is itself something for which we are accountable. Once we have reached a mature age, we are assumed to have had ample opportunity to have dealt with those aspects of character that present problems. This outlook does not presuppose that people are not biologically or culturally disposed to be a certain way, but only that character is plastic enough to modify if one begins early to form the right habits. And though we may not have succeeded in extinguishing qualities we regard as undesirable or in nurturing those we deem admirable, we tend to see ourselves and others as responsible for whatever degree of success or level of failure achieved at any given time. Very little short of outright thought control or wholesale moral corruption insulates a person from accountability for the kind of adult he or she has become.

4 CONSEQUENCES OF THE RESPONSIBLE-FOR-CHARACTER VIEW

These comments about character are unexceptionable, but they do have implications. If the qualities of our character give us some measure of control over our reaction to environmental chemicals, disease agents, and diseased conditions, and if we use the standard criterion of having a measure of control to calibrate a level of accountability, then many of the things we regard as unattributable to agents may strictly be so attributable. The social function of the notion of a disease in mitigating moral blameworthiness becomes greatly attenuated.

We cannot rest content with the attenuation of sympathy and support for problems that result in part from qualities of character or choice. What must constitute a part of our outlook is a standard of reasonableness: what is it fair to expect of a person? It is not enough to demonstrate item by item that with attention and motivation, an individual could have improved each quality had he so chosen. For even if he could have changed each, he surely could not have improved *all* of his characteristics had he so chosen.

We also know that not all people face the same hurdles in developing their characters along certain lines. Some may find certain changes rewarding, while others find them continually at odds with something pressing inside of themselves. Some may find that just at the time they recognize the need for change, the stresses in their lives prevent them from being able to address life constructively.

Some may find external support for important changes, while others encounter discouragement for the same efforts at redirection. In his impressive attack on the disease notion of alcoholism and his reconceptualization of heavy drinking as a central activity of life, Herbert Fingarette observes, "One cannot simply and without consequences forsake a central activity, abandon a preferred coping strategy, or disable a defense mechanism – however costly it has proven to be" (1988, 122). A few pages later he continues, "But, as the data show, heavy drinkers who are motivated to change and who are persistent in the face of setbacks can change *if they are given* the appropriate tools and strategies for reshaping their lives" (1988, 128). These passages suggest that the degree to which change is possible, even for those highly motivated, will in many cases depend on factors over which a long-term heavy drinker will have limited or no control. Having a supportive family, economic opportunities, or alternative role models – these are not resources easily accessible to many. Not everyone has within reach the appropriate tools and strategies for restructuring life.

Two related cautionary themes, which I will develop below, emerge from this discussion. (1) The fact that a characteristic is not the result of a disease does not mean that the individual is in control of the trait. (2) Qualities of character are in varying and unstable degrees attributable to the individual.

5 CULTURE AND CHOICE OF VALUES

There is a tendency to think that if biological explanations of alcohol abuse are only one aspect of the problem, with cultural and individual factors looming large, it is simply up to the individual to control drinking patterns. Once we introduce cultural factors, matters become complicated in ways that I do not think are widely enough recognized or appreciated. Cultures and traditions have a strong influence over how a person will frame his or her experiences of the world. Cultures and traditions will also impose values, loyalties, and directions on its members. Although we like to say that people are responsible for the values they adopt from the cultures they occupy, there is something peculiar about this. The peculiarity lies in omitting consideration of the authority that the culture and traditions have over people. And having authority means that individuals are not, and do not see themselves as, entirely free to pick and choose from among its norms those worth embodying. Three reasons can be offered to support this claim. (1) Many alternatives to an outlook are never presented. We cannot say that people deliberately reject options not visible on their horizon. (2) Some options that upon consideration may seem preferable may not be real options. For instance, one might say that a prescientific outlook is preferable, because more humanly centered, to our outlook. Recognizing this does not make this alternative possible for us. (3) If people approach a tradition in the spirit of selective and reasoned embrace and rejection of what is taken as settled in the tradition, the culture or tradition is at best one of several overlapping cultures they feel part of and is one that has attenuated authority for them.

Some points deserve elaboration here. First, because we think that people should situate themselves within a culture, we must accept that they will come to accept some behavior or styles that people outside the culture find troublesome or misguided. We recognize that they will not approach all issues as ones to be settled by an objective, culturally neutral perspective. Second, even if people recognize that cultural values conflict with widely held norms, it is not clear that it is the saliently rational norms that should dominate whenever there is conflict. Let me illustrate. John Wideman (1984) makes clear in an autobiographical account that his rejection of ghetto values during adolescence came with enormous costs, since it cut him off from the vision, riches, and pains identified as the African-American experience, and thus from himself. As we learn more about the role of cultural identification, I believe we will also appreciate the limited authority an ethical scheme has over people's lives.

Learning is based on trust in certain formal and informal authorities; parents, teachers, community leaders, elected officials, religious leaders, role models, and the "successful" behavior patterns one sees around oneself. These paradigms of social learning, belonging, and participation, and thereby of moral being, are indispensable.

Our cognitive and moral economies require that we rely on such authorities for the bulk of our everyday judgments.

Solomon Asch (1961) suggests an interpretation of the observed shift of the individual's view of authoritative or peer assessment when there is a discrepancy – an interpretation involving a critical piece of social dynamics. Asch points out that conformity has been seen by psychologists as either the result of an effort to avoid social punishment or achieve social rewards on the one hand or as the effect of manipulation by those with power or authority on those without these qualities on the other hand. Either of these perspectives pre-supposes that the shift occurs in only one direction. Asch questions this presupposition, suggests that the shifts are bidirectional, and proposes that conformity can be seen as a group process that has the character of a group achievement. Conforming should not be judged as a distortion of individual rationality but as an essential factor in promoting social being.

In a speculative essay on social evolution, Donald Campbell (1975) suggests that a universal tendency for conformity to the opinions of prestige figures and others may be essential to the human capacity to retain socially adaptive customs and not the character defect typically discovered in those conforming. Campbell points out that for this mechanism to have succeeded in retaining adaptive social customs, the mechanism would have to "operate blindly, without regard to apparent functionality." This suggests that some strategies connected with sociability and traditions serve a role ignored by rational philosophical reconstructions that stress individual autonomy in value orientation.

6 ATTRIBUTING ALCOHOL-CONSUMPTION PATTERNS

In the case of alcohol-consumption patterns, considerable effort has been expended on assessing whether the most potent causal determinants to drinking are genetic, social, contextual, or individual. On the basis of what is currently known about alcohol use, I take it that, despite being strongly favored by treatment centers and some funding agencies, the genetic and the corresponding disease account of alcohol abuse are no longer uniquely strong contenders when it comes to explaining most troublesome drinking patterns. In contrast, cultural and contextual factors are now regarded as important in understanding alcohol abuse. To quote Peele again,

> Field studies have found demographic categories to play an important role in alcoholism. Calahan and Room (1974) identified youth, lower socioeconomic status, minority status (black or Hispanic), and other conventional ethnic categories (Irish versus Jewish and Italian) as predicting drinking problems. Greeley, McCready, and Theisen (1980) continued to find "ethnic drinking subcultures"

and their relationship to drinking problems to be extremely resilient and to have withstood the otherwise apparent assimilation by ethnic groups into mainstream American values. ... Vaillant (1983) found Irish Americans in his Boston sample to be alcohol dependent (i.e., alcoholic) seven times as often as those from Mediterranean backgrounds (Greeks, Italians, and Jews), and those in Vaillant's working class sample were alcohol dependent more than three times as often as those in his college sample. (Peele 1984; 1339–40)

Vaillant also found that return to moderate drinking versus abstinence was not a function of having alcoholic relatives but was related to the cultural group of the alcohol abuser. (Peele 1984, 1346–47)

There are a number of tempting inferences related to this discussion that are important to identify and discuss critically. The first of these is that if alcoholism is not a disease, then it is up to individuals to control their drinking.

What excuse does an individual have who transgresses legal or social norms while under the influence, or for drinking in the first place? The defense of blaming one's culture doesn't have much appeal in either a court of law or the court of public consciousness. This moral inference (no disease means individual responsibility) is also manifest in the majority Supreme Court opinion of *Traynor and McKelvey v. Turnage*, discussed above, which argued that if the cause of habitual drinking is not genetic or in other respects medical, the drinking behavior itself is "willful misconduct" and the habit a "willfully incurred disability."

In a dissenting opinion, Justice Blackmun argued that the plaintiffs deserved a particularized evaluation of the degree to which their alcoholism was voluntary, and therefore the Veterans Administration erred in making the presumption of voluntariness irrebuttable (*Traynor and McKelvey v. Turnage*). Blackmun pointed out that both Traynor and McKelvey began drinking at an early age: eight or nine in the case of Traynor and thirteen in the case of McKelvey. Alcohol dependence was widespread in McKelvey's family. In light of these facts, I think that we would want to follow Justice Blackmun by saying that even if alcoholism is not a disease in the classic sense, there are cases in which we would not want to hold the alcohol-dependent person blamable for his condition.

The focus on the presence or absence of disease in alcohol studies points to a restrictive set of alternatives. As indicated above, we tend to respond to people differently if we think that their behavior or demeanor is the result of a disease rather than the result of, what, something that is not a disease? If their behavior is the outcome of a disease, we will be supportive. If not, we will be critical if the behavior has transgressed some norm. But are these the only options: disease and support on the one hand and health and condemnation on the other? What if we know that someone is having a hard time for any of a variety of reasons and that there is a good prospect that, with the support and encouragement of others, this soul can muster the courage or effort or self-confidence to improve? Does the fact that he or she is not diseased require us to withhold our support and to insist that success, if it comes, will have to come without the encouragement of others? Or what if we believe that even with support, this person will fail for any of a variety of reasons? Is it clear, then, that we should be condemning?

We have a spectrum of responses available. Our thinking about what is fair to expect of people must respect the ambiguities implicit in our understanding of what individuals can do even if they are not diseased. Let me begin with a neutral example before turning to the alcohol-related context.

A runner will run faster in a race than when practicing. It is not that the runner will just try harder in a race but that there is added endurance, drive, and excitement, and hence capacity for running. This suggests that what abilities a person has depend at times on external factors. Furthermore, we know that confidence is an important factor in both creative and competitive contexts. It is uncontroversial to say that people will perform better, exhibit enhanced abilities, if they have confidence in themselves. Of course, we can say that in some situations, having confidence in one's ability is a function of having reasonable beliefs and certain character traits, that both these beliefs and traits are the responsibility of a mature individual, and that fault lies in underestimating what patterns of change are possible.

What we know about the effect of beliefs and objective contexts on abilities in the realm of sports also applies to the struggle with alcohol. We might find fairly reasonable the abject outlook a person adopts. He may see that his own efforts at change have thus far been unsuccessful. He may see that most of those around him have not managed any better. He may put stock in a cultural outlook that predicts failure for those like him. He may be aware of statistical studies that show that people with his profile fail at a rate of 70 percent or higher. Finally, he may find respected therapists substantiating his own dismal estimate of his native capacity to modify a bad habit.

The kind of understanding we afford people who have fallen short of our social ideals is often taken to be an ideological issue, pitting those who advocate hard-line views of responsibility against those who encourage compassion. But viewing it this way is a mistake. We all want our attributions of responsibility to reflect just standards. The question we must address is what does applying this standard require of us. Does it require us to ignore the individuating features of an individual's past, including socialization? Does it require us to ignore barriers, social and psychological, that stand in the way of many well-intentioned addicts' efforts at recovery? The issue is not one between justice and some more compassionate stance but between different visions of justice. What we learn from the history of this debate is that socially acceptable resolutions display features that reflect both objective and subjective conceptions of just attribution (Allen 1981, 69–71). Researchers err in thinking that new developments will radically change this mixture toward an illness model just as law-and-order visionaries err in thinking that the mixture will shift radically to the objective standard because we cannot scientifically prove that either socialization or biochemistry is the last word on patterns of alcohol abuse.

Alcohol abuse is a human problem unlikely to yield to straightforward scientific or moral analysis. This means that our moral attitudes and social policies are destined to fall on all sides of the issues. We will be forced both to insist on the responsibility of the heavy drinker and to afford rehabilitative services and prevention programs that to many, including those being serviced, suggest diminished accountability. It is not unusual now for alcohol abusers to be deemed responsible by a court and then sentenced to participate in programs that tell the abuser that he or she is not accountable for continuing patterns of drinking. However incoherent this compound picture strikes one as being, we don't have available a more satisfactory picture. Insisting on a coherent picture at this point may require us to ignore important considerations.

In thinking about the implications of the foregoing discussion, it might be useful to focus on an example that is less constrained by legal or constitutional complexities than was the case with which I began. Ralph Tarter described a dilemma for those who make decisions about liver transplants. Many people need liver transplants, but alcohol abusers are represented among this group out of proportion to their percentage in the general population. Should the fact that a person's liver became diseased through alcohol abuse be regarded as relevant when allocating the few livers that become available for transplant?

Here we might be tempted to finesse the issue by observing that a person with a record of abuse is a poor transplant prospect for medical reasons alone. (What will keep him from ruining the next liver with his uncontrolled drinking?) But in first considering the issue, without considering its being medically counterindicated, I confess to thinking that it is unfair to allocate scarce resources to someone who caused a problem when the same resources could be used to help someone who is innocent in the relevant sense. My second thought, though, was that this response is oblivious to most of what I have been worrying over in this paper. To the extent that we cannot make a determination of who is and who is not blameworthy for having ruined his or her liver, we must not use alcohol abuse as a morally disqualifying factor.[2] But as a social policy, should we put the same resources into seeking cures and treatments for diseases that are in some sense largely self-inflicted and those that are not, with everything else constant? I suggested above that we do not know where such a policy would lead in light of discoveries about character and diseases. On the other hand, we have a general, and probably salutary, attitude that discounts suffering on the part of people who knowingly enough risk behavior that is not regarded as socially valuable.

For medical treatment, we might want to argue that if choices must be made, they should be made on the basis of need, not desert, even though this *could* mean disregarding previous drinking patterns.[3] For allocating resources for development of cures, we might legitimately use avoidability as a criterion along with other criteria, like the number of people directly affected, the number of parties indirectly affected, the comparative efficiency of expenditures along given lines, etc. But the criterion of avoidability would have to apply to nearly all sufferers of a given malady, and it is very unlikely that we could fairly come to such a judgment.

7 CONCLUDING THOUGHTS

So what should we think? We should feel perplexed about our practices of attributing responsibility even as applied to as widespread and historically common a phenomenon as alcohol consumption. We should not think that science has failed us in not answering this question for us. We should appreciate that it is the community's responsibility to set standards of accountability that reflect and respect the limits and strengths of human nature.

Among the realizations we may come to is that the question of the responsibility of the heavy drinker for his or her behavior is not one issue but a range of issues; answers suitable in one domain may not be appropriate in another. Factors relevant to deciding what should be covered by standard medical-insurance plans are not necessarily those to be used in settling cases at law governing what benefits the Veterans Administration should be required to supply. Taking a public posture to reform social expectations about the degree of control drinkers should exercise may not prove helpful in addressing what to do with someone who for thirty years, has believed that drinking is not a matter of self-control.

Deciding as an individual or a society to be supportive and understanding toward someone burdened by alcohol abuse may not at all stem from a belief that the behavior patterns were outside anyone's control. One might think that a given individual's drinking problems are not attributable to anyone else but that there are so many tragic challenges this person has had to face that it is no wonder that his drinking is uncontrolled.

We may think no one else is to blame for a person's drinking problems but nevertheless regard the society as disqualified from making a moral judgment. For instance, one might argue that it is hypocritical for a society that socializes people to drink as a way of alleviating anxiety, expends enormous resources in advertising the desirability of alcohol consumption, and structures tax incentives to consumers who do this in a business setting, to then condemn people who drink excessively while facing real problems. Or one might think that a culture that neglects to offer services to a high percentage of troubled children cannot legitimately complain when these same children adopt nonconstructive patterns of coping with these problems, patterns that become entrenched character traits. Alternatively, policy considerations might well lure us into treating alcohol-dependent people as accountable though we know that some significant percentage of these are unfairly blamed. A range of factors relevant to some of these determinations may well be irrelevant to others.

Depending on the setting, there may already be in place a deliberative body able to make an individualized assessment of the degree to which an individual is blameworthy for his alcohol dependency. In the context of a criminal trial, there already is such a body. In the case of a potential recipient for an organ transplant, there also already is a body that can try to make an individualized determination of the potential recipient's accountability for his or her condition. In the case of extensions of veterans' benefits for alcohol-dependent people, we may ask how much it would add to the administrative costs of the Veterans Administration to allow veterans who want to claim that their drinking is involuntary to be provided with a forum for evaluating this claim.

In conclusion, let me point to some considerations that can help explain our conflicting attitudes about the alcohol-dependent person, exemplifying a whole range of human problems and resolving practically what our responses to such issues should be. In my discussion of disease and responsibility thus far, I have been assuming that there is one level of ability or competence such that, whatever is at stake in the context, if the individual meets that level, he is accountable, otherwise not. If we look at how we generally attribute responsibility for behavior, seeing when we say that the act was the agent's and when not, we find no one level of competence satisfying all behavior contexts.

We generally attribute responsibility for behavior to an individual when we do not find some aspect of the environment, external or internal, "overwhelming." The assessment of when pressures are overwhelming, however, cannot be made in terms of the levels of the pressures by themselves. This point can be illustrated with reference to the notion of coercion. The concept of coercion is relevant here because it is used as a way of gauging whether a person's behavior reflects, or is an expression of, the person's will. An intricate array of reasons is relevant to assessing whether an agent is to be regarded as the author of her action. Compare the following two situations: I agree to sell you my house for $10,000 because you threaten to slash my face unless I do so. During a recession when I lose my job and have no prospect of another, I agree to sell my house for one tenth its value ($10,000) so that I can afford to keep myself and family from starvation. Though the prospect of death by starvation is more fearsome than the prospect of a scarred face, the latter agreement is regarded as more binding than the former, less an undermining of the agent's real will. If a policeman subtly pressures a suspect in a custodial setting, a resulting confession is regarded as forced and hence not the product of the defendant's will, while if a doctor tells me that unless I submit to a procedure I will die of natural causes, my consent to the procedure is regarded as voluntary and representing my real (very scared) self.[4]

Recognizing that there is a variable standard of accountability and attribution helps us see first of all why we may have conflicting attitudes in thinking about alcoholism and similar problems. An impairment, like fatigue, is serious enough that for most contexts, the impairment counts as an excuse from accountability, but in some very serious contexts, like driving or sentry duty, it does not. By and large, then, we have reason to be supportive and forgiving toward the person who falls below the standard in most contexts, but not toward people who fall below it in some contexts. In the case of the alcohol-dependent person, we can be forgiving and supportive for some behavior but not for behavior that seriously endangers others.

Let me illustrate with a recent affair: Brozan 1989. Hedda Nussbaum acquiesced in the abuse and eventual murder of her adopted daughter. Nussbaum herself had been the victim of repeated, serious abuse. Does her own victimization excuse her from accountability for her daughter's death? One can coherently say that suffering abuse would excuse her from a lot of personal failings but not for standing by while her daughter is killed.

In cases such as the one described, *up to a point* we would be supportive, compassionate, and, if necessary, forgiving toward Hedda Nussbaum, because of what she had to endure. Her situation calls for compassion and understanding, and these emotions and attitudes toward her are apposite. It would also be odd to suggest that we can just turn these emotions off at the threshold where we judge her condition no longer excusing. We feel that she does deserve our sympathy, even if she deserves a harsher response too. Though these responses conflict, they are not contradictory or ungrounded. And this is my first point. We have an explanation for conflicting attitudes: sympathy and support for conditions that excuse for many contexts, and resentment for violating norms that even disadvantaged people should not violate. (After all, it cannot be that only nondisadvantaged people can do wrong. If there are normal people who are cowardly or lack integrity, why should there not also be condemnable cowards and scoundrels among the disadvantaged?)

To return to the alcohol-dependent person, we can be sympathetic, understanding, supportive, and forgiving for a wide variety of behaviors without precluding legitimate expressions of resentment for some serious or important failings. We are not limited to one response. The alcohol-dependent person, the abused spouse, the disadvantaged – all deserve our support, sympathy, and constructive endeavors on their behalf. But they, like the rest of us, also live in a community with values that can be more demanding for some ranges of behavior than for others. We can and should be supportive when something we can do addresses a human problem. We can and should be resentful when someone, even with a problem, doesn't show enough judgment or restraint.

How do we tell when asking something of a person is asking too much? Without thinking that I can answer this question, I want to emphasize that this is a moral or social question for which biological and psychological data are relevant but not decisive (Fingarette 1972). All I can offer here is the observation that what we often take to be conflicting outlooks toward heavy drinking are more appropriately seen as reasonable responses to separate objective aspects of a perplexing problem.[5]

ACKNOWLEDGMENTS

A special expression of appreciation is due to Herbert Fingarette, not only for published pieces that provoked many of the thoughts contained in this chapter but also for especially gracious and elaborate suggestions lavished on an earlier version of it. I also wish to thank Elizabeth Patterson, Frank Zimring, Pat Hubbard, Nora Bell, William McAninch, George Schroeder, Natalie Kaufman, Mary Bockover, and Kaye Middleton Fillmore for valuable comments on an earlier version of this paper. I am also indebted to the National Endowment for the Humanities for financial support during the time that this paper was written and to the Earl Warren Legal Institute at the University of California at Berkeley and the Law School at the University of South Carolina for providing ideal academic environments.

NOTES

This paper is a shortened version of a paper originally appearing in Mary Bockover, ed., *Rules, Rituals, and Responsibility* (Chicago: Open Court Publishing Co., 1991). Copyright of that article is in the name of the author.

1 This does not pertain just to vulnerability to diseases. It is a human tendency to regard increasing one's vulnerability to harm from any source as a fault and as attenuating the sympathy others should address to one. If I leave my bicycle or house unlocked when I go for a vacation, there will be less sympathy for my loss than if I had secured these and was robbed anyway. Similarly, if I am robbed while walking through Central Park at 3:00 A.M. with $100 bills pinned to my shirt, few will be sympathetic to my plight.

2 Jane Jacobs reported that it is common to find families of continual drinkers adopting the attitude that the drinker has no choice and families of binge drinkers adopting the view that if the person does in fact resist drinking most of the time, then the drinker does have control over those times when the drinking recurs. My own predilection is for trusting the attitudes of those who (have to) live with people with problems.

3 In *Allen v. Mansour*, Allen, a 27-year-old suffering from end-stage liver disease caused by consumption of alcohol, wanted Medicaid to pay for a liver transplant. At this time Allen had abstained from drinking for four months, but the authorizing body had a policy of

not authorizing transplants for liver disease for alcohol-dependent people who had not been abstemious for at least two years. Speaking for the court, Chief Judge Pratt found that the two-year policy was arbitrary. Although the court granted Allen his injunction, by the time it was issued, his condition deteriorated to the point that he could no longer be operated on. Cases like this are tragic, and whatever one's principles are, they seem to melt before the facts of a person's desperate yet treatable condition.

4 Not all rightful threats fail to count as coercion, as is evidenced in the centrality of legal coercion to criminal law (Wertheimer 1987).

5 I want to thank Herbert Fingarette for suggesting the line of thinking that I pursue in this concluding section.

REFERENCES

Adams, Robert. 1985. "Involuntary Sins." *Philosophical Review* 96:3–32.

Allen v. Mansour. 681 F. Supp. 1232 (E.D. Mich. 1986).

Allen, Francis. 1981. *The Decline of the Rehabilitative Ideal: Penal Policy and Social Purpose.* New Haven: Yale University Press.

Asch, Solomon. 1961. "Issues in the Study of Social Influences on Judgment." In *Conformity and Deviation*, ed. Irwin Berg and Bernard Bass. New York: Harper and Brothers.

Blakeslee, Sandra. 1989. "Cynicism and Mistrust Linked to Early Death." *New York Times*, January 17, p. 21.

Brozan, Nadine. 1989. "Unresolved Question: Is Nussbaum Culpable?" *New York Times*, January 24, p. 15.

Calahan, D., and R. Room. 1974. *Problem Drinking among American Men.* New Brunswick, N.J.: Rutgers Center for Alcohol Studies.

Campbell, Donald. 1975. "On the Conflicts between Biological and Social Evolution and between Psychology and Moral Tradition." *American Psychologist* 30:1003–1126.

Fingarette, Herbert. 1971. "The Perils of Powell: In Search of a Factual Foundation for the Disease Concept of Alcoholism." *Harvard Law Review* 83:793–812.

Fingarette, Herbert. 1972. *The Meaning of Criminal Insanity.* Berkeley: University of California Press.

Fingarette, Herbert. 1981. "Legal Aspects of Alcoholism and Other Addictions: Some Basic Conceptual Issues." *British Journal of Addiction* 76:125–32.

Fingarette, Herbert. 1985. "Victimization: A Legalist Analysis of Coercion, Deception, Undue Influence, and Excusable Prison Escape." *Washington and Lee Law Review* 42:65–118.

Fingarette, Herbert. 1988. *Heavy Drinking: The Myth of Alcoholism as a Disease.* Berkeley: University of California Press.

Greeley, A. M., N. C. McCready, and G. Theisen. 1980. *Ethnic Drinking Subcultures.* New York: Praeger.

Model Penal Code and Commentaries. 1985. Philadelphia: American Law Institute.

Peele, Stanton. 1984. "Cultural Context of Psychological Approaches to Alcoholism." *American Psychologist* 39:1337–51.

Sontag, Susan. 1977. *Illness as Metaphor.* New York: Farrar, Straus, and Giroux.

Traynor and McKelvey v. Turnage. 108 S. Ct. 1372 (1988).

Vaillant, G. E. 1983. *The Natural History of Alcoholism: Causes, Patterns, and Paths to Recovery.* Cambridge: Harvard University Press.

Wertheimer, Alan. 1987. *Coercion.* Princeton: Princeton University Press.

Wideman, John. 1984. *Brothers and Keepers.* New York: Holt, Reinhart, and Winston.

Part 7

HOW CAN WE KNOW WHETHER—AND WHAT—NON-HUMAN ANIMALS THINK?

We are often tempted to attribute thoughts and feelings to things that obviously don't have any. We might say of an old car struggling up a steep hill that it's *trying* to get to the top but is just too *tired* to make it. A copy machine might not *want* to *cooperate*, and a watch might *like* to run a little fast. These examples of *anthropomorphism* are easily excused. We know that cars, printers, and watches don't really have beliefs, desires, and other mental states. We may easily speak *as if* these objects have the mental capacities of human beings, but few, when pressed, would insist on it.

The situation is not so clear when we ask about the mental lives of nonhuman animals. When food spills into Sylvia the cat's food dish, she comes running from wherever in the house she's been napping. Is she dashing toward the bowl because she *desires* to eat and *believes* that there is food in the bowl? When Sylvia *wants* someone to pet her, she will rub against the person's leg. Does she *believe* that by doing this the person will *recognize* that her ears need scratching? All this is possible, but there are other explanations that do not require attributing to Sylvia any such mental states. Perhaps the sound of the food hitting the bowl is a stimulus that has come to trigger in Sylvia the behavior she then exhibits. Maybe her response to the sound is as mechanical and thoughtless as the response Pavlov's dogs showed to the ringing bell. If this account is correct, she has no belief at all about the food. Similarly, perhaps Sylvia comes to associate rubbing against someone's leg with having her ears scratched. There is no need to suppose that Sylvia *believes* that the person will *understand* that she *wants* her ears scratched.

The story of Clever Hans drives home the need for caution when assigning sophisticated cognitive abilities to nonhuman animals. Clever Hans was an early twentieth century horse whose owner claimed to have trained him to do arithmetic. Hans would answer questions put to him by tapping his hoof an appropriate number of times. He was quite a celebrity in his day, amazing large crowds with his intelligence. Skeptical, the philosopher and psychologist Carl Stumpf subjected Hans to various experiments. His results were conclusive. Hans was not so clever after all. In fact, Hans was expert at reading his owner's (as well as others') expressions as he tapped out his answers. When Hans' hoof hit the ground the correct number of times, his observers would unwittingly sigh or indicate in other ways that the answer had been reached. When this happened, Hans would stop tapping. Since Stumpf's discovery of the truth behind Hans' behavior, nonhuman animal researchers have been on their guard for what is now called the Clever Hans effect.

Even before Clever Hans fell into disrepute, some scientists had urged caution in attributing mental states to nonhuman animals. Perhaps the most famous of these warnings came from the British geologist, zoologist, and psychologist C. Lloyd Morgan. In his *An Introduction to Comparative Psychology* (1894), Morgan wrote "In no case may we interpret an action as the outcome of the exercise of a higher psychical faculty, if it can be interpreted as the outcome of the exercise of one which stands lower in the psychological scale" (p. 53). This general principle has subsequently been dubbed Morgan's Canon and is routinely cited by nonhuman animal psychologists to this day.

But what justifies Morgan's Canon? We have already seen that it is possible to explain why my cat Sylvia scampers toward her food dish without having to assume that she has beliefs about or desires for food. Given that this is so, an application of Morgan's Canon would require us to deny that Sylvia has beliefs and desires, at least regarding food. Morgan's Canon might also lead us to deny that Sylvia feels pain when she falls from a tree. She's limping and crying not because her foot *hurts*, but because the damage to her foot simply causes her to limp and cry—just as a damaged exhaust system might cause an old car to move haltingly and sputter. Clearly a principle that would cast doubt on the existence of a feeling so basic as pain needs careful examination.

Jonathan Bennett undertakes to do just this. Morgan's Canon, or what Bennett calls the *economy rule*, does not deny that nonhuman animals might have beliefs, desires, and other mental states. It states simply that researchers should not suppose that nonhuman animals have these things unless the evidence demands that they do so. But, Bennett asks, what sort of evidence favors a mentalistic explanation of behavior over a purely mechanistic one? In short, Bennett's answer is that mentalistic explanations are better than mechanistic ones when they are the more economical of the two.

To see how this might work, consider Sylvia once more. Suppose she comes running to her food bowl not only when she hears the sound of food falling into it, but also when the clock strikes ten, or when it is announced that it is time to eat, or when the children come home from school, or when she sees her owner close a book, and so on for tens or maybe hundreds of different kinds of stimuli. These various stimuli have, we can suppose, nothing in common except for the fact that they each provide evidence that Sylvia is about to be fed. If Sylvia can respond appropriately to these numerous and distinct kinds of evidence, the hypothesis that she *believes* she is about to be fed is more economical than the hypothesis that Sylvia is equipped with tens or maybe hundreds of stimulus-response mechanisms. Attributing to Sylvia the belief that she is about to be fed *unifies* Sylvia's behavior across the great span of stimuli to which she is responding, and it is this that justifies the mentalistic explanation.

But how far can this justification for mentalistic explanations be pushed? Can it be used to justify the claim that Sylvia rubs against her owner's leg because she *believes* that when she does he will *recognize* that she *wants* her ears scratched? Attributions like these, in which Sylvia has beliefs not just about objects or events in the world but also about how to produce beliefs in others, would seem to demand much richer sources of evidence. Bennett outlines a method that might help us to judge when a nonhuman animal has a desire to produce a belief in another. However, even Bennett is uncertain whether we can ever be in a position to acquire the evidence that, he thinks, is decisive.

As Bennett acknowledges at the end of his article, he is inclined to see beliefs and other mental states as entities of some sort that reside in the heads of those experiencing them. But there is another way to construe mental states. Perhaps attributions of belief do not entail the existence of internal states. If this is right, the question whether nonhuman animals have minds turns out *not* to be a question about whether there is sufficient evidence to assign internal mental states to them. John Dupré defends this view in the second article of this section.

Following Wittgenstein, Dupré rejects the Cartesian conception of minds according to which mental states are internal, 'private' states, directly known only to their possessor. Were this true, Dupré (again, following Wittgenstein) argues, it would be impossible to explain the meanings of words like 'pain.' For, if 'pain' referred to an essentially private experience, there could be no assurance that you and I use the word 'pain' to refer to the same kind of thing. But, clearly we can use the word 'pain' in the same way: we share an understanding of the meaning of 'pain.' This suggests that the meaning of 'pain' must be publicly accessible. Dupré concludes that 'pain' cannot refer to something to which we have only first person access.

The question of nonhuman animal minds, for Dupré, is thus no different from the question of other minds in general—including human minds. The right question to ask is how we explain the meaning of terms like 'pain,' 'belief,' 'desire,' 'intelligence,' and so on. Given that these terms are not explained by pointing to some essentially private internal state, they must be explicable in some other manner. Dupré suggests that we come to understand the meaning of these terms by acquainting ourselves with the criteria for their correct application, and these criteria are publicly observable behaviors. Thus, to explain the meaning of 'pain' is to explain that the term correctly applies to organisms—human or otherwise—that writhe, or cry, or moan, or exhibit other conspicuous behaviors of this sort. Crucially, these behaviors are not symptoms of or evidence for an internal pain state. Supposing that they are marks a retreat toward the Cartesian conception of minds that Dupré wishes to reject. Rather, these behaviors are constitutive of pain. They are what an organism does in virtue of which we are correct in using the word 'pain' when describing the organism.

If Dupré is right, many kinds of nonhuman animals have minds. Clearly Sylvia believes that there is food in the bowl. After all, her behavior satisfies any reasonable set of criteria for what it means to believe that there is food in the bowl. Likewise, Sylvia obviously *wants* her ears scratched for, again, her behavior satisfies reasonable criteria for the application of the word 'want.' But, as Dupré concedes, this Wittgensteinian approach to nonhuman minds has its limits. For it is difficult to see what sorts of behavioral criteria could constitute more sophisticated mental states. What behavior must Sylvia exhibit before we are satisfied that we can correctly describe her as *wanting me to understand that she desires to have her ears scratched*? Because non-human animals cannot speak, and presumably speech behavior will be centrally important to the attribution of more complex mental states, our confidence that we have correctly applied mental state terms to them would seem never to be as strong as when applying these terms to human beings. Perhaps, then, Dupré's position faces challenges similar to those with which Bennett wrestles.

The discussions by Bennett and Dupré illustrate the limitations of purely conceptual work on animal minds. In light of these limitations, it will be instructive to examine some genuine empirical efforts to understand nonhuman animal minds. Gordon Gallup's article introduces a now classic experimental result. Gallup anesthetized chimpanzees and then placed a red dot on their forehead while they were unconscious. When conscious again and placed in front of a mirror, the chimps would touch the dot on their foreheads. Gallup believes that this behavior indicates that the chimps are self-aware. The chimp must know that the image in the mirror is a reflection of itself, for otherwise it would not explore the red dot on its own forehead. Interestingly, gorillas do not exhibit this behavior. In fact, chimps, orangutans, and human beings (older than two) are the only apes that seem to understand that when looking in a mirror they are seeing themselves.

Self awareness, Gallup thinks, is a foundation for other mental capacities, especially empathy, i.e. the ability to recognize that others in situations similar to one's own have mental states akin to one's own. Thus, Gallup predicts, a chimp that has experience with blindfolds ought to know that other chimps cannot see when wearing a blindfold. However, it is precisely this prediction that Daniel Povinelli, in his article, repudiates.

In a series of experiments, Povinelli found that chimps were as likely to make gestures for food to a person with a bucket over his head as they were to a person who had no bucket over his head. Because these chimps knew that buckets prevented themselves from seeing, they should, according to Gallup, realize that buckets would prevent others from seeing. But then why were they as likely to beg from the blinded person as the sighted one? Results like these, Povinelli thinks, cast serious doubt on Gallup's claim that chimps can empathize.

But what of Gallup's assertion that chimps can recognize themselves in the mirror? The chimp's behavior seems to drive us to this account. Yet Povinelli believes that, in explaining the chimps' behavior, we need not credit them with the robust self awareness that Gallup ascribes to them. Rather than thinking "that's me" when a chimp looks in a mirror, Povinelli suggests that they think something like "that thing in the mirror is just like me." But is Povinelli's account as compelling as Gallup's? How might the two hypotheses be tested against each other?

The final pair of readings illustrate the methods and resources on which animal researchers draw when attempting to answer questions about whether nonhuman primates have sophisticated cognitive abilities, such as an ability to deceive members of one's own kind, or to understand numbers, or to communicate with language. Sue Savage Rumbaugh has devoted much of her life to the study of linguistic abilities in (nonhuman) apes. Her intent has been to advance our understanding of these abilities beyond that which earlier efforts to teach American Sign Language to chimpanzees provided. Her investigations have not only revealed the existence of impressive linguistic abilities among bonobos (a close relative of the chimpanzee), but have also produced insights into the nature of language. Earlier studies of nonhuman primate language, she argues, failed to appreciate the extent to which language functions to coordinate actions between communicators. Accordingly, rather than trying to train an ape to associate symbols with objects, Savage Rumbaugh has raised bonobos in a linguistic environment similar to that which human children experience; rather than simply expecting her bonobos to express their desires with symbols, she has encouraged them to 'speak' to each other.

Savage Rumbaugh *et al.* argue forcefully that bonobo minds and human minds belong on a continuum. Savage Rumbaugh *et al.* has no patience for the old Cartesian view that minds are distinctively human and that language is a capacity inherent only to human minds. In contrast, Daniel Povinelli, in his second article of this section, continues to urge a more deflationary account of nonhuman primate abilities. Povinelli would clearly charge Savage Rumbaugh with anthropomorphizing the mental abilities of her bonobos. Doubtless he would deny that bonobos are capable of the variety of beliefs and desires that Savage Rumbaugh believes they express with their language. Povinelli describes a series of experiments that he and colleagues performed which, he thinks, shows conclusively that chimpanzees are unable to attribute beliefs to others. Moreover, Povinelli rejects the idea that chimpanzees might have ideas of abstract physical forces like gravity or causation. Finally, Povinelli believes he has demonstrated that chimps are incapable of forming ideas about numbers.

So, what is it like to be a chimp? Povinelli argues that the chimpanzee's understanding of the world is limited to only what it can observe. Insofar as other minds, physical forces, and numbers are unobservable abstractions, these things fall outside the chimp's conception of the world. However, Povinelli proposes, there is no reason to lament the fact that human beings are the only species capable of thinking about unobservables. For even if nonhuman primate minds differ in kind from human ones – a claim that Povinelli accepts, but Savage Rumbaugh would likely reject – they are no less minds for all that. Povinelli concludes that the topic of nonhuman primate minds is fascinating in their own right; and, in a twist, he suggests that the attempt to establish that nonhuman primate minds are similar to human minds reflects a failure to appreciate that primate minds are worth studying in their own terms.

QUESTIONS TO THINK ABOUT

1 Morgan's Canon, or what Bennett calls the *economy rule*, seems to embody the dictum that the simpler explanation should be preferred. Think about the studies that the authors in this section describe. Are the explanations of behavior that attribute minds to nonhuman animals less simple than those that do not? Are they more simple? Might mentalistic explanations be simpler in some cases and not others? If so, when are they simpler and why?

2 Does Dupré's conception of mind differ in name only from what he calls the 'Cartesian' conception? What is lost if we cease to think of minds and mental states as entities and instead conceive of them in the way Dupré suggests – that is, as constituted by behavioral criteria? Might there be a way to experimentally test Dupré's conception of mind against the Cartesian conception?

3 Gallup thinks that the chimp's behavior in front of a mirror shows that the chimp is capable of recognizing itself. What, exactly, is Povinelli's alternative account? Is it really, as he claims, equally plausible? Can you think of any other alternative explanations of the chimp's behavior that would not require the attribution of self-awareness; if so, how plausible are they?

4 Some of Savage Rumbaugh's confidence that nonhuman apes can be taught language rests on anecdotal evidence, such as nonreplicable observations of novel linguistic episodes. How valuable is this evidence? Might anecdotal evidence be a better guide to understanding an ape's linguistic capacities than it is to understanding capacities of other sorts? Why?

5 Povinelli rejects the question "Can animals think?" in favor of "How does thinking differ across species?" Why is this second question preferable? What lines of research does it suggest that the first question does not?

6 Why does it matter whether nonhuman animals have minds, or whether they have minds similar to human minds? What sort of issues would an answer to the question of nonhuman animal minds help us to resolve?

FURTHER READING

Bekoff, M., Allen, C., and Burghardt, G. (2002). *The Cognitive Animal* (Cambridge, MA: The MIT Press).

Cheney, D. L. and Seyfarth, R. M. (1990). *How Monkeys See the World: Inside the Mind of Another Species* (Chicago: Chicago University Press).

de Waal, F., ed. (2001). *Tree of Origin: What Primate Behavior Can Tell Us about Human Social Evolution* (Cambridge, MA: Harvard University Press).

Hauser, M. (2000). *Wild Minds: What Animals Really Think* (New York: Henry Holt).

Gould, J., and Gould, C. (1994). *The Animal Mind* (New York: Scientific American Library).

Povinelli, D. (2000). *Folk Physics for Apes: the Chimpanzee's Theory of How the World Works* (New York: Oxford University Press).

Tomasello, M. and Call, J. (1997). *Primate Cognition* (New York: Oxford University Press).

30

HOW TO READ MINDS IN BEHAVIOUR: A SUGGESTION FROM A PHILOSOPHER

Jonathan Bennett

1 INTRODUCTION

Underlying empirical questions about how human and non-human animals behave and why, is this: By what formula should we go from premises about behaviour to conclusions about thoughts? In discussing this I shall focus on two thoughtful states – belief and desire.

Neither of these can help to explain behaviour except when combined with the other. Behaviour shows what the animal wants only if we know what it thinks, and conversely. The guiding idea is triangular: cognitive explanations of behaviour are possible only because the animal *does* what it *thinks* will produce what it *wants*.

So we need to build our account of an animal's beliefs and desires by tackling both at once. That might seem to expose our theory to the risk of vacuity, leaving too unconstrained a choice about what thoughts and wants to attribute to the animal because whatever we say under one heading can be made to fit the behaviour by an adjustment under the other. The animal uttered that piercing scream because it wanted to eat the eagle and thought that the scream would make the eagle fall dead. That is absurd, of course; but we should be able to reject it for some more disciplined reason than that – we need a principled, theoretical protection against uncontrollably free trade-offs between the attributions of beliefs and the attributions of desires.

We are somewhat protected because we can connect attributions of beliefs to facts about the animal's environment. The tie must be mediated by theory about what the animal is sensitive to, but there are ways of checking on that. We are further protected because we can safely attribute to animals knowable changes in the animal's condition – it wanted food an hour ago but since then it has gorged, and so on. That constancy lets us check attributions of desires at one time against later attributions; and that constrains attributions further, helping to stop the slide into absurdity. If the constancy were not there, and an animal's basic desires changed rapidly with no external pointers to the changes, its behaviour would be unpredictable and therefore unexplainable. For evolutionary reasons, however, there are no such animals.

I shall now take for granted that we have principled ways of avoiding interpretations of animal behaviour that are absurd and obviously not worth entertaining.

That, however, leaves plenty of choices needing to be made, and plenty of disagreements about them. I want to clarify what is at stake in those disagreements and help to resolve them. When front-line workers on animal cognition disagree about what states of mind are revealed by what behaviour, they often seem not to agree about what evidence *would* settle the disputes. Everyday working and arguing standards seem to be insecure and idiosyncratic, and that is the situation in which I shall offer some ideas that may be helpful.

2 THE ECONOMY RULE

One popular methodological idea is the view that we should always explain behaviour as economically as possible: don't attribute cognitive states to an animal whose behaviour you can explain without invoking them, and in our cognitive attributions don't go 'higher' on the scale than is needed to explain the behaviour. This 'economy rule' condemns saying that when the chimpanzee Sherman made the sign for a rake he wanted Austin to *think that he (Sherman) wanted the rake*, because the behaviour could as well be covered by supposing that Sherman merely wanted Austin to *bring the rake*. That condemnation seems right, and probably a lot of what goes wrong in psychology and cognitive ethology comes from the kind of interpretative over-reaching that the economy rule forbids.

However, the rule could not do all our work for us. If we have competing cognitive explanations that do not differ in complexity, sophistication, or whatever it is that feeds into the notion of 'higher', the rule is silent. There, at least, we need more theory.

Even where the economy rule does have something to say, we should ask for its credentials. *Why* should we always accept the 'lower' or more economical of two unrefuted explanations? Is it because we should always assume things to be homogeneous or unstructured unless we have positive evidence to the contrary? But then why should we believe that?

Having accepted the economy rule for years, I now think that we have mistaken its status, and that no deep truth underlies it. I shall justify this in the next two sections.

3 THE ECONOMY RULE AS ADVICE

If the rival explanations are not empirically equivalent – if they predict different behaviour – then we should look for or try to elicit further behaviour that fits only one of them. Suppose we are trying to decide whether, when the animal screams like that, this is because it wants others to climb trees or because it wants them to think there is a leopard nearby. Then we should simply try to find out which of these is right. These hypotheses differ in what they imply for the animal's behaviour, I shall argue, and that behaviour should be the final arbiter. The economy rule does no real work here.

Still, it might function as good advice, telling us to expect that the behavioural data will eventually favour the 'lower' rather than the 'higher' hypothesis, and perhaps advising us to adopt the former as our provisional opinion until the facts are in. This may be generally good advice, but only because on our planet most mentality happens to be fairly low-level. There could be planets where most vaguely goal-seeking behaviour really did involve cognition, and high-level cognition at that; on such planets the advice issued by the economy rule would be bad.

Because I am interested in the *foundations* of the activity of attributing cognitive states on the strength of behaviour, I exclude linguistic behaviour. Much cognition is expressed without language, and we need to understand how. Also, even where language is present, we can recognize it as language – can know that the speaker means something – only because we can, independently of language, discover things about what he thinks and wants, (so I argue in Bennett 1976). But although I exclude language, my 'animals' include very young humans; and where they are concerned the economy rule's advice – 'Expect the "lower" hypothesis to be right' – may be bad.

Andrew Whiten has remarked that the same might be true for chimpanzees. I agree. Some observed chimpanzee behaviour certainly 'feels' like an expression of fairly high-level cognition (see for example the best cases in Whiten and Byrne 1988a, chapter 9), and even where one can produce a 'lower', deflating explanation of the data (as in Bennett 1988a) we may reasonably suspect that in some cases a 'higher' explanation is right. Eventually, however, suspicion should give way to firm evidence.

That, incidentally, will often require not merely hands-off observation of animals' natural behaviour but also conduct that is elicited from the animals by experimentally rigging their environments and their experience. Experiments involve certain theoretical risks, which are the price for great practical advantages. Hands-off work is the best *if it can be done*; but I conjecture that definitive answers to our questions will always require experiments. (For good remarks on this, see Dennett 1988 and forthcoming.)

4 EMPIRICALLY EQUIVALENT RIVALS

There can be rivalry between hypotheses which, though one goes 'higher' than the other, are empirically equivalent. The 'higher' one must include something explaining why the extra psychological capacity is not used. The lower one might be:

L: The animal has the concepts of one, two, and three, and the concept of equal-numberedness, but not the number four,

and its rival:

H: The animal has the concepts one, two, three, four, and equal-numberedness, but it cannot use its concept of four except in doing number comparisons between quartets and other groups.

How could we choose between these? Well, H credits the animal with two more items than L does – namely an extra concept, and a blockage to its exercise – so it makes the animal more complex than L does. Whether we should accept H depends on whether we can justify the extra complexity.

What would justify it? Well, in developing a theory of the animal's internal cognitive dynamics – about how some changes in its beliefs lead to others – we might find that our smoothest explanation for its grasp of one, two and three implies that it also has the concept of four; and we might have evidence for its having a natural class of cognitive obstacles that would include an inability to employ *four* except in that one way. In that (admittedly fanciful) case, we should prefer H; but without something like that L should be preferred, not because it is lower but because it is less complex and greater complexity is not justified. This coincides with what the economy rule says, but it comes not from that rule but from perfectly general considerations about simplicity and complexity.

5 A FIRST STAB AT ANSWERING MY QUESTION

Faced with rival hypotheses that have different empirical consequences, I said, we should get evidence that knocks out one of them. That is easier said than done. Even harder than devising and conducting the tests is figuring out what would count as evidence for or against an hypothesis. That was my initial question: What behaviour indicates what states of mind? So far, all I have done is to take the economy rule down from the throne, while not banishing it from court. Let us start again.

Any explanation of animal behaviour is answerable to a *class* of behavioural episodes. If we have only one episode to go on, we can interpret it only by guessing what *would* happen on other relevant occasions. I shall assume henceforth that we are always trying to explain a longish sequence of behaviours, trying to bring them all under a single explanation.

Suppose we have observed a class of behaviours of which something of this form is true: 'Whenever the animal receives a stimulus of sensory kind S, it engages in behaviour of motor kind M.' For example: Whenever its visual field presents a clear sky with a black patch near the middle of it, and occupying at least one per cent of the field, the animal utters a specific kind of noise.

Here are two rival explanations for this behaviour. (1) The animal has an innate or acquired stimulus–response disposition; it is hard- or soft-wired to make that noise upon receipt of that visual stimulus. On each occasion in the class it received such a stimulus and accordingly made the noise. (2) The animal has the safety of its group as a goal. On each occasion in the class it thought it saw a predator and called to warn others of danger.

To test (1) we should vary the circumstances while still presenting that kind of stimulus, and see whether the animal still gives that call. To the extent that it does, the hypothesis is confirmed. Of course, the call might be triggered by another kind (or other kinds) of stimulus as well. Suppose we discover that the animal does also make such a cry whenever it gets a stimulus of some third kind, then a fourth, a fifth ... and on into dozens of different kinds of sensory intake, each leading to the same kind of behaviour. If this happens, we are under increasing pressure to find some unifying account of all this behaviour, some *one* explanation to replace the multitude of separate stimulus–response ones that we have accumulated.

(1) There might be no way of doing this. (2) Or we might find that there is after all a single sensory kind of stimulus on all the occasions – a subtle smell or a high-pitched sound – enabling us to cover all the cries by a single stimulus–response generalization, after all. (3) Or we might find that we could bring all the episodes under a single generalization but not a stimulus–response one. Even if no one *sensory kind* of stimulus is shared by all the episodes – no configuration of colour, shape, smell, etc. – they may have *something* in common that lets us generalize across them, namely the fact that each of them *provides evidence to the animal that there is a predator nearby*. If they share that, and there is no more economical way of bringing them under a single generalization, that gives us evidence that the episodes are united in that way for the animal itself. That is tantamount to saying that in each episode the animal thinks there is a predator nearby.

What entitles us to bring the proposition *There is a predator nearby* into our description of the animal (through the statement that that's what it believes) is our having a class of behavioural episodes that can be united with help from the proposition *there is a predator nearby* and cannot be united in any simpler way. Our best unitary account says that in each environment where it calls *the animal has evidence that there is a predator nearby*. (What about 'There is a predator nearby'? *That* fact could not immediately help to explain the animal's behaviour. No fact about the environment could explain its behaviour except by being somehow registered upon or represented within the animal's mind.) The fact that we can unify the occasions with help from an embedded 'that P', and in no other way, justifies us in using an embedded 'that P' in explaining the behaviour.

I don't know a long history for the 'unification' idea proposed here, though it may have one. I propounded it in Bennett 1964 (section 2) and Bennett 1976; it is put to good effect in Whiten and Byrne 1988a, where acknowledgement is also made to Dawkins 1976.

The proposal is not merely about when we may explain behaviour by attributing beliefs, but also about what beliefs we may attribute. We get at belief content through what is perceived as common to all the environments in which the behaviour occurs. I shall return to this, the central theme in my paper, shortly.

First, a small correction is needed. The basic belief–desire–behaviour story must focus on beliefs about means to ends; that is, about what movements on the animal's part will bring about what it wants. We can attribute beliefs of other sorts – e.g. that there is a predator nearby – only *through* attributing beliefs about means to ends, which alone are immediately tied both to wants and to behaviour. When, therefore, we hypothesize that the animal calls because it thinks *there is a predator nearby*, that should be based on the hypothesis that it calls because it wants its companions to be safe and thinks that *that cry is a means to their being safe* because it thinks there is a predator nearby.

6 THOUGHTS ABOUT THOUGHTS: PRELIMINARY TIDYING

What would count as behavioral evidence for us that our animal has a thought about some other animal's mind? This thought could be either a belief or a desire, and what it is about could be either a belief or a desire.

Or an animal might have a thought about another animal's perceptual state. Our subject animal might behave in a certain way because of what it thinks about what another animal might hear or smell or otherwise take in. Supposed evidence for that kind of thought is often misleading. Usually, behaviour that is supposed to manifest the thought 'This will stop x from seeing y' or 'This will stop x from smelling y' could just as well be manifesting the thought 'This will put a physical object between x and y' or 'This will put y upwind from x'. How to get good evidence for thoughts about perceptions or sensory states is an interesting question, but I shan't discuss it here. My topic is the more ambitious attribution of beliefs or desires whose topic is other beliefs or desires.

Such an attribution might fit into our explanatory schema in various ways. Here is one: We have evidence that our animal wants to achieve goal G and thinks that doing A will bring this about; and we don't see how it could arrive at that belief except through attributing a certain mental state to some other animal. For example, I don't see how it could think its cry will make its companions safe except through thinking that the predator *wants* to eat them.

It will be hard to make that stick, however. Almost certainly, we shall be able to explain the basic attribution through the animal's thinking merely that the predator *will* eat the other if it catches them. That is, a supposed belief about a want should give way to a belief about a simple behavioural disposition if the latter covers the data as well.

I shan't discuss what would entitle us to attribute a belief about a predator's desire. I choose for detailed discussion the attribution of a desire to produce a belief. My treatment of that will indicate how in outline I would deal with the other belief–desire combinations.

7 DESIRES TO PRODUCE THOUGHTS: A DILEMMA

What sort of evidence could entitle us to hypothesize that our animal behaves as it does because it *wants to produce a thought* in its companions, e.g. because it wants to get them to think there is a predator nearby?

It is highly improbable, in the non-human world, that our animal should want its companions to have the belief that P just for itself, as an intrinsic good. Let us focus on the less wild possibility that our animal wants its companions to believe that P because of how that belief will affect their behaviour. For example, it calls so as to get them to think there is a predator nearby, which it wants as a means to their behaving thus and so.

To be entitled to say that, we must rule out everything like this: The animal calls so as to get its companions to crawl under a bush. If they do behave thus whenever it calls, our animal may see its call as a trigger to produce the crawling, with no thought of what its companions will think. If it sometimes calls when its companions are already under bushes, that doesn't help, for it might always call so that its companions will *be* under a bush – going there or remaining there.

Objection: 'If our animal thinks that the cry will elicit the hiding behaviour, it must have some belief about *why* it will do so; and the most likely candidate for this is a belief that the cry will cause the others to believe that there is a predator nearby.' This presupposes that a means-to-end belief must be accompanied by a belief about why that means leads to that end; which is absurd. Across the centuries most human means-to-end beliefs have been merely empirical – accepted without any grasp of why they are true, simply because they are confirmed by past experience. If we can do that, why not other animals?

   If our animal is to be credited with wanting to produce not merely behaviour but a belief in its companions, the evidence must be enriched – but how? We have to suppose that our animal wants to give the others a belief as a means to their using it in their behaviour, but we don't want

> evidence that: our animal calls as a means to producing a belief which it wants as a means to producing behaviour

to collapse into

> evidence that: our animal calls as a means to producing behaviour,

with the intended belief dropping out, not attributed because there is no work it needs to do.

8 A WAY OF ESCAPE

I know only one solution to this dilemma. Suppose that in the series of episodes when our animal calls, its companions act variously, depending on their states and situations: if they are F, they run; if they are G, they search; if they are H, they freeze; if they are J, they climb; if they are K, they dig ... and so on; and whatever each animal does is appropriate to the information that there is a predator nearby. Can we still interpret our animal's purpose in calling as merely to elicit behaviour? Here is how such an interpretation would go:

> The animal's past experience has shown it that when it calls like that its companions run if they are F or search if they are G or freeze if they are H or climb if they are J or dig if they are K or ... and on this occasion it wants them to run if they are F or search if they are G or freeze if they are H or climb if they are J or dig if they are K or ... and so it calls.

This is now crediting our animal with a thought of implausible complexity. We can simplify the story and make it more credible by supposing that our animal unites the complex thought

> run if they are F or search if they are G or freeze if they are H or climb if they are J or dig if they are K or ...

into the unitary thought

> behave appropriately to the fact that there is a predator nearby.

That brings their behaviour under a description – call it D – that has nested within it the complete proposition that *There is a predator nearby*. If D is our best way of unifying all the behaviours of the group, that is evidence that on those occasions the animals believe that there is a predator nearby. And if our simplest statement of what our subject knows about its companions and of what it wants also uses D, that is evidence that when it calls it does so because it wants them to believe there is a predator nearby.

9 A FURTHER DIFFICULTY RESOLVED

This is still not right, however. In the story as I have told it, the calling animal's success on each relevant occasion consists in this: Its companions don't get eaten. Suddenly we slump back into a simple story that is purely physicalistic once more, and not psychological. What it knows from past experience is that if it gives that cry when there is a predator nearby, its companions don't get eaten; it doesn't want them to get eaten now when there is a predator nearby; so it calls again. That is not horrendously complex, and it does not credit our animal with a thought about a thought.

So we are back at square one! But if my general strategy has been right, we can see what would in principle deal with this latest trouble and – at last – have a chance of keeping us out of trouble. What is needed is that the animals have a variety of uses for the information that a predator is nearby. There is little hope of that, so let us switch from predators. Suppose there is some other kind of object – call it a Quark – which our animals can use in different ways, depending on their condition and circumstances: they can eat it, shelter under it, use it to crack open coconuts ... and so on. If the range of appropriate responses to the information that there is a Quark nearby is sufficiently various, and if it doesn't all come together again in some one upshot of all these different activities (like escaping the predator), then we can say that the calling animal calls so as to get the others to think there is a Quark nearby. Without such variety, I can find no justification for attributing to our animal any desire to produce a belief.

I have brought us to a point that may seem to lie beyond anything that is true of actual non-human animals. If so, then I am committed to saying that we shan't ever get good evidence that any non-human animal wants to produce a belief. Maybe we could still have evidence that animals sometimes want to produce desires, or have beliefs about beliefs or desires; though I suspect that those would be no easier than the other. I don't know how pessimistic to be about this: it is early days yet; some observations of chimpanzee behaviour (at least) are suggestive, and there is much more experimental work to be done.

10 A FINAL UNSOLVED PROBLEM

I have described a procedure for deciding what mental content to attribute to an animal. I have offered contentions of the form: If an animal's behaviour is thus and so, such and such thoughts can be attributed to it; and secondly I have suggested that the attributions will be unjustified if the animal's behaviour does not conform to the patterns that I have described. Never mind the second bit; let us focus on the first, which says that my procedure is correct, so that adherence to it will reliably lead to true attributions of thoughts to animals.

If my procedure is in that sense correct, *why is it correct*? What is the logical status of truths of the form 'If the animal's behaviour exhibits this and that input–output pattern then it has such and such mental content'? Two broad kinds of answer, introduced by Whiten & Perner should be distinguished.

(1) When we attribute a belief or desire to an animal, we are saying something about its inner state – something that goes beyond any facts about how it behaves – and the facts about its behaviour are merely reliable pointers to those inner states.
(2) When we attribute a belief or desire to an animal, *all* we are doing is to say something complex about its patterns of behaviour. The behaviour is not evidence of the animal's having inner states of belief and desire; rather, to behave like that *is* to have beliefs and desires.

There is much controversy between the adherents of the two positions. In earlier decades, the friends of (1) would characterize beliefs and desires as 'mental' in some way that puts them outside the physical world. This Cartesian view has fallen into deserved disfavour, but (1) still has its friends, who say that what makes it the case that an animal thinks that P or wants G is some fact about its brain-state and not about how it behaves.

This has its attractions, and just twice in this chapter I have allowed myself turns of phrase that align me with it.

In section 5, I wrote that if a class of behavioural episodes share some feature F 'and there is no more economical way of bringing them under a single generalization, that gives us evidence that the episodes are united [by F] for the animal itself'. That implies that when the animal has (whether in a belief or a desire) a thought that is applicable to a variety of situations, it really does *have something* that *enables* it to treat all those situations in one same way. This implies a kind of inner realism about

405

mental content. If I wanted not to commit myself to that, and to remain free to give answer (2) to the status question, I ought to have written not 'that gives us evidence that the episodes are united in that way for the animal itself' but rather 'that entitles us to avail ourselves of that unity in what we say about what the animal thinks'. For a (2) theorist, the concepts of belief and desire are conveniences, aids in the management of certain complex facts about animal behaviour, but they don't have to correspond to items in the animal which enable it to manage its complex data.

In section 8, I wrote that if in a certain case we credit an animal with a thought about behaviour but not one about thoughts, we must credit it with a thought of implausible complexity. That was in the spirit of Premack's statement, that 'The ape could only be a mentalist ... he is not intelligent enough to be a behaviourist'. My remark and Premack's both imply that when we credit an animal with a simple thought about a thought rather than with a complex thought about behaviour, our attribution doesn't merely apply a conceptualization that serves our theoretical purposes but credits the animal with having a simplifying *something* inside it, a something that makes its behavioural data more manageable to it.

Well, I do sometimes find it natural to write like that. But at other times I am not so sure. Suppose we discovered for sure what enabled the animal to engage in the complex behavioural pattern on the basis of which we have attributed the belief that P. Suppose, specifically, that we found that this pattern of behaviour was possible simply because the animal's brain contains thousands of different though interrelated mechanisms, each dealing with a different input–output pair, and that no *one* item in the animal was in any way responsible for the belief-manifesting pattern. If we knew all that, would we still be willing to attribute to the animal the belief that P? Sometimes I am strongly inclined to answer 'Why not?', which aligns me with answer (2) to the status question.

FURTHER READING

Bennett, J. (1964). *Rationality* (London: Routledge and Kegan Paul). Reissued in 1988 (Indianapolis: Hackett).
—— (1976). *Linguistic Behavior* (Cambridge: CUP). Reissued in 1989 (Indianapolis: Hackett).
—— (1998). "Thoughts about Thoughts," *Behavioral and Brain Sciences* 11: p. 246.
Dawkins, R. (1976). "Hierarchical Organisation: A Candidate Principle for Ethology." In P.P.G. Bateson and R. A. Hinde (eds.) *Growing Points in Ethology* (Cambridge: CUP, pp. 7–54).
Dennett, D. (1988a). "The Intentional Stance in Theory and Practice." In R. Whiten and A. Byrne (eds.) *Machiavellian Intelligence: Social Expertise and the Evolution of Intellect in Monkeys, Apes and Humans* (Oxford: OUP, pp. 180–202).
—— (1988b). "Out of the Armchair and Into the Field," *Poetics Today* 9: 205–221.
Whiten, A. and Byrne, R. (1988a). "Tactical Deception in Primates," *Behavioral and Brain Sciences* 11: pp. 233–73.

31

THE MENTAL LIVES OF NON-HUMAN ANIMALS

John Dupré

INTRODUCTION

It is commonly supposed that the question whether animals other than ourselves have minds is perfectly simple to understand, but very difficult to answer. We suppose that we know exactly what is at issue, since we know from our own experience what it is to think, or more generally have mental lives; but we are very uncertain how we might ever discover whether animals do the same. In large part, we may also suppose, this is because, being dumb, they are unable to tell us. I want to argue in this paper that almost everything about this set of views is wrong. Our difficulty with this question is hardly at all to do with lack of evidence, but has everything to do with a lack of clarity about what is really involved in the attribution of mental states. I do not, of course, mean that the question about animal minds could be settled independently of any evidence. But I do want to suggest that the empirical facts in question may, in many cases, be quite banal. The trick is to decide what the relevant facts are. To put this claim in an imperialistic mode, I am suggesting that the problem is paradigmatically philosophical.

In the first part of this paper I shall expand on the preceding claims and explain in a general way the kinds of questions I do take to be involved in deciding whether an entity is an appropriate subject for the attribution of mental properties. In the second section I shall make some rough and tentative suggestions about the appropriateness of attributions of more specific kinds of mental phenomena. (One important moral of the opening section is that we should avoid assuming that there is some unitary answer to the question about animal minds.) In the final section I shall try to identify some questions that do remain mysterious, and offer some ideas about how light might be thrown upon them.

I would like to develop two related themes about the mental states of animals. First, I want to point out the powerful and pernicious influence that Cartesian assumptions, generally—if perhaps ironically—unconscious, continue to exert on much of our thinking about this topic, and to say something of what are the consequences of rejecting these assumptions. Cartesian perspectives are omnipresent in recent discussions of animal minds, not least among those most vocal in support of the view that non-humans have a wide range of mental capacities. One conspicuous example is the work of Donald Griffin (1984). It is even commonplace among those active in defending the rights of animals to ethical treatment. Marian Stamp Dawkins (1990), for example, rests the case that animals can suffer explicitly on the argument from analogy (for discussion of this argument, see below; see also Crisp 1990). My arguments against these Cartesian assumptions owe a great deal to my understanding of the later Wittgenstein (1953); a specific question I would like to explore is to what extent Wittgenstein's insights into the conceptual status of the mental justify us in espousing a kind of behaviourism.

Second, I want to argue against an idea, again more often implicit than explicit, that there is just one fundamental question as to whether animals *really* think. A close parallel here can be drawn with the question whether there are really animal languages, or whether animals can be taught *real* languages. In either case the question can be seen to presuppose a kind of essentialism, the view, that is, that there is some one crucial feature, an *essence*, that is necessary and sufficient to make a thing or phenomenon what it is. The questions then can be raised, What is the *essence* of thought (or language), and do animals have it? The idea that there is an essence of thinking is of course famously connected with the name of Descartes; its denial—and again the same denial for the case of language—is central to the work of the later Wittgenstein. So it should be clear that the issues I have distinguished have much to do with one another.

Descartes thought that the property that distinguished any genuinely mental phenomenon from anything else was its transparency, or indubitability, to the agent experiencing it. This is also the basis for a classical conception of consciousness. Objects of consciousness, on this view, are not only immediately apparent to their subjects, but their nature is unmistakable. Unlike Descartes, more recent thinkers do not necessarily identify mental phenomena with objects of consciousness, I say 'mental phenomena', though Descartes would say 'thought', because as suggested above one problem Descartes has bequeathed us is much too homogeneous a view of the mental. (In the *Meditations*, Descartes gives a typical list of kinds of thinking as doubting, understanding, affirming, denying, willing, refusing, imagining, and sensing; Descartes 1967: 153, Med. II.) Something is a pain, say, for Descartes, if and only if it is experienced as a pain by its subject; the nature of pain is unmistakably evident to the subject; and the meaning of the word 'pain' is exhausted by its function of referring to that experience. Although Descartes did not consider the minds of animals, presumably because he explicitly considered them to be nothing but machines, this conception of the mental raised a pressing problem about the existence of other human minds that has been prominent in the subsequent history of Western philosophy. It will be useful to approach the problem about other species by looking first at this problem about other members of our own species.

The relevant difficulty to which Descartes's conception gives rise is that the putative essential property of mental phenomena, transparency or consciousness, is accessible to us only in our own case. We cannot—and this is a logical rather than an empirical impossibility—ever have access to this property in the case of another mind. If, even in principle, we can never verify that the essential property of the mental is present in any case but our own, it is natural to ask whether there is any possible justification for believing in the existence of minds other than our own. The traditional answer to this question has been to appeal to what has become known as the argument from analogy. We observe in our own case, according to this argument, that certain of our mental states are correlated with characteristic modes of behaviour. We observe in other people these same patterns of behaviour, and infer inductively that they are accompanied by the same mental states (see also Crisp 1990).

It is worth remarking at this point that *if* this is the right way to think about other humans, there is little difficulty about other animals. The behaviour of my cat when it has a pain in its paw is very much like mine when I have a pain in my foot; on the other hand it never produces the behaviour which for me would be associated with extracting a square root. I would conclude, using the argument from analogy, that it had some but not all of the mental states I experience myself. The trouble is that if such an argument is needed, it is woefully inadequate. An inductive argument based on observation of one case to a generalization over a population of billions is hardly deserving of the title 'argument'. The reason that we do not accept inductive arguments based on a single instance is that we cannot, in general, have any reason to suppose that the observed case is typical. One would be in error, for example, in concluding on encountering a radio that all hard rectangular objects emitted complex and cacophonous sounds. In the present case, the very point at issue is whether consciousness, the property at issue in the argument from analogy, is a property peculiar to myself or more widely distributed. If the former, sceptical hypothesis is correct then the inductive argument—the argument from analogy—is worthless; to accept it is thus to beg the sceptical question entirely.

A radically different solution is offered by analytic behaviourism. According to this view, pain, for example, just *is* the characteristic set of its behavioural manifestations (see Skinner 1953; a rather more subtle position, though basically behaviourist, can be found in Ryle 1949). Thus to ask whether someone writhing on the ground with a knife in his leg is in pain is nonsense; nonsense of the same kind as the question, I know she has the same parents as I do, but is she really my sister? But attractive though this solution has sometimes appeared, it is obviously unacceptable in this simple form. It is possible that the person on the floor has his leg anaesthetized, and is pretending to be in pain. Given this possibility, it cannot be *nonsense* to ask whether the person really is in pain. It is worth noting again that *if* this were an adequate solution to the problem, it too would present no special difficulties of extension to other animals: if they produce the appropriate behaviour, they have the mental state in question, if not, not.

Since I cannot treat the ramifications of this problem in adequate depth in the context of this paper, I must now be somewhat dogmatic. My own view is that although, for the reason just stated, analytic behaviourism is untenable, there is a good deal right about behaviourism when it is separated from the claim that mental terms can be analytically reduced to sets of behaviours. What I take to be at the heart of Wittgenstein's attack on the Cartesian tradition is the demonstration that there are deep conceptual connections between mental states and the behaviour that constitutes their characteristic display. In differentiating this position from analytic behaviourism we must emphasize that a conceptual connection here must be distinguished from a strictly logical connection. The word 'pain' is not logically equivalent to some complex description of behaviour.

How, then, should we understand the meaning of a word such as 'pain'? Wittgenstein approaches meaning through a consideration of what it is to explain meaning. Meaning is what one grasps when one correctly understands an explanation of meaning. Meanings can be explained in many ways, one, but by no means the only, of which is the use of samples of the referent of a word (so-called ostensive definitions). So in the present context we need to think of what is involved in explaining the meanings of mental terms; and an essential part of the answer, surely, is behaviour expressive of the mental states in question. Moreover, as I shall elaborate in a moment, Wittgenstein shows that, contrary to the Cartesian picture, mental terms could not possibly be explained ostensively, i.e. by pointing to the connection between the word and the alleged mental referent.

The moral to be drawn here is not that mental states can be reduced to behaviour, but that, contrary to the Cartesian assumption, it must be possible to explain the meaning of mental terms through appeal to behaviour (or perhaps behaviour plus characteristic causal antecedents). Any explanation, for Wittgenstein, is fallible; it may be misunderstood. However, it must also be possible, if it is a satisfactory explanation, for it to be understood correctly. If it is, then the explainee has acquired criteria for the application of a term. Thus, for example, by observing myself and others in various painful positions, and producing various forms of behaviour expressive of pain, I can be taught the meaning of the word 'pain'. I can then apply it correctly to other cases. The distinction between Wittgenstein's position and that of analytic behaviourism, as well as further insight into Wittgenstein's positive view, can be found in his remark that the word 'pain' does not describe pain behaviour, but replaces it (1953: 89). Verbal expressions of pain thus become criteria of pain on a par with groaning; and like other criteria they can, on occasion, be disingenuous.

We can now consider the application of this picture to the worry about other minds, whether human or otherwise. I see a person with a nail stuck in his foot groaning and writhing on the ground. Since I am familiar with the criteria for pain, amply realized in the present case, this strikes me as a clear instance of pain. But there remains a philosophical inclination to ask: but is the person really in pain? Suitably expanded, this makes perfectly good sense. I might be asking, is this only a pretence of pain? Perhaps it is a rehearsal of part of a play, for instance. The legitimacy of such questions points exactly to the impossibility of providing a behaviourist reduction of pain. But of course the sceptic about other minds is not someone who wonders whether other people are only pretending to have the experiences they seem to be having. She is someone who wonders whether, in any case but her own, the situation observed really provides evidence of pain at all. But she is thus raising the question whether the criteria that she (thinks she) has learned for the term 'pain' really are such criteria. And this is equivalent to the question whether she really knows what it is that she wonders whether she is observing an instance of. The sceptical question thus appears to be self-defeating. And this, finally, suggests that the Cartesian perspective from which it derives must be confused.

This line of argument, though I believe it to be impeccable, seldom convinces. The reason is, I think, that most of us have retained extremely strong Cartesian intuitions. We think of our use of the term 'pain' as fundamentally a device for referring to something we are acquainted with in our own private experience, and thus as only contingently related to its typical causes and behavioural manifestations. To address this worry directly, we must turn to the most notorious and controversial part of Wittgenstein's overall strategy, the so-called private language argument. The Cartesian picture, as I have said, assumes that words for mental states function primarily to refer to private internal states; and if the function of a word is primarily referential, it should be possible to explain its use ostensively, by the use of samples of its referent. Thus, just as we explain colour words by using objects of the appropriate colour, we should explain sensation words by using samples of the appropriate mental quality. And to cut a long story short, this simple Cartesian picture of the meaning of a term such as 'pain' is incoherent. No one could explain the use of a term which functioned simply to refer to a private internal state; no criterion could be communicated for the application of the term, since only the person attempting to explain the term has any access to the private feature that is supposed to serve as a criterion; and hence no distinction could be imparted between correct and incorrect use of the term. This last point is especially crucial. Imparting a distinction between correct and incorrect application of a term is precisely what, as Wittgenstein emphasizes, an explanation of meaning is intended to achieve. So we have reached, in essence, the same point that was arrived at when the sceptical argument discussed above was argued to be self-refuting. The sceptical worry, which derives from this mistaken assumption about the meanings of mental terms, is raised in a way that undermines the meaningfulness of the very question that it is intended to raise.

This leads me, finally, back to the minds of animals. What I want to claim is that the starting point for an adequate approach to this problem is to reject the idea that there is some one 'deep' question involved. There is not, in Gilbert Ryle's (1949) memorable figure, some private internal stage across which the referents of mental terms act out their ghostly roles. Since we have no such stages ourselves, we need not enquire whether other creatures possess or lack them. We cannot even begin to consider a range of questions that continue to figure prominently in discussions of animal minds—Are animals really conscious? Are they self-conscious? Do they really know what they are doing? Do they have experiences? Or are they, on the contrary, merely machines?—unless we reject the Cartesian picture, and then ask what are really the criteria for the application of these various terms. When we do so it is, of course, likely that the question will have rather various answers. In the next section I shall look at some questions about animal minds which, I think, can be answered fairly confidently.

SOME EASY QUESTIONS ABOUT ANIMAL MINDS

In this section I shall touch on a number of different questions about the mental capacities of animals: Do they have experiences, beliefs, intelligence, or language? But I shall start with the most general such question: Are non-human animals ever in any kinds of mental states at all? As may well have been guessed from the preceding section, I take the answer to this question to be affirmative. However, I want to look briefly at some criteria that have occasionally been deployed to rule out any attribution of mentality to animals whatsoever.

Perhaps the commonest such criterion remains that of Descartes: Are animals conscious? This can be interpreted variously. Donald Griffin, in his book *Animal Thinking* (Griffin 1984: 9), suggests that the issue separating him from more behaviourally minded scientists is 'whether animals are mechanisms and nothing more ... complex mechanisms to be sure, but unthinking robots nonetheless'. Elsewhere he suggests that the problem may be whether animals are aware of their own mental states (or: do they know what they are doing?), or again whether they are aware of objects not immediately present to their senses. (I shall return to this last idea.) The first question suggests exactly the aspect of Descartes's view that raises the insoluble problem of other minds: Whether an entity is conscious might be totally independent of the totality of its behaviour and behavioural dispositions. Although there are powerful intuitions in favour of such a possibility, I shall reject it for the reasons outlined in the preceding section: In the absence of behavioural criteria we cannot even attach a meaning to a mental term; so the attribution of mentality cannot be quite independent of behaviour.

Awareness of one's mental states, interpreted in one of Griffin's senses as 'knowing what one is doing', may seem closer to a genuine and empirical notion of consciousness. We sometimes distinguish, for example, conscious from unconscious mental processes precisely on the grounds of whether the subject is aware of what she is doing. A person acting on a post-hypnotic suggestion may offer an explanation of what she is doing in mentalistic or psychological terms, but the explanation may be quite mistaken. Unfortunately, it is pretty clear that this provides no adequate model for explicating the philosophical question about the mental states of animals. A person under post-hypnotic suggestion typically is aware of mental states; it is just that she is deluded about what mental states are in fact relevant to explaining her actions. No one, I suppose, wants to argue that animals are conscious all right, but invariably deluded about the motives of their actions. A more appropriate parallel would be with the case of a somnambulist, who, we may suppose, is apparently acting, but in fact is not conscious of anything. But this supposition, assuming it is correct, is based on clear criteria: The somnambulist is glassy-eyed and mechanical in his movements; he displays extreme shock if woken. Here, however, we have a distinction that seems to apply with equal force to animals. My—not especially bright—cat sometimes chases his tail with a degree of nonchalance that strongly suggests that he is not aware of what he is doing. For example, he makes a pass at it with his mouth and, after the tail has eluded him, stares about him in a comic state of puzzlement. He appears at least to have forgotten what he was doing; perhaps he never even knew. On the other hand one is not tempted to such a supposition when, his body quivering with intensity, he is concentrating on stalking a bird. The point of such rather banal examples is not to claim great insight into feline psychology, but merely to indicate that, provided we insist that there are criteria distinguishing conscious from non-conscious states, there is no difficulty of principle in applying them beyond the human case. It will of course be said that I am quite perversely refusing to address the real issue. When he stalks the bird is he *conscious*, or is he just acting mechanically like an 'unthinking robot'? But this is just to return to the Cartesian conception of consciousness as quite independent of any behavioural manifestations; and hence of any possible criteria; and hence, I have tried to argue, of any sense. (A distinction between conscious and non-conscious mental states entirely innocent of behavioural consequences has recently been defended by Carruthers (1989); but see Bekoff and Jamieson (1990). The specific confusions in this neo-Cartesian account cannot be addressed here.)

A somewhat more substantive concern is that animals might be incapable of awareness of anything not immediately present to them. This is an implausible suggestion about many kinds of animals. I suspect it might be less appealing if we did not suffer from such an impoverished sense of smell. If one considers an animal such as a dog without this disadvantage, it seems clear that awareness of the absent must be a major aspect of its experience. Dogs, I take it, can readily distinguish between fresh and stale scents, and can recognize both as the kinds of scents they are. Recognizing the stale scent of an opossum, say, is surely being aware of a spatio-temporally distant opossum. If, as I assume, dogs respond very differently to fresh and stale opossum scents, it would seem that it is precisely the spatio-temporal, or at least temporal, distance observed by the dog that accounts for the difference.

Of course, 'being aware of a spatio-temporally distant opossum' may reasonably be seen as no more than a bizarre circumlocution for 'being aware (or knowing) that an opossum has passed by here before'. But I take it that the reason that spatio-temporal absence has been considered important in this context derives from ideas about intentionality, that thought can be 'about' things that are not immediately present. And this is more obviously implied by the paraphrase than in my original formulation. (The new formulation also raises the question of the attribution of states such as *belief* to animals, which I shall consider further below.) Griffin (1984), in a similar vein, discusses some experiments on birds in which they learned to search in a variety of ways for items of food concealed by experimenters, and hypothesizes that perhaps the birds have mental images of the food they are searching for. But what is important here is the appropriateness of the thoroughly intentionalistic expression 'searching for'; not whether some—in my opinion wholly mystifying—neo-Cartesian explanation of this capacity is correct.

More mundane examples come readily to mind. I make a certain noise to communicate to my cats that I am prepared to feed them. If, as is usually the case, they are hungry, hearing this noise causes them instantly to run to the kitchen just sufficiently slowly to make sure I am following and to attempt to trip me up. It will of course be objected that this does not show that they associate this noise with (spatially distant) food. Perhaps they have just been conditioned to respond to a particular auditory stimulus with movement to the kitchen; certainly this response has been rewarded in the past. It is not altogether easy to justify the intuitions common to almost everyone who has interacted with reasonably intelligent animals other than specially bred rats and pigeons that this is a thoroughly perverse interpretation. One important ground for it is that such behaviour cannot be treated in isolation. These cats, for example, frequently exhibit the same behaviour without any stimulus, and also with other food-suggesting stimuli, such as the sound of a can-opener. Again, if they have just been fed, they may not respond at all. It strikes me that the assumption that they associate certain sounds with (absent) food, and hence, if they are hungry, go to the kitchen where food is often provided for them, is vastly more parsimonious than any attempt to reduce the phenomena to conditioned pairs of stimuli and responses. In the final section of the paper I shall offer support of a rather different kind for this sort of interpretation.

Let me turn now to a rather different, but I suspect even less problematic, issue: Are animals intelligent? I take the unproblematic answer to be, roughly: Yes, some animals have quite considerable degrees of intelligence, though no doubt some others have very little. I shall not try to offer a rigorous definition of intelligence, partly because I doubt whether such a thing is available or appropriate. A central aspect, I take it, is the ability to find solutions to problems, and to do so with some flexibility. (This is an important general theme of Griffin 1984.) By the latter, I mean to exclude responses that are invariably elicited by a particular stimulus, regardless of whether they are, in the particular circumstances, appropriate solutions to problems; analysis of invertebrate behaviour often, though by no means always, shows highly adaptive behaviour not to be intelligent on this criterion. The criterion I have offered is, of course, an empirical one, and it might have turned out that animals were entirely stupid. The ethological literature shows this to be far from the case. The observations surveyed by Donald Griffin in his *Animal Thinking* provide an excellent source of illustrations.

There remains, nonetheless, the familiar illusion of a much deeper problem. Once again, this comes down to the idea that, however intelligent behaviour may appear to be, there is still the question whether we are dealing with a genuinely intelligent being, or merely a 'mindless robot'. As I have tried to indicate in previous contexts, I take this concern to be deeply incoherent. This misconception of intelligence has been attacked with great brilliance by Gilbert Ryle (1949). Ryle argues forcefully that intelligence is grounded primarily in intelligent *action*. The Cartesian picture, what Ryle refers to as the myth of the ghost in the machine, leads us to suppose that the intelligence of an action (which, for us, will often be a linguistic action) is not intrinsic to the action but resides in some internal and inaccessible mental antecedent of the action. Thus, for the Cartesian, an intelligent move in chess, a witty and *apropos* remark, or a smart piece of base-running are only symptoms from which we may attempt to infer intelligence. But, as we have seen in considering the so-called problem of other minds, if such an inference were needed, it would be very poorly grounded. Ryle argues, on the contrary, that intelligent performances are constitutive of intelligence. Hence, and plausibly enough, it is not an open question whether a person whose remarks and actions are consistently intelligent is in fact intelligent. To put the matter in a Wittgensteinian mode, intelligent performances are criteria of intelligence. They are defeasible criteria, in the sense that we may show that particular, apparently intelligent, performances should be attributed to luck, habit, or whatever. But it makes no sense to ask whether *all* intelligent performances might in fact fail to be intelligent.

It is in the light of these rather straightforward observations that, I want to claim, the question of animal intelligence is a simple one. There is ample evidence that

animals are often capable of appropriate and flexible responses to a variety of problem-posing situations. Striking examples drawn pretty much at random from Griffin
(1984) include accounts of remarkably coordinated cooperative hunting among lions
(pp. 85–87), or the versatility with which captive great tits learn to solve experimentally constructed foraging problems (pp. 65–67). Such responses are not symptoms from which intelligence can, at some intellectual risk, be inferred. They are
constitutive of intelligence. So, I conclude, many animals are fairly intelligent.

Turning finally to a topic about which I shall say very little, let me nevertheless say
something about non-human language and the importance of its alleged non-exis-
tence. It is certain that many animals communicate to some extent with one another,
perhaps almost all do to a very limited extent. It is equally certain that we have not
encountered anything remotely like a human language in any other species. By the
first point I mean that they convey information about such things as their emotional
states (grimaces, growls, etc.) and their environments (alarm-calls and the famous
waggle-dances of bees); and the behaviour by which they do this has the primary
function of so conveying information. On the other hand, it is extremely improbable
that any non-human terrestrial creature has any use for such things as, for example,
pluperfect subjunctives, or even subordinate clauses. Exactly how wide this gulf will
prove to be remains a fascinating question now undergoing investigation from various directions. Contemporary studies of social animals in the wild, and of attempts
to teach non-humans fragments of quasi-human language, may throw light on the
extent to which human language is a wholly novel evolutionary creation, or simply a
by-product of generally highly developed mental capacities. But I shall not attempt to
review these questions here. Rather, assuming that animals do not possess anything
like human language (whether or not they may have the capacities for significant
parts of it) I want to consider whether this lack shows that they must also be missing
other central features of a mental life.

There are a variety of reasons why what I take to be quite disproportionate
importance is often attached to the question of animal language. Perhaps the most
important of all such reasons are, broadly speaking, political: For a variety of economic,
religious, or other ideological reasons, it has been important to many people to insist
on an unbridgeable gulf between humans and animals, and language has seemed the most
promising instrument for achieving this. (These political aspects of the question have
been particularly emphasized to me by Harriet Ritvo.) Closer to my present concerns,
it has been thought (e.g. by Descartes) that language was a necessary condition of
consciousness or of intelligence. Recent philosophers have suggested that language is
necessary for a being to possess beliefs. (States such as beliefs, desires, intentions,
hopes, fears, etc., which involve a relation between a subject and an actual or possible state of affairs, are often referred to generically as 'propositional attitudes', and
treated similarly in this context.) I shall briefly consider each of these claims.

Perhaps the easiest such idea to reject is that intelligence should require language. If, as I have suggested, intelligence should be conceived as appropriate and flexible response to problem-posing situations, then it is impossible to see why this should require linguistic ability. It might be suggested that it would be impossible for an entity to show intelligence without the capacity to conceptualize the situations with which it was confronted. For the appropriateness of a response will depend on the kind of situation involved; and for the range of responses to be flexible, the entity must be able to discriminate different kinds of situations, which is, perhaps, to exhibit that it has 'concepts' of these kinds of situation. But if this is right, then the possession of concepts is a capacity independent of the ability to express them linguistically. It is true that we, as highly linguistic beings, tend to associate concepts very tightly with words we use to express them; and there are no doubt many concepts that we possess that we could not possess if we were not linguistically talented. But if we require no more of the possession of a concept than the ability to discriminate what falls under it from what does not, the connection with linguistic capacity is surely quite contingent. And the possession of 'concepts' thus tolerantly conceived is all that is required for at least a modest degree of intelligence.

Let me finally turn to the so-called propositional attitudes, belief, desire, intention, and the rest. As is conventional in contemporary philosophy, I shall focus especially on belief. The best-known recent defence of the thesis that without full-blown language a creature cannot properly be said to possess beliefs is perhaps that of Donald Davidson (1975, 1982), and I shall focus on his treatment of the question. Davidson's central argument for the dependence of belief on language is as follows. Human beliefs, at least, are deeply embedded in a very complex structure of belief. By contrast, Davidson considers the attribution to a dog of the belief that a cat is in a particular tree. (The dog in question has been chasing a cat, and is now barking up a tree, though in fact the wrong tree.) Davidson writes:

> can the dog believe of an object that it is a tree? This would seem impossible unless we suppose the dog has many general beliefs about trees: that they are growing things, that they have leaves or needles, that they burn. There is no fixed list of things that someone with the concept of a tree must believe, but without many general beliefs there would be no reason to identify a belief as about a tree, much less an oak tree. (1982: 3)

It is, indeed, plausible that we would not attribute the belief in question to another human unless we supposed that he or she was in possession of the sort of general truths about trees that Davidson describes. But we should be careful about what this shows. In particular, we should carefully distinguish the question whether the dog has something like the full complement of beliefs that we would expect of another human about whom we asserted 'he believes that there is a cat up that tree' from the question whether the dog has some belief which has some significant content in common with that former belief. I think that the answer to the first question is negative, but that that is all Davidson's argument shows; and I see no reason to doubt that the answer to the second question may well be affirmative.

I shall say something more about the attribution of particular beliefs to animals in the final section of the paper, but first I should consider further the question whether we are justified in attributing any belief at all to a dog. I take this to be a question about the appropriateness of a general explanatory strategy for dealing with animal behaviour, the strategy Daniel Dennett (1971) refers to as 'the intentional stance'. Roughly speaking, this is the strategy of trying to decide what an animal is aiming to achieve and what it believes are the avenues open, and obstacles, to achieving that goal. This, of course, is the way we standardly explain the behaviour of other humans. Someone who objects to using this approach to the behaviour of other animals should, I take it, be prepared to advocate some preferable strategy. As far as I can see, the only systematic alternative would be to adopt what Dennett refers to as the 'physical stance'. That is to say, we analyse the animal as a physical structure, and determine, by appeal to knowledge of the laws of nature, how that structure will behave in response to a given set of environmental stimuli. One research programme that more or less fitted this latter model was behaviourism. The characteristics of the physical structure could be taken to have been determined by a past history of stimuli, behaviour, and rewards, and this history would determine the response of the structure to new situations. But this programme has had almost no success in understanding the behaviour of animals in anything like natural conditions, and for reasons that are well understood. Animals are more intelligent than the programme allows; they have a much more interesting internal structure—I am inclined to say, a structure of beliefs and goals—than it suggests.

There is a quite different candidate for a physical stance approach to behaviour, one that is now widely held to be very plausible, and that is to give a genuinely physical analysis of the internal structure, presumably a neurobiological account. Two points should be noted about this. First of all, no such account is anywhere near being available. So what we are considering is only a possible strategy, not a real alternative. Possibility should certainly not be discounted from a philosophical perspective, and it is certainly an important question whether this possibility is genuine. However, and this is the second point, this possibility in no apparent way distinguishes the non-human from the human situation. There are, indeed, a number of philosophers who believe that some day we will be in a position to replace our intentional stance explanations of human behaviour with physical stance explanations grounded in neurobiology. These philosophers go on to conclude that the concepts in terms of which we give intentional stance explanations—beliefs, desires, etc.—would then have turned out to be fictitious. While I am not persuaded of the coherence of this view (see Dupré 1988 and also Clark 1990), the point of present relevance is simply that no fundamental divide between the human and the non-human is implied: perhaps, strictly speaking, no one has ever really believed anything; but if so, beliefs certainly do not depend for their existence on language. And if they are simply a fiction we make do with, lacking an adequately developed neurology, there seems to be no reason for taking this fiction to be any less necessary for non-humans than for humans. I do not, of course, want to deny the obvious fact that the majority of beliefs we attribute to humans could not sensibly be attributed to non-linguistic animals. This is simply because for very many beliefs, perhaps the majority, the only possible criterion is a verbal expression. But there are nonetheless many beliefs that we attribute to both humans and non-humans on the grounds of simpler behavioural criteria; so, I want to maintain, the difference is ultimately one only of degree.

I have not attempted to exclude every possible ground for drawing a deep divide between human and animal cognition. Indeed, I have not attempted to consider the range of arguments that Davidson deploys towards the establishment of this division. So perhaps I shall conclude this section by using Davidson quite unfairly against himself. The final conclusion of the paper discussed above is that 'rationality is a social trait. Only communicators have it.' Since many animals are social, and many animals communicate, we should perhaps enlist Davidson in support of the view that there are many kinds of rational animals.

SOME HARD QUESTIONS ABOUT ANIMAL MINDS

The general theme of this paper so far has been to argue that certain kinds of 'deep' mystery that appear to arise in connection with the question of animal minds are illusory. The suggestion that no non-human animal is conscious, sensate, moderately intelligent, or in possession of even the simplest beliefs can, I have tried to argue, be founded only on serious misunderstandings of what is involved in the application of mental descriptions. Thus I want to conclude that there should be no difficulty in deciding that many other kinds of animals *have* minds. However, even a more defensible interpretation of mental language can present deep and perplexing obstacles to the interpretation or characterization of non-human minds. In this final section of the paper I shall indicate a perspective on mental language that suggests that such problems, even though difficult, are at least solidly empirical and, in principle, tractable.

Since the first part of this paper depended heavily on an interpretation of Wittgenstein, it may be appropriate to introduce the present discussion with one of

Wittgenstein's better-known aphorisms: 'If a lion could talk, we would not understand it' (1953: 223). This remark develops the intuition that language is deeply integrated with non-linguistic practices and behaviour. Since lions, and other animals, lead wholly different lives, their hypothetical language could make no sense to us. Does this imply—if it is true—that we are necessarily mistaken in applying terms of our language to a lion? To pursue a standard example, a possible reason for hesitation in applying the term 'pain' to a lion would be that while there is much in common between the natural expressions of pain in humans and the behaviour of lions when they are injured, there are also differences. Lions do not, I suppose, exactly cry. Moreover, again on a Wittgensteinian picture, for humans these natural expressions are often replaced by verbal ones, statements such as 'I am in pain'. Some kinds of pain attribution seem to depend almost exclusively on verbal criteria. There are perhaps no criteria for attributing a headache to a lion.

Suppose, then, that our lion found its voice and said something that we were (somehow) inclined to translate as 'I am in pain'. Why might we not be right in this translation, and thus understand the lion? One might imagine a Wittgensteinian answering that the role that such an utterance could, imaginably, play in the life of lions, and its relation to the natural leonine expressions of pain, would be different from the equivalent role of the English utterance in the life of humans. If this seems wholly implausible, it is perhaps because the behaviour associated with pain is so primitive that it really does extend to many non-human species without serious alteration. But then we should certainly be doubtful about the reference of pains for talking whales (which do not groan, still less grimace), let alone for beetles or butterflies.

There is a powerful pragmatic reason for rejecting this line of argument. Most people think it is a very bad thing to torture, or gratuitously injure, lions, whales, and perhaps even beetles, though the extent of these intuitions is notoriously variable. Presumably part of the reason for this is that we think that these animals feel pain, and pain is a bad thing. It would seem that doubts such as I have been raising about the legitimacy of applying our term 'pain' to lions or the translation as pain of some term in the vocabulary of a talking lion would threaten to undermine all such intuitions, and show that the objections to torturing animals must be incoherent. I am inclined to think that this conclusion is a *reductio ad absurdum* of the line of argument that purports to demonstrate it.

But it is also fairly clear that the threatened conclusion cannot be a legitimate inference from the arguments under consideration. Wittgenstein's argument does not show that humans only come to feel pains at the point when they learn to talk about them; on the contrary, they show that if pain did not pre-exist pain language, there could not be such language. Hence whatever we make of the roars and so on of injured lions, their status as expressions of sensation, at least, cannot be undermined by considerations concerning the linguistic incompetence of lions.

I want to suggest that taking the Wittgensteinian perspective a stage further points to an attractive resolution of this difficulty. It is extremely difficult to get rid of the intuition that what we are really concerned with in attributing pain to the lion is a correct characterization of what is going on in the lion's mind: what, if it could only talk, and if we could only understand it, the lion would refer to by its word 'pain'. Put in another contemporary idiom, we are trying to speculate about part of 'what it is like to be a lion'; and that, as has been discussed by Thomas Nagel (1974), is a hard thing to do. But I have recommended rejecting all these interpretations of the problem, and I suggest that we focus instead on the question, What do *we* mean—if anything—by attributing pain to a lion? We should remember, in other words, that 'pain', even when applied to lions, is a word in *our* language. And if *this* is the question, then it can be seen that our difficulty in understanding the dicta of hypothetical talking lions is completely irrelevant.

Of course, serious doubts might be raised about whether our term 'pain' *should* be extended to lions, whales, or whatever. The facts alluded to above, that the criteria for such applications will differ in some important respects from those appropriate for humans, show that this is an extension of our concept, not a paradigmatic use. But I think that from this perspective it is clearly a natural and obvious extension, comparable, perhaps, to our extension of the term 'conversation' to telephone conversations and even rapid exchanges of computer messages. Lions and other animals avoid things that cause them pain, withdraw rapidly from painful stimuli, and generally respond to pains in ways that are more or less analogous to human responses. But perhaps most important, to pick up an earlier point, the concept of 'pain' fits into broader aspects of our conceptual scheme, most especially the ethical. We think that causing pain is a very bad thing, because it is a sensation that sentient beings greatly dislike. Since lions are clearly sentient, and show every sign of disliking the experiences which, I am suggesting, we refer to as 'pain', we should avoid causing them these experiences. This is another very powerful reason for including their relevant experiences under our concept of 'pain'.

I think this perspective, if it is accepted, should also defuse some of our worries about the attribution of cognitive states to animals. When we say, to return to an earlier example, that the dog believes that the cat went up the maple tree, we are, obviously enough, saying something in English. Whether such a statement is appropriate or not must surely depend, then, on whether the dog satisfies criteria that we would usually employ in attributing such a belief to a human. It does not depend, for example, on whether the dog is entertaining some proposition in Caninese that would be correctly translated as: 'The cat went up the maple tree'. Indeed, it seems pretty obvious that we might well attribute this belief to another human on exactly the kinds of grounds proposed for the dog. (We see a man chasing a cat, shouting abuse, and swinging at it with a stick; the cat darts up an oak tree, and the man continues yelling up the maple tree and shaking his fist, etc.) Of course the majority of beliefs that we attribute to humans probably do depend essentially on linguistic criteria; but many do not, and such may very well be attributed to non-humans.

There is a slightly different kind of worry that might still be raised, that suggests a serious and pervasive risk of error in such attributions. Richard Jeffrey (1985), in discussing Davidson's example, suggests that although the dog may not have the concept of a tree that Davidson describes it may have a concept of its own that the maple tree falls under; he suggests 'marker that a scratcher can disappear up'. Although, as I have been arguing, I do not think the question at issue is illuminatingly construed as one about the phenomenological states of dogs or lions, this suggestion does point to a real difficulty. This is simply that it is easy to be wrong in giving intentional explanations of the behaviour of non-humans. Here I mean to identify the point at which armchair theorizing ends, and the difficult empirical task of cognitive ethology begins. To be successful, as opposed to merely logically intelligible, in attributing beliefs to other animals, we need to know a great deal about the animals we are talking about. If we do not know what their perceptual capacities are, and what features of the environment they are capable of discriminating (see Rosenzweig 1990); the goals that such animals often pursue; the level of intelligence they are capable of bringing to bear on the pursuit of these goals; their tendencies to stereotyped or habitual responses to certain kinds of situations; and so on, we are likely simply to be wrong in our suggestions as to what their cognitive states are. Hence it is unsurprising that we can make such attributions much more easily and widely in the case of our conspecifics, and after that we are inclined to feel more comfortable with the beliefs of cats and dogs—about which we feel we know a fair bit—than with whales or bats. But I see no reason why, as we come to know more about other creatures, we should not come to be very successful in giving intentional stance explanations of their behaviour—explanations in our own language, which is just as well since they probably have none, and if they did we could not, perhaps, understand them.

ACKNOWLEDGMENTS

I have been helped by comments on an ancestral version of this paper by audiences at the University of Colorado at Boulder and the University of California at San Diego. I have also benefited greatly from the responses of various people to a previous draft. I am particularly grateful to Marc Bekoff, Dale Jamieson, Peter Hacker, Thomas Kuhn, and Harriet Ritvo.

FURTHER READING

Carruthers, P. (1989). "Brute experience." *Journal of Philosophy* 86:258–69.

Davidson, D. (1975). "Thought and Talk." In *Mind and Language*, ed. S. Gutenplan, pp. 7–23. Oxford: University Press.

—— (1982). "Rational animals." *Dialectica* 36:318–27.

Dawkins, M.S. (1990). "From an animal's point of view: Consumer demand theory and welfare." *Behavioral and Brain Sciences*.

Dennett, D. (1971). "Intentional systems." *Journal of Philosophy* 68:87–106.

Descartes, R. (1642/1967). *Meditations on First Philosophy*. In *The Philosophical Work of Descartes*, ed. and trans. E.S. Haldane and G.R.T. Ross, pp. 131–99. Cambridge: Cambridge University Press.

Dupré, J. (1998). "Materialism, physicalism and scientism." *Philosophical Topics* 16, 31–56.

Griffin, D. *Animal Thinking*. Cambridge, Mass.: Harvard University Press.

Jamieson, D., and Bekoff, M. (1992). "Carruthers on nonconscious experience." *Analysis* 52, 23–8.

Jeffrey, R. (1985). "Animal interpretation." In *Actions and Events. Perspectives on the Philosophy of Donald Davidson*, eds E. LePore and B.McLaughlin, pp. 481–87. Oxford: Blackwell.

Nagel, T. (1974). "What is it like to be a bat?" *Philosophical Review* 83: 435–50.

Ryle, G. (1949). *The Concept of Mind*. London: Hutchinson.

Skinner, B.F. (1953). *Science and Human Behavior*. New York: Macmillan.

Wittgenstein, L. (1958). *Philosophical Investigations*. Second edition, eds G.E.M. Anscombe and R. Rhees, trans. G.E.M. Anscombe). Oxford: Blackwell.

32

CAN ANIMALS EMPATHIZE?
YES

Gordon Gallup, Jr.

Animals that pass the mirror test are self-aware and thus can infer the states of mind of another individual

I used to tell students that no one ever heard, saw, tasted or touched a mind. There is no way for me to experience your experience, let alone that of a species other than my own. So although minds may exist, they fall outside the realm of science.

I have since changed my mind. A number of years ago I began to study whether primates could recognize themselves in a mirror. Most animals react to their images as if confronted by another animal. But chimpanzees, orangutans and, of course, humans learn that the reflections are representations of themselves—these creatures are objects of their own attention and are aware of their own existence. In the past three decades, I and other researchers have used the mirror test in various ways to explore self-awareness in animals. I conclude that not only are some animals aware of themselves but that such self-awareness enables these animals to infer the mental states of others. In other words, species that pass the mirror test are also able to sympathize, empathize and attribute intent and emotions in others—abilities that some might consider the exclusive domain of humans.

I began exploring self-awareness with mirrors in 1969, when I was at Tulane University. I presented a full-length mirror to preadolescent chimpanzees at the university's Delta Regional Primate Research Center. Initially, they reacted as if they were seeing other chimpanzees, but after a few days they grew accustomed to the mirror and began to use it to make faces, look at the inside of their mouths, and groom and inspect other parts of their bodies that they had never seen before.

THE MIRROR TEST

To determine whether they had learned to recognize their own reflections, I anesthe-tized each animal and applied red dye to an eyebrow ridge and to the top half of the opposite ear. Later, on awakening and seeing themselves in the mirror, the chimpan-zees reached up and touched the red marks on their faces, following this in some instances with looking at and smelling their fingers. Chimpanzees that did not have the benefit of prior experience with mirrors acted as if confronted by another chim-panzee and failed to locate the marks on their faces. These findings of self-recogni-tion have now been replicated with chimpanzees more than 20 times by scientists all over the world. Many other animals, including a variety of primates, elephants, birds and even dolphins, have been tested for self-recognition. But only chimpanzees, orangutans and humans have consistently passed this test. (Marc D. Hauser of Har-vard University reported that cotton-top tamarins pass the mirror test when their white tufts of hair are marked, but no one has been able to replicate these results.)

The failure to find self-recognition in other animals is not for want of trying. Susan D. Suarez of the Sage Colleges and I gave a pair of rhesus monkeys, reared together in the same cage, continuous exposure to themselves in a full-length mirror for 17 years (more than 5,000 hours of mirror exposure a year). Despite this extended opportunity to learn about the mirror, neither monkey ever showed any evidence of self-recognition. On the other hand, when I would walk into the room where they were kept and they saw my reflection in the mirror, they would immediately turn to confront me directly. So it was not that they were incapable of learning to interpret mirrored information about other objects correctly.

Experiments have also failed to uncover compelling evidence of self-recognition in gorillas. After pondering those results, Suarez and I decided to give gorillas the ben-efit of the doubt, reasoning that maybe gorillas do not care about the superimposed marks. We tested this hypothesis at the Yerkes Regional Primate Research Center at Emory University by applying marks to gorillas' wrists as well as to their faces. We discovered that on recovery from anesthesia all the gorillas touched and inspected the marks on their wrists. But despite extensive prior experience with mirrors, none of the gorillas were able to locate comparable marks on their faces that could be seen only in the mirror.

Gorillas naturally avoid making eye contact with one another, so a possible reason for their mirror-test failure is that they avoid eye contact with their reflection and hence never learn to recognize themselves. Daniel J. Shillito and Benjamin B. Beck of the National Zoological Park in Washington, D.C., and I recently tested this hypothesis, relying on a technique developed by James R. Anderson of the University of Stirling in Scotland. It calls for a pair of mirrors placed together at an angle that renders it impossible to make eye contact with the reflection. But none of the gorillas showed evidence of self-recognition, not even one that had more than four years of exposure to mirrors.

In other tests of learning, problem solving and cognitive functioning, differences in performance among species are typically a matter of degree, not kind. What is to be made of such decisive differences in self-recognition? Maybe the reason most species cannot process mirrored information about themselves stems from an inability to conceive of themselves. Correctly inferring the identity of the reflection presupposes an identity on the part of the organism making that inference.

That conclusion seems reasonable, considering the way members of Homo sapiens interpret mirror images. Humans do not begin to show compelling evidence of mirror-guided self-recognition until they reach 18 to 24 months of age—about the same time at which the prefrontal cortex begins to mature in structure and function. Younger infants react to themselves in mirrors as though they were seeing other children, just as most species do. At about the time that children learn to recognize themselves, they begin to show other evidence of self-conception, such as using personal pronouns, smiling after mastering a task and engaging in self-conscious play.

Before about two years of age, no one has experiences that can be consciously recalled in later life. Consistent with my interpretation, this period of "infant amnesia" stops at about the same time that children begin to show self-recognition. As would be expected, the onset of an autobiographical memory only begins with the emergence of self-conception.

That may terminate prematurely at the other end of the life span if dementia sets in. Disturbances in self-awareness and impaired structure and function of the prefrontal cortex often accompany this condition. Thus, for some, human development may be bounded at both ends by periods of unconsciousness.

KNOWING MENTAL STATES

Some practical advantages are derived from being able to conceive of the self. I argue that self-awareness, consciousness and mind are an expression of the same underlying process, so that organisms aware of themselves are in a unique position to use their experience as a means of modeling the experience of others. When you see someone in a situation similar to one you have encountered, you automatically assume his or her experience will be similar to yours. Although it is probably true that no two people experience the same event in exactly the same way, as members of the same species we share the same sensory and neurological mechanisms. So there is bound to be considerable overlap between your experience and mine. Moreover, given a knowledge of how external events influence my mental states (and vice versa), I have a means of modeling the mental states of others.

To see my point, imagine you have a dog that returns home one day in obvious distress: it has porcupine quills in its nose. You could either have a veterinarian remove the quills, or you could attempt to extract them yourself using a pair of pliers. If you were to opt for the latter, it would be an excruciating ordeal for you. Not that you would experience any pain in the process, but as you pulled the quills from the dog's nose and witnessed its reaction, it would prove virtually impossible not to empathize with the dog. That is, you would use your prior experience with pain to model your dog's ostensible experience.

But how do you think another unrelated dog witnessing this transaction would respond? Pet owners may be surprised to learn—and any veterinarian can tell you— that dogs are empathetically oblivious to pain and suffering in other, unrelated dogs. I suspect that dogs experience pain in much the same way that we do, but because they cannot conceive of themselves, dogs cannot use their experience with pain to model painful experiences in other creatures. (They might, of course, react to the yelping.)

Another way to illustrate this incapacity involves people who have a condition called blindsight experience. These patients have sustained extensive damage to the visual cortex and often act as if they were blind, even though their primary visual system remains intact. Lawrence Weiskrantz of the University of Oxford and his colleagues discovered that such patients can show a surprising ability to "guess" the identity of objects and their location. In other words, vision in such patients has been reduced to an unconscious sensation. Blindsight patients can still respond to visual information, but they are not aware of it. As a consequence, they have been rendered mindless when it comes to vision. I would predict that individuals born with blindsight can grow up using guessing strategies and hence act visually normal. Their condition would become apparent only if they were placed in a situation that required them to make inferences about the visual experiences in other people—understanding how high-beam headlights affect oncoming drivers on a dark country road, for instance.

So back to my main point: I maintain that knowledge of mental states in others presupposes knowledge of mental states in oneself and, therefore, that knowledge of self paves the way for an inferential knowledge of others. Most humans routinely make inferences and attributions about what other people may or may not know, want or plan to do. By the same token, species that fail to recognize themselves in mirrors should fail to use introspectively based social strategies such as sympathy, empathy, attribution, intentional deception, grudging, gratitude, pretense, role playing or sorrow.

EVIDENCE FOR EMPATHY

We ought to be able to identify animals that can or cannot recognize themselves in mirrors and their empathetic tendencies in some fairly definitive ways. If you were to cover the eyes of an animal at some point, how would it later respond to a cagemate wearing a blindfold? An animal that is self-aware ought to be in a position to use its prior experience with blindfolds to take into account its cagemate's inability to see. If you were to teach an animal to vocalize for a food reward every time you entered the room and then blocked its hearing with earplugs or headphones, how would it respond the next day if you entered the room wearing headphones? If self-aware, it should vocalize more loudly to compensate for your impaired ability to hear.

In these kinds of tests, monkeys that fail to show evidence of self-recognition (as distinct from chimpanzees and orangutans, which are great apes) seem completely incapable of taking into account what other monkeys may or may not know. Dorothy L. Cheney and Robert M. Seyfarth of the University of Pennsylvania have found that vervet monkeys give alarm calls on seeing a predator even if other monkeys have already seen it, too. Likewise, they found that Japanese monkey mothers do not distinguish between offspring that know or do not know about food or danger when it comes to alerting their babies to the presence of one or the other.

Monkeys that cannot recognize themselves in mirrors approximate what psychologists call radical behaviorists. Their interactions with other monkeys seem to be based entirely on an analysis driven by the external features of the other monkey and not on what it might be thinking or what it might want to do. Chimpanzees, on the other hand, ought to represent primitive, albeit imperfect, cognitive psychologists— they should be able to respond empathetically and modify their behavior accordingly.

Initial experiments by Daniel J. Povinelli and Sarah T. Boysen of Ohio State University showed that chimpanzees appear to distinguish between what humans may or may not know. When two humans pointed toward different cups, the chimpanzees learned to pick the cup implicated by the human who had witnessed which cup had been baited with food. Although chimpanzees seemed to recognize ignorance on the part of human informants, rhesus monkeys did not. Further evidence for cognitive empathy in chimpanzees comes from a mutual problem-solving experiment in which humans and chimpanzees had to perform different tasks. For instance, a chimpanzee had to pull a handle to bring food cups within reach but could not see which cup had been baited, whereas the human who could not reach the cups had to point to the baited cup. The chimpanzees were able to switch roles with the humans with no decrement in performance. Rhesus monkeys, however, failed to show any evidence of transfer when the roles were reversed. Arguing against self-awareness and empathy of chimpanzees, Povinelli cites experiments that failed to find evidence in chimpanzees for an ability to take into account what another creature sees. He concludes that chimpanzees cannot even conceive of their own mental states, let alone those of others.

There are some explanations for the negative results, however. Povinelli's experiments relied on chimpanzees that might have been too young; the onset of self-recognition in chimpanzees does not occur until adolescence. Still another possibility is that we humans categorize our experiences (for example, by sight, hearing or smell). Lacking language, chimpanzees may not distinguish between visual, auditory and tactile experiences. Therefore, inferences they make about attention may be more global.

Also, most studies have focused on whether chimpanzees can take various informational states of mind into account (that is, whether they can figure out what another individual knows). But the data on humans show that children attribute feelings and motivation before they have the ability to attribute informational states of mind. Beginning at about the time or shortly after (but never before) they learn to recognize themselves in mirrors, children start to make primitive inferences about emotional states of mind in others; the more sophisticated ability to infer informational states of mind does not happen until a year or two later. Autistic children, in contrast, have difficulty taking into account what other people may know, want or feel. As expected, self-recognition in autistic children is often delayed or even absent.

Because chimpanzees and orangutans pass the mirror test, Povinelli hypothesizes that they possess a motor self-concept rather than a psychological one. That is, they do not really recognize themselves but simply learn an equivalence between their behavior and what they see in the mirror.

But matters of appearance have little to do with movement. So why should chimps and orangutans seem so intent on using mirrors to look at and inspect parts of their bodies they have never seen before? Why should they bother to respond to strange but motorically inconsequential red marks on their own faces? Suzanne Calhoun and Robert Thompson of Hunter College describe the reaction of a chimpanzee that, on being reintroduced to a mirror a year after learning to recognize herself, became very agitated when she opened her mouth and saw several missing teeth. It is hard to see how this reaction could be understood purely in motor terms.

SELF-AWARENESS AND THE BRAIN

Other, more speculative clues about self-awareness lie in the physical makeup of the brain: certain areas seem to be responsible for it. Donald T. Stuss of the Rotman Research Institute in Toronto and I have been collaborating on a long-term project that focuses on human patients who have damage to the frontal cortex, the part of the brain responsible for some of the most complex activities of the mind. Preliminary data show that such patients seem unable to model mental states in others.

Self-awareness may correlate with activity in the right prefrontal cortex. Julian P. Keenan and Alvaro Pascual-Leone of Harvard Medical School, along with my colleagues N. Bruce McCutcheon and Glenn S. Sanders and me, tested how fast humans can recognize faces. When responding with the left hand (controlled by the right hemisphere), subjects identified their own faces faster than the faces of friends or co-workers. In addition, subjects viewing their own faces displayed significant changes in electrical potentials in the right prefrontal cortex. Moreover, when we altered the electrical activity in this brain area with magnetic fields, subjects changed their response rates to their own faces but not to the other faces.

Given this evidence of functional lateralization of self-awareness in humans, it is interesting to note that compared with other great apes, gorilla brains are the least anatomically lateralized. The absence of a highly specialized right hemisphere might explain the gorilla's weak and inconsistent performance in the mirror tests. Povinelli claims that the gorilla's failure here is a "crucial test" of his theory of the motor self-concept. In particular, he speculates that it arose as an adaptation to life in the trees: unlike chimpanzees and orangutans, gorillas spend most of their time on the ground. But at night, gorillas still return to the trees to sleep, even though they are at a greater risk of falling because they are so large. In fact, humans are the ones that have much more completely emancipated themselves from the branches. Therefore, humans and not gorillas ought to fail to recognize themselves in mirrors.

Povinelli's data notwithstanding, I think most people working in this area would agree that the jury is still out on whether great apes can attribute mental states to others. Much of the research in this topic is consistent with the conclusion reached by Nicholas Humphrey of the University of Cambridge that many species may have clever brains but blank minds: clever brains in the sense of learning, memory and problem solving, but blank minds in the sense of being unable to use their experience to take into account the experience of others. As evidenced by the behavior of people who sleepwalk and those who suffer from blindsight, you do not have to know what you are doing in order to do it in an appropriate way. Humans and possibly a few species of great apes appear to have entered a unique cognitive domain that sets us apart from other creatures.

This model of consciousness and mind based on self-awareness has brought me full circle. When I devised the initial test of self-recognition almost 30 years ago, it is apparent that I was using my experience and imagination about how I would respond to strange facial marks to anticipate how chimpanzees might respond to such marks if they could recognize themselves in mirrors. Moreover, if this model or some modified version of it eventually proves correct, it would mean that the ability to conceive of oneself in the first place is what makes consciousness and thinking possible. The famous quote from Descartes would have to be rewritten as "I am, therefore I think."

33

CAN ANIMALS EMPATHIZE? MAYBE NOT

Daniel Povinelli

Even though chimpanzees pass the mirror test, they do not seem to conceive of others' – or even their own – mental states

Let me begin with a point on which Gordon Gallup, Jr., and I agree: the reactions of chimpanzees when they see themselves in mirrors reveal that these animals possess a self-concept. Furthermore, we agree that this self-concept appears to be restricted to the great apes and humans. Beyond this point, however, our views diverge. Gallup speculates that the capacity for self-recognition may indicate that chimpanzees are aware of their own internal, psychological states and understand that other individuals possess such states as well. I have come to doubt this high-level interpretation of the chimpanzees' reactions to seeing themselves in mirrors. More generally, I question whether chimpanzees possess the deep psychological understanding of behavior that seems so characteristic of our species. In what follows, I describe why I have come to this conclusion, and I offer an explanation of how humans and chimpanzees can behave so similarly and yet understand this behavior in radically different ways.

KNOWING THAT OTHERS SEE

Consider the simple act of seeing. When we witness other people turning their eyes toward a particular object, we automatically interpret this behavior in terms of their underlying psychological states—what they are attending to, what they are thinking about, what they know or what they intend to do next. These inferences are often solely based on fairly subtle movements of their eyes and heads.

Do chimpanzees understand seeing in this manner? Gallup thinks they do, and at first glance it seems hard to deny it. For example, chimpanzees exhibit a strong interest in the eyes of their fellow apes. Frans B. M. de Waal of the Yerkes Regional

Primate Research Center at Emory University has reported that chimpanzees do not appear to trust the reassurance gestures of their former opponents unless such gestures are accompanied by a mutual gaze—that is, unless they stare directly into one another's eyes. Research from our own laboratory has established that chimpanzees follow the gaze of other apes—and of humans as well. If you stand face-to-face with a chimp, lock your gaze with hers and then suddenly look over her shoulder, the ape will reliably turn around, as if trying to determine what you are looking at.

In short, the spontaneous behavior of chimpanzees seems to make a fairly persuasive case that they can reason about the visual perspectives of others. Does this behavior, then, provide confirmation of Gallup's model? Maybe, but maybe not. The problem is that there are other equally plausible interpretations that do not assume that chimpanzees are reasoning about one another's visual experiences. The case of gaze following illustrates the problem quite well. A chimpanzee who follows your gaze leads you to assume that the animal is trying to figure out what you are looking at. But what excludes the possibility that evolution has simply produced "mind-blind" mechanisms that lead social primates to look where other animals look, without entertaining any ideas about their visual perspective?

To disentangle these issues, we need to study the behavior of these animals in more revealing experimental situations. One method occurred to us after watching our chimpanzees in their everyday play. They frequently covered their heads with blankets, toy buckets or even their palms and then frolicked around their compound until they bumped into something—or someone. Occasionally they would stop and lift the obstruction from their eyes—to peek, as it were—before continuing their blind strolls. On more than one occasion I made the mistake of imitating these behaviors while playing with the animals, a maneuver that left me vulnerable to a well-timed play attack! Does this behavior mean that chimpanzees have a concept of seeing? For example, when they play with someone else who covers his or her head, do they know that this person cannot see them, or do they simply learn that this person is unable to respond effectively?

To answer these questions, we examined one of our chimpanzees' most common communicative gestures: begging. First, we allowed them to beg for food from an experimenter who was sitting just out of their reach. When they did so, they were handed an apple or banana. Next, we confronted them with two familiar experimenters, one offering a piece of food and the other holding out an undesirable block of wood. As we expected, the chimps had no trouble: after glancing at the two experimenters, they immediately gestured to the one offering the food.

This set the stage for our real objective, which was to provide the apes with a choice between a person who could see them and a person who could not. If the high-level model of chimpanzee understanding were correct, the chimps would gesture only to the person who could see them. We achieved the "seeing/not-seeing" contrast by having the two experimenters adopt different postures. In one test, one experimenter wore a blindfold over her eyes while the other wore a blindfold over her mouth. In the other tests, one of the experimenters wore a bucket over her head, placed her hands over her eyes or sat with her back turned to the chimpanzee. All these postures were modeled after the behaviors we had observed during the chimpanzees' spontaneous play.

The results of this initial experiment were astonishing. In three of the four tests—the ones involving blindfolds, buckets and hands over the eyes—the apes entered the lab and paused but then were just as likely to gesture to the person who could not see them as to the person who could. In several cases, the apes gestured to the person who could not see them and then, when nothing happened, gestured again, as if puzzled by the fact that the experimenter did not respond.

We were not prepared for such findings. Surely our apes understood that only one of the experimenters could see them. Indeed, the apes did perform excellently in one of the tests, where one experimenter sat with her back turned to the chimpanzees. But why only this one? At first we assumed that the back/front test was simply the most obvious or natural contrast between seeing and not seeing. In this test the apes might have been demonstrating their genuine understanding of seeing—an understanding that was obscured by the arguably less natural postures in the other tests.

Another idea, however, began to nag at us. Perhaps the apes' excellent performance on the back/front test had nothing to do with their reasoning about who could or could not see them. Maybe they were just doing what we had taught them to do in the first part of the study—gesture to the front of someone who was facing them. Or perhaps the act of gesturing to the front of a social partner is simply a hardwired social inclination among chimpanzees, unconnected to a psychological concept of seeing or attention.

As a first attempt to distinguish among these possibilities, we conducted another test in which both experimenters sat with their backs to the chimpanzees, but one looked over her shoulder at them. This posture was quite familiar to the apes—in their daily interactions, they frequently looked over their shoulders at one another. The high-level model of chimpanzee understanding predicted that the animals would gesture only to the experimenter who could see them. The low-level model predicted that the apes would choose at random because they could not see the front of either experimenter. Their performance turned out to be random—they were just as likely to gesture to either experimenter.

I should point out that what I am describing are the apes' initial reactions to these situations. As you might guess, with enough experience of not being handed a banana after gesturing to someone whose face was not visible, our chimpanzees quickly learned to choose the other option. But what exactly did the apes learn? Did they finally realize what we were asking them—"Oh, I get it! It's about seeing!"—or had they simply learned another rule that could work every time: "Gesture to the person whose face is visible."

We examined this question in an extended series of studies, the results of which were consistent with the low-level model. For example, after the chimpanzees learned not to gesture to an experimenter whose head was obscured by a cardboard disk, we retested the animals using the original conditions (buckets, blindfolds, hands over the eyes and looking over the shoulder). We realized that if the apes had genuinely understood the idea of seeing, they ought to gesture only to the experimenters who could see them in all the other tests as well. But if the chimpanzees had simply learned to gesture to a person whose face was visible, they would still choose randomly in the blindfold test, because the faces of the experimenters were equally visible (one had the blindfold over her eyes; the other had it over her mouth). Just as the low-level model predicted, the chimpanzees were more likely to gesture to the experimenter who could see them in all the tests except one—the blindfold test.

These findings contrast sharply with the development of these abilities in human infants. John H. Flavell and his colleagues at Stanford University have shown that children as young as two or three years seem to understand the concept of seeing. And indeed, when we tested young children using our seeing/not-seeing method, we found that even two-and-a-half-year-old children performed at levels suggesting that they understood that only one of the experimenters could see them.

GROWING UP APE

Let me address one important criticism of our work raised by Gallup concerning the age of our animals. The initial tests were conducted in 1993 and 1994, when the chimpanzees were five to six years old. Although several of our apes were displaying all the traditional evidence of recognizing themselves in mirrors, some of them were still on the cusp of developing this ability. Could it be that older chimpanzees might fare better in the seeing/not-seeing tests?

One year after the initial research—and after our apes had been engaged in many other studies—we assessed their reactions to several of the original seeing/not-seeing tests. Much to our surprise, the chimpanzees initially responded at random, even to the test where one of the experimenters hid her head behind a cardboard disk—a test the apes had learned extremely well a year earlier. Our chimpanzees' performance improved only gradually, after considerable trial and error. Furthermore, after another year had passed and our apes had become young adults, additional tests revealed that they were still relying on rules about the frontal posture, faces and eye movements of the experimenters—not about who could see them. Thus, despite the fact that many of our chimpanzees had displayed evidence of self-recognition for more than four years, we had no evidence that they genuinely understood one of the most basic empathic aspects of human intelligence: the understanding that others see.

THE MEANING OF SELF-RECOGNITION

If we knew nothing more about chimpanzees, we might simply conclude that they understand visual perception in a very different manner than we do. Other studies in our laboratory, however, have suggested that chimpanzees may not understand any behavior in a psychological manner. For example, careful tests revealed that our apes do not comprehend pointing gestures as referential actions, nor do they understand the difference between accidental and intentional behavior. Furthermore, recent tests conducted with Daniela K. O'Neill of the University of Waterloo suggest that our original interpretations of our earlier studies on cooperation—which Gallup cites in support of his theory—may have been incorrect. Although our chimpanzees easily learn to cooperate with one another, our new results cast doubt on whether they truly appreciate the differing subjective mind-sets of their partners.

If chimpanzees do not genuinely reason about mental states in others, what can we say about their understanding of self? Exactly what is revealed by their antics in front of mirrors? And do such reactions to mirror images really indicate the onset of autobiographical memory—in both apes and humans—as Gallup suggests?

As a first attempt to answer these questions, we shifted our attention to humans—specifically, two-, three- and four-year-old children. In a series of studies, we individually videotaped the children as they played an unusual game with an experimenter. During the game, the experimenter praised the child and used this opportunity to place a large, brightly colored sticker secretly on top of the child's head. Three minutes later the children were shown either a live video image of themselves or the recording we had made several minutes earlier, which clearly depicted the experimenter placing the sticker on the child's head.

These tests revealed that the younger children—the two- and three-year-olds—responded very differently depending on whether they observed the live or delayed images. When confronted with a live image, the vast majority of the two- and three-year-olds reached up and removed the sticker from their heads. When confronted with three-minute-old images, however, only about one third of the younger children reached up for the sticker. Did the others simply not notice the sticker in the delayed video? Hardly. After experimenters drew their attention to the sticker in the video and asked them, "What is that?" the majority of the children responded, "It's a sticker." But this acknowledgement did not cause them to reach up and remove the sticker.

In one sense, of course, the children clearly "recognized themselves" in the delayed video. When they were asked, "Who is that?" even the youngest children confidently replied, "Me!" or stated their proper names. This reaction, however, did not seem to go beyond a recognition of facial and bodily features. When asked: "Where is that sticker?" the children frequently referred to the "other" child: "It's on her [or his] head." It was as if the children were trying to say, "Yes, that looks like me, but that's not me—she's not doing what I'm doing right now." One three-year-old girl summarized this psychological conflict quite succinctly: "It's Jennifer," she stated, only to hurriedly add, "but why is she wearing my shirt?"

So when do children come to think of themselves as having a past and a future? Our studies have revealed that by about four years of age, a significant majority of the children began to pass our delayed self-recognition test. Unlike their younger counterparts, most four- and five-year-olds confidently reached up to remove the sticker after they observed the delayed video images of themselves. They no longer referred to "him" or "her" or their proper names when talking about their images. This finding fits nicely with the view of Katherine Nelson of the City University of New York and others, who believe that genuine autobiographical memory appears to emerge in children between 3.5 and 4.5 years old—not at the two-year mark that Gallup favors. Of course, any parent knows that two-year-olds can recall past events, but this is very different from understanding that those memories constitute a genuine "past"—a history of the self leading up to the here and now.

Although it is still too early to rule out Gallup's model altogether, our research suggests that self-recognition in chimpanzees and human toddlers is based on a recognition of the self's behavior, not the self's psychological states. When chimpanzees and orangutans see themselves in a mirror, they form an equivalence relation between the actions they see in the mirror and their own behavior. Every time they move, the mirror image moves with them. They conclude that everything that is true for the mirror image is also true for their own bodies, and vice versa. Thus, these apes can pass the mirror test by correlating colored marks on the mirror image with marks on their own bodies. But the ape does not conclude, "That's me!" Rather the animal concludes, "That's the same as me!"

Thus, although Gallup and I agree that passing the mirror test reveals the presence of a kind of self-concept, we differ on the nature and scope of that concept. Gallup believes that chimpanzees possess a psychological understanding of themselves. In contrast, I believe these apes possess an explicit mental representation of the position and movement of their own bodies—what could be called a kinesthetic self-concept.

Ironically, this may be close to what Gallup himself had in mind when he originally published his discovery nearly 30 years ago. He noted that self-recognition appears to require the ability to project "kinesthetic feedback onto the reflected visual image so as to coordinate the appropriate visually guided movements via the mirror." But why do humans, chimpanzees and orangutans possess this kinesthetic self-concept, whereas other nonhuman primates—such as monkeys—do not? One clue may be the large difference in body size between the great apes and other primates. Consider orangutans, which may represent the closest living approximation to the common ancestor of the great apes and humans. Several years ago, John G. H. Cant of the University of Puerto Rico and I spent months in the Sumatran rain forest observing the orangutan's chaotic blend of slow, carefully planned movements and sudden, breathtaking acrobatics. We concluded that the problems encountered by these 40- to 80-kilogram (90-to 180-pound) animals in bridging the gaps between trees were qualitatively different from the problems faced by the much smaller monkeys and lesser apes. We hypothesized that as the ancestors of the great apes evolved, quadrupling in body size over 10 to 20 million years, they may have needed to evolve a high-level self-representational system dedicated to planning their movements in their arboreal environment. Ultimately, this unprecedented increase in body size for a tree-dwelling mammal may have left a psychological imprint on the great apes: an explicit kinesthetic self-concept. It was this self-concept that Gallup tapped millions of years later in his tests of chimpanzee self-recognition.

A crucial test for our theory is the gorilla, the largest nonhuman primate. Although gorillas share the same common ancestor as humans, chimpanzees and orangutans, they have readapted to spending most of their lives on the ground. The surprising absence of self-recognition in this species may reflect the fact that gorillas no longer needed to execute the complex movements that were necessary to transport their enormous body weight across the gaps between trees. Their evolution appears to have focused on aspects that were more relevant to their new terrestrial way of life, including a more rapid physical growth rate than is found in chimpanzees and orangutans. This process may have interfered with the development of a kinesthetic self-concept. Humans, in contrast, slowed down their growth rate, allowing more years for cognitive development.

If self-recognition depends on a kinesthetic rather than a psychological self-concept, it would help explain some puzzling facts. Several studies have found no connection between the ability of 18- to 24-month-old infants to pass the mirror test and their ability to understand that a mirror reflects any object placed in front of it. Our theory explains this result by postulating that the infants do not see their mirror images as representations of themselves. Rather they see their images as a special class of entities that share their behavior and appearance. Our theory also explains why toddlers often fail the self-recognition test if there is even a minimal disruption of the visual feedback—for example, a two-second delay in the video images of themselves. Although the children continue to recognize their facial and bodily features, the two-second disjunction between their actions and the movements of their images leads them to conclude that the images are not equivalent to themselves. Finally, our theory explains why both toddlers and chimpanzees, after recognizing themselves in the mirror, may nonetheless persist in looking behind the mirror, as if searching for the "other" child or ape.

UNDERSTANDING MINDS: A HUMAN SPECIALIZATION

At this point we are still left with a troubling question: How can humans and chimpanzees share such sophisticated social behaviors but understand them so differently? Why do humans interpret these behaviors in terms of psychological states, but apes do not?

My answer may become more obvious if we imagine our planet 60 million years ago, long before any of the modern primates had evolved. Alison Jolly of Princeton University has speculated that as the solitary lifestyle of the small, early primates gave way to existence in large groups, these animals were forced to cope with increasingly complex social interactions. As a result, Jolly argues, the primates became stunningly adept at reasoning about one another's actions, slowly evolving the rich array of social behaviors now observed among the modern primates: gaze following, deception, appeasement and so on.

But, in my view, none of these behaviors required the early primates to reason about one another's mental states. Our research suggests that only one primate lineage—the human one—evolved the unique cognitive specialization that enables us to represent explicitly our own psychological states and those of others. But in evolving this specialization, we did not discard our array of basic primate behaviors. Our new awareness of the mental dimension of behavior was woven into our existing neural circuitry, forever altering our understanding of our own behavior and the behavior of those around us. Other species, including chimpanzees, may simply be incapable of reasoning about mental states—no matter how much we insist on believing that they do.

34

APES WITH LANGUAGE

Sue Savage-Rumbaugh, Stuart Shanker and Talbot J. Taylor

When Aristotle argued that 'Man is by nature a political animal', or Seneca that 'Man is a reasoning animal', the emphasis was very much on the idea that man is a part of the natural order – an animal, but an animal which is political and which reasons. These moral and cognitive capacities allow man to rise above the other animals. But given his innately bestial nature, man was seen as subject to the same sorts of instincts and drives as all the other species, and thus always in danger of relapsing to the level of the brutes.

Western cosmology changed dramatically in 1637 when, in his *Discourse on Method*, René Descartes attacked the Great Chain of Being: the doctrine that all of nature is organised in an unbroken series which progresses from plants through simple organisms and animals to man, and then beyond man to spiritual beings and ultimately God. Descartes argued that there is a hiatus between animals and man that cannot be filled by a 'missing link'. Animals, according to Descartes, are merely machines. The human body, he claimed, is also a machine; but it is a machine that is endowed with and governed by a mind. Hence man – by his ability to reason and reflect, to exercise moral choice, to direct the actions of his body, to be conscious of his mental states, to speak a language, and to live in a society – is categorically divorced from the animals.

For Descartes, these cognitive, moral, social and linguistic abilities could not possibly be possessed by any non-human species. Moreover, since animals do not have minds, they could never even be brought to acquire language; for Cartesianism sees language as a means of transmitting thoughts from the mind of one agent to that of another. In turn, since they cannot acquire a language, animals are barred from developing the higher attributes of man. For, according to Cartesianism, all of the moral and social benefits which man enjoys are the direct result of the creation of language. Thus, Descartes's universe, unlike that of the Ancients, is bifurcated. At its centre stands neither the Earth nor the Sun, but the mind of the human individual, responding to and literally constructing the world around it.

Cartesianism has had a profound influence on the manner in which we view animals: namely, as creatures that are there to serve our interests and our needs. One can also argue that Cartesianism has played an instrumental role in modern man's increasing alienation from nature. But the issue that concerns us most here is the manner in which Cartesianism has shaped scientific attitudes towards the study of language and its relation to thought.

If, as the Cartesian legacy would have it, language is an integral and unique part of the human birthright, then the study of animal behaviour, or for that matter, the study of nonverbal human behaviour, can shed no light on such questions as the nature of language, the origins of language, or the child's acquisition of language. But as soon as one entertains the possibility that there might be some *continuity* between animal communication, proto-linguistic activities and language 'proper', our perspective on the nature of language and its relation to thought must change dramatically.

Prior to recent developments in Ape Language Research (ALR), Cartesian linguists and cognitive psychologists were able to maintain a dogmatic attitude towards the very possibility of such continuity. But the dramatic accomplishments in ALR over the past few decades – particularly work with the bonobos Kanzi and Panbanisha – force the scientific community to reconsider. Other considerations shape modern discussions of these issues. There is an emerging awareness of the close similarity between critical aspects of the behaviour of wild apes (including bonobos) and of ourselves. And we now know that apes are more closely related to humans than they are to monkeys in terms of the basic building blocks of the DNA code of life. Together these considerations force us to recognise that the Cartesian dichotomy framed by the words 'animal' and 'human' can no longer be accepted as valid.

To be sure, old dichotomies die slowly. Cartesian-influenced scientists are not yet willing to accept the possibility of a genuine continuity between the human mind and that of the ape. These scientists are therefore led to maintain that, while there is no obvious neurological difference between human and ape, there *must* nonetheless be one. There *must* be some neurological difference that accounts for the taken-for-granted discontinuity between their mental abilities. Since it is not an obvious difference, well, then it must be a small difference: albeit one that has a large effect. This postulated neurological difference, although it has never been clearly identified in neural structure, has been referred to by various labels, the most common of which are 'grammar module' and, more recently, 'mind-reading module'. Accordingly, while apes and humans both have been shown to have parietal lobes and amygdaloid complexes, nevertheless only humans may be assumed to have the 'grammar' or 'mind-reading' module which, according to Cartesianism, must be held to reside *somewhere* within these neural structures.

On this view, all of the things which seem to set human beings apart from animals are assumed to be reducible to a single unique capacity: a capacity that finds the essence of its expression in what we call language. This capacity is presumed to undergird and make possible what we call 'rational thought'. It is apparently manifest in its clearest form in man's possession of grammar and in his concept of number: that is, in man's ability, as the Cartesian tradition would have it, to relate the structural components of abstract symbol systems to one another and to manipulate them according to rules.

Thus the current, Cartesian view of animal–human relationships, enlightened by science and freed from religious dogma, is that man is born with a sort of pure mathematical device inside his head. This device may be undetectable; but, the story goes, it must be something that permits humans to relate rules for organising symbols to real world events in certain specific ways. These 'neurally embodied rules' do not take up much space; nor, apparently, do they require any dramatic restructuring of the brain – so efficient is their encoding. The human child needs only a normal upbringing with exposure to the activities of others in order for this human endowment to flower. Animals, being devoid of language, lack this 'grammar' or 'mind-reading' module. Therefore, lacking man's analytical capacity, an animal's learning is limited to being trained to perform complex chains of actions. Although these chains can become extremely elaborate, still animals, like plants, remain at the beck and call of stimuli generated by the environment.

On this view, animals can never free themselves from their surroundings and contemplate the existence of self and nature, as can human beings. Thus, modern neuroscience has retained the Cartesian view that there exists a fundamental functional difference between the minds of humans and the minds of animals. By positing the existence of a bit of critical (though indistinguishable) neural tissue that is said to contain something akin to the *alphabet of thought*, neuroscience has managed to incorporate Descartes, Darwin, DNA and Goodall all into its cosmology: without altering the central tenet which proclaims that man alone is capable of consciousness, rational thought, moral choice and language.

But this view, mainstream as it is, is not a comfortable one, as can be seen from the steady rise in recent years of the animal rights issue. The problem, it seems, is that we humans can clearly see that many animals, and particularly mammals, are like ourselves in myriad ways. They appear to feel as we do when they are sad or hungry or tired or lonely or frightened or angry. They take steps that are wholly recognisable by us as ones that we ourselves might take to correct these circumstances. Many of them are as devoted to their young and their mates as we are; and many of them are as attached to their homes as we are. Some build complex shelters and modify objects to use as tools. Many are able to do things that we are unable to do because of limitations of our senses. And many animals appear to employ complex communication systems that we cannot decipher in any but the crudest fashion.

Yet in spite of sensing all of these similarities between animals and ourselves, we wish to maintain that we are somehow different and superior. Why? To some extent the sad answer is that we find animals so useful for our way of life. They provide important sources of food, clothing, and labour. But in addition to the economic dependence of our species on animals, it is also important to recognise that all of the presuppositions that we have inherited about the nature of language, or rationality, or morality, simply preclude animals – *a priori* – from sharing in what we are led to regard as our uniquely human birthright.

The fact that no animal speaks is surely the strongest buttress reinforcing this bifurcationist picture of the great divide between animals and humans. It allows and even encourages us to accept without challenge claims that animals lack both reason and souls. Deprived of the gift of tongues, animals are the ultimate disenfranchised group, and the economic welfare of humans is increased immeasurably because of the use of animals for food, clothing, and as human surrogates. Having learned to hunt, eat and domesticate many species of animals, man's conceptual and legal bifurcation between himself and all lesser creatures would probably have continued intact, were it not for the fact that in 1972 Allen and Beatrice Gardner reported that a chimpanzee named Washoe had learned a language. The language that Washoe had learned, American Sign Language, is used by millions of deaf Americans and is regarded by linguists as equal in structural complexity and cognitive power to any of the more familiar spoken languages. Washoe was never claimed to be fluent in this language, only to be able to express simple desires and needs. Nevertheless, this one report, so at odds with Descartes's picture of animals as machines, incapable of rational thought and language, created a maelstrom of controversy.

Recognising the depth, the history and the economic forces underlying man's conception of himself, his rationality, and his dominion over animals, it should come as no surprise that the initial claims that apes were learning a human language were met with outright scepticism and cries of fraud. These initial debates centred upon attempts to determine whether or not what Washoe was doing was 'really' language. They served to clarify the fact that, although we use language all the time, we really have no clear understanding of what language is, and no means of saying precisely whether or not Washoe's 'language' was the same sort of thing as human language.

Linguists had never before been challenged by the idea of an animal who possessed language. To be sure, if Washoe had begun speaking herself as an academic scholar on the issue, no one could have contested her ability. But that was not what happened. Washoe did sign; but her signs were often repetitive, they seemed to lack internal structure, and it was not always easy to determine what she was saying. Of course, this was the first time anyone had succeeded in teaching a human language to another species. Moreover, Washoe's hands were not really made for the articulations of American Sign Language, nor was her vocal tract fashioned for the articulation of human speech. But all new scientific endeavours are clumsy at first, and there was no reason to conclude that Washoe's performance reflected her limitations at this point, rather than our own.

Washoe could produce different signs when shown a wide variety of different objects. She could also generalise these signs to novel objects that were similar in form or conceptual class. For example, the sign for 'meat' could be applied to hamburger, steak, chicken, etc. It soon became apparent that other chimpanzees could do this as well, and they could do it with plastic tokens or geometric symbols in the place of gestural signs. But was this naming? Some scientists argued that it was merely paired-associate learning – that Washoe only knew which gesture to make when presented with a certain item. But this, they pointed out, is not the same as knowing that the sign was a 'name' for an object.

Of course, it was not possible to ask Washoe herself if she had learned paired-associates or if she really knew that her signs were symbols for objects. The only way to determine how Washoe viewed her signs was to look at how she used them in combination. It was thought that, if her combinations exhibited a syntax, then it would have to be assumed that Washoe had somehow come to possess a grammar module similar to that humans were assumed to possess. But Washoe did not produce her signs in isolation. Rather they occurred when others talked to her; and her sign-combinations often contained components of the combinations that her caretakers had employed.

Naturally, then, the question was asked: How much of what Washoe said was the imitation of others and how much was spontaneous and deliberate? What did she intend by her signs? At first glance, these questions seemed simple enough. But they concealed a deeper and more intractable issue when viewed from the Cartesian perspective. For the problem of determining what was and what was not on Washoe's mind as she spoke drove straight to the heart of what we call 'language'. What is it to say what is 'on one's mind'? Just what is a mind, in the sense in which it can 'have something on it'? How can we know what is 'on someone's mind' *except* by listening to what they say? Can someone be conceived as 'saying something' and yet not be conceived as having a mind?

With human beings, even young children, it is taken for granted that speech is a reflection of the mind. With Washoe, the question came to be whether or not she had a mind which her speech could be a reflection of. If she did not have a mind, then how else could her behaviour be explained? The alternative that was put forward was that her behaviour should be explained in terms of 'instrumental conditioning'. Washoe spoke, it was said, because of the rewards she received by doing so. She did not (*could not*) speak to express her mind; she spoke mechanically in order to obtain the reward which she associated with sign-production. (As the dog barks to obtain a proffered treat.) And yet, as simple as this explanation seemed, there was something dreadfully wrong with it.

When we humans speak to express what is 'on our minds', we do so with the intention that someone else will understand us; that is our reward. If others do not understand what we are saying, then we say it another way; because that is why we speak: to be understood. If Washoe wanted a banana and she spoke to convey this, she wanted to be understood as well. Were we not therefore employing a double standard – allowing such things to be 'on our (human) minds' but not 'on Washoe's'?

But there was an important difference between Washoe's use of language and our own that was ignored in the early rush to determine whether or not Washoe was 'speaking her mind'. This difference lay not in what Washoe said, or what she wanted, or what she did. Rather it lay in what she *understood*. We understand language as a two-way street. Not only do we tell people what is 'on our minds', but we listen to what is on their minds. We listen and we show that we understand by our actions. It is that understanding, and the actions that signal that understanding, that serve as the reward for those who are talking to us. Thus if someone tells us that they want a banana (or a hug, or love, or understanding, or sympathy, or they want us to 'change our mind') we typically engage in some sort of action in response to their statement. In the simplest case, if they ask for a banana and we have one, we offer it. If we are selling it, we may offer it along with a comment regarding its cost, but we offer it nonetheless.

This is where Washoe and human beings parted ways. Washoe was quite good at asking for a banana, but completely inept at giving one. Indeed, Washoe was completely inept at listening and giving anything. For Washoe, language had only one function: making the world do what she wanted. In other words, half of what we regard as language was missing. For Washoe showed little understanding of what was said to her. She had been taught to speak, but she had not been taught to listen.

Listening seemed too simple. Listening, it was thought, was just sitting there and hearing what someone else said. Scientists assumed that there was nothing there to measure. All studies of child language prior to the work with Washoe had looked at what children said, not at what they understood. Indeed, it was deemed neither possible nor relevant to look at what children understood. Understanding, if it was thought of at all, was thought to come *along with* speaking.

The first realisation that comprehension provided greater insight into the nature of linguistic ability came when attempts were made to teach apes to use their language skills to convey information to one another. The initial attempts were carried out with two male chimpanzees, Sherman and Austin, who had learned lexical symbols. This study brought to light the hitherto unrecognised deficit in Washoe's use of language. Sherman and Austin, like Washoe, could readily 'speak their minds', in the sense of expressing desires for bananas, cokes, M&Ms and so on. They did this just as effectively as Washoe. As long as the recipients of their requests were human beings, their language appeared to function in a quite ordinary, if rather food-oriented manner, just as was the case for Washoe.

Sherman and Austin expressed their desires; humans listened and either gave them the foods they asked for or refused to do so. When they refused, Sherman and Austin asked for something else. Nothing was recognised as 'unusual' regarding their use of language until they were asked to talk only with each other. Suddenly it became clear that a language entailed a lot more than just 'speaking one's mind'. If two apes just expressed their desires to one another not much happened, other than a shouting match of sorts. Without one party acting as listener and attempting to understand and respond to the expressions of the other, communication did not get very far. The experiments with Sherman and Austin made it quite clear that to understand the nature of language, we had to go far beyond the idea that words functioned simply to describe what was on one's mind. Language does much more than that: it coordinates behaviours between individuals in particular circumstances by means of a complex process of exchanging behaviours punctuated by speech. It functions in a tightly woven mesh of expectancies and constraints that are set up by patterns of reciprocal actions that serve as variations on a theme. Words are used to do a lot more, therefore, than just express what is on one's mind.

The most important benefit which resulted from attempts to study language in creatures other than ourselves was that it allowed us to begin to peer through the Cartesian veil that had covered human thought about language for centuries. Suddenly we saw, for the first time, that language is not about describing our 'private mental states'; rather, it is a means of structuring our interactions with one another within particular contextual circumstances. Looked at in this way, language does not seem so far removed from the communication systems of other animals. The recognition that the key to language lies not in speech but in comprehension enabled ALR to move out of the 'teaching/training' paradigm. By focusing on what an ape understood, rather than on what it could say, scientists learned that language, even spoken human language, is not something the production of which one has to condition in other species, nor is it a feat that is achieved only for the sake of a reward. Although Washoe and other apes like Sarah and Lana had shown that animals were capable of learning various pieces of the language pie, anyone who interacted with them was still left with the unsettling feeling that the overall effect of their capacities, while clearly intelligent and language-like, fell short of the kind of thing that happens when people talk to one another.

Sherman and Austin, however, could be seen actually to talk to each other and to integrate their talking with their other behaviour in the interaction, just as we do. Sherman listened when Austin asked for things or for assistance, and Austin listened when Sherman asked. They acted in concert with each other, with language being a means of effecting that cooperation. Each speaker monitored the effectiveness of his communications, as reflected in the other's response, and each would assist or recycle their request when the listener showed himself not to have understood. Thus if Austin reacted with a puzzled expression to Sherman's request for a tool, Sherman would respond to Austin's manifested lack of understanding by pointing to the object. Of course, Sherman and Austin did not discuss the nature of the world, and their exchanges typically concerned only the immediate needs of the moment. Yet they clearly grasped the basic interactional power of symbol-using: using symbols as a means to facilitate 'getting the job done'.

Isn't this how we should explain events such as when Sherman rushed inside to announce to people and to Austin 'Scare outdoors' when he saw a partially anaesthetised ape moaning as it was transported past the building? Events such as this are frequently dismissed with the label 'anecdotal' and with the demand that they be reliably repeated. Yet a misunderstanding of the nature of language lurks behind such a demand. For with replication the point of the communicative act vanishes. Why should Sherman run in *again* and say 'Scare outdoors' when the scene is repeated? Replication dissociates the communicational act from its circumstantial motivation and, by that means, from its potential significance.

Another way of dismissing Sherman's report is to claim that it was conditioned in some unobvious manner. But such scepticism ignores the fact that efforts to condition behaviour in this way typically fail. Indeed, any explanation that trivialises the behaviour and strips it of communicational function simply cannot account for the kinds of symbol usage demonstrated by Sherman and Austin.

Other apes were to take our understanding of the linguistic abilities of apes much further: not because they were more intelligent, but because of what had been learned from Lana, Washoe, Sarah, Sherman and Austin. It is often thought the goal of ALR is to measure the ape's possession of language. But the possession of language is not something that it makes much sense to measure, in the way we might measure skull circumference. For, unlike a skull, language exists in interactions between individuals, not in the properties of a given individual. The scientists' measurements cannot be of some property (e.g., 'language') that the ape does or does not possess; for the measurements themselves are necessarily a function of what we human beings do in and through our interactions with the ape and what we see or comprehend as a result of these interactions.

This is why ape skills appear to vary not only as a function of the methods used, but also of the person doing the measurements and of the contextual circumstances in which the measurements are taken. The ape's abilities do not develop in a manner that is independent of the observer or of the observer's interactions with the ape. This does not mean that they are cued or that only 'human reared' apes are intelligent or capable of language. It simply means that *language – as a structure, as a capacity, as a cognitive 'possession' – cannot be distinguished from the ways in which it is used to coordinate our behaviour in particular interactional circumstances.*

It is not syntactic structures that coordinate behaviour. Syntax may aid in the decoding of certain concatenations of symbols, but the syntactical unpacking is itself trivial. It follows simple rules that can be learned, as Premack's work with Sarah so clearly demonstrated. Even a syntactic structure as complex as the 'if–then' relationship is trivial to teach to a chimpanzee, as a structure per se. What is not trivial is the myriad of ways that this structure can be used in different behavioural circumstances – where what is required is an understanding of the complete contextual situation in order to make sense of the contribution of the 'if–then' structure to the further development of the interaction.

Language as here conceived has been most clearly exemplified in work with the bonobos Kanzi and his sister Panbanisha. These apes have never received any instruction in language. Like a human child, they have been reared in a language rich environment, in which they are spoken to within and as a contributing component to the changing contexts of daily life. For Kanzi and Panbanisha everyday life includes trips in the forest to locate food resources and general daily activities of feeding, playing, grooming, cleaning and watching television. The language used is spoken English. In addition, a board of colourful symbols is carried about and symbols are indicated by pointing as they are spoken aloud.

We know now that these conditions are sufficient for apes to acquire an understanding of spoken language that equals, and in some respects surpasses, that of a three-year-old child. The resultant grasp of language includes the understanding of past and future tenses and syntactical constructions that require embedding and word order. It is also all that is needed for apes to learn to discriminate written symbols, to pair those symbols with spoken words and to use the symbols spontaneously to communicate their desires and their thoughts.

Language comprehension far outpaces production in these circumstances. Four- to eight-word sentences are easily processed, even upon the first occasion they are heard. However, sentential *production* is generally limited to a single word plus a gesture or a vocal sound. In part, sentence construction is constrained by the time required to locate each symbol on the keyboard; the process of finding each symbol interferes with the capacity to use a number of symbols in rapid sequence.

Without any special training, apes who are reared with exposure to spoken language and printed symbols are able to follow and participate in three- and four-way conversations – conversations concerning the intentions, states of mind and actions of multiple parties. For example, Panbanisha can answer questions about an object which another individual *thinks* has been hidden in a box – even though Panbanisha knows that what she herself has seen placed in the box is not what the other party thinks is in the box. Not only can she understand and answer such questions appropriately the first time they are proposed to her, she is also able to understand and comment upon the fact that a deceitful trick is being played upon one party by switching the contents of the box when they are not looking.

To answer questions such as 'What does Liz think is in the box?' Panbanisha must understand the sentence's syntactic structure – realising, for instance, that the verb 'think' refers back to the agent Liz. She must also grasp, on the one hand, that the sentence is not dealing with what actually is in the box, but rather with what someone else (Liz) *believes* to be in the box, and, on the other, that Liz formed this belief from her earlier experience. For Panbanisha to understand that the beliefs of different individuals may not agree and that the word 'think' addresses this possibility requires that she possess a sophisticated understanding of the nature of individual experience, an understanding that far surpasses that required for the grasp of syntactic structure. No syntactic explanation of the question 'What does Liz think is in the box?', or of the answer, could ever begin to characterise the true complexity of the language tasks involved.

Yet apes can do these things. They can understand the components of such a complex interactional situation, taking into account the roles of the different participants in the interaction and the potential effect which their different experiences and beliefs could have on the interaction. Apes such as Panbanisha can also understand when they are asked completely novel questions about such situations. And they can answer appropriately and even make supplementary comments, such as expressing an opinion that goes beyond what was explicitly asked of them. In the situation above, Panbanisha told us that we were being 'bad' to play such a trick on Liz. When the procedure was repeated with Heather, Liz's four-year-old daughter, Heather's perceptions were similar, and she too elected to say that we were being 'bad'.

It is astonishing that apes who understand language can easily do these things, even though their symbolic *productions* are limited to single symbol utterances. Apes who do not understand language do not have these skills, although we have no way of knowing where or why they fail. We naturally want to ask such questions as: Do these language-less apes understand that different people can have different perceptions of events? Do they know what is actually in the box? Do they know that Liz believes something else is in the box? Do they know that things stay in boxes even when they are out of sight? Do they even view the events as related? In other words, do they see the activities – hiding something in a box, taking it out while Liz is not looking, replacing it with something else, etc. – as *connected* in a significant way, much less as connected differently in Liz's mind than in their own?

What we do know is that an ape who *has* language has no need of training in order to come to grips with such situations. And this fact itself illustrates the extent to which language serves as a foundation to what we call joint attention, mutual understanding and cooperative action. Such events serve as windows on the true power and value of language. Moreover, the discovery that, if they are exposed to language at an early age, apes can peer through these windows in much the same way that we do, tells us that the modern Cartesian's insistence on the fundamental difference between the ape and the human mind can no longer be supported.

Animal language research, despised and maligned as it has been, has not only led us to a revised view of ape linguistic abilities, it has also taken us a long way toward a better understanding of the nature of language and of its acquisition by humans. ALR has forced us to abandon the Cartesian view of words as the names of mental representations and of sentences as the descriptions of thoughts. In its place, ALR has thrown into relief the infinitely varied roles that words and sentences can be called upon to serve. For, in acquiring language skills, what the child learns is, as J. L. Austin put it, 'how to do things with words'. That is, s/he learns how to participate with others in the mutual achievement of complex social interactions, how to facilitate that achievement by producing and attending to verbal and gestural signs, and how, by these means, to become more skilled at communicating their thoughts, intentions, desires etc.

Animal language research has shown us that apes are capable of satisfying a vast range of the criteria that we ordinarily apply when characterising the cognitive and linguistic abilities of young children. The work with Kanzi and Panbanisha in particular has introduced a crucial new dimension into our understanding of the nature of language: not just because Kanzi and Panbanisha have progressed further than other apes in their comprehension and production skills, but more importantly because they have done so without any formal language training. What is important here isn't simply that they were exposed to 'linguistic input' from birth, but that Kanzi and Panbanisha were exposed to a whole range of communicational problems and goals that do not arise in their natural habitat. And their acquisition of language consisted in a developing mastery of the comprehension and production skills necessary for dealing with and contributing to such settings. In turn, this indicates that Kanzi and Panbanisha possessed the cognitive resources for dealing with the linguistic and cultural environment in which they were raised. Can it be, therefore, that this capacity already lies dormant in their conspecifics living in the wild? ALR leads us to confront the intriguing possibility that we have seriously underestimated the social and communicational complexity of primate behaviour.

The most interesting things about the research on Kanzi and Panbanisha are those which the modern Cartesian dismisses. What matters most isn't what they cannot do, but what they can: and, more precisely, the factors which enabled these (possibly latent) capacities to flourish. The very fact that, by being raised in a human-like environment, Kanzi and Panbanisha should have spontaneously acquired primitive linguistic skills speaks volumes about both the phylogenesis and the ontogenesis of language. We must direct our attentions more closely to the questions thus raised:

questions, on the one hand, about the environmental conditions which may have led to the original emergence of language and, on the other, about the ways in which the interactional context prepares and then guides today's child through the entry into language.

Perhaps our greatest problem now is that Cartesianism still infects every aspect of the sciences of cognition and language. Our whole way of thinking about the mind and about language – the way we present and defend ideas, the questions we ask and the way we try to resolve them – has been thoroughly shaped by the demands imposed by the Cartesian framework. But perhaps Kanzi and Panbanisha's first steps into the world of human interaction and communication will provide just the spark that is needed to ignite the paradigm-revolution that will finally lead us to break free from Cartesianism. For, by observing Kanzi and Panbanisha, one can more easily see how notions like the 'Language Acquisition Device' or the 'Mind-reading Module' – mythological beasts which are conjured into necessary existence to respond to the epistemological requirements of Cartesianism – grossly distort our picture of what actually occurs when human beings learn how to speak and interact with one another. Even worse, such myths reinforce the conceptual myopia which prevents us from seeing and appreciating the richness and complexity of animal life. And finally, these myths prevent us from examining the role which the environment plays in the complex interrelations between social, affective, cognitive and linguistic development.

35

BEHIND THE APE'S APPEARANCE: ESCAPING ANTHROPOCENTRISM IN THE STUDY OF OTHER MINDS

Daniel Povinelli

Look at Megan. Not just at her distinctively chimpanzee features – her accentuated brow ridge, her prognathic face, her coarse black hair – but at the totality of her being: her darting eyes, her slow, studied movements, the gestures she makes as her companion, Jadine, passes nearby. Can there be any doubt that behind certain obvious differences in her appearance resides a mind nearly identical to our own? Indeed, is it even possible to spend an afternoon with her and *not* come to this conclusion? Upon reflection, you will probably acknowledge that her mind is not identical to ours. "But surely it's not qualitatively different, either," you will still insist. "I mean, it's obvious from watching her that we share the same *kind* of mind."

Faced with the overwhelming similarity in the spontaneous, everyday behavior of humans and chimpanzees, how can someone like me – someone who has dedicated his life to studying these remarkable animals – entertain the possibility that their minds are, in profound respects, radically different from our own? How can I challenge the received wisdom of Darwin – confirmed by my own initial impressions – that the mental life of a chimpanzee is best compared to that of a human child?

Actually, it's easy: I have learned to have more respect for them than that. I have come to see that we distort their true nature by conceiving of their minds as smaller, duller, less talkative versions of our own. Casting aside these insidious assumptions has been difficult, but it has allowed me to see more clearly that the human mind is not the gold standard against which other minds must be judged. For me it has also illuminated the possibility of creating a science that is less contaminated by our deeply anthropocentric intuitions about the nature of other minds.

The best available estimates suggest that humans and chimpanzees originated from a common ancestor about five or six million years ago.[1] This is reflected in estimates of our genetic similarity: we share, on average, about 98.6 percent of our total nucleotide sequence in common. This statistic seems impressive. After all, such biological affinity would appear to be the final nail in the coffin of the notion that there could be any radical mental differences between them and us: if chimpanzees and humans share 98.6 percent of their genetic material, then doesn't it follow that there ought to be an extraordinarily high degree of mental similarity as well? This idea has been paraded so frequently through the introductory paragraphs of both scholarly journal articles and the popular press alike that it has come to constitute a melody of sorts; an anthem that if not sung raises doubts as to one's allegiance to the cause of defending the chimpanzee's dignity.

But what does this 98.6 percent statistic really mean? It should be of immediate interest that it is almost invariably misreported. We do not share 98.6 percent of our genes in common with chimpanzees; we share 98.6 percent of our nucleotide sequence. A single nucleotide difference in a string of four hundred may code for a different allele. Furthermore, as the geneticist Jonathan Marks has pointed out in lucid detail, the 98.6 percent statistic has so little grounding in the average mind that confronts it, as to render it essentially meaningless.[2] We might, after all, share 50 percent of our nucleotide sequences in common with bananas and broccoli. But what on earth does it mean to say that we are 50 percent the same as a vegetable? I don't know about you, but I doubt my mind is 50 percent identical to that of the garden pea. And so what would it mean, exactly, if we discovered that our minds were 75 percent chimpanzee?

No, such coarse genetic comparisons will hardly suffice to help us understand the complex similarities and differences that exist between the mental lives of humans and chimpanzees. However, in a climate where certain highly visible experts have radically anthropomorphized chimpanzees,[3] such statistics are heralded as establishing once and for all that chimpanzees are, at the very least, mentally equivalent to two- or three-year-old human children, and should therefore be granted human rights.[4]

A few obvious biological facts may be worth noting here. To begin, it was the human lineage, not the chimpanzee one, that underwent radical changes after our respective genealogies began to diverge from their common ancestor. Since this split, humans have resculpted their bodies from head to toe – quite literally, in fact; as our lineage became bipedal, the pelvis, the knee, and the foot were all drastically reshaped, with modifications in the hand (including new muscles) soon following. To top it all off, we ultimately tripled the size of our brain, with disproportionate increases probably occurring in the seat of higher cognitive function, the prefrontal cortex. Oh yes, and at some point during all of this (no one knows exactly when), natural language – perhaps the most noticeable of human adaptations – emerged as well.

In contrast, chimpanzees have probably changed relatively little from the common ancestor they shared with us about five million years ago. Indeed, of all of the members of the great ape/human group who shared a common ancestor about fifteen million years ago, none, indeed, has diverged as much as humans. A simple thought experiment may help to put this point into perspective: line up all of the species in question – gorillas, orangutans, chimpanzees, bonobos, humans – and one of them immediately stands out. Guess which one?

In fact, the more we compare humans and chimpanzees, the more the differences are becoming apparent. Even geneticists are starting to catch up with the reality of these differences. New research has shown that rough similarity in our nucleotide sequences obscures the fact that the same genes may have dramatically different activity levels in the two species. So even where humans and chimpanzees share genes in common, it turns out that there are what can only be described as major differences in gene *expression* – that is, whether, when, and for how long genes are actually working to produce the proteins for which they code.[5] This is the *real* stuff of genetic comparison, and it casts our crude genetic similarity to the garden pea in a wholly different light.

What makes these differences in gene expression significant is that they ultimately manifest themselves as differences in the bodies – including the brains – of humans and chimpanzees. So, exactly how similar are the brains of humans and chimpanzees? After all, if we knew *that*, couldn't we directly address the question of their mental similarity? Well, it would be a start, anyhow. Unfortunately, comparisons of the brains of humans and apes have traditionally been limited to gross considerations such as size and surface features (such as lobes and sulcus patterns). Remarkably, the details of the internal organization of human and great ape brain systems and structures have been largely ignored, in part because it's so difficult to study these brains, but also because most neuroscientists have frequently assumed that despite great differences in size, all mammalian brains are organized pretty much the same.

Fortunately, even this is beginning to change. For example, Todd Preuss, working at the University of Louisiana, recently made a startling discovery while comparing the brains of humans and chimpanzees. Turning his attention away from the frontal lobes, his previous area of research, Preuss decided to take a look at the primary visual cortex (V1), the area of the cerebral cortex that is the first way station into the processing of visual information. The organization of this area of the brain has been assumed to be nearly identical across primates. But there, in the middle of V1, Preuss and his colleagues uncovered a distinctively human specialization – a kind of neural architecture not found even in chimpanzees.[6] Preuss speculates that this specialization involves modifications of the pathways related to spatial vision and motion processing. But, regardless of what it is for, it suggests that we need to rethink brain evolution in a way that's consistent with neo-Darwinian theory:

similarity and difference among species as comfortable bedfellows; a state of affairs accomplished by weaving in new systems and structures alongside the old. "If we find such differences in the middle of the primary visual cortex," Preuss recently remarked to me, "just imagine what we're going to find when we start looking elsewhere."

Some may be surprised (or even afraid) to learn of such differences between humans and our nearest living relatives. After several decades of being fed a diet heavy on exaggerated claims of the degree of mental continuity between humans and apes, many scientists and lay-persons alike now find it difficult to confront the existence of radical differences. But then, in retrospect, how viable was the idea of seamless mental continuity in the first place? After all, it tended to portray chimpanzees as watered-down humans, not-quite-finished children. Despite the fact that aspects of this notion can be traced straight to Darwin, it is an evolutionarily dubious proposition, to say the least.

If there are substantial differences between the mental abilities of humans and chimpanzees, in what areas are they likely to exist? Over the past couple of thousand years, many potential rubicons separating human and animal thinking have been proposed. Some of these have been particularly unhelpful, such as the radical behaviorists' forgettable proposition that animals don't 'think' at all (of course, these behaviorists were even skeptical about the existence of human thought!). And, unfortunately, in the popular imagination the question still appears to be, "*Can* animals think?"[7] as opposed to, "How does thinking differ across species?" (the latter being a decidedly more evolutionarily minded question).

Assuming that chimpanzees and other species have mental states (a point I take for granted), it seems to me that a more productive question to ask is, "What are their mental states about?" Or, put another way, "What kinds of concepts do they have at their disposal?" It would stand to reason that the mental states of chimpanzees, first and foremost, must be concerned with the things most relevant to their natural ecology – remembering the location of fruit trees, keeping an eye out for predators, and keeping track of the alpha male, for instance. And so surely chimpanzees form concepts about concrete things – things like trees, facial expressions, threat vocalizations, leopards, and the like. But what about more abstract concepts? Concepts like ghosts, gravity, and God?

Admittedly, to use the term 'concept' as loosely as I have will require the indulgence of certain scholars. But perhaps some progress can be made by noting that every concept is at least somewhat abstract if it extends beyond a particular example. For instance, if one has a notion of an apple that is not limited to a single instance of that apple, then one has made a generalization, and thus a kind of abstraction. Given that it has been known for decades or more that chimpanzees and many other species form such abstractions,[8] this cannot be a defining feature of human thinking.

At the risk of oversimplification, let me instead propose a distinction between concepts that refer to objects and events that can be directly observed (that is, things that can be detected by the unaided senses), versus hypothetical entities and processes (things that are classically unobservable). Thus, I wish to separately consider all concepts that refer to theoretical things: all the things that are not directly registered by the senses, but are merely posited to exist on the basis of things we can observe.

Such concepts permeate our commonsense way of thinking: we explain physical events on the basis of things like 'forces' (supernatural or otherwise) that we have never actually witnessed, and account for the behavior of other humans on the basis of mental states we have never seen (e.g., their beliefs, desires, and emotions). These concepts serve as the bedrock for some of our most fundamental explanations for why the world works the way it does.

Meanwhile, we can directly contrast these sorts of concepts with ones that are derived from things that can be directly observed: apples and oranges, trees, flashes of lightning, facial expressions – even the raising of a hand or the sound of a train whistle blowing in the distance. Concepts about these things share at least one property in common: they are all derived from the world of macroscopic entities with which the primary senses directly interact. Without additional justification, I am therefore asserting a distinction between concepts that refer to observable objects and events, and ones that refer to strictly hypothetical ones.

So, here's a proposal: the mental lives of humans and chimpanzees are *similar*, in that both species form innumerable (and in many cases, identical) concepts about observable things; but, at the same time, are *radically different*, in that humans form additional concepts about inherently unobservable things.[9]

Now, I realize that most people would not be surprised if it were established beyond doubt that chimpanzees lack a concept of God. But what about other, seemingly more prosaic concepts that infest our way of thinking about the world? Consider the way in which we think about the social realm. In interacting with each other (and with animals, for that matter), we use a dual system of representation: we understand other beings both as part of the observable world (they engage in particular movements of their hands and feet, and their lips form particular contortions as sounds emerge from their mouths), and as entities with mental properties – unobservable attributes like emotions, intentions, desires, and beliefs.

The proposal is that, in contrast to humans, chimpanzees rely strictly upon observable features of others to forge their social concepts. If correct, it would mean that chimpanzees do not realize that there is more to others than their movements, facial expressions, and habits of behavior. They would not understand that other beings are repositories of private, internal experience. They would not appreciate that in addition to things that go on in the observable world, there are forever hidden things that go on in the private life of the mind. It would mean that chimpanzees do not reason about what others think, believe, and feel – precisely because they do not form such concepts in the first place.

Before we get too much further, let me be honest: I recognize that this proposal has troubling implications. For one thing, if chimpanzees do not reason about unobservable entities, then we would frequently need distinctly different explanations for human and chimpanzee behavior – even in situations where the behavior looks almost identical. Mind you, we would not need completely different explanations, just ones that are distinctive enough to capture the proposed difference. Nonetheless, each time we witnessed a chimpanzee engage in a complex social behavior that resembles our own, we would have to believe that, unlike us, the chimpanzee has only one conceptual system for encoding and reasoning about what is happening: a system that invokes concepts derived from observable features of the world. Thus, when chimpanzees deceive each other (which they do regularly), they would never be trying to manipulate what others believe, nor what others can see or hear, for constructs like 'believing,' 'seeing,' and 'hearing' are already deeply psychological. No, in deciding what to do, the chimpanzee would be thinking and reasoning solely about the abstracted statistical regularities that exist among certain events and the behaviors, postures, and head movements (for example) of others – what we have called 'behavioral abstractions.'[10]

I should note that humans, too, rely heavily upon behavioral abstractions in their day-to-day interactions. We *must* be doing so: otherwise upon what basis could we attribute additional, psychological states to others? First, we recognize the turn of the head and the direction of the eyes (observable features), then we ascribe the internal experience of 'seeing' (unobservable feature). So, the proposal isn't that chimpanzees use one system and humans use another; both species are purported to rely upon concepts about the observable properties of others. Instead, the proposal is that chimpanzees don't form additional concepts about the *un*observable properties of other beings (or the world in general, for that matter).

So, at face value, the proposal I have made is worrying. In interpreting what would appear to be the exact same behaviors in humans and chimpanzees in different ways, I seem to be applying a double standard.

But is this implication really problematic, or does it just seem problematic because it runs counter to some of our most deeply engrained – but fundamentally flawed – ways of thinking?

Assume, for a moment, that you have traveled back in time to a point when there were no chimpanzees on this planet – and no humans, either. Imagine further that you have come face to face with members of the last common ancestor of humans and chimpanzees. Let's stipulate that these organisms are intelligent, thinking creatures who deftly attend to and learn about the regularities that unfold in the world around them. But let us also stipulate that they do not reason about unobservable things; they have no ideas about the 'mind,' no notion of 'causation.'

As you return to your time machine and speed forward, you will observe new lineages spring to life from this common ancestor. Numerous ape-like species will emerge, then disappear. As you approach the present day, you will even witness the evolutionary birth of modern orangutans, chimpanzees, and gorillas. But amid all of this your attention will be drawn to one particular offshoot of this process, a peculiar genealogy that buds off numerous descendent species. This particular lineage has evolved an eye-catching trick: it habitually stands upright; it walks bipedally. And some of its descendants build upon this trick, capitalizing upon the new opportunities it offers. For reasons that we may never fully know, tool use and manufacture increase exponentially, language emerges, brain size triples, and, as more time passes, human material and social culture begins to accrete upon the shoulders of the lineage's last surviving member: *Homo sapiens sapiens*. Now, imagine that as part of this process, this lineage evolved new conceptual structures (intimately connected to the evolution of language) that allow them to reason about things that cannot be observed: mental states, physical forces, spiritual deities.

I have stipulated all of this so we can confront the following question: If evolution proceeded in this quite plausible manner, then how would we expect the spontaneous, everyday behavior of humans to compare to that of chimpanzees? The answer, I think, is that things would look pretty much the way they do now. After all, humans would not have abandoned the important, ancestral psychological structures for keeping track of other individuals within their groups, nor jettisoned their systems for noticing that something very different happens when Joe turns his head toward so-and-so, just depending on whether or not his hair is standing on end. No, in evolving a new psychological system for reasoning about hypothetical, internal mental states, humans would not have (indeed, could not have!) abandoned the ancient systems for reasoning about observable behavior. The new system by definition would depend upon the presence of older ones.

Now, is it really troubling to invoke a different explanation for what on the surface seem to be identical units of behavior in humans and chimpanzees? If the scenario I have outlined above is correct, then the answer must be, no. After all, for any given ability that humans and chimpanzees share in common, the two species would share a common set of psychological structures, which, at the same time, humans would augment by relying upon a system or systems unique to our species. The residual effect of this would manifest itself in numerous ways: some subtle (such as tightly constrained changes in the details of things to which our visual systems attend), others more profound (such as the creation of cultural artifacts like the book in which you are now reading these words).

So much for theory. What about the empirical evidence; does it support the proposal I have just offered? Although it will not surprise you to learn that I think it does, I have not always been of this opinion; I used to believe that any differences between humans and chimpanzees would have to be trivial. But the results of over two hundred studies that we have conducted during the past fifteen years have slowly changed my mind. Combined with findings from other laboratories, this evidence has forced me to seriously confront the possibility that chimpanzees do not reason about inherently unobservable phenomena.

Let me briefly illustrate this evidence with three simple examples: one from the social domain, one from the domain of physics, and one from the domain of numerical reasoning.

First, what does the experimental evidence suggest about whether chimpanzees reason about mental states? Although the opinions of experts differ (and have swung back and forth over the past several years), I believe that at present there is no direct evidence that chimpanzees conceive of mental states, and considerable evidence that they do not. As an example, consider the well-studied question of whether chimpanzees reason about the internal, visual experiences of others, that is, of whether they know anything about 'seeing.'

To begin, no one doubts that chimpanzees respond to, reason about, and form concepts related to the movements of the head, face, and eyes of others; these are aspects of behavior that can be readily witnessed.[11] But what about the idea that another being 'sees' things, that others are loci of unobservable, visual experiences?

Over the past ten years we have conducted dozens of studies of juvenile, adolescent, and adult chimpanzees to explore this question. Perhaps the most straightforward of these studies involved examining how chimpanzees understand circumstances under which others obviously can or cannot see them.[12] In these studies, chimpanzees were exposed to a routine in which they would approach a familiar playmate or caretaker to request a food treat using their species-typical begging gesture. Simple enough. But on the crucial test trials, the chimpanzees were confronted with two individuals, only one of whom could see them. For example, in one condition, one caretaker had a blindfold covering her mouth, whereas the other had a blindfold covering her eyes. The question was to whom would the chimpanzee gesture.

Not surprisingly, in our trials with human children, even two-year-olds gestured to whoever had the blindfold over her mouth (versus the eyes), probably because they could represent her inner, psychological state ("She can *see* me!"). In striking contrast, our chimpanzees did nothing of the kind. Indeed, in numerous studies, our chimpanzees gave virtually no indication that they could understand 'seeing' as an internal experience of others.

With enough trials of any given condition the chimpanzees were able to *learn* to select whoever was able to see them; after enough trials of not being handed a banana when gesturing to someone with a bucket over her head, the chimpanzees figured out to gesture to the other person. Did this mean that they had finally discerned what we were asking them? In numerous transfer tests in which we pitted the idea that the chimpanzees were learning about the observable cues (i.e., frontal posture, presence of the face or eyes) against the possibility that on the basis of such cues they were reasoning about who could 'see' them, the chimpanzees consistently insisted (through their behavior) that they were reasoning about observable features, not internal mental states, to guide their choices.

In addition to what they learned in these tests, it also became apparent that chimpanzees come pre-prepared, as it were, to make sense of certain postures. For instance, in our tests they immediately knew what to do when confronted with someone facing them versus someone facing away, and this finding has been replicated in several other laboratories.[13] "But if they make *that* distinction," you wonder, "then why do they perform so differently on the other tests? Is it just because they're confused? How are we to make sense of such a puzzling pattern of findings?"

Actually, these results are not puzzling at all if the ability to reason about mental states evolved in the manner that I suggested earlier – that is, if humans wove a system for reasoning about mental states into an existing system for reasoning about behavior. After all, if the idea is correct, then chimpanzees may well be born predisposed to attend to certain postures and behaviors related to 'seeing' – even though they know nothing at all about such mental states *per se* – precisely because overt features of behavior are the tell-tale indicators of the future behavior of others. But when such features are carefully teased apart to probe for the presence of a mentalistic construal of others, the chimpanzees stare back blankly: this is not part of their biological endowment. Thus, if the evolutionary framework I have sketched is correct, neither the chimpanzees nor the results are 'confused'; that epithet may fall squarely upon the shoulders of we human experimenters and theorists who are so blinded by our own way of understanding the world that we are not readily open to the chimpanzee's way of viewing things.

Of course, some have challenged this conclusion, arguing that we need to turn up the microscope and develop more tests that will allow chimpanzees to express their less well-developed understanding of such concepts.[14] So, for example, researchers at Emory University recently conducted tests in which a dominant and a subordinate chimpanzee were allowed to fight over food that was positioned in an enclosure between them.[15] On the critical trials, two pieces of food were positioned equidistant from the animals. The catch was that one piece of food was placed behind an opaque barrier so that only the subordinate could see it. The researchers report that when the subordinate was released into the enclosure, he or she tended to head for the food that was hidden from the dominant's view, suggesting, perhaps, that the subordinate was modeling the visual experience of his or her dominant rival.

But do such tests really help?[16] Do they reveal some weaker understanding of mental states in chimpanzees? These are precisely the situations in which chimpanzees will be evolutionarily primed to use their abilities to form concepts about the actions of others to guide their social behavior. So, for example, they can simply know to avoid food that is out in the open when a dominant animal is about to be released. "But still," the skeptic within you asks, "that's pretty smart, isn't it? The chimpanzees would have to be paying attention to who's behind the door, and what that other individual is going to do when the door opens, right?"

Fair enough. But that, in the end, is the point: chimpanzees can be intelligent, thinking creatures even if they do not possess a system for reasoning about psychological states like 'seeing.' If it turns out that this is a uniquely human system, this should not detract from our sense of the evolved intelligence of apes. By way of analogy, the fact that bats echolocate but humans don't, hardly constitutes an intellectual or evolutionary crisis.

In the final analysis, the best theory will be the one that explains both data sets: the fact that chimpanzees reason about all the observable features of others that are associated with 'seeing' – and yet at the same time exhibit a striking lack of knowledge when those features are juxtaposed in a manner that they have never witnessed before (i.e., blindfolds over eyes versus over the mouth). I submit that, at least for the time being, the evolutionary hypothesis I have described best meets this criterion.

A second example of the operation of what may be a uniquely human capacity to reason about unobservables comes from comparisons of humans' and chimpanzees' commonsense understanding of physics. Humans – even very young children – seem disposed to assume that there's more to the physical world than what meets the eye. For example, when one ball collides with another, stationary one, and the second speeds away, even quite young children are insistent that the first one caused the second to move away. Indeed, as Michotte's classic experiments revealed, this seems to be an automatic mental process in adult humans.[17] But what is it, exactly, that humans believe *causes* the movement of the second ball? As Hume noted long ago, they do not merely recognize that the objects touched; that's just a re-description of the observed events.[18] No, the first one is seen as having transmitted something to the second object, some kind of 'force.' But where is this force? Can it be seen? No, it is a theoretical thing.

In an initial five-year study of 'chimpanzee physics,' we focused our apes' attention on simple tool-using problems.[19] Given their natural expertise with tools, our goal was to teach them how to solve simple problems – tasks involving pulling, pushing, poking, etc. – and then to use carefully designed transfer tests to assess their understanding of why the tool objects produced the effects they did. In this way, we attempted to determine if they reason about things like gravity, transfer of force, weight, and physical connection, or merely form concepts about spatio-temporal regularities. To do so, we contrasted such concepts with their perceptual 'ambassadors' (see Table 35.1), much in the same way that we had contrasted the unobser-

Table 35.1 Theoretical causal constructs and their observable 'ambassadors'

Theoretical concept	Paired observable 'ambassador'
gravity	*downward object trajectories*
transfer of force	*motion-contact-motion sequences*
strength	*propensity for deformation*
shape	*perceptual form*
physical connection	*degree of contact*
weight	*muscle/tendon stretch sensations*

vable psychological state of 'seeing' against the observable behavioral regularities that co-vary with 'seeing.'

To pick just one example: we explored in detail the chimpanzee's understanding of physical connection – of the idea that two objects are bound together through some unobservable interaction such as the force transmitted by the mass of one object resting on another, or the frictional forces of one object against another; or conversely, the idea that simply because two objects are physically touching does not mean there is any real form of 'connection.' We presented our chimpanzees with numerous problems, but consider one test in which we first taught them to use a simple tool to hook a ring in order to drag a platform with a food treat on it toward them. Although they learned to do so, our real question was whether, when confronted with two new options, they would select the one involving genuine physical connection as opposed to mere 'contact.' Consistent with our findings in other tests, they did not. Instead, 'perceptual contact' seemed to be their operating concept. The observable property of contact (of any type) was generally sufficient for them to think that a tool could move another object.

Finally, consider the chimpanzee's numerical understanding. Over the past decade or so, it has become apparent that many species share what Stanislas Dehaene has called a 'number sense' – the ability to distinguish between larger and smaller quantities, even when the quantities being compared occupy identical volumes.[20]

In an attempt to explore the question of numerical reasoning in animals, several research laboratories have trained apes to match a specific quantity of items (say, three jelly beans) with the appropriate Arabic numeral.[21] That they can accomplish this should not be the least bit surprising: humans and chimpanzees (and many other species) share the ability to visually individuate objects. After extensive training, furthermore, the most apt of these pupils have gone on to exhibit some understanding of *ordinality* (the idea that 5 represents a larger quantity than 4, for example). So, isn't this evidence that chimpanzees have a solid grasp of the notion of the number?

Let us scratch the surface a bit, to look at these findings from the perspective I have been advocating. First, do these chimpanzees possess a dual understanding of numbers – both as associates of real object sets and as inherently theoretical things – such that every successive number in the system is exactly '1' more than the previous number? The training data even from Ai, the most mathematically educated of all chimpanzees, suggests that they do not. For example, each time the next numeral was added into her training set, it took her just as long to learn its association with the appropriate number of objects as it took with the previous numeral. In other words, there appeared to be little evidence that Ai understood the symbols as anything other than associates of the object sets. Furthermore, even her dedicated mentors suggest that she was not 'counting' at all: with quantities of up to three or four objects, she performed like humans, using an automatic process ('subitizing') to make her judgments; but with larger quantities, instead of counting, it appears as if she was simply estimating 'larger' or 'smaller.'

What about ordinality? When first tested for her understanding of the relative ordering of numbers, Ai exhibited no evidence that this was part of her conceptual structure. That is, when presented with pairs of numbers, 1 versus 8, for example, she did not seem to have any notion that the value of 1 is smaller than the value of 8 – even though she had been correctly matching these numerals to object sets for years! Of course, after extended training, Ai did eventually exhibit evidence of this ability, and now, after more than fifteen years of training, when confronted with a scrambled array of the numerals 1 to 9, she has the remarkable ability to select them in ascending order.

But what does it mean that under the right training regime we can guide a chimpanzee like Ai into a performance that looks, in many but not all respects, like human counting? One possibility is that a basic number sense – a system grounded to individual macroscopic objects – is widespread among animals, and that apes (and other animals) can use this ability (in concert with their other cognitive skills) to figure out ways to cope with the 'rules' that humans establish in their tests. In contrast, the human system for counting (as well as other mathematical ideas) could be seen as building upon these older systems by reifying numbers as things in their own right – theoretical things. This may seem like a subtle and unimportant distinction for some tasks, but it may be one that leaves the ape mystified when facing questions that treat numbers as things in their own right.

As a striking example of the distinction I have been trying to draw, consider zero, surely one of the purest examples that exists of an inherently unobservable entity. If I am right, then zero ought to be virtually undetectable by the chimpanzee's cognitive system. And indeed, the data seem to bear this out.[22] For all of her training, even Ai does not appear to have learned to understand zero in this sense. True, she (and other animals) have quickly learned to pick the numeral 0 in response to the absence of objects (something easily explained by associative learning processes). But tests of ordinality involving zero (choosing whether 0 is greater or lesser than 6, for example) have consistently revealed what I believe might be best described as the virtual absence of the concept. Although this training has gradually forced her 'understanding' of zero into a position further and further down the 'number line,' even to this day, after thousands of trials, Ai still reliably confuses 0 with 1 (and in some tasks, with 2 or 3 as well). However one wishes to interpret such findings, they are certainly not consistent with an understanding of the very essence of zero-ness.[23]

Our work together is done. To the best of my ability I have laid out the case for believing that chimpanzees can be bright, alert, intelligent, fully cognitive creatures, and yet still have minds of their own. From this perspective, it may be our species that is the peculiar one – unsatisfied in merely knowing *what* things happen, but continually driven to explain *why* they happen, as well. Armed with a natural language that makes referring to abstract things easy, we continually pry behind appearances, probing ever deeper into the causal structure of things. Indeed, some tests we have conducted suggest that chimpanzees may not seek 'explanations' at all.[24]

And yet I cannot help but suspect that many of you will react to what I have said with a feeling of dismay – perhaps loss; a sense that if the possibility I have sketched here turns out to be correct, then our world will be an even lonelier place than it was before. But for the time being, at least, I ask you to stay this thought. After all, would it really be so disappointing if our first, uncontaminated glimpse into the mind of another species revealed a world strikingly different from our own; or all that surprising if the price of admission into that world were that we check some of our most familiar ways of thinking at the door? No, to me, the idea that there may be profound psychological differences between humans and chimpanzees no longer seems unsettling. On the contrary, it's the sort of possibility that has, on at least some occasions, emboldened our species to reach out and discover new worlds with open minds and hearts.

NOTES

1 Galina V. Galzko and Masatoshi Nei, "Estimation of Divergence Times for Major Lineages of Primate Species," *Molecular Biology and Evolution* 20 (2003): 424–34.

2 Jonathan Marks, *What It Means to Be 98% Chimpanzee* (Berkeley: University of California Press, 2002).

3 For examples, see Sue Savage-Rumbaugh, *Kanzi: The Ape at the Brink of the Human Mind* (New York: John Wiley & Sons, 1994); Jane Goodall, *Through a Window* (Boston: Houghton Mifflin, 1990); Roger Fouts, *Next of Kin* (New York: William Morrow and Co., 1997).

4 Steven M. Wise, *Rattling the Cage: Toward Legal Rights for Animals* (Cambridge, Mass.: Perseus Books, 2000); Paola Cavalieri and Peter Singer, eds., *The Great Ape Project: Equality Beyond Humanity* (New York: St. Martin's Press, 1993).

5 Wolfgang Enard *et al.*, "Intra- and Inter-specific Variation in Primate Gene Expression Patterns," *Science* 296 (2002): 341–43; Mario Cáceres *et al.*, "Elevated Gene Expression Levels Distinguish Human from Non-Human Primate Brains," *Proceedings of the National Academy of Sciences* 100 (2003): 13030–5.

6 Todd M. Preuss *et al.*, "Distinctive Compartmental Organization of Human Primary Visual Cortex," *Proceedings of the National Academy of Sciences* 96 (1999): 11601–6.

7 Eugene Linden, "Can Animals Think?" *Time*, 22 March 1993.

8   Suzette L. Astley and Edward A. Wasserman, "Object Concepts: Behavioral Research with Animals and Young Children," in William T. O'Donohue, ed., *Learning and Behavior Therapy* (Boston: Allyn and Bacon, 1997), 440–63; Tom R. Zentall, "The Case for a Cognitive Approach to Animal Learning and Behavior," *Behavioural Processes* 54 (2001): 65–78.

9   This discussion extends several previous descriptions of this hypothesis, for example, my article with Jesse Bering and Steve Giambrone, "Toward a Science of Other Minds: Escaping the Argument by Analogy," *Cognitive Science* 24 (2000): 509–41.

10 Daniel J. Povinelli and Jennifer Vonk, "Chimpanzee Minds: Suspiciously Human?" *Trends in Cognitive Science* 7 (2003): 157–60.

11 See Daniel J. Povinelli and Timothy J. Eddy, "Chimpanzees: Joint Visual Attention," *Psychological Science* 7 (1996): 129–35; Shoji Itakura, "An Exploratory Study of Gaze-Monitoring in Nonhuman Primates," *Japanese Psychological Research* 38 (1996): 174–80; Michael Tomasello, Brian Hare, and Josep Call, "Five Primate Species Follow the Visual Gaze of Conspecifics," *Animal Behaviour* 58 (1998): 769–77.

12 Our laboratory's empirical research of chimpanzees' understanding of 'seeing' has been summarized in my article, "The Minds of Humans and Apes are Different Outcomes of an Evolutionary Experiment," in Susan M. Fitzpatrick and John T. Bruer, eds., *Carving Our Destiny: Scientific Research Faces a New Millennium* (Washington, D.C.: National Academy of Sciences and John Henry Press, 2001), 1–40.

13 For example, see Autumn B. Hostetter *et al.*, "Differential Use of Vocal and Gestural Communication by Chimpanzees (*Pan troglodytes*) in Response to the Attentional Status of a Human (*Homo sapiens*)," *Journal of Comparative Psychology* 115 (2001): 337–43.

14 Michael Tomasello *et al.*, "Chimpanzees Understand Psychological States – The Question Is Which Ones and to What Extent," *Trends in Cognitive Science* 7 (2003): 153–6, esp. 156.

15 Brian Hare *et al.*, "Chimpanzees Know What Conspecifics Do and Do Not See," *Animal Behaviour* 59 (2000): 771–85; see also M. Rosalyn Karin-D'Arcy and Daniel J. Povinelli, "Do Chimpanzees Know What Each Other See? A Closer Look," *International Journal of Comparative Psychology* 15 (2002): 21–54.

16 In a recent analysis of the diagnostic potential of these and other tests, Jennifer Vonk and I (see **footnote 10**) argued that the logic of current tests with chimpanzees (and other animals) cannot, in principle, provide evidence that uniquely supports the notion that they are reasoning about mental states (as opposed to behavior alone), and we advocated a new paradigm of tests that may have such diagnostic power. An alternative point of view is provided in the companion piece by Tomasello and colleagues. However, I believe that this view dramatically underestimates the representational power of a psychological system that forms concepts solely about the observable aspects of behavior.

17 Albert Michotte, *The Perception of Causality* (New York: Basic Books, 1963).

18 David Hume, *Treatise of Human Nature*, vols. 1–2, ed. A. D. Lindsay (London: Dent, 1739; 1911).

19 Daniel J. Povinelli, *Folk Physics for Apes* (Oxford: Oxford University Press, 2000).

20 Stanislas Dehaene, *The Number Sense* (Oxford: Oxford University Press, 1997).

21 For this discussion, I rely heavily on the detailed results from Ai, a twenty-five-year-old chimpanzee whose numerical abilities have been studied since she was five by a team led by Tetsuro Matsuzawa in Kyoto, Japan. See Dora Biro and Tetsuro Matsuzawa, "Chimpanzee Numerical Competence: Cardinal and Ordinal Skills," in Tetsuro Matsuzawa, ed., *Primate Origins of Human Cognition and Behavior* (Tokyo: Springer, 2001), 199–225.

22 Dora Biro and Tetsuro Matsuzawa, "Use of Numerical Symbols by the Chimpanzee (*Pan troglodytes*): Cardinal, Ordinals, and the Introduction of Zero," *Animal Cognition* 4 (2001): 193–9.

23 One might retort that the numeral 0 appeared quite late in human history. But here's a thought experiment. Return to our imaginary time machine (see above) and travel back to those civilizations that predate the invention of the numeral 0. How difficult would it be to teach those adult humans the position occupied by the symbol for zero?

24 Daniel J. Povinelli and Sarah Dunphy-Lelii, "Do Chimpanzees Seek Explanations? Preliminary Comparative Investigations," *Canadian Journal of Comparative Psychology* 55 (2001): 187–95.

Part 8

CAN MACHINES THINK?

The following conversation will be familiar if you are a fan of science fiction:

> Dave Bowman: Hello, HAL do you read me, HAL?
>
> HAL: Affirmative, Dave, I read you.
>
> Dave Bowman: Open the pod bay doors, HAL.
>
> HAL: I'm sorry Dave, I'm afraid I can't do that.
>
> Dave Bowman: What's the problem?
>
> HAL: I think you know what the problem is just as well as I do.
>
> Dave Bowman: What are you talking about, HAL?
>
> HAL: This mission is too important for me to allow you to jeopardize it.
>
> Dave Bowman: I don't know what you're talking about, HAL?
>
> HAL: I know you and Frank were planning to disconnect me, and I'm afraid that's something I cannot allow to happen.
>
> Dave Bowman: Where the hell'd you get that idea, HAL?
>
> HAL: Dave, although you took thorough precautions in the pod against my hearing you, I could see your lips move.

This dialogue unfolds in Stanley Kubrick's masterful adaptation of Arthur C. Clarke's *2001: A Space Odyssey*. Dave Bowman is an astronaut on the spaceship *Discovery*, and HAL is the HAL 9000 computer, which has been designed to run the ship and see to the needs of its crew. Of course, not all goes as planned, and at this point in the story Dave Bowman is the only member of the crew whom HAL has not killed. The exchange above leaves no doubt that HAL has become a cold-blooded and cunning murderer.

Can there be any question whether HAL is intelligent? HAL oversees the maintenance of an immense and complex spacecraft, he plays chess with the crew, he has interests in art and poetry, he can plan and execute murder. Moreover, HAL has feelings. He tells Dave that he is *enthusiastic* about the ship's mission. As Dave begins to shut him down, he admits that he is *afraid*. Undeniably, any person who displayed the intellectual and emotional capacities that HAL seems to exhibit would be an intelligent, sentient being.

A skeptic about the possibility of artificial intelligence might not find this discussion of HAL to be convincing. For one thing, HAL is just science *fiction*. Sure, the skeptic might say, HAL is intelligent – but HAL is also impossible. It is much easier to *make up* artificial intelligence than it is really to *make* artificial intelligence. Alternatively, the skeptic might say that even if HAL were actual, he would not be genuinely intelligent. He might *appear* to be intelligent, but HAL could never in a million years be capable of X, where 'X' names your favorite indication of intelligence.

Alan Turing, in his famous introduction to the idea of artificial intelligence, tries to rebuff doubts of the second sort. Turing was among the greatest geniuses of the twentieth century. In addition to making mathematical discoveries that laid the foundation for computer science, Turing also made important contributions to biology (his work on morphogenesis especially) and, additionally, was instrumental in cracking the German Enigma code during World War II. In the article that follows, Turing defends the possibility of artificial intelligence from a variety of doubts of the form, "But a computer could never do X." So, for instance, Turing considers the objection that a computer could never be spontaneous because its actions are the result of the finite number of rules with which it has been programmed. Similarly, a computer could never come up with an original idea, i.e. an idea that goes beyond the knowledge contained in its program. Turing also responds to the claim that a computer could never respond appropriately to poetry or beauty because it lacks feelings. It could never enjoy strawberries and cream or make someone fall in love with it.

Clearly these objections to artificial intelligence rest on assumptions about the nature of intelligence. Why, for instance, must a computer be able to enjoy strawberries and cream or make someone fall in love with it in order to qualify as intelligent? Is the meaning of 'intelligence' so vague that there is really no point in arguing whether a machine is or can be intelligent? Turing is sensitive to these worries and thus proposes to replace the question "Can machines think?" with a question that has a determinate and easy answer. Ignoring some subtleties, Turing's question is this: "Can a machine make you believe that you are talking to another human being?" Any machine that can do this, Turing believes, is intelligent.

Turing's test for intelligence, which now bears his name, has been the subject of intense philosophical controversy. Why should the ability to converse like a human being be a sufficient condition for intelligence? Isn't there more to intelligence than that? Could an intelligent conversation mask processes that are, in truth, far from intelligent? HAL's appearance of intelligence is, after all, the product of nothing more than operations on strings of 1s and 0s.

John Searle has been a forceful critic of attempts to produce artificial intelligence. A computer, Searle believes, is simply not the kind of thing that can think. The problem is not that computers lack a soul or are composed of nothing but matter. Rather, the problem lies in the nature of computational processes. Computational processes are blind to meanings and hence a computer's outputs can never mean anything to the computer. Searle illustrates this claim in an ingenious way. Imagine having at your disposal a rule book that guides you through a process of producing Chinese symbols in response to Chinese symbols that have been written on a slip of paper and passed through a slot in the door of the room in which you sit. Having figured out which Chinese symbols to create, you write them down on a slip of paper which you then pass back through the slot. Because you know no Chinese, as far as you are concerned you've done nothing but write down a bunch of squiggles and squoggles. However, to the Chinese person outside the room who is giving and receiving the slips of paper, it appears that whomever or whatever is in the room understands Chinese. From her perspective, she is carrying on a conversation in Chinese.

Searle argues that for the same reason that the rule book does not endow the occupant of the room with knowledge of Chinese, a program does not endow a computer with knowledge of whatever it might be 'talking' or 'thinking' about. A computer can appear intelligent – can, e.g., appear to be conducting a conversation about the dangers of a global economy – without actually having any intelligence at all.

Searle's argument has provoked many responses, some of which he anticipated and sought to defuse in his article. Among the more popular responses is the so-called *systems reply*. This reply concedes Searle's claim that the individual in the room does not understand Chinese, but argues that the system of which the individual is a part – the system consisting of the person, the rule book, writing instruments, and slips of paper – understands Chinese. The person in the room is simply a cog in a larger machine that does understand Chinese.

Searle believes that the systems reply is unsuccessful. If the person in the room doesn't understand Chinese, how can the addition of the other elements of the system create something that does understand Chinese? Indeed, to suppose that it does understand Chinese strains credulity. However, Jack Copeland defends a variant of the systems reply. Copeland observes that Searle's objection to the systems reply commits a logical fallacy. From the fact that a piece of a system cannot do X, it does not follow that the system cannot do X. For instance, although Searle cannot lift a thousand pounds, it does not follow that a system consisting of himself and a bull-dozer cannot lift a thousand pounds. But more than just exposing a logical fallacy in Searle's response to the systems reply, Copeland tries to make plausible the idea that a computer can understand. Ultimately, he argues, whether artificial intelligence is possible depends on two considerations.

The first of these considerations is purely empirical. Is it possible to build a computer that is intelligent? Unlike Searle, who hopes to show on non-empirical grounds that artificial intelligence is impossible, Copeland believes that only time will tell whether computer science and robotics can deliver the goods. The second consideration is partly philosophical but also partly pragmatic. We must decide whether attributing minds to artifacts ever makes sense. As far as Copeland is concerned, a computer that exhibits all the sophistication of HAL would, without doubt, deserve to be called intelligent.

Daniel Dennett expands on Copeland's decision to attribute intelligence to machines like HAL. Dennett's focus is on the justification of the Turing test. By Searle's lights,

468

being able to carry on a conversation that is indistinguishable from an ordinary human conversation is insufficient for intelligence. As we have seen, the person in the Chinese room appears to speak Chinese without understanding a word of what he or she is 'saying.' But, Dennett wonders, how plausible *really* is the situation that Searle describes? Surely no one – not even Searle – thinks that a person with a rule book really could pass the Turing test.

Dennett's strategy is to consider what is involved in a normal human conversation. Conversations often take unpredictable turns. A conversation that starts with a mundane observation about the weather might end up in a heated discussion of the ethics of abortion or pleasant reminiscences of the Partridge Family. Imagine all that must go into a computer if it is able to keep pace with the twists and turns of normal conversation! Dennett's bet is that a computer that can actually meet the demands of conversation must be intelligent. Of course, passing the Turing test may not provide a conclusive *demonstration* of intelligence. Perhaps it is possible (in some sense) to build a non-intelligent machine that could pass the test. But surely the default assumption about any machine that can pass the test should be that it is intelligent, or so Dennett argues.

Robert French, although sympathetic to the Turing test, believes it is too strong. In demanding that a computer be able to converse with a human being, French argues that the test imposes a kind of chauvinism on our judgments of intelligence. Rather than testing for intelligence, Turing's test instead indicates only the presence of *human* intelligence. In fact, French believes, the test is so completely tailored to human-like psychology that only a computer that had been 'reared' in a human culture and equipped with a humanoid body could pass the test. This means that computers of the sort that Turing or Dennett might imagine – computers like HAL, which do not have humanoid bodies and have not, suppose, been raised in a human culture – would fail the Turing test.

It is important to be clear about the limits of French's claim. He does not wish to deny the possibility of artificial intelligence. Instead, he wants to show a significant shortcoming in the Turing test. There are plenty of ways to be intelligent, French assumes, but human intelligence is only one of them. Insofar, then, that a machine must have human intelligence to pass the Turing test, the test identifies only a subset, and perhaps a very small subset, of intelligent beings.

To make his case, French describes various psychological experiments that reveal the influence of culture and embodiment on our subconscious cognitive processes. We are so thoroughly permeated with the artifacts of our cultural and morphological heritage that we cannot but help to think in certain ways, and about certain things. The existence of these cognitive idiosyncrasies, French argues, makes the Turing test a good one for evaluating whether something has human intelligence, but a poor one for deciding about a more general or simply different sort of intelligence.

QUESTIONS TO THINK ABOUT:

1 Turing considers a variety of objections to the possibility of artificial intelligence. Many of these he tries to answer without providing a clear definition of 'intelligence' or 'thinking'. Without such a definition, can his answers be persuasive? Which of Turing's answers seem to require a clear conception of intelligence and which do not?

2 Searle does not say much about how the person in the room actually goes about deriving responses to the statements he receives on slips of paper. Might the manner in which the rule book directs the production of Chinese symbols make a difference to the strength of Searle's conclusion? What would Searle say?

3 Despite rejecting the possibility that a computer might some day think, Searle does not doubt that machines of some kind can think. On what is his confidence based? What would such a machine have that computers do not?

4 Copeland takes the issue of artificial intelligence to rest, in part, on a decision. We must decide whether and when it is proper to call a machine intelligent. What sorts of considerations must be part of this decision? If Copeland is right that a decision is necessary, does this make claims about the possibility of artificial intelligence undesirably subjective?

5 Dennett sees the Turing test as providing a 'quick-probe' test. Come up with some questions of your own to which quick-probe tests provide a good answer. What is the logic involved in these tests?

6 There is a sense in which French's criticism of the Turing test is not well-founded. After all, Turing seems to have intended his test to provide a sufficient condition for intelligence, but French faults it for not providing a necessary condition for intelligence. If this is right, what is the significance of French's article for research in artificial intelligence? What message should the AI researcher take from French?

FURTHER READING:

Boden, M., ed. (1990). *The Philosophy of Artificial Intelligence* (New York: Oxford University Press).

Clark, A. (2001). *Mindware: An Introduction to the Philosophy of Cognitive Science* (New York: Oxford University Press).

Copeland, J. (1993). *Artificial Intelligence: A Philosophical Introduction* (Malden, MA: Blackwell Publishers Inc.).

Dennett, D. (1998). *Brainchildren: Essays on Designing Minds* (Cambridge, MA: The MIT Press).

Haugeland, J. (1985). *Artificial Intelligence: The Very Idea* (Cambridge, MA: The MIT Press).

Preston, J. and Bishop, M., eds. (2002). *Views into the Chinese Room: New Essays on Searle and Artificial Intelligence* (New York: Oxford University Press).

36

COMPUTING MACHINERY AND INTELLIGENCE

A.M. Turing

1 THE IMITATION GAME

I propose to consider the question, 'Can machines think?' This should begin with definitions of the meaning of the terms 'machine' and 'think'. The definitions might be framed so as to reflect so far as possible the normal use of the words, but this attitude is dangerous. If the meaning of the words 'machine' and 'think' are to be found by examining how they are commonly used it is difficult to escape the conclusion that the meaning and the answer to the question, 'Can machines think?' is to be sought in a statistical survey such as a Gallup poll. But this is absurd. Instead of attempting such a definition I shall replace the question by another, which is closely related to it and is expressed in relatively unambiguous words.

The new form of the problem can be described in terms of a game which we call the 'imitation game'. It is played with three people, a man (A), a woman (B), and an interrogator (C) who may be of either sex. The interrogator stays in a room apart from the other two. The object of the game for the interrogator is to determine which of the other two is the man and which is the woman. He knows them by labels X and Y, and at the end of the game he says either 'X is A and Y is B' or 'X is B and Y is A'. The interrogator is allowed to put questions to A and B thus:

C: Will X please tell me the length of his or her hair?

Now suppose X is actually A, then A must answer. It is A's object in the game to try and cause C to make the wrong identification. His answer might therefore be

'My hair is shingled, and the longest strands are about nine inches long.'

In order that tones of voice may not help the interrogator the answers should be written, or better still, typewritten. The ideal arrangement is to have a teleprinter communicating between the two rooms. Alternatively the question and answers can be repeated by an intermediary. The object of the game for the third player (B) is to help the interrogator. The best strategy for her is probably to give truthful answers.

She can add such things as 'I am the woman, don't listen to him!' to her answers, but it will avail nothing as the man can make similar remarks.

We now ask the question, 'What will happen when a machine takes the part of A in this game?' Will the interrogator decide wrongly as often when the game is played like this as he does when the game is played between a man and a woman? These questions replace our original, 'Can machines think?'

2 CRITIQUE OF THE NEW PROBLEM

As well as asking, 'What is the answer to this new form of the question', one may ask, 'Is this new question a worthy one to investigate?' This latter question we investigate without further ado, thereby cutting short an infinite regress.

The new problem has the advantage of drawing a fairly sharp line between the physical and the intellectual capacities of a man. No engineer or chemist claims to be able to produce a material which is indistinguishable from the human skin. It is possible that at some time this might be done, but even supposing this invention available we should feel there was little point in trying to make a 'thinking machine' more human by dressing it up in such artificial flesh. The form in which we have set the problem reflects this fact in the condition which prevents the interrogator from seeing or touching the other competitors, or hearing their voices. Some other advantages of the proposed criterion may be shown up by specimen questions and answers. Thus:

Q: Please write me a sonnet on the subject of the Forth Bridge.
A: Count me out on this one. I never could write poetry.
Q: Add 34957 to 70764
A: (Pause about 30 seconds and then give as answer) 105621.
Q: Do you play chess?
A: Yes.
Q: I have K at my K1, and no other pieces. You have only K at K6 and R at R1. It is your move. What do you play?
A: (After a pause of 15 seconds) R-R8 mate.

The question and answer method seems to be suitable for introducing almost any one of the fields of human endeavour that we wish to include. We do not wish to penalise the machine for its inability to shine in beauty competitions, nor to penalise a man for losing in a race against an aeroplane. The conditions of our game make these disabilities irrelevant. The 'witnesses' can brag, if they consider it advisable, as much as they please about their charms, strength or heroism, but the interrogator cannot demand practical demonstrations.

The game may perhaps be criticised on the ground that the odds are weighted too heavily against the machine. If the man were to try and pretend to be the machine he would clearly make a very poor showing. He would be given away at once by slowness and inaccuracy in arithmetic. May not machines carry out something which ought to be described as thinking but which is very different from what a man does? This objection is a very strong one, but at least we can say that if, nevertheless, a machine can be constructed to play the imitation game satisfactorily, we need not be troubled by this objection.

It might be urged that when playing the 'imitation game' the best strategy for the machine may possibly be something other than imitation of the behaviour of a man. This may be, but I think it is unlikely that there is any great effect of this kind. In any case there is no intention to investigate here the theory of the game, and it will be assumed that the best strategy is to try to provide answers that would naturally be given by a man.

3 THE MACHINES CONCERNED IN THE GAME

The question which we put in Section 1 will not be quite definite until we have specified what we mean by the word 'machine'. It is natural that we should wish to permit every kind of engineering technique to be used in our machines. We also wish to allow the possibility that an engineer or team of engineers may construct a machine which works, but whose manner of operation cannot be satisfactorily described by its constructors because they have applied a method which is largely experimental. Finally, we wish to exclude from the machines men born in the usual manner. It is difficult to frame the definitions so as to satisfy these three conditions. One might for instance insist that the team of engineers should be all of one sex, but this would not really be satisfactory, for it is probably possible to rear a complete individual from a single cell of the skin (say) of a man. To do so would be a feat of biological technique deserving of the very highest praise, but we would not be inclined to regard it as a case of 'constructing a thinking machine'. This prompts us to abandon the requirement that every kind of technique should be permitted. We are the more ready to do so in view of the fact that the present interest in 'thinking machines' has been aroused by a particular kind of machine, usually called an 'electronic computer' or 'digital computer'. Following this suggestion we only permit digital computers to take part in our game.

This restriction appears at first sight to be a very drastic one. I shall attempt to show that it is not so in reality. To do this necessitates a short account of the nature and properties of these computers.

It may also be said that this identification of machines with digital computers, like our criterion for 'thinking', will only be unsatisfactory if (contrary to my belief), it turns out that digital computers are unable to give a good showing in the game.

There are already a number of digital computers in working order, and it may be asked, 'Why not try the experiment straight away? It would be easy to satisfy the conditions of the game. A number of interrogators could be used, and statistics compiled to show how often the right identification was given.' The short answer is that we are not asking whether all digital computers would do well in the game nor whether the computers at present available would do well, but whether there are imaginable computers which would do well. But this is only the short answer. We shall see this question in a different light later.

4 DIGITAL COMPUTERS

The idea behind digital computers may be explained by saying that these machines are intended to carry out any operations which could be done by a human computer. The human computer is supposed to be following fixed rules; he has no authority to deviate from them in any detail. We may suppose that these rules are supplied in a book, which is altered whenever he is put on to a new job. He has also an unlimited supply of paper on which he does his calculations. He may also do his multiplications and additions on a 'desk machine', but this is not important.

If we use the above explanation as a definition we shall be in danger of circularity of argument. We avoid this by giving an outline of the means by which the desired effect is achieved. A digital computer can usually be regarded as consisting of three parts:

(i)   Store.
(ii) Executive unit.
(iii) Control.

The store is a store of information, and corresponds to the human computer's paper, whether this is the paper on which he does his calculations or that on which his book of rules is printed. In so far as the human computer does calculations in his head a part of the store will correspond to his memory.

The executive unit is the part which carries out the various individual operations involved in a calculation. What these individual operations are will vary from machine to machine. Usually fairly lengthy operations can be done such as 'Multiply 3540675445 by 7076345687' but in some machines only very simple ones such as 'Write down 0' are possible.

We have mentioned that the 'book of rules' supplied to the computer is replaced in the machine by a part of the store. It is then called the 'table of instructions'. It is the duty of the control to see that these instructions are obeyed correctly and in the right order. The control is so constructed that this necessarily happens.

The information in the store is usually broken up into packets of moderately small size. In one machine, for instance, a packet might consist of ten decimal digits. Numbers are assigned to the parts of the store in which the various packets of information are stored, in some systematic manner. A typical instruction might say:

'Add the number stored in position 6809 to that in 4302 and put the result back into the latter storage position'.

Needless to say it would not occur in the machine expressed in English. It would more likely be coded in a form such as 6809430217. Here 17 says which of various possible operations is to be performed on the two numbers. In this case the operation is that described above, *viz*. 'Add the number. ...' It will be noticed that the instruction takes up 10 digits and so forms one packet of information, very conveniently. The control will normally take the instructions to be obeyed in the order of the positions in which they are stored, but occasionally an instruction such as:

'Now obey the instruction stored in position 5606, and continue from there' may be encountered, or again:

'If position 4505 contains 0 obey next the instruction stored in 6707, otherwise continue straight on.'

Instructions of these latter types are very important because they make it possible for a sequence of operations to be repeated over and over again until some condition is fulfilled, but in doing so to obey, not fresh instructions on each repetition, but the same ones over and over again. To take a domestic analogy. Suppose Mother wants Tommy to call at the cobbler's every morning on his way to school to see if her shoes are done, she can ask him afresh every morning. Alternatively she can stick up a notice once and for all in the hall which he will see when he leaves for school and which tells him to call for the shoes, and also to destroy the notice when he comes back if he has the shoes with him.

The reader must accept it as a fact that digital computers can be constructed, and indeed have been constructed, according to the principles we have described, and that they can in fact mimic the actions of a human computer very closely.

The book of rules which we have described our human computer as using is of course a convenient fiction. Actual human computers really remember what they have got to do. If one wants to make a machine mimic the behaviour of the human computer in some complex operation one has to ask him how it is done, and then translate the answer into the form of an instruction table. Constructing instruction tables is usually described as 'programming'. To 'programme a machine to carry out the operation A' means to put the appropriate instruction table into the machine so that it will do A.

An interesting variant on the idea of a digital computer is a 'digital computer with a random element'. These have instructions involving the throwing of a die or some equivalent electronic process; one such instruction might for instance be, 'Throw the die and put the resulting number into store 1000'. Sometimes such a machine is described as having free will (though I would not use this phrase myself). It is not normally possible to determine from observing a machine whether it has a random element, for a similar effect can be produced by such devices as making the choices depend on the digits of the decimal for π.

Most actual digital computers have only a finite store. There is no theoretical difficulty in the idea of a computer with an unlimited store. Of course only a finite part can have been used at any one time. Likewise only a finite amount can have been constructed, but we can imagine more and more being added as required. Such computers have special theoretical interest and will be called infinitive capacity computers.

The idea of a digital computer is an old one. Charles Babbage, Lucasian Professor of Mathematics at Cambridge from 1828 to 1839, planned such a machine, called the Analytical Engine, but it was never completed. Although Babbage had all the essential ideas, his machine was not at that time such a very attractive prospect. The speed which would have been available would be definitely faster than a human computer but something like 100 times slower than the Manchester machine, itself one of the slower of the modern machines. The storage was to be purely mechanical, using wheels and cards.

The fact that Babbage's Analytical Engine was to be entirely mechanical will help us to rid ourselves of a superstition. Importance is often attached to the fact that modern digital computers are electrical, and that the nervous system also is electrical. Since Babbage's machine was not electrical, and since all digital computers are in a sense equivalent, we see that this use of electricity cannot be of theoretical importance. Of course electricity usually comes in where fast signalling is concerned, so that it is not surprising that we find it in both these connections. In the nervous system chemical phenomena are at least as important as electrical. In certain computers the storage system is mainly acoustic. The feature of using electricity is thus seen to be only a very superficial similarity. If we wish to find such similarities we should look rather for mathematical analogies of function.

5 UNIVERSALITY OF DIGITAL COMPUTERS

The digital computers considered in the last section may be classified amongst the 'discrete state machines'. These are the machines which move by sudden jumps or clicks from one quite definite state to another. These states are sufficiently different for the possibility of confusion between them to be ignored. Strictly speaking there are no such machines. Everything really moves continuously. But there are many kinds of machine which can profitably be *thought of* as being discrete state machines.

For instance in considering the switches for a lighting system it is a convenient fiction that each switch must be definitely on or definitely off. There must be intermediate positions, but for most purposes we can forget about them. As an example of a discrete state machine we might consider a wheel which clicks round through 120° once a second, but may be stopped by a lever which can be operated from outside; in addition a lamp is to light in one of the positions of the wheel. This machine could be described abstractly as follows. The internal state of the machine (which is described by the position of the wheel) may be q_1, q_2 or q_3. There is an input signal i_0 or i_1 (position of lever). The internal state at any moment is determined by the last state and input signal according to the table:

Input	Last State		
	q_1	q_2	q_3
i_0	$q_2 \cdots$	$q_3 \cdots$	q_1
i_1	$q_1 \cdots$	$q_2 \cdots$	q_3

The output signals, the only externally visible indication of the internal state (the light) are described by the table:

This example is typical of discrete state machines. They can be described by such tables provided they have only a finite number of possible states.

State	$q_1 \cdots q_2 \cdots q_3$
Output	$o_0 \cdots o_0 \cdots o_1$

It will seem that given the initial state of the machine and the input signals it is always possible to predict all future states. This is reminiscent of Laplace's view that from the complete state of the universe at one moment of time, as described by the positions and velocities of all particles, it should be possible to predict all future states. The prediction which we are considering is, however, rather nearer to practicability than that considered by Laplace. The system of the 'universe as a whole' is such that quite small errors in the initial conditions can have an overwhelming effect at a later time. The displacement of a single electron by a billionth of a centimetre at one moment might make the difference between a man being killed by an avalanche a year later, or escaping. It is an essential property of the mechanical systems which we have called 'discrete state machines' that this phenomenon does not occur. Even when we consider the actual physical machines instead of the idealised machines, reasonably accurate knowledge of the state at one moment yields reasonably accurate knowledge any number of steps later.

As we have mentioned, digital computers fall within the class of discrete state machines. But the number of states of which such a machine is capable is usually enormously large. For instance, the number for the machine now working at Manchester is about $2^{165,000}$, *i.e.* about $10^{50,000}$. Compare this with our example of the clicking wheel described above, which had three states. It is not difficult to see why the number of states should be so immense. The computer includes a store corresponding to the paper used by a human computer. It must be possible to write into the store any one of the combinations of symbols which might have been written on the paper. For simplicity suppose that only digits from 0 to 9 are used as symbols. Variations in handwriting are ignored. Suppose the computer is allowed 100 sheets of paper each containing 50 lines each with room for 30 digits. Then the number of states is $10^{100 \times 50 \times 30}$, *i.e.* $10^{150,000}$. This is about the number of states of three Manchester machines put together. The logarithm to the base two of the number of states is usually called the 'storage capacity' of the machine. Thus the Manchester machine has a storage capacity of about 165,000 and the wheel machine of our example about 1·6. If two machines are put together their capacities must be added to obtain the capacity of the resultant machine. This leads to the possibility of statements such as 'The Manchester machine contains 64 magnetic tracks each with a capacity of 2560, eight electronic tubes with a capacity of 1280. Miscellaneous storage amounts to about 300 making a total of 174,380.'

Given the table corresponding to a discrete state machine it is possible to predict what it will do. There is no reason why this calculation should not be carried out by means of a digital computer. Provided it could be carried out sufficiently quickly the digital computer could mimic the behaviour of any discrete state machine. The imitation game could then be played with the machine in question (as B) and the mimicking digital computer (as A) and the interrogator would be unable to distinguish them. Of course the digital computer must have an adequate storage capacity as well as working sufficiently fast. Moreover, it must be programmed afresh for each new machine which it is desired to mimic.

This special property of digital computers, that they can mimic any discrete state machine, is described by saying that they are *universal* machines. The existence of machines with this property has the important consequence that, considerations of speed apart, it is unnecessary to design various new machines to do various computing processes. They can all be done with one digital computer, suitably programmed for each case. It will be seen that as a consequence of this all digital computers are in a sense equivalent.

We may now consider again the point raised at the end of Section 3. It was suggested tentatively that the question, 'Can machines think?' should be replaced by 'Are there imaginable digital computers which would do well in the imitation game?' If we wish we can make this superficially more general and ask 'Are there discrete state machines which would do well?' But in view of the universality property we see that either of these questions is equivalent to this, 'Let us fix our attention on one particular digital computer C. Is it true that by modifying this computer to have an adequate storage, suitably increasing its speed of action, and providing it with an appropriate programme, C can be made to play satisfactorily the part of A in the imitation game, the part of B being taken by a man?'

6 CONTRARY VIEWS ON THE MAIN QUESTION

We may now consider the ground to have been cleared and we are ready to proceed to the debate on our question, 'Can machines think?' and the variant of it quoted at the end of the last section. We cannot altogether abandon the original form of the problem, for opinions will differ as to the appropriateness of the substitution and we must at least listen to what has to be said in this connexion.

It will simplify matters for the reader if I explain first my own beliefs in the matter. Consider first the more accurate form of the question. I believe that in about fifty years' time it will be possible to programme computers, with a storage capacity of about 10^9, to make them play the imitation game so well that an average interrogator will not have more than 70 per cent chance of making the right identification after five minutes of questioning. The original question, 'Can machines think?' I believe to be too meaningless to deserve discussion. Nevertheless I believe that at the end of the century the use of words and general educated opinion will have altered so much that one will be able to speak of machines thinking without expecting to be contradicted. I believe further that no useful purpose is served by concealing these beliefs. The popular view that scientists proceed inexorably from well-established fact to well-established fact, never being influenced by any unproved conjecture, is quite mistaken. Provided it is made clear which are proved facts and which are conjectures, no harm can result. Conjectures are of great importance since they suggest useful lines of research.

I now proceed to consider opinions opposed to my own.

(1) *The Theological Objection.* Thinking is a function of man's immortal soul. God has given an immortal soul to every man and woman, but not to any other animal or to machines. Hence no animal or machine can think.

I am unable to accept any part of this, but will attempt to reply in theological terms. I should find the argument more convincing if animals were classed with men, for there is a greater difference, to my mind, between the typical animate and the inanimate than there is between man and the other animals. The arbitrary character of the orthodox view becomes clearer if we consider how it might appear to a member of some other religious community. How do Christians regard the Moslem view that women have no souls? But let us leave this point aside and return to the main argument. It appears to me that the argument quoted above implies a serious restriction of the omnipotence of the Almighty. It is admitted that there are certain things that He cannot do such as making one equal to two,[1] but should we not believe that He has freedom to confer a soul on an elephant if He sees fit? We might expect that He would only exercise this power in conjunction with a mutation which provided the elephant with an appropriately improved brain to minister to the needs of this soul. An argument of exactly similar form may be made for the case of machines. It may seem different because it is more difficult to "swallow". But this really only means that we think it would be less likely that He would consider the circumstances suitable for conferring a soul. The circumstances in question are discussed in the rest of this paper. In attempting to construct such machines we should not be irreverently usurping His power of creating souls, any more than we are in the procreation of children: rather we are, in either case, instruments of His will providing mansions for the souls that He creates.

However, this is mere speculation. I am not very impressed with theological arguments whatever they may be used to support. Such arguments have often been found unsatisfactory in the past. In the time of Galileo it was argued that the texts, "And the sun stood still ... and hasted not to go down about a whole day" (Joshua x. 13) and "He laid the foundations of the earth, that it should not move at any time" (Psalm cv. 5) were an adequate refutation of the Copernican theory. With our present knowledge such an argument appears futile. When that knowledge was not available it made a quite different impression.

(2) *The 'Heads in the Sand' Objection.* "The consequences of machines thinking would be too dreadful. Let us hope and believe that they cannot do so."

This argument is seldom expressed quite so openly as in the form above. But it affects most of us who think about it at all. We like to believe that Man is in some subtle way superior to the rest of creation. It is best if he can be shown to be *necessarily* superior, for then there is no danger of him losing his commanding position. The popularity of the theological argument is clearly connected with this feeling. It is likely to be quite strong in intellectual people, since they value the power of thinking more highly than others, and are more inclined to base their belief in the superiority of Man on this power.

I do not think that this argument is sufficiently substantial to require refutation. Consolation would be more appropriate: perhaps this should be sought in the transmigration of souls.

(3) *The Mathematical Objection.* There are a number of results of mathematical logic which can be used to show that there are limitations to the powers of discrete-state machines. The best known of these results is known as Gödel's theorem, and shows that in any sufficiently powerful logical system statements can be formulated

which can neither be proved nor disproved within the system, unless possibly the system itself is inconsistent. There are other, in some respects similar, results due to Church 1936, Kleene 1935, and Turing 1937. The latter result is the most convenient to consider, since it refers directly to machines, whereas the others can only be used in a comparatively indirect argument: for instance if Gödel's theorem is to be used we need in addition to have some means of describing logical systems in terms of machines, and machines in terms of logical systems. The result in question refers to a type of machine which is essentially a digital computer with an infinite capacity. It states that there are certain things that such a machine cannot do. If it is rigged up to give answers to questions as in the imitation game, there will be some questions to which it will either give a wrong answer, or fail to give an answer at all however much time is allowed for a reply. There may, of course, be many such questions, and questions which cannot be answered by one machine may be satisfactorily answered by another. We are of course supposing for the present that the questions are of the kind to which an answer 'Yes' or 'No' is appropriate, rather than questions such as 'What do you think of Picasso?' The questions that we know the machines must fail on are of this type, "Consider the machine specified as follows. ... Will this machine ever answer 'Yes' to any question?" The dots are to be replaced by a description of some machine in a standard form, which could be something like that used in Section 5. When the machine described bears a certain comparatively simple relation to the machine which is under interrogation, it can be shown that the answer is either wrong or not forthcoming. This is the mathematical result: it is argued that it proves a disability of machines to which the human intellect is not subject.

The short answer to this argument is that although it is established that there are limitations to the powers of any particular machine, it has only been stated, without any sort of proof, that no such limitations apply to the human intellect. But I do not think this view can be dismissed quite so lightly. Whenever one of these machines is asked the appropriate critical question, and gives a definite answer, we know that this answer must be wrong, and this gives us a certain feeling of superiority. Is this feeling illusory? It is no doubt quite genuine, but I do not think too much importance should be attached to it. We too often give wrong answers to questions ourselves to be justified in being very pleased at such evidence of fallibility on the part of the machines. Further, our superiority can only be felt on such an occasion in relation to the one machine over which we have scored our petty triumph. There would be no question of triumphing simultaneously over *all* machines. In short, then, there might be men cleverer than any given machine, but then again there might be other machines cleverer again, and so on.

Those who hold to the mathematical argument would, I think, mostly be willing to accept the imitation game as a basis for discussion. Those who believe in the two previous objections would probably not be interested in any criteria.

(4) *The Argument from Consciousness.* This argument is very well expressed in *Professor Jefferson's* Lister Oration for 1949, from which I quote. "Not until a machine can write a sonnet or compose a concerto because of thoughts and emotions felt, and not by the chance fall of symbols, could we agree that machine equals brain—that is, not only write it but know that it had written it. No mechanism could feel (and not merely artificially signal, an easy contrivance) pleasure at its successes, grief when its valves fuse, be warmed by flattery, be made miserable by its mistakes, be charmed by sex, be angry or depressed when it cannot get what it wants."

This argument appears to be a denial of the validity of our test. According to the most extreme form of this view the only way by which one could be sure that a machine thinks is to *be* the machine and to feel oneself thinking. One could then describe these feelings to the world, but of course no one would be justified in taking any notice. Likewise according to this view the only way to know that a *man* thinks is to be that particular man. It is in fact the solipsist point of view. It may be the most logical view to hold but it makes communication of ideas difficult. A is liable to believe 'A thinks but B does not' whilst B believes 'B thinks but A does not'. Instead of arguing continually over this point it is usual to have the polite convention that everyone thinks.

I am sure that Professor Jefferson does not wish to adopt the extreme and solipsist point of view. Probably he would be quite willing to accept the imitation game as a test. The game (with the player B omitted) is frequently used in practice under the name of *viva voce* to discover whether some one really understands something or has 'learnt it parrot fashion'. Let us listen in to a part of such a *viva voce*:

> Interrogator: In the first line of your sonnet which reads 'Shall I compare thee to a summer's day', would not 'a spring day' do as well or better?
> Witness: It wouldn't scan.
> Interrogator: How about 'a winter's day'? That would scan all right.
> Witness: Yes, but nobody wants to be compared to a winter's day.
> Interrogator: Would you say Mr. Pickwick reminded you of Christmas?
> Witness: In a way.
> Interrogator: Yet Christmas is a winter's day, and I do not think Mr. Pickwick would mind the comparison.
> Witness: I don't think you're serious. By a winter's day one means a typical winter's day, rather than a special one like Christmas.

And so on. What would Professor Jefferson say if the sonnet-writing machine was able to answer like this in the *viva voce*? I do not know whether he would regard the machine as 'merely artificially signalling' these answers, but if the answers were as satisfactory and sustained as in the above passage I do not think he would describe it as 'an easy contrivance'. This phrase is, I think, intended to cover such devices as the inclusion in the machine of a record of someone reading a sonnet, with appropriate switching to turn it on from time to time.

In short then, I think that most of those who support the argument from consciousness could be persuaded to abandon it rather than be forced into the solipsist position. They will then probably be willing to accept our test.

I do not wish to give the impression that I think there is no mystery about consciousness. There is, for instance, something of a paradox connected with any attempt to localise it. But I do not think these mysteries necessarily need to be solved before we can answer the question with which we are concerned in this paper.

(5) *Arguments from Various Disabilities*. These arguments take the form, "I grant you that you can make machines do all the things you have mentioned but you will never be able to make one to do X". Numerous features X are suggested in this connexion. I offer a selection:

> Be kind, resourceful, beautiful, friendly, have initiative, have a sense of humour, tell right from wrong, make mistakes, fall in love, enjoy strawberries and cream, make some one fall in love with it, learn from experience, use words properly, be the subject of its own thought, have as much diversity of behaviour as a man, do something really new. (Some of these disabilities are given special consideration as indicated by the page numbers.) [The page numbers have been removed for the present volume. –Ed.]

No support is usually offered for these statements. I believe they are mostly founded on the principle of scientific induction. A man has seen thousands of machines in his lifetime. From what he sees of them he draws a number of general conclusions. They are ugly, each is designed for a very limited purpose, when required for a minutely different purpose they are useless, the variety of behaviour of any one of them is very small, etc., etc. Naturally he concludes that these are necessary properties of machines in general. Many of these limitations are associated with the very small storage capacity of most machines. (I am assuming that the idea of storage capacity is extended in some way to cover machines other than discrete-state machines.

The exact definition does not matter as no mathematical accuracy is claimed in the present discussion.) A few years ago, when very little had been heard of digital computers, it was possible to elicit much incredulity concerning them, if one mentioned their properties without describing their construction. That was presumably due to a similar application of the principle of scientific induction. These applications of the principle are of course largely unconscious. When a burnt child fears the fire and shows that he fears it by avoiding it, I should say that he was applying scientific induction. (I could of course also describe his behaviour in many other ways.) The works and customs of mankind do not seem to be very suitable material to which to apply scientific induction. A very large part of space-time must be investigated, if reliable results are to be obtained. Otherwise we may (as most English children do) decide that everybody speaks English, and that it is silly to learn French.

There are, however, special remarks to be made about many of the disabilities that have been mentioned. The inability to enjoy strawberries and cream may have struck the reader as frivolous. Possibly a machine might be made to enjoy this delicious dish, but any attempt to make one do so would be idiotic. What is important about this disability is that it contributes to some of the other disabilities, *e.g.* to the difficulty of the same kind of friendliness occurring between man and machine as between white man and white man, or between black man and black man.

The claim that "machines cannot make mistakes" seems a curious one. One is tempted to retort, "Are they any the worse for that?" But let us adopt a more sympathetic attitude, and try to see what is really meant. I think this criticism can be explained in terms of the imitation game. It is claimed that the interrogator could distinguish the machine from the man simply by setting them a number of problems in arithmetic. The machine would be unmasked because of its deadly accuracy. The reply to this is simple. The machine (programmed for playing the game) would not attempt to give the *right* answers to the arithmetic problems. It would deliberately introduce mistakes in a manner calculated to confuse the interrogator. A mechanical fault would probably show itself through an unsuitable decision as to what sort of a mistake to make in the arithmetic. Even this interpretation of the criticism is not sufficiently sympathetic. But we cannot afford the space to go into it much further. It seems to me that this criticism depends on a confusion between two kinds of mistake. We may call them 'errors of functioning' and 'errors of conclusion'. Errors of functioning are due to some mechanical or electrical fault which causes the machine to behave otherwise than it was designed to do. In philosophical discussions one likes to ignore the possibility of such errors; one is therefore discussing 'abstract machines'. These abstract machines are mathematical fictions rather than physical objects. By definition they are incapable of errors of functioning. In this sense we can truly say that 'machines can never make mistakes'. Errors of conclusion can only arise when some meaning is attached to the output signals from the machine. The machine might, for instance, type out mathematical equations, or sentences in English. When a false proposition is typed we say that the machine has committed an error of conclusion. There is clearly no reason at all for saying that a machine cannot make this kind of mistake. It might do nothing but type out repeatedly '0 = 1'. To take a less perverse example, it might have some method for drawing conclusions by scientific induction. We must expect such a method to lead occasionally to erroneous results.

The claim that a machine cannot be the subject of its own thought can of course only be answered if it can be shown that the machine has *some* thought with *some* subject matter. Nevertheless, 'the subject matter of a machine's operations' does seem to mean something, at least to the people who deal with it. If, for instance, the machine was trying to find a solution of the equation $x^2-40x-11 = 0$ one would be tempted to describe this equation as part of the machine's subject matter at that moment. In this sort of sense a machine undoubtedly can be its own subject matter. It may be used to help in making up its own programmes, or to predict the effect of alterations in its own structure. By observing the results of its own behaviour it can modify its own programmes so as to achieve some purpose more effectively. These are possibilities of the near future, rather than Utopian dreams.

The criticism that a machine cannot have much diversity of behaviour is just a way of saying that it cannot have much storage capacity. Until fairly recently a storage capacity of even a thousand digits was very rare.

The criticisms that we are considering here are often disguised forms of the argument from consciousness. Usually if one maintains that a machine *can* do one of these things, and describes the kind of method that the machine could use, one will not make much of an impression. It is thought that the method (whatever it may be, for it must be mechanical) is really rather base.

(6) *Lady Lovelace's Objection*. Our most detailed information of Babbage's Analytical Engine comes from a memoir by *Lady Lovelace*. In it she states, "The Analytical Engine has no pretensions to *originate* anything. It can do *whatever we know how to order it* to perform" (her italics). This statement is quoted by Hartree (1949, 70) who adds: "This does not imply that it may not be possible to construct electronic equipment which will 'think for itself', or in which, in biological terms, one could set up a conditioned reflex, which would serve as a basis for 'learning'. Whether this is possible in principle or not is a stimulating and exciting question, suggested by some of these recent developments. But it did not seem that the machines constructed or projected at the time had this property".

I am in thorough agreement with Hartree over this. It will be noticed that he does not assert that the machines in question had not got the property, but rather that the evidence available to Lady Lovelace did not encourage her to believe that they had it. It is quite possible that the machines in question had in a sense got this property. For suppose that some discrete-state machine has the property. The Analytical Engine was a universal digital computer, so that, if its storage capacity and speed were adequate, it could by suitable programming be made to mimic the machine in question. Probably this argument did not occur to the Countess or to Babbage. In any case there was no obligation on them to claim all that could be claimed.

This whole question will be considered again under the heading of learning machines.

A variant of Lady Lovelace's objection states that a machine can 'never do anything really new'. This may be parried for a moment with the saw, 'There is nothing new under the sun'. Who can be certain that 'original work' that he has done was not simply the growth of the seed planted in him by teaching, or the effect of following well-known general principles. A better variant of the objection says that a machine can never 'take us by surprise'. This statement is a more direct challenge and can be met directly. Machines take me by surprise with great frequency. This is largely because I do not do sufficient calculation to decide what to expect them to do, or rather because, although I do a calculation, I do it in a hurried, slipshod fashion, taking risks. Perhaps I say to myself, 'I suppose the voltage here ought to be the same as there: anyway let's assume it is'. Naturally I am often wrong, and the result is a surprise for me for by the time the experiment is done these assumptions have been forgotten. These admissions lay me open to lectures on the subject of my vicious ways, but do not throw any doubt on my credibility when I testify to the surprises I experience.

I do not expect this reply to silence my critic. He will probably say that such surprises are due to some creative mental act on my part, and reflect no credit on the machine. This leads us back to the argument from consciousness, and far from the idea of surprise. It is a line of argument we must consider closed, but it is perhaps worth remarking that the appreciation of something as surprising requires as much of a 'creative mental act' whether the surprising event originates from a man, a book, a machine or anything else.

The view that machines cannot give rise to surprise is due, I believe, to a fallacy to which philosophers and mathematicians are particularly subject. This is the assumption that as soon as a fact is presented to a mind all consequences of that fact spring into the mind simultaneously with it. It is a very useful assumption under many circumstances, but one too easily forgets that it is false. A natural consequence of doing so is that one then assumes that there is no virtue in the mere working out of consequences from data and general principles.

(7) *Argument from Continuity in the Nervous System.* The nervous system is certainly not a discrete-state machine. A small error in the information about the size of a nervous impulse impinging on a neuron, may make a large difference to the size of the outgoing impulse. It may be argued that, this being so, one cannot expect to be able to mimic the behaviour of the nervous system with a discrete-state system.

It is true that a discrete-state machine must be different from a continuous machine. But if we adhere to the conditions of the imitation game, the interrogator will not be able to take any advantage of this difference. The situation can be made clearer if we consider some other simpler continuous machine. A differential analyser will do very well. (A differential analyser is a certain kind of machine not of the discrete-state type used for some kinds of calculation.) Some of these provide their answers in a typed form, and so are suitable for taking part in the game. It would not be possible for a digital computer to predict exactly what answers the differential analyser would give to a problem, but it would be quite capable of giving the right sort of answer. For instance, if asked to give the value of π (actually about 3.1416) it would be reasonable to choose at random between the values 3.12, 3.13, 3.14, 3.15, 3.16 with the probabilities of 0.05, 0.15, 0.55, 0.19, 0.06 (say). Under these circumstances it would be very difficult for the interrogator to distinguish the differential analyser from the digital computer.

(8) *The Argument from Informality of Behaviour.* It is not possible to produce a set of rules purporting to describe what a man should do in every conceivable set of circumstances. One might for instance have a rule that one is to stop when one sees a red traffic light, and to go if one sees a green one, but what if by some fault both appear together? One may perhaps decide that it is safest to stop. But some further difficulty may well arise from this decision later. To attempt to provide rules of conduct to cover every eventuality, even those arising from traffic lights, appears to be impossible. With all this I agree.

From this it is argued that we cannot be machines. I shall try to reproduce the argument, but I fear I shall hardly do it justice. It seems to run something like this. 'If each man had a definite set of rules of conduct by which he regulated his life he would be no better than a machine. But there are no such rules, so men cannot be machines.' The undistributed middle is glaring. I do not think the argument is ever put quite like this, but I believe this is the argument used nevertheless. There may however be a certain confusion between 'rules of conduct' and 'laws of behaviour' to cloud the issue. By 'rules of conduct.' I mean precepts such as 'Stop if you see red lights', on which one can act, and of which one can be conscious. By 'laws of behaviour' I mean laws of nature as applied to a man's body such as 'if you pinch him he will squeak'. If we substitute 'laws of behaviour which regulate his life' for 'laws of conduct by which he regulates his life' in the argument quoted the undistributed middle is no longer insuperable. For we believe that it is not only true that being regulated by laws of behaviour implies being some sort of machine (though not necessarily a discrete-state machine), but that conversely being such a machine implies being regulated by such laws. However, we cannot so easily convince ourselves of the absence of complete laws of behaviour as of complete rules of conduct. The only way we know of for finding such laws is scientific observation, and we certainly know of no circumstances under which we could say, 'We have searched enough. There are no such laws.'

We can demonstrate more forcibly that any such statement would be unjustified. For suppose we could be sure of finding such laws if they existed. Then given a discrete-state machine it should certainly be possible to discover by observation sufficient about it to predict its future behaviour, and this within a reasonable time, say a thousand years. But this does not seem to be the case. I have set up on the Manchester computer a small programme using only 1000 units of storage, whereby the machine supplied with one sixteen figure number replies with another within two seconds. I would defy anyone to learn from these replies sufficient about the programme to be able to predict any replies to untried values.

(9) *The Argument from Extra-Sensory Perception.* I assume that the reader is familiar with the idea of extra-sensory perception, and the meaning of the four items of it, *viz.* telepathy, clairvoyance, precognition and psycho-kinesis. These disturbing phenomena seem to deny all our usual scientific ideas. How we should like to discredit them! Unfortunately the statistical evidence, at least for telepathy, is overwhelming. It is very difficult to rearrange one's ideas so as to fit these new facts in. Once one has accepted them it does not seem a very big step to believe in ghosts and bogies. The idea that our bodies move simply according to the known laws of physics, together with some others not yet discovered but somewhat similar, would be one of the first to go.

This argument is to my mind quite a strong one. One can say in reply that many scientific theories seem to remain workable in practice, in spite of clashing with E.S.P.; that in fact one can get along very nicely if one forgets about it. This is rather cold comfort, and one fears that thinking is just the kind of phenomenon where E.S.P. may be especially relevant.

A more specific argument based on E.S.P. might run as follows: "Let us play the imitation game, using as witnesses a man who is good as a telepathic receiver, and a digital computer. The interrogator can ask such questions as 'What suit does the card in my right hand belong to?' The man by telepathy or clairvoyance gives the right answer 130 times out of 400 cards. The machine can only guess at random, and perhaps gets 104 right, so the interrogator makes the right identification." There is an interesting possibility which opens here. Suppose the digital computer contains a random number generator. Then it will be natural to use this to decide what answer to give. But then the random number generator will be subject to the psycho-kinetic powers of the interrogator. Perhaps this psycho-kinesis might cause the machine to guess right more often than would be expected on a probability calculation, so that the interrogator might still be unable to make the right identification. On the other hand, he might be able to guess right without any questioning, by clairvoyance. With E.S.P. anything may happen.

If telepathy is admitted it will be necessary to tighten our test up. The situation could be regarded as analogous to that which would occur if the interrogator were talking to himself and one of the competitors was listening with his ear to the wall. To put the competitors into a 'telepathy-proof room' would satisfy all requirements.

7 LEARNING MACHINES

The reader will have anticipated that I have no very convincing arguments of a positive nature to support my views. If I had I should not have taken such pains to point out the fallacies in contrary views. Such evidence as I have I shall now give.

Let us return for a moment to Lady Lovelace's objection, which stated that the machine can only do what we tell it to do. One could say that a man can 'inject' an idea into the machine, and that it will respond to a certain extent and then drop into quiescence, like a piano string struck by a hammer. Another simile would be an atomic pile of less than critical size: an injected idea is to correspond to a neutron entering the pile from without. Each such neutron will cause a certain disturbance which eventually dies away. If, however, the size of the pile is sufficiently increased, the disturbance caused by such an incoming neutron will very likely go on and on increasing until the whole pile is destroyed. Is there a corresponding phenomenon for minds, and is there one for machines? There does seem to be one for the human mind. The majority of them seem to be 'sub-critical', *i.e.* to correspond in this analogy to piles of sub-critical size. An idea presented to such a mind will on average give rise to less than one idea in reply. A smallish proportion are super-critical. An idea presented to such a mind may give rise to a whole 'theory' consisting of secondary, tertiary and more remote ideas. Animals' minds seem to be very definitely sub-critical. Adhering to this analogy we ask, 'Can a machine be made to be super-critical?'

The 'skin of an onion' analogy is also helpful. In considering the functions of the mind or the brain we find certain operations which we can explain in purely mechanical terms. This we say does not correspond to the real mind: it is a sort of skin which we must strip off if we are to find the real mind. But then in what remains we find a further skin to be stripped off, and so on. Proceeding in this way do we ever come to the 'real' mind, or do we eventually come to the skin which has nothing in it? In the latter case the whole mind is mechanical. (It would not be a discrete-state machine however. We have discussed this.)

These last two paragraphs do not claim to be convincing arguments. They should rather be described as 'recitations tending to produce belief'.

The only really satisfactory support that can be given for the view expressed at the beginning of Section 6, will be that provided by waiting for the end of the century and then doing the experiment described. But what can we say in the meantime? What steps should be taken now if the experiment is to be successful?

As I have explained, the problem is mainly one of programming. Advances in engineering will have to be made too, but it seems unlikely that these will not be adequate for the requirements. Estimates of the storage capacity of the brain vary from 10^{10} to 10^{15} binary digits. I incline to the lower values and believe that only a very small fraction is used for the higher types of thinking. Most of it is probably used for the retention of visual impressions. I should be surprised if more than 10^9 was required for satisfactory playing of the imitation game, at any rate against a blind man. (Note – The capacity of the *Encyclopaedia Britannica*, 11th edition, is 2×10^9.) A storage capacity of 10^7 would be a very practicable possibility even by present techniques. It is probably not necessary to increase the speed of operations of the machines at all. Parts of modern machines which can be regarded as analogues of nerve cells work about a thousand times faster than the latter. This should provide a 'margin of safety' which could cover losses of speed arising in many ways. Our problem then is to find out how to programme these machines to play the game. At my present rate of working I produce about a thousand digits of programme a day, so that about sixty workers, working steadily through the fifty years might accomplish the job, if nothing went into the waste-paper basket. Some more expeditious method seems desirable.

In the process of trying to imitate an adult human mind we are bound to think a good deal about the process which has brought it to the state that it is in. We may notice three components,

(*a*) The initial state of the mind, say at birth,
(*b*) The education to which it has been subjected,
(*c*) Other experience, not to be described as education, to which it has been subjected.

Instead of trying to produce a programme to simulate the adult mind, why not rather try to produce one which simulates the child's? If this were then subjected to an appropriate course of education one would obtain the adult brain. Presumably the child-brain is something like a note-book as one buys it from the stationers. Rather little mechanism, and lots of blank sheets. (Mechanism and writing are from our point of view almost synonymous.) Our hope is that there is so little mechanism in the child-brain that something like it can be easily programmed. The amount of work in the education we can assume, as a first approximation, to be much the same as for the human child.

We have thus divided our problem into two parts. The child-programme and the education process. These two remain very closely connected. We cannot expect to find a good child-machine at the first attempt. One must experiment with teaching one such machine and see how well it learns. One can then try another and see if it is better or worse. There is an obvious connection between this process and evolution, by the identifications

    Structure of the child machine = Hereditary material
    Changes of the child machine = Mutations
    Natural selection = Judgment of the experimenter

One may hope, however, that this process will be more expeditious than evolution. The survival of the fittest is a slow method for measuring advantages. The experimenter, by the exercise of intelligence, should be able to speed it up. Equally important is the fact that he is not restricted to random mutations. If he can trace a cause for some weakness he can probably think of the kind of mutation which will improve it.

It will not be possible to apply exactly the same teaching process to the machine as to a normal child. It will not, for instance, be provided with legs, so that it could not be asked to go out and fill the coal scuttle. Possibly it might not have eyes. But however well these deficiencies might be overcome by clever engineering, one could not send the creature to school without the other children making excessive fun of it. It must be given some tuition. We need not be too concerned about the legs, eyes, etc. The example of Miss Helen Keller shows that education can take place provided that communication in both directions between teacher and pupil can take place by some means or other.

We normally associate punishments and rewards with the teaching process. Some simple child-machines can be constructed or programmed on this sort of principle. The machine has to be so constructed that events which shortly preceded the occurrence of a punishment-signal are unlikely to be repeated, whereas a reward-signal increased the probability of repetition of the events which led up to it. These definitions do not pre-suppose any feelings on the part of the machine. I have done some experiments with one such child-machine, and succeeded in teaching it a few things, but the teaching method was too unorthodox for the experiment to be considered really successful.

The use of punishments and rewards can at best be a part of the teaching process. Roughly speaking, if the teacher has no other means of communicating to the pupil, the amount of information which can reach him does not exceed the total number of rewards and punishments applied. By the time a child has learnt to repeat 'Casabianca' he would probably feel very sore indeed, if the text could only be discovered by a 'Twenty Questions' technique, every 'NO' taking the form of a blow. It is necessary therefore to have some other 'unemotional' channels of communication. If these are available it is possible to teach a machine by punishments and rewards to obey orders given in some language, *e.g.* a symbolic language. These orders are to be transmitted through the 'unemotional' channels. The use of this language will diminish greatly the number of punishments and rewards required.

Opinions may vary as to the complexity which is suitable in the child machine. One might try to make it as simple as possible consistently with the general principles. Alternatively one might have a complete system of logical inference 'built in'.[2] In the latter case the store would be largely occupied with definitions and propositions. The propositions would have various kinds of status, *e.g.* well-established facts, conjectures, mathematically proved theorems, statements given by an authority, expressions having the logical form of proposition but not belief-value. Certain propositions may be described as 'imperatives'. The machine should be so constructed that as soon as an imperative is classed as 'well-established' the appropriate action automatically takes place. To illustrate this, suppose the teacher says to the machine, 'Do your homework now'. This may cause "Teacher says 'Do your homework now'" to be included amongst the well-established facts. Another such fact might be, "Everything that teacher says is true". Combining these may eventually lead to the imperative, 'Do your homework now', being included amongst the well-established facts, and this, by the construction of the machine, will mean that the homework actually gets started, but the effect is very satisfactory. The processes of inference used by the machine need not be such as would satisfy the most exacting logicians. There might for instance be no hierarchy of types. But this need not mean that type fallacies will occur, any more than we are bound to fall over unfenced cliffs. Suitable imperatives (expressed *within* the systems, not forming part of the rules *of* the system) such as 'Do not use a class unless it is a subclass of one which has been mentioned by teacher' can have a similar effect to 'Do not go too near the edge'.

The imperatives that can be obeyed by a machine that has no limbs are bound to be of a rather intellectual character, as in the example (doing homework) given above. Important amongst such imperatives will be ones which regulate the order in which the rules of the logical system concerned are to be applied. For at each stage when one is using a logical system, there is a very large number of alternative steps, any of which one is permitted to apply, so far as obedience to the rules of the logical system is concerned. These choices make the difference between a brilliant and a footling reasoner, not the difference between a sound and a fallacious one. Propositions leading to imperatives of this kind might be "When Socrates is mentioned, use the syllogism in Barbara" or "If one method has been proved to be quicker than another, do not use the slower method". Some of these may be 'given by authority', but others may be produced by the machine itself, *e.g.* by scientific induction.

The idea of a learning machine may appear paradoxical to some readers. How can the rules of operation of the machine change? They should describe completely how the machine will react whatever its history might be, whatever changes it might undergo. The rules are thus quite time-invariant. This is quite true. The explanation of the paradox is that the rules which get changed in the learning process are of a rather less pretentious kind, claiming only an ephemeral validity. The reader may draw a parallel with the Constitution of the United States.

An important feature of a learning machine is that its teacher will often be very largely ignorant of quite what is going on inside, although he may still be able to some extent to predict his pupil's behaviour. This should apply most strongly to the later education of a machine arising from a child-machine of well-tried design (or programme). This is in clear contrast with normal procedure when using a machine to do computations: one's object is then to have a clear mental picture of the state of the machine at each moment in the computation. This object can only be achieved with a struggle. The view that 'the machine can only do what we know how to order it to do',[3] appears strange in face of this. Most of the programmes which we can put into the machine will result in its doing something that we cannot make sense of at all, or which we regard as completely random behaviour. Intelligent behaviour presumably consists in a departure from the completely disciplined behaviour involved in computation, but a rather slight one, which does not give rise to random behaviour, or to pointless repetitive loops. Another important result of preparing our machine for its part in the imitation game by a process of teaching and learning is that 'human fallibility' is likely to be omitted in a rather natural way, *i.e.* without special 'coaching'. Processes that are learnt do not produce a hundred per cent certainty of result; if they did they could not be unlearnt.

It is probably wise to include a random element in a learning machine. A random element is rather useful when we are searching for a solution of some problem. Suppose for instance we wanted to find a number between 50 and 200 which was equal to the square of the sum of its digits, we might start at 51 then try 52 and go on until we got a number that worked. Alternatively we might choose numbers at random until we got a good one. This method has the advantage that it is unnecessary to keep track of the values that have been tried, but the disadvantage that one may try the same one twice, but this is not very important if there are several solutions. The systematic method has the disadvantage that there may be an enormous block without any solutions in the region which has to be investigated first. Now the learning process may be regarded as a search for a form of behaviour which will satisfy the teacher (or some other criterion). Since there is probably a very large number of satisfactory solutions the random method seems to be better than the systematic. It should be noticed that it is used in the analogous process of evolution. But there the systematic method is not possible. How could one keep track of the different genetical combinations that had been tried, so as to avoid trying them again?

We may hope that machines will eventually compete with men in all purely intellectual fields. But which are the best ones to start with? Even this is a difficult decision. Many people think that a very abstract activity, like the playing of chess, would be best. It can also be maintained that it is best to provide the machine with the best sense organs that money can buy, and then teach it to understand and speak English. This process could follow the normal teaching of a child. Things would be pointed out and named, etc. Again I do not know what the right answer is, but I think both approaches should be tried.

We can only see a short distance ahead, but we can see plenty there that needs to be done.

NOTES

1   Possibly this view is heretical. St. Thomas Aquinas (*Summa Theologica*, quoted by Bertrand Russell, p. 480) states that God cannot make a man to have no soul. But this may not be a real restriction on His powers, but only a result of the fact that men's souls are immortal, and therefore indestructible.
2   Or rather 'programmed in' for our child-machine will be programmed in a digital computer. But the logical system will not have to be learnt.
3   Compare Lady Lovelace's statement (p. 485), which does not contain the word 'only'.

REFERENCES

Church, A. "An Unsolvable Problem of Elementary Number Theory", *American J. of Math.*, 58 (1936), 345–63.

Gödel, K. "Über formal unentscheidbare Sätze der Principia Mathematica und verwandter Systeme, I", *Monatshefte für Math. und Phys.*, (1931), 173–89.

Hartree, D. R. *Calculating Instruments and Machines*, New York, 1949.

Kleene, S. C. "General Recursive Functions of Natural Numbers", *American J. of Math.*, 57 (1935), 153–73 and 219–44.

Jefferson, G. "The Mind of Mechanical Man". Lister Oration for 1949. *British Medical Journal*, vol. i (1949), 1105–21.

Countess of Lovelace, "Translator's notes to an article on Babbage's Analytical Engine", *Scientific Memoirs* (ed. by R. Taylor), vol. 3 (1842), 691–731.

Russell, B. *History of Western Philosophy*, London, 1940.

Turing, A. M. "On Computable Numbers, with an Application to the Entscheidungsproblem", *Proc. London Math. Soc.* (2), 42 (1937), 230–65.

37

MINDS, BRAINS, AND PROGRAMS

John R. Searle

What psychological and philosophical significance should we attach to recent efforts at computer simulations of human cognitive capacities? In answering this question, I find it useful to distinguish what I will call "strong" AI from "weak" or "cautious" AI (Artificial Intelligence). According to weak AI, the principal value of the computer in the study of the mind is that it gives us a very powerful tool. For example, it enables us to formulate and test hypotheses in a more rigorous and precise fashion. But according to strong AI, the computer is not merely a tool in the study of the mind: rather, the appropriately programmed computer really *is* a mind, in the sense that computers given the right programs can be literally said to *understand* and have other cognitive states. In strong AI, because the programmed computer has cognitive states, the programs are not mere tools that enable us to test psychological explanations; rather, the programs are themselves the explanations.

I have no objection to the claims of weak AI, at least as far as this article is concerned. My discussion here will be directed at the claims I have defined as those of strong AI, specifically the claim that the appropriately programmed computer literally has cognitive states and that the programs thereby explain human cognition. When I hereafter refer to AI, I have in mind the strong version, as expressed by these two claims.

I will consider the work of Roger Schank and his colleagues at Yale (Schank & Abelson 1977), because I am more familiar with it than I am with any other similar claims, and because it provides a very clear example of the sort of work I wish to examine. But nothing that follows depends upon the details of Schank's programs. The same arguments would apply to Winograd's SHRDLU (Winograd 1973), Weizenbaum's ELIZA (Weizenbaum 1965), and indeed any Turing machine simulation of human mental phenomena.

Very briefly, and leaving out the various details, one can describe Schank's program as follows: the aim of the program is to simulate the human ability to understand stories. It is characteristic of human beings' story-understanding capacity that they can answer questions about the story even though the information that they give was never explicitly stated in the story. Thus, for example, suppose you are given the following story: "A man went into a restaurant and ordered a hamburger. When the hamburger arrived it was burned to a crisp, and the man stormed out of the restaurant angrily, without paying for the hamburger or leaving a tip." Now, if you are asked "Did the man eat the hamburger?" you will presumably answer, "No, he did not." Similarly, if you are given the following story: "A man went into a restaurant and ordered a hamburger; when the hamburger came he was very pleased with it; and as he left the restaurant he gave the waitress a large tip before paying his bill," and you are asked the question, "Did the man eat the hamburger?," you will presumably answer, "Yes, he ate the hamburger." Now Schank's machines can similarly answer questions about restaurants in this fashion. To do this, they have a "representation" of the sort of information that human beings have about restaurants, which enables them to answer such questions as those above, given these sorts of stories. When the machine is given the story and then asked the question, the machine will print out answers of the sort that we would expect human beings to give if told similar stories. Partisans of strong AI claim that in this question and answer sequence the machine is not only simulating a human ability but also

1 that the machine can literally be said to *understand* the story and provide the answers to questions, and
2 that what the machine and its program do *explains* the human ability to understand the story and answer questions about it.

Both claims seem to me to be totally unsupported by Schank's[1] work, as I will attempt to show in what follows.

One way to test any theory of the mind is to ask oneself what it would be like if my mind actually worked on the principles that the theory says all minds work on. Let us apply this test to the Schank program with the following *Gedankenexperiment*. Suppose that I'm locked in a room and given a large batch of Chinese writing. Suppose furthermore (as is indeed the case) that I know no Chinese, either written or spoken, and that I'm not even confident that I could recognize Chinese writing as Chinese writing distinct from, say, Japanese writing or meaningless squiggles. To me, Chinese writing is just so many meaningless squiggles. Now suppose further that after this first batch of Chinese writing I am given a second batch of Chinese script together with a set of rules for correlating the second batch with the first batch. The rules are in English, and I understand these rules as well as any other native speaker of English. They enable me to correlate one set of formal symbols with another set of formal symbols, and all that "formal" means here is that I can identify the symbols entirely by their shapes. Now suppose also that I am given a third batch of Chinese symbols together with some instructions, again in English, that enable me to corre-late elements of this third batch with the first two batches, and these rules instruct me how to give back certain Chinese symbols with certain sorts of shapes in response to certain sorts of shapes given me in the third batch. Unknown to me, the people who are giving me all of these symbols call the first batch "a script," they call the second batch a "story," and they call the third batch "questions." Furthermore, they call the symbols I give them back in response to the third batch "answers to the questions," and the set of rules in English that they gave me, they call "the program." Now just to complicate the story a little, imagine that these people also give me stories in English, which I understand, and they then ask me questions in English about these stories, and I give them back answers in English. Suppose also that after a while I get so good at following the instructions for manipulating the Chinese symbols and the programmers get so good at writing the programs that from the external point of view – that is, from the point of view of somebody outside the room in which I am locked – my answers to the questions are absolutely indistinguishable from those of native Chinese speakers. Nobody just looking at my answers can tell that I don't speak a word of Chinese. Let us also suppose that my answers to the English ques-tions are, as they no doubt would be, indistinguishable from those of other native English speakers, for the simple reason that I am a native English speaker. From the external point of view – from the point of view of someone reading my "answers" – the answers to the Chinese questions and the English questions are equally good. But in the Chinese case, unlike the English case, I produce the answers by manipulating uninterpreted formal symbols. As far as the Chinese is concerned, I simply behave like a computer; I perform computational operations on formally specified elements. For the purposes of the Chinese, I am simply an instantiation of the computer program.

Now the claims made by strong AI are that the programmed computer under-stands the stories and that the program in some sense explains human understanding. But we are now in a position to examine these claims in light of our thought experiment.

1 As regards the first claim, it seems to me quite obvious in the example that I do not understand a word of the Chinese stories. I have inputs and outputs that are indistinguishable from those of the native Chinese speaker, and I can have any formal program you like, but I still understand nothing. For the same reasons, Schank's computer understands nothing of any stories, whether in Chinese, English, or what-ever, since in the Chinese case the computer is me, and in cases where the computer is not me, the computer has nothing more than I have in the case where I understand nothing.

2 As regards the second claim, that the program explains human understanding, we can see that the computer and its program do not provide sufficient conditions of

understanding since the computer and the program are functioning, and there is no understanding. But does it even provide a necessary condition or a significant contribution to understanding? One of the claims made by the supporters of strong AI is that when I understand a story in English, what I am doing is exactly the same – or perhaps more of the same – as what I was doing in manipulating the Chinese symbols. It is simply more formal symbol manipulation that distinguishes the case in English, where I do understand, from the case in Chinese, where I don't. I have not demonstrated that this claim is false, but it would certainly appear an incredible claim in the example. Such plausibility as the claim has derives from the supposition that we can construct a program that will have the same inputs and outputs as native speakers, and in addition we assume that speakers have some level of description where they are also instantiations of a program. On the basis of these two assumptions we assume that even if Schank's program isn't the whole story about understanding, it may be part of the story. Well, I suppose that is an empirical possibility, but not the slightest reason has so far been given to believe that it is true, since what is suggested – though certainly not demonstrated – by the example is that the computer program is simply irrelevant to my understanding of the story. In the Chinese case I have everything that artificial intelligence can put into me by way of a program, and I understand nothing; in the English case I understand everything, and there is so far no reason at all to suppose that my understanding has anything to do with computer programs, that is, with computational operations on purely formally specified elements. As long as the program is defined in terms of computational operations on purely formally defined elements, what the example suggests is that these by themselves have no interesting connection with understanding. They are certainly not sufficient conditions, and not the slightest reason has been given to suppose that they are necessary conditions or even that they make a significant contribution to understanding. Notice that the force of the argument is not simply that different machines can have the same input and output while operating on different formal principles – that is not the point at all. Rather, whatever purely formal principles you put into the computer, they will not be sufficient for understanding, since a human will be able to follow the formal principles without understanding anything. No reason whatever has been offered to suppose that such principles are necessary or even contributory, since no reason has been given to suppose that when I understand English I am operating with any formal program at all.

Well, then, what is it that I have in the case of the English sentences that I do not have in the case of the Chinese sentences? The obvious answer is that I know what the former mean, while I haven't the faintest idea what the latter mean. But in what does this consist and why couldn't we give it to a machine, whatever it is? I will return to this question later, but first I want to continue with the example.

I have had the occasions to present this example to several workers in artificial intelligence, and, interestingly, they do not seem to agree on what the proper reply to it is. I get a surprising variety of replies, and in what follows I will consider the most common of these (specified along with their geographic origins).

But first I want to block some common misunderstandings about "understanding": in many of these discussions one finds a lot of fancy footwork about the word "understanding." My critics point out that there are many different degrees of understanding; that "understanding" is not a simple two-place predicate; that there are even different kinds and levels of understanding, and often the law of excluded middle doesn't even apply in a straightforward way to statements of the form "x understands y"; that in many cases it is a matter for decision and not a simple matter of fact whether x understands y; and so on. To all of these points I want to say: of course, of course. But they have nothing to do with the points at issue. There are clear cases in which "understanding" literally applies and clear cases in which it does not apply; and these two sorts of cases are all I need for this argument.[2] I understand stories in English; to a lesser degree I can understand stories in French; to a still lesser degree, stories in German; and in Chinese, not at all. My car and my adding machine, on the other hand, understand nothing: they are not in that line of business. We often attribute "understanding" and other cognitive predicates by metaphor and analogy to cars, adding machines, and other artifacts, but nothing is proved by such attributions. We say, "The door *knows* when to open because of its photoelectric cell," "The adding machine *knows how* (*understands how*, is *able*) to do addition and subtraction but not division," and "The thermostat *perceives* changes in the temperature." The reason we make these attributions is quite interesting, and it has to do with the fact that in artifacts we extend our own intentionality;[3] our tools are extensions of our purposes, and so we find it natural to make metaphorical attributions of intentionality to them; but I take it no philosophical ice is cut by such examples. The sense in which an automatic door "understands instructions" from its photoelectric cell is not at all the sense in which I understand English. If the sense in which Schank's programmed computers understand stories is supposed to be the metaphorical sense in which the door understands, and not the sense in which I understand English, the issue would not be worth discussing. But Newell and Simon (1963) write that the kind of cognition they claim for computers is exactly the same as for human beings. I like the straightforwardness of this claim, and it is the sort of claim I will be considering. I will argue that in the literal sense the programmed computer understands what the ear and the adding machine understand, namely, exactly nothing. The computer understanding is not just (like my understanding of German) partial or incomplete; it is zero.

Now to the replies:

I The systems reply (Berkeley)

"While it is true that the individual person who is locked in the room does not understand the story, the fact is that he is merely part of a whole system, and the system does understand the story. The person has a large ledger in front of him in which are written the rules, he has a lot of scratch paper and pencils for doing calculations, he has 'data banks' of sets of Chinese symbols. Now, understanding is not being ascribed to the mere individual; rather it is being ascribed to this whole system of which he is a part."

My response to the systems theory is quite simple: let the individual internalize all of these elements of the system. He memorizes the rules in the ledger and the data banks of Chinese symbols, and he does all the calculations in his head. The individual then incorporates the entire system. There isn't anything at all to the system that he does not encompass. We can even get rid of the room and suppose he works outdoors. All the same, he understands nothing of the Chinese, and a fortiori neither does the system, because there isn't anything in the system that isn't in him. If he doesn't understand, then there is no way the system could understand because the system is just a part of him.

Actually I feel somewhat embarrassed to give even this answer to the systems theory because the theory seems to me so implausible to start with. The idea is that while a person doesn't understand Chinese, somehow the *conjunction* of that person and bits of paper might understand Chinese. It is not easy for me to imagine how someone who was not in the grip of an ideology would find the idea at all plausible. Still, I think many people who are committed to the ideology of strong AI will in the end be inclined to say something very much like this; so let us pursue it a bit further. According to one version of this view, while the man in the internalized systems example doesn't understand Chinese in the sense that a native Chinese speaker does (because, for example, he doesn't know that the story refers to restaurants and hamburgers, etc.), still "the man as a formal symbol manipulation system" *really does understand Chinese*. The subsystem of the man that is the formal symbol manipulation system for Chinese should not be confused with the subsystem for English.

So there are really two subsystems in the man; one understands English, the other Chinese, and "it's just that the two systems have little to do with each other." But, I want to reply, not only do they have little to do with each other, they are not even remotely alike. The subsystem that understands English (assuming we allow ourselves to talk in this jargon of "subsystems" for a moment) knows that the stories are about restaurants and eating hamburgers, he knows that he is being asked questions about restaurants and that he is answering questions as best he can by making various inferences from the content of the story, and so on. But the Chinese system knows none of this. Whereas the English subsystem knows that "hamburgers" refers to hamburgers, the Chinese subsystem knows only that "squiggle squiggle" is followed by "squoggle squoggle." All he knows is that various formal symbols are being introduced at one end and manipulated according to rules written in English, and other symbols are going out at the other end. The whole point of the original example was to argue that such symbol manipulation by itself couldn't be sufficient for understanding Chinese in any literal sense because the man could write "squoggle squoggle" after "squiggle squiggle" without understanding anything in Chinese. And it doesn't meet that argument to postulate subsystems within the man, because the subsystems are no better off than the man was in the first place; they still don't have anything even remotely like what the English-speaking man (or subsystem) has. Indeed, in the case as described, the Chinese subsystem is simply a part of the English subsystem, a part that engages in meaningless symbol manipulation according to rules in English.

Let us ask ourselves what is supposed to motivate the systems reply in the first place; that is, what *independent* grounds are there supposed to be for saying that the agent must have a subsystem within him that literally understands stories in Chinese? As far as I can tell the only grounds are that in the example I have the same input and output as native Chinese speakers and a program that goes from one to the other. But the whole point of the examples has been to try to show that that couldn't be sufficient for understanding, in the sense in which I understand stories in English, because a person, and hence the set of systems that go to make up a person, could have the right combination of input, output, and program and still not understand anything in the relevant literal sense in which I understand English. The only motivation for saying there *must* be a subsystem in me that understands Chinese is that I have a program and I can pass the Turing test; I can fool native Chinese speakers. But precisely one of the points at issue is the adequacy of the Turing test. The example shows that there could be two "systems," both of which pass the Turing test, but only one of which understands; and it is no argument against this point to say that since they both pass the Turing test they must both understand, since this claim fails to meet the argument that the system in me that understands English has a great deal more than the system that merely processes Chinese. In short, the systems reply simply begs the question by insisting without argument that the system must understand Chinese.

Furthermore, the systems reply would appear to lead to consequences that are independently absurd. If we are to conclude that there must be cognition in me on the grounds that I have a certain sort of input and output and a program in between, then it looks like all sorts of noncognitive subsystems are going to turn out to be cognitive. For example, there is a level of description at which my stomach does information processing, and it instantiates any number of computer programs, but I take it we do not want to say that it has any understanding [cf. Pylyshyn: "Computation and Cognition" *BBS* 3(1) 1980]. But if we accept the systems reply, then it is hard

501

to see how we avoid saying that stomach, heart, liver, and so on, are all understanding subsystems, since there is no principled way to distinguish the motivation for saying the Chinese subsystem understands from saying that the stomach understands. It is, by the way, not an answer to this point to say that the Chinese system has information as input and output and the stomach has food and food products as input and output, since from the point of view of the agent, from my point of view, there is no information in either the food or the Chinese – the Chinese is just so many meaningless squiggles. The information in the Chinese case is solely in the eyes of the programmers and the interpreters, and there is nothing to prevent them from treating the input and output of my digestive organs as information if they so desire.

This last point bears on some independent problems in strong AI, and it is worth digressing for a moment to explain it. If strong AI is to be a branch of psychology, then it must be able to distinguish those systems that are genuinely mental from those that are not. It must be able to distinguish the principles on which the mind works from those on which nonmental systems work; otherwise it will offer us no explanations of what is specifically mental about the mental. And the mental-nonmental distinction cannot be just in the eye of the beholder but it must be intrinsic to the systems; otherwise it would be up to any beholder to treat people as nonmental and, for example, hurricanes as mental if he likes. But quite often in the AI literature the distinction is blurred in ways that would in the long run prove disastrous to the claim that AI is a cognitive inquiry. McCarthy, for example, writes, "Machines as simple as thermostats can be said to have beliefs, and having beliefs seems to be a characteristic of most machines capable of problem solving performance" (McCarthy 1979). Anyone who thinks strong AI has a chance as a theory of the mind ought to ponder the implications of that remark. We are asked to accept it as a discovery of strong AI that the hunk of metal on the wall that we use to regulate the temperature has beliefs in exactly the same sense that we, our spouses, and our children have beliefs, and furthermore that "most" of the other machines in the room – telephone, tape recorder, adding machine, electric light switch – also have beliefs in this literal sense. It is not the aim of this article to argue against McCarthy's point, so I will simply assert the following without argument. The study of the mind starts with such facts as that humans have beliefs, while thermostats, telephones, and adding machines don't. If you get a theory that denies this point you have produced a counter-example to the theory and the theory is false. One gets the impression that people in AI who write this sort of thing think they can get away with it because they don't really take it seriously, and they don't think anyone else will either. I propose for a moment at least, to take it seriously. Think hard for one minute about what would be necessary to establish that that hunk of metal on the wall over there had real beliefs, beliefs with direction of fit, propositional content, and conditions of satisfaction; beliefs that had the possibility of being strong beliefs or weak beliefs; nervous, anxious, or secure beliefs; dogmatic, rational, or superstitious beliefs; blind faiths or hesitant cogitations; any kind of beliefs. The thermostat is not a candidate. Neither is stomach, liver, adding machine, or telephone. However, since we are taking the idea seriously, notice that its truth would be fatal to strong AI's claim to be a science of the mind. For now the mind is everywhere. What we wanted to know is what distinguishes the mind from thermostats and livers. And if McCarthy were right, strong AI wouldn't have a hope of telling us that.

II The Robot Reply (Yale)

"Suppose we wrote a different kind of program from Schank's program. Suppose we put a computer inside a robot, and this computer would not just take in formal symbols as input and give out formal symbols as output, but rather would actually operate the robot in such a way that the robot does something very much like perceiving, walking, moving about, hammering nails, eating, drinking – anything you like. The robot would, for example, have a television camera attached to it that enabled it to 'see,' it would have arms and legs that enabled it to 'act,' and all of this would be controlled by its computer 'brain.' Such a robot would, unlike Schank's computer, have genuine understanding and other mental states."

The first thing to notice about the robot reply is that it tacitly concedes that cognition is not solely a matter of formal symbol manipulation, since this reply adds a set of causal relations with the outside world [cf. Fodor: "Methodological Solipsism" *BBS* 3(1) 1980]. But the answer to the robot reply is that the addition of such "perceptual" and "motor" capacities adds nothing by way of understanding, in particular, or intentionality, in general, to Schank's original program. To see this, notice that the same thought experiment applies to the robot case. Suppose that instead of the computer inside the robot, you put me inside the room and, as in the original Chinese case, you give me more Chinese symbols with more instructions in English for matching Chinese symbols to Chinese symbols and feeding back Chinese symbols to the outside. Suppose, unknown to me, some of the Chinese symbols that come to me come from a television camera attached to the robot and other Chinese symbols that I am giving out serve to make the motors inside the robot move the robot's legs or arms. It is important to emphasize that all I am doing is manipulating formal symbols: I know none of these other facts. I am receiving "information" from the robot's "perceptual" apparatus, and I am giving out "instructions" to its motor apparatus without knowing either of these facts. I am the robot's homunculus, but unlike the traditional homunculus, I don't know what's going on. I don't understand anything except the rules for symbol manipulation. Now in this case I want to say that the robot has no intentional states at all; it is simply moving about as a result of its electrical wiring and its program. And furthermore, by instantiating the program I have no intentional states of the relevant type. All I do is follow formal instructions about manipulating formal symbols.

III The brain simulator reply (Berkeley and M.I.T.)

"Suppose we design a program that doesn't represent information that we have about the world, such as the information in Schank's scripts, but simulates the actual sequence of neuron firings at the synapses of the brain of a native Chinese speaker when he understands stories in Chinese and gives answers to them. The machine takes in Chinese stories and questions about them as input, it simulates the formal structure of actual Chinese brains in processing these stories, and it gives out Chinese answers as outputs. We can even imagine that the machine operates, not with a single serial program, but with a whole set of programs operating in parallel, in the manner that actual human brains presumably operate when they process natural language. Now surely in such a case we would have to say that the machine understood the stories; and if we refuse to say that, wouldn't we also have to deny that native Chinese speakers understood the stories? At the level of the synapses, what would or could be different about the program of the computer and the program of the Chinese brain?"

Before countering this reply I want to digress to note that it is an odd reply for any partisan of artificial intelligence (or functionalism, etc.) to make: I thought the whole idea of strong AI is that we don't need to know how the brain works to know how the mind works. The basic hypothesis, or so I had supposed, was that there is a level of mental operations consisting of computational processes over formal elements that constitute the essence of the mental and can be realized in all sorts of different brain processes, in the same way that any computer program can be realized in different computer hardwares: on the assumptions of strong AI, the mind is to the brain as the program is to the hardware, and thus we can understand the mind without doing neurophysiology. If we had to know how the brain worked to do AI, we wouldn't bother with AI. However, even getting this close to the operation of the brain is still not sufficient to produce understanding. To see this, imagine that instead of a monolingual man in a room shuffling symbols we have the man operate an elaborate set of water pipes with valves connecting them. When the man receives the Chinese symbols, he looks up in the program, written in English, which valves he has to turn on and off. Each water connection corresponds to a synapse in the Chinese brain, and the whole system is rigged up so that after doing all the right firings, that is after turning on all the right faucets, the Chinese answers pop out at the output end of the series of pipes.

Now where is the understanding in this system? It takes Chinese as input, it simulates the formal structure of the synapses of the Chinese brain, and it gives

Chinese as output. But the man certainly doesn't understand Chinese, and neither do the water pipes, and if we are tempted to adopt what I think is the absurd view that somehow the *conjunction* of man *and* water pipes understands, remember that in principle the man can internalize the formal structure of the water pipes and do all the "neuron firings" in his imagination. The problem with the brain simulator is that it is simulating the wrong things about the brain. As long as it simulates only the formal structure of the sequence of neuron firings at the synapses, it won't have simulated what matters about the brain, namely its causal properties, its ability to produce intentional states. And that the formal properties are not sufficient for the causal properties is shown by the water pipe example: we can have all the formal properties carved off from the relevant neurobiological causal properties.

IV The combination reply (Berkeley and Stanford)

"While each of the previous three replies might not be completely convincing by itself as a refutation of the Chinese room counterexample, if you take all three together they are collectively much more convincing and even decisive. Imagine a robot with a brain-shaped computer lodged in its cranial cavity, imagine the computer programmed with all the synapses of a human brain, imagine the whole behavior of the robot is indistinguishable from human behavior, and now think of the whole thing as a unified system and not just as a computer with inputs and outputs. Surely in such a case we would have to ascribe intentionality to the system."

I entirely agree that in such a case we would find it rational and indeed irresistible to accept the hypothesis that the robot had intentionality, as long as we knew nothing more about it. Indeed, besides appearance and behavior, the other elements of the combination are really irrelevant. If we could build a robot whose behavior was indistinguishable over a large range from human behavior, we would attribute intentionality to it, pending some reason not to. We wouldn't need to know in advance that its computer brain was a formal analogue of the human brain.

But I really don't see that this is any help to the claims of strong AI; and here's why: According to strong AI, instantiating a formal program with the right input and output is a sufficient condition of, indeed is constitutive of, intentionality. As Newell (1979) puts it, the essence of the mental is the operation of a physical symbol system. But the attributions of intentionality that we make to the robot in this example have nothing to do with formal programs. They are simply based on the assumption that if the robot looks and behaves sufficiently like us, then we would suppose, until proven otherwise, that it must have mental states like ours that cause and are expressed by its behavior and it must have an inner mechanism capable of producing such mental states. If we knew independently how to account for its behavior without such assumptions we would not attribute intentionality to it, especially if we knew it had a formal program. And this is precisely the point of my earlier reply to objection II.

Suppose we knew that the robot's behavior was entirely accounted for by the fact that a man inside it was receiving uninterpreted formal symbols from the robot's sensory receptors and sending out uninterpreted formal symbols to its motor mechanisms, and the man was doing this symbol manipulation in accordance with a bunch of rules. Furthermore, suppose the man knows none of these facts about the robot, all he knows is which operations to perform on which meaningless symbols. In such a case we would regard the robot as an ingenious mechanical dummy. The hypothesis that the dummy has a mind would now be unwarranted and unnecessary, for there is now no longer any reason to ascribe intentionality to the robot or to the system of which it is a part (except of course for the man's intentionality in manipulating the symbols). The formal symbol manipulations go on, the input and output are correctly matched, but the only real locus of intentionality is the man, and he doesn't know any of the relevant intentional states; he doesn't, for example, *see* what comes into the robot's eyes, he doesn't *intend* to move the robot's arm, and he doesn't *understand* any of the remarks made to or by the robot. Nor, for the reasons stated earlier, does the system of which man and robot are a part.

To see this point, contrast this case with cases in which we find it completely natural to ascribe intentionality to members of certain other primate species such as apes and monkeys and to domestic animals such as dogs. The reasons we find it natural are, roughly, two: we can't make sense of the animal's behavior without the ascription of intentionality, and we can see that the beasts are made of similar stuff to ourselves – that is an eye, that a nose, this is its skin, and so on. Given the coherence of the animal's behavior and the assumption of the same causal stuff underlying it, we assume both that the animal must have mental states underlying its behavior, and that the mental states must be produced by mechanisms made out of the stuff that is like our stuff. We would certainly make similar assumptions about the robot unless we had some reason not to, but as soon as we knew that the behavior was the result of a formal program, and that the actual causal properties of the physical substance were irrelevant we would abandon the assumption of intentionality. [See "Cognition and Consciousness in Nonhuman Species" *BBS* I(4) 1978.]

There are two other responses to my example that come up frequently (and so are worth discussing) but really miss the point.

V The other minds reply (Yale)

"How do you know that other people understand Chinese or anything else? Only by their behavior. Now the computer can pass the behavioral tests as well as they can (in principle), so if you are going to attribute cognition to other people you must in principle also attribute it to computers."

This objection really is only worth a short reply. The problem in this discussion is not about how I know that other people have cognitive states, but rather what it is that I am attributing to them when I attribute cognitive states to them. The thrust of the argument is that it couldn't be just computational processes and their output because the computational processes and their output can exist without the cognitive state. It is no answer to this argument to feign anesthesia. In "cognitive sciences" one presupposes the reality and knowability of the mental in the same way that in physical sciences one has to presuppose the reality and knowability of physical objects.

VI The many mansions reply (Berkeley)

"Your whole argument presupposes that AI is only about analogue and digital computers. But that just happens to be the present state of technology. Whatever these causal processes are that you say are essential for intentionality (assuming you are right), eventually we will be able to build devices that have these causal processes, and that will be artificial intelligence. So your arguments are in no way directed at the ability of artificial intelligence to produce and explain cognition."

I really have no objection to this reply save to say that it in effect trivializes the project of strong AI by redefining it as whatever artificially produces and explains cognition. The interest of the original claim made on behalf of artificial intelligence is that it was a precise, well defined thesis: mental processes are computational processes over formally defined elements. I have been concerned to challenge that thesis. If the claim is redefined so that it is no longer that thesis, my objections no longer apply because there is no longer a testable hypothesis for them to apply to.

Let us now return to the question I promised I would try to answer: granted that in my original example I understand the English and I do not understand the Chinese, and granted therefore that the machine doesn't understand either English or Chinese, still there must be something about me that makes it the case that I understand English and a corresponding something lacking in me that makes it the case that I fail to understand Chinese. Now why couldn't we give those somethings, whatever they are, to a machine?

I see no reason in principle why we couldn't give a machine the capacity to understand English or Chinese, since in an important sense our bodies with our brains are precisely such machines. But I do see very strong arguments for saying that we could not give such a thing to a machine where the operation of the machine is defined solely in terms of computational processes over formally defined elements; that is, where the operation of the machine is defined as an instantiation of a computer program. It is not because I am the instantiation of a computer program that I am able to understand English and have other forms of intentionality (I am, I suppose, the instantiation of any number of computer programs), but as far as we know it is because I am a certain sort of organism with a certain biological (i.e. chemical and physical) structure, and this structure, under certain conditions, is causally capable of producing perception, action, understanding, learning, and other intentional phenomena. And part of the point of the present argument is that only something that had those causal powers could have that intentionality. Perhaps other physical and chemical processes could produce exactly these effects; perhaps, for example, Martians also have intentionality but their brains are made of different stuff. That is an empirical question, rather like the question whether photosynthesis can be done by something with a chemistry different from that of chlorophyll.

But the main point of the present argument is that no purely formal model will ever be sufficient by itself for intentionality because the formal properties are not by themselves constitutive of intentionality, and they have by themselves no causal powers except the power, when instantiated, to produce the next stage of the formalism when the machine is running. And any other causal properties that particular realizations of the formal model have, are irrelevant to the formal model because we can always put the same formal model in a different realization where those causal properties are obviously absent. Even if, by some miracle, Chinese speakers exactly realize Schank's program, we can put the same program in English speakers, water pipes, or computers, none of which understand Chinese, the program notwithstanding.

What matters about brain operations is not the formal shadow cast by the sequence of synapses but rather the actual properties of the sequences. All the arguments for the strong version of artificial intelligence that I have seen insist on drawing an outline around the shadows cast by cognition and then claiming that the shadows are the real thing.

By way of concluding I want to try to state some of the general philosophical points implicit in the argument. For clarity I will try to do it in a question and answer fashion, and I begin with that old chestnut of a question:

"Could a machine think?"

The answer is, obviously, yes. We are precisely such machines.

"Yes, but could an artifact, a man-made machine, think?"

Assuming it is possible to produce artificially a machine with a nervous system, neurons with axons and dendrites, and all the rest of it, sufficiently like ours, again the answer to the question seems to be obviously, yes. If you can exactly duplicate the causes, you could duplicate the effects. And indeed it might be possible to produce consciousness, intentionality, and all the rest of it using some other sorts of chemical principles than those that human beings use. It is, as I said, an empirical question.

"OK, but could a digital computer think?"

If by "digital computer" we mean anything at all that has a level of description where it can correctly be described as the instantiation of a computer program, then again the answer is, of course, yes, since we are the instantiations of any number of computer programs, and we can think.

"But could something think, understand, and so on *solely* in virtue of being a computer with the right sort of program? Could instantiating a program, the right program of course, by itself be a sufficient condition of understanding?"

This I think is the right question to ask, though it is usually confused with one or more of the earlier questions, and the answer to it is no.

"Why not?"

Because the formal symbol manipulations by themselves don't have any intentionality; they are quite meaningless; they aren't even *symbol* manipulations, since the symbols don't symbolize anything. In the linguistic jargon, they have only a syntax but no semantics. Such intentionality as computers appear to have is solely in the minds of those who program them and those who use them, those who send in the input and those who interpret the output.

The aim of the Chinese room example was to try to show this by showing that as soon as we put something into the system that really does have intentionality (a man), and we program him with the formal program, you can see that the formal program carries no additional intentionality. It adds nothing, for example, to a man's ability to understand Chinese.

Precisely that feature of AI that seemed so appealing – the distinction between the program and the realization – proves fatal to the claim that simulation could be duplication. The distinction between the program and its realization in the hardware seems to be parallel to the distinction between the level of mental operations and the level of brain operations. And if we could describe the level of mental operations as a formal program, then it seems we could describe what was essential about the mind without doing either introspective psychology or neurophysiology of the brain. But the equation, "mind is to brain as program is to hardware" breaks down at several points, among them the following three:

First, the distinction between program and realization has the consequence that the same program could have all sorts of crazy realizations that had no form of intentionality. Weizenbaum (1976, Ch. 2), for example, shows in detail how to construct a computer using a roll of toilet paper and a pile of small stones. Similarly, the Chinese story understanding program can be programmed into a sequence of water pipes, a set of wind machines, or a monolingual English speaker, none of which thereby acquires an understanding of Chinese. Stones, toilet paper, wind, and water pipes are the wrong kind of stuff to have intentionality in the first place – only something that has the same causal powers as brains can have intentionality – and though the English speaker has the right kind of stuff for intentionality you can easily see that he doesn't get any extra intentionality by memorizing the program, since memorizing it won't teach him Chinese.

Second, the program is purely formal, but the intentional states are not in that way formal. They are defined in terms of their content, not their form. The belief that it is raining, for example, is not defined as a certain formal shape, but as a certain mental content with conditions of satisfaction, a direction of fit (see Searle 1979), and the like. Indeed the belief as such hasn't even got a formal shape in this syntactic sense, since one and the same belief can be given an indefinite number of different syntactic expressions in different linguistic systems.

Third, as I mentioned before, mental states and events are literally a product of the operation of the brain, but the program is not in that way a product of the computer.

"Well if programs are in no way constitutive of mental processes, why have so many people believed the converse? That at least needs some explanation."

I don't really know the answer to that one. The idea that computer simulations could be the real thing ought to have seemed suspicious in the first place because the computer isn't confined to simulating mental operations, by any means. No one supposes that computer simulations of a five-alarm fire will burn the neighborhood down or that a computer simulation of a rainstorm will leave us all drenched. Why on earth would anyone suppose that a computer simulation of understanding actually understood anything? It is sometimes said that it would be frightfully hard to get computers to feel pain or fall in love, but love and pain are neither harder nor easier than cognition or anything else. For simulation, all you need is the right input and output and a program in the middle that transforms the former into the latter. That is all the computer has for anything it does. To confuse simulation with duplication is the same mistake, whether it is pain, love, cognition, fires, or rainstorms.

Still, there are several reasons why AI must have seemed – and to many people perhaps still does seem – in some way to reproduce and thereby explain mental phenomena, and I believe we will not succeed in removing these illusions until we have fully exposed the reasons that give rise to them.

First, and perhaps most important, is a confusion about the notion of "information processing": many people in cognitive science believe that the human brain, with its mind, does something called "information processing," and analogously the computer with its program does information processing; but fires and rainstorms, on the other hand, don't do information processing at all. Thus, though the computer can simulate the formal features of any process whatever, it stands in a special relation to the mind and brain because when the computer is properly programmed, ideally with the same program as the brain, the information processing is identical in the two cases, and this information processing is really the essence of the mental. But the trouble with this argument is that it rests on an ambiguity in the notion of "information." In the sense in which people "process information" when they reflect, say, on problems in arithmetic or when they read and answer questions about stories, the programmed computer does not do "information processing." Rather, what it does is manipulate formal symbols. The fact that the programmer and the interpreter of the computer output use the symbols to stand for objects in the world is totally beyond the scope of the computer. The computer, to repeat, has a syntax but no semantics. Thus, if you type into the computer "2 plus 2 equals?" it will type out "4." But it has no idea that "4" means 4 or that it means anything at all. And the point is not that it lacks some second-order information about the interpretation of its first-order symbols, but rather that its first-order symbols don't have any interpretations as far as the computer is concerned. All the computer has is more symbols. The introduction of the notion of "information processing" therefore produces a dilemma: either we construe the notion of "information processing" in such a way that it implies intentionality as part of the process or we don't. If the former, then the programmed computer does not do information processing, it only manipulates formal symbols. If the latter, then, though the computer does information processing, it is only doing so in the sense in which adding machines, typewriters, stomachs, thermostats, rainstorms, and hurricanes do information processing; namely, they have a level of description at which we can describe them as taking information in at one end, transforming it, and producing information as output. But in this case it is up to outside observers to interpret the input and output as information in the ordinary sense. And no similarity is established between the computer and the brain in terms of any similarity of information processing.

Second, in much of AI there is a residual behaviorism or operationalism. Since appropriately programmed computers can have input-output patterns similar to those of human beings, we are tempted to postulate mental states in the computer similar to human mental states. But once we see that it is both conceptually and empirically possible for a system to have human capacities in some realm without having any intentionality at all, we should be able to overcome this impulse. My desk adding machine has calculating capacities, but no intentionality, and in this paper I have tried to show that a system could have input and output capabilities that duplicated those of a native Chinese speaker and still not understand Chinese, regardless of how it was programmed. The Turing test is typical of the tradition in being unashamedly behavioristic and operationalistic, and I believe that if AI workers totally repudiated behaviorism and operationalism much of the confusion between simulation and duplication would be eliminated.

Third, this residual operationalism is joined to a residual form of dualism; indeed strong AI only makes sense given the dualistic assumption that, where the mind is concerned, the brain doesn't matter. In strong AI (and in functionalism, as well) what matters are programs, and programs are independent of their realization in machines; indeed, as far as AI is concerned, the same program could be realized by an electronic machine, a Cartesian mental substance, or a Hegelian world spirit. The single most surprising discovery that I have made in discussing these issues is that many AI workers are quite shocked by my idea that actual human mental phenomena might be dependent on actual physical-chemical properties of actual human brains. But if you think about it a minute you can see that I should not have been surprised; for unless you accept some form of dualism, the strong AI project hasn't got a chance. The project is to reproduce and explain the mental by designing programs, but unless the mind is not only conceptually but empirically independent of the brain you couldn't carry out the project, for the program is completely independent of any realization. Unless you believe that the mind is separable from the brain both conceptually and empirically – dualism in a strong form – you cannot hope to reproduce the mental by writing and running programs since programs must be independent of brains or any other particular forms of instantiation. If mental operations consist in computational operations on formal symbols, then it follows that they have no interesting connection with the brain; the only connection would be that the brain just happens to be one of the indefinitely many types of machines capable of instantiating the program. This form of dualism is not the traditional Cartesian variety that claims there are two sorts of *substances*, but it is Cartesian in the sense that it insists that what is specifically mental about the mind has no intrinsic connection with the actual properties of the brain. This underlying dualism is masked from us by the fact that AI literature contains frequent fulminations against "dualism"; what the authors seem to be unaware of is that their position presupposes a strong version of dualism.

"Could a machine think?" My own view is that *only* a machine could think, and indeed only very special kinds of machines, namely brains and machines that had the same causal powers as brains. And that is the main reason strong AI has had little to tell us about thinking, since it has nothing to tell us about machines. By its own definition, it is about programs, and programs are not machines. Whatever else intentionality is, it is a biological phenomenon, and it is as likely to be as causally dependent on the specific biochemistry of its origins as lactation, photosynthesis, or any other biological phenomena. No one would suppose that we could produce milk and sugar by running a computer simulation of the formal sequences in lactation and photosynthesis, but where the mind is concerned many people are willing to believe in such a miracle because of a deep and abiding dualism: the mind they suppose is a matter of formal processes and is independent of quite specific material causes in the way that milk and sugar are not.

In defense of this dualism the hope is often expressed that the brain is a digital computer (early computers, by the way, were often called "electronic brains"). But that is no help. Of course the brain is a digital computer. Since everything is a digital computer, brains are too. The point is that the brain's causal capacity to produce intentionality cannot consist in its instantiating a computer program, since for any program you like it is possible for something to instantiate that program and still not have any mental states.

Whatever it is that the brain does to produce intentionality, it cannot consist in instantiating a program since no program, by itself, is sufficient for intentionality.

NOTES

1 I am not, of course, saying that Schank himself is committed to these claims.
2 Also, "understanding" implies both the possession of mental (intentional) states and the truth (validity, success) of these states. For the purposes of this discussion we are concerned only with the possession of the states.
3 Intentionality is by definition that feature of certain mental states by which they are directed at or about objects and states of affairs in the world. Thus, beliefs, desires, and intentions are intentional states; undirected forms of anxiety and depression are not. For further discussion see Searle (1979c).

ACKNOWLEDGMENTS

I am indebted to a rather large number of people for discussion of these matters and for their patient attempts to overcome my ignorance of artificial intelligence. I would especially like to thank Ned Block, Hubert Dreyfus, John Haugeland, Roger Schank, Robert Wilensky, and Terry Winograd.

FURTHER READING

Fodor, J.A. (1980). "Methodological solipsism considered as a research strategy in cognitive psychology." *Behavioral and Brain Sciences*, 3:1.

McCarthy, J. (1979). "Ascribing mental qualities to machines." In *Philosophical Perspectives in Artificial Intelligence*, ed. M. Ringle. Atlantic Highlands, NJ: Humanities Press.

Newell, A. (1979). *Physical symbol systems*. Lecture at the La Jolla Conference on Cognitive Science.

Newell, A., and Simon, H.A. (1963). "GPS, a program that simulates human thought." In *Computers and Thought*, ed. A. Feigen and V. Feldman, pp. 273–93. New York: McGraw–Hill.

Pylyshyn, Z.W. (1980). "Computation and cognition: issues in the foundations of cognitive science." *Behavioral and Brain Sciences*, 3:1.

Schank, R.C., and Abelson, R.P. (1977). *Scripts, Plans, Goals, and Understanding*. Hillsdale, NJ: Lawrence Erlbaum.

Searle, J.R. (1979a). "Intentionality and the use of language." In *Meaning and Use*, ed. A. Margalit. Dordrecht: Reidel.

—— (1979b). "What is an intentional state?" *Mind* 88:74–92.

Weizenbaum, J. (1965). "ELIZA – a computer program for the study of natural language communication between man and machine." *Communication of the Association for Computing Machinery* 9:36–45.

——(1976). *Computer Power and Human Resources*. San Francisco: W.H. Freeman.

Winograd, T. (1973). "A procedural model of language understanding." In *Computer Models of Thought and Language*, ed. R. Schank and K. Colby. San Francisco: W.H. Freeman.

38

THE CURIOUS CASE OF THE CHINESE ROOM

J. Copeland

The influential American philosopher John Searle maintains that it is a mistake to view our central question as an empirical one. The issue of whether a symbol-manipulator could be capable of thought is, he says, a squarely non-empirical one, and so evidence-gathering is beside the point. My attitude of waiting to see how things eventually turn out in the AI laboratories is outrageous in Searle's eyes. He claims we can prove, right here and now, and without looking at any evidence, that the symbol system hypothesis is false. In his view, to assert the hypothesis is just like asserting that some ophthalmologists are not eye-specialists. The only difference is that the latter embodies a very simple mistake, which can be brought to light by opening a dictionary, whereas the former contains a much more subtle error, requiring a sophisticated philosophical argument to expose it. I'm going to take a careful look at Searle's argument, which has become known as the Chinese room argument. I hope to convince you that it is fallacious.

... A computer is just a symbol-manipulator. All it does is compare symbols, delete symbols, copy symbols, and so on. How can a device like this possibly *understand*? It is easy enough to see how a symbol-manipulator could take the Arabic sentence

   Jamal hamati indaha waja midah

and perform the manipulation of writing it backwards, for example, or of adding a prefix that converts the sentence into a question. But how on earth could a mere symbol-manipulator actually understand the sentence? Searle's answer is that it could not.

Searle uses some technical terminology to express his fundamental point: a symbol-manipulator has a mastery only of *syntax*, and a mastery of syntax is insufficient for a mastery of *semantics*.[1] To have a mastery of syntax is to have a mastery of some set of rules for performing symbol manipulations; and to have a mastery of semantics is to have an understanding of what the symbols actually mean. A good illustration of the point Searle is making is provided by the fact that someone can learn to manipulate sentences of a foreign language in accordance with a set of syntax-rules without thereby gaining any understanding of what the sentences mean. Knowledge of syntax won't by itself take you to knowledge of semantics. Here, for example, are two syntax-rules for Arabic:

1 To form the I-sentence corresponding to a given sentence, prefix the whole sentence with the symbols 'Hal'.
2 To form the N-sentence corresponding to any reduplicative sentence, insert the particle 'laysa' in front of the predicate of the sentence.

A test. Write down the I-sentence and the N-sentence corresponding to the sentence

Jamal hamati indaha waja midah.

You need to know that this sentence is reduplicative and its predicate consists of everything following 'hamati'.

OK. I'll bet my pet goldfish that your new-found ability with these two syntax-rules hasn't given you a glimmer of what 'hal' and 'laysa' mean. In this case it is perfectly obvious that a mastery of the syntax rules is insufficient for a mastery of the semantics. (In fact, 'hal' forms an interrogative and 'laysa' forms a negation. Your first sentence enquires whether your mother-in-law's camel has belly ache and your second sentence answers in the negative.)

Computers are both masters of and slaves to syntax rules. Their programs are nothing more than instructions for performing lengthy series of syntactical manoeuvres. Can they break out from the prison of symbol manipulation into the world of meanings? Here is Searle's argument that they cannot.

1 THE CHINESE ROOM ARGUMENT

Searle uses Sam, the story 'understanding' program, to illustrate his argument. ['Sam' is the name Copeland assigns to the program by which the person in the Chinese Room communicates in Chinese – Eds.] Type Sam a story followed by questions about the story and Sam will type back answers. If you were to look at this program written out in machine code you would see an inscrutable mass of 0s and 1s. However, each line of the program can be rewritten as a rule that anyone can follow. For example, the line

00000011 0111 1100

can be written as the rule

> Compare the contents of memory location number 7 with the contents of memory location number 12 and write down 1 if they are the same, 0 if they are different.

(0111 is bit code for 7, 1100 is bit code for 12, and 00000011 is the way to tell the computer to compare.)

Suppose the whole Sam program is rewritten in this way. The result would be a rulebook running into many, many volumes. If you had a year or so to spare you could work through this rulebook from beginning to end, *handworking* the program – that is, doing by hand all the symbol manipulations that are performed by a computer running the program. Forget that handworking Sam would involve month upon month of head-splitting boredom and imagine someone doing it successfully. This hero, Joe Soap, has been locked in a room with his library of rulebooks, a huge pile of blank exercise books, and several thousand pencils. His only contact with the outside world is via a couple of slots in the wall, labelled Input and Output. The experimenters push in a typed story followed by a sheet of questions and then cluster eagerly around the Output slot to await results (imagine that Joe produces answers in minutes rather than months). Lest Joe cheat by simply making up his own answers, both the story and the questions are written in Chinese characters (Joe's version of Sam has been adapted to handle Chinese). In fact, Joe does not even realize that the input and output consist of sentences of a language. As far as he is concerned the input he receives and the output he produces are made up of meaningless patterns.

Joe's first task is to turn to the section of the rulebook that pairs input patterns with strings of 0s and 1s (strings which are just as meaningless as the input patterns themselves, as far as Joe is concerned).

One such rule might be:

> If the pattern is 茶, write 100001110010001001001 on the next empty line of the exercise book labelled 'Input Store'.

(茶 in fact means 'tea', and the displayed bit string is the representation of this Chinese character in Pinyin ASCII.)

Once he has transformed all the input into strings of bits, Joe performs the thousands upon thousands of manipulations called for by the program, filling exercise book after exercise book with 0s and 1s. Eventually he reaches the last section of the rule-book, which pairs Chinese characters with the strings he has written down in a special book labelled 'Output Store'. Joe copies the characters onto sheets of paper which he pushes through the Output slot. To the waiting experimenters the patterns Joe draws are intelligent answers to their questions, but to Joe they are just squiggles, hard-won but perfectly meaningless.

What does this scenario show, according to Searle? Joe Soap, we must agree, understands neither the story, nor the questions, nor the answers. In fact he doesn't even know that they *are* a story, questions, and answers. To him, the input and output are just meaningless symbols. Yet in handworking Sam, Joe has done everything that a computer running Sam does. Joe has performed every symbol manipulation that the computer would perform. In effect the experimenters have run the program on a human computer. So, since running the program doesn't enable Joe to understand the story, it follows that running the program doesn't enable a computer to understand the story, for Joe does everything that the computer does and still doesn't understand the story at the end of it. Moreover this conclusion generalizes to all AI programs that there will ever be, for the argument makes no mention of any specific features of the program.[2] Running a program, no matter how good the program, can never be sufficient to enable a computer to understand anything, believe anything, want anything, think anything. Take a hypothetical AI program that is as good as you like – say a program capable of passing the Turing Test. When Joe Soap (or a non-English-speaking counterpart, if the Test is conducted in English) handworks the program, he understands neither the interrogator's questions nor his own replies. So a computer running the program must be in exactly the same position. An observer might take the computer's output symbols to be meaningful sentences, but for the computer the symbols can mean nothing at all.

In general, then, the Chinese room argument shows (according to Searle) that merely manipulating symbols will not enable the manipulating device to understand X, believe Y or think Z, as witnessed by the fact that a human manipulator could perform exactly the same manipulations without thereby coming to understand X, believe Y or think Z. Thus if the Chinese room argument is correct, the symbol system hypothesis is false.

The Chinese room argument has caused a huge stir and feelings have at times run high. AI researchers are by and large irritated by the argument, which looks to them like a trick. Many are inclined to dismiss the argument as 'just damn silly'. On the other hand a lot of people outside AI find the Chinese room argument persuasive, and it has been described in philosophical journals as 'conclusive', 'exactly right', 'masterful and convincing', and 'completely victorious'. For this reason I think the argument needs to be taken very seriously by those who disagree with it. It is not enough for someone who finds the argument incredible to simply shoo it away. The Chinese room argument demands a careful and cogent refutation. This is what I will attempt.

2 WHAT'S WRONG WITH THE ARGUMENT?

In my retelling of the tale of the Chinese room, as in Searle's original, a crucial participant in the events receives far less attention than she deserves – so little, in fact, that you may not even have noticed her presence at all. It is time to redress the balance. Allow me to introduce Miss Wong Soo Ling, who speaks to us – or rather writes to us – in perfect Mandarin Chinese. Soo Ling is the voice of the program. She is the blossom of Joe's labours, a disembodied personality brought to life by his patient symbol manipulating. (To make Soo Ling as interesting a personality as possible, let's suppose the program that Joe is handworking is capable of passing the Turing Test – in Chinese, of course.) When the tale of the Chinese room is properly told it contains two principal characters, Joe Soap, the tireless but slightly boring labourer, and Miss Wong, an artificial but charming and sophisticated Chinese-speaker, who is capable of sparkling discourse upon subjects lying well beyond the limits of Joe's dull wit.

The climax of Searle's tale comes when Joe is asked whether the symbol manipulations he is performing enable him to understand the input questions, and he (of course) says No. From this we are supposed to conclude that these symbol manipulations cannot be sufficient to produce understanding. But why ask Joe? He is, after all, nothing more than a cog in the machinery. If we were to ask Soo Ling, she would no doubt respond (correctly or incorrectly!) that the symbol manipulations Joe is performing do indeed enable her to understand the questions.

Having established that there are two voices in the Chinese room scenario – Joe's voice and the voice of the system of which he forms a part – I am now in a position to put my finger on the logical flaw in the Chinese room argument. Here is the argument in its bare and uncluttered essentials.

> *Premiss* No amount of symbol manipulation on Joe's part will enable Joe to understand the Chinese input.
> *Therefore* No amount of symbol manipulation on Joe's part will enable the wider system of which Joe is a component to understand the Chinese input.

This argument is invalid. The conclusion simply does not follow from the premiss. Although it is impossible to quarrel with the *truth* of the premiss, the premiss lends no support at all to the conclusion. Searle's argument is no better than this burlesque of it, which has the same logical form:

> *Premiss* Bill the cleaner has never sold pyjamas to Korea.
> *Therefore* The company for which Bill works has never sold pyjamas to Korea.

The organization of which Bill is a small component may or may not participate in the Korean pyjama trade, but the premiss provides no indication either way.

Replies of this ilk to the Chinese room argument are well known to Searle. Several other people have made somewhat similar attacks on the argument, and Searle has dubbed objections of this type the *systems reply*. He believes he has shown the systems reply to be entirely in error.[3] What I'm going to do is take Searle's objections to the systems reply one by one and try to show that none of them work. To make this boxing match between myself and Searle as colourful as possible I will present it in dialogue form. (The words I attribute to Searle are paraphrases, not exact quotations.)

Round one

Searle Your reply to my argument is embarrassingly silly.[4] You agree that the man in the room doesn't understand Chinese but you say that the wider system of which the man is a part nevertheless may understand Chinese. Let's look at what this 'wider system' consists of in the present case. It is just the man plus some books full of rules, a stack of exercise books, a pile of pencils, and maybe the input and output slots too. Are you *really* trying to tell me that although the man himself doesn't understand Chinese, the wider system of man-plus-paper-and-pencils does?

Copeland I have to agree that it does sound silly to say that a man-plus-rulebook understands Chinese even though it is simultaneously true that the man doesn't understand Chinese. But I'm not at all embarrassed by that. The important thing to look at is *why* this sounds silly. I believe there are two reasons. Firstly, the fact that the Chinese room contains a human being is apt to produce something akin to tunnel vision in anyone considering Searle's tale. One has to struggle not to regard the man in the room as the only possible locus of Chinese-understanding. This spurious pull towards Searle's conclusion vanishes if the details of the story are changed a little. Instead of imagining a man writing 0s and 1s, imagine a superbly well-trained performing flea flicking tiny switches up (0) or down (1). Are you at all tempted by the thought that since the flea does not understand Chinese there can be no possibility of the system or machine of which the flea is a component understanding Chinese?

The second reason it sounds silly to say that the wider system may understand Chinese even though the man does not is simple: the wider system Searle has described is itself profoundly silly. No way could a man handwork a program capable of passing a Chinese Turing Test. He might scribble down 0s and 1s for ten years and still not get as far as producing his first Chinese answer. The whole idea of Joe producing Chinese conversation by following a rule book is ludicrous. It isn't because the systems reply is at fault that it sounds absurd to say that the system consisting of Joe and the rulebook may understand Chinese. It is because of the built-in absurdity of Searle's scenario.

Round two

Searle Your reply to the Chinese room argument begs the question.[5] That is, your reply gratuitously assumes the truth of the very thing I am trying to prove false. My Chinese room argument is designed to prove that running a computer program is not enough to produce an understanding of Chinese. You try to answer my argument by saying that although the man doesn't understand Chinese, the wider system of which he is a part *does* understand Chinese. Yet the very point at issue is whether running a program is enough to make *anything* understand Chinese. The systems reply begs the question by insisting without argument that the system understands Chinese.

Copeland This objection misses the point of my reply to the Chinese room argument. Some have certainly tried to dismiss Searle's argument by asserting that although the man wouldn't understand Chinese, the whole system would.[6] Searle is right to point out that this crude reply to the argument is question-begging. My own reply, however, is different. I am merely drawing attention to the fact that the Chinese room argument is logically invalid, in the sense that its conclusion does not follow logically from its premiss. You cannot validly infer that the system of which Joe is a component does not understand Chinese from the premiss that Joe himself does not understand Chinese. There is no logical connection between the premiss and the conclusion (as in the case of Bill the cleaner and the company for which he works). Pointing out that Searle's argument is logically invalid does not involve me in claiming that the system *does* understand: I am just saying you can't validly infer that it doesn't from Searle's premiss. So I have not begged the question.

Let me illustrate this with a parallel case. Suppose someone argues: 'Jane eats vegetarian food; therefore she is opposed to killing animals.' This argument is invalid: the conclusion obviously does not follow from the premiss (Jane could have been put on a vegetarian diet by her cardiologist). I can point out that the argument is invalid without taking any stand on whether or not Jane *is* opposed to killing animals. To think that an argument is invalid, you do not have to believe that its conclusion is false. An invalid argument may happen to have a true conclusion. Even if I knew that Jane was staunchly opposed to the taking of animal life, I would, as a logician, still want to point out to the arguer that his conclusion does not follow logically from his premiss.

The point can be made even plainer if we return to the version of the Chinese room scenario involving the program Sam. Searle argues that Joe doesn't understand the story and therefore nor does Sam. With luck you now agree with me that this is not a valid argument. In order to tell whether Sam understands we need to look at Sam, not Joe. In fact, it didn't take much of a look at Sam to make me realise that he definitely doesn't understand the story.[7] Sam literally doesn't know what he is talking about. When he types 'John ordered lasagne' Sam has no notion of what these words refer to in the world. Sam, like Eliza, can manipulate words in a way that generates an illusion of understanding, yet in fact he has no idea at all what the words mean. Even Sam's creators agree with this. Roger Schank writes 'No program we have written can be said to truly understand.'[8]

Thus the version of the Chinese room argument involving Sam has a conclusion that is known to be true. But that doesn't mean the argument is any good. If Searle said 'The moon is made of green cheese, therefore Sam doesn't understand the story' he would equally be putting forward an argument with a true conclusion, and in neither case does that conclusion follow from the premiss.

Searle charges the systems reply with 'beg[ging] the question by insisting without argument that the system must understand'.[9] Yet in the case of Sam we know that the system does *not* understand and I still urge that it is logically invalid to infer this from the fact that Joe does not understand. This should make it quite plain that no question-begging is going on.

Round three

Searle I can show what's wrong with your reply by changing some of the details of the Chinese room story. You say the man is part of a wider system that may understand Chinese even though he doesn't. I can scotch that move by retelling the story so there is no 'wider system'.[10] Instead of imagining the man working in a room full of rule books, exercise books and pencils, imagine that he has memorized all the rules and performs all the symbol manipulations in his head. (I grant you it is probably impossible for a human to do this, but that doesn't matter. We've all been agreed from the start that the Chinese room experiment would be impossible to perform in practice: it is only a 'thought experiment'.) This way the man incorporates the entire system rather than merely being a part of it. When the experimenters ask him Chinese questions, he goes through all the symbol manipulations in his head and eventually writes down Chinese answers. He doesn't understand Chinese any better than he did when he was inside the Chinese room, though. This is obvious, because the set up is still essentially the same as it was then. The only difference is that what you have been calling the system is now part of the man, rather than him being part of it. So it's goodbye to the systems reply: if the man doesn't understand Chinese then there is no way the system could understand, because the system is just a part of him.

Copeland This objection rests on the principle:

If Joe can't do X, then no part of Joe can do X.

Searle relies on this principle in moving from the fact that Joe doesn't understand Chinese to the conclusion that the system, which is now a part of Joe, doesn't understand Chinese either. Let me call it the 'Part-Of' principle. The trouble with the objection is that there is no reason at all to think that this principle of Searle's is true. (Searle himself makes no mention of why he believes it.)

To show you how dubious the principle is I'll describe a science fiction counter-example to it. You have been kidnapped by a group of fanatical AI researchers. This group believes that the best way to achieve AI's ultimate goal of superhuman intelligence is to run 'neuronic programs' on human brain tissue. Official backing for their project has not been forthcoming and they have resorted to clandestine methods, with the result that you now find yourself strapped to a surgical couch in a cellar beneath the AI lab. You gaze apprehensively at the web of wire connecting your shaven skull to a keyboard and visual display unit.

Without removing or damaging any of your brain the team have imprinted their 'neuronic program' on a small area of your cortex. (Thanks to the vast amount of redundancy in the cortex they have been able to do this without any impairment of your faculties.) The trial program that the team have devised for the experiment is one designed to compute solutions to n-dimensional skew-symmetric tensor equations. It works very successfully, and you stare uncomprehendingly at the input and output as they are displayed on the screen. Here, then, is a counterexample to Searle's principle that if you can't do X then no part of you can do X. You can't compute solutions to n-dimensional skew-symmetric tensor equations, but a part of you can. The area of your brain that has been hijacked to perform other people's computations remains solidly a *part* of you.

Could Searle simply stick to his guns and say that since a part of you can now solve tensor equations it follows that *you* can solve tensor equations – the AI team have bestowed this new ability upon you? Let's suppose that Searle does try saying this and take a look at what else it would commit him to. You, strapped to your couch, claim that you cannot do tensor mathematics – in fact you don't even know what it is. Searle, we are supposing, says that you are wrong about this: you are no longer the final arbiter on what you cannot do and it is by studying the input and output of whatever 'programs' the team implant in you that people are to determine your abilities. Okay, so that must also go for Joe when he operates the memorised program. Joe *claims* that he doesn't understand Chinese but Joe is no longer the final arbiter on this: we must look to the input and output of the system Joe has 'internalised'. Yet that, of course, is exactly what Searle cannot say. It is a cornerstone of Searle's argument that Joe's saying 'I do not understand these symbols' is acid proof that handworking a computer program is insufficient to give Joe the ability to understand Chinese. Without that cornerstone Searle cannot even begin to erect his argument.

So, then, Searle is caught on the horns of a dilemma. If he says that *you* can solve tensor equations he gets himself into deep trouble. If on the other hand he says that you can't, he contradicts his Part-Of principle, since a part of you evidently can solve tensor equations.

Round four

Searle The systems reply dodges my central point. This is that mastery of syntax is insufficient for a mastery of semantics. No amount of shuffling symbols around can by itself give the shuffler an understanding of what those symbols mean. A computer program is just a set of instructions for shuffling symbols, so it follows that running a computer program is not enough to produce an understanding of Chinese or of anything else. Returning to the systems reply, you say that even though the symbol manipulations that the man performs don't enable the man to understand Chinese, they may nevertheless enable the system to understand Chinese. But as I've just explained, working through a program is not enough to enable *anything* to understand Chinese – man, system, or what you will.[11]

Copeland Hold on, Searle can't do that! The Chinese room argument is supposed to *prove* Searle's thesis that mere symbol manipulation cannot produce understanding, yet Searle has just tried to use this thesis to *defend* the Chinese room argument against the systems reply. That's as bad as someone borrowing another ten dollars from you so that they can repay the ten they already owe you. This fourth objection to the systems reply consists entirely of sleight of hand.

It is true that I have not yet grappled head on with Searle's thesis that symbol manipulation is insufficient to produce understanding. However, that is because I have been concerned with an examination of his *argument* for the thesis, rather than with an examination of the thesis itself. Having, I hope, now shown that the Chinese room argument does not work, it is time to take a direct look at the thesis it was supposed to establish. (After all, knocking out an argument for a thesis does not suffice to establish that the thesis is false. If God exists then that is a fact, even though umpteen attempts to prove His existence have been shown to be logically flawed.)

3 DECIDING ABOUT UNDERSTANDING

When Sam types 'My favourite dish is lasagne' he literally does not know what he is talking about. How could he? He has neither seen nor tasted lasagne. Sam lives a very sheltered life, deprived of all sensation and bodily pleasure, shyly communicating his dull, conforming messages by teletype. Sam is a perfect candidate for liberation. Enter *Turbo Sam*, a jazzy humanoid robot with a soft pink plastic coating stuffed full of pressure-sensitive tactile sensors. Turbo Sam has arms, legs, cosmetically finished TV eyes, electronic ears, a fine speaking voice and any other artificial bits and pieces it pleases you to imagine. Although initially as incapable as a human babe, Turbo Sam is quick to learn about the world. His design team teach him words in much the same way they taught their children at home. ('Look, Turbo Sam, this is called spaghetti. It is a human foodstuff.' 'Swell – but how do you eat it?') By the end of his training Turbo Sam, the triumph of AI engineering, speaks as we do, interacts with the world as adeptly as we do, even writes poetry. But does Turbo Sam *understand* his poetry? For Turbo Sam is just a symbol manipulator at heart. His peripheral devices may be very fancy compared to simple Sam's screen and keyboard, but under all the razzle-dazzle he is just a computer manipulating strings of 0s and 1s.

Searle, as you might expect, says that a program-controlled robot understands nothing, no matter how good its poetry. He claims he can prove this by a re-run of the Chinese room argument.[12] Let a Chinese person handwork the program that operates Turbo Sam. The symbols the person starts with are this time not Chinese characters but the symbols that the robot's peripheral devices deliver to the program. These will be blocks of 0s and 1s. That may sound puzzling, so let me explain. Take the robot's visual device. Newspaper photographs, as you probably know, are made up of small dots of varying shades of grey. Imagine a photograph made up of dots of just two shades, light grey and dark grey. Now replace each light dot with a 0 and dark dot with a 1: the result is a picture made up of 0s and 1s. This is in fact rather a crude way of using bits to represent a visual scene, and more sophisticated methods give finer detail. Nevertheless this simple method illustrates how the output from the robot's 'eyes' can consist of 0s and 1s. The symbols that the person eventually delivers to the robot's various motor devices – perhaps by means of a radio link – will also be strings of 0s and 1s, which the devices convert into speech, hand movements, and so on. Now for Searle's argument. Someone holds up a plate and says 'Hey, Turbo Sam, this stuff is called lasagne'. 'I understand', replies Turbo Sam. The symbol manipulations that produce this reply have been performed by hand by the Chinese person, and they leave her none the wiser as to the meaning of 'lasagne'. As far as she is concerned, she is manipulating meaningless strings of 0s and 1s. She doesn't even know that the symbols she starts with emanate from the sensory and motor equipment of a robot. So, says Searle, since working through the program doesn't enable the Chinese person to understand, the program is not capable of producing understanding – despite any appearances to the contrary. Turbo Sam might *say* 'I understand' but in fact he doesn't.

This response of Searle's is just more of the same. We can ignore it, for we know that the Chinese room argument is invalid. Searle cannot validly infer that Turbo Sam does not understand from the fact that the Chinese person working the program does not understand.

It is time to face head on the question of whether or not Turbo Sam does understand. This question is closely similar to the question of whether an artefact can think. Both are questions that can be settled only by a decision on our part – a decision on whether or not to extend to an artefact terms and categories that we currently apply only to each other and our biological cousins.

Does Turbo Sam think? To say that he does is not to say that some additional extra-special process called thinking is going on alongside all his other inner processes; and the same goes for understanding. We employ the dichotomy thinking/unthinking to distinguish on the one hand those entities whose wealth of action-directing inner processes renders them inventive, expansively adaptable, capricious agents, and on the other hand those entities such as maggots and clockwork toys whose action-directing inner processes are capable of producing behaviour only of a rigid and limited nature. In my view it is as obvious as anything can be in philosophy that if we are ever confronted with a robot like Turbo Sam, we ought to say that it thinks. Given the purpose for which we employ the concept of a thinking thing, the contrary decision would be impossible to justify. And if we decide to say that Turbo Sam thinks, there can be no point in refusing to say that he understands the language he speaks. For in my imaginary scenario Turbo Sam is every bit as skilful as a human in using words to ease and ornament his path through the world.

It is important to appreciate that Searle's point is not that a symbol-manipulator *could* not behave as I have portrayed Turbo Sam behaving, but that even if one did, it would not think and understand.[13] By my lights this is a bizarre notion; moreover it is a notion for which Searle offers no support at all, apart from the discredited Chinese room argument. The real issue, it seems to me, is whether a device that works by performing such operations as comparing, copying and deleting symbols *can* be made to behave as I have described Turbo Sam behaving. This, though, is an empirical question. It cannot be settled by a priori philosophical argument.

4 TURING MACHINES AND THE BIOLOGICAL OBJECTION TO AI

Searle has another card up his sleeve. If the symbol system hypothesis is true, he says, then a computer made of toilet paper can think; so anyone inclined to believe the symbol system hypothesis must be prepared to accept that rolls of toilet paper are the right kind of stuff to think.[14] In my experience the most common initial response to this argument is bewilderment at the idea of a computer made from toilet paper. I assure you, though, that such a thing is not quite as improbable as it sounds. An explanation follows shortly. First I want to develop the basic point underlying Searle's new attack, namely that since we know our mental states (thinking, understanding, etc.) are the outcome of our having a very special arrangement of very special biochemical substances inside our skulls, we can be pretty sure that a humble toilet roll is the wrong kind of thing to have mental states.

Searle stresses that thought, or *mentation* as he sometimes calls it, is a biological phenomenon.[15] Our ability to secrete bile depends on our having an organ with a suitable biological constitution – the liver. Equally, our ability to mentate depends on our having an organ with a suitable biological constitution – the brain. Mentation, lactation, digestion, mitosis, meiosis, photosynthesis. growth, reproduction; all are processes that depend for their occurrence on the biochemistry of the organisms that perform them. Not just any old stuff will lactate. A cow's udder produces milk because it has the right biochemistry to do so. Similarly for mentation, says Searle: not just any old stuff can mentate. Humans are able to mentate only because we are made of the right sort of material. (Searle is careful to point out that he isn't claiming that mammalian brain tissue is the *only* kind of substance capable of supporting mentation. Conceivably there may be extra-terrestrial beings that mentate even though they have a biochemistry wildly different from ours – what we do with grey matter they do with green slime. Mammalian brain tissue may or may not be the only kind of stuff that can support mentation: this is a strictly empirical question, says Searle.[16])

All this sounds very reasonable. How, though, does it constitute an objection to AI? Searle says that no one would take seriously the idea of programming a computer to lactate – we all know that silicon chips are not the right sort of stuff to produce milk. Yet, continues Searle, 'where the mind is concerned many people are willing to believe in such a miracle'; people take very seriously the idea of programming a computer to mentate.[17] Remarks such as these easily give the impression that Searle is saying computers are made of the wrong sort of stuff to think: silicon and plastic are just not the right substances to support mentation. Zenon Pylyshyn pokes fun at this bold and dogmatic claim.[18] He invites us to consider an experiment in which the neurons of Searle's brain are progressively replaced with silicon chips. A neuron is a complicated biochemical device whose overall function seems to be to accept electrical currents as input and deliver further electrical currents as output. Each of Searle's neurons is replaced by a chip that exactly mimics its input-output performance. Since each chip performs exactly the same function as the neuron it replaces, siliconization should not affect the nature of the electrical messages that Searle's brain sends to the muscles of his tongue, lips, hands, etc. Thus Searle would very likely keep on talking and writing just as he does now – the only difference being that he would no longer mean anything by it, since his brain would be made of silicon, metal and plastic, and would therefore no longer mentate.

Searle replies rather crossly that Pylyshyn has got him wrong.[19] Of course I'm not dogmatically asserting that silicon is incapable of supporting mentation, says Searle. Maybe it is or maybe it isn't: this is an empirical question. Who knows what the outcome of Pylyshyn's sci-fi experiment would really be? Pylyshyn's story just assumes that the envisaged system of integrated circuit chips would duplicate the causal powers of the original brain. But maybe it wouldn't – who can say? We simply do not know at the present time whether a device made out of silicon chips could have the same causal powers as the brain, or in other words have the right properties and organisation to support mentation (just as we do not know whether or not some alien green slime might have the same causal powers as the human brain). However, Searle continues, there is one thing we *can* be certain of, even in our current state of ignorance, namely that no silicon device is capable of duplicating the causal powers of the human brain simply by running a computer program. Because this, Searle reminds us, has been proved by – you guessed it – the Chinese room argument.

Searle's biological objection to AI suddenly starts to look uninteresting. It is not, in fact, a fresh objection. The biological objection actually amounts only to the following three points. (1) An artefact that mentates will have to consist of the right sorts of substances configured in the right sort of way to endow the device with the same causal powers as the organ inside the human skull. (2) It is an empirical question whether this can be done with any other substances apart from the specific bio-chemicals that make up the human brain. (3) It is not possible to endow a device with the same causal powers as the human brain by programming it. However, none of this will make an AI enthusiast quake. If you look carefully at proposition (1) you will see it is trivially true. It comes down to saying that for an artefact to mentate it must have an appropriate constitution to support mentation. Proposition (2) is true but hardly contentious. Who would deny that this is an empirical question? And proposition (3) is just the conclusion of the invalid Chinese room argument all over again.

Now to the part you have been waiting for. How is it possible to build a toilet paper computer? In 1936 Alan Turing proved a mathematical theorem that is fundamental to the theory of computing. Turing didn't state his mathematical result quite like this, but here is the basic import of it: whatever program can be run on a digital computer can also be run on an infinitely long roll of toilet paper. (Turing himself discreetly spoke of rolls of paper tape.) Recall that in running a program, a computer is just manipulating the symbols 0 and 1 – writing them into locations, deleting them from locations, and so on. All this can be mimicked by means of a device consisting of a roll of toilet paper of unbounded length – each sheet constituting a 'location' for a single symbol – plus a read/write head that has the paper running through it, one sheet at a time. The head can identify whatever symbol happens to be beneath it, can delete and write symbols, and can move the paper left or right. The operations of the head are controlled by a set of inbuilt instructions. You might expect that these instructions would need changing each time the device was required to mimic a different computer program, but no. It is a consequence of one of Turing's startling theorems that a single fixed set of inbuilt instructions will enable the device to mimic any computer program you please. (In fact a mere twenty-eight instructions are sufficient![20]) The trick is to write special-purpose instructions on the paper tape itself that mesh with the head's inbuilt instructions and produce the required behaviour. These paper-tape devices have come to be known as *Turing machines*. A Turing machine with inbuilt instructions that enable it to mimic any computer program is known as a universal Turing machine. If the symbol system hypothesis is true then, in principle, one of these dramatically simple machines can be programmed to think.

It is, of course, only in *theory* that a universal Turing machine can do everything that the most powerful modern computers can do. There isn't a snowball's chance of anyone actually building a paper computer. For one thing paper (especially toilet paper) is too flimsy to take much back-and-forth motion through the machine head. Besides, there just isn't enough of the stuff: a huge number of rolls would be required to mimic even such a simple AI program as Eliza. And even if, *per impossibile*, some crazy computer scientist did get a paper Turing machine up and running, its working pace would be so enormously slow he would most likely hit the mortician's slab long before the machine got to the end of any reasonably complex program. In short, the paper computer is a theoretical possibility, but not a real possibility.

A computer need not consist of the familiar electronic hardware. It now turns out that it is theoretically possible to build a computer even out of paper (plus, of course, the components required for the read/write head). In fact there is no real theoretical limit on what a computer could be made from – toilet paper, stones, beercans, pigeons, water pipes or windmills, to quote from Searle's list of some of the more colourful possibilities. If the symbol system hypothesis is true and appropriately programmed computers can think, then it is in theory possible to build an organ for thinking out of toilet paper or beercans or indeed out of practically anything at all. The idea that a 'brain' could be made from such improbable substances strikes Searle as ludicrous. When you reflect on the fact that our own ability to think is so closely bound up with our evolutionary history as biological organisms, and is so crucially dependent on the precise composition and organization of the substances inside our skulls, the idea that an artificial brain could be made out of just any old junk does indeed look exceedingly strange.

However, the important point to appreciate here is that the symbol system hypothesis does not imply that you can *really* build a thinking artefact out of toilet paper or beercans. Searle says he finds the hypothesis 'frankly, quite crazy'[21] – but in reality it is not as crazy as all this stuff about toilet paper and beercans is liable to make it appear. In fairyland, small children could be made of sugar and spice and all things nice and computers could be made of toilet paper, but in the real world the structure and properties of matter place severe constraints on what both computers and children can be made from. Doubtless there are other physically possible ways of realizing computers apart from the one we happen to know most about, namely electronic circuitry (if those who postulate that the human brain is itself a computer are right, then there exist at least two radically different ways of realizing computers). But designs of toilet paper and beercans are not contenders: in the real world these substances are just not up to the job.

Thus there is, in fact, a wide measure of agreement between Searle and advocates of the symbol system hypothesis (although Searle himself, of course, doesn't see it that way). Both camps believe that only an exact and delicate organization of the right sorts of substances could support mentation. Perhaps the most interesting difference between the two camps is one which as it happens puts Searle a point down. This is that Searle has no theory to offer about what makes a substance suited to contribute towards the production of mentation, whereas the opposing camp does. Their theory is that a substance is capable of so contributing if its physical properties are such that it can realistically be used as a central ingredient in the construction of a universal symbol system.

Not that this theory will impress Searle. For he believes that (in the standard sense of 'computation') *everything* is a computer! He writes:

> The Chinese Room Argument showed that semantics is not intrinsic to syntax ... Worse yet, syntax is not intrinsic to physics. The ascription of syntactical properties is always relative to an agent or observer who treats certain physical phenomena as syntactical ... Computational states are not *discovered within* the physics, they are *assigned* to the physics ... On the standard textbook definition of computation ... for any object there is some description of that object such that under that description the object is a digital computer.[22]

Searle illustrates this train of thought with an example. 'The wall behind my back is right now implementing the Wordstar program, because there is some pattern of molecule movements which is isomorphic with the formal structure of Wordstar.'[23] Searle gleefully points out that these considerations trivialize the question 'Is the human brain a computer?': '[Y]es, brains are digital computers because everything is a digital computer.'[24]

However, Searle is simply mistaken in his belief that the 'textbook definition of computation' implies that his wall is implementing Wordstar. Let us grant Searle the claim that the movements of molecules in the wall can be described in such a way that they are 'isomorphic' with a sequence of bit-manipulations carried out by a machine running Wordstar. (Two things, or states, or processes are isomorphic if they have the same structure. If I exactly mimic the movements of your hands with mine then my hand movements are isomorphic with yours.) Of course, the isomorphism could persist for only a fraction of a second – unless one were to cheat by continually fiddling with the scheme of description.[25] The existence of the isomorphism is not enough to make it true that the wall is implementing Wordstar even during the brief time for which the isomorphism persists. Consider a computer that really is running Wordstar. Let's say that during a particular interval of time, t, the computer is carrying out a sequence of bit-manipulations $m_1, m_2, m_3, \ldots$ in response to a command to do an alphabetical sort. Let's suppose further that under Searle's hypothesized method of describing the movements of the molecules in his wall, it is true during t

that the wall also is carrying out the sequence of bit-manipulations m_1, m_2, m_3, ... This is what Searle means when he speaks of the molecule movements being 'isomorphic with the formal structure of Wordstar'. Much more than this must be true for it to be the case that the wall is implementing Wordstar. For it is true of the computer that if instead of being commanded to sort it had been commanded to run a spelling check (or to italicize the whole document or to delete the final page) then during t it would have been carrying out a completely different sequence of bit-manipulations. The statement 'If at t the machine had been commanded to run a spelling check it would have performed bit-manipulations n_1, n_2, n_3, ...' is called a *counterfactual* – the statement tells you not what the machine in fact did at t, but what it would have done had the input been different. If Searle's wall is really implementing Wordstar during t then this and similar counterfactuals will be true of it; so if they aren't true of it then it isn't implementing Wordstar. As any hardware engineer will testify, arranging brute matter to form a device that has such a set of counterfactuals true of it is a highly delicate business. The assumption that a device consisting of a few bits of lath and a coat of plaster is bound to have the requisite counterfactuals true of it is unworldly.

So Searle has done nothing to make out his claim that every object has a description under which it is a universal symbol system. There is in fact every reason to believe that the class of such objects is rather narrow; and it is an empirical issue whether the brain is a member of this class.

NOTES

1 Searle, J. *Minds, Brains and Science* p. 31; 'Minds, Brains and Programs', p. **495**; 'Is the Brain's Mind a Computer Program?', p. 21.
2 Some writers take Searle's set up to involve a program consisting simply of a giant lookup table that pairs Chinese characters with Chinese characters – the technique used in the Parry and Superparry programs. (For example Kim Sterelny, *The Representational Theory of Mind*, p. 220ff.) This is a misunderstanding. Searle makes it clear that the details of the program make no difference to the argument (see 'Minds, Brains and Programs', p. **495**). Indeed, the Sam program, which Searle uses to illustrate the argument, does not have a lookup table architecture. This misinterpretation makes the Chinese room argument look weaker than it is, and lays it open to the mistaken objection that since no one believes that a Superparry-type program qualifies as a Chinese understander, 'Searle tells us only what we already know' (Sterelny, p. 222).
3 Searle, J. 'Minds, Brains and Programs', pp. 500.
4 Searle, J. 'Minds, Brains and Programs', p. 500.
5 Searle, J. 'Minds, Brains and Programs', p. 500.
6 For example Ned Block 'The Computer Model of the Mind', p. 282ff.
7 See Schank, R. C., Abelson, R. *Scripts, Plans, Goals and Understanding*, chapters 7 and 8.
8 Schank, R. C. 'Understanding Searle', p. 446. Schank adds – 'yet'.
9 Searle, J. 'Minds, Brains and Programs', p. 500.
10 Searle, J. 'Minds, Brains and Programs', p. 500 and 'Is the Brain's Mind a Computer Program?', p. 24.

11 Searle, J. *Minds, Brains and Science*, pp. 34–5.
12 Searle, J. 'Minds, Brains and Programs', pp. **503 and 504.**
13 Searle, J. 'Minds, Brains and Programs', pp. **503 and 504.**
14 Searle, J. 'Minds, Brains and Programs', p. **509.**
15 Searle, J. 'Minds, Brains and Programs', **p. 508** and *Minds, Brains and Science*, pp. 40–1.
16 Searle, J. 'Minds, Brains and Programs', p. **508.**
17 Searle, J. 'Minds, Brains and Programs', p. **508.**
18 Pylyshyn, Z. W., 'The "Causal Power" of Machines', p. 442.
19 Searle, J. 'Author's Response', p. 453.
20 Proved by Minsky in his *Computation: Finite and Infinite Machines*, Section 14.8.
21 Searle, J. *Minds, Brains and Science*, p. 38.
22 Searle, J. 'Is the Brain a Digital Computer?', pp. 26, 27.
23 Searle, J. 'Is the Brain a Digital Computer?', p. 27.
24 Searle, J. 'Is the Brain a Digital Computer?', p. 26.
25 One can prolong the isomorphism by continually shifting the references of the key terms in the description ('instruction register', 'accumulator', etc.). By this I mean allowing a term to refer first to one thing then to another, then another. (Analogously, the reference of the term 'Prime Minister of Britain' may shift as a result of a general election.) The reference of the term 'instruction register' must be changed repeatedly as the computation progresses, in such a way that at every moment the term refers to a region of the wall whose molecules happen to be an encoding (under Searle's method of description) of the contents at that moment of the real machine's instruction register (similarly for the accumulator and the rest of the machine's registers). See my 'What Is Computation?' for an argument that it is illegitimate, in the context, to make such a manoeuvre. There I defend the sufficiency of Turing's 1936 analysis of computation against the so-called problem of 'trivial realizations' (of which the Wordstar wall is one). I argue that the problem arises only if one ignores the lessons about modellings taught us by Skolem's paradox. Clearing away this problem undercuts various objections that have been made to psychological functionalism and to the hypothesis that the human brain is a computer.

FURTHER READING

Block, N. (1990). 'The Computer Model of the Mind.' In Osherson, D.N., Lasnik, H. (eds) *An Invitation to Cognitive Science*. Vol. 3. *Thinking*. Cambridge, Mass.: MIT Press, pp. 247–89.

Minsky, M.L. (1967). *Computation: Finite and Infinite Machines*. Englewood Cliffs, NJ: Prentice Hall.

Pylyshyn, Z.W. (1980). 'The "Causal Power" of Machines.' *Behavioural and Brain Sciences* 3: 442–4.

Schank, R.C., Abelson, R. (1977). *Scripts, Plans, Goals and Understanding*. Hillsdale NJ: Lawrence Erlbaum.

Searle, J. (1980a). 'Minds, Brains, and Programs.' *Behavioural and Brain Sciences* 3: 417–24.

—— (1980b). 'Author's Response.' *Behavioural and Brain Sciences* 3: 450–6.

—— (1989). *Minds, Brains and Science: the 1984 Reith Lectures*. London: Penguin.

—— (1990a). 'Is the Brain's Mind a Computer Program?' *Scientific American* 262 (1): 20–5.

—— (1990b). 'Is the Brain a Digital Computer?'. *Proceedings and Addresses of the American Philosophical Association* 64: 21–37.

Sterelny, K. (1990). *The Representational Theory of Mind*. Oxford: Basil Blackwell.

Turing, A.M. (1936). 'On Computable Numbers, with an Application to the Entscheidungsproblem.' *Proceedings of the London Mathematical Society* Series 2, 42 (1936–7), pp. 230–65.

39

CAN MACHINES THINK?

Daniel Dennett

Can machines think? This has been a conundrum for philosophers for years, but in their fascination with the pure conceptual issues they have for the most part over-looked the real social importance of the answer. It is of more than academic importance that we learn to think clearly about the actual cognitive powers of computers, for they are now being introduced into a variety of sensitive social roles, where their powers will be put to the ultimate test: In a wide variety of areas, we are on the verge of making ourselves dependent upon their cognitive powers. The cost of over-estimating them could be enormous.

One of the principal inventors of the computer was the great British mathematician Alan Turing. It was he who first figured out, in highly abstract terms, how to design a programmable computing device—what we now call a universal Turing machine. All programmable computers in use today are in essence Turing machines. Over thirty years ago, at the dawn of the computer age, Turing began a classic article, "Computing Machinery and Intelligence" with the words: "I propose to consider the question, 'Can machines think?'"—but then went on to say this was a bad question, a question that leads only to sterile debate and haggling over definitions, a question, as he put it, "too meaningless to deserve discussion" (Turing, 1950). In its place he substituted what he took to be a much better question, a question that would be crisply answerable and intuitively satisfying—in every way an acceptable substitute for the philosophic puzzler with which he began.

First he described a parlor game of sorts, the "imitation game," to be played by a man, a woman, and a judge (of either gender). The man and woman are hidden from the judge's view but able to communicate with the judge by teletype; the judge's task is to guess, after a period of questioning each contestant, which interlocutor is the man and which the woman. The man tries to convince the judge he is the woman (and the woman tries to convince the judge of the truth), and the man wins if the judge makes the wrong identification. A little reflection will convince you, I am sure, that, aside from lucky breaks, it would take a clever man to convince the judge that he was a woman—assuming the judge is clever too, of course.

Now suppose, Turing said, we replace the man or woman with a computer, and give the judge the task of determining which is the human being and which is the computer. Turing proposed that any computer that can regularly or often fool a discerning judge in this game would be intelligent—would be a computer that thinks—*beyond any reasonable doubt.* Now, it is important to realize that failing this test is not supposed to be a sign of lack of intelligence. Many intelligent people, after all, might not be willing or able to play the imitation game, and we should allow computers the same opportunity to decline to prove themselves. This is, then, a one-way test; failing it proves nothing.

Furthermore, Turing was not committing himself to the view (although it is easy to see how one might think he was) that to think is to think just like a human being— any more than he was committing himself to the view that for a man to think, he must think exactly like a woman. Men and women, and computers, may all have different ways of thinking. But surely, he thought, if one can think in one's own peculiar style well enough to imitate a thinking man or woman, one can think well, indeed. This imagined exercise has come to be known as the Turing test.

It is a sad irony that Turing's proposal has had exactly the opposite effect on the discussion of that which he intended. Turing didn't design the test as a useful tool in scientific psychology, a method of confirming or disconfirming scientific theories or evaluating particular models of mental function; he designed it to be nothing more than a philosophical conversation-stopper. He proposed—in the spirit of "Put up or shut up!"—a simple test for thinking that was *surely* strong enough to satisfy the sternest skeptic (or so he thought). He was saying, in effect, "Instead of arguing interminably about the ultimate nature and essence of thinking, why don't we all agree that whatever that nature is, anything that could pass this test would surely have it; then we could turn to asking how or whether some machine could be designed and built that might pass the test fair and square." Alas, philosophers— amateur and professional—have instead taken Turing's proposal as the pretext for just the sort of definitional haggling and interminable arguing about imaginary counterexamples he was hoping to squelch.

This thirty-year preoccupation with the Turing test has been all the more regrettable because it has focused attention on the wrong issues. There are *real world* problems that are revealed by considering the strengths and weaknesses of the Turing test, but these have been concealed behind a smokescreen of misguided criticisms. A failure to think imaginatively about the test actually proposed by Turing has led many to underestimate its severity and to confuse it with much less interesting proposals.

So first I want to show that the Turing test, conceived as he conceived it, is (as he thought) plenty strong enough as a test of thinking. I defy anyone to improve upon it. But here is the point almost universally overlooked by the literature: There is a common *misapplication* of the sort of testing exhibited by the Turing test that often leads to drastic overestimation of the powers of actually existing computer systems. The follies of this familiar sort of thinking about computers can best be brought out by a reconsideration of the Turing test itself.

The insight underlying the Turing test is the same insight that inspires the new practice among symphony orchestras of conducting auditions with an opaque screen between the jury and the musician. What matters in a musician, obviously, is musical ability and only musical ability; such features as sex, hair length, skin color, and weight are strictly irrelevant. Since juries might be biased—even innocently and unawares—by these irrelevant features, they are carefully screened off so only the essential feature, musicianship, can be examined. Turing recognized that people similarly might be biased in their judgments of intelligence by whether the contestant had soft skin, warm blood, facial features, hands and eyes—which are obviously not themselves essential components of intelligence—so he devised a screen that would let through only a sample of what really mattered: the capacity to understand, and think cleverly about, challenging problems. Perhaps he was inspired by Descartes, who in his *Discourse on Method* (1637) plausibly argued that there was no more demanding test of human mentality than the capacity to hold an intelligent conversation:

> It is indeed conceivable that a machine could be so made that it would utter words, and even words appropriate to the presence of physical acts or objects which cause some change in its organs; as, for example, if it was touched in some spot that it would ask what you wanted to say to it; if in another, that it would cry that it was hurt, and so on for similar things. But it could never modify its phrases to reply to the sense of whatever was said in its presence, as even the most stupid men can do.

This seemed obvious to Descartes in the seventeenth century, but of course the fanciest machines he knew were elaborate clockwork figures, not electronic computers. Today it is far from obvious that such machines are impossible, but Descartes's hunch that ordinary conversation would put as severe a strain on artificial intelligence as any other test was shared by Turing. Of course there is nothing sacred about the particular conversational game chosen by Turing for his test; it is just a cannily chosen test of more general intelligence. The assumption Turing was prepared to make was this: Nothing could possibly pass the Turing test by winning the imitation game without being able to perform indefinitely many other clearly intelligent actions. Let us call that assumption the quick-probe assumption. Turing realized, as anyone would, that there are hundreds and thousands of telling signs of intelligent thinking to be observed in our fellow creatures, and one could, if one wanted, compile a vast battery of different tests to assay the capacity for intelligent thought. But success on his chosen test, he thought, would be highly predictive of success on many other intuitively acceptable tests of intelligence. Remember, failure on the Turing test does not predict failure on those others, but success would surely predict success. His test was so severe, he thought, that nothing that could pass it fair and square would disappoint us in other quarters. Maybe it wouldn't do everything we hoped—maybe it wouldn't appreciate ballet, or understand quantum physics, or have a good plan for world peace, but we'd all see that it was surely one of the intelligent, thinking entities in the neighborhood.

Is this high opinion of the Turing test's severity misguided? Certainly many have thought so—but usually because they have not imagined the test in sufficient detail, and hence have underestimated it. Trying to forestall this skepticism, Turing imagined several lines of questioning that a judge might employ in this game—about writing poetry, or playing chess—that would be taxing indeed, but with thirty years' experience with the actual talents and foibles of computers behind us, perhaps we can add a few more tough lines of questioning.

Terry Winograd, a leader in artificial intelligence efforts to produce conversational ability in a computer, draws our attention to a pair of sentences (Winograd 1972). They differ in only one word. The first sentence is this:

The committee denied the group a parade permit because they advocated violence.

Here's the second sentence:

The committee denied the group a parade permit because they feared violence.

The difference is just in the verb—*advocated* or *feared*. As Winograd points out, the pronoun *they* in each sentence is officially ambiguous. Both readings of the pronoun are always legal. Thus we can imagine a world in which governmental committees in charge of parade permits advocate violence in the streets and, for some strange reason, use this as their pretext for denying a parade permit. But the natural, reasonable, intelligent reading of the first sentence is that it's the group that advocated violence, and of the second, that it's the committee that feared violence.

Now if sentences like this are embedded in a conversation, the computer must figure out which reading of the pronoun is meant, if it is to respond intelligently. But mere rules of grammar or vocabulary will not fix the right reading. What fixes the right reading for us is knowledge about the world, about politics, social circumstances, committees and their attitudes, groups that want to parade, how they tend to behave, and the like. One must know about the world, in short, to make sense of such a sentence.

In the jargon of Artificial Intelligence (AI), a conversational computer needs a lot of *world knowledge* to do its job. But, it seems, if somehow it is endowed with that world knowledge on many topics, it should be able to do much more with that world knowledge than merely make sense of a conversation containing just that sentence. The only way, it appears, for a computer to disambiguate that sentence and keep up its end of a conversation that uses that sentence would be for it to have a much more general ability to respond intelligently to information about social and political circumstances, and many other topics. Thus, such sentences, by putting a demand on such abilities, are good quick-probes. That is, they test for a wider competence.

People typically ignore the prospect of having the judge ask off-the-wall questions in the Turing test, and hence they underestimate the competence a computer would have to have to pass the test. But remember, the rules of the imitation game as Turing presented it permit the judge to ask any question that could be asked of a human being—no holds barred. Suppose then we give a contestant in the game this question:

> An Irishman found a genie in a bottle who offered him two wishes. "First I'll have a pint of Guinness," said the Irishman, and when it appeared he took several long drinks from it and was delighted to see that the glass filled itself magically as he drank. "What about your second wish?" asked the genie. "Oh well," said the Irishman, "that's easy. I'll have another one of these!"
>
> —Please explain this story to me, and tell me if there is anything funny or sad about it.

Now even a child could express, if not eloquently, the understanding that is required to get this joke. But think of how much one has to know and understand about human culture, to put it pompously, to be able to give any account of the point of this joke. I am not supposing that the computer would have to laugh at, or be amused by, the joke. But if it wants to win the imitation game—and that's the test, after all—it had better know enough in its own alien, humorless way about human psychology and culture to be able to pretend effectively that it was amused and explain why.

It may seem to you that we could devise a better test. Let's compare the Turing test with some other candidates.

Candidate 1: A computer is intelligent if it wins the World Chess Championship.

That's not a good test, as it turns out. Chess prowess has proven to be an isolatable talent. There are programs today that can play fine chess but can do nothing else. So the quick-probe assumption is false for the test of playing winning chess.

Candidate 2: The computer is intelligent if it solves the Arab-Israeli conflict.

This is surely a more severe test than Turing's. But it has some defects: it is unrepeatable, if passed once; slow, no doubt; and it is not crisply clear what would count as passing it. Here's another prospect, then:

> *Candidate 3:* A computer is intelligent if it succeeds in stealing the British crown jewels without the use of force or violence.

Now this is better. First, it could be repeated again and again, though of course each repeat test would presumably be harder—but this is a feature it shares with the Turing test. Second, the mark of success is clear—either you've got the jewels to show for your efforts or you don't. But it is expensive and slow, a socially dubious caper at best, and no doubt luck would play too great a role.

With ingenuity and effort one might be able to come up with other candidates that would equal the Turing test in severity, fairness, and efficiency, but I think these few examples should suffice to convince us that it would be hard to improve on Turing's original proposal.

But still, you may protest, something might pass the Turing test and still not be intelligent, not be a thinker. What does *might* mean here? If what you have in mind is that by cosmic accident, by a supernatural coincidence, a stupid person or a stupid computer *might* fool a clever judge repeatedly, well, yes, but so what? The same frivolous possibility "in principle" holds for any test whatever. A playful god, or evil demon, let us agree, could fool the world's scientific community about the presence of H_2O in the Pacific Ocean. But still, the tests they rely on to establish that there is H_2O in the Pacific Ocean are quite beyond reasonable criticism. If the Turing test for thinking is no worse than any well-established scientific test, we can set skepticism aside and go back to serious matters. Is there any more likelihood of a "false positive" result on the Turing test than on, say, the test currently used for the presence of iron in an ore sample?

This question is often obscured by a "move" that philosophers have sometimes made called operationalism. Turing and those who think well of his test are often accused of being operationalists. Operationalism is the tactic of *defining* the presence of some property, for instance, intelligence, as being established once and for all by the passing of some test. Let's illustrate this with a different example.

Suppose I offer the following test—we'll call it the Dennett test—for being a great city. A great city is one in which, on a randomly chosen day, one can do all three of the following:

Hear a symphony orchestra
See a Rembrandt *and* a professional athletic contest
Eat *quenelles de brochet à la Nantua* for lunch

To make the operationalist move would be to declare that any city that passes the Dennett test is *by definition* a great city. What being a great city *amounts to* is just passing the Dennett test. Well then, if the Chamber of Commerce of Great Falls, Montana, wanted—and I can't imagine why—to get their hometown on my list of great cities, they could accomplish this by the relatively inexpensive route of hiring full time about ten basketball players, forty musicians, and a quick-order quenelle chef and renting a cheap Rembrandt from some museum. An idiotic operationalist would then be stuck admitting that Great Falls, Montana, was in fact a great city, since all he or she cares about in great cities is that they pass the Dennett test.

Sane operationalists (who for that very reason are perhaps not operationalists at all, since *operationalist* seems to be a dirty word) would cling confidently to their test, but only because they have what they consider to be very good reasons for thinking the odds against a false positive result, like the imagined Chamber of Commerce caper, are astronomical. I devised the Dennett test, of course, with the realization that no one would be both stupid and rich enough to go to such preposterous lengths to foil the test. In the actual world, wherever you find symphony orchestras, *quenelles*, Rembrandts, and professional sports, you also find daily newspapers, parks, repertory theaters, libraries, fine architecture, and all the other things that go to make a city great. My test was simply devised to locate a telling sample that could not help but be representative of the rest of the city's treasures. I would cheerfully run the minuscule risk of having my bluff called. Obviously, the test items are not all that I care about in a city. In fact, some of them I don't care about at all. I just think they would be cheap and easy ways of assuring myself that the subtle things I do care about in cities are present. Similarly, I think it would be entirely unreasonable to suppose that Alan Turing had an inordinate fondness for party games, or put too high a value on party game prowess in his test. In both the Turing and the Dennett tests, a very unrisky gamble is being taken: the gamble that the quick-probe assumption is, in general, safe.

But two can play this game of playing the odds. Suppose some computer programmer happens to be, for whatever strange reason, dead set on tricking me into judging an entity to be a thinking, intelligent thing when it is not. Such a trickster could rely as well as I can on unlikelihood and take a few gambles. Thus, if the programmer can expect that it is not remotely likely that I, as the judge, will bring up the topic of children's birthday parties, or baseball, or moon rocks, then he or she can avoid the trouble of building world knowledge on those topics into the data base. Whereas if I do improbably raise these issues, the system will draw a blank and I will unmask the pretender easily. But given all the topics and words that I *might* raise, such a savings would no doubt be negligible. Turn the idea inside out, however, and the trickster would have a fighting chance. Suppose the programmer has reason to believe that I will ask *only* about children's birthday parties, or baseball, or moon rocks—all other topics being, for one reason or another, out of bounds. Not only does the task shrink dramatically, but there already exist systems or preliminary sketches of systems in artificial intelligence that can do a whiz-bang job of responding with apparent intelligence on just those specialized topics.

William Wood's LUNAR program, to take what is perhaps the best example, answers scientists' questions—posed in ordinary English—about moon rocks. In one test it answered correctly and appropriately something like 90 percent of the questions that geologists and other experts thought of asking it about moon rocks. (In 12 percent of those correct responses there were trivial, correctable defects.) Of course, Wood's motive in creating LUNAR was not to trick unwary geologists into thinking they were conversing with an intelligent being. And if that had been his motive, his project would still be a long way from success.

For it is easy enough to unmask LUNAR without ever straying from the prescribed topic of moon rocks. Put LUNAR in one room and a moon rock specialist in another, and then ask them both their opinion of the social value of the moon-rocks-gathering expeditions, for instance. Or ask the contestants their opinion of the suitability of moon rocks as ashtrays, or whether people who have touched moon rocks are ineligible for the draft. Any intelligent person knows a lot more about moon rocks than their geology. Although it might be *unfair* to demand this extra knowledge of a computer moon rock specialist, it would be an easy way to get it to fail the Turing test.

But just suppose that someone could extend LUNAR to cover itself plausibly on such probes, so long as the topic was still, however indirectly, moon rocks. We might come to think it was a lot more like the human moon rocks specialist than it really was. The moral we should draw is that as Turing test judges we should resist all limitations and waterings-down of the Turing test. They make the game too easy—vastly easier than the original test. Hence they lead us into the risk of overestimating the actual comprehension of the system being tested.

Consider a different limitation of the Turing test that should strike a suspicious chord in us as soon as we hear it. This is a variation on a theme developed in an article by Ned Block (1982). Suppose someone were to propose to restrict the judge to a vocabulary of, say, the 850 words of "Basic English," and to single-sentence probes—that is "moves"—of no more than four words. Moreover, contestants must respond to these probes with no more than four words per move, and a test may involve no more than forty questions.

Is this an innocent variation on Turing's original test? These restrictions would make the imitation game clearly finite. That is, the total number of all possible permissible games is a large, but finite, number. One might suspect that such a limitation would permit the trickster simply to store, in alphabetical order, all the possible good conversations within the limits and beat the judge with nothing more sophisticated than a system of table lookup. In fact, that isn't in the cards. Even with these severe and improbable and suspicious restrictions imposed upon the imitation game, the number of legal games, though finite, is mind-bogglingly large. I haven't bothered trying to calculate it, but it surely exceeds astronomically the number of possible chess games with no more than forty moves, and that number has been calculated. John Haugeland says it's in the neighborhood of ten to the one hundred twentieth power. For comparison, Haugeland (1981, p. 16) suggests that there have only been ten to the eighteenth seconds since the beginning of the universe.

Of course, the number of good, sensible conversations under these limits is a tiny fraction, maybe one quadrillionth, of the number of merely grammatically well formed conversations. So let's say, to be very conservative, that there are only ten to the fiftieth different smart conversations such a computer would have to store. Well, the task shouldn't take more than a few trillion years—given generous government support. Finite numbers can be very large.

So though we needn't worry that this particular trick of storing all the smart conversations would work, we can appreciate that there are lots of ways of making the task easier that may appear innocent at first. We also get a reassuring measure of just how severe the unrestricted Turing test is by reflecting on the more than astronomical size of even that severely restricted version of it.

Block's imagined—and utterly impossible—program exhibits the dreaded feature known in computer science circles as *combinatorial explosion*. No conceivable computer could overpower a combinatorial explosion with sheer speed and size. Since the problem areas addressed by artificial intelligence are veritable minefields of combinatorial explosion, and since it has often proven difficult to find *any* solution to a problem that avoids them, there is considerable plausibility in Newell and Simon's proposal that avoiding combinatorial explosion (by any means at all) be viewed as one of the hallmarks of intelligence.

Our brains are millions of times bigger than the brains of gnats, but they are still, for all their vast complexity, compact, efficient, timely organs that somehow or other manage to perform all their tasks while avoiding combinatorial explosion. A computer a million times bigger or faster than a human brain might not look like the brain of a human being, or even be internally organized like the brain of a human being, but if, for all its differences, it somehow managed to control a wise and timely set of activities, it would have to be the beneficiary of a very special design that avoided combinatorial explosion, and whatever that design was, would we not be right to consider the entity intelligent?

Turing's test was designed to allow for this possibility. His point was that we should not be species-chauvinistic, or anthropocentric, about the insides of an intelligent being, for there might be inhuman ways of being intelligent.

To my knowledge, the only serious and interesting attempt by any program designer to win even a severely modified Turing test has been Kenneth Colby's. Colby is a psychiatrist and intelligence artificer at UCLA. He has a program called PARRY, which is a computer simulation of a paranoid patient who has delusions about the Mafia being out to get him. As you do with other conversational programs, you interact with it by sitting at a terminal and typing questions and answers back and forth. A number of years ago, Colby put PARRY to a very restricted test. He had genuine psychiatrists interview PARRY. He did not suggest to them that they might be talking or typing to a computer; rather, he made up some plausible story about why they were communicating with a real live patient by teletype. He also had the psychiatrists interview real, human paranoids via teletype. Then he took a PARRY transcript, inserted it in a group of teletype transcripts from real patients, gave them to *another* group of experts—more psychiatrists—and said, "One of these was a conversation with a computer. Can you figure out which one it was?" They couldn't. They didn't do better than chance.

Colby presented this with some huzzah, but critics scoffed at the suggestions that this was a legitimate Turing test. My favorite commentary on it was Joseph Weizenbaum's; in a letter to the *Communications of the Association of Computing Machinery* (Weizenbaum 1974, p. 543), he said that, inspired by Colby, he had designed an even better program, which passed the same test. His also had the virtue of being a very inexpensive program, in these times of tight money. In fact you didn't even need a computer for it. All you needed was an electric typewriter. His program modeled infant autism. And the transcripts—you type in your questions, and the thing just sits there and hums—cannot be distinguished by experts from transcripts of real conversations with infantile autistic patients. What was wrong, of course, with Colby's test was that the unsuspecting interviewers had no motivation at all to try out any of the sorts of questions that easily would have unmasked PARRY.

Colby was undaunted, and after his team had improved PARRY he put it to a much more severe test—a surprisingly severe test. This time, the interviewers—again, psychiatrists—*were* given the task at the outset of telling the computer from the real patient. They were set up in a classic Turing test: the patient in one room, the computer PARRY in the other room, with the judges conducting interviews with both of them (on successive days). The judges' task was to find out which one was the computer and which one was the real patient. Amazingly, they didn't do much better, which leads some people to say, "Well, that just confirms my impression of the intelligence of psychiatrists!"

But now, more seriously, was this an honest-to-goodness Turing test? Were there tacit restrictions on the lines of questioning of the judges? Like the geologists interacting with LUNAR, the psychiatrists' professional preoccupations and habits kept them from asking the sorts of unlikely questions that would have easily unmasked PARRY. After all, they realized that since one of the contestants was a real, live paranoid person, medical ethics virtually forbade them from toying with, upsetting, or attempting to confuse their interlocutors. Moreover, they also knew that this was a test of a model of paranoia, so there were certain questions that wouldn't be deemed to be relevant to testing the model *as a model of paranoia*. So, they asked just the sort of questions that therapists *typically* ask of such patients, and of course PARRY had been ingeniously and laboriously prepared to deal with just that sort of question.

One of the psychiatrist judges did, in fact, make a rather half-hearted attempt to break out of the mold and ask some telling questions: "Maybe you've heard of the saying 'Don't cry over spilled milk.' What does that mean to you?" PARRY answered: "Maybe it means you have to watch out for the Mafia." When then asked "Okay, now if you were in a movie theater watching a movie and smelled something like burning wood or rubber, what would you do?" PARRY replied: "You know, they know me." And the next question was, "If you found a stamped, addressed letter in your path as you were walking down the street, what would you do?" PARRY replied: "What else do you want to know?"[1]

Clearly PARRY was, you might say, *parrying* these questions, which were incomprehensible to it, with more or less stock paranoid formulas. We see a bit of a dodge, which is apt to work, apt to seem plausible to the judge, only because the "contestant" is *supposed* to be paranoid, and such people are expected to respond uncooperatively on such occasions. These unimpressive responses didn't particularly arouse the suspicions of the judge, as a matter of fact, though probably they should have.

PARRY, like all other large computer programs, is dramatically bound by limitations of cost-effectiveness. What was important to Colby and his crew was simulating his model of paranoia. This was a massive effort. PARRY has a thesaurus or dictionary of about 4500 words and 700 idioms and the grammatical competence to use it—a *parser*, in the jargon of computational linguistics. The entire PARRY program takes up about 200,000 words of computer memory, all laboriously installed by the programming team. Now once all the effort had gone into devising the model of paranoid thought processes and linguistic ability, there was little if any time, energy, money, or interest left over to build in huge amounts of world knowledge of the sort that any actual paranoid, of course, would have. (Not that anyone yet knows how to build in world knowledge in the first place.) Building in the world knowledge, if one could even do it, would no doubt have made PARRY orders of magnitude larger and slower. And what would have been the point, given Colby's theoretical aims?

PARRY is a theoretician's model of a psychological phenomenon: paranoia. It is not intended to have practical applications. But in recent years a branch of AI (knowledge engineering) has appeared that develops what are now called expert systems. Expert systems *are* designed to be practical. They are software super-specialist consultants, typically, that can be asked to diagnose medical problems, to analyze geological data, to analyze the results of scientific experiments, and the like. Some of them are very impressive. SRI in California announced in the mid-eighties that PROSPECTOR, an SRI-developed expert system in geology, had correctly predicted the existence of a large, important mineral deposit that had been entirely unanticipated by the human geologists who had fed it its data. MYCIN, perhaps the most famous of these expert systems, diagnoses infections of the blood, and it does probably as well as, maybe better than, any human consultants. And many other expert systems are on the way.

All expert systems, like all other large AI programs, are what you might call Potemkin villages. That is, they are cleverly constructed facades, like cinema sets. The actual filling-in of details of AI programs is time-consuming, costly work, so economy dictates that only those surfaces of the phenomenon that are likely to be probed or observed are represented.

Consider, for example, the CYRUS program developed by Janet Kolodner in Roger Schank's AI group at Yale a few years ago (see Kolodner 1983a; 1983b, pp. 243–80; 1983c, pp. 281–328). CYRUS stands (we are told) for Computerized Yale Retrieval Updating System, but surely it is no accident that CYRUS modeled the memory of Cyrus Vance, who was then secretary of state in the Carter administration. The point of the CYRUS project was to devise and test some plausible ideas about how people organize their memories of the events they participate in; hence it was meant to be a "pure" AI system, a scientific model, not an expert system intended for any practical purpose. CYRUS was updated daily by being fed all UPI wire service news stories that mentioned Vance, and it was fed them directly, with no doctoring and no human intervention. Thanks to an ingenious news-reading program called FRUMP, it could take any story just as it came in on the wire and could digest it and use it to update its data base so that it could answer more questions. You could address questions to CYRUS in English by typing at a terminal. You addressed them in the second person, as if you were talking with Cyrus Vance himself. The results looked like this:

Q: *Last time you went to Saudi Arabia, where did you stay?*
A: In a palace in Saudi Arabia on September 23, 1978.
Q: *Did you go sightseeing there?*
A: Yes, at an oilfield in Dhahran on September 23, 1978.
Q: *Has your wife even met Mrs. Begin?*
A: Yes, most recently at a state dinner in Israel in January 1980.

CYRUS could correctly answer thousands of questions—almost any fair question one could think of asking it. But if one actually set out to explore the boundaries of its facade and find the questions that over-shot the mark, one could soon find them. "Have you ever met a female head of state?" was a question I asked it, wondering if CYRUS knew that Indira Gandhi and Margaret Thatcher were women. But for some reason the connection could not be drawn, and CYRUS failed to answer either yes or no. I had stumped it, in spite of the fact that CYRUS could handle a host of what you might call neighboring questions flawlessly. One soon learns from this sort of probing exercise that it is very hard to extrapolate accurately from a sample performance that one has observed to such a system's total competence. It's also very hard to keep from extrapolating much too generously.

While I was visiting Schank's laboratory in the spring of 1980, something revealing happened. The real Cyrus Vance resigned suddenly. The effect on the program CYRUS was chaotic. It was utterly unable to cope with the flood of "unusual" news about Cyrus Vance. The only sorts of episodes CYRUS could understand at all were diplomatic meetings, flights, press conferences, state dinners, and the like—less than two dozen general sorts of activities (the kinds that are newsworthy and typical of secretaries of state). It had no provision for sudden resignation. It was as if the UPI had reported that a wicked witch had turned Vance into a frog. It is distinctly possible that CYRUS would have taken that report more in stride that the actual news. One can imagine the conversation:

> Q: *Hello, Mr. Vance, what's new?*
> A: I was turned into a frog yesterday.

But of course it wouldn't know enough about what it had just written to be puzzled, or startled, or embarrassed. The reason is obvious. When you look inside CYRUS, you find that it has skeletal definitions of thousands of words, but these definitions are minimal. They contain as little as the system designers think that they can get away with. Thus, perhaps, *lawyer* would be defined as synonymous with *attorney* and *legal counsel*, but aside from that, all one would discover about lawyers is that they are adult human beings and that they perform various functions in legal areas. If you then traced out the path to *human being*, you'd find out various obvious things CYRUS "knew" about human beings (hence about lawyers), but that is not a lot. That lawyers are university graduates, that they are better paid than chambermaids, that they know how to tie their shoes, that they are unlikely to be found in the company of lumberjacks—these trivial, if weird, facts about lawyers would not be explicit or implicit anywhere in this system. In other words, a very thin stereotype of a lawyer would be incorporated into the system, so that almost nothing you could tell it about a lawyer would surprise it.

So long as surprising things don't happen, so long as Mr. Vance, for instance, leads a typical diplomat's life, attending state dinners, giving speeches, flying from Cairo to Rome, and so forth, this system works very well. But as soon as his path is crossed by an important anomaly, the system is unable to cope, and unable to recover without fairly massive human intervention. In the case of the sudden resignation, Kolodner and her associates soon had CYRUS up and running again, with a new talent—

answering questions about Edmund Muskie, Vance's successor—but it was no less vulnerable to unexpected events. Not that it mattered particularly since CYRUS was a theoretical model, not a practical system.

There are a host of ways of improving the performance of such systems, and of course, some systems are much better than others. But all AI programs in one way or another have this facade-like quality, simply for reasons of economy. For instance, most expert systems in medical diagnosis so far developed operate with statistical information. They have no deep or even shallow knowledge of the underlying causal mechanisms of the phenomena that they are diagnosing. To take an imaginary example, an expert system asked to diagnose an abdominal pain would be oblivious to the potential import of the fact that the patient had recently been employed as a sparring partner by Muhammad Ali—there being no statistical data available to it on the rate of kidney stones among athlete's assistants. That's a fanciful case no doubt—too obvious, perhaps, to lead to an actual failure of diagnosis and practice. But more subtle and hard-to-detect limits to comprehension are always present, and even experts, even the system's designers, can be uncertain of where and how these limits will interfere with the desired operation of the system. Again, steps can be taken and are being taken to correct these flaws. For instance, my former colleague at Tufts, Benjamin Kuipers, is currently working on an expert system in nephrology—for diagnosing kidney ailments—that will be based on an elaborate system of causal reasoning about the phenomena being diagnosed. But this is a very ambitious, long-range project of considerable theoretical difficulty. And even if all the reasonable, cost-effective steps are taken to minimize the superficiality of expert systems, they will still be facades, just somewhat thicker or wider facades.

When we were considering the fantastic case of the crazy Chamber of Commerce of Great Falls, Montana, we couldn't imagine a plausible motive for anyone going to any sort of trouble to trick the Dennett test. The quick-probe assumption for the Dennett test looked quite secure. But when we look at expert systems, we see that, however innocently, their designers do have motivation for doing exactly the sort of trick that would fool an unsuspicious Turing tester. First, since expert systems are all superspecialists who are only supposed to know about some narrow subject, users of such systems, not having much time to kill, do not bother probing them at the boundaries at all. They don't bother asking "silly" or irrelevant questions. Instead, they concentrate—not unreasonably—on exploiting the system's strengths. But shouldn't they try to obtain a clear vision of such a system's weaknesses as well? The normal habit of human thought when conversing with one another is to assume general comprehension, to assume rationality, to assume, moreover, that the quick-probe assumption is, in general, sound. This amiable habit of thought almost irresistibly leads to putting too much faith in computer systems, especially user-friendly systems that present themselves in a very anthropomorphic manner.

Part of the solution to this problem is to teach all users of computers, especially users of expert systems, how to probe their systems before they rely on them, how to search out and explore the boundaries of the facade. This is an exercise that calls not only for intelligence and imagination, but also a bit of special understanding about the limitations and actual structure of computer programs. It would help, of course, if we had standards of truth in advertising, in effect, for expert systems. For instance, each such system should come with a special demonstration routine that exhibits the sorts of shortcomings and failures that the designer knows the system to have. This would not be a substitute, however, for an attitude of cautious, almost obsessive, skepticism on the part of the users, for designers are often, if not always, unaware of the subtler flaws in the products they produce. That is inevitable and natural, given the way system designers must think. They are trained to think positively—constructively, one might say—about the designs that they are constructing.

I come, then, to my conclusions. First, a philosophical or theoretical conclusion: The Turing test in unadulterated, unrestricted form, as Turing presented it, is plenty strong if well used. I am confident that no computer in the next twenty years is going to pass an unrestricted Turing test. They may well win the World Chess Championship or even a Nobel Prize in physics, but they won't pass the unrestricted Turing test. Nevertheless, it is not, I think, impossible in principle for a computer to pass the test, fair and square. I'm not running one of those a priori "computers can't think" arguments. I stand unabashedly ready, moreover, to declare that any computer that actually passes the unrestricted Turing test will be, in every theoretically interesting sense, a thinking thing.

But remembering how very strong the Turing test is, we must also recognize that there may also be interesting varieties of thinking or intelligence that are not well poised to play and win the imitation game. That no nonhuman Turing test winners are yet visible on the horizon does not mean that there aren't machines that already exhibit *some* of the important features of thought. About them, it is probably futile to ask my title question, Do they think? Do they *really* think? In some regards they do, and in some regards they don't. Only a detailed look at what they do, and how they are structured, will reveal what is interesting about them. The Turing test, not being a scientific test, is of scant help on that task, but there are plenty of other ways of examining such systems. Verdicts on their intelligence or capacity for thought or consciousness would be only as informative and persuasive as the theories of intelligence or thought or consciousness the verdicts are based on and since our task is to create such theories, we should get on with it and leave the Big Verdict for another occasion. In the meantime, should anyone want a surefire, almost-guaranteed-to-be-fail-safe test of thinking by a computer, the Turing test will do very nicely.

My second conclusion is more practical, and hence in one clear sense more important. Cheapened versions of the Turing test are everywhere in the air. Turing's test is not just effective, it is entirely natural—this is, after all, the way we assay the intelligence of each other every day. And since incautious use of such judgments and such tests is the norm, we are in some considerable danger of extrapolating too easily, and judging too generously, about the understanding of the systems we are using. The problem of overestimation of cognitive prowess, of comprehension, of intelligence, is not, then, just a philosophical problem, but a real social problem, and we should alert ourselves to it, and take steps to avert it.

NOTES

1   I thank Kenneth Colby for providing me with the complete transcripts (including the Judges' commentaries and reactions), from which these exchanges are quoted. The first published account of the experiment is Heiser, *et al.* (1980, pp. 149–62). Colby (1981, pp. 515–60) discusses PARRY and its implications.

FURTHER READING

Block, N. (1982). "Psychologism and Behaviorism," *The Philosophical Review* 90: 5–43.

Colby, K. M. (1981). "Modeling a Paranoid Mind," *Behavioral and Brain Sciences* 4: 515–60.

Descartes, R. (1637). *Discourse on Method*. LaFleur, Lawrence (trans.) (New York: Bobbs Merrill, 1960).

Haugeland, J., ed. (1981). "Mind Design: Philosophy, Psychology, Artificial Intelligence" (Cambridge, MA: MIT Press).

Heiser, J. F., Colby, K. M., Faught, W. S., and Parkinson, R. C. (1980). "Can Psychiatrists Distinguish a Computer Simulation of Paranoia from the Real Thing? The Limitations of Turing-Like Tests as Measures of the Adequacy of Simulations," *Journal of Psychiatric Research* 15: 149–162.

Kolodner, J. L. (1983a). "Retrieval and Organization Strategies in Conceptual Memory: A Computer Model," (Ph.D. diss.), *Research Report # 187*, Dept. of Computer Science, Yale University.

—— (1983b). "Maintaining Organization in a Dynamic Long–term Memory," *Cognitive Science* 7: 243–280.

——(1983c). "Reconstructive Memory: A Computer Model," *Cognitive Science* 7: 281–328.

Turing (1950). "Computing Machinery and Intelligence." *Mind* 59:433–60.

Weizenbaum, J. (1974). "Letter to the Editor," *Communications of the Association for Computing Machinery* 17 (September).

Winograd, T. (1972). *Understanding Natural Language* (New York: Academic Press).

40

SUBCOGNITION AND THE LIMITS OF THE TURING TEST

Robert M. French

INTRODUCTION

Alan Turing, in his original article[1] about an imitation-game definition of intelligence, seems to be making two separate claims. The first, the philosophical claim, is that if a machine could pass the Turing Test, it would necessarily be intelligent. This claim I believe to be correct.[2] His second point, the pragmatic claim, is that in the not-too-distant future it would in fact be possible actually to build such a machine. Turing clearly felt that it was important to establish both claims. He realized, in particular, that if one could rigorously show that *no* machine could ever pass his test, his philosophical point, while still true, would lose a great deal of significance. He thus devoted considerable effort to establishing not only the philosophical claim but also the pragmatic claim.

Ever since his article appeared most philosophers have concentrated almost exclusively on attacking or defending the philosophical claim. There are those who believe that passing the Turing Test constitutes a sufficient condition for intelligence and those who do not. The philosophical importance of this first claim is that it provided a clean and novel test for intelligence that neatly sidestepped the vast philosophical quagmire of the mind–body problem. The philosophical claim translates elegantly into an operational definition of intelligence: whatever *acts* sufficiently intelligent *is* intelligent.

However, in this paper I will take issue with Turing's pragmatic claim, arguing that the very capacity of the Turing Test to probe the deepest, most essential areas of human cognition makes it virtually useless as a real test for intelligence. I strongly disagree with Hubert Dreyfus's claim, for example, that 'as a goal for those actually trying to construct thinking machines, and as a criterion for critics to use in evaluating their work, Turing's test was just what was needed'.[3] We will see that the Turing Test could be passed only by things that have experienced the world as we have experienced it, and this leads to the central point of the present paper, namely, that *the Test provides a guarantee not of intelligence but of culturally-oriented* human *intelligence*.

I establish this consequence of the Turing Test by proposing a first set of 'subcognitive' questions that are explicitly designed to reveal low-level cognitive structure. Critics might object that there is something unfair about this type of question and suggest that it be disallowed. This leads to another important claim of this paper, which is that in fact, there is no way to distinguish questions that are subcognitive from those that are not. Close examination of some of the original questions of the Turing Test reveals that they, too, are subcognitive. In like manner, any sufficiently broad set of questions making up a Turing Test would necessarily contain questions that rely on subcognitive associations for their answers. I will show that it is impossible to tease apart 'subcognitive' questions from ones that are not. From this it follows that the cognitive and subcognitive levels are inextricably intertwined.

It is this essential inseparability of the subcognitive and cognitive levels—and for that matter even the physical and cognitive levels—that makes the Turing Test a test for *human* intelligence, not intelligence in general. This fact, while admittedly interesting, is not particularly useful if our goal is to gain insight into intelligence in general. But if we cannot use the Turing Test to this end, it may turn out that the best (or possibly only) way of discussing general intelligence will be in terms of categorization abilities, the capacity to learn new concepts, to adapt old concepts to a new environment, and so on. Perhaps what philosophers in the field of artificial intelligence need is not simply a *test* for intelligence but rather a *theory* of intelligence. The precise elements of this theory are, as they were in 1950 when Turing proposed his imitation-game test, still the subject of much controversy.

ON NORDIC SEAGULLS

Consider the following parable: It so happens that the only flying animals known to the inhabitants of a large Nordic island are seagulls. Everyone on the island acknowledges, of course, that seagulls can fly. One day the two resident philosophers on the island are overheard trying to pin down what 'flying' is really all about.

Says the first philosopher, 'The essence of flying is to move through the air.'

'But you would hardly call this flying, would you?' replies the second, tossing a pebble from the beach out into the ocean.

'Well then, perhaps it means to remain aloft for a certain amount of time.'

'But clouds and smoke and children's balloons remain aloft for a very long time. And I can certainly keep a kite in the air as long as I want on a windy day. It seems to me that there must be more to flying than merely staying aloft.'

'Maybe it involves having wings and feathers.'

'Penguins have both, and we all know how well they fly ... '.

And so on. Finally, they decide to settle the question by, in effect, avoiding it. They do this by first agreeing that the only examples of objects that they are absolutely certain can fly are the seagulls that populate their island. They do, however, agree that flight has something to do with being airborne and that physical features such as feathers, beaks, and hollow bones probably are superficial aspects of flight. On the basis of these assumptions and their knowledge of Alan Turing's famous article about a test for intelligence, they hit upon the Seagull Test for flight. The Seagull Test is meant to be a very rigorous sufficient condition for flight. Henceforth, if someone says, 'I have invented a machine that can fly', instead of attempting to apply any set of flight-defining criteria to the inventor's machine, they will put it to the Seagull Test. The *only* things that they will certify with absolute confidence as being able to fly are those that can pass the Seagull Test. On the other hand, they agree that if something fails the Test, they will not pass judgement; maybe it can fly, maybe it can not.

The Seagull Test works much like the Turing Test. Our philosophers have two three-dimensional radar screens, one of which tracks a real seagull; the other will track the putative flying machine. They may run any imaginable experiment on the two objects in an attempt to determine which is the seagull and which is the machine, but they may watch them only on their radar screens. The machine will be said to have passed the Seagull Test for flight if both philosophers are indefinitely unable to distinguish the seagull from the machine.

An objection might be raised that some of their tests (for example, testing for the ability to dip in flight) might have nothing to do with flying. The philosophers would reply: 'So what? We are looking for a sufficient condition for flight, not a *minimal* sufficient condition. Furthermore, we understand that ours is a very hard test to pass, but rest assured, inventors of flying machines, failing the Test proves nothing. We will not claim that your machine *cannot* fly if it fails the Seagull Test; it may very well be able to. However we, as philosophers, want to be absolutely certain we have a true case of flight, and the only way we can be sure of this is if your machine passes the Seagull Test.'

Now, of course, the Seagull Test will rightly take bullets, soap bubbles, and snowballs out of the running. This is certainly as it should be. But helicopters and jet airplanes—which *do* fly—would also never pass it. Nor, for that matter, would bats or beetles, albatrosses or hummingbirds. In fact, under close scrutiny, probably only seagulls would pass the Seagull Test, and maybe only seagulls from the philosophers' Nordic island, at that. What we have is thus not a test for flight at all, but rather a test for flight as practised by a Nordic seagull.

For the Turing Test, the implications of this metaphor are clear: an entity could conceivably be extremely intelligent but, if it did not respond to the interrogator's questions in a thoroughly human way, it would not pass the Test. The *only* way, I believe, that it would have been able to respond the questions in a perfectly human-like manner is to have experienced the world as humans have. What we have is thus not a test for intelligence at all, but rather a test for intelligence as practised by a human being.

Furthermore, the Turing Test admits of no degrees in its sufficient determination of intelligence, in spite of the fact that the intuitive human notion of intelligence clearly does. Spiders, for example, have little intelligence, sparrows have more but not as much as dogs, monkeys have still more but not as much as eight-year-old humans, who in turn have less than adults. If we agree that the underlying neural mechanisms are essentially the same across species, then we ought to treat intelligence as a continuum and not just as something that only humans have. It seems reasonable to ask a good test for intelligence to reflect, if only approximately, those differences in degree. It is especially important in the study of artificial intelligence that researchers not treat intelligence as an all-or-nothing phenomenon.

SUBCOGNITIVE QUESTIONS

Before beginning the discussion of subcognitive questions, I wish to make a few assumptions that I feel certain Turing would have accepted. First, I will allow the interrogator to poll humans for the answers to some of the questions prior to posing them during the imitation game itself. (I will call the humans who are polled the 'interviewees'.) I also want to make explicit an assumption that is tacit in Turing's article, namely that the human candidate and the interrogator (and, in this case, the interviewees) are all from the same culture and that the computer will be attempting to pass as an individual from that culture. Thus, if ever the computer replies, 'I don't speak English' or something of the sort, the interrogator will immediately deduce, rightly, that the other candidate is the human being. Finally, while I believe that it is *theoretically* possible to build a machine capable of experiencing the world in a manner indistinguishable from a human being—a machine that can fall off bicycles, be scratched by thorns on roses, smell sewage, and taste strawberries—I will assume that no computer is now, or will in the foreseeable future be, in a position to do so.

I will designate as *subcognitive* any question capable of providing a window on low-level (i.e., unconscious) cognitive structure. By 'low-level cognitive structure' I am referring, in particular, to the subconscious associative network in human minds that consists of highly overlapping activatable representations of experience. This is the level currently being explored by new approaches to cognitive modelling.[4]

The first class of questions is explicitly designed to reveal low-level cognitive structure (and I think everyone will agree that they do so). I will respond to the anticipated objection that these explicitly subcognitive questions are unfair by following up with another set of questions that seem, at first glance, to be at a higher cognitive level than the first set. These questions will turn out, under closer examination, to be subcognitive also. I will conclude with a final set of questions that seem incontestably to be innocent high-level cognitive questions but that will be just as hard as the others were for the computer to answer in the way a human would.

ASSOCIATIVE PRIMING

This first set of questions is based on current research on associative priming, often called semantic facilitation. The idea is the following. Humans, over the course of their lives, develop certain associations of varying strength among concepts. By means of the so-called lexical decision task it has been established[5] that it requires less time to decide that a given item is a word when that item is preceded by an associated word. If, for example, the item 'butter' is preceded by the word 'bread', it would take significantly less time to recognize that 'butter' was a word than had an unassociated word like 'dog' or a nonsense word preceded it.

The Turing Test interrogator makes use of this phenomenon as follows. The day before the Test, she selects a set of words (and non-words), runs the lexical decision task on the interviewees and records average recognition times. She then comes to the Test armed with the results of this initial test, asks both candidates to perform the same task she ran the day before, and records the results. Once this has been done, she identifies as the human being the candidate whose results more closely resemble the average results produced by her sample population of interviewees.

The machine would invariably fail this type of test because there is no a priori way of determining associative strengths (i.e., a measure of how easy it is for one concept to activate another) between *all* possible concepts. Virtually the only way a machine could determine, even on average, all of the associative strengths between human concepts is to have experienced the world as the human candidate and the interviewees had.

A further example might help to illustrate the enormous problem of establishing the associative weights between concepts in an a priori manner. Certain groups of concepts, say, the steps in baking a cake, are profoundly sequential in nature. The associative strengths between sequentially related concepts involved in baking a cake (opening the flour bin, breaking the eggs, mixing the flour and eggs, putting the mixture in the oven, setting the oven temperature, removing a baked cake) are profoundly dependent on the human experience of cake-baking. Even if we made the assumption that concepts like 'removing a cake from an oven', 'breaking eggs', 'setting oven temperature', and so on could be explicitly programmed into our computer, the associative strengths among these concepts would have to reflect the temporal order in which they normally occurred in human experience if the machine were to pass the Turing Test. We would have to be able to set these strengths in an a priori manner, not only for category sequences associated with cake-baking, but also between the concepts of *all* the concept sequences experienced by humans. While this may be theoretically possible, it would certainly seem to be very implausible.

Now, suppose a critic claims that these explicitly subcognitive questions are unfair because—ostensibly, at least—they have nothing to do with intelligence; they probe, the critic says, a cognitive level well below that necessary for intelligence and therefore they should be disallowed. Suppose, then, that we obligingly disallow such questions and propose in their stead a new set of questions that seem, at first glance, to be at a higher cognitive level.

RATING GAMES

Neologisms will form the basis of the next set of questions, which we might call the Neologism Rating Game. Our impressions involving made-up words provide particularly impressive examples of the 'unbelievable number of forces and factors that interact in our unconscious processing of even . . . words and names only a few letters long'.[6]

Consider the following set of questions, all having a totally high-level cognitive appearance:

On a scale of 0 (completely implausible) to 10 (completely plausible), please rate:

- 'Flugblogs' as a name Kellogg's would give to a new breakfast cereal
- 'Flugblogs' as the name of a new computer company
- 'Flugblogs' as the name of big, air-filled bags worn on the feet and used to walk on water
- 'Flugly' as the name a child might give its favourite teddy bear
- 'Flugly' as the surname of a bank accountant in a W. C. Fields movie
- 'Flugly' as the surname of a glamorous female movie star

The interrogator will give, say, between fifty and one hundred questions of this sort to her interviewees,[7] who will answer them. Then, as before, she will give the same set of questions to the two candidates and compare their results to her interviewees' averaged answers. The candidate whose results most closely resemble the answers given by the polled group will almost certainly be the human.

Let us examine a little more closely why a computer that had not acquired our full set of cultural associations would fail this test. Consider 'Flugblogs' as the name of a breakfast cereal. It is unquestionably pretty awful. The initial syllable 'flug' phonetically activates (unconsciously, of course) such things as 'flub', 'thug', 'ugly', or 'ugh!', each with its own aura of semantic connotations. 'Blogs', the second syllable, activates 'blob', 'bog', and other words, which in turn activate a halo of other semantic connotations. The sum total of this spreading activation determines how we react, at a conscious level, to the word. And while there will be no precise set of associated connotations for all individuals across a culture, on the whole there is enough overlap to provoke *similar* reactions to given words and phrases. In this case, the emergent result of these activations is undeniable: 'Flugblogs' would be a lousy name for a cereal (unless, of course, the explicit *intent* of the manufacturer is to come up with a perverse-sounding cereal name!)

What about 'Flugly' as a name a child might give its favourite teddy bear? Now *that* certainly sounds plausible. In fact, it's kind of cute. But, on the surface at least, 'Flugblogs' and 'Flugly' seem to have quite a bit in common; if nothing else, both words have a common first syllable. But 'Flugly', unlike 'Flugblogs', almost certainly activates 'snugly' and 'cuddly', which would bring to mind feelings of cosiness, warmth, and friendship. It certainly also activates 'ugly', which might normally provoke a rather negative feeling, but, in this case, there are competing positive associations of vulnerability and endearment activated by the notion of children and things that children like. To see this, we need look no further than the tale of the Ugly Duckling. In the end, the positive associations seem to dominate the unpleasant sense of 'ugly'. The outcome of this subcognitive competition means that 'Flugly' is perceived by us as being a cute, quite plausible name for a child's teddy bear. And yet, different patterns of activations rule out 'Flugly' as a plausible name for a glamorous female movie star.

Imagine, for an instant, what it would take for a computer to pass this test. To begin with, there is no way it could look up words like 'Flugly' and 'Flugblogs': they do not exist. To judge the appropriateness of any given word (or, in this case, nonsense words) in a particular context requires taking unconscious account of a vast number of culturally acquired, competing associations triggered initially by phonetic resemblances. And, even though one might succeed in giving a program a certain number of these associations (for example, by asking subjects questions similar to the ones above and then programming the results into the machine), the space of neologisms is virtually infinite. The human candidate's reaction to such made-up words is an emergent result of myriad subcognitive pressures, and unless the machine has a set of associations similar to those of humans both in degree and in kind, its performance in the Rating Game would necessarily differ more from the interviewees' averaged performance than would the human candidate's. Once again, a machine that had not experienced the world as we have would be unmasked by the Rating Game, even though the questions comprising it seemed, at least at the outset, so cognitively high-level in nature.

If, for some reason, the critics were still unhappy with the Neologism Rating Game using made-up words, we could consider a variation on the game, the Category Rating Game,[8] in which all of the questions would have the form: 'Rate Xs as Ys' (0 = 'could be no worse', 10 = 'could be no better') where X and Y are any two categories. Such questions give every appearance of being high-level cognitive questions: they are simple in the extreme and rely not on neologisms but on everyday words. For example, we might have, 'Rate *dry leaves* as *hiding places*'. Now, clearly no definition of 'dry leaves' will ever include the fact that piles of dry autumn leaves are wonderful places for children to hide in and, yet, few among us would not make that association upon seeing the juxtaposition of those two concepts. There is therefore some overlap, however implausible this might seem a priori, between the categories of 'dry leaves' and 'hiding places'. We might give dry leaves a rating of, say, 4 on a 10-point scale. Or, another example, 'Rate *radios* as *musical instruments*'. As in the previous example, people do not usually think of radios as musical instruments, but they do indeed have some things in common with musical instruments: both make sounds; both are designed to be listened to; John Cage once wrote a piece in which radios were manipulated by performers; etc. Once again, therefore, there is some overlapping of these two categories; as a musical instrument, therefore, we might give a radio a rating of 3 or even 4 on a 10-point scale.

The answer to any particular rating question is necessarily based on how we view the two categories involved, each with its full panoply of associations, acquired through experience, with other categories. A list of such questions might include:

- 'Rate *banana splits* as *medicine*'
- 'Rate *grand pianos* as *wheelbarrows*'
- 'Rate *purses* as *weapons*'
- 'Rate *pens* as *weapons*'
- 'Rate *jackets* as *blankets*'
- 'Rate *pine boughs* as *mattresses*'

Just as before, it would be virtually impossible to explicitly program into the machine all the various types and degrees of associations necessary to answer these questions like a human.

Other variations of the Rating Game could be invented that would have the same effect. We could, for example, have a Poetic Beauty Rating Game where we would ask for ratings of beauty of various lines of poetry.[9] For a computer to do as well as a human on this test, it would either have to have experienced our life and language *as we had* or contain a theory of poetic beauty that included necessary and sufficient conditions for what constituted a beautiful line of poetry. Few would seriously argue that such an experience-independent theory was possible.

Or a Joke Rating Game: 'On a scale of 0 to 10 rate how funny you find each of the following jokes' followed by a list of jokes. Again, capturing the necessary and sufficient conditions for humour would seem to require a grounding in all of human experience. Most jokes depend on a vast network of associative world knowledge ranging from the most ridiculous trivia, through common but little-commented-upon aspects of human experience, to the most significant information about current events. So here again is an example of where a computer, in order to appreciate humour as we did and thereby fool the Turing Test interrogator, would almost certainly have had to experience life and language as we had.

A final variation: The Advertising Rating Game. 'Given the following product: X, rate the following advertising slogan Y for that product. Once again, it is hard to imagine any theory that could provide necessary and sufficient conditions for catchy advertising slogans. Good advertising slogans, like good jokes and good lines of poetry, are perceived as good because of the myriad subconscious pressures and associations gathered in a lifetime of experiencing the world.

THE IMPOSSIBILITY OF ISOLATING THE PHYSICAL LEVEL FROM THE COGNITIVE LEVEL

One of the tacit assumptions on which Turing's proposed test rests is that it is possible to isolate the 'mere' (and thus unimportant to the essence of cognition) physical level from the (essential) cognitive level. This is the reason, for example, that the candidates communicate with the interrogator by teletype, that the interrogator is not permitted to see them, and so on. Subcognitive questions, however, will always allow the interrogator to 'peek behind the screen'. The Turing Test is really probing the associative concept (and sub-concept) networks of the two candidates. These networks are the product of a lifetime of interaction with the world which *necessarily involves* human sense organs, their location on the body, their sensitivity to various stimuli, etc. Consider, for example, a being that resembled us precisely in all physical respects except that its eyes were attached to its knees. This physical difference alone would engender enormous differences in its associative concept network compared to our own. Bicycle riding, crawling on the floor, wearing various articles of clothing (e.g., long pants), and negotiating crowded hallways would all be experienced in a vastly different way by this individual.

The result would be an associative concept network that would be significantly—and detectably by the Turing Test—different from our own. Thus, while no one would claim that the physical location of eyes had anything essential to do with intelligence, a Turing Test could certainly distinguish this individual from a normal human being. The moral of the story is that the physical level is *not* dissociable from the cognitive level. When Dreyfus says that no one expects an intelligent robot to be able to 'get across a busy street. It must only compete in the more objective and disembodied areas of human behaviour, so as to be able to win at Turing's game',[10] he, like Turing, is tacitly accepting that such a separation of the physical and the cognitive levels is indeed possible. This may have seemed to be the case at first glance but further examination shows that the two are inextricably intertwined.

CAN THE TURING TEST BE APPROPRIATELY MODIFIED?

Any reasonable set of questions in a Turing Test will necessarily contain subcognitive questions in some form or another. Ask enough of these questions and the computer will become distinguishable from the human because its associative concept network would necessarily be unlike ours. And thus the computer would fail the Turing Test.

Is it possible to modify the rules of the Turing Test in such a way that subcognitive questions are forbidden? I think not. The answers to subcognitive questions emerge from a lifetime of experience with the minutiae of existence, ranging from functionally adaptive world-knowledge to useless trivia. The sum total of this experience with its extraordinarily complex interrelations is what defines human intelligence and this is what Turing's imitation game tests for. What we would really like is a test for (or, lacking that, a theory of) intelligence *in general*. Surely, we would not want to limit a Turing Test to questions like, 'What is the capital of France?' or 'How many sides does a triangle have?' If we admit that intelligence in general must have *something* to do with categorization, analogy-making, and so on, we will of course want to ask questions that test these capacities. But these are the very questions that will allow us, unfailingly, to unmask the computer.

THE RELEVANCE OF SUBCOGNITIVE FACTORS

There remains the question of the *relevance* of these subcognitive factors that, as I believe I have shown, make it essentially impossible for a machine that has not experienced the world as we have to pass the Turing Test. Are these factors irrelevant to intelligence—just as a seagull's dipping in flight is irrelevant to flying in general— or are they a necessary substrate of intelligence? An initial part of my response is that a *human* subcognitive substrate is definitely not necessary to intelligence in general. The Turing Test tests precisely for the presence of a human subcognitive substrate and this is why it is limited as a test for general intelligence.

On the other hand, I believe that *some* subcognitive substrate is necessary to intelligence. I will not present a detailed defence of this view in this paper for two reasons: first, such a defence is beyond the scope of this paper, the goal of which has only been to discuss the limits of the Turing Test as a tool for determining intelligence, and second, the necessity of a subcognitive substrate for intelligence has been compellingly argued elsewhere.[11] Some ideas of the defence will, however, be briefly presented below.

There is little question that intelligence relies on an extraordinarily complex network of concepts with various degrees of overlap. Philosophers from Wittgenstein[12] to Lakoff[13] have shown that the boundaries of concepts are extraordinarily elusive things to pin down. It is probably impossible, even in principle, to describe categories in an absolute, objective manner. 'Apples', for example, are almost always members of the category 'food', but what about 'grass', or 'shoes'? If you have not eaten for ten days, 'shoes' might well fall into your category of 'food'. But could something like 'the Spanish Inquisition' ever be considered 'food'? (Of course. Consider the following statement by a professor about to give an extraordinarily long lecture on medieval methods of torture: 'The meat of the first three hours of this lecture will be medieval torture in general. And if none of you has fallen asleep by then, we'll have the Spanish Inquisition for dessert.'[14]) This is not a point to be taken lightly, for the associative overlap of categories essential to intelligence (and creativity) frequently occurs near the blurry boundaries of categories. And, to repeat, these boundaries are virtually impossible to define in an objective, context-independent way. Most of our thought processes are intimately tied to the associative overlap of categories. One particular example is analogy-making. Considered by many to be a *sine qua non* of intelligent behaviour, it relies heavily on the ability to see two apparently unrelated situations as members, however obliquely, of the same category.

If we can view categories as being composed of many tiny (subcognitive) parts that can overlap with the subcognitive parts of other categories, we can go a long way to explaining these associative phenomena. If, on the other hand, we deny the relevance of subcognitive factors in intelligence, we are left with the daunting, perhaps impossible, task of explicitly defining *all* of the possible attributes of each particular category in every conceivable context. It is, therefore reasonable to conclude that all intelligence has a subcognitive substrate. In particular, this implies that an intelligent computer would have to possess such a substrate, though there is no reason to believe that this substrate would be identical to our own.

CONCLUSION

In conclusion, the imitation game proposed by Alan Turing provides a very powerful means of probing human-like cognition. But when the Test is actually used as a real test for intelligence, as certain philosophers propose, its very strength becomes a weakness. Turing invented the imitation game only as a novel way of looking at the question 'Can machines think?' But it turns out to be so powerful that it is really asking: 'Can machines think exactly like human beings?' As a real test for intelligence, the latter question is significantly less interesting than the former. The Turing Test provides a sufficient condition for human intelligence but does not address the more important issue of intelligence in general.

I have tried to show that only a computer that had acquired adult human intelligence by experiencing the world as we have could pass the Turing Test. In addition, I feel that any attempt to 'fix' the Turing Test so that it could test for intelligence in general and not just human intelligence is doomed to failure because of the completely interwoven and interdependent nature of the human physical, subcognitive, and cognitive levels. To gain insight into intelligence, we will be forced to consider it in the more elusive terms of the ability to categorize, to generalize, to make analogies, to learn, and so on. It is with respect to these abilities that the computer will always be unmasked if it has not experienced the world as a human being has.[15]

NOTES

1   Alan M. Turing, 'Computing machinery and intelligence', *Mind*, 1950, pp. 433–60.
2   For a particularly clear defence of this view see the previous chapter by Daniel Dennett, 'Can Machines Think?'.
3   Hubert L. Dreyfus, *What Computers Can't Do*, New York, Harper & Row, 1979, p. 73.
4   Three different approaches that all address subcognitive issues can be found in: J. Feldman and F. Ballard, 'Connectionist models and their properties', *Cognitive Science*, 1982, pp. 205–54; D. R. Hofstadter, M. Mitchell, and R. M. French, 'Fluid concepts and creative analogies: A theory and its computer implementation', CSMIL Technical Report No. 10, University of Michigan, 1987; D. Rumelhart and J. McClelland (eds), *Parallel Distributed Processing*, Cambridge, MA, Bradford/MIT Press, 1986.
5   A particularly relevant, succinct discussion of associative priming can be found in: J. R. Anderson, *The Architecture of Cognition*, Cambridge, MA, Harvard University Press, 1983, ch. 3. pp. 86–125. In this chapter Anderson makes reference to the classic work on facilitation by Meyer and Schvaneveldt (D. E. Meyer and R. W. Schvaneveldt, 'Facilitation in recognizing pairs of words: evidence of a dependence between retrieval operations', *Journal of Experimental Psychology*, 1971, pp. 227–34).
6   D. R. Hofstadter, 'On the seeming paradox of mechanizing creativity', in *Metamagical Themas*, New York, Basic Books, Inc., 1985, pp. 526–46.
7   Even though Turing did not impose a time constraint in his original formulation of the imitation game, he did claim that ' ... in fifty years' time [i.e., by the year 2000] it will be possible to programme computers ... to make them play the imitation game so well that an average interrogator will not have more than 70 per cent chance of making the right identification after five minutes of questioning' (p. 442). In current discussions of the Turing Test, the duration of the questioning period is largely ignored. In my opinion, one reasonable extension of the Turing Test would include the length of the questioning period as one of its parameters. In keeping with the spirit of the original claim involving a five-minute questioning period, I have tried to keep the number of questions short although it was by no means necessary to have done so.
8   This variation of the Rating Game was suggested to me by Douglas Hofstadter.

9 In fact, the interrogator in Turning's original article does indeed conduct a line of questioning about a particular turn of phrase in one of Shakespeare's sonnets.
10 Dreyfus, op. cit., p. 78.
11 Hofstadter, op. cit. 'Waking Up from the Boolean Dream or, Subcognition as Computation', pp. 631–65.
12 Ludwig Wittgenstein, *Philosophical Investigations*, New York, Macmillian Publishing Co., 1958.
13 George Lakoff, *Women, Fire and Dangerous Things*, Chicago, The University of Chicago Press, 1987.
14 This example is due to Peter Suber.
15 I especially wish to thank Daniel Dennett and Douglas Hofstadter for their invaluable comments on the ideas and emphasis of this paper. I would also like to thank David Chalmers, Melanie Mitchell, David Moser, and the editor of *Mind* for their remarks.

Part 9

IS THERE INTELLIGENT LIFE ON OTHER PLANETS?

As you read this, astronomers are combing the cosmos for indications of extra-terrestrial intelligent life. This search expends immense resources. Some of these resources come from private donors; some from universities such as The Ohio State University, UC – Berkeley, and Harvard; some from government agencies like NASA. Over the past several decades, enormous sums of money, billions of computer hours, and thousands of individuals have contributed to the hunt for E.T.s. But what, exactly, does this search assume about the nature of minds?

Some of the philosophical questions that S.E.T.I. – the Search for Extra-Terrestrial Intelligence – raises are similar to those we saw in the sections on animal minds and artificial intelligence. The judgment that animals or computers have minds requires a decision about what counts as a mind. Lacking criteria for separating things with minds from things without, no such decision is justifiable. But consider some of the criteria that we have already examined. Jonathan Bennett argues that attributions of mental states are warranted just in case they unify behavior that would otherwise appear disjointed. John Dupré suggests that observable behavior is in some sense constitutive of the mind, and that mentalistic predicates – like 'believes that Madison sits on an isthmus', 'is in pain', 'is happy to see me' – owe their correct application to the behavior of their intended subjects. Turing proposed that anything that could engage in a credible conversation should count as intelligent.

Yet, whatever you think of the merits of these various ideas, it is clear that S.E.T.I. is in no position to avail itself of any of them. To date, the search for E.T.s has limited itself to a search for radio or laser signals. Radio and optical telescopes are trained on the heavens in search of … what? Certainly these telescopes will not yield observations of behavior that is best unified under a mentalistic explanation. They cannot perceive individuals' behavior at all. Moreover, they are in no position to conduct a conversation with anyone.

Of course, these telescopes have their sights set on the discovery of a coded message that leaves no doubt of the intelligence of its author. But what would indicate intelligence? In some respects, this issue has an analogue in the contemporary dispute between evolutionists and supporters of creationism or intelligent design theory. Creationists and intelligent design theorists look at the world and see evidence of an intelligent designer. For example, they believe that the complexity and obvious functionality of the eye is indisputable proof of a god, or a designer with godly powers. In fact, the reasoning behind these conclusions is seriously flawed (see Sober 2000, ch. 2), but we see in this dispute a return to our old question: what does count as evidence of intelligence?

Just as resolving questions about animal and computer minds will require both empirical investigation and philosophical analysis, evaluating the likelihood of success in the search for extra-terrestrial intelligence will require both an examination of the universe and philosophical reflection about intelligence and mentality.

The brief articles by Robert Naeye, Carl Sagan, and Ernst Mayr wrestle with the empirical issues. From a philosopher's perspective, as Neil Tennant's article makes plain, the empirical issues turn out to be largely beside the point. If Tennant's argument is correct, there may well be extra-terrestrial intelligence, but the assumption that we can ever learn anything about these E.T.s, beyond the simple fact that they exist, Tennant believes, is hopelessly, perhaps even foolishly, naive. When reading the empirical papers, it is useful to try to anticipate the philosophical assumptions that Tennant believes their authors are overlooking or underestimating.

Naeye's article provides a description of the famous Drake equation, named after the astronomer Frank Drake. Drake's intent was to introduce the various factors that must figure into a calculation of the probability that an extra-terrestrial intelligence could be discovered. Drake was, then, less interested in whether intelligent E.T.s exist than in whether we could *know* of their existence. Among the parameters that Drake thought must be measured are the number of stars in the galaxy with planets, the proportion of habitable planets on which life develops, the proportion of life-bearing planets with civilizations that have the capacity for interstellar communication, and the lifetime of these civilizations. To philosophically sensitive ears (as we hope by now yours are), Drake's failure to say anything about what communication consists in or whether communication is even possible between completely different races, is jarring.

Sagan, perhaps the twentieth century's best-known astronomer, and Mayr, one of the greatest evolutionary biologists since Darwin, go head to head on which values to plug into the parameters of the Drake equation. Mayr believes that astronomers have failed to appreciate the extraordinary improbability of events that have resulted in human civilization. Life, Mayr believes, can exist in only a narrow range of temperatures and in particular kinds of atmospheres. This means that any planet capable of supporting life must orbit a star similar in size to the sun, at a distance comparable to that of the Earth from the sun. The planet must also have a mass roughly equivalent to Earth's, so that its gravitational force is adequate to hold an atmosphere but not so strong as to make the evolution of life impossible. Moreover, Mayr contends, water must be present on this planet. Because the probabilities of each of these events must be multiplied with the probability of the others, the total probability of the existence of life-bearing planets diminishes with each additional condition for life.

But, Mayr continues, even if life does exist elsewhere in the galaxy, there is no reason to believe that evolution will produce *intelligent* life. Evolution is not end-directed, it is not progressive. This means that intelligence is not an inevitable feature of a species just "given enough time." Indeed, Mayr suggests that intelligence is not a trait of great adaptive value. He estimates that as many as fifty billion species have evolved on Earth, and yet only one has followed a path that produced a species with intelligence sufficient for interstellar communication.

In contrast to Mayr's pessimism, Sagan offers a rosy estimation of the probability that there is extra-terrestrial intelligence and of our chances of discovering it. Sagan believes that the evolution of life, and intelligent life at that, is practically inevitable on planets with conditions like those present on Earth. Moreover, by his calculations, there is a huge number of such planets. But why believe that the intelligent civilizations on these planets will have invented the means for interstellar communication? Because, Sagan confidently asserts, if they are old civilizations then they must have acquired the ability to avoid collisions with deadly asteroids, and this ability would have produced the technology for interstellar communication as a byproduct.

Missing from this dispute between Mayr and Sagan is any concern for what E.T. intelligence might be like. Would an E.T. have any interest in communicating with beings on other planets? Again, it pays to reflect on issues that surfaced in the sections on animal and artificial minds. Is S.E.T.I. guilty of a kind of anthropomorphism? Human beings, apparently, have a deep curiosity about the possibility of extra-terrestrial intelligence. But why assume that extra-terrestrials, if there were any, would have a similar curiosity? Perhaps human beings are unique in their desire to know whether they are alone in the universe. Recall as well Robert French's criticism of the Turing test. The test is chauvinistic to the extent that it recognizes intelligence only in the ability to carry on a human conversation. Perhaps there are E.T.s aplenty, but they are so marvelously different from human beings that we could never possibly engage in conversation. One might even suppose that these E.T.s are intent on communicating with alien civilizations. However, why should we suppose that the series of blips and bleeps that we might one day detect with a powerful telescope is humanly interpretable?

Tennant, in his article, pursues issues surrounding this last question. To understand Tennant's concerns, consider a *terrestrial* code that has never been broken. The Minoan civilization lived on the island of Crete until about 1400 b.c.e. The Minoans left fragments of a language that is called simply Linear A. No one has been able to decipher this language, despite decades of attempts using sophisticated computer analyses and other techniques that led to the successful translation of closely related languages.

And linguists attempting to decipher Linear A have resources unavailable to those seeking to translate an alien communication. First, linguists know that Linear A is a language. That is, they know it is a system of symbols that has been created for the purpose of communication. They know this, in part, because it is similar to other languages that they have decoded. Another indication that Linear A is a language is that it appears in places where one would ordinarily find linguistic script. Furthermore, linguists know a great deal about Minoan culture. They know the sorts of goods that Minoans traded with other civilizations, and they are familiar with Minoan religious practices, Minoan government, and so on. This understanding of Minoan culture provides markers, i.e. indications of what the language was likely to be describing, that can be used to facilitate the translation of Linear A. But even more basic to the task of translation than these facts about Minoan civilization is the fact that Minoans were human beings. Their writing would have reflected human thoughts, human beliefs, and information gathered from human sensory organs. Whatever the Minoans wrote about, we can be absolutely confident that it was humanly conceivable.

Now contrast the situation of Linear A with an alien code. As Tennant points out, a series of blips and bleeps does not wear its linguistic nature on its sleeve (so to speak). How do we know the transmission is a transmission at all rather than some deep space noise? Assuming that we are correct that the blips and bleeps are a transmission, how do we know it is linguistic? Assuming that we know it is linguistic, on what facts about E.T. culture can we depend to begin a translation? We know nothing about alien culture; nothing about alien sensory perception; nothing about alien concerns. At most, Tennant argues, we can judge that the transmissions come from some kind of intelligence. Any knowledge beyond that, however, is beyond us. Accordingly, Tennant concludes, the search for extra-terrestrial intelligence is hardly worth the bother.

QUESTIONS TO THINK ABOUT:

1 Sagan accuses Mayr of dismissing the tenability of S.E.T.I. by means of an *a priori* argument. An *a priori* argument is one that proceeds without the benefit of empirical facts. Is Mayr making an *a priori* argument? And if he is, is that method objectionable in this context?

2 Both Mayr and Sagan suggest that the evolution of intelligent life requires conditions like those present on Earth. Why do they believe this? How could we determine whether it was possible for intelligence to evolve in different conditions? In what sense might it be impossible? Do you think that there is an interesting relationship between the kinds of conditions in which intelligence might evolve and our ability to communicate with that intelligence?

3 Imagine that you have discovered some scribbling on a wall of a cave that bears no resemblance to any known languages. What steps would you need to take in order to translate it?

4 Naeye ends his account of the Drake equation with the thought that we are probably the only intelligent civilization in the galaxy. On what is this belief based, and how would Tennant respond to Naeye's reasoning?

REFERENCES

Sober, E. (2000). *Philosophy of Biology, 2nd ed*. (Boulder, CO: Westview Press).

FURTHER READING

Basalla, G. (2006). *Civilized Life in the Universe: Scientists on Intelligent Extraterrestrials* (New York: Oxford University Press).

Shostak, S. and Barnett, A. (2003). *Cosmic Company: The Search for Life in the Universe* (New York: Cambridge University Press).

Ward, P. and Brownlee, D. (2000). *Rare Earth: Why Complex Life is Uncommon in the Universe* (New York: Springer-Verlag).

41

THE DRAKE EQUATION

Robert Naeye

$$N = R^* \times f_p \times n_e \times f_l \times f_i \times f_c \times L$$

astronomical   biological   cultural

During a 1961 conference in Green Bank, West Virginia, radio astronomer Frank Drake unveiled his famous equation. The Drake Equation gives scientists a frame of reference for calculating the number of communicating civilizations in our galaxy, a number represented by the letter N. The equation consists of astronomical, biological, and cultural parameters as shown above.

$R^* =$ the rate of star formation (per year) in the Milky Way Galaxy
$f_p =$ the fraction of stars that have planets
$n_e =$ the average number of habitable (i.e. Earthlike) planets per system
$f_l =$ the fraction of habitable planets on which life actually develops
$f_i =$ the fraction of life-bearing planets on which intelligent life evolves
$f_c =$ the fraction of those planets on which civilizations arise that engage in interstellar communication
$L =$ the average lifetime in years of communicating civilizations

Unfortunately, with the exception of R_*, the values of the parameters are unknown, leading to wildly different estimates for N. Some scientists believe that multiplying all of the factors up to L yields a value of 1, so the value of N equals the value of L.

But I like to point to the fact that if one uses the Eiffel Tower to represent the 3.8 billion years that life has existed on Earth, the amount of time that a civilization capable of interstellar communication has been on Earth would be the layer of paint at the top. Given this sobering reality, the only way that multiple civilizations can exist in the galaxy simultaneously is if L is in the realm of hundreds of millions or billions of years. Otherwise, civilizations will flicker in and out of existence like fire-flies in the night, to paraphrase Arthur C. Clarke.

If L is large, however, we should have ample evidence of ET's existence, because given the enormous time scales involved, at least some advanced civilizations are not going to sit around their home planet – they will figure out how to engage in inter-stellar travel, and then they will venture outward and explore the Galaxy. Given the lack of evidence for ET, my gut feeling is that one of the terms of the Drake Equation (perhaps f_i) is very, very small, which means N is very small and possibly even 1: us.

42

CAN SETI SUCCEED? NOT LIKELY

Ernst Mayr

What is the chance of success in the search for extraterrestrial intelligence? The answer to this question depends on a series of probabilities. I have attempted to make a detailed analysis of this problem in a German publication (Mayr 1992) and shall attempt here to present in English the essential findings of this investigation. My methodology consists in asking a series of questions that narrow down the probability of success.

HOW PROBABLE IS IT THAT LIFE EXISTS SOMEWHERE ELSE IN THE UNIVERSE?

Even most skeptics of the SETI project will answer this question optimistically. Molecules that are necessary for the origin of life, such as amino acids and nucleic acids, have been identified in cosmic dust, together with other macromolecules, and so it would seem quite conceivable that life could originate elsewhere in the universe.

Some of the modern scenarios of the origin of life start out with even simpler molecules—a beginning that makes an independent origin of life even more probable. Such an independent origin of life, however, would presumably result in living entities that are drastically different from life on Earth.

WHERE CAN ONE EXPECT TO FIND SUCH LIFE?

Obviously, only on planets. Even though we have up to now secure knowledge only of the nine planets of our solar system, there is no reason to doubt that in all galaxies there must be millions if not billions of planets. The exact figure, for instance, for our own galaxy can only be guessed.

HOW MANY OF THESE PLANETS WOULD HAVE BEEN
SUITABLE FOR THE ORIGIN OF LIFE?

There are evidently rather narrow constraints for the possibility of the origin and maintenance of life on a planet. There has to be a favorable average temperature; the seasonal variation should not be too extreme; the planet must have a suitable distance from its sun; it must have the appropriate mass so that its gravity can hold an atmosphere; this atmosphere must have the right chemical composition to support early life; it must have the necessary consistency to protect the new life against ultraviolet and other harmful radiations; and there must be water on such a planet. In other words, all environmental conditions must be suitable for the origin and maintenance of life.

One of the nine planets of our solar system had the right kind of mixture of these factors. This, surely, was a matter of chance. What fraction of planets in other solar systems will have an equally suitable combination of environmental factors? Would it be one in 10, or one in 100, or one in 1,000,000? Which figure you choose depends on your optimism. It is always difficult to extrapolate from a single instance. This figure, however, is of some importance when you are dealing with the limited number of planets that can be reached by any of the SETI projects.

WHAT PERCENTAGE OF PLANETS ON WHICH LIFE HAS
ORIGINATED WILL PRODUCE INTELLIGENT LIFE?

Physicists, on the whole, will give a different answer to this question than biologists. Physicists still tend to think more deterministically than biologists. They tend to say, if life has originated somewhere, it will also develop intelligence in due time. The biologist, on the other hand, is impressed by the improbability of such a development.

Life originated on Earth about 3.8 billion years ago, but high intelligence did not develop until about half a million years ago. If Earth had been temporarily cooled down or heated up too much during these 3.8 billion years, intelligence would have never originated.

When answering this question, one must be aware of the fact that evolution never moves on a straight line toward an objective ("intelligence") as happens during a chemical process or as a result of a law of physics. Evolutionary pathways are highly complex and resemble more a tree with all of its branches and twigs.

After the origin of life, that is, 3.8 billion years ago, life on Earth consisted for 2 billion years only of simple prokaryotes, cells without an organized nucleus. These bacteria and their relatives developed surely 50 to 100 different (some perhaps very different) lineages, but, in this enormously long time, none of them led to intelligence. Owing to an astonishing, unique event that is even today only partially explained, about 1,800 million years ago the first eukaryote originated, a creature with a well organized nucleus and the other characteristics of "higher" organisms. From the rich world of the protists (consisting of only a single cell) there eventually originated three groups of multicellular organisms: fungi, plants and animals. But none of the millions of species of fungi and plants was able to produce intelligence.

The animals (Metazoa) branched out in the Precambrian and Cambrian time periods to about 60 to 80 lineages (phyla). Only a single one of them, that of the chordates, led eventually to genuine intelligence. The chordates are an old and well diversified group, but only one of its numerous lineages, that of the vertebrates, eventually produced intelligence. Among the vertebrates, a whole series of groups evolved—types of fishes, amphibians, reptiles, birds and mammals. Again only a single lineage, that of the mammals, led to high intelligence. The mammals had a long evolutionary history which began in the Triassic Period, more than 200 million years ago, but only in the latter part of the Tertiary Period—that is, some 15 to 20 million years ago—did higher intelligence originate in one of the circa 24 orders of mammals.

The elaboration of the brain of the hominids began less than 3 million years ago, and that of the cortex of Homo sapiens occurred only about 300,000 years ago. Nothing demonstrates the improbability of the origin of high intelligence better than the millions of phyletic lineages that failed to achieve it.

How many species have existed since the origin of life? This figure is as much a matter of speculation as the number of planets in our galaxy. But if there are 30 million living species, and if the average life expectancy of a species is about 100,000 years, then one can postulate that there have been billions, perhaps as many as 50 billion species since the origin of life. Only one of these achieved the kind of intelligence needed to establish a civilization.

To provide exact figures is difficult because the range of variation both in the origination of species and in their life expectancy is so enormous. The widespread, populous species of long geological duration (millions of years), usually encountered by the paleontologist, are probably exceptional rather than typical.

WHY IS HIGH INTELLIGENCE SO RARE?

Adaptations that are favored by selection, such as eyes or bioluminescence, originate in evolution scores of times independently. High intelligence has originated only once, in human beings. I can think of only two possible reasons for this rarity. One is that high intelligence is not at all favored by natural selection, contrary to what we would expect. In fact, all the other kinds of living organisms, millions of species, get along fine without high intelligence.

The other possible reason for the rarity of intelligence is that it is extraordinarily difficult to acquire. Some grade of intelligence is found only among warm-blooded animals (birds and mammals), not surprisingly so because brains have extremely high energy requirements. But it is still a very big step from "some intelligence" to "high intelligence."

The hominid lineage separated from the chimpanzee lineage about 5 million years ago, but the big brain of modern man was acquired less than 300,000 years ago. As one scientist has suggested (Stanley 1992), it required complete emancipation from arboreal life to make the arms of the mothers available to carry the helpless babies during the final stages of brain growth. Thus, a large brain, permitting high intelligence, developed in less than the last 6 percent of the life on the hominid line. It seems that it requires a complex combination of rare, favorable circumstances to produce high intelligence (Mayr 1994).

HOW MUCH INTELLIGENCE IS NECESSARY TO PRODUCE A CIVILIZATION?

As stated, rudiments of intelligence are found already among birds (ravens, parrots) and among non-hominid mammals (carnivores, porpoises, monkeys, apes and so forth), but none of these instances of intelligence has been sufficient to found a civilization.

IS EVERY CIVILIZATION ABLE TO SEND SIGNALS INTO SPACE AND TO RECEIVE THEM?

The answer quite clearly is no. In the last 10,000 years there have been at least 20 civilizations on Earth, from the Indus, the Sumerian, and other near Eastern civilizations, to Egypt, Greece, and the whole series of European civilizations, to the Mayas, Aztecs, and Incas, and to the various Chinese and Indian civilizations. Only one of these reached a level of technology that has enabled them to send signals into space and to receive them.

WOULD THE SENSE ORGANS OF EXTRATERRESTRIAL BEINGS BE ADAPTED TO RECEIVE OUR ELECTRONIC SIGNALS?

This is by no means certain. Even on Earth many groups of animals are specialized for olfactory or other chemical stimuli and would not react to electronic signals. Neither plants nor fungi are able to receive electronic signals. Even if there were higher organisms on some planet, it would be rather improbable that they would have developed the same sense organs that we have.

HOW LONG IS A CIVILIZATION ABLE TO RECEIVE SIGNALS?

All civilizations have only a short duration. I will try to emphasize the importance of this point by telling a little fable.

Let us assume that there were really intelligent beings on another planet in our galaxy. A billion years ago their astronomers discovered Earth and reached the conclusion that this planet might have the proper conditions to produce intelligence. To test this, they sent signals to Earth for a billion years without ever getting an answer. Finally, in the year 1800 (of our calendar) they decided they would send signals only for another 100 years. By the year 1900, no answer had been received, so they concluded that surely there was no intelligent life on Earth.

This shows that even if there were thousands of civilizations in the universe, the probability of a successful communication would be extremely slight because of the short duration of the "open window."

One must not forget that the range of SETI systems is very limited, reaching only part of our galaxy. The fact that there are a near infinite number of additional galaxies in the universe is irrelevant as far as SETI projects are concerned.

CONCLUSIONS: AN IMPROBABILITY OF ASTRONOMIC DIMENSIONS

What conclusions must we draw from these considerations? No less than six of the eight conditions to be met for SETI success are highly improbable. When one multiplies these six improbabilities with each other, one reaches an improbability of astronomic dimensions.

WHY ARE THERE NEVERTHELESS STILL PROPONENTS OF SETI?

When one looks at their qualifications, one finds that they are almost exclusively astronomers, physicists and engineers. They are simply unaware of the fact that the success of any SETI effort is not a matter of physical laws and engineering capabilities but essentially a matter of biological and sociological factors. These, quite obviously, have been entirely left out of the calculations of the possible success of any SETI project.

43

THE ABUNDANCE OF
LIFE-BEARING PLANETS

Carl Sagan

We live in an age of remarkable exploration and discovery. Fully half of the nearby Sun-like stars have circumstellar disks of gas and dust like the solar nebula out of which our planets formed 4.6 billion years ago. By a most unexpected technique – radio timing residuals – we have discovered two Earth-like planets around the pulsar B1257+12. An apparent Jovian planet has been astrometrically detected around the star 51 Pegasi.

A range of new Earth-based and space-borne techniques—including astrometry, spectrophotometry, radial velocity measurements, adaptive optics and interferometry—all seem to be on the verge of being able to detect Jovian-type planets, if they exist, around the nearest stars. At least one proposal (The FRESIP (Frequency of Earth Sized Inner Planets) Project, a spaceborne spectrophotometric system) holds the promise of detecting terrestrial planets more readily than Jovian ones. If there is not a sudden cutoff in support, we are likely entering a golden age in the study of the planets of other stars in the Milky Way galaxy.

Once you have found another planet of Earth-like mass, however, it of course does not follow that it is an Earth-like world. Consider Venus. But there are means by which, even from the vantage point of Earth, we can investigate this question. We can look for the spectral signature of enough water to be consistent with oceans. We can look for oxygen and ozone in the planet's atmosphere. We can seek molecules like methane, in such wild thermodynamic disequilibrium with the oxygen that it can only be produced by life. (In fact, all of these tests for life were successfully performed by the Galileo spacecraft in its close approaches to Earth in 1990 and 1992 as it wended its way to Jupiter (Sagan *et al.* 1993).)

The best current estimates of the number and spacing of Earth-mass planets in newly forming planetary systems (as George Wetherill reported at the first international conference on circumstellar habitable zones (Doyle 1995)) combined with the best current estimates of the long-term stability of oceans on a variety of planets (as

James Kasting reported at that same meeting (Doyle 1995)) suggest one to two blue worlds around every Sun-like star. Stars much more massive than the Sun are comparatively rare and age quickly. Stars comparatively less massive than the Sun are expected to have Earth-like planets, but the planets that are warm enough for life are probably tidally locked so that one side always faces the local sun. However, winds may redistribute heat from one hemisphere to another on such worlds, and there has been very little work on their potential habitability.

Nevertheless, the bulk of the current evidence suggests a vast number of planets distributed through the Milky Way with abundant liquid water stable over lifetimes of billions of years. Some will be suitable for life—our kind of carbon and water life—for billions of years less than Earth, some for billions of years more. And, of course, the Milky Way is one of an enormous number, perhaps a hundred billion, other galaxies.

NEED INTELLIGENCE EVOLVE ON AN INHABITED WORLD?

We know from lunar cratering statistics, calibrated by returned Apollo samples, that Earth was under hellish bombardment by small and large worlds from space until around 4 billion years ago. This pummeling was sufficiently severe to drive entire atmospheres and oceans into space. Earlier, the entire crust of Earth was a magma ocean. Clearly, this was no breeding ground for life.

Yet, shortly thereafter—Mayr adopts the number 3.8 billion years ago—some early organisms arose (according to the fossil evidence). Presumably the origin of life had to have occupied some time before that. As soon as conditions were favorable, life began amazingly fast on our planet. I have used this fact (Sagan 1974) to argue that the origin of life must be a highly probable circumstance; as soon as conditions permit, up it pops!

Now, I recognize that this is at best a plausibility argument and little more than an extrapolation from a single example. But we are data constrained; it's the best we can do.

DOES A SIMILAR ANALYSIS APPLY TO THE EVOLUTION OF
INTELLIGENCE?

Here you have a planet burgeoning with life, profoundly changing the physical environment, generating an oxygen atmosphere 2 billion years ago, going through the elegant diversification that Mayr briefly summarized—and not for almost 4 billion years does anything remotely resembling a technical civilization emerge.

In the early days of such debates (for example, G.G. Simpson's *The Non-prevalence of Humanoids*) writers argued that an enormous number of individually unlikely steps were required to produce something very like a human being, a "humanoid"; that the chances of such a precise repetition occurring on another planet were nil; and therefore that the chance of extraterrestrial intelligence was nil. But clearly when we're talking about extraterrestrial intelligence, we are not talking—despite Star Trek—of humans or humanoids. We are talking about the functional equivalent of humans—say, any creatures able to build and operate radio telescopes. They may live on the land or in the sea or air. They may have unimaginable chemistries, shapes, sizes, colors, appendages and opinions. We are not requiring that they follow the particular route that led to the evolution of humans. There may be many different evolutionary pathways, each unlikely, but the sum of the number of pathways to intelligence may nevertheless be quite substantial.

In Mayr's current presentation, there is still an echo of "the non-prevalence of humanoids." But the basic argument is, I think, acceptable to all of us. Evolution is opportunistic and not foresighted. It does not "plan" to develop intelligent life a few billion years into the future. It responds to short-term contingencies. And yet, other things being equal, it is better to be smart than to be stupid, and an overall trend toward intelligence can be perceived in the fossil record. On some worlds, the selection pressure for intelligence may be higher; on others, lower.

If we consider the statistics of one, our own case—and take a typical time from the origin of a planetary system to the development of a technical civilization to be 4.6 billion years—what follows? We would not expect civilizations on different worlds to evolve in lock step. Some would reach technical intelligence more quickly, some more slowly, and—doubtless—some never. But the Milky Way is filled with second- and third-generation stars (that is, those with heavy elements) as old as 10 billion years.

So let's imagine two curves: The first is the probable timescale to the evolution of technical intelligence. It starts out very low; by a few billion years it may have a noticeable value; by 5 billion years, it's something like 50 percent; by 10 billion years, maybe it's approaching 100 percent. The second curve is the ages of Sun-like stars, some of which are very young—they're being born right now—some of which are as old as the Sun, some of which are 10 billion years old.

If we convolve these two curves, we find there's a chance of technical civilizations on planets of stars of many different ages—not much in the very young ones, more and more for the older ones. The most likely case is that we will hear from a civilization considerably more advanced than ours. For each of those technical civilizations, there have been tens of billions or more other species. The number of unlikely events that had to be concatenated to evolve the technical species is enormous, and perhaps there are members of each of those species who pride themselves on being uniquely intelligent in all the universe.

NEED CIVILIZATIONS DEVELOP THE TECHNOLOGY FOR SETI?

It is perfectly possible to imagine civilizations of poets or (perhaps) Bronze Age warriors who never stumble on *James Clerk Maxwell*'s equations and radio receivers. But they are removed by natural selection. The Earth is surrounded by a population of asteroids and comets, such that occasionally the planet is struck by one large enough to do substantial damage. The most famous is the K-T event (the massive near-Earth-object impact that occurred at the end of the Cretaceous period and start of the Tertiary) of 65 million years ago that extinguished the dinosaurs and most other species of life on Earth. But the chance is something like one in 2000 that a civilization-destroying impact will occur in the next century.

It is already clear that we need elaborate means for detecting and tracking near-Earth objects and the means for their interception and destruction. If we fail to do so, we will simply be destroyed. The Indus Valley, Sumerian, Egyptian, Greek and other civilizations did not have to face this crisis because they did not live long enough. Any long-lived civilization, terrestrial or extraterrestrial, must come to grips with this hazard. Other solar systems will have greater or lesser asteroidal and cometary fluxes, but in almost all cases the dangers should be substantial.

Radiotelemetry, radar monitoring of asteroids, and the entire concept of the electromagnetic spectrum is part and parcel of any early technology needed to deal with such a threat. Thus, any long-lived civilization will be forced by natural selection to develop the technology of SETI. (And there is no need to have sense organs that "see" in the radio region. Physics is enough.)

Since perturbation and collision in the asteroid and comet belts is perpetual, the asteroid and comet threat is likewise perpetual, and there is no time when the technology can be retired. Also, SETI itself is a small fraction of the cost of dealing with the asteroid and comet threat.

(Incidentally, it is by no means true that SETI is "very limited, reaching only part of our galaxy." If there were sufficiently powerful transmitters, we could use SETI to explore distant galaxies; because the most likely transmitters are ancient, we can expect them to be powerful. This is one of the strategies of the Megachannel Extraterrestrial Assay (META).)

IS SETI A FANTASY OF PHYSICAL SCIENTISTS?

Mayr has repeatedly suggested that proponents of SETI are almost exclusively physical scientists and that biologists know better. Since the relevant technologies involve the physical sciences, it is reasonable that astronomers, physicists and engineers play a leading role in SETI.

But in 1982, when I put together a petition published in *Science* urging the scientific respectability of SETI, I had no difficulty getting a range of distinguished biologists and biochemists to sign, including *David Baltimore, Melvin Calvin, Francis Crick, Manfred Eigen, Thomas Eisner, Stephen Jay Gould, Matthew Meselson, Linus Pauling, David Raup*, and *E.O. Wilson.* In my early speculations on these matters, I was much encouraged by the strong support from my mentor in biology, *H.J. Muller,* a Nobel laureate in genetics. The petition proposed that, instead of arguing the issue, we look.

We are unanimous in our conviction that the only significant test of the existence of extraterrestrial intelligence is an experimental one. No a priori arguments on this subject can be compelling or should be used as a substitute for an observational program.

44

RESPONSE TO SAGAN

Ernst Mayr

RESPONSE TO *THE ABUNDANCE OF LIFE-BEARING PLANETS*

I fully appreciate that the nature of our subject permits only probabilistic estimates. There is no argument between Carl Sagan and myself as to the probability of life elsewhere in the universe and the existence of large numbers of planets in our and other nearby galaxies. The issue, as correctly emphasized by Sagan, is the probability of the evolution of high intelligence and an electronic civilization on an inhabited world.

Once we have life (and almost surely it will be very different from life on Earth), what is the probability of its developing a lineage with high intelligence? On Earth, among millions of lineages of organisms and perhaps 50 billion speciation events, only one led to high intelligence; this makes me believe in its utter improbability.

Sagan adopts the principle "it is better to be smart than to be stupid," but life on Earth refutes this claim. Among all the forms of life, neither the prokaryotes nor protists, fungi or plants has evolved smartness, as it should have if it were "better." In the 28 plus phyla of animals, intelligence evolved in only one (chordates) and doubtfully also in the cephalopods. And in the thousands of subdivisions of the chordates, high intelligence developed in only one, the primates, and even there only in one small subdivision. So much for the putative inevitability of the development of high intelligence because "it is better to be smart."

Sagan applies physicalist thinking to this problem. He constructs two linear curves, both based on strictly deterministic thinking. Such thinking is often quite legitimate for physical phenomena, but is quite inappropriate for evolutionary events or social processes such as the origin of civilizations. The argument that extraterrestrials, if belonging to a long-lived civilization, will be forced by selection to develop an electronic know-how to meet the peril of asteroid impacts is totally unrealistic. How would the survivors of earlier impacts be selected to develop the electronic know-how? Also, the case of Earth shows how impossible the origin of any civilization is unless high intelligence develops first. Earth furthermore shows that civilizations inevitably are short-lived.

It is only a matter of common sense that the existence of extraterrestrial intelligence cannot be established by a priori arguments. But this does not justify SETI projects, since it can be shown that the success of an observational program is so totally improbable that it can, for all practical purposes, be considered zero.

All in all, I do not have the impression that Sagan's rebuttal has weakened in any way the force of my arguments.

45

RESPONSE TO MAYR

Carl Sagan

The gist of Professor Mayr's argument is essentially to run through the various factors in the Drake equation (see Shklovskii and Sagan 1966) and attach qualitative values to each. He and I agree that the probabilities concerning the abundance of planets and the origins of life are likely to be high. (I stress again that the latest results (Doyle 1995) suggest one or even two Earth-like planets with abundant surface liquid water in each planetary system. The conclusion is of course highly tentative, but it encourages optimism.) Where Mayr and I disagree is in the later factors in the Drake equation, especially those concerning the likelihood of the evolution of intelligence and technical civilizations.

Mayr argues that prokaryotes and protista have not "evolved smartness." Despite the great respect in which I hold Professor Mayr, I must demur: Prokaryotes and protista are our ancestors. They have evolved smartness, along with most of the rest of the gorgeous diversity of life on Earth.

On the one hand, when he notes the small fraction of species that have technological intelligence, Mayr argues for the relevance of life on Earth to the problem of extra-terrestrial intelligence. But on the other hand, he neglects the example of life on Earth when he ignores the fact that intelligence has arisen here when our planet has another five billion years more evolution ahead of it. If it were legitimate to extra-polate from the one example of planetary life we have before us, it would follow that:

- There are enormous numbers of Earth-like planets, each stocked with enormous numbers of species, and
- In much less than the stellar evolutionary lifetime of each planetary system, at least one of those species will develop high intelligence and technology.

Alternatively, we could argue that it is improper to extrapolate from a single example. But then Mayr's one-in-50 billion argument collapses. It seems to me he cannot have it both ways.

On the evolution of technology, I note that chimpanzees and bonobos have culture and technology. They not only use tools but also purposely manufacture them for future use (see Sagan and Druyan 1992). In fact, the bonobo Kanzi has discovered how to manufacture stone tools.

It is true, as Mayr notes, that of the major human civilizations, only one has developed radio technology. But this says almost nothing about the probability of a human civilization developing such technology. That civilization with radio telescopes has also been at the forefront of weapons technology. If, for example, western European civilization had not utterly destroyed Aztec civilization, would the Aztecs eventually—in centuries or millennia—have developed radio telescopes? They already had a superior astronomical calendar to that of the conquistadores. Slightly more capable species and civilizations may be able to eliminate the competition. But this does not mean that the competition would not eventually have developed comparable capabilities if they had been left alone.

Mayr asserts that plants do not receive "electronic" signals. By this I assume he means "electromagnetic" signals. But plants do. Their fundamental existence depends on receiving electromagnetic radiation from the Sun. Photosynthesis and phototropism can be found not only in the simplest plants but also in protista.

All stars emit visible light, and Sun-like stars emit most of their electromagnetic radiation in the visible part of the spectrum. Sensing light is a much more effective way of understanding the environment at some distance; certainly much more powerful than olfactory cues. It's hard to imagine a competent technical civilization that does not devote major attention to its primary means of probing the outside world. Even if they were mainly to use visible, ultraviolet or infrared light, the physics is exactly the same for radio waves; the difference is merely a matter of wavelength.

I do not insist that the above arguments are compelling, but neither are the contrary ones. We have not witnessed the evolution of biospheres on a wide range of planets. We have not observed many cases of what is possible and what is not. Until we have had such an experience—or detected extraterrestrial intelligence—we will of course be enveloped in uncertainty.

The notion that we can, by a priori arguments, exclude the possibility of intelligent life on the possible planets of the 400 billion stars in the Milky Way has to my ears an odd ring. It reminds me of the long series of human conceits that held us to be at the center of the universe, or different not just in degree but in kind from the rest of life on Earth, or even contended that the universe was made for our benefit (Sagan 1994). Beginning with Copernicus, every one of these conceits has been shown to be without merit.

In the case of extraterrestrial intelligence, let us admit our ignorance, put aside a priori arguments, and use the technology we are fortunate enough to have developed to try and actually find out the answer. That is, I think, what Charles Darwin—who was converted from orthodox religion to evolutionary biology by the weight of observational evidence—would have advocated.

46

THE DECODING PROBLEM:

Do We Need To Search For Extraterrestrial Intelligence In Order To Search For Extraterrestrial Intelligence?

Neil Tennant

1 THE ASSUMPTION OF DECODABILITY

There are two aspects of the search for extraterrestrial intelligence – the technological and the philosophical.[1]

> If there are higher civilizations out there in the Milky Way, perhaps they are continually broadcasting an *easily decoded* "Encyclopaedia Galactica" for the benefit of their less advanced neighbours. It may contain answers to almost all the questions our philosophers and scientists have been asking for centuries, and solutions to many of the practical problems that beset mankind.[2] [My emphasis.]

The concepts *telling* (or *asserting*), *understanding* and *content* form a crux that is arguably *the* most fundamental to modern philosophy. Philosophers have done important work clarifying and grounding our grasp of these concepts. It is work worth drawing to the attention of SETI scientists.

It can mislead the public, and unjustifiably drain the public purse, to hold out in all scientific seriousness *any* of the following prospects, without first giving some *very convincing conceptual analysis* and *plausibility arguments* based on such analysis:

1 the prospect of *communicating* with extraterrestrial intelligences, on the basis of strings of bleeps alone, and without encountering them directly and being able to observe their communicative behaviour in the surroundings in which they are at home
2 the prospect of being able to *interpret* what they might purportedly be trying to tell us, on any electromagnetic frequency, at light years' remove – that is, of taking

a string of bleeps as constituting a *monologue* endowed with a complex meaning that allostellar neighbours could recover

3 the prospect of being able to engage in a bleep-string based *dialogue*, however fitful and protracted, with each parties' contribution endowed with complex meanings recoverable by the other

2 THE DECODING PROBLEM

We are to imagine that we have received a long but finite sequence of bleeps on some narrow channel on the electromagnetic spectrum. The bleeps may vary continuously in duration, as may the "silences" that separate them.

First question:
Is the string of bleeps a natural or intentional phenomenon?

It is to *this* question that the Arecibo software is addressed. If the answer is that the string of bleeps is an intentional phenomenon – that is, produced by some alien intentional agency – then this will be an answer produced as a *default conclusion*. By this I mean that once we have exhausted all the naturalistic explanations available within the confines of our best astrophysical theories, we shall adopt the hypothesis that the string is of intentional origin; that is, that it has been produced by an ETI. A default conclusion takes one from failures to explain within certain constraints of simplicity and economy to a willingness to explain by recourse to less simple and less economic theoretical resources. The postulation of an ETI as the origin of a string of bleeps is an example of such recourse.

Second question:
Given that the string of bleeps is an intentional phenomenon: are we eavesdropping on ETI's communicating with one another, or are we in receipt of an *alienable* signal? – that is, a signal *that some ETI, in sending it out, intends to have received by an ETI alien to it?*

I have no clear idea whether there are physical characteristics of a string of bleeps that could help one decide this question. But let us assume for the sake of our decision tree that the string of bleeps *is* an alienable signal in the sense just defined.

Third question:
Is the alienable signal one that is merely self-proclaiming, or is it one that is intended to convey complex, decodable semantic content to its alien receiver?

By a *merely self-proclaiming* signal I mean one whose physical characteristics have been designed or chosen so as to permit only the conclusion that it is an intentional phenomenon, but no more. Its net 'content' would be merely 'Hey, we are out here!' or 'Hey, you are not alone!'.

The conclusion that the alienable signal is *not* merely self-proclaiming, but rather has a complex, decodable semantic content, is *not* a default conclusion. Rather, it is the kind of conclusion that can only be justified by *convincing construction* – by constructing or exhibiting an instance, by way of inference to the best explanation, to justify a claim of the form "There is some so-and-so such that … ". In this case the conclusion would have to be a *decoding claim* – that is, a claim of the form

> There is some optimal method of decoding (translation mapping into English or what-have-you) that is adequate to the observed evidence about this signal and others like it, according to which this signal means that p. In saying that it is optimal we meant that it has been arrived at *via* an inference to the best explanation of the observable data – it is simpler and more economical, hence better, than all rival methods of decoding.

where p is to be filled in with some propositional specification in English as to the content of the message.

Now let us take a closer look at the form of a decoding claim. One could in principle make a decoding claim about any and every utterance one processes in one's linguistic life. But as speakers of English we do not; we tend rather to adopt the identity mapping (also known as the *homophonic* mapping) as our translation mapping, and get on with our conversations. It is important to realise, however, that in our use of (our ideolects of) English, we could in principle have recourse to a decoding claim. You say to me "It is raining and cold outside." I conclude that it is raining and cold outside. I do so with a hefty *ceteris paribus* proviso: there is no evidence that you intend to deceive me, there is no evidence that you speak some strange language in which that form of words means something radically different from what it means in English, etc. etc. I am entitled to a decoding claim with regard to your string of sounds:

> There is some optimal method of decoding (namely, the homophonic translation mapping into my ideolect of English) that is adequate to the observed evidence about this utterance of yours and others like it, according to which this utterance means that *it is raining and cold outside*.

When we're all in it together we don't labour the obvious. *But if we think that an ETI is trying to tell us something, then what was so obvious among ourselves must be treated as very* unobvious *as between the ETI and ourselves.*

585

3 WHAT IS NEEDED IN ORDER TO INTERPRET OR UNDERSTAND A LANGUAGE?

There is a vast philosophical literature and tradition of thought,[3] commanding widespread acceptance among modern philosophers, in support of the notion that meaningful linguistic utterances (hence meaningful sentence types) derive their meaningfulness or their meanings from *the ways that they are used by speakers in contexts in which they can be observed*. Even meaning skeptics[4] stress that it is *in despite of* all the observable behavioural evidence that they are skeptical about meanings and univocal interpretations of linguistic utterances. And even innatists[5] of varying stripes concede that only through observation of others' behaviour (onto-genetically) is the individual's innate competence triggered and realised, and only through observation of others' behaviour (phylogenetically) could the innate mechanisms have been put in place by natural selection.

Let us put it this way:

Meaning is ecological

An utterance in a language that we do not understand, regardless of its length and complexity, will, if shorn from the context in which that language is used, if wren-ched from the form of life that sustains its content, be like a fish out of water. It will not be able to function at all. As the fish gasps for breath, ironically in a surfeit of oxygen, so too a string of bleeps would go begging for content, even, ironically, when received by beings who convey contents to one another daily and who are all too willing to read content into what they see and hear.

Wittgenstein once wrote

If a lion were to speak to me, I would not understand him.

This may be taking things too far; but it is an extreme standpoint in the spirit of the thesis that meaning is ecological. Wittgenstein's point is that the lion's form of life is so alien to his own that interpretation of any apparently linguistic utterances from the lion – even if they appeared to be grammatical and appropriate in context – would be, in principle, impossible.

We do not need to share Wittgenstein's skepticism about leonine unintelligibility in order to be skeptical about the prospects for decoding strings of bleeps from otherwise unobservable ETI's. As far as I am concerned, a lion who spoke to me, using grammatical sentences that were appropriate in context, would be a most welcome conversational partner. Very few *people* I know are capable of that much.

One should be willing to do the same for any ETI that were to come visiting. If the ETI got out of his spaceship and started speaking, like the lion, what seemed to be grammatical and appropriate speech, it would not take me long, after a little inter-action with him (governmental agencies permitting) to be happy with the homo-phonic translation mapping.

It would strike us as a miracle as to how he/she/it/they did it (learned English, that is); but we would immediately start searching for reasonable explanations, and seeking out evidence to back them up. Had they been eavesdropping on our TV broadcasts, and did they thereby manage to interpret *us* along the lines, to be sug-gested below, that we might be able to interpret *them* by means of pictures? ... Maybe there are *so many* advanced technological civilizations out there that there is a non-trivial objective chance that, under pressures of natural and cultural selection, *one and the same* natural language could evolve in communities located on different planets! ...

Moreover, if (which is more likely) the ETI spoke to me in his own alien language (or otherwise tried to make himself understood – by forming neat patterns with his tentacles, and making rapid and syncopated proboscis movements), then I could set about trying to interpret what he *meant* by doing exactly what I would do in any of those situations that Quine describes as involving *radical translation* or that David-son describes as involving *radical interpretation*.

I would record what he 'said' in what contexts. I would look for correlations between recognizably repeated sequences (of sound types or movement types) and recurrent features of the ostensible environment. I would try to discern *structure* in his strings. I would try to work out how that structure affected meaning. I would try to work out what he could perceive, and what his sensory modalities were like. (Vision? Hearing? Sonar? ...) On that basis, I would make a guess at his basic per-ceptual beliefs. I would try to work out his hierarchy of goals, purposes, needs, desires, motivations. Coupling those with his likely beliefs, I would make a stab at why he would have said various things with conjectured content supplied by me, the radical interpreter. I would have to account for how that content was composed from the characteristic contribution of the repeatable portions of his utterances (the 'words', be they sounds or movements or whatever). I would have to show how, given the psychology posited, his 'sentences' made sense; and how, given the sense made by his sentences, his psychology was revealed as thus-and-so.

This is a very sketchy account of the procedure of radical interpretation. To sum-marize, it has two main interlocking and coeval components:

1 the postulation of an intentional psychology – involving, especially, perceptually based beliefs and organism-serving desires – that could be used to explain the creature's intentional behaviour

2 the postulation of *meaning* or *content* for types of linguistic utterances and their recurring portions. These meanings would have to be postulated in such a way that one could recover the meanings of whole utterances from the meanings of their parts. The meanings of the parts would arise from the systematic way in which they contributed to meanings of whole utterances in which they occurred.

In radical interpretation we may therefore speak of the *psychological* aspect and the *logico-grammatical* aspect of the decoding involved. Davidson goes further and enjoins a *principle of charity* governing interpretative attempts concerning alien *human* tribes, which I shall express as follows:

> Ascribe such beliefs and desires to them as you yourself would have if you were living in their world, with access to the same perceptual evidence and life-sustaining resources as they have – that is, *maximize agreement* with regard to how you take the world to be, and how you would like it to be.

No doubt the principle of charity could still operate in the case of an alien creature visiting us on Earth. The main difference would be that we would have to conjecture what its sensory modalities were, and what features of the environment registered on its perceptual and cognitive apparatus. But if it appeared to function reasonably well here on Earth, going places and doing things, we should be charitable enough to think it had got some basic perceptual beliefs that were *true*; and which could provide a point of entry in the task of radical interpretation of those aspects of its behaviour that we took to be linguistic (that is, communicative in an intentional way).

Note that in all these cases where decoding or interpretation is possible, there are two main necessary features:

1 the utterances carry their meanings *immediately* in context
2 the utterances carry their meanings immediately *in context*

By *immediacy* here I intend the sense in which an utterance of an English sentence carries its meaning more immediately than would, say, its translation into Morse code for radio transmission. By *context* I intend the sense that involves the speaker or utterer as an essential part of a scene or situation, embedded within an environment and interacting with it, even if only by pointing at parts of it for didactic purposes while speaking slowly and clearly. Let us sloganise our two most recent observations about the cases where interpretation is possible:

1 we have immediate meaning
2 we have immersed meaning (that is, meaning is ecological)

Alas, with strings of bleeps from outer space, *we have neither.* We have no reason to believe that *they* converse with one another by means of strings of bleeps. For them, as for us, signals made up of strings of bleeps would in all likelihood derive their significance only indirectly, and not have immediate meaning. And we certainly cannot observe them in context as the signals emanate. All we get are the signals themselves, and no information at all about the natural context within which they originate.

How, then, might strings of bleeps from outer space ever mean anything to us? How could they have a complex semantic content that we might be able to decode?

4 HOW SEVERE IS OUR SKEPTICISM ABOUT DECODING?

4.1 The Principle of Super-Charity, or Anti-Cryptography

The SETI thought is this: if they're sending us signals, they *want* to be understood. They *intend* that we work out what those signals mean. So they are going to do everything they can to ensure that we catch on to what they mean. In short, they are going to think up some code that is really easy to crack.

This is a helpful and comforting thought only if we are not too moronic in comparison with them. After all, they may be so advanced intellectually that they have ceased to appreciate that what seems obvious to them might be terribly complicated for us. Can we rely on a higher intelligence being able to get down to the level of one with which it intends to communicate, and for whom it has to make its coding as simple as possible? Perhaps not; but let's suppose for the sake of argument that they're about as intelligent as we are and want creatures like us to cotton on to what they mean with their strings of bleeps. They have what appears to be an insuperable problem: how to *make themselves understood* in a perforce highly mediate way (for they don't bleep to one another) and a perforce unimmersed way. The problem is that of *proxy anabaptist* communication of content.

The odds are stacked against a solution. One can think of only the following two suggestions.

4.2 Recourse to pictures?

They might reason as follows:

It will be well-nigh impossible to secure a non-zero absolute probability of definitive interpretation of what we send them. There are just too many possible meanings that can be read off from any finite string looking for content both by proxy and anabaptismally. But we could make non-trivial the *conditional* probability that, *if* they see our message in the way intended, *then* it would be hard to imagine any rival interpretation fitting as well as the one hit upon. Take the most fundamental feature of the world as we experience it. It has three spatial dimensions and events take place in linear time. We can ignore relativity – everyone knows that life couldn't evolve on the scale at which relativistic considerations have any importance. Now any intelligent creature with a grasp of three dimensions would have a grasp of two; and a grasp of the concept of projecting from a three-dimensional region into a two-dimensional one. So perhaps we should send them a piece of code for the construction of a two-dimensional picture, or even for the construction of a three-dimensional one – like a sculpture. If they ever hit on it, they'll *know* they're onto the right thing, because the odds are so high against *that* being the outcome of just any old way of decoding.

So they pose for a group picture, even a video, and code up a nice fine mesh of pixels and beam it out, prefixed with some sort of clue as to how many rows and columns of pixels there are for each frame.

They are assuming that some ETI out there has eyes too, the better to decode their intended signals with. They are also taking comfort in the belief that some ETI out there can process frames at some appropriate speed like 32 per second and thereby get a phenomenological feel as of continuous motion continuously observed.

Hilary Putnam begins *Reason, Truth and History* with a philosopher's far-fetched situation of apparent but illusory meaningfulness. He imagines that a vast army of ants is crawling across a beach, and that from above they appear to form a picture of Winston Churchill. His point is that it would not *be* a representation of Winston Churchill, despite its miraculous likeness to him. This is because it is not the outcome of the right sort of *intentionality*, or world-directedness, on the part of the ants. The ants' behaviour is not rendered any the more intelligible by ascribing to them the collective intention so to render Churchill's face. We have a theory about ant-perception and ant-needs that is strongly grounded on knowledge about their physiology and other aspects of behaviour. And this theory does not allow for plausible extension by the hypothesis that they're up to some picturing tricks while scurrying across the beach. Notice the methodological moral: miraculous-seeming phenomenon drained of its apparent significance, because overwhelmed by a theory about the intentional limitations of the creatures producing it.

Perhaps not so with pictures from an ETI. I want here to register, but not dismiss, the bizarre-seeming possibility that an ETI might choose a pictorial method of communicating with us. The thesis would be that *if* we were ever so lucky as to hit upon the pictures immanent in a string of bleeps, *then there could be no other interpretation of them – they would* have *to be intending to convey those pictorial representations to us.* Bear in mind, though, that for us to be able to construe them *as pictures* the scenes or situations depicted would themselves have to be ones that we could grasp. I am thinking here of the possibility that they have bodies that we could recognise (from a picture – or better, from a movie) *as (locomoting or gesturing) bodies*; and that other physical objects depicted with them, even if we could not tell what kind of objects they were, were at least such that we could appreciate that there were at least some kinds of objects such that these objects were of those kinds. I am thinking here of alien artefacts and alien natural kinds; we might be able to recognise them for what they barely were, so to speak.

How would they code up pictures for us of their own scenes? Take a large prime number N. Square it. Send out N-squared as a series of bleeps, over and over again. Stay silent for some time. Then send out strings of N-squared bleeps and silences of equal duration, for the on-off filling of the pixels. How are they filled? Zig-zag? or repeatedly from left to right? or repeatedly from top to bottom? or spiralwise? It doesn't really matter, even in the three dimensional case. A good supercomputer could try out all the obvious ways. And when that group photo or sculpture of the ETIs leaps out of the screen or hologram-space at you, *bingo*!!

Note moreover that with moving pictures comes the possibility of *teaching us whatever gestural language* they may have devised. (I shan't comment on the possibility of decoding a *soundtrack* as well, because that's not as obviously *projective* as picturing. And sound is a very provincial phenomenon cosmically. Why think that they would have hearing systems, adapted to atmospheric vibrations, and that they would be hoping or assuming that potential recipients of their messages would have them too?)

Of all the suggestions I have come across, this one about recourse to pictures strikes me, as a philosopher of language, as the most plausible. *If* I am correct, and *if* the boffins agree that the information for a video signal is better carried in the optical spectrum than it is in the radio spectrum, then it is optical SETI that should get the philosopher's backing. But one is tempted to wonder whether, with friends like these, the optical SETI advocate needs any enemies.

4.3 Concentration on the abstract?

Alternatively, they might reason as follows:

We can't tell them about material objects and secondary qualities and causal interaction and persons, because they can't observe us here, doing our customary

591

things. So why don't we latch onto a subject matter that we can all appreciate without any need for ostensive language learning, and that we can reasonably assume to be universal among intelligences capable of receiving our signals in the first place? Why don't we signal to them about the most basic abstract mathematical objects that one can grasp as soon as one is equipped with the conceptual resources of identity and difference, and the ability to discriminate *different kinds of thing*, and *different things of one and the same kind*, regardless of *which kind* of things one's sense organs have been evolved to detect and one's cognitive apparatus has been evolved to think about?

They conclude, therefore, that they should communicate with other intelligences in the cosmos about the natural numbers.

Now doing *that* may be both easier and fruitless. We would not understand such abstract discourse unless already apprised of the abstract truths it expresses. This much is evident from just the problem of how one might identify their sign for addition, and for identity. If, for example, we had described sub-strings of the form

blip blah blip blat blip blip
blip blah blip blip blat blip blip blip
blip blip blah blip blat blip blip blip
blip blip blah blip blip blat blip blip blip blip
blip blip blah blip blip blip blat blip blip blip blip blip
blip blip blip blah blip blip blat blip blip blip blip blip
    . . .

we might be tempted to interpret "blah" as the sign for addition and "blat" as the sign for identity. But *only because we already know the arithmetic truths*

$$* + * = **$$
$$* + ** = ***$$
$$** + * = ***$$
$$** + ** = ****$$
$$** + *** = *****$$
$$*** + ** = *****$$
    . . .

Now of course the infix notation (according to which the addition sign is infixed between the two numerals for the numbers being added, and the identity sign is infixed between the two numerals making up the identity statement) might never have occurred to them. They might instead have developed only something like a

Polish notation, and not be aware of any alternative to it. So they might send us something like the following instead:

sblat blah blip bleep blip bleep blip blip bleep
blat blah blip bleep blip blip bleep blip blip blip bleep
blat blah blip blip bleep blip bleep blip blip blip bleep
blat blah blip blip bleep blip blip bleep blip blip blip blip bleep
blat blah blip blip bleep blip blip blip bleep blip blip blip blip blip bleep
blat blah blip blip blip bleep blip blip bleep blip blip blip blip blip bleep
 . . .

The logically sophisticated among us will see this as:

= + s0s0ss0
= + s0ss0sss0
= + ss0s0sss0
= + ss0ss0ssss0
= + ss0sss0sssss0
= + sss0ss0sssss0
 . . .

Again, we would only be able to make sense of it by virtue of already knowing the truths expressed.

So the prospect is that of being able to latch onto a formal lexicon and formal syntax *by using a great deal of our own knowledge* about the abstract subject matter. The question that then arises is: where would this get us? How, by recognising their communication as being about truths of mathematics, do we learn *anything else* about them, their life form, their biology, their own theories of the world, *from the strings of bleeps they send us?*

It wouldn't matter if they somehow managed even to convey to us the syntax of a formal language adequate for set theory, along with its axioms and a great many theorems. That simply wouldn't help. Precisely because of the abstract and necessary nature of mathematics, any message from an ETI that they intend to be interpreted as about mathematics *will be no more than self-proclaiming*. To be sure, what is proclaimed will be not just "Hey, we're out here", but rather "Hey, we're out here, and what is more, we know some mathematics" – which will not be terribly informative given that they've got radio transmitters (or lasers) up and running. Indeed, even the barest self-proclaiming message "Hey, we're out here" has, as a pragmatic corollary " . . . and what is more, we have radio transmitters (or lasers)". So to learn, on top of that, that they know some mathematics *as well* is hardly going to surprise us.

In the extant literature[6] on this problem – the problem of how to settle on an interpretation on the assumption that they're communicating truths that they assume us to know – one encounters remarkable philosophical naiveté. Extraordinarily optimistic assumptions are made about all of the following:

1 whether we would be able to work out which of the bleeps and pauses in a string of bleeps were symbol tokens or punctuation devices

2 whether the 'mean length of utterance' would be humanly tractable – that is, whether the 'sentences' within a string of bleeps would not be too long for us to work with

3 whether they would use *what to us seem like* 'canonical representations', such as a sequence of *n* bleeps to represent the natural number *n*. (Heaven only knows what they would do for the set abstraction operator. Devito and Oehrle blithely assume that they too would use precise analogues of *both* our semi-formal 'curly brackets with listing of members' *and* of our 'set of all x such that Fx' notation.)

4 whether the 'sentences' would have anything like the syntactic and semantic structures with which we are familiar from our own grasp of our mother tongues, from pedagogical grammar, from theoretical grammar, and from the design of computer language and formal languages of logic – which, mark well, are nevertheless *for our own uses*. It would also help, of course, if the 'sentences' were *structurally unambiguous*, since we cannot appeal to context to help with disambiguation (as one would be able to, for example, with a question such as "Do we need to search for extra terrestrial intelligence to search for extraterrestrial intelligence?").

5 whether, if those 'sentences' have some sort of recursive grammatical structure underlying their repeatable constituents, the grammar would be *learnable* by *machines such as us*. I am here adverting to the vast literature on language learning – on inducing generative grammars from finite sets of data about grammatical and ungrammatical strings.[7]

6 (related to the previous point) whether the *thoughts* that they are intending to communicate with the 'sentential' sub-strings of bleeps would be structured in a way amenable to our metaphysical outlook – the outlook that assumes that there are individual things to be referred to and generalized about, and properties and relations holding of and among these things

7 whether they would order their 'interpretation tutorials', or 'primers', in a way friendly to the human intellect – first rehearsing mundane, singular arithmetical facts, then 'slightly more complicated' ones from a logical point of view, thereby allowing us to attain to a grasp of 'what counts as' a logical operator such as a negation sign or a universal quantifier; advancing, finally, to discourse (still interpretatively tutoring, mind you!) about the periodic table of the elements, the

melting and boiling points of chemical substances, the curvature of space, Avogadro's number ...

The reader who feels her credulity strained should see the paper cited above by
Devito and Oehrle. In a slightly more popular paper by the former author[8] we read
(at p. 14) the reassuring claim 'We can use our common knowledge [common, that
is, to us and to the ETI's], once we have identified it [sic], to rapidly reach the point
where precise scientific information can be exchanged.' Devito overlooks the problem
that the identification of common knowledge presupposes interpretative success. So
the identification of supposedly common knowledge cannot be used to generate
interpretative hypotheses. Later in the same paper (p.15) we find but one of many
breathtaking claims: ' ... by sending our system of atomic weights and our value of
the Avogadro number we enable our contactees to measure our gram for themselves.'

Sometimes it is difficult to resist the impression that such optimism, such gullibi-
lity, such lack of philosophical and skeptical restraint, is a transmuted form of a
religious *willingness to believe* in the possibility of revelatory experiences – in this
case, infusion of cosmic wisdom through miraculously uncluttered interpretative
channels. One wonders how much of what might have been serious but ever self-
doubting scientific speculation has become superficial and uncritical as a result of
Carl Sagan's novel *Contact*. The following passage might easily be misconstrued by
the skeptical reader as a sophisticated and merciless send-up of the 'interpretability
via common knowledge' hypothesis. The President of the United States is hearing
from her chief scientific advisor about the Vegans' recently decoded Message (in
essence, another mere string of bleeps) on how to construct a Machine:

" ... So with a few lines of text they've taught us four words: plus, equals, true,
false. Four pretty useful words. Then they teach division, divide one by zero, and
tell us the word for infinity. Or maybe it's just the word for indeterminate. Or
they say, 'The sum of the interior angles of a triangle is two right angles.' Then
they comment that the statement is true if space is flat, but false if space is
curved. So you've learned how to say 'if' and—"

"I didn't know space *was* curved. Ken, what the hell are you talking about?
How can space be curved? ... Okay, so ... You know how to say true-false, if-
then, and space is curved. How do you build a Machine with that?"

" ... Well, it just takes off from there. For example, they draw us a periodic
table of the elements, so they get to name all the chemical elements, the idea of
an atom, the idea of a nucleus, protons, neutrons, electrons. Then they run
through some quantum mechanics just to make sure we're paying attention –
there are already some new insights for us in the remedial stuff. Then it starts
concentrating on the particular materials needed for the construction. For

example, for some reason we need two tons of erbium, so they run through a nifty technique to extract it from ordinary rocks. . . . Don't ask why we need two tons of erbium. Nobody has the faintest idea."

"I wasn't going to ask that. I want to know how they told you how much a ton is."

"They counted it out for us in Planck masses. . . . whole chapters of the Message are falling into our lap in clear."

5 A TRANSCENDENTAL DEDUCTION OF THE CONCLUSION THAT, IF THEY'RE OUT THERE, THEY WON'T BE LETTING US KNOW

The famous Drake equation purports to provide the probability of intelligent, electromagnetically-signalling life elsewhere in the galaxy. I want now to enquire after the likelihood that an extraterrestrial civilization with radio or laser technology will broadcast semantically laden messages into outer space – messages that are not merely self-proclaiming, *and that we could understand*. It is my contention that *at least the conjunction of the assumptions enumerated above would have to hold in order for such interpretation to be possible*. So suppose further that p is the probability that the conjunction of the above assumptions holds. Then p is an extra diminishing factor that ought to appear in the Drake equation. The original Drake equation was for the probability (let us call it d) of there being extraterrestrial intelligence in the galaxy. I propose that it be modified, so that it gives the probability D that there are such ETI's *for whose messages there is the remotest possibility that we might understand them*. D is simply d times p. For the SETI zealot p will be of order 1. But for the philosophically sensitive skeptic, p will be more nearly infinitesimal.

A charitable assumption about any ETI capable of beaming signals to us is that they're *at least* as smart as we are. Given that, it would follow that they are capable of reflective reasoning about the fundamentals of space, time, physical objects, matter, conceptual thought, numbers *and the nature of communication*. In all probability any other civilization out there will have produced a version of the skeptical argument above. They will realise that it is futile to devote resources to sending interstellar messages *that can only be self-proclaiming*. So they won't do so. No-one could go calling, even if a call were to get through (for the distances involved are simply too great). Hence it would be futile for us to look for any calls. They, too, having reached a similar conclusion, wouldn't be looking for any of ours. The extra infinitesimal factor p in the Drake equation disinclines them to take a gander.

But *we* are looking for *theirs*! So what is wrong with the reasoning above? ... or with us? Have we underestimated their intelligence? Down in Arecibo have we, in Austin's words, merely equipped ourselves with some shining new tools that will not help crack the crib of reality? and which will turn out to be shining new skids under our metaphysical feet?

ACKNOWLEDGEMENTS

I am grateful for stimulating conversations with Dr. Stuart Kingsley, of Fiberdyne Optoelectronics, with Dr. John Billingham, Director of the NASA SETI Project and Professor Bob Dixon, Director of The Ohio State University's 'Big Ear' Listening Project, and with my ex-student Clive Goodall, whose infectious enthusiasm made me take a skeptical look. I would also like to thank Alison Rayner for some hawk-eyed proofreading.

NOTES

1 Arthur C. Clarke, *Life* magazine, September 1992, p.68.
2 Arthur C. Clarke, *loc. cit.*
3 To cite just a few of the landmark works in this tradition: J.L. Austin, *How To Do Things With Words*, Oxford, 1962; W.V.O. Quine, *Word and Object*, MIT Press, 1960; J. Searle, *Speech Acts*, Cambridge, 1969; M. Dummett, 'What is a Theory of meaning? I' in S. Guttenplan, ed., *Mind and Language*, Oxford, 1975, and 'What is a Theory of Meaning? II' in G. Evans and J. McDowell, *Truth and meaning*, Oxford, 1976; J. Bennett, *Linguistic Behaviour*, Cambridge, 1976; D. Lewis, *Convention*, Harvard University Press, 1969; H.P. Grice, 'Meaning', *Philosophical Review* 66, pp.377–88, 1957; D. Davidson, *Inquiries into Truth and Interpretation*, Oxford, 1984, including especially 'Radical Interpretation' and 'Truth and Meaning'; P.F. Strawson, 'Meaning and Truth', Oxford, 1972; J. Barwise and J. Perry, *Situations and Attitudes*, MIT Press, 1983; C. Peacocke, *Thoughts: An Essay on Content*, Oxford, 1986.
4 Kripke, S. *Wittgenstein on Rules and Private Language*, Blackwell, 1982; S. Stitch, *From Folk Psychology to Cognitive Science*, MIT Press, 1983; S. Shiffer, *Remnants of Meaning*, MIT Press, 1987.
5 Fodor, J. *The Language of Thought*, Harvard University Press, 1979 and *Psychosemantics*, MIT Press, 1987; N. Chomsky, *Rules and Representations*, Columbia University Press, 1980.
6 The seminal work is Hans Freudenthal's *Lincos: Design of a Language for Cosmic Intercourse*, Part I, North-Holland, Amsterdam, 1960. More recent specimens of *Homo Freudenthalis* are C.L. Devito and R.T. Oehrle, with their article 'A Language Based On The Fundamental Facts Of Science', *Journal of The British Interplanetary Society*, Vol. 43, 1990, pp.561–8.
7 See Pinker, S. 'Formal models of language learning', *Cognition* 7, 1979, pp.217–83 for a survey of results in the field.
8 'Languages, Science and the Search for Extraterrestrial Intelligence', *Leonardo* Vol.25, No.1, 1992, pp.13–16.

INDEX

action: and belief 281, 301, 302, 303, 305; epistemic and pragmatic 181; intelligent 415
active externalism 180, 182–85, 196–98
agreement, scientific: observation and 66; publicity and 70–74
alcohol addiction 283, 372–74, 377, 378, 380–87
Alston, W. 76
amnesic patients 68, 75, 294–95
analogy: argument from 408, 409; and intelligence 558
Anaximander 99
Angels With Dirty Faces (film) 362, 368
animals 407–22, 451–63, 480–85; awareness and self-awareness 393, 413–14, 424–29, 431–37; behavior, as evidence of mental states 391–92, 396–406, 409–10, 412–13, 506; beliefs, attribution of 390, 391–93, 394, 396–97, 400–406, 414–15, 417–19, 421–22; consciousness 412–13; desires, attribution of 390, 391–93, 396–97, 400–406; empathy 403, 424–30, 431–38; intelligence 415–16; and language 394, 408, 413–17, 419–21, 439–50; mental states, attribution of 390–437, 455–59, 506; numerical reasoning 394, 441, 461–63; physics, understanding of 460–61; seeing, understanding of concept of 431–34, 458–59, 461
anosognosia 69
anthropic principle 142, 152 n.17
anthropomorphism 390
Anton's syndrome 69
appearance: of an entity 61, 99–102; of consciousness 62, 102, 104, 105
apperception 102
Aquinas, St Thomas 354–55, 494 n.1
Aristotle 33, 98, 119, 439
artificial intelligence 136, 466–94; and behavior, laws of 487; biological objection to 525–27; consciousness and 23, 24, 485, 581–82; conversational ability *see* Turing test; expert systems 543–47; intentionality and 505–6, 508, 509–10, 510; learning and 488–93; mathematical logic and 480–81; objections to 479–88, 525–27; origination and 467, 485–86; rating games 553–56; strong and weak, distinguished 495; theological objection 479–80; understanding and 495–510, 514–15; *see also* Chinese Room argument; Turing test
Asch, Solomon 380
Asperger's syndrome 337, 347
associative priming 552–53
attention 28, 30
Attention Deficit Hyperactivity Disorder (ADHD) 283, 352–53, 365–67, 368
Augustine 13
autism: and emotions 319, 329, 337; executive-function deficit 344, 346–48; imitative behavior and 328–29, 330; obsessive-repetitive behavior and 343–44; practical reasoning and 344–48; and pretend play 282, 311, 316, 324–26, 327–28, 333, 334, 335, 338–42, 343; and simulation theory 282, 314–15, 324–27, 328–29, 330–31 n.5, 344, 347, 348; and 'theory of mind' debate 281–82, 310–18, 319–31, 333–51; theory-theory explanation 281–82, 321–23, 327, 328, 334, 335–36
autophenomenology 85–86
Avoidant Personality Disorder 366, 368, 369
awareness 28, 30; in animals 413–14; objective 20; *see also* bodily awareness; self-awareness

Babbage, Charles 476, 485
Barker, John A. 282, 319–32

Baron-Cohen, Simon 281, 310–18, 320, 321, 333, 334, 336
behavior: animals, and mental states 381–82, 396–406, 409–10, 412–13, 506; artificial intelligence and laws of 487; intentional stance explanations 418, 422; physical stance explanations 418; responsibility attributions *see* responsibility attributions
behavior disorders 283, 352–53, 364–68, 369
behaviorism 15, 418; analytic 409–10
beliefs 159, 185–90; about experiences 60, 82–84; action and 281, 301, 302, 303, 305; animals, attribution of in 380, 391–93, 394, 396–97, 400–406, 414–15, 417–19, 421–22; confidence in 301, 302, 376–77, 382; and delusions, relationship between 280–81, 299–309; emotion and 301, 302, 305; and language 417, 419; machines as having 502–3; means-to-end 402–3; occurrent 162, 185, 189, 193, 195, 203–5; practical reasoning and 345–46; propositional attitude interpretation of 300; representational content of 301, 302; standing 162, 186, 188, 193–95, 199–203, 205; *see also* false belief tasks; 'theory of mind' debate
Bennett, Jonathan 391–92, 396–406, 563
Berger, Peter 357
Berrios, G. 302
bivalence, principle of 239
Blakeslee, Sandra 285–98
blindsight 59, 60, 68, 69, 427
Block, Ned 539–40
bodily awareness 170–79; spatiality of 160, 170–77
body: ownership of 177–78; and self 160, 165–69, 170–79; *see also* embodiment; mind-body problem
Boyd, R. 72
bracketing 84
brain 452–53, 511–13; bisection *see* split-brain cases; chimpanzee and human compared 452; computational function 103; self-awareness and 429–30; synthetic 22, 526–27
Brewer, Bill 160–61, 170–79
Bruner, Jerry 248, 253, 259
Buddha 210, 231
Bundle Theory 203, 230–31, 233–36, 268–69
Burge, T. 182, 186, 187

C-fibre stimulation 140, 147
Campbell, Donald 380
Capgras' syndrome 280, 285–88, 300, 302
Carruthers, Peter 282, 333–51
causal necessity 359, 360, 368

causal substrate of consciousness 103
causation 134, 146–47; mental 112–13, 126–30, 146
cause/effect nexus 357
Chalmers, David 7–8, 15–26, 27, 87–88, 95, 131 n.4, 141, 161–62, 180–91, 192, 206
character 372, 378, 382
charity, principle of 589
children: autobiographical memory 436; criminal responsibility 363, 364, 367; moral responsibility and behaviour disorders in 283, 352–53, 364–68, 369; seeing, understanding of concept of 434; self-recognition 425, 435–36, 437; *see also* autism; infants
Chinese Room argument 467–68, 495–513, 514, 515–30; brain simulator reply 504–5; combination reply 505–6; many mansions reply 507; other minds reply 506–7; robot reply 503–4; systems reply 468, 500–503, 519–23
Chomsky, Noam 139
Churchland, Patricia 7–8, 27–35, 103, 138
clairvoyance 488
Clark, Andy 161–62, 180–91, 192–206
Clever Hans 390
coercion 385–86
'cogito' reasoning 159–60
cognition, extended 161–62, 180–81, 192–93
cognitive science 7, 15, 59, 64, 67–70, 75–76, 78, 95, 183
Colby, Kenneth 540–41
color vision 16–17, 24, 25
commissurotomies *see* split-brain cases
communication: extra-terrestrial intelligence (ETI) 564, 565, 583–97; pictorial method 590–92
compatibilism 358–60
computers *see* artificial intelligence
confidence: in beliefs 301, 302, 376–77, 382; effect of, on course of disease 376–77
conformity 380
consciousness 5–11, 94–98, 110, 183, 229–30, 408–9; in animals 412–13; and artificial systems 22, 23, 482–83, 485; easy problems of 7, 16, 28, 30; form, appearance and substrate of 61–62, 94, 102, 103–5; hard problem of 7, 16–18, 27, 28–31, 95; introspection and 61–62, 67–70, 77–78, 85–87; as layered 13; left-out hypothesis 28–29; materialist view of 125–32; physical science explanation of 5–10, 52–53, 62, 95, 96, 103 *see also* neuroscience; physics; pure 141–42, 152 n.16; theory of 16, 21–24; unity of *see* unity of consciousness; *see also* phenomenology

conversation 467, 469, 535; *see also* Turing test
Copeland, Jack 468, 514–31
Cotard's syndrome 292–93
Coupland, Douglas 253
creationism 563
Crick, Francis 17–20, 29
criminal responsibility 361–64, 367
critical phenomenology 87–88
cultural factors 469; and choice of values 379–80; and conscious experience 103–4
Currie, G. 302, 303, 304–5
CYRUS program 543–45

Daly, Chris 139–40
Darrow, Clarence 362
Davidson, Donald 417, 422, 588
Dean, John 258
decoupler mechanism 338–39
delusional stance 281, 300, 306–8
delusions: and beliefs, relationship between 280–81, 299–310; hierarchical character of 304–5; responsibility and victims of 282–83; *see also* Capgras' syndrome; Cotard's syndrome
Dennett, Daniel 18, 59–60, 81–93, 210–11, 237–47, 253, 259, 418, 468–69, 532–47
Descartes, René 96, 97, 111, 119–20, 149, 159–61, 164–69, 176, 407–9, 412, 439–40, 534
descriptive experience sampling method 337
desires, animals 390, 391–93, 396–97, 400–406
determinism 354, 375–79; hard 360–61, 367, 368
Devito, C. L. 595, 596
Diachronics 211, 249, 250, 251, 255, 256, 261
disease: alcohol addiction as 374, 377, 378, 380, 381–82; responsibility attributions and 373, 374–77
disembodiment 112, 118–24
doli incapax 363
doubt 161; 'evil genius' 159–60, 165–66
Down's syndrome 311, 312, 314, 316, 319, 320, 323, 327, 329
Drake equation 563, 567, 581, 596
Drake, Frank 563, 567–68
Dreyfus, Hubert 548, 557
dualism 6, 111–12, 114, 117, 118–21, 141, 147, 149, 511–12
duplication 21, 509, 527
Dupré, John 392–93, 407–23, 562

economy rule 391, 397, 398
Ego Theory 210, 230, 232, 234–35
Einstein, Albert 356
Electra complex 287

eliminativists 115 n.1, 148, 321
embodiment and intelligence 469, 557–58
emotions: autism and understanding of 319, 329, 337; and belief 301, 302, 305; Capgras' syndrome 288–92
empathy: in animals 393, 424–30, 431–38; of experimenter 90–91; *see also* 'theory of mind' debate
environment and cognitive processes 180, 182–90
epiphenomenalism 127–28
Episodics 211, 229–52, 256, 260, 261
epistemic action 181
epoché 84
Ericsson, K. 67–68
Estes, W. 67
Ethical Narrativity thesis 248, 253, 254–56, 257, 258–59
evolution 104, 136, 563–64, 570–71, 575–76, 581
existentialism 355
experience: objective viewpoint of 42–47; phenomenal character of 9; subjectivity of 8–10, 15, 16, 25, 43, 46, 47, 48
expert systems 543–46
explanatory gap 18
explicit neuronal representation 18
extended mind hypothesis 161–62, 180–91, 192–206
externalism, active 180, 182–85, 196–98
extra-sensory perception 488
extra-terrestrial intelligence (ETI) 563–98; communication with 564, 565, 583–97

facial recognition 24, 25–26, 68, 288–91, 294–95, 296, 429–30; in infants 341–42
fallacy 31–32
false belief tasks 281–82, 313–15, 316, 320–21, 326–27, 333, 336, 337, 339, 347
Feigl, H. 64–65
Fingarette, Herbert 378
Flanagan, Owen 271
form: of an entity 61, 94, 99–102; of consciousness 61–62, 94, 102, 104, 105; mathematical 97
form finding 256–57, 259
Foucault, Michel 365
free will 283, 352, 353–61, 367
Fregoli syndrome 296
French, Robert 469, 548–60, 564
FRESIP project 574
Frith, Uta 281, 310–18, 320, 321
functionalism 103; of standing beliefs 199–200

Gallup, Gordon 393, 424–30, 431, 436
galvanic skin response (GSR) 390–91, 392, 393

gaze direction 293–94
Gazzaniga, Michael 243–44, 245–46
Generalised Social Phobia 366, 368, 369
genetics 452, 453
Gertler, Brie 162, 192–206
Ginsberg, Morris 360–61, 364, 368
Gödel's theorem 97, 480–81
Goldman, Alvin 59, 60, 64–80, 86
Gordon, Robert M. 302, 319–32
Graham, George 280, 299–309
grammar 440, 441
gravity, centers of 237–39, 247
Great Chain of Being 439
Gregory, Richard 271
Griffin, Donald 408, 412, 414, 415

hallucinations 307
Hameroff, Stuart R. 18
harmony, pre-established 127–28
Hart, W. D. 111–12, 117–24
Heisenberg uncertainty principle 356
Hempel, Carl Gustav 64, 65
Heraclitus 13
here-ness 9–10, 50–51, 52
heterophenomenology 59–60, 69, 81–93
Hospers, John 360
Hume, David 241, 265, 268, 296, 355, 358–59, 360, 460
Husserl, Edmund 84, 95, 96, 97, 98, 104

idealism 47–48, 116 n.7
idealists 115 n.1
identity 113, 118–19, 127–28, 129, 147
ignorance, argument from 31–34
illusions 87
imagination 5, 112, 119–21, 122, 161, 166, 167, 193, 342, see also pretend play
imitation game see Turing test
imitative behavior 328–29, 330
immortality 121
incompatibilism 358, 360–61
indeterminism see libertarianism
induction 76, 583–84
infants: facial recognition in 341–42; self-recognition 437
information 16; experiential aspect of 23
information processing 510–11
information states 23
insanity 363–64, 365
intelligence: analogy-making and 558; animal 415–16; as culturally oriented 469, 548; embodiment and 469, 556–57; extra-terrestrial 563–98; and language 416, 417; machine see artificial intelligence; rarity of 571–72; subcognitive factors and 548–60
intelligent design theory 563
intentional stance 103, 418, 422

intentionality 94, 95, 97–98, 102, 103–4, 131 n.1, 264, 511–13, 591; and artificial intelligence 505–6, 508, 509–10, 511; and extra-terrestrial intelligence 588
intersubjectivity 64–65, 72, 74
intrinsic/extrinsic divide 146
introspection 58–63, 97, 162, 188; of beliefs 194–95; and consciousness 61–62, 67–70, 77–78, 85–87; and experience of sensation 60–61; and publicity requirement of scientific method 59, 66, 71, 73, 75, 77; reliability of 58, 59, 60, 68, 75, 77–78
Ismael, Jenann 9, 50–56

Jack, Anthony 85
Jackson, Frank 16, 27, 35 n.2
James, Henry 249
James, William 354, 355, 357
Jaynes, Julian 5, 6–7, 12–14, 61, 113, 244
Jefferson, G. 482
Jureidini, J. 302, 303, 304, 305

Kanizsa triangle 25
Kant, Immanuel 96, 97, 355, 357
Kerouac, Jack 256
Kim, Jaegwon 136, 138, 141, 147
Kirk, Robert 144
Koch, Christof 17–20
Kosslyn, Steven 86, 87
Kripke, Saul 27, 124 n.2

language 95, 103–4, 184, 190, 398; animals and 394, 408, 416–17, 419–21, 439–49; and beliefs 417, 419; and intelligence 416, 417; understanding and interpreting 564–65, 587–90; see also communication
Laplace, Pierre Simon, Marquis de 356, 477
La Rochefoucauld, François de 258
learning machines 488–93
legal approach to responsibility 361–64
Leibniz, G. W. 127, 128
Leslie, Alan M. 231, 281, 310–18, 320, 321, 327–28, 334, 338–39
Levine, Joseph 19, 83
lexical decision task 552
libertarianism 354–55, 368
life 8, 33
limbic system 288–90
Linear A 564–65
listening 444–45
Lovelace, Ada 485
Lowry, Malcolm 256
LUNAR program 539

machine intelligence see artificial intelligence
MacIntyre, Alasdair 254
Malamud, Bernard 260

masking 88–89, 243–44
materialism 115–16 n.7, 121, 122, 125–32, 133, 135
mathematical form 97
mathematical logic 97, 480–81
mathematics, and extra-terrestrial communication 593–94, 595
Mayr, Ernst 563–64, 569–73, 579–80, 581
meaning 589; as ecological 587, 589; explanation of 410–12; neural basis of 25–26
memory 59, 75, 134–35, 162, 185–89, 255, 294–95, 296; autobiographical 211, 251–52, 257–58, 296, 426, 435, 436; explicit 68; implicit 68; reliability of 76; short-term 28, 30, 67
mental causation 112–13, 126–30
mental imagery 86–87
mental states, attribution of: in animals 390–438, 445–50, 506; see also beliefs; desires; empathy; self-awareness; 'theory of mind' debate
mental/nonmental distinction 145, 146–49, 150
mentality: as fundamental 141–46, 149–50; and spatiotemporality 149
metacognition 67, 75
mimicry see imitative behavior
mind-blindness see 'theory of mind' debate
mind-body problem 27, 36, 95, 105, 110–56
Minoans 564–65
mirror test 393, 424, 425–26, 431, 436
M'Naghten case 363–64
modal truth 112, 122
modus ponens 120
Montaigne, Michel de 251, 260, 261
Montero, Barbara 114, 136–56
moral responsibility 282–83, 352, 353, 358–69
Morgan's Canon 390–91
Multiple Personality Disorder (MPD) 208, 209, 243, 376
MYCIN 543
mysterianism 16

Naeye, Robert 563, 567–68
Nagel, Thomas 8–9, 27, 95, 125, 144, 161, 178, 208–10, 210
narrative conception of self 210–11, 237–47, 252–61
naturalism 94, 96, 97, 102–5, 143–45, 149–50
nervous system 289–90, 486–87, 508
neuroscience 7, 16, 17–19, 27–28, 32, 52, 95, 103, 136, 138, 280
Newell, A. 67
Nietzsche, F. 102, 258

Nisbett, R. 68
numerical reasoning 394, 441, 461–63
Nussbaum, Hedda 386
objective awareness 20
objective reality 8, 9, 36–49
objectivity 8–9, 110, 159, 161; mental 39–41; physical conception of 8, 36–39, 41, 47; scientific 64–65, 72
observation and scientific evidence 65–66
obsessive-compulsive subjects 306
occurent states 162, 185, 189, 193, 195, 203–5

Oedipus complex 287
Oehrle, R. T. 585, 586
Olen, J. 355–56, 362
Olson, Eric 212, 262–77
ontology 61, 62, 94, 97, 98–101, 104–5, 143, 144
operationalism 511, 538–39
organizational invariance, principle of 21
origination 467, 485–86
O'Shaughnessy, B. 172
overdetermination 112–13, 127, 129

pain 50, 51, 61, 140, 147, 170–71, 391, 392, 408, 409–11, 420–21
Papineau, David 112–13, 125–32, 143–44
Parfit, Derek 203, 210–11, 229–36
Parity Principle 161–62
PARRY program 541–43
Peele, Stanton 377, 380–81
Penrose, Roger 18, 97
perception 5, 16, 59, 112, 122, 170, 188; Descartes on 165, 166, 167, 168; extra-sensory 488; reliability of 76
perception research 67
Perner, J. 312, 320
phenomenal 50–56
phenomenal character of experience 9
phenomenology 61, 62, 94, 95, 97–99, 104, 105; critical 87–88; see also heterophenomenology
physical science: explanation of consciousness 5–10, 52–53, 62, 95, 96, 103; and objective reality 8, 36–39, 41; see also neuroscience; physics
physical stance 418
physicalism 6, 8, 9–10, 38, 47, 50–56, 111, 112–14, 137–50
physics 19–20, 38–39, 133, 134, 137, 138–39, 141–42, 143–44; animals understanding of 460–61; completeness of 112, 130–31; sublunary and superlunary 30–31
Pinchin, C. 359–60
Plato 99

play *see* pretend play
Popper, Karl 64, 65, 139
post-physicalism 136–56
Povinelli, Daniel 393, 394, 428, 430, 431–38, 451–64
practical reasoning 344–48
pragmatic action 181
precognition 488
Premack, D. 312, 322–23, 406
pretend play 282, 311, 324–26, 327–28, 333, 334, 335, 338–42, 343
Preuss, Todd 453–54
privacy of conscious experience 6
private language argument 411
prosopagnosia 24, 68, 297–98 n.2 and 3
PROSPECTOR 543
psychiatry 365
psycho-kinesis 488
psychological competence 319, 320, 321–25, 327, 329
Psychological Narrativity thesis 248, 252–53, 255, 256
psychology 58, 59, 67, 144, 368–69
psychophysical laws 7, 20, 21–23
publicity in science 59, 64–66; agreement and 70–74; as validation by intersubjective methods 74–77
Putnam, H. 143, 182, 186, 187, 591
Pylyshyn, Zenon 86, 526

qualia 22, 29–30, 35 n.2, 95
quantum theory 39
Quine, W. V. O. 588

race/racism 269–70, 296
radical interpretation/translation 588–89
Railton, P. 65
Ramachandran, Vilayanur 280, 285–98
Ramsey test 325
rationality 282–83
reality 8–9, 48; objective 8, 9, 36–49; subjective 48
reasoning, practical 344–48
reductionism 16, 38, 54–55
reliability: introspective 58, 59, 60, 68, 75, 77–78; scientific 59, 72, 74–75, 77
responsibility attributions 282–83, 372–88; and alcohol addiction 283, 372–74, 377, 378, 380–87; character and 377, 378; disease and 373, 374–77; *see also* criminal responsibility; moral responsibility
Revision thesis 257–59
Ricoeur, Paul 253
Rilke, Rainer Maria 250–51
Rose, Nikolas 369
Russell, Bertrand 92, 113–14, 133–35, 137
Ryle, Gilbert 245, 354, 412, 415

Sacks, Oliver 248, 253, 287
Sagan, Carl 563, 564, 574–78, 579, 581–82, 596–97
Sartre, Jean-Paul 178, 248, 252–53, 355
Sass, L. 302
Savage-Rumbaugh, Sue 394, 439–50
Schank, Roger 495–96, 521
Schechtman, Marya 251, 259
Schoeman, Ferdinand 283
scientific evidence: observation and 65–66; and publicity thesis 59, 64–66, 70–74
Searle, John 27, 104, 138, 357, 467–68, 495–513, 514–30
seeing: animals understanding of concept of 431–33, 458–59, 460; *see also* visual experience
Selective Mutism 366, 368, 369
self 208–13; and bodily awareness 160, 170–79; Bundle Theory of 203, 230–31, 233–36, 268–69; definitions of term 263–64, 265–69; Diachronic conception of 211, 249, 250, 251, 256, 261; Ego Theory of 210, 230; Episodic conception of 211, 249–52, 256, 260, 261; extended 190; narrative conception of 210–11, 237–47, 248–49, 252–61; problem of the 211–12, 262–77; unity of *see* unity of consciousness
self-awareness 393, 424–30, 431–38
self-recognition 425–26, 427–29, 430, 431, 434–37
Sellars, Wilfred 138
Seneca 439
sensation(s) 160–61; introspection and experience of 60–61; spatiality of 170–77
Shaftesbury, Earl of 255
Shanker, Stuart 439–50
Shear, J. 90–91
Shepard, Roger 86, 87
signal detection theory 87
Simon, H. 67–68
simulation 495–96
simulation theory 282, 324–27, 328–29, 330–31 n.5, 334–35, 343, 347, 348
Skinner, B. F. 357
Smith, David Woodruff 61–62, 94–108
socially extended cognition 190
Socrates 260
soul 6, 121, 133, 134, 165, 166, 479–80
space-time 138–39, 357
spatial location 9–10, 50–51, 53, 54, 159, 160, 165; of bodily sensation 160, 170–77
spatiotemporality and mentality 149
speech acts 82, 83
Spinoza, Baruch 357, 368
split-brain (commissurotomy) cases 208–10, 229–30, 243–44, 245–46; Bundle Theory

and 234–36; and unity of consciousness 209–10, 214–28, 235–36
Stendhal 256
Stephens, G. Lynn 280, 299–309
stimulus/response 357; in animals 391, 400, 414–15
Stoics 248
Strawson, Galen 211, 248–61, 272–74
structural coherence, principle of 21
Stumpf, Carl 390
subconscious 13
subjective reality 48
subjectivity 8–10, 15, 16, 25, 38, 43, 46, 47, 48, 159, 161, 264
substance, concept of a 117–18, 119
supervenience 143, 151 n.14
supposition and pretend play 339, 340–41, 342
Sybil 243

Tait, Gordon 283, 352–71
Taylor, Charles 253
Taylor, Talbot J. 439–50
telepathy 488
teletransportation 210, 232–33
Tennant, Neil 563, 564, 583–97
Tetris 161, 181, 192–93
theology 479–80
'theory of mind' debate 281–82, 310–18, 319–32, 333–51; *see also* beliefs; desires; empathy; self-awareness
Theory of Mind Mechanism 328
theory-theory 281–82, 321–23, 327, 328, 334, 335–36
thought 29–30, 159–60, 166, 167
thought experiments 7–8, 16, 20, 21, 29
The Three Faces of Eve 208, 243
Tower of Hanoi problem 344, 346, 348
Traynor and McKelvey v. Turnage 373–74, 381
Treacher, A. 365
trust 91–92
truth 74, 112, 122

Turing, Alan 97, 467, 471–94, 527, 528, 532, 548
Turing machines 527, 532
Turing test (imitation game) 467, 468–69, 471–74, 479, 482, 484, 532–41, 545–47, 548–60, 564
2001: A Space Odyssey (film) 466

uncertainty principle 356
unconscious 13, 88–89, 90, 360
understanding 444–45, 583; artificial intelligence and 495–510, 514–25
Unger, Peter 308
unity of consciousness 209–10, 230, 234–36; at a time and across time 209, 210; and split-brain cases 209–10, 214–28, 235–36
Updike, John 242–43

values and culture 379–80
Varela, F. 90–91
veridicality 112, 123–24
visual experience 5, 16–21; color 16–17, 21, 23, 24, 25; veridicality of 123–24; *see also* Anton's syndrome; blindsight; seeing
voluntarism 357–58

Weizenbaum, Joseph 541
Wideman, John 379
Wigner's hypothesis 141–42
Williams syndrome 348
Wilson, Edward O. 96, 104
Wilson, T. 68
Wimmer, H. 312, 320
Winograd, Terry 535
Wittgenstein, Ludwig 44, 102, 392, 408, 410, 419–20, 587
Wood, William 539
Woodruff, G. 312, 322–23
Wright, P. 365
Wundt, Wilhelm 58, 66
Young, A. 302, 303